The

History of Beech

by

WILLIAM H. McDANIEL

Published by

McCormick-Armstrong Co., Incorporated
Publishing Division

1501 East Douglas Ave., Wichita, Kansas 67206

Copyright 1982 by Beech Aircraft Corporation

HD9711.U63B42   338.7'62'9133340973
ISBN 0-911978-00-3
Library of Congress Catalog Card Number 82-81640

*The medal on the
title page was struck
to commemorate the
Fiftieth Anniversary of the
Beech Aircraft Corporation.
The portraits are of
Walter H. Beech,
O. A. Beech,
Frank E. Hedrick
and E. C. Burns.*

Beech

Fifty Years of Excellence

Walter H. Beech
(1924)

Preface

TEAMWORK is named by Chairman O. A. Beech as the major factor in the growth of the Beech enterprises from Travel Air to the Beech Aircraft Corporation of today. Rightly so; but the historian must also take note of other special elements. The writer has been privileged to observe the inner workings of Beech Aircraft closely for more than forty years, and to compare its operations with those of many other corporations. We have seen no other business that more fully embodies the better qualities of the American free enterprise system: Initiative, responsibility, and loyalty. Initiative in creating new designs that have significantly advanced the state of the aircraft and aerospace arts. Responsibility in meeting the many obligations of the modern corporation. And loyalty, in every respect. Loyalty to the government of the United States . . . in war and peace. Loyalty to and from Beech customers . . . among whom are consistent buyers of Beech-built airplanes from early Travel Air days onward. Loyalty to and from Beech employees . . . expressed in a noteworthy pattern of harmony in management-employee relationships. All of these are elements in a record of effective teamwork that makes the history of Beech an object lesson in the study of free enterprise at work. To this end our book is dedicated . . . and to the thousands of Beech employees, past and present, who have made the company what it is . . . to the memory of Walter H. Beech, aviation pioneer and founder . . . and to co-founder O. A. Beech and her associates in the management of the Beech Aircraft Corporation.

William H. McDaniel

Contents

CHAPTER 1: Early times . . . Walter H. Beech founds Travel Air, wins Ford Reliability Tour . . . "Woolaroc" wins Dole race . . . Sales grow.   1

CHAPTER 2: Travel Air leads the world in sales . . . "Mystery S" smashes speed records . . . Depression ends production in Wichita.   9

CHAPTER 3: First Beechcraft biplane tops 200 mph . . . 240 mph with higher power . . . Production begins in original Travel Air factory.   13

CHAPTER 4: Sales grow . . . a B17R flies around the world . . . a C17R wins the Bendix Trophy . . . the Beech Aircraft Corporation is formed.   18

CHAPTER 5: Beech buys its home . . . the Model 18 Twin Beechcraft is born . . . a D17W wins the Macfadden Race . . . The N. Y. Curb Exchange lists Beech stock.   24

CHAPTER 6: Beech sales top $1 millions . . . Feeder airlines buy Model 18 . . . Governments order Beechcrafts . . . A Beech sets altitude record.   28

CHAPTER 7: An 18S twin wins Macfadden Trophy . . . Government defense orders pour in . . . Beech expands for vastly increased production.   34

CHAPTER 8: A hard winter . . . Beech creates the AT-10 twin trainer . . . Contract backlog quadruples . . . Production steadily increases.   38

CHAPTER 9: Pearl Harbor finds Beech ready . . . 1942 volume tops $60 millions . . . Beech promotes subcontracting . . . Earns its first "E" Award.   43

CHAPTER 10: Gross 1943 volume tops $126 millions . . . Production shifts from AT-10 to A-26 wings . . . Beech helps redistribute surplus materials.   50

CHAPTER 11: Beech XA-38 "Grizzly" flies . . . Beech designs a practical "V" empennage . . . qualifies for a $50 million revolving credit fund.   54

vi

CHAPTER 12: Victory ends war production: Score, 7,400 Beechcrafts, 1635 sets of A-26 wings . . . Peacetime production and deliveries resume.   60

CHAPTER 13: Refined Model D18S Beechcrafts pour from the production lines . . . The Model 35 V-tail Bonanza makes its first flight.   65

CHAPTER 14: The Bonanza passes accelerated service tests and wins its ATC . . . Model 18s make over-ocean delivery flights.   71

CHAPTER 15: Beech beats a gas shortage . . . starts mass deliveries on 1500 Bonanza orders . . . designs the "Mentor" pilot trainer.   80

CHAPTER 16: Bonanza and Odom set a world flight distance record . . . Beech shows off the Mentor . . . designs the Model 50 Twin Bonanza.   89

CHAPTER 17: Walter H. Beech passes away . . . Korean conflict renews defense preparations . . . T-36A design wins Air Force production contract.   98

CHAPTER 18: New plant constructed for T-36A production . . . Twin-Bonanza and Mentor enter military service . . . Korean truce ends T-36A.   111

CHAPTER 19: "Super 18" introduced . . . Beech builds ground service units, and more T-34 Mentors for the services . . . Wings for Lockheed jets.   125

CHAPTER 20: Beech examines purejets . . . extends its aerospace work . . . flies the new Travel Air Twin . . . founds Beech Acceptance Corporation, Inc.   133

CHAPTER 21: Silver Anniversary brings 10% stock dividend . . . doubling of Beech - Boulder aerospace site . . . 1957 sales top $103 millions.   147

CHAPTER 22: Travel Air light twin Beech finds a ready market . . . Pat Boling flies a J35 Bonanza to a new 7,090-mile non-stop flight record.   159

vii

CHAPTER 23: Super 18 adds JATO thrust . . . Beech - Boulder wins a $1 million thermal heat study contract . . . Bonanza No. 6,000 is delivered. 171

CHAPTER 24: Beech declares a 5% stock dividend and 3-for-1 split . . . introduces the Model 55 Baron . . . builds the 500th Super 18. 185

CHAPTER 25: Beech accelerates propjet studies . . . declares a 2% stock dividend . . . introduces the low-priced Model 23 Musketeer. 196

CHAPTER 26: Beech - Boulder wins $4 million life support system contract for NAA/NASA Apollo spacecraft . . . "Three Musketeers" tour the USA. 212

CHAPTER 27: Beech builds new plant at Boulder . . . offers tricycle gear Super 18 . . . T-34 Mentor sets new records in U. S. Navy service. 223

CHAPTER 28: King Air passes first flight tests . . . Stockholders equity shows 250% increase since 1954 . . . Musketeer II Series is introduced. 237

CHAPTER 29: Beech promotes "Zero Defects" program, introduces "Magic Hand", pressurized Model 88 Queen Air . . . produces its 8,000th Bonanza. 252

CHAPTER 30: Beech establishes new plant at Salina . . . delivers the 100th King Air . . . flies the new Model 60 pressurized twin-engine Duke. 264

CHAPTER 31: Beech names Mrs. O. A. Beech Chairman of the Board, Frank E. Hedrick President . . . wins $75 million Bell contract . . . sells $30 million in debentures . . . sets new sales records. 280

CHAPTER 32: Beech helps put man on the moon . . . Mrs. O. A. Beech receives NBAA Award . . . Beech presents the King Air 100 and enters business jet market with the Beechcraft-Hawker 125. 293

CHAPTER 33: Beechcraft 99A wins London-to-Sydney Air Race . . . Air Force orders Beech HAST target missiles . . . Beech delivers 30,000th production airplane . . . follows with 500th Beechcraft King Air . . . celebrates 25th anniversary of Beechcraft Bonanza.   310

CHAPTER 34: Beech presents advanced Beechcraft King Air A100 . . . contributes to Apollo 14 and 15 space missions . . . receives U. S. Army's first order for pressurized aircraft . . . introduces refined Aero Center Beechcrafts.   325

CHAPTER 35: Beechcrafts set new world speed records . . . Lyndon B. Johnson gets a new Beechcraft King Air A100 . . . Beech wins U. S. Army contract competition with MQM-107 Variable Speed Training Target . . . celebrates 40th anniversary . . . introduces speedy new King Air E90 . . . reorganizes domestic distribution . . . contributes to Apollo 16 and 17 space missions.   343

CHAPTER 36: John H. Shaffer joins Beech board of directors . . . Mrs. O. A. Beech named one of "Ten Highest Ranking Women in American Business" . . . Beech systems perform in Skylab space missions . . . Beech presents new Beechcraft Super King Air . . . sets new sales and earnings records.   362

CHAPTER 37: Beech earns NASA/Rockwell International Space Shuttle contract . . . University of Kansas honors Mrs. O. A. Beech . . . Beech wins Army/Air Force utility aircraft competition . . . announces Garrett-powered Beechcraft King Air B100 . . . previews new Model 76 Aero Center light twin . . . sets new sales and earnings records.   387

CHAPTER 38: Beech delivers 1,000th commercial Beechcraft King Air . . . receives U. S. Navy contract for Beechcraft Turbo Mentor T-34C trainers . . . celebrates 20th anniversary of Beech-Boulder . . . hails dedication of Walter H. Beech Hangar at Staggerwing Museum with Mrs. O. A. Beech as honor guest . . . sends "Waikiki Beech" Bonanza to Smithsonian Institution for permanent display . . . observes 30th anniversary of first Beechcraft Bonanza flight . . . breaks all past sales and earnings records.   415

CHAPTER 39: Beech wins major U. S. Navy VTAM-X competition . . . celebrates U. S. Bicentennial . . . applauds "Uncommon Citizen" award to Mrs. O. A. Beech . . . ranks 76th among top 100 defense contractors . . . sets new sales and earnings records.   434

CHAPTER 40: Beech builds 10,000th Model 35 V-tail Beechcraft Bonanza . . . celebrates 45th anniversary . . . sets new world speed records . . . Walter H. Beech enshrined in Aviation Hall of Fame . . . Beech delivers 1,500th commercial Beechcraft King Air, 2,000th Bell JetRanger helicopter airframe and 40,000th Beechcraft . . . sets new sales and earnings records.   450

CHAPTER 41: Beechcraft Bonanza sets around-the-world speed record . . . Beech introduces "Executive Flight Plan" charter service . . . delivers 2,000th Beechcraft King Air . . . graduates 20,000th student from Beechcraft Training Center . . . receives 15,000th P & W gas turbine engine . . . opens Selma, Ala. facility . . . sets new sales and earnings records.   468

CHAPTER 42: Beech wins U. S. Customs contract competition . . . delivers first Beechcraft Baron A36TC, 500th Beechcraft Duke and 85th Beechcraft purchased by Marathon Oil . . . Mrs. Beech is honor guest at Navy Pensacola, Fla. graduation . . . Beech announces new Beechcraft Commuter C99 and 1900 models . . . assents to merger with Raytheon Company . . . sets new sales and earnings records.   487

CHAPTER 43: Beech completes merger with Raytheon Company . . . Mrs. O. A. Beech and Frank E. Hedrick elected as Raytheon directors . . . Raytheon Chairman T. L. Phillips and President D. Brainerd Holmes elected as Beech Aircraft directors . . . Prototype Beechcraft Commuter C99 makes first flight . . . Beechcraft Training Center graduates 25,000th student . . . Boulder Division celebrates 25th anniversary . . . Beech founds Alternative Energy Division . . . Mrs. O. A. Beech receives Wright Brothers Memorial Trophy and "Sands of Time" Kitty Hawk awards . . . Beech breaks past records for 8th consecutive year, Raytheon for 10th consecutive year. 508

CHAPTER 44: Beech names Edward C. Burns company's fourth president . . . dedicates new $1 million Plant Four at Beech Field with delivery of 3,000th Bell JetRanger helicopter airframe . . . introduces new higher-performance Beechcraft Super King Air B200 . . . shares in first and second space flights of Space Shuttle "Columbia" . . . Mrs. O. A. Beech honored at Staggerwing Museum dedication of Olive Ann Beech Gallery and Chapel at Tullahoma, Tenn.; enshrined with Walter H. Beech in Aviation Hall of Fame, Dayton, Ohio; receives Distinguished Achievement Award from Wings Club, New York City . . . Alternative Energy Division receives first liquefied methane fuel system automotive fleet order, sponsors world's first methane-fueled flight with Beechcraft Sundowner . . . Selma Division delivers first Beechcraft Commuter C99s and Japan's 13th Maritime Patrol Beechcraft Super King Air . . . Frank E. Hedrick honored at West Point Military Academy . . . Beech delivers 400th Beechcraft Baron 58P . . . Beech breaks past records for 9th consecutive year, Raytheon for 11th consecutive year.   523

CHAPTER 45: Beech prepares to celebrate 50th anniversary in April . . . delivers 1,000th Beechcraft Super King Air . . . charts long-range five-year action plan . . . looks forward to next fifty years.   536

Walter H. Beech
(1891-1950)

Olive Ann Beech
Chairman of the Board

Frank E. Hedrick
Vice Chairman of the Board

E. C. Burns
President

The Early Years

Chapter 1

The story of Beechcraft is more than the sum total of the many contributions to aeronautical progress made by thousands of Beechcrafters who have taken part in the company's activities since its founding in 1932. It is also the achievement record of its founder, and of its principal officers, in the years preceding 1932, as well as in the span of time that has followed. A brief survey of that record is helpful to a full understanding of the Beech Aircraft Corporation of today.

Most of Beechcraft's principal officers have been associated together in manufacturing successful and popular aircraft for over thirty years. The aeronautical experience of the company's first president and chairman of the board of directors, Walter H. Beech, extended over more than one-third century. During that time, airplanes designed and built under his supervision — Swallows, Travel Airs, and Beechcrafts — won respect and liking all over the world, wherever men flew.

Born on a farm near Pulaski, Tennessee, on January 30, 1891, Walter H. Beech from childhood onward acquired the familiarity with tools and mechanical devices which is the farm boy's natural heritage. As a youth he performed man-sized jobs of repair and installation of sawmills, and municipal water and power supply plants. Then he became a sales engineer with a motor truck manufacturer, and toured Europe for two years as the manufacturer's representative.

Airplanes naturally attracted his attention, and on July 11, 1914, young Beech made his first solo flight in a primitive Curtiss pusher biplane. When the United States entered World War I in 1917, he enlisted in the Air Corps. For three years

1

he served as an Army pilot, flight instructor, and engineer, gaining first-hand experience with the major types of military aircraft in service at that time. In 1920 he returned to civilian life as a barnstorming exhibition pilot, and toured almost every state in the Union during the three years that followed. The tour was perilous, financially and in every other respect; but it vastly enriched his aeronautical knowledge and experience, and gave him many ideas for improvements in aircraft design and construction.

Walter H. Beech did not let those ideas lie idle. In 1923, he came to Wichita, Kansas, staked out his war-surplus "Jennie" in a pasture, and took a job with the Swallow Airplane Corporation as a designer, test and demonstration pilot, and salesman. He was a busy young man at Swallow. To prove what their products would do, he entered and won numerous races, among them the On-to-Detroit cross-country classic, the Admiral Fullam Derby, and the Aviation Town & Country Club of Detroit efficiency contest. In less than two years, he became general manager of the company.

Eager for complete freedom in putting his ideas about aircraft design into practice, Walter H. Beech resigned from Swallow in 1924, and became president and general manager of his own company — Travel Air Manufacturing Company. The first Travel Air was built in a space just 30 feet square, in a leased portion of an old planing mill building. A three-place biplane, it proved outstandingly efficient in utilizing the OX-5 war surplus engine which was virtually the standard power plant of that day. The Travel Air was the first airplane of its time to be equipped with streamlined, faired-in cowling for the OX-5 and OXX-6 engines, a Beech-originated feature. Flying an OXX-6 Travel Air, Walter H. Beech personally demonstrated the ship by qualifying as a winner in the first Ford Reliability Tour in 1925. Altogether, three Travel Air planes entered this event, and all finished with perfect scores. This showing was a potent sales argument in favor of Travel Air, and the business grew rapidly.

The second Ford Reliability Tour of 1926 was scored on a wholly competitive basis, and Walter H. Beech won first place, flying a J-4 Wright-powered Travel Air. He thus proved the advantages of two then new developments: wheel brakes, for

2

The 1926 Ford
Reliability Tour
was won by
Walter H. Beech
and Brice H.
Goldsborough
flying this
Travel Air.

#105

3

Some of Wichita's earliest aircraft workers assembled components for Travel Air aircraft. Company employed 1,000 at peak in 1929.

The business executive of 1929 could outfit his Travel Air monoplane with complete office equipment.

Travel Air 5000 built for National Air Transport was photographed with the 41,000 square foot Travel Air factory.

4

shorter landings, and the earth inductor compass, for accurate navigation. And he demonstrated the capabilities of the ship he had built. An OX-5 Travel Air flown by Fred D. Hoyt gave further proof by winning the On-to-the-Sesqui cross-country race, flying 2,588 miles from Eureka, California to Philadelphia, Pennsylvania, in 31 hours.

While these and the many other racing victories won in later years by Beech-built planes attracted international attention and recognition, it would be wrong to conclude that racing, in itself, was Walter H. Beech's major interest. It is true that he enjoyed it greatly. But it was only one outlet for the keen competitive spirit which he possessed and passed along to his associates. At Travel Air, as at Beech Aircraft, the people who really belonged in the clan, whether as workmen or executives, were those who felt and demonstrated the urge to excel; to build the best airplanes that human skill could contrive, and to prove their excellence competitively against all others. The faint-hearted and the idly wishful had nothing in common with Walter H. Beech, and his ways and theirs soon parted.

His zest for competition was expressed in every aspect of the enterprises which Beech directed. His demands for peak efficiency were always blunt, forthright, and unrelenting. Whatever was done under his direction had to be the best of its kind; nothing less was acceptable. He got as much pleasure out of closing a tough sale, or winning a design competition, as he received from any racing trophy.

It was a design competition, late in 1926, that sparked the creation of the famous Travel Air six-place high-wing cabin monoplane. National Air Transport, Inc., asked for bids and demonstrations of a monoplane capable of carrying a 1,000-lb. load, with cargo space of 100 cubic feet or more. Walter H. Beech and his men jumped at this chance to show what they could do. Only 38 days after the bid invitations were posted, the first Model 5000 Travel Air was completed, test-flown, and delivered to N.A.T. It was accepted and became the first unit of a Travel Air fleet operating day and night between Chicago and Dallas. Other airlines also bought the Model 5000 in substantial numbers.

5

The new transport monoplane in 1927 dramatically proved the dependability of Beech-built products. That was the ocean-flying year. Lindbergh started it off with his New York-Paris flight. Many others followed. Some succeeded; some were lost at sea. Two of the successful flights were made in Travel Air monoplanes. The first commercial airplane to fly from California to Hawaii was the Travel Air "City of Oakland." On July 14 and 15, it was flown by Ernest L. Smith and Emory B. Bronte from Oakland to Molokai in 25 hours and 36 minutes. A month later, Arthur Goebel and William Davis won the $25,000 Dole prize, flying the Phillips Petroleum Company's Travel Air "Woolaroc" from Oakland to Wheeler Field in 26 hours 17 minutes. Eight planes started in the Dole race. The Travel Air was one of two that reached its goal.

In other speed contests, Travel Air biplanes won important victories. H. C. Lippiatt piloted a Travel Air from San Francisco to Spokane in 8 hours and 16 minutes to win a $1,500 first prize in the Pacific Coast Air Derby on September 21, 1927. Two days later, Eugene Detmer won the Western Flying Trophy at the National Air Races at a speed exceeding 102 mph.

Neither Walter H. Beech nor his company could spare time in 1927 to sponsor racing entries. Within their own plant at Wichita, an exciting race was taking place every day in the year — a race to increase production and keep up with the rising demand for their products. A new factory building was erected on the 160-acre field that was then Wichita's municipal airport. It was the first unit of what was later to become the great Beech Aircraft plant. Scarcely had Travel Air settled in the new location when it became necessary to duplicate the original building. Before the year ended, Travel Air had produced and delivered 158 planes, was working on a backlog of orders for more than 500 ships. The fame of Walter H. Beech was spreading within the industry. He held three important posts in the Aeronautical Chamber of Commerce of America: Kansas state committeeman, and memberships on the engineering standardization, and rules and regulations committees. It was a great year for the Tennessee farm boy and his associates. But it was no more than a good beginning.

Celebrities in all fields have long shown a natural affinity with Beech-built airplanes. This is film star Wallace Beery, taking delivery in 1928 on his Travel Air 6000 from Walter H. Beech.

Travel Air Model 5000 was chosen by National Air Transport airline in 1926 to carry U. S. Mail between Chicago and Dallas.

Art Goebel flew this Travel Air 5000 named "Woolaroc" non-stop from U. S. Mainland to Hawaii in 1927 to win Dole Race. Plane is on display at Woolaroc Museum, Bartlesville, Oklahoma.

Doug Davis won the Thompson Trophy in 1929 flying this Travel Air Mystery S which with a speed of 194.90 mph hopelessly outdistanced all other contestants. It was the first occasion a civilian plane had out-performed military ships in speed competition.

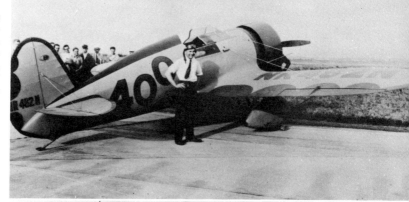

Forerunner of the fleet of King Air Beechcrafts operated decades later by Shell Aviation was the "Shell 400" flown by Jimmy Doolittle (pictured), who called it "The finest airplane I have ever flown".

Flying this "Texaco 13" Travel Air Mystery S for the Texas Company, Capt. Frank Hawks set more than 200 new speed records in America and Europe.

8

Chapter 2

In 1928, the executive group that was later to direct the Beech Aircraft Corporation worked together as a smoothly functioning team at Travel Air, with Walter H. Beech as the quarterback. Its members were Olive Ann Mellor, secretary to the president, office manager of Travel Air, and Walter's wife-to-be; R. K. Beech, Walter's brother, purchasing agent and chief inspector; T. A. Wells, modest engineering genius and pilot; C. G. Yankey, Wichita capitalist and legal counsel to the company; and T. D. Neelands, New York broker and financial advisor, a company director. Only two persons had not yet joined this group who were later to earn positions of top importance with Beech Aircraft: John P. Gaty and Frank E. Hedrick.

The quality of their teamwork is shown by the record. Travel Air became one of the largest producers of commercial aircraft in the United States. Wichita manufacturers built more planes than any plane-builders elsewhere — 927 units out of a national total of 3,781 commercial aircraft. Travel Air dominated Wichita production by delivering more than 400 planes during the year. Walter H. Beech became a governor of the Aeronautical Chamber of Commerce of America; and his planes won such important racing events as the Oakland to Los Angeles Race, and the Civilian Free-for-All at Mines Field. Plant facilities, and the number of employees at Travel Air, were doubled.

In 1929, Travel Air became the world's largest producer of both monoplane and biplane type commercial aircraft. Out of a total U.S. production of 5,357 commercial planes reported by 95 manufacturers, Travel Air produced 547 units. The factory often operated at its peak capacity of 25 airplanes per week that year, and employed 1,000 men. The company became affiliated with the Curtiss-Wright interests, but continued to function independently in its production and design operations.

While Beech and his people were leading the world in output, their products were proving their superiority in almost every race or contest held in America. Little time could be spared for company-sponsored entries, but in the Air Derby from Portland, Oregon to Cleveland, Ohio, T. A. Wells handily won first place. Other Travel Air planes took third and fourth prize money in this event. The Rim of Ohio Derby was won by J. O. Donaldson in a Travel Air. First place in the Toronto to Cleveland race went to a Travel Air flown by Herbert St. Martin. Billy Parker took first prize, flying a Travel Air, in the On-to-Tulsa Derby. The winner of the International Air Derby from Mexico City to Kansas City, Missouri, Arthur Goebel, flew a Travel Air. Victory in the Women's Derby from Santa Monica, California to Cleveland, Ohio went to Louise Thaden in a Travel Air. Warming up for the Derby, Mrs. Thaden set a new U.S. endurance record for women, remaining aloft in a Hisso-powered Travel Air for 22 hours and 3 minutes at Santa Monica. To complete her achievements, Mrs. Thaden flew a Travel Air to a new U.S. altitude record for women of more than 20,000 feet. Even the Travel Air planes powered with World War I surplus engines proved their mettle. At the National Air Races, George H. Shealy won the OX-5 Race in a Travel Air; and first place in the Relay Race also went to an OX-5 Travel Air. And a Travel Air powered with a new type of engine, the Chevrolet D-6, was flown by Douglas Davis to first place in the Experimental Ship Race.

Probably the outstanding racing event of the year was the 50-mile ten-lap closed-course Free-for-All which was the biggest feature of the National Air Races. It was the prototype of the Thompson Trophy Race, a competition which became, according to one historian, "the closed-course classic of two continents." Entrants included Army and Navy pursuit planes, and high-powered privately owned racing craft. Little attention was paid to a new type Travel Air with a 400 hp Wright Whirlwind engine which was entered in this race. Designated as the "Mystery S," it was a one-place low-wing open monoplane, neatly streamlined and utilizing the newly developed NACA cowling. The plane was the creation of two of Beech's young engineers, Herb Rawdon and Walt Burnham. A smart-looking ship, air-wise spectators said, but far out of its class against its much higher-powered competitors. It was a great surprise to everyone but its pilot, Doug Davis, and its builders, when the "Mystery S" showed its flippers to the entire field throughout the race, finishing with a phenomenal average speed exceeding 194 mph.

Throughout 1930 and the years that followed, the "Mystery S" continued a record-smashing career that increased the fame of Travel Air and Walter H. Beech all over the world. The Texas Company bought one of these speedy ships for the use of its chief pilot, Captain Frank Hawks and "Texaco 13," as the ship was designated, established more than 200 new speed records in America and Europe with Hawks at the controls. Existing transcontinental east-west and west-east records were the first to fall. A series of fast inter-city flights followed: Detroit-New York, 2 hours 41 minutes; Boston-New York, 54 minutes; Philadelphia-New York, 20 minutes; New York-Havana and return, 9 hours 21 minutes southbound, 8 hours 44 minutes northbound; Agua Caliente, Mexico-Vancouver, Canada and return, 13 hours 44 minutes round trip. These were only a few of "Texaco 13" American records. In a 20,000-mile European tour in 1931, Hawks and his Travel Air established many records which stood for years. He became known as "the flying epicure — arising in Paris, breakfasting in London, lunching in Berlin, and back to Paris for dinner." The records show that this was no exaggeration: Paris-London (218 miles), 59 minutes; London-Berlin (620 miles), 2 hours 57 minutes; London-Rome (950 miles), 4 hours 38 minutes — to cite some typical examples. One commentator wrote: "The old world had justly prided itself on the achievements of its Schneider fliers — breaking world records over relatively short courses — but it had not a single machine that could stand long flights day after day with the same engine at speeds above 200 miles per hour." His European tour with "Texaco 13" brought Captain Hawks the Ligue Internationale des Aviateurs medal as the world's outstanding airman.

Other "Mystery S" owners and pilots did their share of record-breaking. Montreal-New York was a 115-minute run for Dale Jackson, flying a "Mystery S"; Detroit-Cleveland only a 26½-minute jaunt. Florence Lowe Barnes set a world speed

11

record for women, covering a measured course near Los Angeles in a "Mystery S" at better than 196 mph. In local and regional contests all over the country, "Mystery S" monoplanes consistently took first place.

In the 1931 Year Book, official aviation history compiled annually by the Aeronautical Chamber of Commerce of America, the industry's historian commented: "No new design introduced during the year (1930) surpassed the performance of the Travel Air Mystery Ship, introduced in 1929 and produced during 1930 as high speed sport jobs. Powered with a Wright Whirlwind 300 engine, the Mystery Ship held all transcontinental speed records and hung up many shorter speed marks during the year. . . . Many engineers attributed the year's trend toward low-wing streamlined monoplanes to the early success of this Travel Air model, which consistently attained speeds well in excess of 200 miles an hour. . . ."

Sales of all aircraft during 1930 showed the effects of the 1929 stock market crash. A total of 1,937 commercial planes were built in America; and Travel Air still dominated the market in its class. A merger was completed with the Curtiss-Wright interests, and Travel Air became the Curtiss-Wright Airplane Company. Walter H. Beech, as its president, assumed charge of a large factory in St. Louis, in addition to the Wichita plant, and also became vice president of the Curtiss-Wright Sales Corporation at New York City, assuming charge of all commercial sales.

In 1931, economic conditions worsened, and the entire industry produced only 1,582 commercial aircraft. The Wichita plant was closed and Travel Air production was transferred to St. Louis. Walter H. Beech had to spend practically all of his time in New York fulfilling the duties of a "big-business" executive and director. These activities were not consistent with his constant desire to maintain an active personal part in aircraft design and construction. Late in 1931 he resigned, and soon afterward returned to Wichita.

Chapter 3

America came close to rock bottom in 1932. Crude oil sold for 10¢ a barrel, wheat for 25¢ a bushel, and General Motors stock was quoted at less than $8.00 a share, with no buyers. Bread lines and soup kitchens kept the unemployed from totally starving. The bonus army of jobless war veterans encamped in Washington. The entire aviation industry produced a total of only 549 commercial planes valued at a little more than two million dollars.

If there was ever a time for a man who had any money to hold on to it tightly, that was it. Walter H. Beech had accumulated a tidy sum from the sale of his holdings in Travel Air to the Curtiss-Wright interests. He could have played safe and waited out the depression at his ease, making it an occasion for a long vacation. He did not. He was a man with a fixed idea. Beech wanted to build the finest airplanes in the world; and the most drastic economic slump in history could not stop him.

So, in April, 1932, Walter H. Beech turned away from New York City and the circles of high finance to come home to Wichita. There, he and his wife, the former Olive Ann Mellor, who was his right-hand "man" in managerial and financial matters, organized the Beech Aircraft Company, predecessor to the present corporation. Walter H. Beech was president of the new company, and Olive Ann Beech, who had demonstrated extraordinary business ability as his assistant and office manager since she joined Travel Air in 1925 fresh from business college, was secretary-treasurer and director. Their associates were the people who had made up the management of Travel Air.

In small quarters rented in a depression-closed factory building, Beech and his crew went to work. Objective: to design and build a five-place biplane having the interior luxury and passenger comfort of a fine sedan, a top speed of 200 mph or better, a landing speed no higher than 60 mph, a non-stop range close to 1,000 miles, and easy controllability and sound

13

aerodynamic characteristics. An objective almost fantastically hopeful, considering the state of the aeronautical art in 1932.

Never for a moment conceding the impossibility of producing such an ideal plane, Beech dug deep into his savings to meet the payroll, defray overhead, buy supplies, tools, materials, parts, and instruments, and keep the job moving forward with his money and his own prodigious energy and forcefulness. It was much like the early days of Travel Air, with one important difference. In 1925, Beech could always put on his pilot's helmet and windbreaker, when the financial sledding was tough, and go out and win a race, or put on an exhibition, or fly a charter trip, and come back with enough money in his shirt pocket to meet the payroll. Few such opportunities existed in 1932, and Beech was too busy anyway to take advantage of them. He had a new airplane to build.

The first Beechcraft biplane made its initial flight on November 4, 1932. A week later, it was demonstrated to the public at the Wichita municipal airport. The flight test results showed a top speed of 201 mph, a cruising speed of 180 mph, a landing speed of 60 mph, a takeoff time of 12 seconds, a rate of climb of 1,600 feet per minute, and a ceiling of 21,500 feet. The near-impossible had been accomplished.

Walter H. Beech was gratified, but not completely satisfied. He never was; for he was always striving for perfection. The prototype Beechcraft had shown performance far surpassing anything in its class. But even before the tests were completed, Beech was busy planning improvements. Beechcraft No. 1 was sold to the Ethyl Corporation, and at the Miami Air Races in January 1933, flown by E. H. Wood, it captured the Texaco Trophy in a memorable closed-course race. Meanwhile Beech and his crew were designing a still better Beechcraft.

A full year elapsed — a year of incessant poring over engineering data and drawings, of designing and redesigning, of building and testing and rebuilding almost every part of the airplane — before the new Beechcraft was produced. The work was costly, and a lot more of Walter H. Beech's savings were needed to keep the company going; for most of its bookkeeping was done in red ink. Out of it all, a great airplane was taking shape. Beech and his engineers were making the most

14

First design of the Beech Aircraft Company was this Model 17R powered by a Wright 420 hp engine. Its top speed was 200-plus mph; its landing speed 60 mph. This airplane won the Texaco Trophy at the Miami Air Races in January 1933. Note experimental split-rudder air brake.

Production was well under way when Walter H. Beech posed in 1934 with this 225 hp B17L Beechcraft. The Model 17 has become a classic design; and decades later, dozens of well-kept Beech biplanes are still flying.

Former Travel Air buildings became Beechcraft plant and served as nucleus of present day Plant I and home offices. (Page 17)

15

". . . Devil Was Triumphant"

In early days a few of the settlers had the audacity to ride about in brightly colored coaches. There was no objection to riding in a man-carried sedan chair, or to making a journey on foot . . . but a coach! Heaven forbid! It must be of the devil. But, according to an early history, the devil was triumphant.

"My God! It Talks!"

Of course young Alexander Bell's contraption was "impractical". The customers at the Centennial Exposition (1876) didn't take it seriously. But Emperor Don Pedro of Brazil probably wanted to humor the young inventor. Gingerly he put his ear to the device. Smug. Smiling. These North Americans were a little mad, perhaps. But they were interesting. Suddenly the smile disappeared. Consternation! "My God!" exclaimed the Emperor, "It talks!"

Boys Threw Stones

In 1827 Sir Goldsworthy Gurney patented the steam coach—an early forerunner of the automobile. As the steam coach chugged along farmers dug trenches across the roads to impede its progress and small boys threw stones at it. In 1836 the English Parliament passed a law requiring that a man carrying a red flag should walk ahead of a steam coach to warn the people on the road.

"Better Come Back to the Farm, Son"

Thus did the father of Henry Ford urge his boy who had gone to Detroit and was learning the machinist's trade. Even before Henry Ford went to the farm where, according to his father, he was wasting his time . . . better to raise potatoes and peaches and apples.

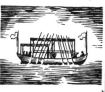

They needed, they had estimated, only eight horsepower. Since no one could provide it except at prohibitive weight, they turned to the...... After six weeks they.... gasoline engine they fou..... horsepow..... sult they..... en the..... Th.....

The propellers—there were two—were just as in the motor, and the Wrights got just as.... side would as they had with...... They were..... such a..... find.....

". . . He Is Crazy"

Long before Robert Fulton's steamships appeared, John Fitch was heard to remark: "Steamboats will be preferred to all other means of conveyance." Peter Brown, a shipsmith, glanced at the toe of his rough boot to cover his embarrassment. He held his tongue until John Fitch had gone back to his steamboat; then spoke Peter: "Poor fellow! What a pity he is crazy." Did you say crazy, Peter?

The propellers..... genius....the motor, an..... little help from the outside wor..... the engine. They didn't expect..... to make an air-screw. propellers on the open market..... almost the first persons who ever wanted such a..... such data.

"Witchcraft . . ."

The man who painted the "Mona Lisa" and the "Last Supper" was also a great scientist. Because of his scientific research he was forced at one time to flee an angry mob that whispered in hissing crescendo: "Witchcraft!" If a study of aerodynamics and gliding surfaces was witchcraft, then Leonardo da Vinci should have been burned with the rest of the witches.

"Just a Freak"

"Both Crazy!"

It was the belief of some of the farmers around Kitty Hawk that the Wright brothers were crazy—"Both crazy!" And yet, there probably never were two brothers who were more sober, level-headed and cautious. The terms "crazy" and "freak" are always quick to appear when someone has the courage to defy conventional beliefs.

"A Knave and a Fool!"

The first steamboat on the Great Lakes was Robert Fulton's "The Walk-in-the-Water" (1818). Surely by that time the people could see more clearly the future of the steamboat. True, there were some who did; but even then many there were who called Fulton "a knave, a fool and an enthusiast." History agrees that he was an enthusiast.

"Foolhardy . . ."

That one word was on the lips of millions on the morning of May 29, 1927. A young air mail pilot by the name of Charles Lindbergh took off from Curtiss Field on his way to Paris, that morning. A number of famous aviators were ready to do that very thing . . . had been waiting for favorable conditions, but here this young punk took off all by himself. And thereby brought interest in commercial aviation to a high pitch.

"Unimportant"

When John Stevens presented plans for an overland steam train before the New Jersey legislature in 1811 they refused to consider it on the grounds that they had important matters to consider and the train was decidedly not an important matter. Not an important matter, gentlemen? With more than two million square miles of land in your very back yard to be settled?

THAT'S what they said three years ago when Walter Beech announced plans for a luxurious cabin airplane that would travel 200 m.p.h., and could be landed on ordinary airports. "Some day, perhaps; not in our generation." *But the first Beechcraft exceeded that speed.* A few months ago when Mr. Beech announced he would build a 225 h.p., four-place cabin airplane that would travel 170 m.p.h. there was again much head shaking. "It will be just a freak." Again Mr. Beech and his engineers exceeded their estimates. The new 225 h.p. Beechcraft has a guaranteed top speed of 175 m.p.h. History is today repeating itself. The early critics of the Beechcraft are now busy trying to imitate its many SUPERIOR FEATURES! The Beechcraft is out in front . . . *and will stay there!*

The BEECH AIRCRAFT CO.

WICHITA, KANSAS

A Beech magazine advertisement published in 1934.

of an excellent basic design so generally overlooked that Beech Aircraft was the only manufacturer ever to use it in quantity production — the negative stagger biplane. To the basic advantages of this design — very favorable stall and recovery characteristics, optimum controllability at all speeds, high visibility for pilot, easy, quick ground servicing, and compactness — they added superlative streamlining, and a highly efficient, fast-acting, fully retractable landing gear.

Flight tests of the new Beechcraft B17L proved that the improvements devised since the prototype was constructed were sound. The plane was ready to go into production, with Walter H. Beech's reputation riding on its wings. So, early in 1934, Beech again became a full-fledged airplane manufacturer. Tooling for production was set up on a modest scale, and the world was told that Beech Aircraft was offering for sale three models of Beechcrafts: the B17L with a 225 hp Jacobs engine, cruising at 152 mph and topping 166; the 17R with a 450 hp Wright engine, designed to better 200 mph; and the A17F with a 650 hp Wright Cyclone engine, designed to top 240 mph.

Of the three models, the B17L proved best suited to the economic climate of those depressed times. Most of the 18 Beechcrafts built during 1934 were of the lowest-powered model. It cost more than other aircraft of equal or greater horsepower and seating capacity; but its higher performance more than made up for the difference. One of the first B17L biplanes went half-way around the world to Mr. M. Thaning, Danish counsel-general at Johannesburg, South Africa. With it Mr. Thaning easily broke almost every existing cross-country flight record in that part of the world.

The Cyclone-powered Beechcraft could show its flippers to the Army's standard pursuit ships any time in a speed contest, since the military service type pursuits of that day were credited with a speed of only 230 mph. But there were few buyers, in 1934, who were willing to invest the $18,000 or more necessary to purchase such extremely high performance.

Beech Aircraft meanwhile had returned to the scene of Walter H. Beech's previous successes — the Travel Air factory and airfield six miles east of downtown Wichita. Closed since 1931, its walls again echoed the sounds of aircraft production from April

17

23rd onward. It has remained Beechcraft's home ever since that date, with many additions which have dwarfed the size of the original buildings.

Chapter 4

Business picked up at Beech Aircraft in 1935, as it did almost everywhere. Production was doubled, 36 Beechcrafts being built during the year. Two new models were introduced: the B17B biplane, with a 285 hp Jacobs engine; and the B17R, an improved version of the 17R using a 420 hp Wright engine. Preliminary engineering work was begun on the Model 18 Beechcraft, a low-wing, all-metal, twin-engine monoplane intended as a six- to eight-place deluxe executive plane or feeder airline transport.

Somewhat reluctantly, Walter H. Beech dropped the Cyclone-powered Beechcraft from his line of aircraft. He liked the idea of building a commercial four-place luxury plane which could outrun the fastest military planes of its time. (The Gloster single-seater pursuit, then credited with being the fastest military ship in service, had an announced speed of 231 mph.) But he was a good enough business man to realize the limited market for such a plane; and he concentrated on delivering superlative performance with power plants economically practical for more widespread use.

A successful flight around the world by a B17R Beechcraft that year enhanced the growing international fame of Beech products. The east-west route was from North Beach, New York to Heston, England, by way of Canada, Alaska, Siberia, China, India, and North Africa. The trip was a pleasure jaunt undertaken by the Beechcraft's owner-pilot, Captain H. L. Farquhar, first secretary of the British legation at Mexico City. The plane was Captain Farquhar's second Beechcraft. He had owned one of the first B17L biplanes. With Mr. Fritz Beiler as his navigator, Captain Farquhar reported a very pleasant and uneventful trip. The Beechcraft was operated on seaplane floats over water, and conventional gear over land.

This achievement was a fitting prelude to Beechcraft's 1936 accomplishments. First, important improvements were made in the aircraft designs. The wing flaps were relocated, and the landing gear legs shortened, resulting in better landing, takeoff, and taxiing qualities. The improved biplanes were designated as the C17L (225 hp Jacobs) topping 166 mph; the C17B (285 hp Jacobs) topping 177; and the C17R (420 hp Wright) topping 202 mph. Among broadened promotion and sales activities was a news-making shipment of a new Model 17 biplane from Lakehurst, N. J. to Germany via a giant dirigible airship for a demonstration tour of Europe.

One of the tokens of this broadening of activities holds a place of honor today in Beech Aircraft's crowded trophy cases. It is the Frank E. Phillips Trophy, emblematic of victory in the Unlimited Race for licensed commercial aircraft which was the feature of the Mile-High Air Races at Denver, Colorado, on July 4th and 5th, 1936. Like the Thompson Trophy Race, this was a 50-mile event, run over a 5-mile closed course. Of the five planes which finished in the money, three were Beechcrafts. First place was taken by a C17R flown by Bill Ong at an average speed of 191.971 mph. Second and fourth place prizes also went to Beechcrafts — a showing which prompted a comment often repeated at later races — "It takes a Beechcraft to beat a Beechcraft."

Then Walter H. Beech played a long shot. Entries opened for Event No. 1 of the National Air Races — the Bendix Transcontinental Speed Dash, from Bendix, New Jersey to Los Angeles, California. Among the participants were veteran pilots flying some of the highest-powered planes in existence, including new twin-engine transports with advertised top speeds of 210 mph. Ignoring advice from conservatives who urged him not to hazard his reputation against such stiff competition, Beech entered the same C17R that had done so well at Denver in the coast-to-coast race. Mrs. Beech had a hand in the matter, too. She persuaded her husband that the demonstration of the Beechcraft's good qualities offered in the gruelling cross-country dash would be even more convincing if a woman were given the job of flying it. This, she argued, would be convincing proof that unlike some airplanes of that day, brute strength was not required to operate a Beechcraft.

Walter H. Beech grumbled a little, but finally consented. Mrs. Beech's candidate was Louise Thaden. Almost ten years before, Mrs. Thaden had made her first contact with aviation at the Travel Air factory, when she was working as secretary to J. H. Turner, a large stockholder of that company. From that moment on, tall, dark-haired Louise knew that she was born to fly. Mr. and Mrs. Beech arranged a job for her with the Travel Air distributor on the Pacific coast, in which she could learn to fly. She was an apt pupil. She broke altitude and endurance records in 1929 and 1932, and won many races flying Beech-built Travel Air planes. To warm up for the Bendix race, she set a national speed record for women on May 29th at St. Louis, Missouri, flying the C17R Beechcraft at a speed of 197.958 mph for a distance of 100 kilometers.

As her navigator, Mrs. Thaden chose another skilled woman pilot, Blanche Noyes. Aside from its racing identification markings, the only equipment which distinguished her plane from any other commercial C17R Beechcraft, when it crossed the starting line at the Bendix airport on the morning of the Bendix Race, was extra gasoline tankage in the rear seat.

Taking off from Bendix early on the morning of September 4th, Louise Thaden set the C17R Beechcraft down on the Los Angeles airport exactly 14 hours, 55 minutes and 1 second later, almost three-quarters of an hour sooner than her nearest competitor. She had won first place, and the coveted Bendix Trophy, in America's most famous cross-country race. She had set a new transcontinental speed record for women pilots, almost four hours better than the previous record. She earned $10,000 in prize money, and received the Harmon Trophy, awarded by the Ligue Internationale des Aviateurs, as "the outstanding woman pilot in the United States in 1936."

The results of the 1936 Bendix race were dramatic proof of what a commercial Beechcraft could do, in open competition with higher-powered and supposedly much faster aircraft. The Beechcraft was flown at only 68% of its rated horsepower throughout the race. Its total fuel consumption was 318 gallons

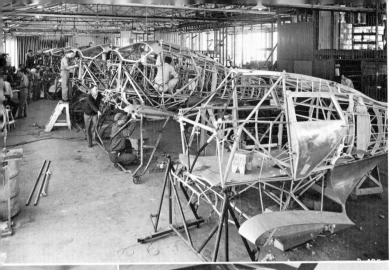

Each Beechcraft biplane that came from the assembly line was a product of painstaking and meticulous craftsmanship.

Louise Thaden changed from the leather jacket of open cockpit Travel Air days to a modish travel costume — and kept on winning races and setting new records in Beechcrafts. She won the 1936 Bendix Race in Model C17R.

Beech Aircraft built a total of five 600 hp Model 17 biplanes. Two were A17F models — like this speedy executive plane flown for Sanford Mills by Bob Fogg . . .

Three were D17W models — like this plane owned and flown by Jacqueline Cochran in setting new women's speed and altitude records and taking third place in the 1937 Bendix Race. (Pages 26, 27, 33)

Daily "Belly Landing" of C17B Beechcraft by pilot Bill Ong to demonstrate safety was staged at 1936 National Air Races and 1937 Miami Air Show.

A fleet of white ambulance-equipped D17R biplanes was de-livered to the government of the Republic of China in 1938. Camou-flage finish re-placed white on later deliveries. (Page 30)

The D17S Beech-craft won a 1938 Air Corps evalua-tion competition — and an order for biplanes to serve military and naval attaches at U. S. legations. (Page 30)

The day was clear and mild on Janu-ary 15, 1937 when Walter H. Beech approved the first flight of the new Model 18 — a design that endured for more than thirty years. (Pages 24, 25, 26)

— an average of better than 8 miles per gallon of fuel, against the constantly prevailing west-east head-winds. Its pilot and passenger reported that they were no more fatigued, after their one-day dash across the entire United States from ocean to ocean, than they would have been on a train or motor trip of equal duration.

Less sensational than the Bendix racing victory, but fundamentally more important as a demonstration of a safety feature exclusive to Beechcraft in its power class, was a special exhibition staged daily at the National Air Races of "belly landing" a C17B biplane with its landing gear entirely retracted. One of the major attractions of the entire show for pilots and airwise spectators, both at Los Angeles and at the 1937 Miami Air Show where it was repeated, it consisted of a quick climb to about 2,000 feet, where the engine was cut off and the propeller locked in a horizontal position. A dead stick landing was then made on the hard ground in front of the grandstand, the Beechcraft sliding to a halt after a run of 170 feet or less. The whole affair required less than five minutes to perform. The plane was a standard commercial biplane, carrying as extra equipment only a pair of sled-like steel runners mounted on the bottom of the fuselage, to protect the fabric covering from damage, and a simple propeller brake, controlled from the cockpit, to lock the propeller and thus prevent its tips from striking the earth and bending upon contact with the ground. After each demonstration, the plane was hoisted up from the turf, the landing gear was extended, and it taxied away, ready to repeat the show on the next day.

This demonstration publicly proved what some Beechcraft owners had already learned — that under emergency conditions, the Beechcraft biplane could safely be landed with gear retracted on almost any kind of terrain, no matter how rough, or in water, without major damage to the plane or injury to its occupants. Experience with landings of this kind had shown that the repair expense rarely exceeded 4% of the cost of the airplane. The damages generally were confined to bent propeller blades, scratched fuselage bottom and lower wing underside covering, and sometimes deformed lower cowling and fairings. It was a very cheap form of insurance for both plane and passengers. The extremely short landing run following a belly landing enabled the Beechcraft to be landed in almost any halfway open area; even a city lot would suffice. Successful belly landings were made on plowed ground, on hillsides, and even in pine woods where trees eight inches in diameter were mowed down by the airplane in its landing run. This was another advantage of Beechcraft's retractable landing gear over the fixed type gear used on other aircraft, in addition to its gains in aerodynamic efficiency.

In keeping with the improvements made in its products, and its daringly aggressive promotional demonstrations, Beech Aircraft revised its corporate structure. On September 16, 1936, the Beech Aircraft Corporation became the successor of the former company. The same group of people, headed by Walter H. Beech, remained in full active control of the new corporation's affairs; but capitalization was increased from $25,000 to an immediate paid-in total exceeding $100,000, and an eventual authorized total capital stock structure of a half-million dollars, at par of $1.00 per share. Thus a strong financial foundation was provided for future growth.

Chapter 5

Whether in the case of a family or a corporation, ownership of the home it lives in implies a degree of stability and permanence not otherwise attainable. The Beech Aircraft Corporation attained this goal on January 6, 1937, buying the former Travel Air factory at Wichita from the Curtiss-Wright interests lock, stock and barrel for $150,000. Beechcraft had a home of its own.

From its hangar doors emerged, for its first public flight demonstration on January 15th, a new kind of Beechcraft — the Model 18 all-metal twin-engine monoplane. Walter H. Beech's bid for leadership in the executive and feeder airline transport field, the Model 18 was another expression of his constant conviction that high speeds and brilliant performance could be attained at no sacrifice of the desirable control and slow landing qualities inherent without structural complications only in consistently low or at most, moderate wing loadings. His engineers had achieved this goal with the Beechcraft biplane by the use of lightweight but strong wood wing, and steel tubing fuselage construction, plus extremely thorough streamlining and a landing gear that practically melted into the fuselage, producing no drag whatever when it was retracted. They achieved the same results with the monoplane largely through applying the same principles of reducing weight, carefully streamlining all exposed structures, and retracting both main landing wheels and tail wheel into neat, self-fairing nacelle and fuselage housings during flight.

The backbone of the Model 18 Beechcraft was a truss type center section built up by welding together high-strength chrome molybdenum steel tubing into virtually a one-piece structure, which was heat-treated to a strength of 180,000 p.s.i. This single structure carried all of the concentrated loads imposed on the aircraft in flight and on the ground. To it were attached the engine mounts, landing gear and wing root fittings, and fuselage main load fittings. So light in weight that one man could lift it, this center section saved hundreds of pounds over any alternate means of construction, and proved so strong that no failures were ever reported in service.

Heat-treating, long used in highly stressed members of the biplane structure such as the landing gear truss and members, was also liberally applied elsewhere in the monoplane as a weight-saving and strength-boosting device. The main wing spar was a truss-type heat-treated structure built up by welding chrome molybdenum tubing. It carried the major wing loads. The major landing gear and tail wheel elements were also heat-treated chrome molybdenum structures. One of the busiest items of special equipment in the Beech factory was the gas-fired vertical heat-treat furnace, for a long time the largest unit of its kind west of the Mississippi river, accommodating charges ten feet in length and four feet in diameter. Such equipment was expensive both to set up and operate; but it more than paid its way in terms of higher Beechcraft performance and greater owner satisfaction with the finished product.

The first Model 18 Beechcraft showed excellent performance with engines of economical size. Powered with two 350 hp Wright engines, it had a top speed of better than 200 mph, a cruising speed of 192 mph, a range of more than 1,000 miles with full load of pilot, co-pilot, and six passengers, and a landing speed of less than 60 mph.

A dramatic demonstration of efficiency and safety was offered by a Model 18 Beechcraft equipped with two 285 hp Jacobs engines. Fully loaded, it was flown on a round trip, Philadelphia-New York, on only one engine at cruising power with the propeller in high pitch. The left engine propeller was completely stopped by a propeller brake.

While production was getting under way on the Model 18 monoplane, Walter H. Beech did not neglect his program of constantly improving the biplane in every way possible. During 1937, experiments and flight tests proved the desirability of using aileron type, full length flaps mounted on the trailing edge of the lower wing, and relocating the ailerons on the upper wing. Redesign of the empennage on models of 350 hp and upward was also completed, providing a full cantilever type horizontal and vertical stabilizer structure of greater cleanness and higher control efficiency. The biplanes incorporating these improvements were designated as the D17A (350 hp Wright), the D17R (420 hp Wright), and the D17S, a new model using the 450 hp Wasp Junior engine. The improved Jacobs-powered biplanes became the E17B (285 hp) and the F17D models.

The D17W biplane, another of the new series, was an experiment, commercially speaking, intended to test the market for a modernized version of the Cyclone-powered Beechcraft offered for sale in 1934. Results were much the same as before. Only three D17W biplanes were sold, largely because Beech had achieved such a high standard of performance with the 450 hp biplanes that the plus offered by the 600 hp engine was not sufficient to justify its additional cost.

One of those D17W Beechcrafts, however, managed to make quite a record for itself. Flown by its owner, Miss Jacqueline Cochran, it was used to set new U. S. women's speed records of 203.895 mph over a course of 1,000 kilometers, on July 26,

1937. Two days later, Miss Cochran with the D17W set another record of 200.712 mph over a 100-kilometer course. Its performance in these trial runs was so pleasing that Miss Cochran did not hesitate to enter the Beechcraft in the 1937 Bendix Race, against formidable opposition which included special racing planes and one-place military pursuit monoplanes having double the horsepower of her ship. The running of the race, from Burbank, California to Cleveland, Ohio, proved that at last the military and racing plane designers had caught up with the speed standards set up by Walter H. Beech with his economically powered commercial Beechcrafts. A single-place pursuit and a single-place racer, each with 1,200 hp engines, led Miss Cochran's 600 hp Beechcraft across the finish line. Trailing her, however, were another 1,200 hp pursuit plane, a twin-engine transport, and a racing ship, to say nothing of a couple of others that dropped by the wayside. Merely to finish the gruelling transcontinental dash in such fast company would have been a distinct moral victory; but winning third place was a real accomplishment, both for Miss Cochran and Beechcraft.

The same D17W, flown by Max Constant, was the winner in a thrilling finish to the 1,120 mile cross-country Macfadden Race from Floyd Bennett Field, New York to Miami, Florida on January 7, 1938. Less than one minute after the Beechcraft crossed the finish line at Miami to win first place a twin-engine transport streaked past the judges' stand in second place. The winning Beechcraft averaged 204.277 mph; its competitor 204.069 mph. In the 1938 Bendix Race, the D17W, again piloted by Max Constant, competed with its owner, Jacqueline Cochran, who flew a pursuit plane to win first place. Second place went to another pursuit ship; third place to a commercial monoplane rebuilt for racing purposes; fourth place to the D17W; and fifth prize money to a D17S Beechcraft with a 450 hp Wasp Jr. engine flown by Ross Hadley. On January 7, 1939 the D17W again proved its mettle, winning the New York to Miami Sports record with Max Constant as pilot, flying 1,195 miles in 5 hours 43 minutes.

While widely publicized, these and other racing victories were, of course, minor in importance compared with Beech Aircraft's more solidly constructive accomplishments. The rate of production was steadily rising, and Beechcrafts were being delivered with constantly increasing frequency to individual and corporate owners not only throughout the United States, but all over the world. Above the African veldt, the open ranges of New Zealand, the jungles of the Philippines, the frozen lands of Alaska and the Canadian Northwest, the plains of Patagonia — wherever men needed fast, safe transportation without regard to the terrain below, Beechcrafts flew.

An important addition was made to Beech Aircraft's official family on March 1, 1937, when John P. Gaty joined the company as vice president and director of sales. With an excellent background as an engineer, sales executive, and pilot, he brought to Beech a combination of abilities highly valuable for aggressive exploitation of its then well-developed line of aircraft. He was a commercial pilot with an instrument rating, and owned the fourth B17L Beechcraft built — a circumstance which resulted in his acquaintance with Walter H. Beech.

The company's financial position also was further strengthened that year, when the New York Curb approved the listing of 239,049 shares of Beech common stock, at a par value of $1 per share, with authority to add 45,951 shares upon official notice of issuance. Beech Aircraft was commanding respect in financial circles, as well as among airmen.

Chapter 6

Walter H. Beech and his associates had worked long and hard for the day when Beechcraft sales would exceed the million-dollar-a-year mark. In 1938 that goal was reached, with $141,398 to spare. The company was growing up. The biplane models were dominating the private-owner and commercial market in the 285 to 450 hp class. And Model 18 twin-engine Beechcrafts were finding favor with airlines and executive users.

There was at that time no market among airlines in the United States for the Model 18, because theirs were trunk-line operations requiring larger equipment, and feeder lines were almost non-existent. Beechcraft biplanes were purchased by foreign airlines and by many charter operators, who found that their speed and comfort possessed a great deal of profitable appeal to their customers. Very few operators, however, could make the investment needed for modern twin-engine equipment.

The airline picture was different outside the United States. In Canada, feeder lines had long existed to serve territories located away from the single east-west transcontinental rail and air route. A fleet of Model 18 Beechcrafts went to Prairie Airways, of Edmonton, Alberta, in 1938. An 18A, operated on interchangeable ski or float landing gear, joined the fleet of Starratt Airways and Transportation Ltd., at Hudson, Ontario, which already owned an E17B biplane and a Beech-built Travel Air. Another 18A went to Aerovias de Puerto Rico. Operated on seaplane floats, this plane often landed on the open sea, in inter-island service, when waves five and six feet high were being kicked up by the wind. Its service records were perfect, even under these exigent conditions.

As an executive transport, the twin-engine Beechcraft also found a good market. The first Model 18 built went to Mr. Harry K. Coffey, an Oregon insurance executive who used it extensively to visit his branch offices in Alaska and throughout the Pacific Northwest. Another one went to Sucesion J. Serralles, Puerto Rican sugar growers and refiners, as the third unit of a fleet of Beechcrafts used in supervising their plantations throughout the islands. John David Eaton, Canadian department store magnate, bought an 18D Beechcraft for business use. These were typical of the buyers who found the Model 18 Beechcraft best suited to their needs.

An item in the Wichita newspapers of July 29, 1938 told of a visit to the Beech factory by Lieutenant Colonel Dwight Eisenhower, chief of staff of the American military mission to the Philippine Commonwealth, for the purpose of inspecting a Model 18 Beechcraft purchased by the Philippine Army Air Corps and specially equipped for aerial photography. There was a prophetic note in this visit by the officer who was later to liberate Europe, and become the 34th U. S. President; for the Philippine Army Beechcraft was the first of many thousands of Model 18 twins produced for the armed services of the United Nations.

The fast-gathering war clouds brought other orders also to supplement the steadily growing commercial sales. A fleet of D17R biplanes fitted out with ambulance equipment — stretcher and medicine kit — was built for the Chinese government, fighting its then undeclared war with Japan. Painted pure white, with the Red Cross emblem in red on the fuselage the Beechcrafts of this fleet made a striking appearance. It developed that Japanese pursuit pilots found the Red Cross emblem to be an excellent aiming point for their machine guns, and took great delight in trying to shoot down the unarmed ambulance planes. The white paint was soon replaced with a less conspicuous color; and a later group of Beechcrafts built for ambulance use in China was painted in camouflage finish at the factory.

Evaluation competitions were held by the U. S. Army Air Corps in November 1938 to select single-engine aircraft for use by military and naval attaches stationed at the American legations at London, Rome, Paris, and Mexico City, and in March 1939 to select twin-engine planes for top-ranking personnel transport. The first of these competitions was won by a D17S Beechcraft biplane, and the second by an 18S twin-engine Beechcraft. Work was started in 1939 on the Government contracts, which totaled more than a million dollars altogether. These were Beechcraft's first orders from the armed services of the United States, the only previous Government business having been for biplanes ordered by the Civil Aeronautics Authority. Walter H. Beech had never sought to enter the field of specialized military aircraft design, preferring to build commercial aircraft offering optimum performance. The results of the evaluation competitions were excellent evidence of his success, and the fact that the Beechcrafts delivered to the Air Corps were standard commercial planes, with only slight modifications in some details, was further corroboration.

Also ordered by the Air Corps were 18S Beechcrafts modified for high altitude aerial photography. Designated as type F-2, these Beechcrafts were required to operate for several hours at altitudes of 25,000 feet and above. Surveying vital

To expedite his business travel, insurance executive Harry K. Coffey bought the first Model 18 built — the flagship of what was to be the twin Beech "Air Fleet of American Business". (Page 29)

The Model 18 performed brilliantly on floats — operating with Aerovias de Puerto Rico on open seas with waves five to six feet high. (Page 29)

This was one of a fleet of Model 18A transports built for Prairie Airways of Edmonton, Canada for use in Canada. (Page 29)

Starratt Airways and Transportation, Ltd. enlarged their Beech-built fleet serving the Canadian bush country with this Model 18A on skis and floats. (Page 29)

31

Pioneer and victor — this 18S Beech-craft won a 1939 Air Corps evaluation competition, and the 1940 Mac-fadden Trophy. (Pages 34, 35)

"Limousine of generals" was the Air Corps' first fleet of C-45 (Model 18S) Beechcrafts ordered in 1940. (Page 30)

A fleet of Air Corps F-2 (18S) Beechcrafts mapped the route of the vital Alaska Highway from 25,000-ft. altitudes. (Pages 30, 33)

The Republic of China ordered a fleet of 18R twin Beechcrafts equipped for advanced bombing and gunnery training and tactical use. (Pages 35, 36)

areas of the North American continent, they played an important part in preparations for national defense, including mapping the route of the Alaska highway. Theirs was an important part in aerial reconnaissance, an art which was to prove its inestimable value in World War II and in the decades of the cold war to follow.

Beech sales continued to increase as a result of normal commercial activities during 1939, net delivered sales at the end of the fiscal year on September 30 totaling $1,328,296. Only a few biplanes for the Army and Navy were included in this total. Export sales increased to such an extent that at the end of the year, Beechcrafts were being flown by owners in 23 foreign countries all over the world, from the tropics to the polar regions.

The popularity of Beechcrafts in remote areas of the earth arose from several factors, among them Walter H. Beech's own background and experiences. Born and raised on a farm in the Tennessee hills, many miles away from the nearest large city, Beech had seen that machinery and equipment should be simple in design, sturdy, and easy to repair, in order to be of utmost usefulness to its owner. His European experience as a salesman for the White Company added to this impression. And as an early-day "barnstorming" pilot, flying all over the United States at a time when aircraft repair stations were few and far between, Beech had personally performed many "bed-sheet and bailing wire" repair jobs, and learned the bread-and-butter importance to a pilot of an airplane that could be restored to flyable condition by the use of whatever materials were at hand. He had seen the importance, too, of mechanism, structures, and finishes that could stand up equally well under the bitter sub-zero cold of the western plains states, and the semi-tropical heat and humidity of the deep Southland. The airplanes which he built reflected this hard-earned knowledge. In addition to their ability to carry large payloads safely and swiftly non-stop for long distances, Beechcrafts were designed with rugged sturdiness, and maximum possible ease of adjustment and maintenance, always in mind. Manufacturing standards included the liberal use of special protective finishes and processes, affording protection to the airplanes under all climatic extremes, from tropical heat and humidity to polar cold. The first cost of this method of construction was high, but it paid handsome dividends in the long run to Beechcraft owners.

For example, a Model 18 Beechcraft was purchased by the Hudson's Bay Company of Canada, for use in contacting fur trading posts located in the Canadian Northwest Territory, sometimes north of the Arctic Circle. During one of these trips a landing was made on snow-covered frozen muskeg, and a wing tip was torn off by a concealed stump. Hundreds of miles from civilization, the airplane crew hammered out a replacement from sheet metal taken from an oil barrel, fastened it in place with stove bolts and wood screws, and flew the Beechcraft safely back to Winnipeg. It was then flown on to the factory at Wichita, where inspection showed the plane to be in excellent condition, except for the damaged wing tip, despite the rough landing and the hundreds of hours of arduous service which had preceded it.

There was little time in those busy days for racing or record-smashing flights; but Beechcrafts consistently made headlines whenever the chance was offered. Miss Jacqueline Cochran set a national women's altitude record on March 24, 1939 at Palm Springs, California, attaining an officially recorded altitude of 30,052.43 feet in a D17W Beechcraft biplane. In a demonstration tour of Central America, Beechcraft set a new record for flight between Bogota and Barranquilla, Colombia, in a standard production Model 18S twin engine Beechcraft, covering the 450-mile distance in one hour and 54 minutes at an average speed of 237 mph. It was then flown non-stop from Maracay, Venezuela to Miami, Florida, 1,350 miles, in exactly six hours. This was the first known direct flight between these two points. Again, Beechcraft had pioneered new trails in the skies.

Chapter 7

It was fitting that at the beginning of 1940, a standard commercial engine Beechcraft scored the most impressive victory

34

ever achieved by any commercially licensed airplane in open racing competition. Before the year was over, Beech Aircraft became an important entrant in the most serious competition of all history . . . the race against time to overcome more than a decade of preparation for world conquest by the fascist powers, and to equip the United States air services with the vast numbers of modern aircraft needed for victory in World War II.

The racing event which auspiciously opened this fateful year was the On-to-Miami Race for the Macfadden Trophy. On the morning of January 6, the sleek cream and crimson-colored twin-engine commercial Model 18S Beechcraft which had won the Air Corps Wright Field evaluation competitions in 1939 took off from snow-covered Lambert Field at St. Louis, Missouri, with Chief Pilot H. C. Rankin at the controls and Walter H. Beech as co-pilot. Just 4 hours and 37 minutes later, the Beechcraft crossed the finish line at Miami, Florida, completing the 1,084-mile cross-country non-stop run at an average speed of better than 234 mph. Its Wasp Jr. engines were operated at an average of 52½% of their rated 450 horsepower for the duration of the race, and although 330 hours had been logged on each engine up to that time, with only routine servicing, the total oil consumption for both engines during the race was 1½ quarts. Total fuel consumption was 208 gallons, for an average of 5.22 miles per gallon.

Victory in the Macfadden race heightened the interest of commercial and private buyers in the 18S and all other types of Beechcrafts. As a result, commercial sales continued to increase. Governmental agencies were likewise interested in the proof of efficient performance offered by the results of the race. The Brazilian government ordered a fleet of Beechcraft biplanes for its naval air transport and patrol service. Additional biplanes were ordered by the U. S. Army and Navy for personnel transport use. And the Chinese government, which had acquired firsthand experience with Beechcraft performance through operating its fleet of ambulance transport biplanes, placed a ¾ million dollar order in February for a group of Model 18 Beechcrafts equipped as advanced training and light tactical bombers. Work on the Chinese bombers was started immediately.

The importance of this Chinese order soon became apparent. In April, an economy-minded Congress, influenced by the illusory stalemate of the European war at the Maginot line, passed an appropriations bill providing funds for a total of only 47 new airplanes for the U. S. Air Forces for the fiscal year of 1941. Only a few days later, the Nazis loosed their blitzkrieg on the low countries. Their attacks spearheaded by overwhelming mass airpower, Hitler's hordes soon overran Denmark, Norway, the Netherlands, Belgium, Luxembourg, and France. The Luftwaffe made a shambles of England's industrial cities and ports; and only the Nazis' mad preoccupation with London as an aerial target prevented the total collapse of British industries.

The lesson was clear. On May 16, President Roosevelt called on the aircraft industry to build the then enormous amount of 50,000 airplanes. The way was opened for the Air Corps to negotiate for the planes needed to oppose fascist airpower. Because of various legal and financial obstacles, however, it was not until August and September that Beech's first large contracts could be signed. Meanwhile, commercial production had been suspended, except for priority orders, in July; and the company strained its resources and its credit standing to the utmost limits, in an effort to expand its facilities to meet impending production demands. Capital for operating funds and expansion of the plant was finally obtained from the Reconstruction Finance Company, after the company had risked all its resources to start the expansion program moving.

The experience gained from designing and building the Chinese bombers meanwhile proved its worth. On an inspection tour of aircraft factories, the Commanding General of the Air Forces, H. H. Arnold, saw the Chinese bomber version of the Model 18 Beechcraft, and at once ordered 150 airplanes similarly equipped for use as bomber trainers. This was the first of several orders for the plane which became the Army AT-11, or Navy SNB-1, bombing and gunnery trainer. In the AT-11, more than 90% of the Air Forces bombardiers were to learn their skills during World War II. Other Air Forces contracts awarded in 1940 called for AT-7, or Navy SNB-2, navigation trainers, in which 90% or more of Air Forces navigators learned how to direct American bombers to the target, and home again. Additional C-45 personnel transports were also ordered, for top-ranking officers. Almost two years before Pearl Harbor, the Model 18 Beechcraft was well on the way to becoming one of the most versatile types of aircraft in military service throughout the war.

During the last three months of 1940, while engineering and tooling for vastly multiplied production was rushed to completion, the company's new buildings were erected. The weather was an implacable enemy; for the fall and winter of 1940 were the wettest recorded in the history of the Wichita weather bureau. The construction area was a sea of almost bottomless mud. But the work was pushed forward nevertheless; and in a period of 83 days, two large assembly buildings, each having a clear span of 140 feet, and two fabrication buildings, each having a clear span of 100 feet, comprising a total floor area exceeding 300,000 square feet, were constructed. The buildings were of wood, being at that time among the largest structures ever built with 140-foot wood trusses. This type of construction reduced cost, saved steel vitally needed for other National Defense purposes, and reduced construction time. There was nothing fancy about them; Walter H. Beech and his associates never went in for needless extravagance. But they were well and strongly built; had all the furnishings and accessories needed for efficient production of airplanes and employee comfort; and farsightedly (and very fortunately) were designed so that additional working area could be gained by installing mezzanine floors and balconies. Jokes were made, at the time of their construction, about the usefulness of these buildings after the National Defense emergency had passed. "Splendid headquarters for an owl farm," was a favorite proposal of the jesters. Seriously, however, it was the management's hope that the new facilities would be useful to the company after the war clouds had rolled away. To that end every effort was made to keep down expense and avoid over-expansion, mindful always, however, of the company's commitments under the Defense program, which amounted at the end of the year to a backlog of orders exceeding 22½ million dollars.

Chapter 8

On January 2, 1941, a typical raw, cold Kansas winter day, the company's new buildings were first put into use for assembly of AT-7 and AT-11 Beechcrafts. Still uncompleted, the assembly areas lacked heating, and lighting was temporary. The temperature within the buildings was kept barely above freezing by improvised salamanders — oil barrels pierced with holes and filled with burning coke. They gave forth more fumes and smoke than heat; but they did serve to keep the workmen's hands from freezing fast to the cold dural skins of the airplanes. Not a man complained. Personal discomfort was waved aside, in the knowledge that there was a vitally important job to be done; that the Air Forces needed training planes more urgently than any other types of aircraft in existence, to school a mighty air army for America's defense. The parking lots, too, could not be surfaced because of the continuous wet weather; and employees' cars had to be towed into and out of the muddy parking areas with tractors. Beechcrafters accepted this condition philosophically and uncomplainingly, and cheerfully put in long hours of overtime in order to get the job done.

The coming of spring eased these conditions. In spite of a 100% dilution of skilled employees with new personnel untrained in aircraft manufacture, the average monthly production in pounds of airframe had by April, 1941 tripled the average monthly production during 1940. The production rate continued to rise steadily throughout the year.

Beech engineers were very busy with design changes intended to speed production, and adapt the basic commercial designs for the most effective military usage. In addition to the AT-11 and AT-7 designs, and variations therefrom for different uses, they produced a unique special-purpose variant of the Model

38

More than 90%
of the U. S.
bombardiers in
World War II
received their
training in the
Beechcraft AT-11.

SNB-1, Navy
version of the
AT-11, would
continue in active
service years after
the war ended.

Beechcraft C-45A
transports were
ordered to carry
military and
government
leaders.

Three shifts of employees worked around the clock to build AT-11 bombing and gunnery trainers during the war years.

JRB-1 Special Observation and Utility Transport for the Navy was another wartime version of the versatile Twin Beech.

Beechcraft trainers and transports could be seen on the flight lines of most U. S. military bases.

18 for the Navy. Designated as the JRB-1 utility transport, it served as a "mother ship" or flying control point for pilotless radio-controlled target aircraft, which were eventually evolved into tactically useful controllable flying bombs. A special extension of the cockpit roof provided visibility in all directions for the JRB-1 co-pilot, who controlled the target aircraft.

At the request of the Air Forces, T. A. Wells and his engineers also created an entirely new type of aircraft, the AT-10 Beechcraft twin-engine advanced pilot trainer. In it at least 50% of the Army's multi-engine pilots received their transitional training. Designed at a time when aluminum was critically scarce, the AT-10 Beechcraft was constructed entirely of plywood, except for the cowlings and cockpit enclosure. Ease and speed of manufacture on a large scale was also a prime factor in its design; yet it proved to have superior performance to that of similar airplanes and became the favorite trainer of its type.

Throughout this expansion of facilities and personnel for production of twin-engine Beechcrafts, the biplane was not overlooked. The demonstrated efficiency of the Model 17, with its high cruising and low landing speed, ample range, and comfortable passenger accommodations, made it an ideal light personnel and utility transport. The D17S biplane became the Army's UC-43, and the Navy's GB-1 and GB-2 transport. Identical in all but slight details with the commercial version, it went into accelerated production in a factory of its own of 50,000 square feet at the south end of the Beech airport, which had been increased in size to an area of 320 acres, permitting a runway nearly a mile long into the prevailing winds.

Together with the enlargement of the company's physical plant and number of employees, its program of employee training courses, begun in 1940, was enlarged. At its peak, more subjects were offered under this program than is customary in universities, enabling employees to increase their skills in all possible phases of their work. This was the company's solution of the problem common in those days to the entire aircraft industry, of raising the knowledge and skill level of inexperienced personnel to the extent needed to meet production demands. The Beech policy had always been to upgrade its own people by helping them to make the most of their own capabilities; and throughout the war years, as in normal times, this policy was upheld consistently.

It was fortunate that the policies and methods hastily determined for expansion were soundly conceived; for on May 29th, an avalanche of orders descended upon Beech Aircraft that quadrupled the backlog to a total exceeding $82 million. The Army Air Forces wanted more AT-7s, AT-11s, and AT-10s by the hundreds; and the Netherlands goverment obtained Air Forces approval for the purchase of a fleet of AT-11 bombing trainers. Up to that time, the job Beech had undertaken to do seemed difficult. Now, it appeared almost impossible. In fact, one of America's foremost production authorities, visiting the Beech plant on an inspection tour soon afterward, bluntly declared that it would be impossible for the company to meet its delivery schedules. That, as the record proved, was one of the few wrong guesses he made in a long and distinguished career; and he apologized handsomely, some months later, for under-estimating the ability of Beechcrafters and their management to rise to an emergency.

The quadrupling of the company's contractual obligations did not result in a corresponding multiplication of its facilities. Additional useful space was gained within the existing buildings by installation of mezzanine and balcony floors; and the only major addition of any size was a flight hangar of about 45,000 square feet. Receiving, warehousing, shipping, and other autonomous activities were housed in warehouses, storerooms, and vacant buildings all over Wichita, which were occupied on leases expiring at the end of the war emergency period. At the peak of production, almost as much leased space was being utilized in this manner as the working area of the main factory. Efficiency was sustained by close coordination of the satellite operations with those at the Beech airport; and over-expansion of the permanent facilities was avoided, with a resulting saving of time, materials, and many dollars of American taxpayers' money.

The War Years

Chapter 9

The Japanese attack on Pearl Harbor on December 7, 1941 found Beechcrafters and their company ready in all respects to meet the demands of total war. Plant expansion was virtually completed. Nearly 6,000 men and women, the majority without experience but eager to do their part, were working together as a team. Even while learning the complex arts of aircraft building, they increased the output in pounds of airframe to four times the 1940 production; and the production rate was rising steadily as their skills increased.

The knowledge that their country was at last irrevocably committed to fight for its existence, of course, provided a great patriotic stimulus to the efforts of all employees. To this incentive a further motive was added when, a few days after America entered the war, the Beech Efficiency Incentive Plan was adopted. Unique in American industry in its particulars, this plan in effect made every employee a partner with whom the company shared the fruits of his and its resultful labors. As first conceived, the plan was based on a division every three months of 50% of the company's profits among all employees, each one participating without regard to rank, position, or duties, in direct proportion to his earnings during the quarter. Assuming, for example, that half of the profits earned during a given three-month period amounted to 20% of the total payroll for that period, an employee whose wages during the period totaled $600 received 20% of that amount, or $120, as his Beech Efficiency Incentive Plan earnings. If his wages or salary totaled $900, his incentive earnings came to $180; and so on.

Inauguration of the Beech Efficiency Incentive Plan resulted in a tremendous increase in operating efficiency. Every employee exerted the utmost efforts to reduce waste and spoilage, to increase output, and to cooperate with all other employees, for the obvious reason that he had a direct personal stake in the results of the whole operation. The effect was to quicken delivery of thousands of Beechcrafts needed for the prosecution of the war. And, because at the insistence of the Beech management, all of the company's contracts were negotiated on a fixed price basis, the incentive plan substantially reduced the cost of those airplanes to the taxpayers, by enabling the company to reduce voluntarily the contract price per unit.

As a result of the workings of contract renegotiation, it later became necessary to change the basis for incentive plan payments, from profit-sharing to a percentage of payment based on increase in pounds of airframe produced per man-hour compared with a base quarterly period. But throughout the war, and afterward, the Beech Efficiency Incentive Plan continued in operation and provided an unfailing motive for employees to do their best at all times. The plan proved so successful that with suitable adaptations, it was adopted, with Government approval, by several other highly regarded aircraft manufacturers.

At the beginning of 1942, therefore, the outlook was excellent for production achievements exceeding all past performances. Dollar volume had jumped upward from about 2½ million dollars in 1940 to almost 14 million (including work in process) in 1941, when emphasis was as much on expansion of facilities as on actual production. It was to reach far more than 60 million dollars before the calendar year of 1942 ended; and unit deliveries of completed Beechcrafts were to run well into the thousands. In terms of pounds of airframe produced, 1942 results showed an increase of more than 8.6 times over 1941 output.

A very substantial factor in this attainment was the spirit of loyalty, cooperation, and willingness shown by all employees. In no enterprise directed by Walter H. Beech had there ever been any excessive paternalism or sentimentality; but the people who worked with him, unexpressive though he was, knew that their interests and his were always closely linked, not opposed. The inauguration of the Beech Efficiency Incentive Plan was conclusive proof. Beechcrafters expressed their feelings not only in doing their jobs efficiently, but in many other ways, all helpful to production and to the war effort. In 1942, and every

44

Walter H. Beech
and Olive Ann
Beech view war-
time production
lines at Plant I.

Because aluminum
was scarce, the
AT-10 multi-
engine pilot trainer
was built of
plywood, except
for cowlings and
cockpit enclosure.

AT-11 production
line photo was
published through-
out the Allied
countries to show
America's strength.

In Spring 1943, Beech completed its AT-10 contracts with the delivery of its 1,771st plywood trainer to the Air Corps. (Page 51)

At least 50% of the Army's multi-engine pilots received their transitional training in the Beechcraft AT-10.

Victory formation included air crews and Beechcraft AT-11 trainers.

year thereafter during the war, they invested 20% or more of their earnings in War Bonds. They staged a voluntary drive to boost production to a new high figure during the first week in April, naming the occasion "MacArthur Week" in honor of the heroic defenders of the Philippines. In their very few leisure hours, they produced a two-day carnival which netted more than $10,000 donated to military service organizations. More than 1,000 employees, men and women alike, volunteered to serve on their own time in the Beech Reserve Guards, Guardettes, and Volunteer Fire Department, to help protect the plant and company property in the event of any emergency.

As the velocity of production increased progressively from week to week, various ingenious methods developed for swift, efficient manufacture in facilities of minimum size and cost proved their merit. The large number of types of Beechcrafts produced simultaneously on the same premises, and the scarcity of materials, prompted the choice of a lot production system rather than straight-line mass production. Under lot production, sub-assemblies and major parts were built in lots of 20 to 50, rather than in the total quantities necessary to complete hundreds of airplanes. Production quantities of smaller parts were in appropriate amounts. The finished parts were stored in stockrooms carrying a minimum possible inventory to keep ahead of final assembly requirements. The day-to-day needs of the assembly lines were supplied from position line stockrooms, each carrying only the parts needed for installation at a given position on the lines. As a logical corollary of this system, employees were permanently assigned to each position, and thus quickly gained specialized experience in the installations made at their position. At the same time, their work was sufficiently varied to avoid fatigue induced by monotony.

The lot production system worked splendidly. Under it, an excellent balance of use of all facilities was attained. Fabrication and sub-assembly departments were free to meet the continuous needs of the final assembly lines, and no "bottlenecks" occurred as they might if work had been concentrated on hundreds or thousands of one item, to the neglect of other essential components of the complete airframes. Design changes, which were not infrequent as the varying needs of the Air

Forces became apparent from service experience, could be made with maximum ease. Close scheduling and control of production, and a high degree of interdepartmental coordination and cooperation, were essential to the success of the system. These were forthcoming as the joint result of alert management and the willing and helpful spirit of all employees. There was no buck-passing, and every employee, regardless of his departmental affiliation, served as a voluntary production expediter to prevent any impedance to the smooth flow of production.

The importance of another device adopted by Beech Aircraft to do a big job with relatively small permanent facilities was also demonstrated as output of completed Beechcrafts steadily rose. That device was subcontracting, on a scale which previously had not been attempted by any aircraft manufacturer. Its importance in the Beech way of getting the job done is shown by the fact that of all the parts and assemblies that could possibly be constructed outside the company's plant, 85% were made by subcontractors on the AT-10 pilot trainer, and more than 40% on the various versions of the all-metal Model 18 twin — the AT-7, the AT-11, the UC-45, and other types. In terms of dollar volume, more than 100 million dollars worth of parts, sub-assemblies, and tooling were accepted by Beech from subcontractors, compared with a total Beech war production dollar volume of about 425 million.

The small size of the Beech machine shop, to which almost no new equipment was added at any time from 1939 onward, was a source of constant surprise to Government and Air Forces officials who visited the factory during the war. "How can you possibly keep such large assembly lines going with a machine shop of this size?" was their inevitable question. Subcontracting was the answer. Almost all machined parts needed for regular production were purchased from subcontractors, freeing Beech's equipment for tooling and die work and emergency jobs. Again, this system followed the company's consistent policy of minimizing expansion, and rendered unnecessary the purchase of millions of dollars worth of expensive and critically scarce machine tools.

The decision to make the fullest possible use of subcontracting was basic in the company's earliest plans for increased pro-

48

duction. Beech's first subcontracts were placed in the fall of 1939, when there was no actual necessity for going outside the company's own shops for fabrication of any parts, in order to test the practicality of such a system. The tests were successful. The parts built by subcontractors passed rigid inspection, and proved equally serviceable with those built on the company's premises. As a result, a survey was begun covering the territory from the Mississippi river westward to the Rocky Mountains, and from the Canadian border south to the Gulf of Mexico. It was decided to concentrate subcontracting within this area, to avoid conflict with war production demands made upon the more highly industrialized regions of the nation. The survey disclosed an amazing reservoir of industrial capacity. Many millions of square feet of floor space, many thousands of skilled workers, and machinery and equipment of all kinds, were potentially available.

It appeared to be a simple matter to tap this reservoir of auxiliary power when the call came for multiplied aircraft production. Many potential subcontractors were operating at a fraction of capacity, or had closed down their factories entirely, when the demands of total war restricted or cut off the manufacture of civilian goods. The apparent simplicity was however, deceiving. Few, if any subcontractors had any knowledge of aircraft parts production, and many were inexperienced in working to the required standards of precision. Beech's Outside Production Department, which had been set up to place and administer all subcontracts under the supervision of the company's general manager, had its hands full educating its suppliers in their work. In most cases, Beech furnished tooling, in addition to all materials and supplies for fulfillment of subcontracts, and supplied advice and help wherever necessary to assist the subcontractors' managements in doing the job. Beech factory inspectors also took up residence in the plants of the larger subcontractors, providing inspection at the source of many items. Thus, with only a fraction of the expenditure for man-power, working area, and machinery which would otherwise have been required, Beech gained the services of thousands of additional workers. At the peak of production, Beech subcontractors employed nearly 10,000 persons on Beech work, and used almost a million and a half square feet of floor space on Beech contracts.

The subcontracting setup especially proved its value on an emergency assignment in the summer of 1942. On June 8th, the managements of Wichita's three major aircraft companies, Beech, Boeing, and Cessna, received word from the Air Forces that they were scheduled jointly to deliver 1,500 CG-4A troop-carrying gliders before October 1st; that the glider program superseded all others in importance, and had to be performed whether or not any other airplanes were built and delivered during that period. Beech assumed the responsibility for building all inner wing panels, all tail surfaces, and all finished forgings and castings for these 1,500 gliders. A great part of this work was subcontracted, with Beech providing tooling, material, inspectors, instructors, and everything else required except space and labor. The non-subcontractable part of Beech's share was done in a circus tent erected adjoining the company's assembly buildings, which were already over-crowded with work. Beech-built glider parts were delivered according to schedule; and at the same time, finished Beechcrafts continued to roll off the assembly lines precisely as scheduled.

As a result of their demonstrated efficiency, Beechcrafters and their company were honored by the receipt of the Army-Navy "E" Award, conferred upon them at ceremonies held on October 10, 1942. At regular intervals thereafter, a renewal of this award came to Beech from the Government; and at the end of the war, Beechcraft's "E" Award banner carried four stars, signifying that among the 5% of war contractors who received the "E" award for their work during World War II, Beech had qualified for the award five times in succession.

Chapter 10

Throughout the opening months of 1943, production of Beechcrafts continued at constantly accelerating velocity. The Army and Navy air services continued to find additional uses for the versatile Model 18 Beechcraft, and their demands for these planes continued to increase. At the end of the year, an increase in actual production of 227% was registered over the 1942 totals. In dollars and cents, sales exceeded 126 million dollars, prior to provision for refunds to the Government on its purchases.

This record was made in spite of a major shift in type of production during the year. In the spring of 1943, Beech completed its contracts for the AT-10 Beechcraft plywood pilot trainer, having fulfilled the Air Forces needs for aircraft of this special type. Incidentally, the company had supplied engineering and production data, and extended other forms of assistance, to the Globe Aircraft Corporation, Fort Worth, Texas, which enabled that company to fulfill successfully a contract for 600 AT-10 Beechcrafts, in addition to the 1,771 AT-10s built by Beech Aircraft.

At that time the Douglas Aircraft Company was in search of an aircraft production facility having about one million square feet of space to supply all of the complete wing and nacelle assemblies needed by its Tulsa, Oklahoma plant for the new A-26 Invader attack bomber, which was to be assembled at Tulsa and other Douglas factories. By taking utmost advantage of the designed flexibility of the assembly buildings and other areas devoted to AT-10 production, Beech's management figured that they could put together about a third of the amount of space called for. However, they also had a thorough knowledge of what Beech could accomplish in the way of doing a big job in small quarters through its subcontracting system. Without hesitancy, therefore, Beech shouldered the job of supplying Douglas-Tulsa with all of the wings and nacelles needed to keep the line going — assemblies that comprised more than 40% of the complete A-26 Invader.

A great deal of ingenuity, perspiration, and sound engineering of production facilities new to Beech Aircraft's experience went into that job.

The Invader wings were built like a battleship — heavy, complicated, beautifully designed, and necessarily constructed to the highest precision standards throughout. Each wing, in fact, outweighed a complete Model 18 Beechcraft. The only possible way to build these units on a mass production scale

51

was on a mechanized assembly line. Their concentrated mass, unlike that of Beechcrafts which could most economically be built on the floor, with the line moving manually every few hours at shift change and rest periods, demanded such a facility. It was installed quickly, and before many months had passed, was moving at full speed. A-26 Invaders took to the air at Tulsa on Beech-built wings by the hundreds, and played their part in the freeing of Europe and the downfall of the Japanese Empire.

The shift from building all-wood AT-10 Beechcrafts to complex, all-metal Invader wings called for practically a 100% reconversion, not only of facilities and machinery, but also of employee skills. Men and women who had learned the art of woodworking in building the AT-10s had to acquire new skills, to do their part in the Invader wing program. Again Beech's employee training program was called on for full throttle effort; and again the job was done, and retraining completed, while the wing line was being set up.

The same transition was required of subcontractors on the wing program. A prime example was that of the American Seating Company, Grand Rapids, Michigan, which, as an experienced furniture manufacturer, had logically been chosen to supply complete wood wings and other components for the AT-10 Beechcraft. This subcontractor installed metal-working machinery and supplied all of the massive spar caps — complexly shaped tapering members machined from solid aluminum alloy billets — for Invader wings. Other subcontractors proved their adaptability, and with help from Beech when needed, they got the parts out on time.

The problem of safely transporting the large, heavy wings from Wichita to Tulsa was solved by reworking automobile transports — lengthy tractor-trailer combinations which in peacetime had been used for hauling new automobiles from assembly plants to dealers. One pair of wings (right and left) was hauled per trip in each transport, snugly held in place by special fittings. The engine nacelles were so long, exceeding in length the fuselage of many light airplanes, that headroom remaining after the wings were lowered, leading edge down, into the racks was inadequate to clear several railroad underpasses on the only direct highway route. The detachable aft portions of the nacelles were therefore removed for shipping. This was typical of many ingenious methods originated to save time and money and speed up the job.

The record accomplished on the Invader wing program paralleled that of the company in producing Beech-designed aircraft. At all times up to the end of the war in August, 1945, Invader wing production was ahead of the requirements of the Douglas-Tulsa factory. It was an excellent example of adaptability, efficiency, and cooperation among all concerned — Douglas, Beech Aircraft, Beechcrafters who cheerfully underwent retraining and took up new types of work, and Beech subcontractors who met the challenge of their changed assignments successfully.

In December 1943, the company inaugurated a new activity unique, as far as is known, at that time in the aircraft industry. It organized a wholly-owned Beech subsidiary, Material Distributors, Inc., to dispose of its own surplus and obsolete materials, and to assist other manufacturers in getting their surpluses into use. Beech officers and employees directed this activity, which was separately incorporated only for maximum operating efficiency. Actually it was an outgrowth and logical extension of the Beech Conservation and Salvage department, which since 1940 had been highly active at the Beech plant, reclaiming and returning for productive use large amounts of material which might otherwise have ended up on the scrap pile, valueless for war production purposes. This activity was coupled with that of a neighborly custom which had come into some usage among aircraft producers, of borrowing or buying material from other manufacturers whenever supplies ran short of meeting urgent needs.

Beech's experience had shown that often fairly large amounts of material or purchased parts were left on its hands, as a result of design changes and other causes. Much of this material, analysis of other manufacturers' requests showed, could be used elsewhere in war production. The problem was to bring together the holders of such surpluses, and their potential users. Material Distributors, Inc., was therefore organized as a clearing house service, to redistribute surplus materials.

From the outset, this activity proved successful, as well as useful to the total war production effort. Not only did it dispose of Beech's own surplus, but it promoted the movement of other surplus inventories to a total volume of almost five million dollars in its first year of existence. More important, the redistribution service offered by Material Distributors in at least one instance prevented the total shutdown of a major warplane production line, and in many other situations averted production slowdowns, by making critically scarce materials available to needful manufacturers from surpluses held by others. A further effect of this service was to reduce the amount of newly manufactured materials necessary to sustain production, and to reduce the inventories carried over at the end of the war, resulting in a net saving to the taxpayers who footed the cost of all production.

Chapter 11

The pioneering spirit always so characteristic of the Beech enterprises found several important modes of expression during 1944. While production of Invader wings increased during the opening months of the year, as hundreds of employees finished their transitional training and took their places as metalworkers on the wing line, and construction of Model 18 Beechcrafts went steadily forward, the Engineering and Experimental departments worked long hours to complete important confidential projects.

The first of these projects to see the light of open day, although under strict secrecy, was an entirely new Beechcraft — the XA-38 "Grizzly" attack bomber. On May 7th, the "Grizzly" was testflown for the first time, and passed the test with flying colors. Under subsequent testing by Army Air Forces acceptance boards, the "Grizzly" proved acceptable in every detail and was highly commended by Air Forces officials. Its performance in these tests exceeded that of any other similar airplane which was either in production or on an experimental status at that time. On one of its cross-country test flights, a

First Army-Navy "E" Award accepted for all Beechcrafters by Mr. and Mrs. Beech in October 1942 was one of five "E" Awards earned during World War II.

Beechcraft XA-38 Grizzly attack bomber was a distinct contribution to art of aircraft design, though lack of suitable engines prevented quantity war production.

Mary Lynn and Suzanne Beech helped their father observe his 52nd birthday in 1943.

Beechcraft main factory and general offices in Wichita had grown to this modern complex from the old Travel Air plant by 1945.

pursuit plane reputed to be one of the Air Forces' fastest aircraft was assigned to pace the "Grizzly." Soon, however, the "Grizzly" was pacing the pursuit ship. That incident showed the performance of which the "Grizzly" was capable.

The first Beechcraft ever designed expressly for tactical military service, the "Grizzly" was a remarkable airplane. It was the answer to the artilleryman's dream of a "flying gun platform," mounting in its nose an automatic rapid-firing 75-mm. cannon capable of wreaking havoc upon enemy tanks, armored vehicles, shipping, and ground installations. The bore of the cannon represented a perfect extension of the thrust line of the airplane, making it extremely easy for the pilot to attain accuracy of fire by simply aiming the entire plane at the target, with no parallax error whatever.

In addition, it mounted four 50-calibre machine guns in remotely controlled turrets covering a 360° sphere of fire, for attack and defensive purposes, and two fixed forward firing "50s." Crew and vital installations were protected by bullet-proof glass and heavy armour plate. Bombs, chemical smoke or gas tanks, auxiliary fuel tanks, or aerial torpedoes could be carried on external racks, as required by the type of mission to be performed.

Aerodynamically, the XA-38 was a typical Beechcraft. It had a distinct family resemblance to the Model 18, and like all Beechcrafts, possessed a very high cruising/landing speed ratio. Relatively slow landing speed was attained by carefully calculated wing design, based on an airfoil section of the NACA-2300 series, tapering sectionally from 18.87% thickness at the root chord to 12% at the tip chord. Large aileron type flaps, and the use of conventional landing gear, fully retractable in flight, enabled the XA-38 to operate from small, rough fields such as were utilized in the forward zones of action. Among its features was a new type of thermal deicing system utilizing heat from the engine exhaust gases. Its wing span was 67.08 feet, its length 51.7 feet, its design gross weight 29,900 pounds, and its alternate gross weight 36,332 pounds. Unavailability of suitable engines in time for the "Grizzly" to be produced in quantities prevented the airplane from seeing service in World War II; but the work performed by Beech in creating the

"Grizzly" represented a distinct contribution to the art of aircraft design, and enhanced the reputation of its builders.

Another Beech advancement in aeronautical design also was first test-flown, and proven to possess merit, at about the same time that the "Grizzly" first appeared. This was the "V-tail," or "Butterfly" tail, so nicknamed because of its resemblance to the half-opened wings of a butterfly at rest. It consisted of a simplified empennage made up of two rather than the conventional three elements. The forward portion of these two elements was fixed, and the aft portions movable in an up-and-down plane. Through a differential control hookup, the two movable elements, working through conventional stick or wheel, and rudder pedal controls, afforded the same controllability and maneuverability as the conventional empennage. The "V-tail" offered several advantages; reduced drag, simplification of manufacture and maintenance, reduced likelihood of damage to the empennage elements while taxiing, and consequent reduction of first cost and upkeep expense. It was disclosed, after the war had ended, that the "Glomb" type of radio-controlled aerial missile developed by the Navy utilized the "V-tail" empennage. This simplified empennage, developed by Beech as part of its continuous program of wartime research, made its reappearance after the war as a distinctive feature of the Model 35 Beechcraft four-place monoplane.

Still another product of the company's constant quest to increase the efficiency of aircraft appeared in 1944. It was the Beechcraft controllable pitch propeller. Based on the Roby patents, this was the first practical propeller affording positive control of propeller pitch at all ranges from low takeoff to high cruising, for lightplane engines. The first Beechcraft propellers produced were for the 65 hp Continental engine. They did their work so well that the Air Forces at once ordered large quantities, for installation on liaison and artillery spotting lightplanes used in all theaters of war. Performance of these lightplanes was so improved by installation of Beechcraft propellers that the factory's entire output was snapped up from the production lines and flown by air to the various fighting fronts for immediate use. Further research by Beech engineers resulted in the development of controllable pitch propellers

58

in horsepower ranges up to 250 hp, and in the origination of electric governors permitting constant speed installations to be made. This was to become another of the features of the postwar Model 35 Beechcraft.

These evidences of sound, alert, aggressive engineering and planning, coupled with the record which Beech was making and had made in war production and the previous years of peace, were factors influencing a potent form of recognition which came to the company during the year. On March 1st, Beech Aircraft became one of the first manufacturers in the Middle West to qualify for financing under the Regulation V loan setup. An agreement was signed with the Fourth National Bank of Wichita, which served as agent for 36 banks in 18 different cities participating in the arrangement, under which Beech Aircraft was extended a revolving credit for fulfillment of its Army contracts to a maximum amount of 50 million dollars. Looking back a little more than a few years to the time when the sale of a single airplane meant the difference between meeting the payroll from current cash, or borrowing on a note secured by Mr. Beech's signature, it was evident that the company had come a long way in a short time.

A review of the roster of employees, toward the end of the year, showed that almost 4,000 Beechcrafters had joined the armed services since the war began. It had been evident to the management from 1940 onward that sooner or later, most of its male employees of military age would be called to the colors; and its personnel policies had therefore been shaped toward the hiring of women, physically handicapped persons, and older men. The response to its calls for people in these categories had been splendid. Grandmothers dropped their knitting; grandfathers came back from retirement; housewives left the dishes in the sink; and girls and women, particularly those with sweethearts or relatives in the services, came running to back up their fighting men on the production front. At the end of the year, more than 40% of Beechcrafters were women. More than 23% of all employees were physically handicapped in one way or another. The problem of making job assignments suitable to the physical strength of women, and of placing handicapped persons where their disabilities would not endanger themselves or their fellow employees, was a large one. Its most vexing aspect was not, as might be supposed, that of bringing forth complaints from the employees because their assignments were too arduous. The reverse was true. The employees were willing to tackle any job given them; and it often required a great deal of diplomacy to persuade them that they were not being discriminated against because of the limitations of their physical capacities. Women were found to be particularly valuable on unavoidable repetitious jobs, requiring great care and patience. More than 80% of the company's riveters, for example, were women. The company's pay rates were identical for male and female employees, in the various classifications. The ladies earned their pay, for they did their jobs, and did them well.

Chapter 12

If Beechcrafters had been minded to look back, when 1945 began, at the year just ended, they would have found many reasons to be satisfied with their past year's work. In spite of a virtual shutdown of a substantial part of the company's facilities during the transition from AT-10 to Invader wing production, they maintained production at better than a 90 million dollar total. There was no time, however, for looking backward. The Invader wing line was putting out all of the wings that Douglas-Tulsa could absorb. And although manufacture of almost all non-tactical aircraft excepting large transports was halted by contract cancellations early in 1945, the demands of the armed services for Model 18 Beechcrafts continued undiminished. The company still had a full-sized war production job to do.

On April 21st a notable production milestone was passed, without fuss or ceremony, when Beech delivered to Douglas-Tulsa the 1,000th pair of complete Invader wings manufactured since the "big wing" contract was signed. The four-figure production mark had been attained just one year after the wing line started functioning on an operational basis.

60

For exactly ten minutes, work came to a halt at Beech Aircraft when the news of Germany's surrender and V-E Day came on May 8th. Then Beechcrafters returned to their jobs with a new air of determination to speed the day of final victory by every means in their power. As they had done throughout the war, they continued a record of near-perfect attendance. Absenteeism remained at a low level equalled by few other war industries. Employees' War Bond purchases continued to exceed 20% of total payroll, as they had done continuously from early 1942 onward. There was no letdown in production or performance.

Victory in Europe, followed before the month had ended by a reduction in military requirements for A-26 wings, had one effect which was soon to prove important. It enabled the Beech management, without interference to the company's war production, to devote additional time and personnel to preparations for peacetime production and sales. It was an unwavering policy of the company that its war work came first, and that no amount of time, manpower, or materials needed in the performance of its war contracts should be diverted under any circumstances to so-called "postwar planning." Of course there was sound common sense, as well as patriotically motivated devotion to the main task at hand, behind this policy. Aeronautical design was making such rapid progress, under the stimulus of war, that products designed in anticipation of postwar sales might have been obsolete before they could have been gotten into production.

Beech's postwar design and planning staff had plenty of material to work on. Throughout the war, the company had kept in close touch with Army and Navy bases where Beechcrafts were in use, and maintained Service Engineering representatives in residence at the principal air training schools all over the United States. Its service engineers, in helping to keep thousands of Beechcrafts always available for use, made the most of their excellent opportunities to suggest changes and modifications that would improve the serviceability or performance of the planes. Wherever possible, their suggestions, submitted to the factory in daily reports, were incorporated in current production models, and served to make good air-

61

planes even better. A considerable backlog of improvements, however, accumulated which could not be put into effect on military Beechcrafts without unduly slowing production. This backlog, based on a vast amount of service experience, was very useful to the designers of the postwar commercial Model 18 and other Beechcrafts, supplementing the skill which they applied to the origination of new commercial designs.

All military production at Beech completely ceased on August 14th — the day of final victory in World War II. Spare parts orders were later received for maintenance of the Beechcrafts which were to continue at work with the occupation forces and the peace-time military establishments. But the big job ended with the surrender of Japan. Beechcrafters could pause at last, with clear consciences, and look back.

They had produced, during the war years, a grand total of 7,400 Beechcrafts, not including spare parts which, in terms of pounds of airframe, equalled many more complete airplanes. They had built 1,635 complete sets of wings for A-26 Invader attack bombers. They had designed, built, and successfully tested the prototypes of the outstanding combat airplane of its class — the XA-38 Beechcraft "Grizzly." They had delivered large numbers of Beechcraft controllable pitch propellers which increased the performance of the Army's lightplanes. Through their subsidiary, Material Distributors, Inc., they had brought about the reuse, in war and essential civilian production, of millions of dollars worth of surplus materials, often thus preventing slowdowns on vital war production lines. They had won the Army-Navy "E" Production Award for outstanding services in the production of war equipment, five consecutive times. The spirit in which they made this record was described by President (then Senator and Vice-President-elect) Harry S. Truman, speaking on the floor of the United States Senate on January 10, 1945, as follows:

"It was my privilege, while acting as chairman of the committee to investigate the National Defense Program, to visit nearly every aircraft factory and nearly all the other factories in the country; and in the (Beechcraft) factory referred to in the letter just read, we found higher morale, from the standpoint of production, labor, and management, than in any other factory."

62

Conversion to peacetime production was swift at Beech. The assembly line was crowded with new Model 18 executive transports by Fall 1945. (Page 65)

This "Million-dollar" lineup of D18S Beechcrafts was ready for fly-away when the improved design was ATC'd on December 7, 1945. (Page 66)

Among early postwar deliveries was this Model D18S Beechcraft for Ohio Oil Company (later Marathon Oil Company) — a very loyal customer who, over the years through 1975, purchased a grand total of 80 Beechcrafts, ranging from two Model 17 biplanes to 12 King Air Beechcrafts.

63

The postwar Model D18S Beechcraft featured many refinements, in addition to an important 20% increase in payload. In background is a Beech-owned lightplane used in developing the Beechcraft controllable pitch propeller. (Page 67)

The postwar Model G17S Beechcraft biplane brought this famous original Beech design to its ultimate stage of refinement. (Page 67)

An important event in aviation history was the first flight in 1945 of the wholly new Model 35 Beechcraft Bonanza. (Page 71)

Post-War Years

Chapter 13

The cessation of all-out war production at Beech Aircraft on V-J Day did not mean that all of the company's activities came to a halt. Often, at especially hectic intervals during the times of expansion, or of tackling difficult problems that had to be overcome to keep output on schedule, management and employees alike had momentarily done a bit of wistful daydreaming about the glorious day when the war would be over, and they could go fishing and forget that such a creation as an airplane ever existed. When the day actually came, however, they put aside the temptations of leisure, and buckled down to the tasks of reconversion with the same earnestness that they had shown during the war.

Only two weeks after V-J Day, a complete physical inventory of the plant and all its contents, including work in process had been completed. While the lengthy job of plant clearance was under way, tooling and facilities for construction of new postwar commercial Beechcrafts were rushed to completion, and simultaneously work was started on the construction of these new models.

Only two months after the end of the war, the first new commercial postwar Beechcraft, an eight-place deluxe executive transport, came off the reconstituted peacetime assembly line, ready for flight testing. Designated as the D18S Beechcraft, it was a highly refined version of the Model 18, more than 5,200 of which had been delivered to the armed services during the war. Basic improvements over the wartime models included a stronger center section, and other structural changes qualifying the airplane to be licensed commercially at more than a 20% increase in gross weight, with corresponding increases in range and payload. A new type of Beech designed landing gear was used, which was softer in action and smoothed out imperfect landings and fast taxiing on rough, unprepared fields. Engine nacelles were lengthened and extended rearward, and flush riveting was used on wing leading edges and other aerodynamically critical areas, to smooth out the flow of air at cruising speeds of 200 mph or more, and improve the handling qualities at slower speeds. A new instrument panel, and relocation of some controls, added further to ease of pilot handling. New types of brakes and tires, engineered in combination for optimum efficiency, improved the taxiing characteristics and eliminated brake "fading" as a potential source of ground handling difficulties.

During the next two months, while rigid testing of the D18S prototype was undertaken under direction of the company pilots and engineers and the Civil Aeronautics Authority, the Model 18 production line filled up again. On December 7th, sixteen weeks after V-J Day, the first CAA Approved Type Certificate to be issued on any postwar commercial airplane was received by Beech — Certificate No. 757, authorizing the D18S Beechcraft to be delivered to buyers with the "NC" designation on its wings. A quantity of D18S executive transports valued at more than a million dollars was then ready for immediate delivery to buyers among whom some of America's foremost business corporations were numbered. Production and deliveries of the D18S models stood at a rate of two airplanes per day, then and for months afterward.

Developmental work and preliminary production went forward at the same time on another new version of the Model 18, the D18C. Intended primarily for feeder airline service, or like operations requiring maximum payload, the D18C offered performance suitable to meet the exacting requirements of the Air Carrier Section 04 of the Civil Air Regulations. It used Continental R9A 525 horsepower engines, in place of the 450 horsepower Pratt & Whitney Wasp Junior engines with which the D18S Beechcraft was powered. Service tests of the D18C model by All American Airways, prior to its certification, indicated the complete suitability of this airplane for feeder line operations. It was equipped with a retractable mail pickup boom

66

and mail dropping device, for use in the type of airmail pickup and delivery operations which All American Aviation had successfully pioneered in its operating territory. The possibilities of this special type of D18C for extension of airmail and passenger service over almost unlimited territory, as well as of the more conventional D18C passenger and cargo type, were extremely promising.

Approved Type Certificates were also obtained on additional versions of the Beechcraft controllable pitch propeller, engineered for easy installation on a number of types of engines and aircraft in the 65 to 250 horsepower classes. Results of tests conducted with this propeller on various makes of aircraft were impressive, showing sharp decreases in length and time of takeoff runs, and increases in rate of climb and cruising speed. Large numbers of orders for Beechcraft propellers were received, and production was stepped up to a rate of hundreds of units per month.

War-deferred revision of the original Beechcraft, the famous Model 17 five-place biplane, was another item on the postwar agenda. Like the Model 18, this airplane incorporated basic improvements in the new version, designated as the G17S Beechcraft. Retaining all of the good qualities which had brought it world-wide popularity for more than a decade, the G17S featured a new type of engine mount, new drag-reducing cowling, a new exhaust system, larger control areas on the empennage for easier and more positive control at all speeds, a new instrument panel and repositioning of some controls, and many additional refinements. Production was resumed of the G17S Beechcraft on a scale consistent with the restricted market for a luxury aircraft of its type and price.

A wholly new Beechcraft also made its way from the drawing boards of the designers into the skies over Wichita soon after the war ended. It was the Model 35, a four-place all-metal monoplane powered with a 165 hp Continental engine, and using a fully retractable, tricycle type landing gear. Among its features were the unique two-element "V-tail," and the Beechcraft controllable pitch propeller. In addition, it was perhaps the only airplane of its class to be offered with all instruments and equipment necessary for cross-country and night flying operation, including two-way radio, included in its selling price of approximately $7,000 to $7,500. An indication of the reputation which Beech had attained is shown by the fact that before any specifications or detailed information of any kind had been released about the Model 35, more than 500 orders had been received, each accompanied by a substantial cash deposit. In its tests, the new Beechcraft gave ample promise of fulfilling the hopes of these buyers and of its designers alike. It was clocked at a level flight speed of 180 miles per hour during testing. Its all-round performance was rated as extremely satisfactory.

Developmental work was also pushed forward rapidly on another entirely new type of Beechcraft, the Model 34 multi-engine airline transport. Designed specifically for feeder airline or short-haul service, with the recommendations made by the Air Transport Association for an ideal feeder type airplane in mind, the Model 34 gave promise, in its wind tunnel and preliminary tests, of developing extremely high efficiency at a very low operating cost. Inherent in its design was the ability to operate in and out of small fields that would not be legally usable by other comparable types of transport aircraft. It could thus solve the problem of offering dependable, safe, economical airline service to small or medium-sized municipalities unable or unwilling to invest large sums of money in large and elaborate airports.

The items enumerated by no means exhausted the list of projects under way in the Beech design and developmental groups. Additional investigations were under way, based on knowledge gained from the accelerated knowledge and experience gained by the company and by the aircraft industry during the war. The company was keeping quiet about these projects, however, in keeping with its long-standing policy of publicly announcing new developments only after they had been thoroughly proven. The wisdom of maintaining silence about its projected new products in a highly competitive commercial market, too, was obvious.

In the process of reconversion, the company's subsidiary, Material Distributors, Inc., proved to be a highly valuable operation. Its experience in the redistribution of surplus materials was a great asset to Beech, both in obtaining scarce materials to sustain a very substantial volume of production on postwar Model 18 Beechcrafts, and in clearing away Government and company-owned surpluses not needed for postwar production. MDI performed like services for many other manufacturers, liquidating millions of dollars worth of Government-owned surpluses at prices that restored large sums of money to the Federal Treasury. At the same time, its services helped buyers to re-enter civilian goods production more quickly, by making available to them materials otherwise unobtainable.

The company's primary postwar objective remained, as always, the design and manufacture of high-performance aircraft. Its exploration and aggressive exploitation of other diversified possibilities for profitable activity, however, made the reconversion period a very busy time for Beech and Beechcrafters. Many of its wartime employees left the plant on V-J Day gladly, with no thought of ever returning. The old folks went back to a life of well-earned leisure, made easier by their savings and cheered by the knowledge that they had done their part to help win the war. The housewives returned to their homes, the clerks to their stores, and the farmers to their farms. They had all done a great job, and they were happy that it was over.

Throughout reconversion, however, prompt action by the management in setting up and enlarging developmental and production programs enabled the company to retain on its payroll an average of more than 4,000 people, which was almost 40% of the average number employed during the war. This was accomplished in the face of statistical estimates by government experts that the aircraft industry would be reduced in 1946 to a scale of only 4% of its wartime peak. Steady increases in the number of employees were anticipated as the company's various new projects reached the production stage. A source of gratification to employees was the fact that after a brief drop during the three months following V-J Day, the rate of earnings under the Beech Efficiency Incentive Plan, which was retained as a basic system of employee compensation for postwar use, showed little decrease from its wartime peak. Under this plan, Beech employees continued to be one

69

of the highest paid, as well as the most efficiently productive groups, in the aircraft industry.

One of the many reasons for the efficiency of Beechcrafters as a working group was highlighted on April 14th. Filling one of Wichita's large theaters to capacity, Beechcrafters and their families gathered for the presentation by Mr. and Mrs. Beech of service award pins to employees having five years or more of continuous service with the company. More than 1,000 Beechcrafters qualified to receive awards for five years or more of service; and more than 50 received ten-year service emblems, not including the company's officers. Awards were given to more than 25% of all employees on the company's payroll. This high percentage of voluntary continuity of service, during a stressful period when an experienced aircraft worker could almost write his own salary check if he chose to seek employment with some manpower starved manufacturers, testified better than words to the mutual confidence and regard existing between the company and its employees.

As the company entered the second half of its 1946 fiscal year in April 1946, it could look back on a record of outstanding war production accomplishment, and a reconversion to peacetime activity which had already restored its deliveries for the single month of December, 1945, to a level exceeding its total deliveries throughout the entire year of 1940. Its developmental projects were progressing rapidly. Its financial standing was excellent. Substantial reserves were on hand in cash to finance its postwar program, and its credit rating was gilt-edged. In spite of extremely heavy outlays for engineering, design, tooling, and other expenses incidental to development work, production had been resumed to such an extent that its interim financial report on March 31st showed an operating deficit of only $150,000 on combined operations of Beech and its wholly-owned subsidiary, Material Distributors, Inc.

The long-standing reputation of the company for building aircraft having outstanding performance and exceptional qualities of stability, safety, and freedom from maintenance difficulties and expense had reached a new peak, as the result of the good service rendered by Beechcrafts in the armed forces of the United States and its allies all over the world. Army and

70

Navy pilots and mechanics, and the people who had ridden in Beechcrafts with them, were unreservedly enthusiastic about the company's products. Beechcrafters and their management looked back upon the past with pride, and faced the future with confidence.

Chapter 14

Throughout 1946, its first full calendar year of postwar activity, Beech Aircraft and its products reinforced the Beech tradition of setting new marks within the aircraft industry. Beech achievements covered a wide range. New flight speed records were established. Trail-blazing transoceanic delivery flights were successfully completed. Approved Type Certificates were obtained on four new models of Beechcrafts, ranging from various improved versions of existing designs to the all-new Beechcraft Bonanza.

The outstanding event of the year was the introduction of the new Model 35 Beechcraft Bonanza, followed by the receipt of its Approved Type Certificate in November. Later developments were to prove its history-making significance to the business and personal aircraft industry. For the Beech Bonanza was destined to blaze a pattern of precedent-shattering non-stop endurance flights; to become probably the best-known of all business aircraft, and certainly the most popular of all high-performance single-engine personal planes in terms of units sold.

Appearance, equipment and performance of the new Bonanza offered ample proof that Beech designers and builders had significantly advanced the state of the art of aircraft construction. Symbolic of this advancement was the unique V or butterfly tail group, which made the Bonanza stand out at any distance from which its outlines could be seen. In practical terms, the "V-tail" offered distinct advantages. It was aerodynamically cleaner, simpler, and lighter in weight than the customary empennage. It was less susceptible to damage when landing

71

in unprepared areas. Yet control manipulation was conventional in every respect.

The Bonanza's cantilever wing configuration and fully retractable tricycle landing gear offered maximum opportunities for aerodynamic cleanness and consequent high efficiency. And Beech engineers made the most of these opportunities, as Bonanza performance was clearly to demonstrate. In addition, other advantages were realized. Low wing design provided fullest use of the "ground cushion" effect to soften the impact of routine landings, and protect the occupants in emergencies. Positioned above the wing, the cabin afforded sky-wide visibility for maximum safety and enjoyment of flight. A sturdy cabin structure and all-metal top protected the occupants in case of turnover. Streamlining was carried to the point of flush riveting of most of the exterior, snug sealing of retractable landing gear doors, and a retractable passenger loading step and flush cabin door handle. All of this careful attention to major and minor aspects of design made the Bonanza, as its name implied, virtually "the airplane with a built-in tail wind."

As for equipment and appointments, Bonanza designers kept constantly in mind some valid criticisms of personal aircraft often voiced by owners and pilots. One typical comment might be: "I drive out to the airport in a $3,000 sedan that's beautifully upholstered and carpeted with the finest materials; soundproofed, spacious, and seating me and my friends in perfect comfort throughout the longest day's drive. I step into my airplane that cost two or three times as much — and what a contrast! Drab, cramped interiors; narrow seats with little or no padding; and a noise level that makes normal conversation impossible."

Another criticism concerned the lack of equipment on many aircraft. Most makes were customarily sold and delivered from the factory with only the bare minimum of equipment and instrumentation necessary for daytime contact flight. For the manufacturer, this provided attractive range and payload specifications and competitive pricing. But the advantages quickly disappeared when the buyer, seeking maximum safety and utility, undertook to equip the airplane for instrument and night flying. His cost at once went up by thousands of dollars.

72

And weight additions of essential equipment and instruments sharply reduced his range or payload, sometimes to the extent that his four-place airplane became licensable only as a three or two-place craft.

These well-founded criticisms were clearly hampering the popularity and the growth of business and personal aviation. While they had little or no application to prior or existing models of Beechcrafts, Bonanza designers were firmly determined that they should not in any way prove valid for the new model. So, even though its price was only about one-third that of the luxurious Model G17S Beechcraft biplane, the Bonanza was offered to buyers as a fully factory-equipped airplane — ready to carry four people and a normal baggage load over its advertised 750-mile range anywhere, any time, day or night, under contact or instrument flight rules. And its interior appointments compared favorably with those of the finest Beechcrafts, past or present — airplanes that had set the highest standards of comfort and luxury for the personal plane industry.

Passenger comfort equal to that of a deluxe sedan was one aim of Bonanza design. By painstaking planning, it was achieved. At cruising speed, it was possible to carry on normal conversations, or enjoy musical programs from commercial radio stations over the built-in cabin loud speaker. Generous use of soundproofing materials excluded excessive noise from the cabin. And the combination of an efficient Beech propeller and a Beech-muffled, smooth six-cylinder engine, producing full cruising power at only 2,050 rpm, made the Bonanza an exceptionally quiet airplane, both for its occupants and for everyone else in its vicinity.

There was ample room for each occupant to stretch out and relax. Each seat was wide, deep and well-padded over non-sag springs. The upholstery was of fine all-wool fabrics. The floor was fully carpeted from wall to wall. Individual ash trays and sun shades were provided for each occupant. To assure comfort in all climates, a Beech-designed ventilating system allowed fresh air to reach each occupant through widely separated ducts, with a choice of ample warmed air from the cabin heater when desired. An exceptionally wide, deep, molded

Lucite ultra-violet-proof windshield and four large cabin windows afforded undistorted visibility. The baggage compartment, back of the rear seats, offered ample space and easy access for loading up to 120 pounds of luggage or cargo through a 24" x 22" door located at waist-high level. And it had an important advantage over the automobile trunk. Its contents were all accessible in flight.

Bonanza instrumentation and equipment likewise established new standards in its field. The design aim was to produce the most useful medium-priced airplane that human skills could provide. Obviously, it had to be capable of safe operation by day or night, and under contact or instrument flight rules. Anything less would have restricted its utility. So the factory-installed instruments included a bank and turn indicator, sensitive altimeter, jeweled clock with sweep second hand for timing instrument turns, outside air temperature thermometer, manifold pressure gauge, and all other standard flight and engine operating gauges and instruments. Built-in communications and navigation equipment included a two-way, three-band radio with auralnull loop and azimuth indicator, automatic retracting trailing antenna, marker beacon antenna, microphone and headset, and cabin loud speaker. Lighting included two landing lights flush-recessed in wing leading edges, position and tail lights, cabin dome and ultra-violet instrument lights, and landing gear and flap position lights.

The Beech concept of factory-installed full equipment produced other benefits to the buyer than that of a "ready-to-go-anywhere" airplane. It permitted the essential extras to be factory-engineered into Bonanza design, with proper regard for their most favorable locations and for weight and balance considerations. They were genuinely built-in, not added on with hacksaw and file as afterthoughts. Being factory-furnished, they gave the buyer the benefit of Beech's mass purchasing power — saving him many hundreds of dollars. Most important of all, they were there, ready for use whenever needed — enhancing the utility and safety of the Bonanza.

Other features of the Bonanza showed advanced thinking. Its all-metal construction, based on Beech experience in building thousands of aircraft of all types of materials, reflected its

74

designers' purpose of constructing each Bonanza to deliver 2,000,000 miles of safe operation without unusual maintenance expense. Its wide-tread tricycle landing gear faired completely and cleanly into the wings and fuselage when electrically retracted. Its large wing flaps were electrically propelled along tracks built into the wing for extension and retraction.

Performance clinched the Bonanza's place in history. Its horizontal opposed-type, six-cylinder Continental engine was conservatively de-rated from 185 hp to 165 hp at 2,050 rpm. Yet its top speed was 184 mph at sea level. Its cruising speed was 175 mph at 115 hp at 10,000 feet. Its range was 750 miles at economy cruise speed of 165 mph. Its fuel consumption compared with that of an automobile. It won praise from pilots as an honest airplane that handled well at all times. Before the year was over, Beechcraft's books showed a backlog of 1,500 firm orders for the Bonanza — each accompanied by a substantial cash deposit.

The unique Bonanza was not the only advanced Beechcraft design of the year. In July, an Approved Type Certificate was received for production of the redesigned Model 17 Beechcraft biplane. The new model G17S, equipped with a 450 hp Wasp Junior P & W radial engine, had a top speed of 212 mph, a cruising speed of 201 mph, and a range of 1,000 miles. This direct lineal descendant of the first Beechcrafts ever built still found favor among owners who wanted the ultimate in single-engine luxury and performance, even though higher postwar costs of materials and labor had unavoidably increased its selling price.

Another advanced design placed in production during the year was a higher-powered version of the Model 18 Beechcraft. Equipped with 525 hp Continental radial engines in place of the 450 hp Wasp Junior power plants, it was designated as the D18C (executive transport) and the D18C-T (aircarrier transport). As a feeder airliner, it was approved under the new and more rigid CAR 04 aircarrier category at a gross weight of 9,000 pounds, and put into service by Florida Airways, Hawaiian Airlines, Ltd., Empire Airlines, and All American Aviation. Equipped with a mailbag pickup reel, it was used by All American as a combination passenger and nonstop airmail carrier. The first birdproof windshield to meet revised CAR requirements was a result of D18C-T development. Working with the Pittsburgh Plate Glass Company, Beech engineers devised an installation that successfully resisted penetration of birds fired from a compressed air cannon in CAA Indianapolis laboratory tests at velocities up to 250 mph.

On the production line, the redesigned Model D18S twin Beechcraft which had been certificated late in 1945 was the company's major product. Throughout the year, the greatest problem was that of matching supply with demand. Beech, in common with many industries, was vexed with recurring shortages of parts and materials, caused by postwar labor unrest and strikes in the plants of its suppliers. This made it impossible to sustain a smooth flow of production, even after calling into play the expedient of routing partially completed airplanes into a "boneyard" which had served to keep the production lines moving when war-time supply shortages occurred. The situation was doubly vexing to Beechcrafters, because their own labor-management relations remained excellent. Wage increases to meet rising costs of living had been negotiated in a spirit of mutual friendship and trust. And the Beech Efficiency Incentive Plan, which had proved so successful in uplifting employee morale and production rates throughout the war, had been continued on terms matched to the needs of the transition period.

Despite difficulties, hundreds of twin-engine Beechcrafts were delivered in 1946 to corporations and individuals in nearly all of the then 48 states of the Union. Beechcraft's world-wide reputation, enhanced by the performance of Beech airplanes serving the armed forces during World War II all over the globe, also brought many orders from governments, airlines, business firms and eminent persons throughout the New World and overseas. A random sampling included the Netherlands Government, the *St. Louis Post-Dispatch*, the United Fruit Company, the Royal Canadian Mounted Police, the Esso Standard Oil Company, Mr. Harold S. Johnson, the Parker Pen Company, the Attlee Burpee Seed Company, and the Irving Airchute Corporation.

Significant non-stop flight records were established by D18S

Beech entered its first year of post-war production with a versatile and well-organized plant . . . and newly refined products in strong demand. The D18S Beechcraft shown here set a new speed record of 235 mph on its delivery flight. (Page 79)

The Royal Canadian Mounted Police anticipated the Canadian Department of Transportation purchase of 7 King Air Beechcrafts of later years, ordering a fleet of D18S twins, two of which are seen above the clouds.

The Model D18C-T twin Beechcraft was designed to meet the rigid requirements of the CAR 04 air-carrier transport category.

On its trans-Atlantic delivery flight, one unit of the D18S fleet built for Misr Airwork, Egyptian airline, exceeded the scheduled speed of four-engine transports over the same flight stage.

Loyal Beech customers and later owners of King Air fleets included the Dow Corporation . . .

and the Sun Oil Company, whose famous "Sunoco" emblem decorated its D18S executive transport.

Deliveries in 1946 were to almost all of the then 48 states and to several foreign customers, including the KLM Dutch Airline school. Walter H. Beech is pictured with one of the Model 18 trainers.

Beechcrafts being flown from the Wichita factory to their operating bases. The first was established in a flight from Wichita to Hartford, Connecticut on April 6. The new Beechcraft covered the 1,410 miles in 6 hours, making an average speed of 235 mph. While not officially attested, the record was genuine, and once more affirmed the pre-war slogan that "It takes a Beechcraft to beat a Beechcraft." The previous cross-country non-stop speed record was established by a Model 18 Beechcraft which covered the 1,084 miles from St. Louis, Missouri to Miami, Florida in the 1940 Macfadden race at an average speed of 234.097 mph.

Even more dramatic proof of Beechcraft efficiency and reliability was demonstrated in a trans-Atlantic delivery flight eight months later. Flown by Beech staff pilot Dean Cunningham, one of a fleet of D18S Beechcrafts purchased by Misr Airwork, S.A.E., Cairo, Egypt, traversed the over-ocean flight leg from Gander, Newfoundland to Vilaporte, Azores, a distance of 1,744.5 statute miles, in 7 hours and 30 minutes. In setting this record, the Beechcraft averaged 232.5 mph — a speed exceeding that of the 228 mph scheduled for large four-engine airliners on contemporary commercial flights.

The Newfoundland-Azores speed record was a fitting follow-up to an earlier Beech trail-blazing achievement. This was the industry's first commercial over-ocean flight delivery of its kind. Completed routinely in March 1946, it comprised a group of three D18S twins equipped for airline service on Near East and Egyptian routes. The buyer was Misr Airwork — the same firm that received the later flight delivery of three more D18S airliners in November. The route for this historic flight was across the south Atlantic from Belem, Brazil to Ascension Island and Dakar. Flying time from Wichita, Kansas, to Cairo, Egypt, was 47 hours and 40 minutes.

Concurrent with aircraft development and production during the year was an increase in certification and production of various types of Beech controllable propellers for use by other lightplane manufacturers. The product range was broadened to make the Beech propeller adaptable to almost any aircraft engine in the 65 to 250 hp classification. This covered twenty different makes of aircraft then in production. Thus the results of Beech pioneering in this field were placed at the disposal of the entire lightplane industry.

The first postwar year was filled with challenges — and opportunities. All were boldly met. The transition to full-scale commercial activity was well under way. Beech was off and climbing into the postwar era.

Chapter 15

Kansas and the Plains states shivered in the grasp of a prolonged bitter cold wave during the opening days of 1947. Throughout the area, natural gas had long been the principal fuel. The abnormal protracted cold weather created needs that exceeded the designed capacity of the distribution systems. Regretfully, the gas companies sent word to their industrial customers that during this emergency, supplies would have to be cut off. Home heating came first.

To Beech Aircraft, racing against time to reestablish full-scale commercial production, this might have been a serious setback. Even the loss of a few working days would have been keenly felt. Its plants were completely dependent on natural gas. Not only for heating the sprawling manufacturing areas, but also for firing the massive heat treating furnaces that added strength without weight to highly stressed aircraft parts and sub-assemblies, gas was an essential raw material.

But Beech had long ago foreseen just such an emergency. It had been the subject of a management study in 1943 — a study followed by prompt action. In that year, Beech had leased drilling rights on tracts near the plant, and had sunk three gas wells which proved productive enough to supply its entire needs. A standby source was thus ready to prevent any interruption to Beech's wartime work. Although not called into use during the war, this example of "planning ahead" was warmly approved by military procurement authorities. It remained for the severe weather that opened Beechcraft's second peacetime year to demonstrate its value. Maintenance men opened the valves that switched the gas supply from the normal public utility lines to Beech's own gas wells — and production continued without pause.

To capture and hold a share of peacetime markets adequate to keep Beech and its people profitably employed, however, called for much more than safeguards against bad weather. There were 1,500 orders on the books for Beech Bonanzas — 1,500 customers waiting for delivery of the airplanes they had ordered. Even though each order was accompanied with a cash deposit, some of those orders might be lost to competitors, if delivery were too long delayed. And there were plenty of competitors — including some of the biggest and most highly respected aircraft manufacturers in America. Everybody, it seemed, wanted to go into the business of building personal airplanes. At the end of the year 1946, there were at least 17 companies producing more than 30 types of personal aircraft — many of them directly competitive, at least in size and price, with the Beech Bonanza.

The reason for this was what one aviation publication described, some years later, as "One of the most phenomenal business failures in the history of this country . . . the postwar boom in aviation." At the time, there seemed to be good reasons for this boom. As of January 1, 1947, there were 400,061 licensed pilots in the United States. Of this total, 203,251 held commercial licenses, many of which had been issued to ex-military pilots. There were some three million veterans who had served with aviation units of the armed forces in World War II, and who might be assumed to have some special interest in personal postwar flying. There were 85,000 certificated aircraft — mostly personal planes.

Predictions were widespread that American families would take to the air in their personal planes, just as they had taken to the highways in their cars after automobiles became popular. There was a 1945 estimate by the Deputy Administrator for Civil Aeronautics that by 1949, there would be 300,000 registered personal airplanes in the United States; a prediction by the Assistant to the Secretary of Commerce for Air that the nation's general aviation fleet would number 450,000 airplanes by 1955, and that the price of a four-place airplane should settle in the $1,500 to $2,000 range.

If the whole situation had a familiar aspect to the people of Beechcraft there was a good reason for that, too: They had been there before. Many had worked at Travel Air in the palmy days of the earlier aviation boom that climaxed the Roaring Twenties. Walter and Olive Ann Beech had kept their heads, and emerged from that boom right side up. In fact, the money that founded Beech Aircraft came from Walter's timely disposal of his interests in Travel Air to Curtiss Wright. Beech possessed experience — and the judgment necessary to profit from it.

One thing Beech had learned was the importance of offering a truly excellent product — one that would stand out above its competitors. They had such a product in the Beechcraft Bonanza. Relentless accelerated service testing of the prototypes had proved it. The airplane was ready for the market.

Another lesson from experience: Make the most of the boom while it lasts. In 1929, for example, Beech-managed Travel Air delivered more than 10% of all commercial airplanes produced in the United States, although it was only one of the 95 manufacturers competing for the market. To speed the Bonanza into competition, Beech traded dollars for time. Tooling, jigs and fixtures for production were designed and built at the same time that the Bonanza prototypes were being refined; tested, and redesigned into their ultimate form. It was a certainty that some of the production equipment would be scrapped, and more would need to be altered, before the airplane design could reach the ultimate state of refinement for manufacture. But it was the only way to telescope years of preparation into months — to speed the Bonanza onto the market. It was worth the cost.

On February 15, 1947 the first commercial deliveries of Beechcraft Bonanzas began. North, south, east and west — from border to border and from ocean to ocean, the gleaming V-tailed monoplanes swiftly sped. Everywhere they went, the story was the same: Enthusiastic interest and hearty approval. The public, the press and the world of aviation alike joined in praise of the newest Beechcraft. Most important of all, the performance of Bonanzas in the hands of their owners was doing a powerful selling job for Beech. Additional orders were coming in — each order accompanied by a substantial cash deposit.

"Order with cash deposit." Another bit of wisdom, this, gleaned from the lessons learned in the wake of the Roaring Twenties aviation boom — when row after row of glistening new airplanes gathered dust on factory fields all over the nation. Standing in the sun, buffeted by winds, washed by rains — waiting. Waiting for buyers who never came. A hard and costly lesson, for manufacturers who built up inventories of finished airplanes without firm orders on hand. Inventories that could only be moved at a sacrifice, after the boom had died. A lesson that was to be repeated in the aftermath of the postwar boom. But not for Beech. A paragraph from Walter H. Beech's report to the company's stockholders for 1947 succinctly explains:

"The management of your company intends to retain its conservative policy to manufacture its products only after firm orders for them have been received. It will continue to be the policy of your company to release for production only such airplanes as are covered by firm orders, accompanied by a substantial down payment, approximately ninety days in advance of delivery. This policy is intended to protect not only your company against the creation of a surplus, but also the customers of your company against the creation of such a surplus, which would depreciate the value of their investment in Beechcraft airplanes. While it is possible that a few additional sales might be made if Beechcrafts were built on speculation, the hazards of such a course would greatly outweigh any benefits that might be obtained therefrom."

It is worthy of note that this policy fulfilled a dual purpose. It protected the company's interests. At the same time, it protected the company's customers from abnormal depreciation of their investments in their Beechcrafts. A keen sense of responsibility toward its customers was a Beech trait of long standing. It was inherent in the nature of the business, as well as in the basic attitudes of management and employees alike. It was typified in one of the first signs to be put up in the Beech factory when the company was just starting in business — an admonition, signed by Walter H. Beech, that said: "People's

83

lives all over the world depend on the quality of our workmanship. Let's be careful!" New employees quickly got the idea. Those who didn't quickly became ex-employees.

The company's sense of responsibility to Beech owners was shown in action shortly after Bonanza production reached its 1947 peak of nine airplanes per day. During the first week in September, the aviation press received the following notice from the company:

"When the Bonanza was first designed, one of our basic requirements was that the airplane should be able to give approximately 2,000,000 miles of safe operation without unusual maintenance expense. All-metal airplanes have long demonstrated the fact that their potential useful life is better than that of almost any other vehicle, measured in miles of safe operation without unusual maintenance expense.

"In order to insure that the Bonanza fulfills these requirements, a very extensive fatigue testing program was carried through to completion prior to putting the Bonanza in production. No other airplane, either military or commercial, ever received such a thorough test as the Bonanza before quantity production. These tests extended over a year and indicated that the Bonanza would give at least 2,000,000 miles of safe and trouble-free operation except for the usual maintenance.

"During one of the most critical phases of our production acceleration we found ourselves short of automatic riveting capacity. In order to maintain production at the planned level, we made some experimental roll-welded skins and installed them on test wings. These tests indicated that the roll-welded skins were equally as good as the riveted skins. However, there was not time sufficient to accumulate a year of testing or a thousand hours in the air on any such unit. For that reason, the roll-welded skins did not receive the thorough testing that was imposed on the riveted skins.

"Periodic inspections of some of the airplanes with the roll-welded skins have shown a minor and relatively unimportant crack in the vicinity of some of the weld spots. Although these cracks are of no structural significance at this time, they do indicate that the roll-welded skins will not stand up over the desired life of the airplane, on a par with the riveted skins. For that reason they are being replaced. We are making the change merely because each customer is entitled to the best possible airplane that we can deliver to him for the price paid . . ."

To the owners of each of the 250 Bonanzas produced with roll-welded skins, Beech offered to replace the complete wings, without charge for either parts or labor. The replacement program was carried out at the factory, where precision jigs were available to assure the accuracy of installation essential for optimum flight characteristics.

Comments on this action were widely favorable. The trade publication *Aviation Week* described it editorially as "a demonstration of integrity." To Beech, the costly program was all in the day's work. The responsibility was theirs, as they saw it; and the company met it.

Meanwhile, Model 18 twin-engine Beechcrafts continued to move off the production lines, in addition to the popular Bonanzas. Most of the 115 post-war twins built in 1947 went to corporate owners, bringing to more than 300 at the year's end the total ownership of new Model 18s. Many companies also bought used Beech twins that had been declared surplus to the needs of the armed services. The Model 18 Beech was well on the way to establishing a position it was long to enjoy as the favorite executive twin-engine airplane of or near its class.

Mid-1947 also marked the start of a program of rebuilding, or perhaps more accurately, re-manufacturing twin Beechcrafts owned by the armed services that was to continue indefinitely, creating millions of dollars in savings for American taxpayers. At the end of the war, the services had thousands of Beechcrafts on hand. Their condition ranged from hopelessly war-weary to very good. The too-worn planes were scrapped. Some of the rest were sold, some were kept.

The versatile Model 18 had won favor during the war for its case of handling, comfort, speed and staunchness. Another of its attributes gained importance under the impact of cutbacks in military peacetime budgets: its economy of operation. In war or peace, it was a very useful airplane for many purposes. So the Navy Bureau of Aeronautics thriftily hand-picked 117 well-used SNB-1 bomber trainers and flew them back to the Beech factory, to be completely rebuilt into a revised and more broadly useful SNB-4 navigation-trainer and general purpose configuration. Beechcrafters took the used planes apart, replaced everything that showed signs of wear, modified the design as prescribed, and returned them to the Navy — good as new, at much less than the cost of all-new airplanes. The rebuild program worked out so satisfactorily that it brought a "Well done!" commendation, backed by more BuAer rebuild orders eventually adding up to several hundred aircraft. Other military Beechcrafts not included in the rebuild program were kept in good flying condition by service maintenance scheduling that involved parts replacements as required. Beech worked closely with the services in setting up these schedules and supplying the necessary parts. It was good business for Beech; good for the military services that thereby gained more hours of flight per dollar of budget; and good for the taxpayers who footed the bills.

The transition from war to peacetime operation that continued throughout 1947 and 1948 had many aspects. One was a cost control program oriented to commercial competitive needs, started in January 1947. Basically it was an extension of the constant drive to uphold maximum efficiency which had always characterized Beech activities, especially throughout the war. The program emphasized the need for continued efficiency, economically achieved through the elimination of waste wherever possible. Beechcrafters could easily understand its importance to the company's survival in a competitive peacetime economy, and to their own job security. Their cooperation was wholehearted, and successful.

Another transition measure was an aggressive drive to enlarge export markets for Beechcraft products. Prior to World War II, Beechcrafts had been sold to owners in 26 foreign countries all over the world. "The world is our market" — an aim announced when the company was first founded — had become a fact. It was reinforced by the world-wide reputation established by Beechcrafts used in all theaters of the global war by the

U. S. and allied armed forces. So the Beech export sales department was enlarged and strengthened. So effective was the work that in 1947, competent distributors were appointed in 21 foreign lands. In spite of great difficulties arising from foreign dollar exchange problems and widespread import restrictions, Beech export sales topped $4.2 million in 1947, and $3.8 million in 1948.

The company's only subsidiary, Material Distributors, Inc., was liquidated in 1947. Its principal reason for existence had largely disappeared, as the distribution of war surplus materials moved toward completion. MDI had rendered valuable service to the wartime aircraft production program, and to manufacturers seeking scarce materials in the early days of postwar operations; but it had never been intended to replace the normal channels of distribution.

An all-new Beechcraft of unique design successfully completed its first test flight from the Beech field on October 1, 1947. It was the Model 34 "Twin-Quad" Beech — an all-metal, high-wing monoplane 20-passenger transport airplane. It was unique in being the first airplane to combine four engines with two propellers; the first equipped with engines completely submerged in the wings; the first built with integral landing keels on the bottom; and the first large plane to use the "V" tail which had proved its merits on the Beech Bonanza. It was quickly convertible from passenger to semi-cargo or all-cargo transport, through the use of foldable seats remaining in place within the cabin. It was designed and built to meet a need which existed then, and still exists today in many areas, for a fast, economical, multi-engine shuttle and feeder airline plane capable of safely using small flying fields. An extensive flight testing program proved the "Twin-Quad" to be the plane the air transport industry was then frantically demanding. But financial problems overtook the airlines; the potential market shrank drastically; and the Model 34 was reluctantly shelved. It was joined in limbo, to the deep regret of many veteran Beechcrafters and of many pilots, by the Model 17 Beechcraft biplane, which was discontinued in 1948. Rising postwar labor costs of the largely hand-built biplane model had forced its price upward to uneconomic levels; and while it was still saleable, volume was lacking to justify its continued production. It is interesting to note that fully 28 years after the Model 17 was discontinued, many of the 781 Beech biplanes built in the period from 1934 to 1948 were still in constant use; and the "stagger wing Beech," as it was popularly known, brought a good price in the used airplane market.

Development of diversified manufacturing was a new program originated during the transition period. Its basis was the common-sense principle of not putting all your eggs in one basket. Essentially, it was a reversal of the subcontracting system which Beech had used so successfully in expanding its war production capacity. Now, Beech sought to become a subcontractor, or a contract manufacturer as the case might be, for other firms that could profitably use its production skills and facilities. The idea was that work performed for others would help build volume and hold the Beech production team together, no matter what might happen in other directions. A division of the company was set up to solicit orders for whatever articles any responsible buyer might want built, within Beech's capacity to produce. It brought in contracts for manufacturing a widely diversified range of items and parts. Complete vending machines, corn harvesters, and components for home refrigerators and dishwashers were typical of its scope. Much of this work came from Beechcraft owners who were presold on Beech craftsmanship through the performance of their airplanes. Of course the most obvious prospect of all was not overlooked — that of building parts and assemblies for other aircraft. A $1 million-plus contract for jettisonable aircraft fuel tanks, negotiated in 1948, got this end of the program off to a brisk start.

Meanwhile, events abroad had shown the need for the United States and other nations of the Free World to maintain airpower adequate to deter aggressors and keep the peace. The blockade of Berlin instigated by Russian dictator Joseph Stalin in June 1948 served clear warning of Communist aims toward ultimate world domination. Airpower broke that blockade. Airpower would plainly have many other tasks to perform in defense of world freedom. Airplanes would be needed, and men to fly them, for a long time to come.

To help meet this need, another new Beechcraft came into being. It was the Model 45 "Mentor," a two-place single-engine pilot training plane using a number of Bonanza design features and components. Its first test flight from the Beech field on December 2, 1948 was a complete success. It was soon to prove itself as an airplane with a future.

At the end of 1948, the Beech transition to peacetime "business as usual" was complete. Through careful control of inventory, the company freed enough cash in mid-1948 to pay off some $8.7 million in debts — $6 million due the government from contract renegotiations, $700 thousand for purchase of manufacturing facilities from the Defense Plant Corporation, and $2 million in bank loans. It was, for all practical purposes, free of debt. Its net income for fiscal 1948 of $2.21 million more than made up for losses incurred in 1946 and 1947, when reconversion, engineering and development costs ran well into the millions.

A comparison of the company's standing at September 30, 1948 with that of its fiscal year 1940 — the most fairly representative pre-war counterpart — showed striking progress. Deliveries had increased in a ratio of better than 10 to 1 — $2.34 million in 1940, $24.1 million in 1948. The company employed nearly 3 times as many people — from 780 up to 2,325. Their wages had gone up in a 2.63 to 1 ratio — from an average $0.5775/hr. in 1940 to $1.52/hr. in 1948. Its total taxes paid had risen from $78.1 thousand to $1.7 million — nearly a 22 to 1 ratio. Its plant facilities had grown by more than 800% — from 116,000 square feet up to 957,750. And its balance sheet, which showed a $16.9 thousand deficit in its surplus account at September 30, 1940, now displayed a healthy $7.2 million on hand in earned surplus for the same date in 1948. Beech had made it over the hump.

Chapter 16

The pilot who stepped out of the Beech Bonanza that landed at the Teterboro, New Jersey airport shortly after noon on

March 8, 1949 might have been almost any rising young executive arriving for a business luncheon in New York City. He was clean-shaven; his double-breasted suit was well-pressed, his Homburg hat conservatively stylish. Except for its wingtip fuel tanks, the airplane he flew might have been any one of the more than 1,900 Bonanzas then in use. There was no apparent reason why a swarm of reporters and photographers, and a cheering crowd of thousands, should be on hand to welcome this arrival.

No reason — except that pilot and plane had just successfully completed the longest non-stop solo flight in the history of aviation. Captain William P. Odom and his Bonanza, the "Waikiki Beech," had spanned the 4,957.24 Great Circle miles (5,273 actual flight miles) from Hickam Field, Honolulu, Hawaii to Teterboro without pause in exactly 36 hours and 2 minutes, at an average ground speed of 146.3 miles per hour. The six-cylinder E-185-1 Continental 185 hp engine had consumed 272.25 gallons of 80-octane aviation gasoline, and six quarts of oil during the flight, averaging 19.37 miles per gallon of gasoline, at a total fuel cost of approximately $75.

Odom's flight smashed every existing lightplane record for non-stop mileage. The previous recognized world record for all lightplanes of all categories had been established December 29-31, 1938 by Horat Pulkowski and Lt. R. Jenett, Germany, flying an Arado Ar 79 airplane with a Hirth HM 504 A2 motor of 3.984 liters cylinder displacement from Bengasi, Libya to Gaya, India — a distance of 3,917.017 miles.

The world record for aircraft in the Bonanza category (defined by the Federation Aeronautique Internationale as Category III — aircraft weighing from 2,204.7 to 3,858 pounds) had long been held by A. Goussarov and V. Glebov, U.S.S.R., with a flight of 2,061.703 miles made on September 23, 1937 from Moscow to Krasnoyarsk in a Moskalev airplane with an M-11 100 hp engine of 8,577 liters cylinder displacement. This 1937 Russian record had fallen on January 12, 1949 when Odom, flying the "Waikiki Beech" in a full-scale dress rehearsal of his latest performance, had covered the 2,406.902 Great Circle miles from Honolulu to Oakland, California in 22 hours and 6 minutes. His landing at Teterboro reaffirmed a saying long

Longest non-stop solo flight in history was flown in 1948 by William P. Odom in this Bonanza. He flew 4,957 Great Circle miles from Honolulu, Hawaii to Teterboro, New Jersey.

Odom's flight broke every lightplane non-stop mileage record. The standard model Bonanza had been equipped with auxiliary fuel tanks for the flight of 36 hours, 2 minutes.

The Model 34 "Twin-Quad" Beechcraft 20-place airliner scored notably successful "firsts" in aviation history, but had to be shelved due to shrinking markets. (Page 87)

Aviation's most distinctive design, the G17S Beechcraft "staggerwing" biplane, was phased out of production in 1948 as costs rose and sales dropped. (Page 87)

91

Petite aerobatic champion Betty Skelton piloted the new Model 45 Beech Mentor through a thrilling array of military combat maneuvers. (Page 97)

The Mentor became the USAF YT-34 primary-basic trainer in 1950 with the receipt of an Air Force trial order for this sleek, economical Beech design. (Page 99)

The Chinese Republic, buyer in 1940 of Beech's first trainer/tactical twins, came back in 1949 for a fleet of 20 Model 18 bomber trainers. (Page 97)

The Brazilian Air Force, a long-time loyal Beech customer, staged a mass flyaway in 1949 of Model 18 twins and Beech Bonanzas. (Page 97) established throughout the world of aviation: "It takes a Beech-craft to beat a Beechcraft."

The flight log showed that except for mildly delaying en-counters with unexpected bad weather, the trip was remarkable only for its lack of eventfulness — if such a term can be applied to a world record flight. Odom's takeoff from Runway 8 at Hickam Field, Honolulu at 12:04 a.m. March 7 (Eastern Stan-dard Time — or 7:04 p.m. March 6, Honolulu time) was ac-complished routinely in a 2,400-ft. run. The takeoff gross weight, of 3,643 pounds, representing a 50% increase over normal gross weight, provided a safe rate of climb of 400 feet per minute. The first 900 miles were flown in company with a B-17 air-sea rescue plane of the Hawaiian Sea Frontier which was making a regulation patrol tour. For the next 1100 miles, Odom and the Bonanza flew alone above the Pacific. At 9:22 a.m., EST, he radioed that he was over the weather ship "Red Head Fox" at 30° N. latitude, 140° W. longitude, nine hours 18 minutes after takeoff.

Radio advice from San Francisco prompted a 100-mile detour south of Odom's planned rhumb line course shortly after over-flying "Red Head Fox" to avoid a weather system containing severe turbulence and hail. Skirting its southern edge, he missed the worst of the disturbance, but caught enough to require flying on instruments for about an hour. He was well clear of the bad weather at 1:12 p.m., EST, and 450 miles off the California coast, when he met a patrolling Coast Guard PBM flying boat that stayed with him until he flew over San Fran-cisco's Golden Gate bridge at 4:51 p.m., EST. Odom and the Bonanza had covered the 2,474 over-water miles from Honolulu in 16.783 hours, using 128 gallons of gasoline. To span the continent from west to east, 160 gallons remained.

From San Francisco, Odom detoured to the north of the direct west-east airway to avoid bad weather reported over the Sierras. His flight path was over Williams, California; Mount Lassen, California; Lakeview, Oregon; Boise, Idaho. But the weather stayed a jump ahead, and closed in on him. Odom coolly rode it out. He went on instruments, and topped the worst of the widespread disturbance at 16,000 feet, wearing an oxygen mask. The Bonanza droned steadily eastward, past Twin

Falls, Malad City, Rock Springs. Outside the warm cabin, snowflakes swirled as night came on. East of the mountains and over Scottsbluff, Nebraska at 1:40 a.m. Tuesday the skies cleared. From that point on, the flight was sheer routine, paralleling the commercial transcontinental skyways. Omaha, 4:42 a.m.; Des Moines, 5:28 a.m.; Moline, 6:28 a.m.; Chicago, 7:15 a.m.; Toledo, 8:42 a.m.; Cleveland, 9:11 a.m.; Sunbury, 11:04 a.m.; touchdown at Teterboro, 12:06 p.m. When the Bonanza landed, its tanks still held 15.75 gallons of gasoline — enough for 372 more miles of nonstop flight.

"The 'Waikiki Beech' Bonanza functioned perfectly throughout the entire flight." This is how Bill Odom summed up his experience with his Beechcraft. The airplane he flew was almost three years old. Its serial number D-4 identified it as the fourth Bonanza built. A standard Bonanza in every respect except for its added fuel tanks, it had been used by the Beech Engineering Department for a large amount of test flying and development work, including radio-controlled dive testing at speeds of over 300 mph with quick pull-outs. The original 165 hp engine was replaced with a new E-185-1 Continental engine, identical with that used in the then current A35 Bonanza series. This validated any comparisons of performance with that of the current models.

Odom had a simple explanation for the reasons behind the flight. "We set out to prove the efficiency and economy of Beechcrafts by breaking the non-stop distance record," he said. Prove it he did; and the proof was hailed all over the world, to the benefit of the industry and of Beech as its record-breaking leader. The serious purpose of the flight, which was planned and carried out as a demonstration of Bonanza efficiency and reliability, was widely understood and appreciated. It was well expressed by the *New York Times:* "Qualities of dependability have been so well developed in the airplane Odom flew that it is now in daily use by scores of large businesses, to speed and simplify the comings and goings of their executive staffs. The new world record is abundant proof that the light plane and its power plant have reached full stature."

For sheer drama, Odom's flight thoroughly deserved the acclaim and the headlines that it earned the world over. In per-

94

spective as a major event in aviation progress, however, it would probably rank second to another event that took place at the Beech factory during the following few months.

On April 6, 1949, a sheet of three-view drawings came to the desk of Walter H. Beech from the Beech Engineering Department. It outlined the configuration of a proposed all-metal, light twin-engine Beechcraft which had been under discussion as a possible new product. "Okay . . . go ahead" came the word from the company's chief. On November 15, 1949 — just 223 calendar days later — the Beechcraft Twin-Bonanza made its first flight from the Beech field. It was a complete success. The new model immediately went into accelerated flight service testing, while its structural components were undergoing Beech's customary dynamic ground testing simulating millions of miles of flying.

From the record of the carefully pre-planned Odom flight, and the even more remarkable swiftly executed design and development program of the Twin-Bonanza, it is obvious that Walter H. Beech and his people wasted no time or energy in reminiscing about the past. All of the effort and thinking at Beech was, as always, dedicated to planning and building for today and tomorrow, and the years ahead. The past could take care of itself. Its only value in the Beechcraft philosophy consisted in the lessons it taught that might be applied to present and future tasks. The competitive benefits that accrued to the company from past achievements that implied the desirability of buying and using its products were plus factors.

If any of Beechcraft's "old hands" who had worked with Walter H. and Olive Ann Beech during the Travel Air days had been moved to engage in retrospection, they could have made some interesting comparisons between the historic events of 1949 and those of more than two decades past. Odom's flight would have recalled the trail-blazing first crossing by any commercial airplane from California to Hawaii of the Beech-built Travel Air monoplane "City of Oakland" on July 14-15, 1927, flown by Ernest L. Smith and Emory B. Bronte from Oakland to Molokai in 25 hours and 36 minutes. Its sequel was another successful ocean crossing from Oakland to Wheeler Field on August 16-17, completed against headwinds in 26 hours, 17 minutes and 33 seconds by Arthur C. Goebel and Lieut. W. V. Davis, USN, flying the "Woolaroc" Travel Air monoplane owned by the Phillips Petroleum Company to win the $25,000 Dole prize.

The first flight of the Twin-Bonanza, less than nine months after the design was proposed, would have found a parallel in the design and construction of the highly successful Travel Air Model 5000 six-place monoplane late in 1926 – a task completed by Walter H. Beech and his men in just 38 days. Considering the phenomenal advances in the state of the art over the 23-year span separating the two designs, the balance would have been overwhelmingly in favor of the Twin-Bonanza completion as a near-miracle of aeronautical achievement. Just as the stresses imposed on an aircraft structure increase in geometric ratio to increases in its speed, so the problems of design for higher performance and economically feasible production had enormously multiplied over the years. Twin-Bonanza No. 1 was winged proof that Beechcraft's capabilities had more than kept pace with Beech's constant drive to produce the finest airplanes of their kind.

The proof of Bonanza efficiency and reliability offered by Odom's record-breaking flight was well timed from the angle of protecting Beech's position in the personal and business single-engine aircraft market. For 1949 was a bad year indeed for manufacturers in that branch of the industry – a year that some did not survive. Personal aircraft production had steadily fallen, year by year. From a 1946 peak of 33,254 units (representing the fulfillment of pent-up demand unsatisfied during the war years), it declined to 15,515 units in 1947; 6,969 units in 1948; and 3,400 units in 1949. The back-log of demand had burned out. Yet Beech, with one of the highest-priced single-engine planes, held onto its share of the market and more. Buyers who did enter the market demanded excellent value for their money; and the Bonanza had proved its claim to the title of "Best buy" in its class.

Service was another factor in sustaining Bonanza and Beechcraft sales. In 1949 Beech inaugurated a "Courtesy Inspection Program," offering its owners an exhaustive inspection of their aircraft at dealer locations throughout the nation. It was carried out by teams of experts dispatched from the factory – men who knew every rivet and bolt in every model. There was no charge to owners for this inspection, and for a minutely detailed report which was given to the owner at its conclusion. The company's customers approved the program enthusiastically; and it became a standard practice which the factory even now continues to repeat each year. To Beech, it was primarily a natural step in carrying out the responsibility the company had always felt toward its customers. The goodwill it created, and the service business it generated for its dealers, were simply added values.

In the press of other events of 1949, the Beechcraft Mentor, military brother of the Bonanza, did not go neglected. The two-place trainer was dispatched on a tour of air bases throughout the United States, and also sent abroad to be put through its paces for the benefit of air officers of the Western European nations. A dramatic demonstration of aerobatic flight was also presented at Chicago's National Air Fair, before hundreds of thousands of spectators at O'Hare International Airport on the Independence Day weekend. Proving that brute strength was not required to put the Mentor through a breath-taking array of maneuvers standard in military combat operations, the pilot was pretty, petite, 100-lb. Betty Skelton — 22-year-old two-time holder of the women's international aerobatic championship. To cheering crowds, the stunts performed by the Mentor were a source of gasps and thrills. To sober-minded military observers, they were a reminder of the need for continued readiness to maintain airpower in being for the defense of the free world — a reminder already accented by the Communist blockade of Berlin.

The Model 18 Beechcraft was also well in the picture. Delivery was made during the year to the air force of the Chinese Nationalist Government on Formosa of a fleet of 20 Model 18 twins equipped for use as military training planes. The Brazilian Air Force staged a mass flyaway delivery of four twins and five Bonanzas, bringing to more than 40 the total number of Beechcrafts which they had placed in service since the end of World War II. Corporations and other buyers in America and abroad also continued to keep the Model 18 production lines busy. Despite continuing difficulties with foreign exchange that caused a scarcity of U. S. dollars abroad, export sales topped a total of $4.3 million for the year. Beech sales for the fiscal year 1949, ending September 30, topped $20.5 million, and produced a net profit of $922,089.

Chapter 17

Throughout most of its first six months, the year 1950 was outwardly uneventful, in world and national affairs as well as at Beechcraft. There was little to hint at the changes it was to bring.

Behind the Iron Curtain, the Communist leaders pondered their Cold War defeat at the hands of the Berlin Airlift, which had incredibly succeeded in supplying the survival needs of West Berlin's 2¾ million inhabitants, and its industries, for 15 months. Secretly they planned their next thrust in testing the will of the Free World to resist aggression, and chose Korea as their next testing ground.

In Washington, lights burned late at the Pentagon as the chiefs of the armed services worked desperately to maintain adequate defenses for the nation, in the face of an economy program slashing Air Force and Navy air strength to the lowest levels since the panic of the 1946 demobilization.

Across America, a peacetime economy was booming to meet consumer demands for housing, automobiles, television sets, and goods of all kinds. All except airplanes. The aircraft industry was in a slump that recalled a remark once made by aviation pioneer Richard Depew: "Flying's greatest hazard is the risk of starving to death."

In general aviation, most of the aircraft being built were sold to business and corporate owners; to shrewd buyers who required the utmost in value and performance for every dollar invested. The situation was one made to order for Beech, which had introduced its improved Model B35 Bonanza at the beginning of the year. With it the company captured more than its proportionate share of the market. To be exact, Bonanza sales represented 53% of the industry's commercial deliveries of high-performance four-place single-engine aircraft for the year. The Model 18 also did better than might be expected.

98

Bonanza sales undoubtedly were aided by the notable performance record of a fleet of 11 Bonanzas owned by Central Airlines, first of the nation's certificated feeder airline operators to offer regularly scheduled passenger and mail service with high performance single-engine aircraft. On May 18, 1950, Central completed more than one million miles of accident-free service in little more than eight months time. Its Bonanzas were flown over 1,320 route miles, serving 25 cities in Texas, Oklahoma, Arkansas and Kansas.

The budget restrictions placed on military aircraft procurement also worked to Beech's advantage. Taking a sharp look at all items of expense, the Air Force placed an order in March 1950 for a pilot quantity of Beechcraft Mentor primary-basic trainers, which they designated as the YT-34 training plane. The built-in economy of the Mentor was a factor in this decision. Military orders for spare parts for Beechcrafts in service, and factory rebuilding and modification of service-worn Beechcrafts, also provided additional work for Beechcrafters, and savings to the services and to the taxpayers.

To keep its people and facilities occupied, Beech also continued its program of diversified production of both aircraft and non-aircraft items and components. And, sensing that the then current stalemate in the Cold War would not endure, the Beech management took an option to lease the inactive former Air Force base at Herington, Kansas, comprising a large airfield with concrete runways, and hangars providing 160,000 square feet of floor space, for the probable duration of any emergency that might arise.

The emergency came swiftly. On June 25, 1950, the Republic of Korea was invaded without warning by more than 60,000 North Korean troops spear-headed by over 100 Russian-built tanks. Again, Communism was on the march. The United Nations Security Council demanded a halt to this aggression; and the U. S. armed forces backed up its demand.

Was this to be the opening action in World War III — the start of the showdown between militant Communism and the Free World? No one could foretell. Uneasily, America recalled President Truman's announcement on September 23, 1949 that U. S. detection devices had recorded the detonation of an atomic explosion in Russia. Our monopoly had ended; the Communists, too, had the A-bomb. Blocked by its own principles of non-aggression from waging all-out war to end the Communist menace permanently, America and the Free World could act only to restore peace in Korea, and strengthen its defenses against further attacks.

Accelerated action for preparedness was the result. Action in Washington to restore the economy-sapped vitality of the armed forces. Action at Beechcraft to prepare the company and its people to do their full part in meeting the nation's needs.

Again, just as in 1940, Beech wasted no time in waiting on formal contracts to provide certified protection for its interests. There would clearly be plenty of work to do in the national defense, for Beech and for other qualified aircraft producers. This was apparent from an emergency order that was placed with Beech only a few days after the Korean flare-up, calling for delivery of 1,000 Beech-designed jettisonable wing-tip fuel tanks in an almost impossibly short span of time. The order was filled — on time as specified. Meanwhile, Beech on its own initiative exercised its option to lease the Herington air base, rehabilitated it, and started up production lines using local labor. The company further made commitments for some $1 million worth of new machine tools and facilities to be installed in its Wichita plants, and arranged for a $5 million line of bank credit to finance its anticipated additional business. The spirit behind these actions was well expressed in the following statement issued by Walter H. Beech:

"One of our most valuable contributions to the defense and rearmament program in the last war was our willingness to stick our necks out and make facilities available in advance of actual contracts requiring them. As a result, Beechcraft reached full scale production many months in advance of the date that would have been otherwise possible. We frankly believe that the present situation is just as serious as that leading to the last war, and we intend to do everything in our power to make a maximum contribution to our country's present rearmament program."

And again, as in 1940, Beech's willingness to take risks in the nation's defense paid off. Before the end of fiscal 1950 on September 30, its backlog of defense orders totalled more than $50 million; and additional large contracts were being negotiated. Beech production commitments covered a wide range of materiel, from the reconstruction of military Model 18 Beechcrafts to parts and assemblies for important tactical aircraft. Many of the fuel tanks Beech had delivered on short notice were in use in Korea, extending the range of U. S. fighter planes in service there. All of this activity was superimposed on a schedule of commercial aircraft production that continued to lead the industry in its class.

At this stressful stage in the company's affairs, there came a harsh reminder of the timeless axiom: "There is no indispensable person." The three people who together made up the continuum of past, present and future Beech management — Walter H. Beech, Olive Ann Beech, Frank Hedrick — were interlinked by more than ties of family. They shared not only a constant striving for excellence, but also an unfailing willingness to face reality. The reality that put this quality to its ultimate test was a stern one.

On the evening of November 29, 1950, Mr. and Mrs. Beech hosted a dinner in their home at 48 Mission Road for some 25 guests. And there Walter H. Beech's heart stopped beating. So quickly, so quietly Walter H. Beech was gone. He had been in good health and had planned to leave the next morning with his sales manager on a business trip. Later, many employees would tell Mrs. Beech how happy he had been and how much interest in their work he had shown all that week.

There was grief at his passing — at Beechcraft, and all over the world. The funeral cortege that carried the Tennessee farm boy to his last resting place in the Old Mission Cemetery, escorted by a formation of Beechcrafts flying overhead, was perhaps the most impressive Wichita had ever known. But grief was tempered by the knowledge that in his less than sixty years of life, Walter H. Beech had dared more, and achieved more, than most other men in his time. He had joined the immortals of aviation. The legacy he left behind was fittingly described in a tribute written by Beech general manager Jack Gaty:

"The thousands of Beechcrafters' jobs; the thousands of Beechcraft airplanes flying over all parts of the world; and the million

101

square feet of Beechcraft factory space; all stand as a monument to Walter H. Beech — the pioneer who was not afraid."

The time of mourning was brief; for, as Walter H. Beech himself would have said, "There's a lot of work to do." There was never any question as to who would take his place. Olive Ann Beech quietly added to her own weighty work load the duties of the company's chief executive; and the members of its board of directors, elected by the stockholders at their annual meeting on December 14, named her as president and chief executive officer of the Beech Aircraft Corporation on that date.

This was in no sense a sentimental gesture. Its logic was inescapable. For the union of Walter H. and Olive Ann Beech was much more than a conventional marriage; it was also a working partnership of two uniquely gifted individuals. Throughout a quarter century of working and building, planning and fulfilling, side by side with Walter H. Beech, the company's new chief had established beyond any doubt her credentials for leadership. It would be a new kind of leadership — soft-voiced but firm, dispassionate, calmly analytical and realistic — and, according to the record, a highly effective one.

In the pressure of "acceleration for preparedness," the new year of 1951 arrived almost unnoticed. Time had meaning only as a measure of how much might be accomplished in each hour. In some ways, it was as if all the clocks in the world had stood still for the past ten years; for the situation at Beech strongly resembled that of its 1940-1941 years of expansion for defense production. There were differences, of course — some helpful, some obstructive.

On the helpful side, foremost was the reputation Beech had earned for on-schedule production of high quality materiel. In its first era of expansion, the company had been a relative newcomer, its abilities in high volume production still unproved and not known even to itself, to say nothing of the outside world. One of America's foremost experts, the production genius of General Motors and chief of war production program, Lieutenant-General William S. Knudsen, had flatly declared that it would be impossible for Beech to meet its commitments — and had handsomely apologized when Beechcrafters proved him wrong. In the peculiar Korean conflict era, when economy remained

102

a factor and contracts had to be won competitively, the general knowledge of what Beech had done in the past was, while not decisive, still a strong point in its favor.

There was also an advantage in having been over the expansion road before. The Beech management had learned how to anticipate some of its twists and turns, its curves and danger spots. Under new and different circumstances, there would be fresh and unexpected hazards; it would be wise to keep the seat belts fastened. But experience was on their side.

The obstructive elements were based on the differences in circumstances. In 1940 and 1941, America's economy was moving forward at much less than full throttle. Unemployment was substantial, and labor was plentiful. The threat of involvement in World War II was widely recognized, adding zeal to production for defense that was kindled to white heat throughout a unified nation after the attack on Pearl Harbor. Thus the seemingly impossible became less difficult to achieve.

In 1950 and later, almost anyone who wanted work could pick and choose freely. Unemployment was down to 3 million, considered to be mostly hard-core unemployables. The production throttle was jammed all the way forward to the firewall, throughout American industry. While aircraft production was expanding toward a target rate of 50,000 warplanes per year, far surpassing that of World War II, Beech and all other producers had to scramble for manpower and materials. The shortage of skilled labor was particularly acute.

Public support was not unanimous for this war that was not a war, but officially a "police action" by the United Nations. The need to arrest the spreading cancer of Communism, and yet to stop short of total victory, was hard to comprehend. Many worked valiantly to back up the 5.7 million members of the armed forces who served during the Korean conflict. But morale on the home front was inevitably lower than during World War II, and maximum efficiency on defense production lines was more difficult to develop.

Regardless of problems, the need and the opportunity for Beech again to serve in the nation's defense was present; and the challenge was wholeheartedly accepted. The working force was enlarged as rapidly as possible. Training programs were set up to teach aircraft skills to inexperienced men and women, and to upgrade the skills of present employees and qualify them for advancement. Management braced itself to accept the unavoidable higher costs of labor turnover, knowing that some of its new people would find themselves unadaptable to aircraft work, and the higher rate of spoilage that would result from insufficient job experience.

At the beginning of the war, another decision had to be made. Should the company abandon its commercial production, or try to go on building Beechcrafts for business and utility purposes? Its record left no room for doubt on a major point: The choice would be based on management's appraisal of what would be best for the nation's needs. It was a free choice. The top-level government attitude was not to discourage "business as usual," except for reasonable limitations in some critical areas. The need for a strong national economy was recognized.

Experience at the outbreak of World War II provided a guide. At that time, all but the very oldest Beechcrafts then flying had been commandeered by the government for essential defense uses, except for those airplanes already in defense-related service. The existence of this ready force of high-performance aircraft in being had proved to be a valuable asset to the war effort. If they had existed, many more Beechcrafts could have been used to excellent advantage in the same way. Obviously, the same thing would hold good in case of another national emergency. The more Bonanzas and twin-engine Beechcrafts were in existence and ready for use, the better off the nation would be. So Beech decided to continue commercial production on as nearly as possible a normal basis. Its decision was announced in the following statement:

"We intend to continue building airplanes for executives as long as we can get materials and components. It is our opinion that such airplanes constitute an invaluable national asset, whatever the course of the cold, warm or hot war. We believe that what helps business cannot fail to benefit our nation."

So, in January 1951, Beech proceeded to introduce a new Model C35 Bonanza which incorporated many refinements over the previous version. It went into production at once, with a backlog of 100 firm orders with cash deposits offering excellent prospects for its success. The Beechcraft Customer Service Program was continued in full force; and development, testing and preparation for production was kept under way for the new Model 50 light Twin-Bonanza. Distributors and dealers were authorized to book provisional orders for the Model 50.

A building boom was under way meanwhile, substantially enlarging the nearly one million square feet of floor space already in use at the Beech Wichita plant. New warehouses and service buildings were going up. Mezzanine floors enlarged the space available for use in existing buildings. A railroad car loading dock with double trackage spanned the 1,020-ft. length of "warehouse row" south of the major plant buildings; and a two-mile rail spur was built to connect Beech Field with the nearest railroad main line. To some "old hands" at Beech, it was a shocking sight to see rail trackage being laid across the flight apron at the north end of the field. They could recall the days when a vendor, hoping to sell something to the company, had better be very sure to arrive in Wichita via airline rather than by rail, if he nourished hopes of a cordial reception. But the industry had outgrown these youthful rivalries; and with a monthly freight bill of over $100,000 attesting the volume of its shipments by rail, it was only good sense and sound economy for Beech to equip with direct-at-factory rail facilities.

Money to pay for the fast-increasing amounts of materials and labor that accelerated production required, until finished goods were delivered to and paid for by customers, came from a doubling of the revolving bank credit arranged with a syndicate of New York City, Chicago, St. Louis, Kansas City and Wichita banks. In February the available total was raised from $5 to $10 million; and later in the year it was redoubled, from $10 to $20 million. A very solid testimonial, this, to the reputation that the Beech Aircraft Corporation had established.

An all-time sales record for commercial aircraft was established in April, when Beech posted a "Sold Out" sign for its anticipated first year's production of $5 million worth of Model 50 Twin-Bonanzas. Since January, Beech distributors and dealers had booked firm orders for 100 of the all-metal six-place twin-engine executive transports — each order accompanied by a non-revocable $5,000 cash deposit. Most remarkable was

Chapter 17
1951

105

the fact that most of the customers who put up their hard cash had never even seen the airplane or taken a ride in it prior to placing their orders. The Twin-Bonanza was certificated by CAA on May 25, 1951; and the first deliveries in August and September went to the Lycoming-Spencer Division of AVCO Corporation, an important defense contractor; and to Carco Airservice (two units), the "atomic airline" then using four-place Beechcraft Bonanzas in shuttle service between Albuquerque and the atomic research center at Los Alamos, New Mexico. The ability of the Model 50 to deliver satisfactory single-engine takeoff performance at the 7,120-ft. elevation of the 2,500-ft. Los Alamos airstrip, often at high surface-level temperatures, was especially important to Carco.

Briefly noted in the company's records was the conferral in May by the Women's National Aeronautical Association of the title "Woman of the Year in Aviation" on its president, Olive Ann Beech. It was the latest in a long series of honors accorded Mrs. Beech. Always more concerned with getting the job done, rather than personal recognition, she received such honors modestly and with quiet pride, sharing them generously with her associates.

On July 10, 1951, the backlog of orders on hand was increased by many millions of dollars, when the U. S. Air Force announced that Beech was the winner of a design competition for a high-speed twin-engine training airplane of advanced design and performance. Designated as the T-36A trainer, the Beech design outlined a twin-engine, all-metal, low-wing, retractable tricycle landing gear aircraft of more than 25,000 pounds maximum takeoff gross weight, with a speed of over 300 miles per hour and a service ceiling of approximately 34,000 feet. Powered by two R-2800 Pratt & Whitney engines, with takeoff ratings at 2300 hp, its design span was 70 feet, its length 52 feet 2 inches, and its height 21 feet 5 inches. Its combat radius was listed as over 650 miles. As a trainer, it was designed for a crew of four: three students and one instructor, with a cockpit arrangement providing space for two seats behind the pilot and co-pilot on the flight deck. As a transport, it was to afford accommodations for a crew of two and twelve passengers.

The Beech T-36A was a design keyed to the needs of its

106

Beechcraft Twin-Bonanza first flew November 15, 1949, just 223 calendar days after Walter H. Beech approved the design. (Page 95)

Winner of Air Force design competition for a twin-engine trainer was this 300 mph Beechcraft, the T-36A.

Wichita Plant III was completed in 1953 as an assembly plant for the T-36A. (Page 112)

107

ERECTED IN HONOR OF
WALTER H. BEECH
AVIATION PIONEER
FOUNDER OF BEECH AIRCRAFT CORP.
WHOSE VISION AND WILL TO DO
ENDEARED HIM TO ALL OF US.
EMPLOYEES OF BEECHCRAFT
1951

Walter H. Beech Memorial was built by employees and dedicated November 11, 1951, by Lieutenant General James H. Doolittle, long a personal friend of Mr. and Mrs. Beech. (Page 110) time. In less than a decade, airplane performance had nearly doubled in almost every category. Bomber speeds had been stepped up to over 600 mph — more than twice the speeds of World War II bombing planes. Altitudes were in the 40,000 to 55,000-foot range — again doubling the 20,000 to 25,000-foot ranges of World War II. Tactical aircraft had correspondingly increased in size and weight. The T-36A trainer was well matched to these increases. It promised the capability of meeting then current Air Training Command requirements in the same way that the versatile Model 18 Beechcraft had efficiently and economically served in training a majority of the air crews during World War II.

Inspired by the design competition victory and the prospect of producing a Beechcraft that would make history just as the Model 18 had done, Beechcrafters tackled the challenging new project with redoubled energy. In less than five months time, they presented to an Air Force Inspection Board headed by Major General K. P. McNaughton a full scale mock-up of the T-36A. It was a beauty — far more handsome and suggestive of efficiency, in its completely detailed life-size simulation, than the design sketches and drawings had promised. Their swift completion of the mock-up brought high praise from Air Force officials.

In a further expansion move, the company enlarged its satellite plant operations which had been inaugurated at the Herington, Kansas former air base late in 1950. The success of the Herington operation, which by October 1951 employed 500 workers, led to the leasing of a major portion of facilities at the deactivated Liberal, Kansas military air base. This action served several useful purposes. It reduced Beech's expansion of its own buildings to a minimum. It eased the burden of the general expansion for defense by all Wichita aircraft manufacturers on the municipal facilities of Wichita. It gave Beech access to additional supplies of high type, willing-to-work manpower. And it provided employment in localities which otherwise might have had little or no participation in defense production.

Amid the bustle of acceleration for preparedness, a famous Beechcraft took off from the Beech airport on a mission identical with that toward which all Beechcrafters were working — the restoration and preservation of world peace. The airplane was the "Waikiki Beech," which Bill Odom had flown to two nonstop world endurance records — "Old Reliable," the fourth Bonanza built. It was brought out of honorable retirement at the Smithsonian Institution to serve a 35-year-old former Navy pilot, Congressman Peter F. Mack, Jr. of Springfield, Illinois, in a solo globe-girdling "Good Will Tour" that would take him to some 45 major world cities in some 30 countries. For this flight, the record-breaking Bonanza was renamed "The Friendship Flame," in keeping with its pilot's purpose of building goodwill among the peoples of the earth, on a "person-to-person" basis.

After the completion of a factory checkup and minor modifications, "The Friendship Flame", flown by Congressman Mack, took off from its home base at Springfield on October 7, 1951. Just 113 days later, it touched down again at home, after more than 35,000 miles of round-the-world flight over land and sea. "Old Reliable" and its pilot had completed their journey, and had been warmly received everywhere they went. Through no fault of either, one purpose had gone unfulfilled. Congressman Mack had requested permission to visit Russia and Moscow on his tour; but his request was denied by the Communist authorities. Goodwill apparently was officially unwelcome behind the Iron Curtain.

Veterans' Day, November 11, 1951, was a time of rededication for Beechcrafters to the tasks they had undertaken for defense, and for a tribute to the company's co-founder, Walter H. Beech. Through voluntary contributions, employees had financed the construction of a masonry and bronze memorial shaft honoring Mr. Beech, on a site adjoining the Administration building. It was unveiled that day by Lieutenant General James H. Doolittle — the "Jimmy" Doolittle who led the famous 1942 bomber raid over Tokyo, long a warm personal friend of Walter H. Beech. General Doolittle's tribute to Mr. Beech, as a man and as a pioneer of aviation, was moving and sincere.

Almost concurrent with the viewing of the T-36A mock-up in early December by the USAF Inspection Mock-up Board, Beech added another branch of the armed services to its list of customers. A contract was received from the U. S. Army Field Forces for four Model 50 Beech Twin-Bonanzas, following Army appraisal of accelerated evaluation tests of the Beech and other planes in its category at Fort Bragg, North Carolina. The four twins, designated by the Army's air arm as Type YL-23, were the first twin-engine airplanes to enter Army service. Informally known as "Flying Staff Cars," they were ordered for use as transports for general and staff officers of Army and Staff Headquarters. Except for minor modifications, they were "off-the-shelf" airplanes, practically identical with the commercial Model 50 Twin-Bonanza.

Summing up at the close of the year, the record of progress was impressive. Fiscal year deliveries ending September 30 topped $32.7 million, practically double those of 1950. Operations were profitable in spite of heavy expenses and outlays for rapid expansion. Owned and leased plant facilities floor space had jumped to some 1,624,000 square feet, compared with 974,000 square feet at the end of 1950. Employment had almost doubled, from 4,400 to more than 8,500 employees. Beech commercial sales of approximately $9 million were more than double those of the next largest utility aircraft manufacturer. Bonanza No. 3000 had been delivered in December, setting an all-time industry sales record for airplanes of its class. The company's backlog of orders on hand topped $180 million. Clearly, there were busy days ahead.

Chapter 18

Beech's twentieth anniversary year of 1952 was good and busy, in every meaning of the phrase. The rate of output in established product categories accelerated tremendously, much as it had done during the early World War II era. Engineering, Planning and Experimental departments rapidly advanced the design and experimental work connected with new models. And the Beech Plant Engineering Department diligently planned and provided for the substantial additional facilities that the company's commitments required.

Because of the great importance attached by the Air Force Training Command to the T-36A advanced twin-engine trainer project, emphasis was foremost on its furtherance; and much of the company's best talent was concentrated on expediting its development and production. Completion of design and construction of the flyable prototypes pressed on without pause in Engineering and Experimental; and an accelerated testing program of components and assemblies simulated flight experience equivalent to ten flights around the world, before the actual flying prototype would ever make its first takeoff.

Readiness for high rates of production of the big, complex, advanced-performance T-36A Beechcraft called for more than staggering amounts of tooling, jigs and fixtures, and the addition of thousands of employees to the Beech working force, many of whom would lack experience and would thus require months of training and experience to reach acceptable levels of proficiency in their duties. A wholly new plant facility would be required for T-36A assembly, to provide the unencumbered floor space needed for a fast-paced assembly line accommodating airplanes that stood better than 21 feet in height, spanned a width of 70 feet, and stretched out 52 feet 2 inches in length. Beech's World War II assembly buildings had been preplanned to be flexible enough for such uses; but they were already in use, down to the last square inch. Much of their once open assembly area had been converted, after completion of contracts for AT-10 Beech advanced pilot trainers in 1943, to specialized facilities for the assembly of massive A-26 Invader wings and nacelles. These were now in use, day and night, assembling complete sets of wings for urgently needed Lockheed T-33 jet trainers and F-94C Starfire fighters. To clear and re-convert these areas for T-36A assembly would have been wasteful and impractical.

So the Beech Plant Engineering Department designed a new assembly building for the T-36A. The big bird would have a home of its own. Located midway between the existing Beech Plants I and II, at the west edge of the mile-long Beech airport, it comprised 96,000 square feet of assembly space, plus 14,700 square feet of air-conditioned office and engineering quarters and 5,300 square feet for utilities. A travelling crane of ten-ton capacity ran the full length of the line. With an eye to the future, the building was planned for wide-range utility; and the rail spur already installed at Plant I was extended along its length. To ease the pressures on working capital, its $1.3 million cost was financed largely by a $1 million chattel mortgage, secured by Beech-owned equipment and machinery. Ground was broken on June 2, with completion scheduled for Spring 1953.

The Air Force continued to show intense interest in the T-34A single-engine trainer originally developed by Beech at its own expense as the Model 45 Mentor. There was a growing urgency for an economical, efficient basic trainer to replace the T-6 used in World War II; and the Beech design looked right for the job. Two formal meetings were held with Air Force boards to iron out various details, and the engineering was practically completed to put the T-34A into volume production early next year.

The U. S. Army found its trial quantity of L-23A transports very satisfactory, and contracted for delivery of Beech's entire production of this military version of the Model B50 six-place Twin-Bonanza for 1952 and 1953. Engineering and production planning for this contract was pressed to completion during the year. The sturdy Twin-Bonanza, built throughout to withstand flight stresses of 8 G's, conformed with the ruggedness requirements of military service, and at the same time had shown its ability to transport its passengers swiftly and comfortably. It delivered the same traditional Beechcraft dividends of swift, safe, comfortable, efficient travel to the executive officers of the Army as those that made Beechcraft ownership profitable to the executives of American business.

Demand for Beechcrafts was not limited to the U. S. armed services. America's neighbor to the north, Canada, was also making ready for defense. As a basic item in its preparations, the Royal Canadian Air Force ordered a large quantity of new Model 18 twin-engine Beechcrafts, equipped for use as pilot and navigator trainers and utility transports, and designated as the RCAF "Expeditor." The contract for these planes was the largest ever negotiated by the aggressive Beech Export Department. On-schedule delivery of the Canadian Expedi-

113

tors called for exceptional effort on the part of Beechcrafters, which they were glad to make; for warm ties of friendship and mutual esteem had always existed between Beech and its Canadian customers, and the good qualities of Beech products were strongly appreciated in the rigorous conditions of service often prevailing north of the border.

Beech 1952 military production included many other items. Of foremost importance in relation to the Korean conflict was its delivery, in quantities as high as 400 per week, of jettisonable aircraft fuel tanks and napalm fire bomb tanks. The fuel tanks served to extend the range of combat aircraft, making it possible to carry out a greater number of tactical missions in support of the ground forces in Korea. The napalm fire bomb tanks many times came to the rescue of U. S. soldiers and marines pinned down by enemy forces, spreading a blazing curtain of fire over the enemy and saving countless numbers of American lives. Tank manufacture was not a major item in terms of dollar volume; but to patriotic Beechcrafters, it was highly rewarding in terms of its end results.

Production of complete sets of wings for Lockheed jet trainers and fighters was also an important activity, accounting for nearly $28 million in volume for the year. It was exacting work, demanding the best in craftsmanship and precision. Each set of wings for the high-performance jets weighed 2700 pounds — a figure matching the gross weight of a fully loaded Beechcraft Bonanza. Beech was also a source for ailerons for the Boeing B-47 "Stratojet" bomber, then in production as a deterrent to further Communist aggression at a rate that far outdid the peak of World War II B-29 output. Engineering was completed at mid-year on the Beech-designed C-26 jet engine startergenerator unit; and the Herington plant was soon turning out the bright yellow self-propelled ground service units at a fast clip, for use in Korea and all over the world. Aging military Model 18 Beechcrafts continued to set down on weary wings at the Herington air base, and fly away a few weeks later, restored to miraculous newness as Air Force C-45G and Navy SNB-5 utility twins. The working force increased to 700 employees at Herington, and 450 at the Liberal, Kansas plant.

Very little time was spent in the observance of the com-

114

pany's twentieth anniversary on April 19, 1952. There was too much work to be done. The growth of Beech Aircraft from 10 to its then 10,500 employees, in two decades, was duly noted in the employee publication, and everyone got on with the job at hand. A new flight record also was placed in the archives, when Paul Burniat of Brussels, Belgium, established an official world speed record for light planes of 225.776 km. per hour, flying a Beech Bonanza.

In the same spirit of concentration on the work at hand, there was a cordial but quiet reception of the 1952 Lady Drummond-Hay Memorial Trophy, awarded to Mrs. Beech on June 29 in recognition for her achievements as president of the Beech Aircraft Corporation. The award was made by the New York branch of the Women's International Association of Aeronautics. Mrs. Beech did not leave her desk to receive the award in person; but the honor was deeply appreciated.

There were two brief but unavoidable interruptions to production during the year. The first was caused by a city-wide shortage of water, following breaks in a 48-inch main supply line on Sunday, June 15. Since the Beech Wichita plants required more than a million gallons of water each day, a two-day shutdown was imperative until service could be restored. Beech had foreseen this possibility and had drilled wells earlier in the year, seeking a stand-by source of water; but these attempts had been unsuccessful. It acted at once to prevent future shutdowns from such emergencies. The Plant Engineering Department surveyed a site one-half mile north of Plant I which seemed suitable for a reservoir; and, before the year was over, a 45-acre man-made lake had been completed, holding a 100-million gallon supply of water in reserve for plant uses. Its construction required the moving of some 100,000 cubic yards of earth from the lake bed, and the provision of supply pumps and pipelines. At any threat to its vital production, Beech once again proved that it could make the dirt fly. As a bonus, the lake was stocked with fish, and landscaped as a recreation area for Beech employees.

The second interruption was beyond human control — a Great Plains blizzard, rare in southern Kansas, that blocked all roads for two days, following ten hours of heavy snowfall driven into

115

fantastic drifts by a 50 mph wind. A standing weather watch maintained routinely by Beech Plant Protection gave enough warning to permit early dismissal of first shift employees on the afternoon of Tuesday, November 25, shortly after the snowfall began, and to cancel later shifts. But the snowstorm worsened so rapidly that hundreds of cars became snowbound on the way home. Motorists stranded on nearby US 54 highway were sheltered in Beech Plant II. Rescue work had top priority, and no lives were lost in the potentially lethal situation. Thanksgiving Day that week had a special meaning for many. By working on the following weekend, Beechcrafters made up for most of the production and income they had lost to the storm.

Fiscal year results at September 30, 1952 showed $90.9 million in sales — an increase of 277% over the $32.8 million of 1951. Even though the company was heavily involved in military work, its distributors and dealers contributed $9.5 million to this total in domestic commercial sales, adding hundreds of units to "The air fleet of American business" produced by Beech. The Beech Export Department and its distributors in foreign lands accounted for $17.4 million, putting Beechcraft in first place for the lightplane industry with 40.1% of all sales to foreign countries. The Bonanza dominated the export market with 73.8% of all sales in its class.

The company's earnings for fiscal 1952 topped $4.8 million, before taxes — 3½ times those of 1951. Under the excess profits tax law, however, its federal income taxes topped $3.1 million, cutting the net income to less than $1.7 million. Clearly Beech had been working for the government throughout the year, in more ways than one.

At the end of December 1952, the total of 13,418 employees on the payroll very nearly equalled the World War II peak figure. The total was not a source of joy to the Beech management. The thousands of new employees added, in a valiant effort to reach and sustain almost impossible levels of production on the T-36A trainer, were more of a liability than an asset. In the current shortage of labor, many had attached themselves to the payroll merely to go along for the ride, with no intention of pulling their weight. And even the willing new hands were, for the most part, unskilled in aircraft work. Experienced Beech-

116

crafters did their best to help assimilate the newcomers; but it was an uphill struggle.

It was with relief, therefore, that the company negotiated with the Air Force a revised and more realistic delivery schedule for the Beech T-36A. A share in its production was allotted to a Canadian manufacturer, Canadair, Ltd. of Montreal; and Beech management gained the leeway critically needed to prune the deadwood and restore efficiency, which had dropped more than 10% in terms of productivity per employee during the desperate months of hiring almost any and all who might apply. The housecleaning, started in January 1953, permitted a reduction in force by June of more than 2,500 employees, with upsloping improvements in morale and output.

The need for efficiency was pressing, for the company's backlog of business, as the year began, stood at $224 million. The U. S. Army Field Forces took delivery of its first regular production model L-23A Beechcraft — the "Flying Staff Car" version of the Model 50 Twin-Bonanza — in January, and urgently requested soonest possible delivery of its 60-plane contract for use in Korea and all over the world. Beech distributors and dealers, at the annual factory sales meeting in the same month, turned in 85 firm orders for the new D35 Bonanza — a refined version of the long-time world leader in its class, offering 22 pounds increase in payload, and many new comfort and appearance features — also for early delivery. They and their customers were also eager for deliveries of commercial Twin-Bonanzas, which had been preempted by Army needs, at the earliest possible moment. An aggressive commercial sales and production program was firmly projected.

Other items in Beech's extensive product mix also demanded fullest utilization of all its manpower and facilities. Their perennial Model 18 remained in demand, both as a commercial executive transport and, in its military SNB-5 configuration, as a trainer and utility plane for the air services of the French and Netherlands governments. The foreign military twins were ordered by the U. S. government and supplied to these European members of the North Atlantic Treaty Organization under the Mutual Defense Assistance Pact to strengthen their air defenses against Communism. Delivery schedules were stringent, and

117

complicated by a need for special radio installations suited to European requirements. The planes were delivered on time as promised.

U. S. Air Force testing of its trial quantity of T-34A trainers (the Beech-developed Model 45 Mentor) had proved it to be the wanted replacement for the obsolescent World War II T-6 trainer; and a letter contract was issued to Beech early in the year to put the T-34A into quantity production. So the job of setting up production lines for this model was added to the work on hand. There were still other items to be continued in large-scale production: Wings for Lockheed jet trainers and fighters, ailerons for B-47 jet bombers, fuel and napalm tanks, military Model 18 rebuilds, and C-26 jet ground service generators.

Beechcrafters racing to meet delivery dates enjoyed a lift in morale from a quadruple racing victory scored by their products in a national event. Beechcraft Bonanzas swept the first four places in the First Annual Jaycee Transcontinental Air Cruise held April 27 to May 2, from Philadelphia, Pennsylvania to Palm Springs, California. "Just like the old days," they told one another. "It takes a Beechcraft to beat a Beechcraft."

Meanwhile, a pattern was taking shape in world and national affairs which would soon make its repercussions felt at Beech. Joseph V. Stalin, premier of the Soviet Union, died at Moscow on March 5. The fanatic leader of world communism was gone. The Korean conflict was at a stalemate. In Washington, demand for curtailment of defense spending was renewed. The target aim of a 143-wing Air Force was cut back.

On the morning of June 10, 1953, Beech was notified by Department of Defense officials in Washington that all production contracts for its T-36A advanced twin-engine trainer were cancelled effective immediately. In one instant, half the company's backlog was eliminated, and a vast amount of work and effort went down the drain. At the time the cancellation was received, the T-36A project was on schedule; and the prototype was being readied for its first test flight on the following day. The flight was never made.

It was a staggering blow, and a crucial test of courage. Beech passed the test. Before the day was over, plans were under way

118

to meet the new situation, and to go out after new business to replace, as far as possible, what had been wiped out. President O. A. Beech's annual report to the company's stockholders expressed its attitude as follows:

"It should be stated at this point that the management of your company never has and never will express any criticism for the cancellation of the T-36 contract by the U. S. Air Force. The interests of the Government are paramount, and no contractor has any legitimate reason for complaint if and when any branch of the Government wishes to revise its planning and amend its purchase contracts for equipment. In our grand country, one of the most valued axioms is the one stating that 'The customer is always right.' We all enjoy exercising this right in our daily lives and none of us can criticize the officials of the Government for taking any action which may seem necessary, providing that fair compensation is offered for efforts which have been expended. Despite the tremendous impact of the T-36 cancellation on the affairs of your company, the management of your company would have no other choice than to repeat the actions which they took in preparing to deliver T-36's, in accordance with their contract with the Government, in the event that the Air Force again requested it to undertake a new and similar program."

The T-36A cancellation was immediately announced to all Beechcrafters under the fighting title of "A change in assignments" — a correct and aptly chosen term planned to sustain morale in the face of a disappointment keenly felt by everyone in the organization. It was pointed out that all other Beech contracts with the U. S. Government and other customers were completely unaffected by the sudden demise of the T-36A. No time was wasted in useless regrets.

Good news came at the same time as the bad. The government of Chile placed an order for more than a million dollars worth of T-34A primary trainers, following an evaluation competition with other American, British and French airplanes. In performance and operational qualities, the Beech Mentor proved to the Chileans that it had what they wanted. Beech was still a winner.

At almost the same time, a production line move was completed which was to accomplish, before the end of the year, increases in efficiency per man hour expended in building Beechcraft Bonanzas of better than 50%. Plant II, at the south end of the Beech flying field, was remodeled and enlarged to serve as a specialized center for Bonanza production exclusively. The move was made without losing a single day's working time; and on June 8, Bonanza No. 3,551 became the first of its model to emerge from the new plant. The building in which Bonanza production was centered had originally been constructed in 1927 to house the operations of Yello Air Cabs, Inc., a company organized during the post-Lindbergh aviation boom to provide nation-wide air taxi and charter service. It had gone out of business after the 1929 crash, and its quarters had stood idle until they were taken over by Beech for World War II production of Beechcraft Model 17 biplanes for military service. Now, at last, it was to revert to very nearly its original purpose — a center of versatile, swift, economical air transportation for America and the world. Removal of Bonanza production to Plant II cleared room in the larger Plant I for efficient assembly of L-23A Twin-Bonanzas for the Army Field Forces, who were already expressing great satisfaction with their Beechcrafts — the Army's largest fixed-wing aircraft.

In July, the management team that had gone out to beat the bushes for more business, following the T-36A cancellation, brought back a substantial subcontract to build flaps and ailerons for the Republic F-84F swept-wing jet fighter plane. They followed up with another very substantial subcontract from McDonnell Aircraft for important components of the USAF F-101 "Voodoo" supersonic jet fighter. The orders were valuable from a dollars-and-cents viewpoint; and they represented a heartening vote of confidence in the Beech organization from fellow aircraft manufacturers.

Beechcraft product performance received a vote of confidence, too, from an enthusiastic Bonanza owner, Mrs. Marion Hart of New York. On August 27 Mrs. Hart and her co-pilot, PAA pilot Wayne Vetterlein, completed one of the first light plane crossings of the Atlantic Ocean since the pioneer days of aviation, flying a 2,500-mile Great Circle course from Torbay, Newfoundland to Shannon Airport, Ireland in 13½ hours. The

61-year-old sportswoman had made previous Bonanza flights over water and jungle terrain to Central and South America. The Bonanza she flew to Europe was the second one she had owned. The flight was made purely as a pleasure trip; and that, she reported, is what it proved to be — "A beautiful crossing in bright moonlight."

The Beechcraft Mentor also continued to bring credit — and business — to its designers. In October, the Republic of Colombia ordered a substantial quantity of the two-place trainers, and later increased its order by ten more Mentors. In Air Force Phase VI flight tests of the T-34A Mentor at Edwards AFB, California, the test plane logged 434 hours of flight in only 32 days. It wrapped up this performance with a 'round-the-clock run of 23 hours 20 minutes of flight in one 24-hour period, making seven quick landings during that interval to refuel and change pilots. This functional development phase of routine USAF testing did much to verify the stamina of Mentor design and construction; but a near accident associated with the testing program provided an even more dramatic demonstration of its in-built Beechcraft toughness. At full cruising speed of 189 mph, a T-34A was inadvertently flown into contact with an aerial cable stretched across a canyon. The cable did not break, but almost stopped the Beechcraft and spun it around in mid-air, 350 feet above the canyon floor. Through skillful handling, the military pilot righted the airplane before it could touch ground, regained flying speed and flew back to the base, where he made a normal landing. Inspection showed that damage was confined to superficial contusions and abrasions of the right wing leading edge, which bore the imprint of the cable it had contacted in mid-flight.

The Navy Bureau of Aeronautics ran its own series of extensive tests on the T-34A Mentor at Corry Field, Pensacola, Florida, from September 28 to December 4; and the Beechcraft came through with flying colors. The principal airplane tested was serial No. G-3, one of the first Mentors produced; and in spite of its age, it came through without ever being out of service due to mechanical failure. Navy requirements for a training plane were in some ways more stringent than those of the Air Force; for the Navy schooled its pilots from the outset

121

in landing techniques necessary for aircraft carrier operations, which called for abrupt stall-outs just above ground level and heavy "drop-in" landings that imposed great strains on the landing gear. Many well-built airplanes had faltered and "washed out" their landing gears under such severe stresses; but the Mentor gear did not fail. One Navy Commander said he could not "wash out" the Mentor gear in testing.

Other nations of the Free World had been watching the Mentor military test programs with keen interest; and in November, an agreement was reached with the National Safety Forces of Japan for eventual production of Beechcraft Mentors in that country under license to the firm of Fuji Heavy Industries of Tokyo. Beech contracted to furnish initial completed Mentors, followed by parts and manufacturing information necessary to enable its licensee to build the airplane in its own plants. Preliminary phases of a similar agreement were concluded also with the Canadian government to produce the Mentor for RCAF training uses in Canada.

As aviation throughout the world observed the 50th anniversary of powered flight on December 17, 1953, Beechcrafters looked back on a very eventful year of their own. It had opened with a blend of problems and promise — promise that ended in part with the shock of the T-36A cancellations at mid-year. It continued with a fighting organization staging an amazing comeback throughout its remaining months. Figures for fiscal 1953 at September 30 showed total sales of $140.4 million, including a $41.1 million T-36A termination claim. The effect of the high-cost buildup for T-36A production was reflected in a net loss after tax allowance of $2.3 million — almost as much as Beech's total sales for its fiscal year of 1940, only thirteen years ago. But, through vigorous effort, its backlog still stood at better than $100 million; and the company was in excellent condition to gain back all it had lost, and more, in the days ahead. Its commercial and export sales topped $17.1 million; and as the world leader in its product categories, Beech looked forward to substantially increasing this part of its business in the year to come. Beech had proved that it could take punishment, and come back fighting harder than ever.

122

Royal Canadian Air Force ordered military version of the Model 18 as pilot and navigator trainer, as well as personnel transport. (Page 113)

L-23A Beechcraft, Army version of the Twin-Bonanza, was the largest fixed wing airplane in the ground forces inventory when ordered. (Page 117)

Naval Air Training Command chose the Beech Mentor as its student trainer, the T-34B, after thorough evaluation tests. (Pages 121, 128)

Newly completed Plant III was used for a $1 million Plane-O-Rama display of new Beechcrafts offered for 1954.

Conventional gear Twin-Beech, completely redesigned in a Super H18 version, continued to serve business, government and military leaders throughout the world.

The 1000th Beech Model D18S went in February 1954 to join Ohio Oil Company's fleet of 9 twin and 12 Bonanza Beechcrafts. Delivery was sealed with a handshake by O. A. Beech and Mike Murphy, Ohio Oil aviation manager.

124

Beech entered the new year of 1954 at full throttle, staunchly confident of its ability to make the future better than the past. Results for the final quarter of 1953 had already shown that it could be done. The company's books showed a good profit on final-quarter sales of $21.1 million. The old-time "Can do" spirit had never been higher throughout the organization; and a working force of 6,867 Beechcrafters — every man and woman fully worthy of that title — was achieving outstanding standards of efficiency and quality.

On the morning of Thursday, January 28, more of the reasons for Beechcraft's confidence in its future were disclosed. The setting was the handsome new Plant III, also identified as Building 36 after the USAF T-36A for the assembly of which it had originally been constructed. The occasion was a "Million-Dollar Plane-O-Rama," displaying to the annual meeting of Beech's 40 U. S. distributors more than a million dollars worth of sparkling factory-fresh new commercial Beechcrafts. The airplanes on view were not only newly produced; they also showed new advances in design and performance that promised the sure fulfillment of the meeting's theme — "Sell More — Make More in '54."

Heading the all-star cast of new commercial Beechcrafts was the "Super 18" — a redesigned, re-engineered version of the classic Model 18 twin that bettered its famous predecessor in every phase of performance, luxury, convenience and beauty. Its gross weight was increased by 550 pounds, with corresponding gains in payload. Yet the cruising speed was also increased to 215 mph, top speed to 234 mph, and the range to a 1455-mile maximum. Enlarged, redesigned wing tips provided increased single-engine rate of climb and single-engine ceiling at the greater gross weight. Although heavier, it was easier to handle. The cabin was bigger, roomier. A larger cabin door dropped down to present a built-in stairway for easy entrance and exit. Many more new design and comfort features were included. Beech had never gone in for grandiose titles for its products;

and the designation of "Super 18" had been the subject of some debate before it was adopted. But the decision of those who saw and flew the new model was unanimous: No lesser term would have been adequate for this Beechcraft.

The Twin-Bonanza became available for civilian purchase, after years of virtually exclusive Army duty in its L-23A configuration. Like many other veterans, it had matured during its military service. Experience gained in thousands of flight hours all over the world had pointed the way to many improvements and refinements on the design that had been originated five years ago. More than a hundred such changes were included in the new Model B50 Twin-Bonanza that made its bow at the Plane-O-Rama. Its gross weight had gone up from 5,500 to 6,000 pounds; its payload was 447 pounds greater, without any loss in its performance or handling qualities. Its top speed was 205 mph; cruising speed, 192 mph at 10,000 feet; rate of climb, 1450 fpm; service ceiling 20,000 feet; range up to 1,088 miles; and single-engine performance, outstanding. It afforded airliner standards of comfort for six passengers; and with six aboard and full fuel tanks, had payload and room to spare for 191 pounds of baggage. It was built to a flight load factor of 8 G's — far in excess of CAA commercial requirements. The reliability and economy of its two 260 hp Lycoming GO-435-G2 engines had been demonstrated in rigorous military service. Appearance, styling and interior accommodations had been refined in the Model B50 to the most exacting standards of luxury and good taste. The many business firms and executives who had waited long for their Twin-Bonanzas would find their patience well rewarded.

The single-engine Beech Bonanzas shown at the Plane-O-Rama had much that was new and better to offer to commercial buyers. A choice of engines could be had in the new Model E35: The long-popular 205 hp Continental E-185-11, or optionally, a more powerful 225 hp Continental E-225-8 engine delivering 9 mph more speed at recommended 65% cruising power at 8,000 feet, together with a 200 fpm faster rate of climb and a 1,000 foot higher ceiling at full load. The buyer who wanted the utmost in single-engine speed and performance would find his wishes gratified in the new model. Many additional refinements attested Beech's determination to make the best airplane of its class even better in every possible way.

Distributors attending the Plane-O-Rama flew away with every airplane the factory could release to them, and placed orders for $2.5 million more — including 15 of the "Super 18" model at $100,000 each. The year was off to a good start. The new model showing was well timed, too; for the business aircraft market was growing fast. Its upper ranges were dominated by Beech, with many thousands of Beechcrafts in service as "The air fleet of American business," out of a total of 21,500 business planes, large and small, in use during 1953. Business twin-engine planes were widely favored, and three other highly respected manufacturers joined Beech in offering light twins during the year, at prices ranging from $32,000 to $70,000. Beech would have competition; and that was all to the good, as Beech saw it. The efforts of every worthy competitor would benefit the entire industry; and Beech had never been backward about pitting its products against the best the other fellows could build.

Good news came from the Air Force early in March. An order for some $4.5 million worth of Beech-designed C-26 starter-generators for jet aircraft was received at about the same time that a follow-on contract for fifty more T-34A trainers reached Wichita. The follow-on order extended production of the Air Force version of the Beech Mentor through July 1955. A few days later, and presumably not unrelated to these events, a notice came from the Air Force Air Materiel Area office at San Antonio, Texas, that their top-echelon survey team had awarded an efficiency rating "Extremely High" in comparison with the aircraft industry as a whole to the Beechcraft quality control program. Beech's exact rating, after evaluation of more than 307 weighted check list items, was 93.9% in efficiency — among the best in the industry. Beechcrafters were obviously doing their part to help the Air Force realize its goal of "More Air Force per Dollar."

On March 29, handsome compliments came from the Chief of the U. S. Navy Bureau of Aeronautics on the completion of Beechcraft's Navy rebuild program for SNB (Model 18) Beechcrafts. Ceremonies held at the Beech-Wichita Plant I marked the delivery of the 1246th and final twin Beech to the Navy.

It was the last rebuild, at the end of a seven-year contract, for a simple reason: The Navy had no more Beechcrafts to be processed. "Well done" was the essence of the Navy's comment.

A happy sequel to this event was a Navy announcement on June 17 that the Beech Mentor had been chosen as its first-step student trainer for use by the Naval Air Training Command, with an initial order calling for several hundred planes. The Beechcraft had won out over two other airplanes, described by the Navy as "excellent," in evaluation tests conducted at Pensacola, Florida. The Navy's reasons for selecting the Mentor, which had been developed by Beech on its own initiative and at its own expense, were identical with those of the Air Force and of foreign air services: It was judged to be the best and the most economical airplane for the job. The Navy trainers would be almost identical with the Air Force T-34A, the most obvious difference being that of high-visibility bright yellow paint which the Navy considered useful in avoiding collisions around crowded training fields. Performance of the Air Force T-34A and Navy T-34B would be identical, though expressed in different terms: High speed, 189 mph (164 knots); cruising speed at 60% of rated 225 hp at 10,000 feet, 173 mph (150 knots); maximum permissible diving speed, 280 mph (243 knots). Both versions would afford an extremely high flight safety factor of 10, permitting unrestricted aerobatic maneuvers. Both weighed in at 2,900 pounds gross, and approximately 2,170 pounds empty, and used a 225 hp Continental engine powering an 88-inch diameter Beech constant speed propeller, affording a rate of climb of 1,230 fpm at sea level, a sea level takeoff run of 780 feet, and a landing run at sea level of 330 feet. Wing span was 32 feet 10 inches; length 25 feet 11 inches; height 9 feet 7 inches; and total wing area including ailerons, 177.6 square feet. The all-metal, low-wing, cantilever monoplane design, stemming from the Beech Bonanza, featured a fully retractable tricycle landing gear with a steerable nose wheel.

Essentially the same design, in the commercial Bonanza version, again led the field that month in the second annual Jaycee Cross-Country Derby from Philadelphia, Pennsylvania to Palm Desert, California. Finishing first, second and third among 52 entrants in the 2,579-mile event were Beechcraft Bonanzas

128

— two of which repeated victories of the previous year. Beech-crafters did not even bother to complete the familiar phrase: "It takes a Beechcraft . . ."

The Air Force meanwhile had ordered new versions of the B-47 Stratojet intercontinental bomber, for use by its Strategic Air Command in fulfilling its aim: "Peace is our mission." The new B-47s would carry vast amounts of radar and other electronic gear; and a source of absolutely reliable standby ground power was needed for these systems, as well as for jet engine starting on both B-47s and other jets in Air Force service. Air Force experience with the hundreds of C-26 generator units designed and built by Beech, and in use all over the world, had been highly satisfactory; and Beech efficiency was equal to the prevailing demand for top quality at competitive prices. So a $7 million order for additional Beech C-26 generators, plus a new and more powerful Beech-designed unit for the new B-47s, identified as the MD-3 generator, was entrusted to the company. Both units used the same primary power source — a Continental PE 15C-2 Packette unit derived from an air-cooled, horizontally opposed six-cylinder aircraft engine design, and developing 200 hp at 2800 rpm. In the C-26, the gasoline engine drove three 30-volt, 500-ampere generators, and supplied both 28-volt DC and 115-volt AC electrical power for ground servicing and jet engine starting. The electrically higher-output MD-3 featured a 60 KVA, 3-phase generator designed to maintain voltage at the exact level necessary for accurate radar adjustment. Its electrical output was equal to that required to fully air-condition 25 five-room homes by present-day standards. Both units were self-propelled by a 3-speed front wheel drive and carried their own integrated heating and cooling systems, controls and instrumentation. Both benefited from a long-standing interest on the part of Beech engineers in gasoline-electrical transducers — an interest which had existed since 1945, when Beech designed and built a prototype of a gas-electric automobile, the Beechcraft "Plainsman," which featured individual electric motor drive on all four wheels. Designed for use as a military command car to travel over rough terrain, it showed great promise. But, since its development would have carried Beech far afield from the company's primary interests in aviation, the "Plainsman" was not advanced beyond the experimental stages. Its reincarnation as an aircraft ground servicing unit, however, was a logical one.

June was also an anniversary month for Plant II, marking the completion of its first year as the center of Bonanza production. In 255 working days, the compact facility had turned out 297 completed Bonanzas; and its production had been stepped up to 1½ Bonanzas per day, to keep up with incoming orders.

Beechcrafters had always been safety-minded. Their constant sense of responsibility to customers all over the world who entrusted their lives to the safe performance built into Beech products carried over into their own work habits; and the management did all it could to encourage their safety-consciousness. The result was the presentation to the Beech Aircraft Corporation on June 10 of the National Safety Council Award of Merit for achieving one of the outstanding safety records in American industry during 1953. The Beech accident severity rate was 93% better than par, and the frequency rate 33% better, according to the record. The lost-time accident rate was a shade over 3% per million man-hours, compared with a national average of 8.4%. The many hand operations involved in aircraft manufacture made building airplanes inherently more hazardous than flying in them; but Beechcrafters were doing their best to promote safety in all directions — and doing it successfully.

Two Bonanza owners, Roy Carver of Muscatine, Iowa, and Thomas H. Danaher of Wichita Falls, Texas, successfully completed separate midsummer trans-Atlantic crossings in their Beechcrafts. Carver crossed from Torbay, Newfoundland to Paris, with one stop enroute for refueling at the Azores. Danaher flew non-stop 3,100 miles from Newfoundland to Shannon, Ireland in 16 hours 58 minutes. Both flights were individual ventures not sponsored by the factory.

The opening days of August were hot, as usual in Kansas. August 12 was doubly so; for on that date, Beech made its first moves into the "hottest" of all aeronautical areas — Aerospace. It was a timely step; for the atmosphere, and the space beyond, was being penetrated by strange new "birds" of many

130

kinds, winged and wingless. The Martin "Matador," designated by the Air Force as its B-61 pilotless bomber, had entered service with the Tactical Air Command in Germany in March. The Sparrow I air-to-air missile was combat-ready in Navy service. Chance Vought had its "Regulus" missile in being for submarine, shipboard and shore launching. Martin's "Viking" had established a world altitude record for single-stage rockets of 158 miles. More than 30 aerospace projects were actively under way. Beech had no intention of abandoning aircraft for missiles, then or at any time in the foreseeable future. But the opportunity was clearly at hand to enlarge the company's scope; and Beech seized it. One of its first moves was to qualify for and receive two then top-secret research contracts in the space-oriented field of cryogenics — the study of extreme cold and its effects on missile materials and fuels. Beech also saw interesting possibilities in the design and manufacture of target airplanes and missiles, and engineering studies were started along those lines. Whatever went up into the air, whether in or out of the atmosphere, or even out of this world, Beech might have a hand in helping to create. The first steps had been taken toward an aim that would some day take its place beside the long-standing slogan: "The World is small when you fly a Beechcraft"... an aim that could be summed up in the phrase: "Space is in reach — with support from Beechcraft."

The score at the end of the Beech fiscal year on September 30 showed sales of $78 million — $57.2 million in military business, $20.8 million in commercial business (up 21.6% over 1953 commercial sales). Net income after taxes was over $3.3 million, wiping out the T-36 losses with more than $1.1 million to spare. The company's position was also substantially improved in other ways. Compared with fiscal 1973, inventories were reduced by more than $11.4 million, and notes payable to banks were down from $15.9 million to only $5 million. Man-hours required to build airplanes and subcontract components were reduced by 14.6% to 38.8%. With wholehearted support from a loyal and efficient organization, President O. A. Beech had more than proved her title to the honorary Doctorate of Science in Business Administration conferred on her by Southwestern University earlier in the year.

131

There was more to come in the remaining quarter of the calendar year. Financing arrangements were worked out with the National City Bank of New York and other banks for the floor planning of business airplanes; and a new leasing plan was arranged with the American Leasing Company for companies that might wish to use Beechcrafts on a rental basis. Both plans promised substantial increases in commercial sales; and results were to fulfill the promise.

October was more than a month of pleasant Indian Summer days. It brought a follow-on Air Force order for $4.3 million more of T-34A trainers, extending production of that model through the next two years. Lockheed added another $1.8 million to the $18 million order it had placed in March for Beech-built wings for the T-33 jet trainer. On October 2, Beech completed deliveries of 99 Model B50 Twin-Bonanzas which had commenced in late January, only eight months ago. Before the month ended, a new 1955 version of the Twin-Bonanza was introduced — the Model C50. It was Beech's answer to the competition offered by a very respectable twin-engine transport of high-wing design that was edging uncomfortably close to the Twin-Bonanza in price and performance. Always realistic, Beech rarely if ever under-estimated its competitors, but concentrated on keeping its own products ahead of the field in performance, quality and value.

The new C50 had what it took to maintain Beech leadership. Its bigger Lycoming GO 480-F6 engines were rated at 275 hp — an increase of 15 hp over the previous model. Its cruising speed at 66.6% power at 10,000 feet was up to 200 mph, making the C50 the first six-place executive transport in its class to achieve so high a speed at full gross weight. Its top speed was 210 mph. Its useful load was 2,040 pounds; its payload, 1,020 pounds. In spite of its higher power, its range was increased to 1,100 miles. Even before it was publicly introduced, C50 production had been sold out through January — a good omen for its success.

Receipt of an order for external fuel tanks for the Republic F-84F jet fighter also brought on a resumption of tank production, which had been discontinued after the Korean truce pact was signed. Beech had built more than 120,000 tanks of

132

various sizes and types, ranging up to 1,700-gallon tanks for B-47 bombers; and at the peak of production, had completed as many as 400 tanks per day. The company's specialized experience in these important items made it a logical first choice source.

As the year came to an end in December, the Navy took delivery on its first T-34B trainer, just six months to the day from the time the contract was signed. Gratified with Beech's on-schedule delivery of a very satisfactory first article, the Navy, traditionally not lavish with praise, issued a "Well done!" commendation for this performance. The Air Force ordered another $6 million worth of MD-3 generator units. And a nine-day survey by Air Force specialists brought Beech the highest rating for quality control ever granted to any aircraft company in the San Antonio Air Materiel Area — a rating of 97.83%. It was a good finish to a good year.

Chapter 20

When the National Beechcraft Distributors Meeting convened at Plant III on January 12, 1955, the company's 200 guests were greeted with congratulations for having qualified as the world's foremost aircraft distributor and dealer sales organization, with over $20 million in sales to their credit for 1954. They were also told that Beech had completed plans for accelerated production, based on market studies that showed good prospects for a 25% increase in commercial sales for the year ahead. And, to reinforce this forecast, they got their first look at a restyled and refined Bonanza — the new Model F35.

In its 1955 version, the Bonanza became a six-window air-sedan. A third window, added aft on each side of the cabin, provided 20% more rearward visibility for the pilot, for greater safety around congested airports, and enhanced a nearly sky-wide range of view for the passengers, at the same time increasing the feel of spaciousness within the cabin. Borrowing a trick from the airlines, the Bonanza top was painted white to reflect heat and keep the cabin interior cooler and more comfortable. Propeller blades were shortened and prop tips were squared, to cut high speed tip power losses and provide greater efficiency at cruising speeds. More effective "air brakes," desirable to slow down the extremely clean Bonanza in landing approaches and under some instrument conditions, were gained by beefing up the landing gear and adding nose ribs to the flaps, thus increasing the allowable air speed for gear and flap extension. Numerous other refinements were made in a design that 4,000 Bonanza owners had come to accept as the last word in performance, style and luxury. According to the Beech philosophy, model changes had no reason for existence unless they gave the customer significantly more for his money. Mere "face-lifts" to give an artificial stimulus to sales were never even remotely considered, and in fact were frowned on as a form of sharp practice unworthy of Beechcraft. By this standard, and in every other way, the new F35 Bonanza was an honest airplane.

New to some who attended was also the Model C50 Twin-Bonanza, first introduced some two months ago. It and its senior twin, the Beech Super 18, just entering its second year on the market, won the kind of praise that counted most — signed, firm orders. When the meeting was over, nothing was left behind but the floral decorations. Distributors flew away with 28 new Beechcrafts, and in the next few days sent orders for $2 million more to the factory for rush delivery.

In civil aviation, 1955 is remembered as "The year of the jets." Not in an operational way, of course; for it would be years before the big jet airlines would roll off the production lines and soar into the airways of the world. But it was a time when the airlines, after much soul-searching and wonder as to how they would ever pay for the costly birds, signed their initial orders for more than $1 billion worth of jet transports.

Alert to the trend of the times, Beech saw an opportunity to capitalize on the widespread interest in jet aircraft, and also to stake out a prior claim in this area if it should attract a sufficient number of buyers of business and executive transport aircraft. The company promptly nailed down the exclusive distributorship for North America of the MS 760 "Paris," a four-place, twin jet low-wing monoplane built by a long-estab-

134

lished French manufacturer, the Morane-Saulnier Company. Beech also got an option on the rights to build the MS 760 under license in this country, and promptly imported a demonstrator to show off the plane and feel out the market. In 90 days the Beech import made 724 demonstration flights from 38 airports, on a nation-wide tour, and compiled an excellent service and performance record. Almost everyone who saw and flew in it echoed the sentiments of one veteran pilot who exclaimed, after flying the MS 760: "Goshalmighty, what a doll!" With a top speed of 410 mph, and a cabin affording pressurized comfort for four persons at its maximum-range altitude of 23,000 feet, it was quite an airplane. The prestige gained by Beech in demonstrating the first authentic jet executive transport actually in being was substantial. But the MS 760 was perhaps a little too far ahead of its time; and the tangible interest it developed that year and later was not sufficient to justify full-scale continuance of the project. None the less, it was a worthy and a useful experiment for Beech.

Another experiment in jet aircraft, begun in 1955, also wound up eventually on the shelf. This involved a two-place jet trainer of Beech's own design, the Model 73 "Jet Mentor." Based on the tried and well-accepted Model 34 propeller-driven T-34 Mentor, and using many of the same components, it was described as "the most economical jet trainer in the world." It logged many successful test and demonstration flights; but in the meantime, the U. S. Air Force settled on a competitive jet trainer with twin engines and unconventional, for a training plane, side-by-side seating. That was the beginning of the end for the "Jet Mentor"; but, to pilots who saw and flew the swift, maneuverable little ship, it remains even today "The airplane I'd like most to own — just for fun!"

These experimental activities by no means distracted attention from the firm business on hand during 1955, which covered many fields. Beech was busy keeping up with delivery schedules on T-34A Air Force and T-34B Navy trainers; building C-26 and MD-3 generators for the Air Force, wings for Lockheed Air Force T-33 and Navy T2V-1 jet trainers, and sundry vital components for the McDonnell F-101A "Voodoo" fighter and the Republic F-84F "Thunderstreak" fighter. Army L-23s also

135

came home to Beechcraft, somewhat bedraggled by long hours of hard service, to undergo a factory overhaul program known as IRAN ("Inspect and repair as necessary") and return to service good as new.

Progress was made in Beechcraft's missile and aerospace activities, when an extension of its main engineering division was opened at Boulder, Colorado on July 25. The beginnings there were modest, comprising leased quarters in a downtown building accommodating a staff of 75 employees. Initial assignments comprised cryogenic propellant and high energy fuel studies for missiles and future space vehicles. Their pioneering investigations of liquid hydrogen tankage and fluid flow systems, at a time when knowledge in these fields was almost entirely theoretical, helped lay the groundwork for later use of the high-energy liquefied gas as the primary propellant for advanced space vehicles. Beech's new Missiles Division also scored its first hit on target, submitting the winning design of nine entries in a Navy competition for a medium-performance type of pilotless radio-controlled target aircraft. Beech's winning entry was designated as the XKDB-1, and was designed to operate at altitudes up to 40,000 feet and speeds up to 320 mph. Two contracts were awarded to Beech in 1955 by the Navy on this item — a $½-million award for design of a prototype, and a $1 million follow-on award for flight evaluation quantities of the fast, compact V-tailed "bird," which had a 12½-ft. span and a 13½-ft. length. It was powered by a six-cylinder, two-cycle 120 hp McCulloch turbo-supercharged engine, and was equipped with a parachute installation permitting its undamaged recovery and reuse after target runs.

Twenty years of constant activity on the part of Beech and a member of its top management team in promoting greater safety in the air were signally recognized on October 5 when John P. Gaty, vice president - general manager, received the 1954 Annual Business Flight Safety Award from the National Business Aircraft Association. The award cited Mr. Gaty's initial publications in 1934 on the effects of lightning, based on studies made when he became the owner of one of the first B17L Beechcraft biplanes built, and continuing with further flight safety publications sponsored by Beech after he joined the company

136

in 1937. The awards committee found that Beechcraft, under Gaty's supervision, had invested about $100,000 in the ten years following World War II in its Safety Suggestion Program, making some 330,000 direct mailings of free safety literature to pilots, U. S. and foreign government agencies, universities and flight safety groups. The studies were appraised as instrumental in saving hundreds of lives, through advancing pilot and industry awareness of flight safety factors, including such weather problems as thunderstorms, standing waves and turbulence. Incisively presented and scientifically sound, they reflected the characteristic Beech attitude of realism and willingness to recognize and face the facts. The award attested the value of the Beech Safety Suggestion Program to the company's most important group of commercial customers as well as to aviation as a whole, and provided a further stimulus toward the continuance of a valuable program which the company still maintains in effect.

The year was a good one for the business and utility aircraft industry. Sales reached a total of $75 million. The business airplane was proving its worth. It was even better for Beech. The company held first place with more than one-third of the industry's total, scoring commercial sales in fiscal '55 that topped $27 million. Beechcrafts swept the field in their brackets. Super 18 sales showed an 84% gain; Twin-Bonanza sales gained 21.6% in units; and the F35 Bonanza had a 20.5% unit gain. Overall commercial volume showed a gain for Beech of some 40%, fulfilling the forecast of a 25% increase with a wide margin to spare. The Beech Floor Plan Financing Plan, well established in other industries with "big ticket" costly items sold by distributors and dealers, but new to the aviation business when it was introduced by Beech, had sparked sales by making it possible to show and demonstrate actual new Beechcrafts to prospective buyers all over the nation. The Beech Retail Finance Plan offered new convenience to buyers by letting their airplanes pay for themselves out of current earnings or savings accruing from ownership. And a third arrangement, the Beechcraft Leasing Plan, placed new Beechcrafts at the service of many more users in return for a prearranged payment per month of use, without capital commitments. Beech was showing the industry not only how to build better airplanes, but also how to market them more efficiently.

Fiscal 1955 ended September 30 with total sales and income topping $77 million, and a $63 million-plus backlog of well diversified business, military and commercial. Outstanding bank loans had been paid in full during the year. All was well. And another good year was ahead, as the record was soon to show.

Never the type of organization to be inhibited by tradition, Beech moved its calendar forward a month and gained a full-speed start into 1956 by holding its annual distributor and dealer sales meeting at the then new Wichita Municipal Airport on December 8 and 9, 1955. The event was renamed as the company's "International Sales Meeting" — quite properly, for Beech representatives were present from seven foreign countries, and from all over the United States. It was a brilliant success. Following the unveiling of new 1956 models, the sales organization was unanimous in agreement that the company's goal of $32 million in commercial sales for 1956 should be attainable; and they showed that they meant business by submitting firm orders for $11.5 million worth of 1956 Beechcrafts before the new year had even begun.

First-magnitude star of the meeting was a new D50 version of the Twin-Bonanza, supplementing the C50 which was also continued in production. The D50 featured higher-powered 295 hp Lycoming engines, driving new Hartzell three-bladed propellers to achieve a cruising speed of 203 mph and a top speed of 214 mph. Non-stop cruising range was increased to 1,650 miles, ample to span more than half the continent; useful load was up to 2,319 pounds. Alternate five or six-place versions were offered, and numerous other refinements appeared.

The Super 18 also offered much that was new for '56. The list included more than thirty items, ranging from chrome-plated engine cylinders for increased service life to more "plush" features in the already deluxe cabin. And the Bonanza, better than ever in its 1956 G35 version, featured further reinforcement of structures which were already widely in excess of CAA requirements, aerodynamic improvements that boosted its cruising speed to 190 mph at 75% power or 184 mph at 65% power, and still more touches to enhance comfort and ease of flight.

KDB-1 propeller driven missile target established Beechcraft firmly in the missile target field. (Page 136)

Burlington Industries, world-wide textile leaders and later owners of 4 King Air Beechcrafts, added a new D50 Twin-Bonanza to their four Beechcrafts then in use. Pictured (left to right) Burlington executive W. F. Sharp, chief pilot Shelby Maxwell; and Beechcraft dealer Ken Brugh.

Weyerhaeuser Co. anticipated its multiple King Air fleet with the purchase of a new Super 18 to replace its 1946 Model D18S Beechcraft. Its crew: Donald A. Bell, pilot (at left) and A. J. Wildhaber, chief pilot.

Beech was ahead of the times with two pure-jet airplanes: The Jet Mentor (left) and the French MS 760 to which it held exclusive North American rights. (Page 135)

This Super 18 went to Tokyo's No. 1 newspaper in a trans-Pacific ferry flight flown by Jack Ford, president of Fleetways, Inc.

Pulled at the end of a line by tow planes travelling at sonic speeds, the Beech Dart served as a target for fighter pilots practicing gunnery. (Page 142)

Multi-purpose ground service vehicle, the MA-3, replaced six different machines on Air Force flight lines. (Page 142)

Model 95 Travel Air was developed to fill the growing market between the Bonanza and Twin-Bonanza for an easy-to-fly, thrifty light twin. (Page 144)

As a further step in its movement into advanced and secret missile and space projects, the company completed the organization early in February of a wholly-owned subsidiary corporation, Beechcraft Research & Development, Inc. It was the second subsidiary operation to be established in the company's history. The first, Material Distributors, Inc., had been liquidated following the close of World War II after its purpose of aiding redistribution of surplus materials had been fulfilled. The new corporation was organized with both immediate and long-range future considerations in mind. Its board of directors was identical with that of the parent company, and it was in every sense all-Beechcraft. Its permanent site was to be a secluded tract of land, originally 760 acres in size, purchased by Beech near Boulder, Colorado on the eastern slope of the Rocky Mountains. Later in February, Beech awarded contracts for construction of the first buildings on that site, comprising some 4,250 square feet of preliminary testing facilities. This was to supplement and, with later additions, eventually to replace the engineering facility occupied in leased quarters in downtown Boulder by a staff then numbering some 60 aviation design engineers, engaged in secret aerospace research.

Two mid-winter delivery flights of new Beechcrafts were worthy of notice for the contradictory reason that they made no news. The first was that of a C50 Twin-Bonanza to its purchaser, the Krupp Company of Essen, West Germany, across the Atlantic Ocean via the northern route. Reporting to Beech on the performance of the C50, which was flawless in spite of encountering "some extremely difficult weather," crew member Ralph A. Rohweder feelingly commented: "The unreserved excellence of Beech craftsmanship takes on vivid new significance over the icy Atlantic in January." The other flight, described as "routine," was the ferrying of two Super 18 Beechcrafts 6,500 miles across the Pacific Ocean for service with the Japanese Coast Guard out of Tokyo. It was the usual "island-hopping" operation familiar to airmen with World War II PTO experience — California to Hawaii, Midway and Wake Islands and Japan.

The "smallest Beechcraft ever built," the pilotless Navy XKDB-1 target drone, made news in March when it was approved in prototype form by a Mock-up Inspection Board comprising more than 70 Navy, Air Force, Army and industry personnel. At the same time, another Beech-built aerial target device was unveiled. It was the "Dart" tow target, originally developed by the Navy Ordnance Test Center at Inyokern, California, and refined by Beech missile engineers. Pulled at the end of a nylon line by tow planes travelling at sonic speeds, the low-drag Dart brought a new simulation of reality to fighter pilots practicing their gunnery skills. "Greatest advance in fighter-gunnery targets in 25 years" is how they described it. More would be heard of the Model 1002 Dart in the future.

Memories of the early post-war Beechcraft Plainsman electric-drive command car were again revived, and lessons learned in its design found useful application, when the Air Force placed a $5.3 million order early in the Spring for a new Beechcraft MA-3 multipurpose aircraft servicing vehicle. A powerhouse on wheels, the MA-3 had a gross weight of 15,700 pounds, four-wheel power steering and four-wheel drive, and a draw bar pull of 10,000 pounds minimum, enabling it to tow heavy multi-engine aircraft on the ground. It had a 225 hp gasoline engine; a gas turbine power plant capable of firing any "air starting" jet engine; electrical power output of 28 continuous or 42 intermittent kilowatts; a 13-ton air conditioning unit for pre-flight cabin cooling and equipment temperature control; and a special 3,500 psi air compressor. It was the fourth Beech-designed ground service unit to go "on the line" for the Air Force — the latest of a series of units indispensable in readying modern combat aircraft for takeoff.

Another Beech specialized activity got a boost in April, when a $7.5 million Air Force contract was received for jettisonable 1,700-gallon external fuel tanks for B-47 Stratojet medium bombers. It enlarged the range and scope of the reactivated fuel tank production program, centered at the Beech satellite plant at Herington, Kansas, well into the following year. To this division, it was a welcome addition to current assignments that included the manufacture of 1,400-gallon tanks for C-130 cargo planes under Beech's first contract with Lockheed's Marietta, Georgia facility, and 282-gallon tanks for Navy F3H-2N Demon jet fighters under a sub-contract for McDonnell Air-

142

craft Corporation at St. Louis, Missouri. Another Beech assignment in this area was an engineering and manufacturing contract for prototype refueling tanker external stores for a new Navy F-3H jet fighter, on which McDonnell held the prime contract.

Also in April, Beech added to its backlog of varied sub-contract production a $7.75 million follow-on order from McDonnell Aircraft for additional rudders, stabilators and other components for the supersonic USAF F-101 "Voodoo" jet fighter-interceptor. The repeat order evidenced customer and Air Force satisfaction with past Beech performance in building F-101 parts. It was exacting work, calling for highest quality craftsmanship to meet very close tolerances and high strength requirements; for the 20-ton, Mach 1.5 Voodoo was then the largest and one of the highest-performance fighters in the Air Force inventory. Production of wings for Lockheed jets, which totalled more than 5,000 sets in the past five years, was also extended forward by a $4 million order for Navy T2V-1 Lockheed SeaStar jet trainer wings. These were modified versions of T-33 jet trainer wings, strengthened to withstand the higher shock loads of carrier deck landings, and featuring slotted leading edges and boundary-layer control provisions providing a slow 80-knot landing speed for aircraft carrier training operations. Another vote of confidence came from Lockheed in the form of a $1 million contract for the manufacture of aft fuselage sections for its F-104 Starfighter, world's fastest fighter of its day. And producibility studies, carried on concurrently with sub-contract production of canopies and windshields for Convair's USAF F-102 jets, resulted in some $11 million in orders for major sub-assemblies for the delta-wing, supersonic F-102A, F-106A and F-106B jet fighters soon afterward. Some of the jet fighter parts were made of titanium, a then critically scarce metal well worth its cost of $20 a pound because of its lightweight high strength, corrosion resistance, and superior strength-to-weight ratio at high temperatures. Beechcrafters handled this near-precious metal with great care, meeting this new challenge with appreciation for the opportunity to enlarge their experience. Flaps and ailerons also continued in production for Republic Aviation's F-84F jet fighter. As a subcontractor, Beech was doing all right.

143

The month of May was a merry one for Beechcraft. The Navy liked its T-34B Beech Mentor trainers so well that it ordered $4 million more added on to its contract then in production. The Army took one look at the new, higher-powered D50 Twin-Bonanza, and ordered a half dozen of the commercial models "off the shelf" for soonest possible delivery, to add to its large fleet of L-23 Twin-Bonanzas in service at home and abroad. And Beech engineers came up with important new optional features for the Super 18 that enlarged its utility and appeal. They worked out an installation package for both newly produced and already-in-use 18's for the Geisse Safety Gear, widely hailed as "the most prominent safety development in 15 years" — a controlled castering device that compensated for drift in cross-wind landings by permitting each main gear landing wheel to caster under hydraulic and spring control. And they devised outboard wing auxiliary fuel tanks that optimally relocated range-stretching extra fuel supplies, and cleared space in the nose compartment for extra baggage and weather radar installation.

In July, the Air Force turned on the heat. With a $12.5 million contract for more MD-3 Beech ground support units came this word: "We know it's practically impossible, but we also know Beech. We must have 105 units before October 31. Can do?" It took some fast running, but Beech could do, and did. For good measure, the Beech generator builders threw in accelerated deliveries of 180 units per month thereafter. Just to make things more interesting, they carried work forward at the same time on the first order Beech received from the Navy for ground support equipment — a contract disclosed July 16 for Beech-designed Model 316 jet aircraft starters.

Monday, August 8, was "First-flight day" for a completely new Beechcraft business airplane — the Model 95 four-place light twin. Powered with two four-cylinder 180 hp Lycoming engines, the compact 4,000-pound twin combined 200 mph cruising speed with quietness of operation unmatched, in scientific noise-level testing, by any other twin-engine aircraft. It was designed to fill a gap existing in the Beech product line between the single and twin-engine Bonanza models; and its subsequent sales performance showed that design purposes had been more than met. In its successful first flight and many subsequent tests, it carried the name of the Beechcraft "Badger" — a name suggesting, like that of the American badger, exceptional qualities of speed, tenacity, toughness, longevity and ability to get the job done. "Badger" was an apt descriptive term, semantically and phonetically, for the Model 95; but an odd coincidence ruled out its use. The U. S. Air Force, without knowledge of the Beech choice, had adopted but not yet announced the name "Badger" as a code term for identification of a then current model of Russian jet bomber by military and civilian aircraft spotters. To avoid any possibility of confusion, Beech gave up the original designation; and the Model 95 became the Beechcraft "Travel Air." Its later performance was to add luster to that famous name.

August also marked the "on schedule" completion of a 40-month program which produced more than 300 T-34A Beechcraft Mentor trainers for the U. S. Air Force. All Air Force aviation cadets were then receiving their primary pilot training in Beechcraft Mentors operated by the nine USAF contract schools. The Mentor was also then serving the military forces of Chile, Colombia, El Salvador and Turkey; and was being produced under license from Beech in Japan and Canada to serve in training Japanese and RCAF pilots. Other foreign governments were also showing great interest in the efficient, economical tandem trainer; and Beech production was continuing at full speed on T-34B Mentors for the U. S. Navy.

Volume for fiscal 1956 added up to $74.5 million — $42.4 million in military sales, $32.1 million in commercial business. The commercial total topped the $30 million goal which had been set at the beginning of the year, and represented a 23% increase over the previous year. Beech management's long-range plans for diversified production were taking effect.

Mid-November was the activation time for a second wholly-owned Beech subsidiary — Beech Acceptance Corporation, Inc. Its purpose was to further the financing programs introduced in the airplane industry by Beech early in 1954, which had proved highly successful for Beechcraft distributors and dealers and advantageous to Beechcraft owners and users. Under complete control of the parent company's directors and officers, it would serve even more fully to finance distributor and dealer floor stocks of ready-to-show, ready-to-deliver Beechcrafts; to offer deferred payment plans to buyers; and to promote leasing arrangements for firms that preferred to rent rather than own Beechcrafts. By making Beechcrafts easier to sell, and easier to buy, it was to add millions of dollars to the company's commercial volume in 1957 and the years to follow.

Chapter 21

In many ways, 1957 was a year to remember — a year that would stand out in the perspective of history. Most notably, it was "The Year of the Sputnik," in the words of the Aircraft Year Book, official publication of the Aircraft Industries Association, Inc. In the long view, it was more than that. Whether the first man-made object launched into space was called "Sputnik" or "Explorer," or whether it carried the initials "U. S." in Roman lettering, or "C.C.C.P." (the Cyrillic equivalent of "U.S.S.R.") was immaterial. What mattered was that man had at last achieved his long-sought conquest of space. From that time on, the moon, the planets and the stars might realistically be regarded as within his eventual reach. His science of aeronautics had pushed past new frontiers; it had become the science of aerospace.

The year brought problems as well as achievement. U. S. Defense planners were trapped in a dilemma. Its roots came from a source familiar to almost every person at one time or another: Insufficient funds. Defenses had to be built in two areas simultaneously — in missiles, and conventional arms. The missile was obviously the weapon of tomorrow. It had to be researched, developed and pushed further into operational status (a $2 billion item during the year) at the same time that existing forces and weapons were maintained in strength. There was only one way out: Cancellations, cutbacks, stretchouts and reductions in progress payments. It was hard on many manufacturers whose business was derived wholly or mainly from defense sources; but it was inevitable.

Fortunately for the Free World, the Communists too had their problems. They had scored first in the race into space; but their political science seemed nowhere near so advanced as their rocketry. The "de-Stalinization" of the U.S.S.R. touched off a struggle for power within the Kremlin that forestalled any large-scale external aggression. Thus the free nations were presented with time to readjust their defenses.

Commercial air transport within the United States was having its troubles. Costs were rising, and traffic and revenues unexplainably declining. And the airlines had placed orders for $2 billion in new equipment, principally jet and turboprop aircraft, which would have to be paid for. The bright spot in the aviation picture was presented by the general and business aircraft segment, which was continuing to grow in size and importance.

The total state of affairs in 1957 was one that promised, on balance, to be of benefit, rather than injury to Beech Aircraft in its 25th Anniversary Year. The company's continuing emphasis on diversity of production, spread over a broad spectrum of aeronautical and aerospace projects, made it very nearly invulnerable to changes occurring in any single area. Its military work was well distributed among many activities, ranging from the building of complete Beechcrafts to subcontracts for components of very important military aircraft; from jetplane ground servicing units to advanced secret research projects in aerospace. A stretchout, or even a cancellation of any of its more than forty current projects, would not be crippling. The company was not involved in the problems of the commercial airlines. And Beech was firmly established, by deliberate design, as the preeminent leader in the industry's growth segment of general and business aircraft. Events were to continue proving the soundness of the company's planning.

Even before the calendar year began, Beech was off to a strong start. Its 1957 annual Distributor-Dealer Sales Meeting, held on December 5 and 6, 1956, was attended by some 300 masters of aircraft salesmanship who came from all over the United States, and eleven foreign countries. Of the organizations represented, 19 qualified as members of the Beech "Million Dollar Club," each having sold more than $1 million worth of

147

Beechcrafts and parts during 1956. After viewing the 1957 Beechcrafts on display, the entire group accepted with enthusiasm a challenge to push commercial sales for the coming year over the $46 million retail level — a goal they were handily to exceed.

There were excellent reasons for Beechcraft's distributors to be enthusiastic. The company's total sales, at the beginning of its 25th year, were in excess of one billion dollars; and its commercial sales were at the highest level in its history. Beech was the leader, by many millions of dollars, in business aircraft manufacture. Its dealers were members of a winning team. And the new 1957 models continued to improve on the industry's highest standards of performance and luxury.

Wholly new for 1957 was a supercharged Beechcraft Twin-Bonanza with a high speed of 240 mph, a cruising speed of 228 mph at 70% power, a service ceiling of 24,800 feet, and a non-stop range up to 1,650 miles. Its compact supercharged Lycoming engines supplied a maximum 340 hp each to high-efficiency three-bladed constant speed propellers, affording takeoff and climb over a 50-ft. obstacle in less than 1,300 feet, and a rate of climb of 1,620 fpm. Together with the D50 Twin-Bonanza which was continued in production, it featured high-density sound-proofing, fast-action cabin heating adequate to warm a five-room house, and many more new refinements.

The single-engine Beechcraft Bonanza gained more power and speed, greater useful load and other betterments in the 1957 H35 model. Maximum horsepower, raised to 240, was more efficiently utilized by a Beech Model 278 hydraulically controlled, constant speed military type propeller, to produce a top speed of 206 mph and a cruising speed of 196 mph at 75% power. And buyers of "the top of the line" — the Super 18 — got more for their money in 1957 with a 12% increase in range, a new 90,000 BTU combustion type cabin heater, and numerous mechanical improvements.

Other events carried over from 1956 helped to start the new year off right. A $4 million production agreement, executed with the government of Argentina on December 29, 1956, enlarged the scale of Beechcraft Mentor production concurrent with the Navy T-34B program. In addition to providing 15

Beech-built Mentors for fly-away delivery to Argentina, the agreement called for 75 more planes to be assembled there, plus licensing and technical assistance for future Mentor production in that country. Argentina thus joined Japan and Canada in gaining rights to build Mentors for its own use.

A Beechcraft owner who was also an aircraft manufacturer in his own right, H. A. Burgerhout of Papendrecht, Holland, brought word on a visit to the Beech plant that his D35 Bonanza had won top honors in the annual "Le Grand Prix de France" air competition held at Paris, France last fall. The Netherlands pilot took first place in the handicap event, which included short landings, short takeoffs and speed races, competing with some fifty pilots from a number of European nations flying all types of American and European airplanes of 3,500 pounds gross weight and more. His was the only Bonanza entered in the meet; so, for once, the saying "It takes a Beechcraft to beat a Beechcraft" did not apply.

A Beech program of eight years' standing was nationally honored with the conferral of the Greer Maintenance Award for 1956 on the Beech Aircraft Corporation at ceremonies held in New York City. A board of three aviation editors chose the Beech Aircraft Service Clinic Program to receive the award, made annually to the individual or company with the best idea or design for solving aircraft maintenance problems. The work of Beech factory inspectors, who had performed over 7,000 exhaustive inspections of Beechcrafts in the field since the program was started in 1949, was highly praised by the awards board.

As the year began, successful results were reported in flight testing of a new jet fighter in-flight refueling system which Beech was developing jointly with the McDonnell Aircraft Corporation. The Beech-designed system enabled one jet fighter to refuel another at speeds up to 350 knots and altitudes up to 40,000 ft. Its potential tactical importance was very substantial, particularly in carrier-based flight operations where "Out of fuel . . . ditching" had all too often been the last message received from pilot and plane. Development of the in-flight refueling system was a logical outgrowth of Beech pioneering in aircraft range extension that stemmed back even prior to the company's fitting out of Bill Odom's Bonanza with wingtip tanks for his 1949 world record nonstop flight, and its design and construction of many thousands of external fuel tanks from 1950 onward. It might well be said to antedate Beechcraft's own history. For, from the first moment of his start in the commercial aircraft industry, as a pilot-salesman for the Swallow Aircraft Company of Wichita in 1923, Walter H. Beech had always insisted that a prime requirement of a useful airplane was the ability to complete any mission its owner required with maximum swiftness and efficiency. Obviously, this ruled out frequent and time-wasting stops for refueling. A basic design requirement of every Beech-built Travel Air, and of every Beechcraft ever built from Serial No. 1 onward, was that of providing ample range for its anticipated service, plus built-in reserves of fuel affording an extra margin of safety against emergencies. Range extension through in-flight refueling, while impractical for general commercial and business aircraft, was well matched to military needs and modes of flight, and compatible with Beechcraft's basic philosophy. Beechcrafters were proud to have a part in its development.

Good news came to Beech stockholders early in the year. Their company was in good condition financially; so good, in fact, that its board of directors authorized a 10% stock dividend on January 10. Some $2 million were transferred from earned surplus to its common stock and capital surplus accounts, and 74,063 additional shares of common stock (the only kind issued by Beech) were distributed to the many hundreds of stockholders. It was a well deserved reward for the investors whose funds supplied the capital that enabled the company to exist; and it strengthened the already favorable standing of Beech Aircraft in financial and investment circles.

Looking toward further growth in its aerospace activities, the company announced on January 25 its purchase of an additional 700 acres of land adjoining the 760-acre tract it owned and occupied north of Boulder, Colorado. This was to provide isolation and security for its then highly classified researches into high-energy fuels and other assignments connected with missiles and rocketry. A week earlier, on January 19, one result of prior Beech work at Boulder in cryogenics and exotic fuels handling

150

became apparent, when the company was awarded a contract to produce Beech-designed 1,200-gallon double-walled "vacuum bottle" type containers for transporting liquid gases at extremely low temperatures. Employment at Boulder had gone up at that time from an original staff of 50 to some 200 employees, of whom 120 were engineers — many with advanced and highly specialized training.

Also in January, the U. S. Army took delivery on the first of a number of Beechcraft L-23D Twin-Bonanza command transport planes ordered under a $2.8 million production contract. This was the Army version of the new supercharged E50 Twin-Bonanza introduced commercially in December; and the new contract assured busy days on that production line for months to come. From the time it entered Army service in 1953, the Beech L-23 had been one of the most heavily utilized airplanes doing military duty, and the Army's fleet showed an average of over 750,000 passenger miles for each of its many Beechcrafts.

What the Army thought of its new supercharged Twin-Bonanzas was best expressed in a $1.71 million contract award to Beech announced on March 25. The contract called for Beech to remanufacture a large number of older L-23A and L-23B twins in the L-23D configuration — with roomy six-place seating, increased 7,000 pound gross weight, and supercharged 340 hp engines. In every way, the rebuilt planes would correspond with new L-23D's fresh from the production line, and the savings to the Army and the taxpayers who footed the bill would be large. The procedure was one thoroughly familiar to Beech from its experience with the extensive Navy Model 18 rebuild program which had won praise from the Navy Bureau of Aeronautics; and the Army rebuild contract was a welcome one in every way.

Beech also passed another production milestone in March, with the delivery from its Plant II of Bonanza No. 5,000. The high-performance H35 went to O. George Tobey of Hartford, Connecticut, who had purchased his first Beechcraft Bonanza in 1954 after owning three other planes. While Bonanzas had been sold for use by almost every imaginable type of business and service enterprise, the one that Bonanza N5000 would mainly serve was perhaps unique in business aircraft annals.

151

Its owner headed the firm of Tobey, Inc., a group of specialists in determining the sex of newly-hatched chicks for immediate shipment from hatcheries located throughout the New England states. It seemed peculiarly appropriate that Article #5,000 of the most advanced airplane of its class should serve a business dedicated essentially to expertly predicting the shape of things to come.

Flight evaluations of the "littlest Beechcraft" — the 120 hp, 12-ft. span XKDB-1 pilotless target aircraft — started soon afterward, and continued during the summer months at the Naval Air Missile Test Center, Point Mugu, California. The tests went well. The 600-pound "bird" with its characteristic Beech V-tail became the first target aircraft of its type to be ground-launched successfully on the very first attempt. It set a new altitude record for remote-controlled medium performance target planes, reaching 38,500 feet from ground launch. And it proved its ability to meet or exceed Navy specifications for stability, controllability, launching and recovery. The Navy placed a $1 million order for additional test quantities of the XKDB-1; and Beech engineers designed an alternate version, the Beechcraft Model 1013, equipped for use as a photographic and television reconnaissance drone.

The Beech facility at Boulder, Colorado, stepped up a notch in rank when, on May 9, it was elevated to full division status, in recognition of its growing importance and great long-range potential. While most of its work was still veiled under tight security wraps, it was disclosed that Boulder was then in production on a second mobile Dewar container for transporting liquid gases at extremely low temperatures — this one of 6,000 gallons capacity, five times larger than the first such Beech-built vehicle. The Boulder location was a strategic one from several viewpoints. It provided ready access to the National Bureau of Standards laboratory at Boulder, supplementing Beech's own facilities there. It facilitated graduate studies at the University of Colorado in Boulder for members of its engineering staff, a useful consideration in recruiting the highly trained talent increasingly vital to sophisticated aerospace research and development. And it was conveniently near the massive Denver-Martin engineering production and test complex, where work was going forward for the U. S. Air Force on the Titan Intercontinental Ballistic Missile.

Sunday, June 2, was the date chosen for the official celebration of the company's Silver Anniversary. Its twenty-fifth birthday actually had been passed on April 19; but the early June date was more convenient with regard to the work on hand, which always had top priority, and ideal with respect to weather. A gala Open House, attended by many thousands, was the principal event of the day. Guests in attendance included many notables, as well as thousands of Beechcrafters and their families and friends. Congratulatory messages were received from from all over the Free World; from highly placed personages and from friends of Beechcraft in all walks of life. It was a heartening and inspiring time of rededication to its goals of universal service for the company and its people. The Beech management paid high tribute to the men and women of Beechcraft, pointing with great pride to the fact that during the year, 60 employees would attain more than 20 years of service; 1,329 would pass the 15-year service mark; 1,609 would be 10-year veterans; and 5,297 would have 5 years of service to their credit. The combined experience of these Beechcrafters would exceed 63,000 years of working together in planning and building the world's finest aircraft. Vice president Frank Hedrick had good reason to state: "The people of Beech Aircraft represent our most valuable asset."

In mid-July, the industry felt the first effects of contract cancellations, cutbacks and stretchouts in deliveries enforced by defense budget limitations. Shortly afterward, the results became apparent at Beech. They did not appreciably affect the company's business; and in the long run, they were to prove beneficial. Faced with the need to squeeze maximum value out of every dollar spent, defense planners openly stated that delinquent high-cost producers would be eliminated and work passed on to efficient on-schedule producers. The challenge was one that Beechcrafters were ready and eager to accept. A further Air Force contract for $10.6 million worth of 1700-gallon B-47 external fuel tanks that came along in September was signed with alacrity. The many diversified projects in which Beech was engaged were proceeding on schedule; nothing of importance had been cancelled. Among efficient Beechcrafters, there was always room for one more assignment, no matter how challenging it might be.

Delivery in September of six new H35 Bonanzas to Central American Airways Flying Service, Inc., of Louisville, Kentucky, brought to light the extensive use of the Bonanza for instrument flight training of U. S. Army aviators. The new Bonanzas joined a fleet of 16 already in use at two contract schools operated for the Army by Central American, in furtherance of an Army program having as its aim the eventual qualification of every Army pilot for instrument flight. Wilbur Paris, president of Central American, described the experience of his schools as follows: "As an instrument trainer, we've had excellent results with the Beechcraft Bonanza and believe it to be one of the best single-engine aircraft types available for this purpose. Our experience has also shown that the Bonanza is exceptionally low on maintenance despite high utilization." Graduates of the contract instrument course became eligible for advanced twin-engine training in Army-operated programs using the high-performance L-23, military version of the commercial Beechcraft Twin-Bonanza.

Further evidence of the Bonanza's outstanding qualities was presented by the results of the 1957 All Woman Transcontinental Air Race, popularly known as the "Powder Puff Derby." For the second straight year, a Bonanza was flown to first place in this notable event. Its pilot was Mrs. Alice Roberts of Phoenix, Arizona; its co-pilot, Mrs. Iris Critchell, Palos Verdes Estates, California. They had previously taken second place in the 1955 and 1956 races. First place in 1956 had gone to a Bonanza flown by Mrs. Fran Bera, Inglewood, California. A handicap event, the race was an excellent test of both piloting skill and aircraft performance; and, as a "For women only" event, a demonstration that modern business aircraft would yield safe high performance under either feminine or masculine control.

The old reliable Model D18S Beechcraft proved its merits as still the best of its class for varied uses, with a routine ocean-crossing flight delivery to Burma of six new D18 twins for the Burmese Air Force. Two were to operate as navigation trainers, and four were modified for aerial photography — one of the

154

first specialized uses to which the Model 18 was put by the
U. S. Army Air Corps in 1939. The Government of Burma
selected the Beechcraft D18S following rigid evaluations of
various twin-engine types of American and foreign aircraft.

On October 31, Beech completed its 40-month production
program on U. S. Navy T-34B Mentor trainers, delivering the
423d and final unit contracted for to the Navy Air Training
Command. Beech performance on this contract brought pleasing comments in a letter from Rear Admiral W. A. Schoech:
"Your ability to maintain your contractual delivery schedules
and in addition to deliver critical spare parts in advance of
schedules is especially noteworthy. This ability reflects great
credit on the labor-management team of Beech Aircraft Corporation. Please accept the congratulations of all of us in the
Bureau of Aeronautics for a job well done."

The Navy commendation had a broader background than
that of satisfaction with deliveries. The Mentor's record in the
primary training programs directed from the Naval Training
Center at Pensacola, Florida, also earned Navy praise. The
Training Command found that its syllabus could be shortened,
and primary flight time cut from 74 to 36 hours — a better than
50% reduction — since students could attain a higher level of
proficiency more quickly in the Mentor. The time required to
solo was cut by more than half; and the accident rate was notably
improved. In brief, the Mentor was a much better teacher than
its bigger, heavier and higher-powered predecessor, and vastly
more economical to fly and maintain into the bargain.

Completion of the Navy contract brought to 723 the total
number of Beech-designed T-34 trainers delivered to U. S.
military flying services, 300 of the T-34A types already having
been built for the U. S. Air Force. With U. S. needs fulfilled,
production of Mentor aircraft and assemblies continued for
export customers.

Shortly before the year's end, first deliveries were made to
Air Force bases operating heavy jet aircraft of the new Beech-
designed MA-3 multi-purpose ground servicing vehicle. The
high-priority program to start this versatile 15,700-pound mobile
power source rolling into the service of the Strategic Air Command was on schedule; so, also, were deliveries of other Beech-

designed jet starting and servicing units. On-schedule deliveries likewise continued on Beech's high-volume subcontracting assignments. For Lockheed, wing-building continued for the USAF T-33 jet trainer, and was completed for the Navy T2V-1 carrier training jet when Navy requirements were reduced. Assemblies for the USAF F-104 Lockheed StarFighter jet continued in production; and add-on orders enlarged work in progress on parts, assemblies and components for Convair's USAF F-102A, F-106A and F-106B supersonic jet fighter-interceptors.

Beechcrafters building major components for McDonnell's Navy F3H-2N and USAF F-101A jets got a lift from the news that on December 12, an Air Force F-101A flown by Major Adrian Drew had won the Thompson Trophy, and established a new world's speed record of 1207.6 mph, flying over a 10.1 mile course at Edwards Air Force Base, California. There was more of Beechcraft in that airplane, they felt, than the Beech-built stabilators, rudder and other components that had helped to sweep away the previous record at twice the speed of sound. There was the will to win, the fighting spirit that had been their legacy from Walter H. Beech — a spirit shared alike by the men and women of Beech Aircraft and of McDonnell.

The company's Annual Report, issued December 16, revealed an outstanding record of accomplishment for its Silver Anniversary Year. Total volume for the fiscal year that ended September 30 stood at $103,904,870 — a figure exceeded in terms of actual production only during the World War II years of 1943 and 1945. More than one-third of that total was made up of business and commercial sales, to the amount of $35,746,094. Beech continued to lead the commercial field in sales volume of business aircraft, and exceeded its own pace-setting 1956 volume in that field by an 11% margin. Its 1957 military sales of more than $68.1 million were distributed over almost the total range of aeronautical and aerospace defense requirements. The proved versatility of Beech skills, which covered a range of more than 60 different projects, was such as to assure the continuance of its contributions to defense and to general aviation alike throughout the years to come. Beechcrafters could look back on their first quarter century with pride, and forward to the next quarter century with confidence.

156

Ready to go: the first of 4 Super 18 twins added in 1957 to three Model 18's operated for Cities Service . . . later replaced by five King Air executive Beechcrafts. Shown left to right: Harold Walker, pilot; J. A. Rogers, chief pilot; Jack Howe, co-pilot.

Approval of JATO thrust augmentation for the Super Twin Bonanza provided an extra margin of safety and performance when most needed.

The California State Department of Fish and Game used a specially equipped Super 18 Beechcraft to air-drop trout, beaver, and game birds into high, remote mountain lakes and areas.

Philippines-to-Oregon flight by Captain Marion "Pat" Boling in a J35 Bonanza established world solo single-engine flight record in 1958. (Page 164)

Pat Boling flew the 6,856 mile Great Circle distance nonstop in 45 hours and 43 minutes.

King Hussein of Jordan personally flew Beechcraft Twin-Bonanza delivered to him in 1958.

Chapter 22

To gain a flying start into the new year of 1958, Beech repeated a technique it had originated in 1956, and again employed successfully in 1957. The company moved the calendar forward, this time even further, and held its 1958 annual International Distributor-Dealer Sales Meeting at Wichita, November 18-19-20, 1957. The results were dramatically satisfactory. Only six days after the meeting had closed, President O. A. Beech was able to announce that firm orders for more than $14.8 million worth of new 1958 Beechcraft business planes had been received — this while the Silver Anniversary Year of 1957 was still more than a month away from its end.

There had never been a better attended nor a more enthusiastic meeting of the world-wide Beechcraft sales clan than this one. From all around the world they came — more than 350 strong — to celebrate the company's biggest year in commercial sales, and to perfect even greater plans for the future. For the first time, all of the major continents on the globe were represented — America, Asia, Africa, Europe and Australia, to the extent of some fifty foreign countries. World-wide Beechcraft sales and service, a concept that had seemed remote indeed in 1934 when a Beech biplane became the first airplane of its kind to complete a successful round-the-world cruise, was a reality; and the company's long-standing slogan "The world is small when you fly a Beechcraft" had taken on a new meaning.

The new twin Beech Travel Air was the natural center of interest among the 1958 Beechcrafts unveiled at the meeting. Designed to fill a price gap in the Beech line between the perennially popular single-engine Bonanza and the large six-place Twin-Bonanza, the quietly efficient, economical Travel Air made an instant hit with the men who were to sell and service it all over the world. In performance, beauty and comfort, it was every inch a Beechcraft. Powered by two 180 hp four-cylinder Lycoming 0-360-A1A engines, its top speed was 208 mph, cruising speed 200 mph, rate of climb 1,350 fpm, and service ceiling 19,300 feet, all at full gross weight of 4,000 pounds and carrying 1,420-pound useful load. Its non-stop range with 112 gallons of fuel was better than 1,400 miles. A single-engine climb rate of 225 fpm, and ability to maintain 8,000-ft. altitude indefinitely on one engine, gave the Travel Air authentic twin-engine performance, and afforded the engine-out margin of safety wanted by prudent buyers. Easy to handle, and the quietest twin on the market, it was the logical step upward for present owners of high-performance single-engine aircraft; and its sales record was to offer the ultimate proof of its excellence.

The 1958 single-engine J35 Bonanza moved into the 200 mph cruising range, nose to nose with the new twin Travel Air, with the adoption of a new six-cylinder Continental IO-470-C engine featuring continuous flow fuel injection, and rated at 250 hp at 2600 rpm for all operations. Representing perhaps the ultimate refinement in piston type power plants, the new fuel injection engine offered improved economy and efficiency, plus complete freedom from carburetor icing. In combination with other refinements, including a hydraulic constant speed propeller governor, the J35 model was able to offer 200 mph cruise at 75% power, 195 mph economy cruise at 65% power, a 21,300-ft. service ceiling, and an increase in useful load to 1,080 pounds, retaining its former gross weight of 2,900 pounds. A new lightweight, low cost three-axis autopilot system was offered as an optional feature. All things considered, the J35 Bonanza looked like a potential record-breaker. It would soon prove its claim to that title.

The Beechcraft Super 18, and the F50 supercharged Twin-Bonanza and its popular sister ship, the D50 Twin-Bonanza, also displayed numerous advancements for 1958 that made them more than ever leaders in their respective categories. The year was off to a good start — more than a month before it began.

The Beechcraft Mentor provided the opening news item of the calendar year, with the flyaway delivery in mid-January of the first Mentors sold for civil use. Four of the versatile Beech two-place trainers were flown from Wichita by officials and staff members of the International Training Center for Civil Aviation, a unique aviation school sponsored by the Government of Mexico and the United Nations to train pilots, mechanics, air traffic controllers and others for civil aviation jobs in Central and South America. Deriving some 75% of its support from the Mexican government, the school provided training for

160

students from nations throughout Latin America in the highest standard procedures established by the UN's International Civil Aviation Organization, thus helping to advance the progress of aviation and flight safety in the lands "south of the border." The ITCCA Mentors were soon to be joined in Mexico by another group of T-34 trainers ordered by the Mexican Navy; and before the year was to end, fleets of Mentors became the choice of the governments of the Republic of Venezuela and of Chile. The economical, efficient Mentor was making friends for Beechcraft throughout the Americas, and all over the world — in foreign lands as far removed as Turkey and Japan.

On January 28, one day before Kansas celebrated the 97th anniversary of its admission into the Union as a state, President O. A. Beech was named as the "Kansan of the Year" by the Native Sons and Daughters of Kansas. She was the third person to receive this award, conferred annually "for distinguished service to Kansas"; and of all the notable national honors she had received, this was probably the most deeply appreciated, since it came from the hands of her own neighbors and friends throughout her native state. A staff writer for the Topeka *Daily Capital* aptly expressed the spirit of the award in these words: "Mrs. Beech's personal contribution might be called pioneer spirit carried into the 20th century — self-reliance, responsibility, plain hard work, and most of all, vision and faith in the future and in herself."

As the U. S. Air Force gained increasing experience with its Beech-designed and Beech-built multi-purpose ground service vehicles, it found the new units even more valuable than expected in supplying essential pre-flight, starting and maintenance services for its more powerful and sophisticated aircraft. The result was the issuance on March 19 of a $2.38 million contract to Beech for MA-3 spare parts and supplies. An Air Force report published in Europe told how the Beech MA-3s in service there had put six different machines out of work. The story stated: "This new mechanical marvel can now do the jobs formerly done by the tractor, the MC-1 air compressor unit, the MA1A gas turbine compressor, the MD-3 generator, the MA-5 air conditioner and the BT-400 heating unit . . . Formerly, two to three men were required to service an aircraft with all

161

the equipment that this one unit embodies. In addition to the man-hours saved in operation, many hours of moving maintenance equipment will now be eliminated. Maintaining the old equipment called for the services of three men, who worked eight hours a day to keep all the equipment operational. The new units will be serviced by their operators, curtailing the number of man-hours expended in maintenance." As a footnote, it might be added that the estimated value of the MA-3 was $100,000, compared with $140,000 for the items it replaced. Production was also going forward on several types of Beech-designed, highly sophisticated mobile electronic analyzers, capable of quickly detecting malfunctions in both ground support units and aircraft electronic systems and components. Beech was making its mark in the vital area of ground support capability.

On April 1 came the news of a $3 million follow-on contract award from the U. S. Army for additional quantities of Beech L-23D Seminole twin-engine transports. Another year's production of the military Twin-Bonanza went onto the books, much to the satisfaction of the workers on the Model 50 production line whose dedicated craftsmanship had produced this new evidence of customer satisfaction.

At about that time, activity in some areas of the nation's economy was showing signs of a slow-down, particularly in purchases of consumer goods. The reduction of pace was to have some effect on Beech's showing for the year, but only to a marginal extent. More to the point, and closer to home, was a general taking up of slack throughout the aircraft industry, striving to deliver more highly advanced products to the government, which provided 82% of its revenues, within the limitations of sharply pared defense budgets. This again had slight effects on Beech; for the company's unceasing dedication to efficiency was such that there was little or no slack to be taken up. A gentle reminder of the general situation was enough; Beechcrafters willingly did their part to keep costs down.

An odd sort of conflict of loyalties came up early in May — one that brought credit to Beech, however, no matter how it was viewed. Beechcrafters had cheered the F-101A McDonnell Voodoo fighter that had set a new world's speed record in December — an airplane for which they had built essential components. On May 2, an F-104 Lockheed StarFighter jet, piloted by Major Howard C. Johnson, broke the world altitude record with a climb to 91,249 feet. The F-104 followed up this feat by setting a new world's speed record of 1,404.19 mph, flown by Captain Walter W. Irwin. Beech was building F-104 components, too. Should the builders applaud the victory of one customer's product over another's? The issue was resolved in the same spirit followed by the competing prime contractors: No matter whose airplane happened to be ahead at the moment, the defense forces of the United States were the ultimate victors. And that was as it should be.

Beech meanwhile continued with its own race against time, working on a great variety of projects all of which carried rigorous progress and completion dates. In addition to building more business aircraft, dollar-wise, than any other manufacturer, Beech was building new L-23D twin-engine transports for the Army, and remanufacturing Army-used L-23's; building Mentors for export; and turning out Beech KDB-1 target aircraft for the Navy. The company was an important subcontractor to Lockheed on its USAF T-33 and F-104 jet aircraft; to McDonnell on its USAF F-101 program; and to Convair on its USAF F-106A and F-106B supersonic interceptor-fighters. It was a major producer of external fuel tanks for jet fighters and bombers, in sizes ranging from 200-gallon pylon tanks for the F-104 Starfighter to huge 1700-gallon tanks for the B-47 bomber. Its facilities at Boulder and Longmont, Colorado, were busy in research and development programs on high energy missile and spacecraft fuels and systems, and massive Dewar transport vehicles for super-cold liquid gases. It was a prime source of ground support vehicles and associated test equipment. A full description of the work then in progress would have filled a thick book.

It was a source of great pride to the company and to all Beechcrafters, therefore, when the following letter of commendation was received from the resident USAF Plant Representative:

"Dear Mrs. Beech:

On 31 July 1958, Beech possessed 118 military contracts, all of which were on schedule. This commendable performance on delivery of products for the Army, Navy, and Air Force exemplifies effectiveness in the Beech organization.

On-schedule position in July for the wide variety of military products supplied by Beech Aircraft Corporation resulted from the concerted effort and initiative of all Beechcrafters; however, the all-out cooperation and effort of production control, procurement, military spares and contract administration personnel were particularly noteworthy.

Congratulations on this demonstration of Beech efficiency: We are looking forward to a continuation of the high standard achieved by your company.

Sincerely,

/s/ LOREN P. MURRAY, JR., Lt. Colonel, USAF
AF Plant Representative"

The reference date of this letter of commendation was notably significant. For on that same date, a third of the way westward around the globe, a Beech Bonanza was winging its way east over the Pacific in a flight that was again, as in 1949, to blazon the name of Beechcraft in headlines all over the world.

The pilot of this flight that would make history was Marion Livingston ("Pat") Boling, a United Air Lines pilot on leave from his customary duties. His takeoff point in a J35 Bonanza "N35U" was Manila International Airport, Luzon, the Philippines; his destination, nonstop, the United States of America. He completed his flight at Pendleton, Oregon, in 45 hours and 43 minutes after takeoff, having covered an actual distance of 7,090 miles, or an official great circle route distance of 6,856.23 miles, at an average ground speed of 155 mph. He had topped by 1,899 miles the previous world record established by Bill Odom flying a Beech Bonanza in 1949 from Honolulu, Hawaii to Teterboro, New Jersey; and pilot and plane had set a mark for stamina in solo, single-engine over-water flight that in all probability would never be surpassed. A long-familiar saying had once again held true: It takes a Beechcraft to beat a Beechcraft.

Boling's Bonanza had taken off from Manila shortly after sunrise with 402 gallons of gasoline in its tanks. It landed at

Pendleton at 11:52 a.m. with 11 gallons of fuel remaining on hand — enough for fully another safe hour of flight. N35U had consumed 391 gallons of gas, averaging 8.55 gallons per hour or about 18.1 miles per gallon for the 7,090 actual flight miles flown. The cost of the gasoline and oil used was $139.85. Serial #5650 off the production line, N35U was a twin brother in design and construction to other J35 Bonanzas then being delivered to businessmen buyers, its only differences being in the necessary arrangements to carry an additional ton of fuel and otherwise to equip it for its unique mission. Its 250 hp Continental I0-470-C six-cylinder fuel injection engine was identical with those in all 1958 production Bonanzas. The gross weight of N35U at takeoff was 4,964 pounds — 2,064 pounds more than the normal 2,900 pound gross weight of the Model J35. Two streamlined wingtip fuel tanks, each holding 62 gallons, were distinguishing features of N35U. They were the same tanks that had been installed on Bill Odom's "Waikiki Beech" when it set the previous world's record; and they worked just as well as they had before.

Just as in 1949, careful planning and preparation preceded the actual flight. When the "Philippine Bonanza" was fitted out and ready to leave the Beech factory at Wichita, Captain Boling took it over and flew it westward across the Pacific to Manila by way of Hawaii, Wake Island and Guam. Thus he gained experience with N35U under various conditions of loading, and with fuel management for optimum range.

The flight itself, according to Pat Boling, "turned out exactly the way we wanted it." Takeoff, originally scheduled for July 30, was postponed one day to allow typhoon "Doris," then athwart the planned flight course, to move aside. The moon was full — a safety factor in case of emergencies that also enhanced the beauty of Boling's two nights aloft. Winds were neutral — no tailwinds worth mentioning, but no headwinds either. The great circle course spanned the north Pacific over open water more than 90% of the way — 6,555 miles over ocean, 535 miles over land — east of Okinawa, over Tokyo, east of Hokkaido and Russia's Kuril Islands, between Attu and Kiska, north of Adak to the Shumagin Islands, then down to Sandspit, Canada, Port Hardy, Seattle and Pendleton. Because of cloud conditions, the pilot had no sight of either land or water from Japan on until he approached Cold Bay. Local sharp turbulence over Japan, in the wake of typhoon Doris, and unexpected icing conditions over Canada's Queen Charlotte Islands, necessitating a descent to a lower altitude, were the only weather conditions encountered. Pat Boling summed it up to perfection: "The two happiest days of my life." Two very happy days, too, for Beechcraft and its people.

The reason why Beech sponsored the new record-breaking flight was succinctly given in a statement by Jack Gaty: . . . "It became obvious that the Bonanza of 1958 was superficially like the Bonanza of 1949, but that many important improvements had been made in the meantime. It was then thought desirable to again demonstrate the great superiority of the Bonanza to all other aircraft in its category by making another long-range flight that would far surpass the original and unbroken Bonanza record flight made by Bill Odom in 1949 . . ." It was not a stunt, not a daredevil feat, but a carefully planned, precisely engineered demonstration of superiority — in the typical Beech tradition of letting the facts speak for themselves.

Excitement still ran high at Beechcraft over the new Boling-Bonanza world record when word came, early in August, of new electronic devices being tested by the Army that would enhance both the military and business flight utility of Beech and other makes of aircraft. Appropriately, the Army's L-23D Beechcrafts were the vehicles chosen for first tests of the new items. A Beech L-23D was the first Army plane to be equipped with RCA's new lightweight AVQ-50 weather avoidance radar, an "electronic eye" with an 80-mile range that could peer ahead through clouds and provide warning for the pilot of weather systems ahead that should be avoided. In addition to its utility in aiding the completion of military missions that could not be deferred, the new radar would obviously be useful in helping business and executive pilots to carry out their flight plans with greater safety and comfort. Another new radar system developed by Motorola, permitting aerial battlefield surveillance for reconnaissance purposes, had also passed its Army tests; and Army Twin-Bonanzas then in production at Beech were modified to mount this military radar, and redesignated as Army Type RL-23D aircraft.

Returning from a summer tour of Europe that included visits with Beech distributors and with many owners and other long-time friends of the company, President O. A. Beech reported from first-hand observation that Beechcraft's foreign market opportunities were indeed excellent. Everywhere, warm friendship and cordial hospitality reflected a high order of esteem for Beech and its products in both commercial and military circles. The Beech export organization had arranged outstanding representation abroad at the hands of widely respected and capable firms in the various nations. Visibly growing prosperity in major areas of the European community completed a list of good reasons for viewing Beechcraft's future in the markets of Europe with realistic optimism and enthusiasm.

On September 2, Beech made aviation history with the delivery of the world's first executive jet airplane, an MS 760 "Paris," to a commercial customer — the Timken Roller Bearing Company of Canton, Ohio. It was the sequel to another "first" for Beech — the CAA certification of the MS 760 jet, which the company had completed in July. Mr. Henry H. Timken, Jr., concurrently became the world's first businessman-pilot to qualify in a private jet, by soloing his firm's new MS 760 after only six hours of dual instruction. Timken's jet went into service more than three months before the first commercial jet airliner was put into use by a scheduled U. S. airline.

The MS 760 certification and delivery were incidents in a continuing long-range developmental and marketing study of executive jet aircraft which Beech had started several years before and would continue in effect. Jets would enter the business aircraft fleet in the future; that much was sure. But when, in what types and numbers, and to whom they might be sold, no one could assuredly predict. To engineer and construct an original prototype jet would cost somewhere between $15 and $30 millions — too large a sum to gamble, even for boldly pioneering Beech. The company's simple, low-cost approach was to take over exclusive North American distribution for the excellent French-built MS 760; develop a one-price "package deal" that included pilot training, a supply of expendable small

167

spare parts, and guaranteed prompt major engine and aircraft servicing; and offer the "package" for sale. Market research in a practical way — the only way with 100% validity.

Results were disappointing, in terms of MS 760 sales volume, probably because several years would be required for the executive and business community at large to perceive the speed and smoothness benefits of jet travel demonstrated by commercial airliners, and then to prefer jet power for their own business aircraft. But an interesting side effect developed. Beech dealers found that the MS 760 proposal made an arresting "door-opener" in calling on executive and business prospects, with the end result of increasing sales for conventional Beechcrafts.

An event with few, if any parallels in the volatile aircraft and aerospace industry, and not many counterparts in industry as a whole, took place on September 8, with the signing of a new labor contract between the company and officers of District Lodge No. 70 of the International Association of Machinists, representing the Beech hourly-rated employees. The agreement extended to 19 years an unbroken sequence of harmonious labor relations between the Beech Aircraft Corporation and the International Association of Machinists. Throughout a quarter of a century, the company and its employees had known lean times and good times together; expansions and cutbacks, hirings and forced layoffs — all without a single day of labor strife. The union was a vigorous entity among its employee members. Its representatives bargained hard in their behalf; and the company stood up for its interests with equal vigor. But, in all the bargaining sessions, mutual respect and understanding consistently prevailed, ending in a meeting of minds that resulted fairly for all parties concerned. The new contract, like others before it, produced additional benefits for all employees: Pay increases, cost-of-living wage adjustments throughout its term, automatic wage rate reviews three times yearly, a company-funded job improvement plan, new retirement benefits under a wholly company-financed program instituted in 1956, and other gains. The company enhanced its standing as a good employer — a key factor in upholding and increasing the efficiency of its operations.

A long-range trend of great significance to the industry and

168

to Beech was highlighted on September 30, when the National Advisory Committee for Aeronautics signalled the broadening of its scope, from an agency of government concerned primarily with aeronautical research to vastly greater areas, with a change of name, and became the National Aeronautics and Space Administration. The fact was thus recognized that the nation's scientific efforts would no longer be confined to the ocean of air that enveloped the earth; they would go beyond into the void of space. This action verified the soundness of Beech's decision, made in 1954, to qualify as a pioneer in the realm of space vehicle research and development with the founding of its Boulder operation. Currently, the company was enlarging its facilities there, and was active in environmental testing under extremes of heat and cold of vital propellant system components for Martin's USAF Titan intercontinental ballistic missile, as well as other space-oriented projects in the fields of missiles, cryogenics, high energy fuels and astronautics.

On October 20 the news was announced of a follow-on contract awarded to Beech by the Convair Division of General Dynamics Corporation for additional aft fuselage sections and other major components for Convair's USAF F-106A and F-106B "Delta Dart" all-weather jet interceptors. More work for Beechcrafters, already engaged on Convair subcontracts that included components for its F-102A, first USAF delta wing interceptor; its USAF B-58 "Hustler" supersonic bomber; and its Convair 880 commercial jet airline transport — and a welcome sign of customer satisfaction.

November brought still more military business. From the Navy Bureau of Aeronautics, an exacting but appreciative customer, came an $8.7 million-plus contract for Beech KDB-1 target aircraft systems, including planes plus necessary ground support equipment and service spares. In tests earlier in the year, the 300-knot KDB-1 had established an unofficial Navy altitude record of 43,500 feet, a new high for target craft in the KD-300 medium performance class, and had operated successfully at control and tracking ranges of over 100,000 yards. Beech's little bird had done well. The Army, too, showed its liking for Beech performance by signing a $2 million follow-on contract for factory rebuilding of more L-23A and L-23B Seminole twin transports in the new L-23D configuration, making the older planes comparable after rebuilding with the newest F50 commercial Twin-Bonanzas.

"Partners in Progress" was the theme of Beechcraft's 1959 International Distributor-Dealer Sales Meeting, advanced in date to November 11, 12 and 13 to gain maximum momentum for the coming year. At this gathering 49 states and nearly 60 foreign countries were represented. A featured speaker was Captain Marion L. (Pat) Boling, who described his record-breaking 7,090-mile crossing of the Pacific in the J35 "Philippine Bonanza" as a "Flight of Faith." Modest and sincere, the veteran airlines pilot won a standing ovation from his audience.

Numerous advancements in the 1959 models of Beechcraft's "Air Fleet of American Business" — the Super 18, the two Twin-Bonanzas, the light twin Travel Air, and the K35 Bonanza — reinforced the assurance of continued leadership for the Beech sales organization. Notable was a new power plant installation for the G50 Twin-Bonanza, offering 340 hp supercharged Lycoming engines with continuous flow fuel injection. The advantages of this superior fuel-air delivery system thus became available to the twin-engine aircraft buyer, just as to the purchaser of the single-engine Bonanza. Word was also passed along of new models under development that would enlarge the Beech business aircraft line, making it eventually the most complete as well as the most advanced showing of business aircraft in the industry. The sales organization won praise for having sold, in fiscal 1958, more than half of the entire business aircraft industry's total of planes priced at $20,000 or more — 53% to be exact — for a three per cent increase over its 1957 share.

President O. A. Beech's annual report to the company's stockholders, issued on December 15, showed total sales of $95,889,733 for the fiscal year 1958 that ended September 30. Of this total, $63,786,164 represented military business, and $32,103,569 commercial sales. Net earnings of $3,324,663 made possible an increase in dividends per share to $1.60, compared with the previous $1.20 per share level. The year had been a good one for the company and its people.

Chapter 23

The year 1959 was less than three weeks old when a "Whoosh" of rockets signalled another first for Beechcraft in aviation history. The event was the approval on January 19 by the Federal Aviation Authority of standby rocket power for the Beechcraft Super 18 — the world's first civil aircraft under 10,000 pounds gross weight to be so equipped. The installation consisted of two Aerojet-General 15NS-250 "Junior JATO" lightweight rocket engines housed in the upper aft part of the regular engine nacelles. Fired instantly by electric switches located within easy reach of the pilot, the solid-fueled rockets each provided 250 pounds of thrust (equivalent to about 100 hp at climb speeds) for a duration of 15 seconds. Their "instant thrust" provided greatly increased safety in emergencies, and increased flexibility in operations. The optional rocket units proved popular from the outset, and were later made available for other Beech twin-engine models.

FAA approval of the historic JATO installation followed by only four days a company announcement of a new follow-on production contract which had a very substantial thrust of its own. It called for Beech to build $23 million more of aft fuselage sections and other components for the USAF F-106 all-weather jet interceptor for the Convair Division of General Dynamics, extending production of these items well into mid-1960. The year was off to a good start.

Improvements announced soon afterward in the "littlest Beechcraft" — the Navy KDB-1 radio-controlled target drone — typified the Beech attitude of unwillingness to settle for anything less than the best the company could design and build, no matter for what purpose the product was intended. Beech engineers pressurized the engine's ignition system, and without major modifications gave the tiny plane a boost in altitude capabilities of two miles or more — from 30,000 feet to an unofficial record of 43,500 feet. They redesigned the parachute canister and simplified the recovery system to reduce handling, simplify storage and operate more reliably. They revised the fuel system plumbing to speed decontamination from salt water after

171

retrieval of the target from the sea. They redesigned its radar reflector pods to improve its radarscope simulation of hostile aircraft, and got improved flight performance as a bonus. It took a lot of hard work to make all these improvements; but the end result was a product that established new high standards of performance and reliability in the KD-300 targetplane class — a typical Beech product. It would please the customer; it would build repeat business; and it would open the way to further and more advanced Beech designs in the field of air defense targets.

Beechcraft's own "Kansan of the Year" for 1958, President O. A. Beech, received on February 3, an important appointment that ranged far beyond the boundaries of her native state and country. She was named by a fellow Kansan, President Dwight D. Eisenhower, to a two-year membership on the 13-man International Development Advisory Board, an economic policy consultative group serving broadly to aid in achieving the purposes of the nation's Mutual Security Act, and sworn in at Washington, D. C. on that date. Mrs. Beech was co-representative with Harvey S. Firestone, Jr., chairman of the Firestone Tire and Rubber Company, of the general business community on the board.

Opening in March of the company's eleventh annual Beechcraft Service Clinic, a free inspection service by factory representatives conducted in 1959 at 40 distributor-dealer locations for Beechcraft owners throughout the United States, was to enlarge by more than 1,500 the total of over 10,000 exhaustive maintenance checks completed since the start of the program in 1949. The only program of its kind conducted by a business plane manufacturer, the clinic was a highlight of Beech's constant concern for the interests of its customers. This concern was also apparent in the broadening at that time of a line of factory-built "modernization kits" offered through Beech distributors and dealers to owners of earlier Model 18 and other types of Beechcrafts for field installation, to bring their older planes into line with current models with respect to performance, ease of handling and comfort. Some business owners had purchased military Model 18's of World War II vintage at government surplus sales; some had bought D18S

172

and early Super 18 models through regular trade channels. Beech saw no reason to discriminate among them. All were Beechcraft owners, no matter how their airplanes had been acquired. All were entitled to the best the company could provide to protect their investments. So, kits were engineered and built to add every possible advancement that had been made in Model 18 design to the earlier products, at minimum cost and with full FAA approval. It was possible, with these kits, to extend range by at least 10%, add up to 20 mph in speed, substantially increase payload, and improve flight characteristics and cabin appearance and comfort. Beech was the first business aircraft manufacturer to offer kits of this kind. It was a form of enlightened self-interest that paid dividends to Beech owners and to the company alike.

The work of the Beechcraft Research and Development Corporation, Beech's wholly-owned subsidiary at Boulder, Colorado, won a million dollars' worth of hard-cash recognition from the USAF Air Materiel Command on April 15. That was the date when Beech was awarded a $1 million USAF competitive facilities expansion contract for the construction on the 1500-acre Beech-Boulder site of a large "transient heat" laboratory for ground testing the effects of high temperatures on prototype rocket and space vehicle propellant systems. The contract was the first of its kind awarded by USAF; the laboratory, the first of its kind in America. It provided a new means of simulating thermal conditions of flight from launch to burn-out, instantly elevating missile and rocket tank skin and other component structures to 1,000 degrees F. or more, just as in very high velocity travel through the atmosphere. Basis for the contract award was the record made by Beech-Boulder since 1954 in this and allied fields of aerospace research and development — cryogenics, high energy fuel studies, and handling and transport systems for rocket propellants. The new laboratory would substantially enhance Beech's capability to play a basic and significant part in many advanced aerospace programs, then and in the years to come.

Another tangible compliment to Beech's far-ranging abilities came little more than a week later, with the receipt from North American Aviation on April 23 of a multi-million dollar contract

173

for the "alert pod" system for the USAF B-70 Valkyrie intercontinental strategic bomber. The contract award followed North American's extensive evaluation of proposals submitted by 14 competing companies, and reflected Beech experience dating back to 1949 in the design and manufacture of aircraft ground support systems. The "pod" was to be perhaps the most highly sophisticated device of its kind ever engineered, matching the standing of the B-70 as the ultimate in manned bomber design, with 2,000 mph speed and 70,000-ft. altitude performance. It was to contain numerous ground support items, including instant starting sources for the B-70's General Electric J-93 engines, and other systems for maintaining all of the plane's complex electronic equipment in "warmup" condition for instant use. And it was to be built for airlift by the plane it serviced, from airfield to airfield, providing complete flexibility for alert action from any base in the world. Later suspension of activity on the total B-70 program was to indefinitely postpone the full completion of the North American-Beech Contract; but the record of the award remained to Beechcraft's credit.

Shortly after dawn on April 24, the first units of a group of 20 new Beechcraft Mentor trainers ordered some time before by the government of Chile took off from the Beech Field on the start of a 6,000-mile ferry flight to El Bosque, Chile's military flying base near Santiago. Flown from Wichita by a party of 30 Chilean Air Force officers and airmen headed by Colonel Rene Ianiszewski, the Beech trainers enlarged a force of 45 Mentors previously purchased by Chile. The efficient, economical Mentor was then in the service of the U. S. Air Force, the Navy Bureau of Aeronautics, the Royal Canadian Air Force, and in Argentina, Colombia, El Salvador, Japan, Mexico, the Philippines, Spain, Turkey and Venezuela, in addition to Chile.

On May 13 Beech qualified to enter the select group of aerospace manufacturers producing vehicles with supersonic speed capabilities, when the company was named by the U. S. Navy and the U. S. Air Force as the winner of a joint services competition for a new high speed expendable missile target. The choice followed a detailed evaluation of design proposals submitted by 18 guided missile and airplane manufacturers. Planned for speed of up to Mach 2 (twice the speed of sound)

174

and operational altitudes up to 70,000 feet, the Beech design offered a realistic low-cost simulation of advanced enemy aircraft for counter-measures systems evaluation and training. Essentially a small-scale version of high-performance manned military aircraft, using a liquid rocket propulsion system and weighing in at about 600 pounds gross, the Beechcraft target plane would enlarge the company's experience in the area of supersonic flight — a gain of potential high importance for the future. Its design featured high swept delta wings with ailerons located inboard at the trailing edge, endplate twin vertical stabilizers outboard, and horizontal canard control surfaces positioned well forward for optimum stabilization and elevation. Essentially a target object for radar-guided or infra-red heat-seeking air-to-air missiles like the Sidewinder, Sparrow and Falcon, it was built to be air-launched from almost any high-performance aircraft. Simple yet sophisticated, its systems included provisions for self-monitoring guidance, hit or miss scoring, and self-destruction. Service-designated as the KD2B-1, it gave promise of repeating the success of its propeller-driven elder, the KDB-1 Beechcraft target plane.

A few days short of mid-year, employees of Beech Plant II advanced their lunch hour ten minutes and stepped outside to pose for a group picture with a Bonanza just completed for delivery to a Kansas business man. Its FAA registration number was N6000E; and it was the 6,000th Bonanza built since deliveries of the V-tailed Beech had begun in February 1947. Its purchase by a neighbor attested the good name the Bonanza had earned, not only all over the world but also in its home state, where Beech and its products were most intimately known.

Midsummer additions to highly specialized manufacturing facilities at Beech enlarged the company's abilities to produce, accurately and at minimum cost, almost anything that the inventive minds of engineers could originate and describe. And they illustrated Beech's peaceful solution of a conflict between design and production. To production people, the design engineer sometimes seemed to be a wild-eyed, savage type whose chief aim in life was to design airplane parts and components that could not possibly be built by any means known to man. To engineers, the shop people now and then

175

appeared as clods unable to square up a simple right angle. Actually, both were working together to create an inherently contradictory product — an airplane, which by its nature had to be light, yet strong; stable, yet maneuverable; and so on, through a long list of opposites. As aircraft and space vehicles moved upward in speed to supersonic ranges and into new and hostile environments, both the design and manufacturing problems inevitably multiplied in severity; but Beechcrafters, working together as a team, generally managed to come up with practical solutions.

For example, the "elevons" (combined aileron and elevator structures) of supersonic fighter-interceptor jets had to be designed to reconcile substantial size with the ability to withstand very high-speed loads, yet pared to absolute minimum weight. One device to accomplish this was to taper the structural members in proportion to the loads imposed on various areas of the necessary complex assembly. Engineering specifications for the load-supporting elevon channels therefore called for a taper from .136 inch down to .071 inch at one end of their six-foot length, and from .136 to .050 inch at the other. Beech was able to meet these critical requirements within plus or minus .005 inch limits, by enlarging its equipment for taper chemical milling — a process that removed metal in desired areas at a closely controlled rate of .001 inch per minute.

For structures too massive to be milled by conventional methods, Beech installed tracer-controlled milling machines that offered three-dimensional control of metal removal to ultimate tolerances as low as .0010 inch. For forming shapes from thick, high-strength metals, special equipment powered by the detonation of explosives was used. And for high-strength bonding of honeycomb-filled structures and metal-to-metal surfaces, a 22-ton, 13.5-ft. diameter clam shell type autoclave was added to like-purpose equipment in use since 1957. All of these items increased Beech's ability to say to the engineers: "You design it — we'll produce it."

A further sign of the long-range change under way in the direction of the industry — a change for which Beech had been planning and preparing since 1954 — became apparent in July. The Aircraft Industries Association, the trade organization in

176

Boulder Administration Building is center of a 1,500-acre aerospace complex in the foothills of the Rocky Mountains.

Complete facilities for testing cryogenic containers were developed at the Beech-Boulder operation.

Transient heat tower and laboratory for ground testing the effects of high temperatures on prototype space vehicle propellant systems was first of its kind. (Page 173)

Growth of aerospace work at the Boulder Division resulted in construction of new plant.

Single-engine
Debonair joined
the product line
as Beechcraft
expanded its mar-
keting programs.

Queen Air 65
executive transport
added to Beech-
craft's dominance
in the twin-
engine market.

Optional JATO
installations on
Beechcraft Super
18's offered
standby rocket
power for
increased safety in
emergencies and
increased flexi-
bility in operations.
(Page 171)

The 6,000th
Bonanza rolled
from the
production lines
of Plant II
in 1959.
(Page 175)

178

which Beech and most other manufacturers in the field held membership, changed its name to Aerospace Industries Association. This was in acknowledgement of the growing emphasis on the guided missile as a primary deterrent against all-out nuclear attack, and of the industry's new role as the supplier of vehicles and equipment for space exploration. A trend toward de-emphasis of manned aircraft was also signalled a little later by Defense Department cancellation of a multi-million dollar contract for the jet-powered Martin P6M-1 Seamaster mine-laying and reconnaissance seaplane. Beech had taken part in this project by performing engineering research on the Seamaster's high speed emergency personnel escape systems — a program that had involved the design of a new telemetry system, instrumentation of anthropomorphic dummies, assistance in conducting rocket sled ejections that simulated conditions of actual flight, and subsequent reduction of telemetric data. It had not been a large contract, in terms of dollars, but it had provided experience that might well have further applications in the future.

Meanwhile, President O. A. Beech revealed further progress in the company's planning for expansion of its business aircraft sales with the announcement that two new models would soon be unveiled — the Beechcraft Model 33 Debonair, a companion single-engine plane to the Bonanza that would sell at a lower price, and the Model 65 Queen Air, a new twin-engine Beechcraft filling a size and performance niche midway between the Super 18 and the Twin-Bonanza. No matter what changes might occur in military and aerospace procurement, Beech was confident that the steadily growing market for strictly business airplanes would continue to provide an outlet for a very substantial amount of its production; and the company meant to increase its already large share of that market by eventually offering a Beechcraft in every important category of size, performance and price that it could profitably enter.

Painstaking developmental work to maximize the performance and utility of the Beech KDB-1 propeller-driven missile target system brought a dividend on July 20, with the news that the U. S. Army had issued a $1.5 million production contract for the "littlest Beechcraft" and its associated ground handling

179

equipment. The Army would use a version very nearly identical with that of the Beech KDB-1 design then in production for the U. S. Navy — a fact that spoke well for the versatility engineered into the sturdy reuseable target plane by Beech designers.

Another Beech project undertaken to meet a specific Army aviation need was disclosed, with the completion of tests by the Army Aviation Board at Fort Rucker, Alabama of a new configuration of its widely used L-23 "Seminole" version of the Beechcraft Twin-Bonanza. The first three units of the new version, Army-designated as the L-23F, were assigned to duty at locations in Virginia and Heidelberg, Germany. Other specialized versions, carrying an "RL-23F" designation, were ordered into production to carry SLAR ("side-looking airborne radar") electronics equipment — a tactical modification which was also applied to some of the L-23D Army Beechcrafts, providing all-weather surveillance capability to provide combat intelligence in support of field forces.

Gross weight of the Beechcraft "Seminole" in the L-23F version was increased to 7,368 pounds. Its fuselage was enlarged, and its interior was extensively redesigned, to provide a high order of versatility for passenger and cargo disposal. The pilot compartment was separated from the main cabin by a sliding door, as in the Beech Super 18, setting apart a "private office aloft" for use during command transport missions. A work desk could be easily added to the normal cabin seating for four persons, or a fifth passenger seat. All cabin seats were quickly removable, to clear space for 1,350 pounds of cargo in a volume of 215 cubic feet. Alternate high density seating provided capacity to carry a total of ten passengers, or to airlift seven fully equipped troops, in addition to the pilot. Panoramic windows, and an exceptionally low cabin noise level, afforded comfort comparable with that of the executive-type commercial Twin-Bonanza. Higher efficiency, greater versatility — these were the end results of the L-23 redesign.

August marked the close of an eight-year program of wing-building at Beech for Lockheed's USAF T-33 two-place jet training aircraft and their Navy counterparts, the T2V carrier-trainer jets. At its peak, Beech had turned out five sets of wings per day, six days a week; and, as the sole supplier of wings

180

for the famous jet, had completed more than 5,600 wings under its sub-contract with Lockheed for the U. S. Air Force, the Navy Bureau of Aeronautics, the Royal Canadian Air Force and the Defense Services of Japan. Production continued then and throughout the year of important assemblies for Lockheed's USAF F-104 Starfighter jet interceptor, and for McDonnell's USAF F-101 Voodoo jet fighter-bomber, Republic's USAF F-105 Thunderchief all-weather jet fighter-bomber, and Convair's USAF F-106 Delta Dart jet interceptor and USAF B-58 Hustler bomber. On-schedule completion was also recorded for Beech production of 1,700-gallon external fuel tanks for USAF Strategic Air Command's Boeing B-47 six-jet bombers; and the Beech tank builders turned to building smaller external fuel stores for USAF F-100 jet fighters.

The second of the nation's good neighbors in South America to acquire new fleets of Beechcraft Mentor trainers during the year completed flyaway deliveries from Wichita in September. Officers and personnel of the Venezuelan Air Force and the Venezuelan government's Ministry of Communications headed for home with the last of 41 Mentors built during 1959 for their respective services — 34 for Air Force training use, 7 for the Ministry's civilian flying school. "Hasta la Vista" was the phrase of leave-taking — "Till we meet again."

Closing of the books for the company's 1959 fiscal year on September 30 showed record-breaking accomplishments. While total sales of $89.5 million were less than in 1958, net income of more than $3.96 million reached the highest level in 15 years. Business and commercial sales exceeding $37.9 million reached a new all-time high, more than making up for the slight drop in this category that had followed the 1958 recession, with an 18% increase over the previous year. Military sales of $51.6 million were reinforced by a substantial backlog extending a year or more ahead. Net worth had increased from $23 million to a shade under $26 million; working capital was up from $20 million to $22.8 million. The record, and the future prospects, fully justified an increase during the year in the quarterly dividend rate from 30¢ to 40¢ per share of stock, plus a 5% stock dividend which was declared on October 6. Without skimping in the fulfillment of its responsibilities to its customers, its

181

employees, its suppliers and its community, Beech was also meeting the primary obligation of any business — the obligation to operate profitably.

A company-wide activity that produced directly traceable cost savings of $241,000 in fiscal 1959 had a part in this favorable showing. It was a continuous conservation program, backed by posters, and cash awards to employees for conservation suggestions, promoting maximum utilization of all production materials and elimination of waste. As a natural concomitant of good craftsmanship and efficient operation, conservation in these ways had always been built into the approach that Beechcrafters took toward their work. The program served to keep this approach in mind, and to sharpen its focus on methods of producing without waste. As a result, total overhead supply expenses for 1959 were down 9.1% over 1958; and substantial savings were made in other areas. The attitude it fostered was one reason for the company's success in bidding for highly competitive military contracts, and winning customers in the equally competitive business aircraft market.

The month of November opened well, with the receipt on November 3 from Republic Aviation Corporation of a $3.6 million follow-on contract for additional USAF F-105 all-weather tactical jet fighter-bomber assemblies. The order extended production of aft fuselage sections and ailerons for the supersonic "Thunderchief" well into mid-1961. A few days later, came the news that a Beech-built Army L-23F twin-engine transport had been assigned to the Federal Aviation Agency for use in its continuous program of in-flight evaluation of America's air traffic control system. The fast, sturdy, comfortable, far-ranging Beechcraft was well suited to this use. Rated for FAA use at a gross weight of 7,700 pounds, it could easily carry the required extra load of electronic navigation and communications gear and recording devices. Its service ceiling of 27,000 feet qualified the L-23F for high altitude operations in mountainous regions. The record it was to make would speak well for Beech in evaluations of aircraft for later FAA purchases.

From Cape Canaveral, Florida, came welcome news indicating that the United States was making progress in closing the existing gap between its own high payload long-range missiles and those of the Soviet Union. On November 28, a Convair Atlas intercontinental ballistic missile successfully completed a 6,000-mile flight down-range over the South Atlantic. It was highly probable that activities at Beech-Boulder had played a part in the missile's successful firing; for the Boulder Division had been engaged for some months in advanced functional testing of both Convair-Atlas and Martin-Titan ICBM propulsion system components, under subcontract to their respective manufacturers. The Beech tests simulated extremes of operation and environment encountered by the 16,000 mph missiles in their long flights through space, and leaving and re-entering the atmosphere. Giant mechanical shakers, the largest capable of inducing motion at 2,000 strokes per second, checked the reliability of vital control valves under in-use conditions. Environmental chambers, simulating flight altitudes of 300,000 feet and capable of swift temperature changes ranging from 750° F. to -80° F., were joined with "cold boxes" using liquid nitrogen to produce cryogenic environments of -300° F., for further testing. This program, and other exhaustive studies of missile propulsion systems, components and fuels at Beech-Boulder, was playing an important part in missile and space vehicle development.

Meanwhile, Beech at Wichita had launched its 1960 sales program on November 18, 19 and 20 at its annual International Distributor-Dealer Sales Meeting, with the challenging theme "$60 Million in '60," Beech's sales goal for the coming year. To bring this goal more surely within reach, the company unveiled the two new models it had promised its dealers earlier in the year — the majestic Model 65 twin-engine Queen Air, and the competitively priced single-engine Model 33 Debonair. For good measure, many new advancements were also offered in existing designs.

In the hierarchy of business aircraft, the new Beechcraft Queen Air took second place only to the Beech Super 18 — and then only in terms of size and corresponding range. Seating six to seven persons in a variety of luxurious custom arrangements, it had all the features, as well as the appearance, of a modern airliner. Its two 340 hp supercharged fuel injection Lycoming engines and three-bladed propellers afforded a top speed of 239 mph — topping the Super 18 by a shade. It was designed to mount "weather avoidance" radar and other advanced electronic equipment, and still have payload to spare, carrying nearly 3,000 pounds useful load at a 7,700 pound gross weight. Filling a spot in the Beech line midway between the Super 18 and the Twin-Bonanza, it was the airplane many customers had long wanted; and they were quick to express their approval — with signed orders.

The new Beech Model 33 Debonair extended the "Air Fleet of American Business" at the low end of the price spectrum, offering traditional Beech quality and performance at a price just under $20,000. Younger brother of the famous Bonanza, it used the same smooth, reliable 225 hp Continental fuel injection engine and hydraulically controlled Hartzell constant speed propeller as earlier Bonanza models. Its high speed was 195 mph; its cruising speed at 65% power, 180 mph. It was designed to be economical to buy, and economical to operate, yet to offer the utmost in luxurious comfort in the four-place, single-engine class. The crucial test of sales in a highly competitive market was to prove its merits.

In its 1960 Super G18 version, the largest Beechcraft offered a completely re-engineered cockpit with many new features for greater visibility, comfort and handling ease. Useful load was increased to 3,750 pounds — highest in Model 18 history. Cabin redesign enhanced passenger comfort. The two Twin-Bonanza versions for 1960 featured the convenient air-stair door, like the Super 18 and Queen Air, new square wing tips for improved aerodynamic efficiency, a greater useful load for the H50 model of 2,820 pounds, and many other refinements. The B95 Travel Air, 1960 style, offered more room than any other plane in its class, with an increase in cabin section length from 83 to 102 inches; a restyled empennage with larger horizontal stabilizer and elevator surfaces; a 100 pound increase in gross weight for a higher useful load of 1,465 pounds; and numerous other betterments. The M35 Bonanza for 1960 was distinguished by new squared Hoerner-type wing tips, new interior styling and other changes for the better. Altogether, the 1960 line was clearly the best yet; and the goal of "$60 Million in '60" a realistic one.

184

Chapter 24

The opening days of Beech's twenty-eighth year were also the start of a decade that was widely and perhaps extravagantly hailed as "The Soaring Sixties." This designation was not one that found its way into the company's vocabulary. Optimism and enthusiasm were perennial Beech traits; but they were always tempered with realism, and with a common-sense avoidance of hyperbole. The company's position was solid, and its prospects for a record-breaking year were excellent. Beyond that point, glittering predictions would have been meaningless and unsound.

Reports came to Wichita early in the year of transoceanic flights by Beechcraft owners that dramatically demonstrated the performance and reliability of Beech products. Mrs. Arlene Davis of Cleveland, Ohio, completed a 16,000 mile round trip pleasure tour of Europe and North Africa in her twin-engine Beech Travel Air N876R in less than 85 flying hours. "It was a perfect flight all the way," said Mrs. Davis, "but what I liked best about the trip was the Travel Air — it's the nicest airplane in the whole world!" Ample experience reinforced her judgment; for Mrs. Davis, a licensed pilot since 1931, was a World War II instrument flying instructor, a competitor in many air races, and an owner of one of the first Beechcraft biplanes built in 1934. Her eastward flight was across the North Atlantic, via the Azores. The return trip, after an aerial tour of Europe, was from Dakar, Africa, to Natal, Brazil, across the South Atlantic. From many miles westward, a cablegram came to Beech on January 1 from the Philippine capital of Manila, reporting the routine arrival there of a new Beechcraft H50 Twin-Bonanza, flown from Wichita across the Pacific by its owner, Colonel Hans Menzi, a Manila industrialist and publisher. The four-leg ocean crossing, via San Francisco, Honolulu, Wake and Guam, covered 7,772 miles and, against headwinds, required 43 hours. "Everything went smoothly," was the word from Colonel Menzi, who had flown Beechcraft Bonanzas and Twin-Bonanzas for seven years in connection with his business enterprises.

Shortly afterward, a factory demonstration of Beechcraft high altitude capability produced a new national and international high altitude record of 34,862 feet for light airplanes in the class C-1.d category. Taking off from the Beech field at Wichita on February 8, company test pilot James D. Webber flew a standard fully equipped Model 65 Beechcraft Queen Air six-place twin nearly a mile and a half higher than its advertised service ceiling of 27,000 feet. Supervised by officials of the National Aeronautic Association, the flight results were confirmed by the Federation Aeronautique Internationale — and another world record for Beech went into the archives of global aviation.

In mid-February, a production mark was set with the delivery to the Koss Construction Company of Des Moines, Iowa of the 500th Super 18 Beechcraft. The new seven-place red and white twin Beech took the place of a single-engine Beechcraft Bonanza which the construction firm had flown some 1,200 hours in the previous two years. Like most Beechcraft owners, Koss had found its plane to be a definite asset in securing new business, and in supervising and coordinating its activities over a widespread geographical area. It was a typical instance that went far to explain Beech's confident enthusiasm in its future prospects. As long as business firms and individuals continued to find Beechcraft ownership to be a profitable investment, Beech would be sure of a market for its business aircraft, assuming that its products remained competitive in performance and price and were competently merchandised. From the record, this appeared very likely.

The month of May brought additional large orders from the U. S. Army Air Services for L-23F Seminole utility twin-engine transports and RL-23F twins mounting combat surveillance radar systems. These extended production in progress on new twins of the same types — Army versions of the commercial Twin-Bonanza models — and modifications by Beech of existing L-23D Seminole transports to the RL-23D configuration.

Completion in June of a new headquarters and engineering building on the Beech-owned 1,500-acre tract north of Boulder, Colorado was the highlight of a program further expanding the facilities of the Boulder Division. This was in addition to the

186

$1 million transient heat laboratory erected under a special U. S. Air Force contract. The unique transient heat test facility comprised a tower some four stories high, housing a giant vacuum bell lined with 3,000 infra-red quartz lamps, and equipped with supporting equipment remotely located to program liquid hydrogen rocket fuel in and out of the systems under test, plus controls and recording instruments. In a typical test, a huge Beech-developed insulated titanium missile boost stage tank was lowered into the vacuum bell, and filled with hydrogen liquefied at a super-cold temperature of −423° F. The outside pressure was then reduced and fuel was programmed out of the tank, at the same time that tank skin temperatures were rapidly elevated to 1,000° F. or more. This procedure simulated the environments and temperatures encountered in actual missile flight, providing accurate measurements of fuel consumption and aerodynamic heating. Much useful information was thus obtained, at a fraction of the cost of full-scale flight testing. Other Beech-Boulder facilities conducted production environmental tests of Atlas and Titan ICBM propulsion systems components, simulating in-flight vibration, temperature and pressure conditions. Programs were also conducted, under contracts with the armed services and with other agencies and manufacturers concerned with advanced weapons systems and space technology, in cryogenic engineering and space vehicle propellant system design studies. Included was the preparation of an advanced design proposal for the Saturn man-in-space program. Beech-Boulder was an important and growing contributor to U. S. missile and space technology.

Another Beech aerospace activity involved the production, under contract to Lockheed, of support equipment for the Polaris intermediate range ballistic missile. Items built under this contract included huge 7,000-pound containers for storing and transporting first stage engines for the Polaris. Measuring 20 feet in length, these massive mobile caissons, constructed to close tolerances, featured built-in humidity and temperature controls to maintain a stable environment for their critically important contents under varying shipping and storage conditions.

Beech and its distributor in Bremen, West Germany, Travelair

G.m.b.H., scored a first in air transport history on July 7, with the first transatlantic airlift of Beechcraft business planes direct from the Wichita factory. A Lockheed Super G transport owned by Lufthansa Airlines took off from the Wichita Municipal Airport on that date, carrying three Beechcraft Debonairs, one Beechcraft Bonanza, and several tons of spare parts in a direct flight from Beechcraft to Bremen. It was, analysis showed, the most desirable means of effecting quick delivery, and on balance, also the most economical.

Delivery that same month to the Los Angeles Division of North American Aviation, Inc. of a three-plane fleet of twin-engine Beechcraft Travel Air executive transports pointed up the extent to which Beech products were favored by the most knowledgeable business aircraft buyers. North American's purchase was made after complete evaluation and flight testing of all the light twins on the business plane market. Its own four-place, all-metal single-engine Navion had been a highly respected competitor of the Beechcraft Bonanza in the early postwar era; and Beech had been the winner of North American's competition as a design and production source of the alert pod for its USAF B-70 Valkyrie Mach 3 bomber. Beech was no stranger to this customer; nor, for that matter, to Lockheed, which had in June replaced its two Model D50 Twin-Bonanzas, operated since 1958, with new H50 Twin-Bonanzas. Many other leaders in the aircraft and aerospace industry were Beechcraft owners; typically, Aerojet-General Corporation; Chance-Vought Aircraft, Inc.; Goodyear Aircraft Corporation; Fairchild Aircraft Division; Hughes Tool Company; and McDonnell Aircraft. Among the people who knew airplanes best, and whose requirements were the most exacting, Beechcrafts were consistently first choice above all other business aircraft.

Changes in the company's top echelon were also announced during the month. On July 6, John P. Gaty, vice president and general manager since 1940, announced his resignation, effective at the end of the fiscal year, to devote full time to personal business interests. His retirement marked the end of more than 23 years of dedicated service as a Beechcrafter. Gaty had joined the company in March 1937 as vice president and director of sales, and had been named general manager by Walter H.

188

Beech in 1940 to take charge of its rapid expansion for defense and World War II production. He had made many contributions to the industry and to Beechcraft, helping tirelessly to build the company and its products to a position of international renown.

Elected to the position of executive vice president was Frank E. Hedrick, who for ten years had been one of the company's three-member executive committee. In this post he was to establish and administer the company's expansion plans for the years ahead — years in which it was confidently and realistically expected that the sales potential for business aircraft was to more than double. Hedrick had joined Beech in September 1940 at the age of 27 as assistant to the general manager and coordinator, following a rapid rise to executive responsibilities with another Wichita concern. In July 1945, he had been promoted by Walter H. Beech to the post of vice president and coordinator, in recognition of outstanding performance. Five years later, in December 1950, Hedrick was elected to the company's board of directors: and at the time of his latest advancement, he was also serving as president and director of its two wholly-owned subsidiaries, Beech Acceptance Corporation, Inc., and Beechcraft Research and Development, Inc.

Implementation of planning for growth followed very soon, with the establishment of a new Marketing Division to centralize responsibility for the worldwide marketing and merchandising of all Beechcraft commercial airplanes and products. This change in organizational structure brought together, under the supervision of the vice president - marketing, all of the departments and activities concerned with commercial product exploitation, including domestic and export sales, parts and service operation, product development, marketing research, public relations and advertising, and related activities. Its purpose was to coordinate all selling efforts for maximum efficiency, and thus to carry out the precepts of the company's founder, Walter H. Beech, who very early in his aircraft career had earned the reputation of being one of the world's best airplane salesmen. He had always realized, as another famous salesman once said, that "Nothing ever happens until somebody sells something"; and Walter H. Beech and his people had never been content merely to sit around and wait for things to happen. They went out and made sales happen, in the markets of the world. The newly structured Marketing Division would enlarge Beechcraft's ability to develop potential markets for business aircraft which, even then, exceeded in size the creative selling capacity of the entire business aircraft industry; and it would help to maintain for Beech a position of leadership in this field.

Meanwhile, additional contracts had enlarged the backlog of business on hand. In July came a contract from the U. S. Army for $3 million worth of Beechcraft Model 1025 missile target systems, a slightly modified version of the Beech KDB-1 propeller-driven Navy target drone and associated equipment; and also a $1.4 million Army order for additional KDB-1 targets, supplementing an earlier $1.5 million contract. In August, Beech sub-contract production of aft fuselage sections for the USAF F-105 Thunderchief fighter-bomber was increased to some $17 million, with the receipt of a follow-on contract amounting to $7.7 million from Republic Aviation. That month the company was awarded a Bureau of Naval Weapons contract of approximately $1 million for development of high performance in-flight refueling systems, as a result of an original design study competition which Beech had won some time before. The Beech study proposed a unique flexible, completely mechanical hose and drogue system driven by ram air to eliminate the usual hydraulic controls, thus simplifying the refueling of one fighter or bomber plane by another. Later testing was to prove its soundness. Still another special assignment called for Beech to furnish anthropomorphic dummies, instrumentation and technical services for rocket sled tests of USAF B-58 seat ejection emergency escape systems.

The first flight of a new Beechcraft missile target was completed successfully September 30 at the White Sands Missile Range in New Mexico. Similar in configuration to the KDB-1 target in use by the U. S. Navy and U. S. Army, the Beechcraft PD 75-4-1 featured a new four-cylinder Continental 145 hp engine, offering higher performance than the prior 120 hp McCulloch-engine version. The new design was privately financed under a research and development program jointly

190

sponsored by Beech and Continental Motors Corporation, in keeping with the company's policy of striving always to give its customers the utmost in performance and value for their money.

Among other means of delivering maximum value was to promote the highest possible efficiency in production and inventory control and analysis. To these ends, Beech installed mechanized equipment of remarkable capacity and scope. Centralized production control was upgraded with Collecta-data office-plant linkage equipment that made it possible to pin-point the location of some 25,000 items in fabrication at any of 97 locations, every 56 minutes throughout the working day. The system handled some 4,000 transmissions per day in connection with some 700 fabrication projects. In itself it accomplished a 75% reduction in shortage delays on the assembly lines, plus further improvements and savings in other areas. Eventually, it was to be integrated into a master plan for control of all Beechcraft production through a factory-wide data processing system with high-speed memory equipment. Another item in this master plan was a RAMAC (Random Access Method of Accounting and Control) system which, through its electronic logic and memory circuitry, saved thousands of man-hours in the analysis of inventory control. The effect of this highly sophisticated equipment, and of later additions which would be made to it, would be not only to mechanize almost countless routine functions, but also to provide a fast-working, accurate basis for advanced methods of control such as "management by exception." Beech management methods were more than keeping up with the times.

In further preparation for long-term growth, President O. A. Beech announced on November 14 the enlargement of the Beech Aircraft Corporation's board of directors, which prior to that time had consisted of five persons — the company's three-member executive committee, its vice president - counsel, Dwight S. Wallace, and its secretary-treasurer, John A. Elliott. Joining Mrs. Beech, Frank E. Hedrick, Dwight Wallace and John Elliott on the enlarged board were A. R. Bell, vice president - general manager, Beech Acceptance Corporation, and three Beech Aircraft officers: Leddy L. Greever, vice president - domestic sales; Wyman L. Henry, vice president - marketing; and James N. Lew,

191

vice president - engineering. Thus the ranking executives responsible for the many aspects of Beechcraft's far-ranging programs were brought together on the company's highest decision-making council, adding their experience and talents intimately to the progressive team-effort that had always been a Beech characteristic at all operating levels.

There was good news in President Beech's report to the stockholders for the 1960 fiscal year that ended September 30. Total sales were $98,873,800 — an increase of 10.4% over fiscal 1959. Business and commercial sales reached an all-time high of $46,570,254, up more than 22% over 1959. Military sales volume of $52.3 million slightly topped the previous year. Beechcraft's slogan for the year for commercial sales had been "60 Million in '60." It was handily over-fulfilled, with actual sales (at retail prices) of $62,285,119. And net income reached an all-time high of $4,854,059 — equal to $5.41 per share of stock — up 23% over fiscal 1959. A stock dividend of 5% was distributed to stockholders on November 30; and, to provide for wider ownership and greater marketability of its shares, a three-for-one stock split was effected on November 23. Regular quarterly dividends totalling $1,403,030 were paid during the fiscal year. Foresighted additions to the company's earned surplus of nearly $2 million brought its total amount to better than $17.5 million at the end of fiscal 1960. It was in good shape to grow — very good.

"Biggest and best ever" was an accurate summing up of the 1961 Beechcraft International Distributor-Dealer Sales Meeting held November 16-17 in Wichita. More than 500 members of the Beech world-wide sales and service organization were there. That the company's realigned Marketing Division had been active was well attested by the presence of representatives from 120 domestic Beech dealerships (compared with a total of 90 for the year before) and 60 export dealerships. The membership list of the "Beechcraft Millionaires" — distributors who individually sold $1 million or more in Beechcraft planes and parts in 1960 — was up to 27, an increase of nine over the previous year. "Here we Grow Again" was a main theme of the the meeting; and there was ample foundation, in every area of aircraft sales and service, to justify it.

Activities of the Beech Acceptance Corporation, Inc., since

This Model 65 Queen Air climbed above Kansas farmlands to an international high altitude record of 34,862 feet in its class C-1d category. (Page 186)

A Beech "first" in air cargo history was this airlift of three Model 33 Debonairs and a Model 35 Bonanza from Wichita to its distributor in Germany, Travelair G.m.b.H. (Pages 187-188)

Governor Winthrop Rockefeller of Arkansas was typical of American leaders who found the Beech Super 18 ideally adapted to "VIP" transportation needs.

Beechcraft Baron, with a 236 mph top speed, became a top seller almost immediately upon its introduction into the light twin market.

John Morrell & Co., a constant Beech customer since the purchase of its first Travel Air in 1930, added this new Baron to its 1961 fleet of three Beechcrafts.

Volkswagen, a later multiple King Air owner, speeded its American sales as O. A. Beech handed over a new Travel Air twin to Hubert L. Brundage (left), VW Florida distributor.

The J. P. Stevens & Co. Inc. 1961 fleet of five Model 18 Beechcrafts was superseded in later years by five King Air executive transports.

194

this wholly-owned subsidiary was formed in December 1956, were reported to have produced a volume of some $18 million during 1960, and a grand total of over $60 million in new business since its founding. Plans were revealed for this financing organization to expand its operations into underwriting Beechcraft owner purchases of modernization kits, factory-distributed accessories and exchange engines. It was also to assist in enlarging and improving Beech Aircraft's network of sales outlets, by helping new dealers to qualify for fully equipped facilities with a relatively low cash investment. The dealer plan was tied in with a new "package dealership" originated by Beech, offering a choice of several different facilities, complete with furnished buildings and all necessary equipment to start in business in typical Beech first-class style. Many factory advisory services were included in the "package" greatly enhancing the prospects of success and growth for any dealer who would contribute intelligent hard work and responsibility as his part of the effort. Designated as "Operation Turnkey," the immediate purpose of this plan was to enlarge the number of Beech dealerships in the United States to a total of 200, as rapidly as possible, and eventually to establish well-qualified dealers in every community where the sales potential would justify such a step.

Outstanding single event of the 1961 meeting was the introduction of the new Beechcraft Model 55 Baron, a fast, sleek, four to five place twin-engine plane designed for the businessman-pilot. Ruggedly strong, yet extremely trim in appearance, with a swept tail and compact, flat-decked engine nacelles, the Baron offered a high useful load of 1,920 pounds and a top speed of 236 mph. Its two 260 hp Continental 10-470-L fuel injection engines combined fast-cruise and high performance capabilities with anti-icing safety and fuel economy to permit a non-stop range of more than 1,200 miles with reserve. The Baron filled a spot in the Beech line midway between the Twin-Bonanza and the Travel Air twins; and it was soon to prove one of the most popular airplanes in its class.

The twin Beechcraft Queen Air, and the single-engine Debonair, both of which had won enthusiastic market acceptance in their first sales year of 1960, offered many refinements in design and appearance for 1961. So did the other Beechcraft 1961

195

models — the Super G18 twin, the two Twin-Bonanzas, and the always distinguished single-engine Bonanza. Beech distributors and dealers showed their approval of the 1961 line in a very practical way. As of November 22, their orders on hand for the newest Beechcrafts reached a total list value of more than $15.5 million. Year 1961 was off to a good start.

Chapter 25

The routine sale of a new Beechcraft Bonanza early in 1961 by Atlantic Aviation Service, Beech distributor at Philadelphia, Pennsylvania, might by reasonable extension be taken to summarize the company's broad range of activities and interests, not only for that year but for a decade or more into the future. The buyer was Leroy Gordon Cooper, Jr. — his profession, astronaut. One of the seven military test pilots chosen for America's first manned satellite program, Cooper planned to use his Bonanza for travel in connection with his Project Mercury astronaut training. It would expedite his business, as thousands of other Beechcrafts were doing for their owners. He and his fellow astronauts would fly an F-106 from time to time, to maintain pilot proficiency — an airplane for which important components were built by Beech. In his eventual flight into space, some of the research and development work carried on at Beech-Boulder would almost inevitably play a part; and support equipment and hardware built by the Beech Aerospace Division might come into use. Whether cruising 200 mph in his Bonanza, or 17,500 mph in orbital flight, Cooper would have support from Beechcraft. That was how it had been planned to be; and Beech's plans were working out.

Applying what it described as "Imaginuity" in the fields of space exploration, and also of weapon system technology, Beech through its Boulder Division was deeply involved in continuing studies related to some of the nation's most advanced aerospace programs, including the Apollo manned spacecraft program, the Centaur orbital space probe launch vehicle, and the government's Space Plane program. The results of these studies were to become apparent later. Meanwhile, Beech early in the year applied to the top-level control of its wholly-owned subsidiary, Beechcraft Research and Development, Inc. the same principle of advanced planning for growth that it had followed in November, 1960 when the board of directors of the parent company was enlarged. It added to the directorate of Beechcraft R & D the ranking executives responsible for its subsidiary's principal fields of operation, thereby strengthening the teamwork at the highest decision-making level.

Never an organization to be hampered by tradition, Beech in April adopted an improved procedure for the introduction of new models of Beechcrafts to the commercial market. In place of the former practice of presenting an entire new line at the annual International Distributor-Dealer sales meeting at Wichita, the company's decision was to stagger the announcement of new models throughout the year whenever development and testing of advancements in design was completed. Also for the first time, the new models were to be presented in the field at regional meetings conducted by factory teams of marketing specialists. The new procedure held promise of benefits to buyers and dealers alike, offering economies at factory and retail levels which would be reflected in product pricing, and increasing the effectiveness of national promotional programs.

The first model to be introduced in this way was the all-new 200 mph B95A Travel Air light twin. In its April unveiling, the B95A emerged as more strongly than ever the leader in its weight and power category. Its retail price was $49,500 — a basic list price $2,000 lower than that of the preceding model. Its gross weight was upped to 4,200 pounds, providing an increase of nearly 200 pounds useful load. Yet its excellent flying qualities, easy controllability and Beech dependability remained unchanged. Its two new Lycoming IO-360-B1A fuel injection engines helped deliver a top speed of 210 mph, and a nonstop range of more than 1,000 miles with an average fuel consumption of 18 gallons per hour. New "air cushion" flaps retained the same comfortable landing speeds of the lighter model; and a larger interior of 143 cubic feet capacity, and many new refinements, made the B95A Travel Air an important development in business flying.

May 5, 1961 was a date of great significance to all Americans, and one with a special meaning to Beechcrafters. The historic suborbital flight of United States Astronaut Alan B. Shepard, Jr., aboard the Mercury capsule "Freedom 7" was followed to its successful conclusion by countless millions — every man and woman at Beech Aircraft among them. For the duration of Commander Shepard's flight, production virtually stopped, in a way unmatched since V-J Day in 1945; and no one objected. At its end, the losses would be more than regained. Riding with the astronaut was the work of Beechcrafters' minds and hands. Beech had a part in the manufacture, for McDonnell Aircraft, of specialized radar reflectivity panels for the one-ton Mercury capsules. And, in the background of virtually every aerospace project, at least some trace could be found of the experimentation, the research and development which had gone forward at Beech-Boulder without pause since 1954 — work which was being enlarged in scope and importance through expansion, then under way, of the Boulder facilities. The flight of the "Freedom 7" was a proud event for America and for Beech.

Successful results of another first flight, not so dramatic as that of America's first man into space, but important in its way to the nation's defense and to Beech, were also announced in May. The Beechcraft Model 1025 target missile, an improved and simplified version of the KDB-1 Beech-designed medium performance target drone then operational with the U. S. Navy, met and passed its first tests for U. S. Army service at the Ordnance Department's McGregor range near Ft. Bliss, Texas. The flight confirmed the validity of a new procurement concept applied for the first time in the case of the Beech Model 1025 drone — that of acceptance by a military service prior to flight evaluations — which produced substantial savings in product development costs. The Army also awarded Beech an add-on contract for $674,673, enlarging its original $1.7 million contract for Beech Model 1025 target planes. The "littlest Beechcraft" would have more work to do in helping train anti-aircraft missilemen to deter aggressors.

In a broader area concerned with the sum of Beechcraft's present and future services in defense of the nation and of the free world, the company announced a new organizational structure planned, in the words of Frank E. Hedrick, executive vice president, "To increase our capabilities for the military services, industry and other agencies charged with achieving national goals in the defense and space effort." Over-all responsibility for advance planning, weapon system management, all military projects and contractual performance was assigned to William M. Morgan, who had joined Beech in October 1960 as vice president - military relations, after his voluntary retirement with the rank of major general from the U. S. Air Force. It was a logical assignment; for General Morgan had climaxed a distinguished 31-year military aviation career in operational and materiel commands with service as Commander of the Air Force Cambridge Research Center at Bedford, Massachusetts — a basic research facility that was a counterpart in many ways of Beechcraft's military and aerospace activities.

Looking to the future in other directions, Frank Hedrick was joined by Wyman L. Henry, vice president - marketing, in a late-May business trip to Europe that had several objectives. The Beech executives attended the 24th International Air Salon at Le Bourget Airport in Paris — the world's largest showcase of aerospace products — for a first-hand view of the industry's latest developments. They conferred with Beechcraft distributors and dealers in the fast-growing market areas of England, Ireland, West Germany, France, Switzerland and Italy. And they met in Bordeaux, France with officials of Societe Francaise d'Entretien et de Reparation de Materiel Aeronautique (SFERMA), with which Beech had some time ago signed a technical agreement for cooperative development of turboprop engine installations in several models of Beechcraft airplanes.

Beech had an interest of long standing in turbine power plants, and initial development work with its French colleagues in this field dated back some two and one-half years. Current projects involved the retrofitting of new Beechcraft Baron and Travel Air twins with Turbomeca Astazou engines rated at about 500 hp, and of Model 18 Beech twins with 875 hp Turbomeca Bastan engines. Successful airlines experience with high-speed transport planes using larger propjet engines indicated that business air fleets of the future would almost surely include medium and smaller-size aircraft powered with scaled-down

199

versions of the smooth, practically vibration-free turbine, in both propjet and pure jet versions. The propjet was, in fact, already establishing itself in the topmost category of executive aircraft — the million-dollar plus price bracket; and pure jet executive transports were also being offered in the same price class. Whenever turbine power became competitive with the long-established and highly refined piston engines for a broader range of business aircraft, Beech would be ready to supply it — at its best.

From its shackles beneath the wing of a high-flying Navy F3H-2 McDonnell all-weather jet fighter, a unique Beech-built supersonic vehicle was successfully air-launched on its first powered flight May 31 at the Naval Missile Center, Point Mugu, California. The vehicle was the Beech XKD2B1/Q-12 missile target; and the flight was another step in its progress toward operational status with the U. S. Navy and the U. S. Air Force as an expendable air-to-air and surface-to-air missile training object simulating the speed, altitude and radar appearance of advanced design enemy aircraft. It had been under development by Beech aerospace engineers since May 1959, when the company was named winner of a design contract, in competition with 17 other manufacturers, for a target capable of Mach 2 speed (twice the speed of sound) at controlled altitudes ranging from 5,000 to 70,000 feet. A compact liquid propellant rocket engine only 20 inches long, yet producing more than 600 pounds of thrust, had been developed for this specialized Beechcraft by Rocketdyne, a division of North American Aviation, Inc. The newest space age version of the "littlest Beechcraft" had passed its initial trials with flying colors; more would be heard from it later.

In June, other Beech aerospace activities made news. Production got under way on a Beech-developed TAU/28M portable encapsulated seat escape procedures trainer for the Ogden (Utah) Air Materiel Area, U. S. Air Force. Designed to prepare crew members of the Mach 2 B-58 Hustler bomber in procedures for safe escape in emergency, the trainer was the first of its kind to incorporate capsulated ejection, simulating the sensations of an actual seat ejection, let-down by parachute and landing impact. Under the same contract, Beech was also producing a flotation capsule for survival training in case of ejection over water.

At about this time, movement was beginning of America's long-range nuclear deterrent missiles into underground silo sites. Beech-Boulder in June delivered to Convair Astronautics the first "topping control units" of an initial 75-unit Convair order for assemblies needed to complete the underground installations. These units served to deliver liquid oxygen to the missiles at given volumes and pressures immediately prior to firing, providing exact amounts of oxidizer to insure that flights would be carried out as programmed. The need for precision in construction, and absolute reliability in performance, was obvious. The task offered a challenge that Beechcrafters were well qualified to meet.

June was also the month of high school and college commencements; and these happy occasions marked the second decade of a little-publicized Beech activity in the field of aeronautical engineering education. Again, as in each year since 1950, Walter H. Beech Scholarships in Aeronautical Engineering would be awarded to high-ranking students entering and enrolled in the Aeronautical Engineering School at the University of Wichita. Many talented young men had benefited from the financial assistance provided by these scholarships since the program was inaugurated in memory of the company's founder; and the achievement record of Wichita U's "Beech Scholars" was a proud one. Significant student training and laboratory work was also being conducted in the Walter H. Beech Memorial Wind Tunnel at the University of Wichita — one of the most modern and complete of its kind in America, and a fitting tribute to the man who had founded the Beech Aircraft Corporation.

North of the United States border, a new concept in marketing business airplanes ended its first field test in an aura of success, with the landing on June 25 at Victoria, British Columbia, of a five-plane "Caravan of Beechcrafts" which had toured Canada from east to west in a month-long flight that began May 26 at Montreal, Quebec. The tour was planned to provide a "moving open house" of modern business aircraft for America's good neighbors to the north, displaying the latest models of the Beechcraft Super 18, Queen Air, Twin-Bonanza, Baron and Bonanza. Stopovers were made en route, and flight demonstrations were conducted in nine key cities. For many years, Beech products had been well and favorably known throughout Canada. Some of the Travel Air biplanes built by Walter H. Beech back in the Twenties were still faithfully serving bush pilots in the far north, along with many Beechcrafts of all models, from the earliest stagger-wing biplanes to the newest twins. The Royal Canadian Air Force had in 1951 placed with Beech the largest single export order in the company's history, for a fleet of Beechcraft D18S twin-engine trainer-transports, and these twins were still going strong. The Department of Transport (Canadian government counterpart of the U. S. FAA) and the Royal Canadian Mounted Police were Beechcraft owners of more than twenty years' standing; and many business firms and individuals relied on Beechcrafts for safe, fast air transportation in both wilderness and settled areas of Canada. The "Caravan of Beechcrafts" was warmly welcomed at every port of call.

The steady pattern of growth at Beech-Boulder, then involving additional investments of company funds amounting to one half million dollars in new laboratories and equipment, was emphasized on July 27 with the receipt by the Boulder Division of a U. S. Air Force contract of approximately $800,000 for the manufacture of two types of semi-trailers to transport fuel and oxidizer for Titan II ICBM weapons. The fuel trailer, 35 feet in length, would transport 5,000 gallons of a mixture of anhydrous hydrazine and unsymmetrical dimethyl hydrazine (UDMH) or either separately, at pressures up to 100 psi and delivery flow rates up to 250 gallons per minute. The 30-ft. oxidizer trailer would carry 3,000 gallons of nitrogen tetroxide at pressures up to 225 psi and 250 gpm flow rates. To withstand corrosion and high pressures, and maintain temperature control over the highly toxic fluids and vapors, interior tank walls of both trailers would be made of stainless steel up to three-fourths inch thickness, completely insulated and covered with an outer shell of aluminum. Both would be required to meet environmental test temperatures ranging from 160° F. to -80° F., simulating actual conditions that might be encountered at Titan II launching sites. Both trailers would be Beech-designed to provide the highest possible margin of safety in the event of highway or off-road accidents; and both would be transportable in cargo aircraft. The requirements were stringent. But the design and production tasks were of just the kind that the Boulder engineering and test facilities, and its associated Longmont, Colorado fabrication shops, were well equipped to handle.

News also came from the Naval Air Test Center at Patuxent River, Maryland, that the Beech-designed air refueling system had passed its initial evaluation studies in a series of feasibility tests of its basic concept. Slung beneath a B-26 medium bomber, the 16-foot cigar-shaped pod unit had completed nearly 50 successful connections with five of the Navy's latest fighter and attack aircraft — the F9F, F4H, A4D, A3J and F8U jet aircraft. Quickly attached and capable of quick-drop, the simplified Beech unit was designed to function at temperatures as low as -65° F. and at speeds ranging from 180 to 400 knots. Armed forces reports on another Beech product showed a total of more than 1,000 successful flights for the Beechcraft KDB-1 missile target plane during the past two years. During the closing days of a highly successful Nike-Hercules ground-to-air firing mission off Okinawa, an Army KDB-1 target had been the objective when a new tactical intercept record was established, exceeding the range of all previous "kills" the Hercules had achieved. The pilotless "littlest Beechcraft" had given up its mechanical life in a noble cause.

September brought the completion of two factory-sponsored mobile activities which were doing much to assure reliable performance and competent service to Beechcraft owners throughout the nation. Since April, Beechcraft's 13th annual Service Clinic had completed over 1,600 exhaustive inspections of individual aircraft by factory personnel touring distributor and dealer locations throughout the nation. In 1961, this factory field inspection service, rendered without charge to owners, had been extended to Canada, where increasing numbers of Beechcrafts were coming into use by individual firms and owners, apart from those owned by government agencies and professional air service and charter operators. At its close in September, the Service Clinic had completed a total of nearly 16,000 inspections since its inauguration in 1949. It had been the basis for the awarding of the national Greer Maintenance Award to Beech Aircraft; and it remained the only operation of its kind conducted by a major business aircraft manufacturer. Also completed that month was the fourth annual field tour of the Beech Mobile Training School, another activity exclusive to Beechcraft which trained personnel of certified Beech service centers at key locations in the newest developments related to efficient and dependable servicing. This school conferred on students satisfactorily completing its courses the exclusive Beech-craft Specialist and Master mechanic ratings — an added degree of assurance to owners that servicing of their planes would be proficiently accomplished.

Announcement on October 2 of a new union contract, effective through June 30, 1963, marked the 22d year of unbroken friendly relations between Beech and the International Association of Machinists, the collective bargaining agency for regular hourly paid employees. The new agreement kept in effect prior cost-of-living wage adjustment provisions, and added improved fringe benefits applying to retirement, vacations and hospitalization. The new contract maintained for Beech its favorable wage and fringe benefits position in the aircraft industry, and enhanced the reputation it had long held as "A good place to work."

October also saw the introduction in the field of two new models of Beechcrafts, in keeping with the new concept of staggering new model premieres throughout the year. Entering its third year of production, the Model 65 Queen Air made its debut in an enlarged and refined version that offered 80% more usable cabin volume than its nearest competitor; an increase in useful load to 3,060 pounds; and enrichments in decor and fittings that made it, more than ever, the ultimate aircraft in its class. Although production and material costs had risen sharply, the list price of the new Queen Air remained the same as that of the prior model — $126,000. A fair sum of money, but more than a fair sum of airplane.

The 1962 Model B33 Beechcraft Debonair featured increased optional cruising range to 1,135 miles non-stop (plus reserve), a new swept vertical stabilizer, a superbly functional new instru-

204

ment panel, new color schemes and finishes inside and outside, and numerous other refinements adding to comfort, safety and utility. New also was an optional "Super Utility" accessories package that offered total instrumentation and equipment for long-range autopilot IFR flight at a special low factory-installed price. Still the only plane in its class to be FAA-certificated in the utility category, the fast, sturdy Debonair would be a more formidable competitor than ever among deluxe single-engine business aircraft.

Results of the 1961 All-Woman Transcontinental Air Race (The "Powder Puff Derby") received meanwhile showed another first-place victory for the Beechcraft Bonanza. It was the fourth Bonanza win in this annual classic, and the third scored by Mrs. Frances Bera of Long Beach, California. Mrs. Bera took first place in 1961 flying "solo," without help from a co-pilot or navigator, and thus became only the second pilot in the history of the event to win first prize single-handed. The Bonanza she flew was a seven-year-old E35 model identical with the one she had piloted to win first place in 1956. Prior to the race, it had received only a routine 100-hour inspection and a new set of spark plugs.

Summing up of the Beech fiscal year 1961 that ended September 30 showed earnings after taxes of $2,562,102, providing ample margin for dividends to stockholders that totaled $1,577,643 at an increase of better than 12% above the fiscal 1960 dividend rate. A two percent stock dividend was also declared on October 10; and allocations to earned surplus increased the company's holdings under this heading to better than $18.5 million, compared with a little more than $17.5 million at September 30, 1960.

These results had been achieved on total sales of slightly more than $72 million, compared with over $98 million for the 1960 fiscal year. Beechcraft's enlarged concept of management in depth, strategically positioned at points of control, was paying off in dollars and cents. There was also the influence of a very high order of talent in matters of finance at work — that of President O. A. Beech, who, as co-founder of the company in 1932, had always made its financial welfare her special charge.

In a year when national defense requirements continued to

shift in emphasis from high performance manned aircraft to aerospace projects that often ranged far into the future, the company's military sales of $28.9 million exceeded its projections. It had taken a great deal of hard work, distributed over dozens of varied projects, plus perhaps a dash of good fortune, to attain this volume under the conditions that prevailed. Even more important than the dollar volume for the year was the progress Beech had made in further preparing to meet the long-range trend of military and aerospace requirements, through the organization of its Military and Aerospace Division, the enlargement of its Boulder facilities, and in other ways.

Business and commercial sales totalled $43.1 million, which was somewhat less than the all-time high registered in 1960, but still 13% greater than 1959 sales in this area. America's economy was sluggish, bordering on recession; and the effects were felt throughout the business aircraft industry. Even so, Beech continued to hold first place in business aircraft sales for the first nine months of 1961, among the eight manufacturers reporting to the Utility Aircraft Council, industry trade group, with 30% of the total dollar sales volume. Beechcraft's export markets, in pleasing contrast, were booming; and the company's export sales were up 31% over the previous year, setting an all-time commercial export sales record of better than $10 million. Beech was consistently selling nearly 50% of the world's light twin-engine aircraft. For the first time in history, two export distributors — Transair S.A., in Switzerland, and TravelAir G.m.b.H., in West Germany — led the entire Beech retail sales organization, domestic and export in dollar volume of sales. And the Beech Acceptance Corporation, Inc., the company's wholly-owned aircraft financing and leasing organization, reported the largest volume of transactions in its history — over $20.6 million, for a 15.4% increase over its previous record year of fiscal 1960.

As the calendar year neared its end, the Beech military backlog was reinforced by a follow-on contract from Republic Aviation for $8 million worth of additional aft fuselage sections and ailerons for the USAF F-105 "Thunderchief" supersonic fighter-bomber. The award brought to some $25 million the total dollar volume of work assigned to Beech on Republic's all-weather interceptor.

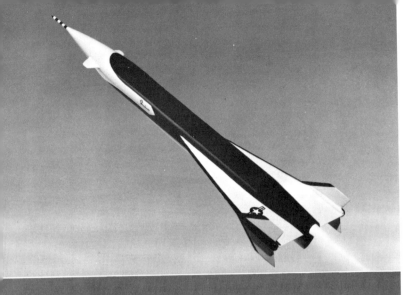

KD2B-1 missile target for both Air Force and Navy used a liquid rocket propulsion system for planned speeds of up to Mach 2. (Page 175)

Beech KD2B–1/Q-12 was launched from beneath the wing of a jet fighter as an expendable air-to-air and surface-to-air missile target. (Page 200)

Model 1025 target helped train anti-aircraft missilemen to deter aggressors. (Page 180)

Semi-trailers to transport fuel and oxidizer under pressure for Titan II ICBM weapons demanded Beechcraft's known quality and precision. (Page 202)

207

Introduction of the four-place Musketeer put Beech salesmen into the lower and medium priced market. Assembly lines for Musketeer were moved to Liberal facility where plane would have complete attention of an entire division. (Page 211)

Queen Air 80 featured swept tail and offered greater speed and capacity than sister ship, Queen Air 65. (Page 213)

Computers became common at Beechcraft as company stayed at the front in adopting new procedures and methods. (Page 215)

Word also came from the Pensacola (Florida) Naval Air Station of notable service marks established by Beechcraft T-34B Mentor single-engine training planes in use there since 1956. Shortly after mid-year, the 9,000th Naval Air cadet successfully completed primary flight training in a Beech-designed Mentor; and the 1,000th inverted spin was performed for the Flight Instruction Indoctrination Group at Pensacola. Restricted to only a few types of Navy aircraft, the inverted spin — an essential item in the instructor training syllabus — often imposed severe stresses that harshly tested the structural integrity of the plane. Pensacola's Mentors had been flown more than 445,000 hours, and had compiled a safety record calculated at five times that of previous Navy trainers over a comparable period. Later, the Saufley Field, Pensacola VT-1 Mentor-equipped squadron reported a new safety record of 75,000 consecutive accident-free flight hours; and the second-stage VT-3 squadron an all-time Navy mark of 80,000 consecutive accident-free hours. Among the more than 1,000 Mentors built by Beech before production came to an end, the Navy's T-34B trainers were adding luster to the Beechcraft name.

Much that was new and promising for the immediate and the long-range future came to light at the 1962 Beechcraft International Distributor and Dealer Management Meeting held at the Wichita factory December 1 and 2. The 1961 change to regional introductions in the field of new Beechcraft models permitted fuller coverage in depth of all aspects of planning and marketing. And the conference activities were conducted for the first time entirely on Beechcraft's own premises — saving many hours of valuable time for the participants who had gathered together from all over the world, and increasing the effectiveness of the sessions.

Scene of the 1962 meeting was the newly completed $600,000 Beechcrafters Activity Center, a handsome native stone and brick block-long building located across the street from the Beech general administration offices. Constructed for and owned by the Beechcraft Employees Club from the proceeds of a building fund established in 1946, its multi-purpose recreational and meeting facilities included a cafeteria seating 490 persons, semi-private dining rooms for smaller groups, and an auditorium, named "Walter H. Beech Hall" by the employee organization, accommodating 1,800 persons seated on individual chairs, or 1,200 at banquet tables. Dominant in the auditorium was a regulation size theatrical stage with a 40-foot-wide opening. Formal dedication of the structure to its primary purpose as a social and indoor entertainment and recreational center for all Beechcrafters came with an Open House and dedication program held on December 3 after the close of the conference.

To offer inspiration for the immediate future to the distributors and dealers in attendance, the company held back the field introductions of two new 1962 models, presenting them for the first time at the conference. These were the new Model A55 twin-engine Beechcraft Baron, and the new single-engine Model P35 Beechcraft Bonanza. Both featured advancements and refinements amply justifying the new-model designations, and sharply increasing their sales appeal. The A55 Baron, for example, offered a normal landing gear extension speed of 175 mph, and partial 15° flap extension, assisting the slowing down of this fast, clean airplane to pattern landing speed. The P35 Bonanza was the most luxurious version yet offered of this famous pace-setting single-engine design. There was general agreement that no matter what economic conditions might prevail in the year ahead, these and other existing models in Beechcraft's "Air fleet of American business" would capture their full share of the business aircraft market.

Offering a preview of the company's planning for progress beyond the immediate year ahead, Frank E. Hedrick, executive vice president, told of a forthcoming broadening of the commercial line which would open new markets to the retail sales organization, and of an expanded, more aggressive marketing program. He introduced a wind tunnel model of a design then under engineering study for an eight to ten-place, pressurized, 300-mph cruise turboprop executive transport — an airplane which would fit into a very promising market above that of the Super 18 Beechcraft, and below the million-dollar-plus price range of larger projects offered by other manufacturers. Further development, he promised, would be continued in this field.

But the highlight of the conference, and an event with his-

210

toric potential for the company and its commercial sales organization, was the dramatic unveiling of a wholly new kind of Beechcraft — the Model 23 Musketeer. It was a full four-place low-wing, fixed gear monoplane with a 160 hp engine affording a high speed of 144 mph, a cruising speed of 135 mph at 75% power, and a nonstop range of 899 miles. Its simplified high-strength construction included metal-bonded, honeycomb components similar to those used in supersonic jets. In performance, handling ease, sturdiness, luxury and advanced styling, it was every inch a Beechcraft. And it would sell, fully factory-equipped with radio and instrumentation for far-ranging business flight, at a package price of $13,300 retail. First deliveries would be made from the Beech production lines in Fall 1962.

"Launching a new way of life with the Beechcraft Musketeer" was the title of the address with which Wyman L. Henry, vice president - marketing, introduced the newest Beechcraft to the company's distributors and dealers; and his thesis was not at all far-fetched. For this new airplane, selling at a price competitive with the lowest-cost four-place business planes on the market, would create wholly new opportunities for the company's sales organization all over the world. It was a simple fact that the name of Beechcraft was respected and honored wherever men flew; and any product bearing that name was sure to find widespread acceptance and demand. Price had been the only barrier to more general ownership of Beech products. Now this barrier was to be removed. As a further gain to Beech, it would be possible for its distributors and dealers to pioneer more widely in developing business aircraft "from the ground up"; to offer, to the businessman who had never flown or owned any airplane, a Beechcraft in which he could start flying from the very first minute of his training in the art of flight. From that point on, as he discovered the benefits of business flying, and moved upward to faster, farther-ranging aircraft, there would be a more advanced Beechcraft ready and waiting for his next stage of progress. A new way of life, indeed, was opening to the Beech sales organization — on the wings of the Beechcraft Musketeer; and the company's projected rate of sales of 1,000 units per year appeared to be a conservative one.

Chapter 26

Greetings, in the form of substantial orders, came to Beech-craft from widely separated sources early in the opening days of the 30th anniversary year of 1962. On January 4 the U. S. Army confirmed its intention to triple its fleet of L-23F Seminole twin-engine Beech transports, with a contract award of more than $4 million for additional L-23F aircraft. The type was later re-designated as the Army U-8F. This and other military versions of the Beech Twin-Bonanza had been prime favorites of the Army Air Service ever since their initial induction in 1953. Almost concurrently, the National Defense Agency of Japan confirmed a large order for deliveries extending years ahead for a fleet of Model 65 Queen Air transports, to be used for air crew navigation training and command personnel trans-portation by the Japanese Maritime Self-Defense Force. The year was starting out nicely.

Exciting good news came soon afterward from the test range at the Naval Missile Center, Point Mugu, California. Beech-craft's first supersonic product, the Navy KD2B-1 U. S. Air Force Q-12 missile target, had recorded on January 11 a near-perfect test flight. On January 22, another of the Beech-designed targets had exceeded operational requirements by flying above 70,000 feet and at more than twice the speed of sound. On the second flight, the rocket-powered Beech "bird" had flown higher and faster than any other known missile target training system in the world. While the exact results of the second test flight were not announced, it seemed certain that the KD2B-1, in its then configuration, would have operational capabilities of flight at altitudes up to 90,000 feet and speeds up to Mach 3.5, speak-ing well for its future worth to the military services.

February 20 was a date that would stand out in aerospace history. It was the day when Astronaut John Glenn success-fully, and happily for all Americans, completed a spectacular three-orbit flight into space around the earth in the spacecraft Friendship 7. As with the prior space flight of Astronaut Shep-ard, Beechcrafters had contributed some measure of support to this latest achievement; and it provided special inspiration

212

for their further work in aerospace research, engineering, development and production.

The same date was a notable one in Beech history, in a less dramatic but far from trivial way. Approved Type Certificates were issued on February 20 by the Federal Aviation Agency simultaneously for two new Beechcrafts — the Model 23 Musketeer, and the new Model 80 Queen Air. Through the combined efforts of many Beechcrafters, both airplanes were qualified for certification well ahead of schedule; and the Musketeer coincidentally had the honor of receiving ATC Number One from the recently redesignated FAA Central Region. It was a good omen for the new design.

The Model 80 Queen Air, Beechcraft's newest twin-engine craft, offered even greater spaciousness, performance, capacity and utility than its sister ship, the Queen Air 65. Two new Lycoming LGSO-540-A1A fuel injection supercharged engines, rated at 380 hp each for takeoff, powered the Queen Air 80 to a high speed of 252 mph and an economical cruising speed of 230 mph. Its higher gross weight of 8,000 pounds boosted the 80's useful load to 3,200 pounds. At normal loadings, its climb rate was 1,485 fpm, its absolute ceiling 30,300 feet, and its nonstop range 1,300 miles with reserve. Its single-engine performance offered a climb rate up to 385 fpm and a ceiling ranging to 15,600 feet. Seating was provided for six to nine persons in a variety of deluxe cabin arrangements. Equipment options made it possible to outfit the Queen Air 80 with virtually every type of system available on the most advanced airliners.

Inauguration in February of the company's first international merchandising fair for retail parts, accessory and service sales representatives pointed up the importance of these items in the Beech pattern of activity. Not only did aggressive merchandising of dependable parts, useful accessories and trustworthy service benefit Beechcraft owners; it also provided a volume of business for the company and its field outlets that totalled some $10 million per year. Beech was increasing its promotional efforts in this area, striving for increases in volume that would increase the utility, and assure the most reliable performance of Beechcrafts to their owners, at the same time that they produced a fair profit.

On March 1, Beech increased to three the total number of its wholly owned subsidiaries. The new operation, Houston-Beechcraft, Inc., would be a commercial distributorship located on the Houston International Airport, and pursuing an aggressive sales and service program throughout southeast Texas and western Louisiana. Its location was highly strategic, since Houston had been designated as the site of the NASA Manned Spacecraft center, in addition to being the focal point of a very active and fast-growing corporate and business aircraft market. It would also provide a controlled environment for factory testing of sales and service merchandising ideas, prior to their release to the distributor and dealer organization at large.

April 19 was the official date of the company's 30th anniversary. It was not made an occasion for any massive ceremonies or wholesale retrospection. Beech was too busy meeting its obligations of the present, and building for the future, to look back at length on the past, however illustrious the record might be. The company's sales since its founding, at its anniversary date, totalled approximately one and one-half billion dollars. The general attitude, however, was not one of self-congratulation on this achievement, but rather of going forward to surpass it in the years ahead.

Recognition of loyal service by individual employees was another matter entirely. The management's appreciation of continuity in the faithful discharge of duties had always been high. At service anniversaries of 5, 10, 15, 20 and 25 years with Beech, company officers had never permitted the pressure of business to interfere with their personal presentation of service awards to eligible employees of all ranks. A point of special pride with Beech was the fact that on the company's 30th anniversary, 3819 employees had been in its service five years or more; 2950, ten years or more; 1233 fifteen years or more; 880, twenty years or more; 33, twenty-five years or more; and one, thirty years.

The one Beechcrafter with 30 years of service was, of course, the company's president and co-founder, Mrs. O. A. Beech. Hers was the rightful honor of being the first Beechcrafter to receive the 30-year Citation of Service; and special recognition

214

was accorded to Mrs. Beech by the company and by her fellow-Beechcrafters on the date of Beech Aircraft's 30th anniversary. It was to her the most significant and deeply touching of all the many honors, some of international scope, that she had received in an illustrious career of leadership.

Control and planning for factually based day-to-day and long-range decisions was expedited in May, with the installation at Beech of a Honeywell 400 electronic computer — the first in the western United States. It was at once put to work, making a variety of vital information quickly available in the areas of procurement reports, accounting and payroll data analysis, inventory and production control systems, and similar tasks involving the processing of complex data. Among the most sophisticated of existing business machine installations, and the first of its kind in the general aviation industry, it would perform, at the speed of light, many tasks helpful to the company's most efficient functioning in the age of space.

In the marketing field, there was the opening in May of the first Beechcraft dealer facility to be completed under the company's recently introduced "Operation Turnkey" plan, which supplied on a small down payment every item needed to operate a dealership, from modern hangar to office furnishings and order blanks. The dealer was Brumos Aviation Corporation at Jacksonville, Florida. Its facility was that of Beechcraft's "B" package plan, which provided an 80-foot by 100-foot clear span hangar, with 1,960 square feet of air-conditioned office and lounge area. Bright red, white and blue stripes in an exclusive Beechcraft pattern identified the building from miles away in the air, as well as from ground level, as a Beech sales and service center. Alternate "package plans" provided larger or smaller facilities in keeping with the immediate volume potential of the dealer's area. All were designed for easy expandability as the need arose for larger space.

Two production marks were achieved as summer neared. The 500th Beechcraft Debonair to be built since this model was introduced in 1959 took off from Beech Field with its new owner, W. B. Morris of Cassidair Services, Inc., Beechcraft dealer in Cassidy, British Columbia, Canada at the controls. The new B33 Debonair was scheduled by Cassidair for a

7,000-mile flight to the Arctic immediately upon reaching its base. And on June 5, Beechcraft Bonanza No. 7,000 came off the Plant II production line on its way to flight test. Since its introduction in 1947, more Bonanzas had been built than any other individual model business aircraft; and the 1962 P35 version was more than ever the world leader for style and performance among all single-engine business aircraft.

Around mid-year, the effects of planning and hard work to assure continued volume on the part of the Military and Aerospace Division came to light in a series of new contracts. From Lockheed-Georgia Company at Marietta came three awards to Beech, following competitive bidding by many well-qualified producers, to build key component parts for the huge USAF C-141 StarLifter Lockheed turbofan jet transport. A giant of the skies measuring 143 feet long, 39 feet high, with a wing span of 160 feet, the logistics support transport had a maximum takeoff weight of 360,000 pounds, and a speed capacity of 500 to 550 mph. The initial Beech contracts for flaps, ailerons and other components totalled some $1.3 million; and prospects for follow-on awards seemed promising.

From the Bell Helicopter Company came production component orders for its U. S. Army HU-1D Iroquois jet-powered high-performance helicopter. Beech's extensive experience in the field of metal bonding assemblies for the "100" series of supersonic jet fighter aircraft was a factor in its selection to produce the HU-1D honeycomb metal bonded side panels — a method of construction also currently in use at Beechcraft in producing sturdy wings for the Beechcraft Musketeer. Bell also called on Beech to design and supply kits for interior styling installations on three of its commercial helicopter models.

Beechcraft's ten-year record of performance as a sub-contractor on high-performance aircraft for McDonnell Aircraft Corporation was not forgotten when the St. Louis firm needed a components source for its 1,500 mph Navy F4H/Air Force F-110 Phantom II jet. Acknowledgment came in the form of an initial $8-million contract from McDonnell for ailerons, speed brakes, spoilers and other critical components for the Phantom II. Then in fleet service, the F4H was the fastest, highest-flying and longest-range fighter operational with the

Navy. Its Navy mission was air defense interception; its work with the U. S. Marines, close support and air superiority; and with the Air Force, tactical strike augmentation and reconnaissance.

Another long-time Beech customer, Republic Aviation, issued a further follow-on contract valued at $3.8 million for additional aft fuselage sections and ailerons for its USAF F-105 Thunderchief fighter. This brought to more than $28 million the total share of F-105 production assigned by Republic to Beech Aircraft.

From the U. S. Army Munitions Command at Picatinny Arsenal, Dover, New Jersey on June 27 came an $.8 million initial contract award for the production of highly classified SUU-7A/A bomb dispensers and containers. Required delivery dates imposed a next-to-impossible schedule on what, owing to extremely close tolerances demanding exacting craftsmanship and critical inspection, was obviously a very difficult undertaking. Beechcrafters not only met these schedules with finished articles that passed final Army inspection without a rejection; they completed deliveries of both pilot and production quantities at rates ranging from 30 to 54 days ahead of schedule. Functional testing of the Beech-produced dispenser at Eglin Air Force Base, Florida brought its unconditional acceptance. After putting the Beech-made containers through "torture tests" at Picatinny Arsenal, the Army called them the best they had tested.

Aerospace work at Beech-Boulder also pressed forward, in the Beech tradition of pioneering in new fields, over a wide range of advanced and often exotic projects. Beech cryogenic engineers initiated experiments with "slush" hydrogen (liquid hydrogen reduced to near-ice consistency by super-chilling) to determine the feasibility of increasing space vehicle fuel capacities without enlarging tank sizes or weights. They worked on positive expulsion systems for delivering cryogenic fluids in zero gravity environments and space rendezvous refueling techniques. Researchers in other disciplines were deeply involved in study and experimentation in low acceleration propulsion modes suitable for vehicles in space, such as electrostatic, electromagnetic and electrothermal power. Beechcrafters in the

217

Boulder Division shops constructed, without a single flaw or repair, the world's largest known titanium assembly — a 460-pound space vehicle fuel tank designed to hold 7,000 gallons of pressurized liquid hydrogen. The metal industry, well aware of the many difficulties involved in working with lightweight, high strength, stubbornly resistive titanium, hailed this as one of the most significant advancements in titanium fabrication yet recorded.

Studies which had been going at Boulder for many months of special requirements relating to gas storage for the command and service modules of the NASA Project Apollo lunar voyage spacecraft were climaxed in July with the receipt of a $4 million contract from North American Aviation for the design, production and testing of the critical gas storage system for this space vehicle. It was an assignment of vital importance; for throughout the lunar voyage of nearly a half-million miles in space, the crew's life support and electric power would depend on the absolute reliability of this system. Its elements would include insulated cryogenic pressure tanks, heat exchangers and valving storing and supplying oxygen and hydrogen, converted from liquid to gaseous states upon delivery, to the environmental control and electrical power systems of the command module. It would need to operate under prolonged periods of weightlessness — possibly for two weeks — and to withstand environmental extremes ranging from earth sea-level to the chill void of space. The technical problems of design and construction would be enormous. But they were exactly the sort of problems Beech-Boulder had been staffed and equipped to solve; and Beechcrafters went at the task with full confidence that the right answers would be found. Beech "Imaginuity" might be stretched to its maximum; but the job would be done.

In the commercial area, summer 1962 was a lively season. Detail parts stocks were being built up, and assembly lines taking shape for the Model 23 Beechcraft Musketeer, in preparation for deliveries of finished planes scheduled to begin in October. Meanwhile, the Marketing Division thought up a promotion plan that looked like — and proved to be — a winner. A transcontinental 90-day tour was set up, featuring Beechcraft's "Three Musketeers" — three new Model 23 airplanes, two of which were flown, not at all as a matter of mere chance, by two very attractive young ladies on the company's staff. Miss Joyce Case and Miss Gene Nora Stumbaugh were the photogenic pilots of the cruise. The third, a male, was seldom noticed. But the airplanes received a large amount of attention from the press, radio, TV and the public wherever they stopped; and that was precisely the object of the plan.

August was the introduction month for the newest and most highly advanced version of Beechcraft's famous Super 18 executive transport — the Beech Super H18. To many it seemed that the ultimate limits of performance and luxury had been reached in this long-refined design; but the Super H18 showed convincingly that Beech engineering skills could continue to improve on near-perfection. The new Super H18 showed very solid gains in the performance areas of speed, range and useful load, plus many new luxury features. Approved gross weight was increased to 9,900 pounds; empty weight was decreased by more than 230 pounds. Result, an all-time useful load of over 4,200 pounds — a gain of 430 pounds over the predecessor Super G18. Maximum speed was up to 236 mph; cruising speed to 220 mph at 65% power for a range of 1,260 nonstop miles with fuel reserve. New smaller landing gear wheels and tires permitted complete enclosure with gear retracted, providing better streamlining to reduce drag, and also saving 50 pounds weight while improving landing and ground handling characteristics. Exhaust stacks and exits were redesigned, and a new single electric cowl flap was added for further performance gains. New exterior paint and interior appointments enhanced the distinctive beauty and luxury of the Super H18. Optional items included a Beechcraft refrigerated cabin air-conditioning system, and a "Skyphone" communications system permitting direct calls from the air to distant cities throughout the nation.

The Super H18 commemorated, in the most fitting possible way, the 25th anniversary year of Model 18 production. The basic Model 18 design had been in continuous production longer than any other airplane in the world. Its nearest competitor in terms of longevity, the Piper Cub two-place lightplane, had been built during a 17-year period, from 1930 to 1947. The third place contender, the renowned Douglas DC-3 airline and cargo transport, had been in manufacture for no more than a ten-year period, from 1935 to 1945. The Beech Model 18 seemed very nearly immortal. Certainly it would continue, in its new Super H18 configuration, as the flagship of the "Air fleet of American business" among many discriminating corporation and business aircraft purchasers.

The shape of what might be things to come, perhaps eventually superseding piston-engine aircraft in the higher performance categories, became apparent when Beech in September unveiled a full-scale, completely detailed mockup of a new Beechcraft turboprop executive transport then under serious consideration as an addition to the line. The completely fitted and instrumented mockup simulated a flyable airplane so realistically that observers commented it seemed ready for flight at its design cruise speed of over 300 mph. While costly to build, it offered the best of all ways to measure the real depth of interest of prospective buyers in purchasing an airplane of its type. If enough prospects were to place orders, after inspecting this close simulation of the real airplane, its future would be assured. If not, the "Caution" signal would be flashed; and the investment of many millions of dollars, and large amounts of time and space required to engineer and equip for production, would need extremely close scrutiny.

Export orders, commercial and military, continued to contribute to Beech volume while other divisions were also busy. The Republic of Switzerland ordered a supply of Beechcraft Model 1001 propeller-driven missile targets, similar to the U. S. Navy KDB-1 target drones. Traditionally neutral and non-combatant, the Swiss would remain prepared to defend their neutrality with modern weapons and training systems. The Federal Republic of Germany also conducted tests on the Beech Model 1001 drone, which resulted in an order late in the year.

Delivery of the first Beechcraft Musketeers from the newly activated production lines started as scheduled in October. More than 300 orders had been received while the company was getting production under way. Demand for Musketeers would exceed supply for some time to come. One of the first planes off the line achieved the distinction of being the first Musketeer to be flown across the Atlantic Ocean. With the addition of auxiliary tanks boosting its normal 60-gallon fuel capacity to 200 gallons, it handily completed the long stages of flight over water and land to Neuchatel, Switzerland.

Aftermath of the highly successful Navy KD2B-1 target missile flight tests in January came in October, with the receipt of a $5 million production contract from the Bureau of Naval Weapons. First production units were to enter fleet service in Summer 1963 — the world's only supersonic target system designed to "go to sea" with the Navy, and needing no support of specialized Navy units. Air launch from any plane was performed as simply as the release of a jettisonable fuel tank. The pilot pulled a lever, and the KD2B-1 was off and flying, as programmed. With minor refinements, surface launch requirements also could be easily met; and speeds up to Mach 3.5 and altitudes up to 90,000 feet were within reach, matching the performance of the most advanced jet aircraft.

Beech astronautic capabilities also received further recognition in October, with the company's selection by McDonnell Aircraft to design, develop and produce essential cryogenic ground support equipment for NASA's two-man Gemini spacecraft. The Beech transportable servicing units would furnish liquid oxygen, hydrogen and nitrogen to Gemini's environmental control and auxiliary power systems during launch preparations. The company's combined experience in the design and manufacture of thousands of jet aircraft ground servicing units, and the "know-how" and facilities extensively developed at Boulder in handling and transporting cryogenic fluids, would be extremely useful in fulfilling the important aerospace assignment.

The annual report to stockholders from President O. A. Beech, issued November 15, showed net earnings for the 1962 fiscal year that ended September 30 that were up 15% over fiscal 1961 returns. For 1962, the total was $2,952,614, compared with 1961's $2,562,102. The company's cost control programs had been rewardingly effective; for 1962 sales of $67.6 millions were about 6% below 1961's $72 millions. On balance, it seemed a remarkable showing for a year of further transition in government and defense aerospace and aviation programs, and of sluggishness bordering on recession in the American economic climate. After distribution of dividends at the same rate as in 1961, Beechcraft's working capital stood at a new high of more than $27.8 million. The company had ample resources for growth — financial and otherwise.

Enthusiasm was in the air, when the Beech Annual International Marketing Conference met December 13-14 at Beech-crafters Activities Center. Distributors and dealers were doing well with the biggest and best line of Beechcrafts ever offered for sale, and looking forward to substantially greater sales and earnings in 1963. New models introduced during the year were making a strong impact on the market. The number of Beech-craft "Million-Airs" — distributors who individually sold $1 million or more in new Beechcrafts, parts and accessories — totalled 23 for the 1962 sales year.

Interest ran high in the beautifully detailed full-size mockup of the proposed Model 120 Beechcraft turboprop executive transport. Marketing Division researchers recorded every word of comment on the new design; for the distributor and dealer management men who viewed it were highly qualified, from first-hand experience on the sales firing line, to appraise the prospects for development of profitable volume on such an item.

Conferees learned, too, of another new development at the top end of the Beechcraft product line. Plans were described to offer a new, fully pressurized executive airplane — the Beech-craft Queen Air Model 85 — to sell at a price around $200,000, with first deliveries starting early in 1964. Development of the new model, which would feature dramatic new styling, complete pressurization for cockpit, cabin and baggage compartment, and a payload approximating that of the Queen Air Model 80's 3,200 pounds, was then well under way.

Beech Field was a busy spot at the end of the 1963 Conference. In addition to other models, distributors and dealers flew home 45 new Beechcraft Musketeers, bringing to about 100 the total of Musketeers delivered since October. Prospects for establishing Beech leadership in new areas of the business and executive aircraft field, and enhancing dominance in long-standing areas of that field, had never looked better.

222

Chapter 27

The opening days of 1963 brought substantial enlargements to Beechcraft's backlog of orders on hand. The Bureau of Naval Weapons issued a $10 million add-on contract for Beech KD2B-1 supersonic missile target systems, less than 90 days after the first production order, amounting to $5 millions, had been received. And the Federal Aviation Agency ordered eight new Queen Air 80 transports, which would join the two Queen Air 65's already in FAA service. The new Queens were to replace 11 Beechcraft ex-Air Force C45H (Model 18) twins which had been in use by the FAA for some years. Their primary use would be for in-flight evaluation of the nation's air traffic control system.

A Navy Beechcraft passed a notable service milestone early in the year. At Saufley Field of the Naval Air Station, Pensacola, Florida, Training Squadron One of the Naval Air Basic Training Command awarded a "gold seal of approval" to Buno 140705, a T-34B Mentor single-engine trainer, on its completion of more than 5,000 hours of flight. First of the Navy's Mentors known to have reached this mark, the durable Beechcraft had been the 39th T-34B to come off the Beech production line. Since its manufacture in September, 1955, Buno 140705 had trained 114 Navy and Marine student aviators; had flown 5,115 hours, made 16,459 landings and performed 4,604 loops, 3,401 spins and 17,904 stalls. In some 700,000 miles of flight, it was refueled 3,325 times. "Beech Aircraft is certainly to be commended for providing us with equipment like the T-34B Mentor," was the comment of Commander H. E. Kendrick, Squadron One commanding officer. Beechcrafters were delighted that the Mentors they had built had earned this praise; for it was almost an axiom in aviation that the only type of airplane that led a harder life than a basic trainer was a target drone.

Beechcraft performance in exceeding delivery schedules and delivering acceptable items on its previous $850,000 contract for Army SUU/7A/A bomb dispensers and containers brought a follow-on contract for more of these classified items in the amount of nearly $4 million on March 6. Army Munitions Command officials at Picatinny Arsenal, Dover, New Jersey, source of the contract awards, expected that still more follow-on awards would be made in keeping with programmed requirements.

At the end of the first half of the Beech fiscal year on March 31, 1963, total volume was $34.8 million, compared with $31.8 million for the same period a year ago. Commercial and business sales totalled better than $23.1 million, sharply up from 1960's first-half $19.3 million. Deliveries of 294 all-new Beechcraft Musketeers, and of the $5.5 million of the Queen Air series, highlighted the commercial sales picture. Starting load costs on major long-range production programs had a temporary effect on first-half earnings which would be offset during the latter half. Estimates of after-tax net at the midway point stood at $1,160,429, or 41¢ per share of stock — amply justifying payment of the regular quarterly dividend at the current 15¢ rate. The company's production programs were on schedule; its long-range plans were being fulfilled, step by step. An experienced, capable and enthusiastic organization, more than 5,500 strong, looked to the future with confidence.

Events of May and June held both immediate and long-range importance. Most notable, from the long-range viewpoint, was the first flight on May 15 of a twin-engine Beechcraft flying test bed fitted with Pratt & Whitney PT6A-6 turboprop engines. It was the first of an almost daily series of test flights that would take place over a six-month interval, providing data for evaluation of power plant performance that would firm up an eventual choice of engines for a wholly new Beechcraft. And it signalled the nearness of a decision on the major question of entering the increasingly promising though highly competitive field of jet aircraft production.

More immediate in impact was the introduction, late in May, of the D95A twin-engine Travel Air. In its newest version, the leader of the high-performance economy twin-engine class moved farther out front, with design changes that increased forward baggage space to 19 cubic feet and rear luggage capacity to 400 pounds, and provided a more favorable location in the nose for most of the radio and electronic gear. New styling, patterned after that of the luxurious Beechcraft Baron, enhanced the appearance of the D95A. Yet the price was held within reach of the market that had already bought more than 500 Travel Air models, at a recommended $49,500.

In a more personal vein, the flying tradition established by Walter H. Beech was carried forward by a member of the second generation. Suzanne, elder daughter of Beechcraft's founder and of its president, successfully completed her first solo flight at Beech Field. The plane she flew was, of course, a Beechcraft — a new Musketeer. Mrs. Beech was on hand at the conclusion of the flight to congratulate her daughter on winning her wings. Again, a Beechcraft was aloft — with a member of the Beech family at the controls.

Clustered in the time span from late spring to early summer, a series of closely related events emphasized the growing prominence of Beech in the missile target field. First was the receipt from the Federal Republic of Germany, through the U. S. Army Materiel Command, of a $1.5 million order for Beech Model 1001 target systems. Virtually identical with previously delivered U. S. Navy KDB-1 and Army 1025 targets in external configuration, the V-tailed, remote-controlled drone simulated the radar image of high-performance military aircraft many times its size, providing excellent air-to-air and ground weapons training. The "littlest Beechcraft," entering the service of a NATO nation for the first time, would have a part in sustaining the defenses of Free World airspace at its frontiers.

Not long afterward came a follow-on contract from the U. S. Army in excess of $2.35 million for additional Model 1025 Cardinal targets, spares and flight service support. It would substantially enlarge the total of more than 1,300 targets of this basic Beechcraft design that had been delivered to the Army and Navy since 1959. And, with its capability of sustained controlled flight at altitudes above 40,000 feet and speeds up to Mach .52, it would continue to offer efficient and economical means of weapon systems training and evaluation.

Meanwhile, another missile target product of the Beech Aerospace Division advanced from research and development to full production and operational status. Four years of intensive work were crowned with success as the U. S. Navy accepted the first production model of the Beechcraft AQM-37A (Navy KD2B-1) supersonic missile target. In subsequent operations,

225

conducted from the U.S.S. Midway, a naval aircraft carrier, the AQM-37A scored two "firsts" for a missile target vehicle in its category — a supersonic launch and a low altitude launch. Both were made from the Navy's new carrier-based McDonnell F-4B jet fighter. The successful launches also marked the first time that a fleet tactical squadron — VF-21 — had handled, serviced and operated AQM class targets at sea.

Achievements of existing Beechcraft target systems provided new incentives to designers working to enlarge the scope and performance of Beech missiles. Models in production covered the range from Mach .52 to Mach 3. New designs well on the way to realization would perform in the Mach 5 and Mach 7 speed ranges, with altitude and other performance factors correspondingly advanced. The impending additions would round out America's most complete target system family — a family that proudly carried the surname of Beechcraft.

Two wholly separate events at mid-year were to demonstrate favorable effects in maintaining production efficiency at peak levels throughout Beechcraft's plants. A new three-year union contract effective July 1, 1963 was signed by representatives of the company and of District Lodge No. 70 of the International Association of Machinists. At almost the same time, the Manufacturing Division introduced a company-wide Work Simplification program, aimed to encourage every Beechcrafter to apply individual creative thinking to better ways of doing the job.

Signing of the labor contract marked the 24th consecutive year of harmonious relations between the company and the International Association of Machinists as the representative of its hourly payroll employees. The new agreement provided for fair but non-inflationary wage increases at yearly intervals through 1965, supplemented with cost-of-living adjustments; establishment of major medical benefits added to existing insurance protection for employees and their dependents; and improvements in employee retirement and vacation plans. Again, the Beech policy of maintaining pay scales compatible with those in its industry produced further gains for Beech employees.

Provision of proper recognition for services above and beyond the normal routine of duty, also a constant policy of Beech management, was a vitalizing feature of the Work Simplifica-

226

"The Three Musketeers" — three new Model 23 Beechcrafts — introduced the new low-priced Beech design to the public with notable success on a 90-day transcontinental tour.
(Pages 218, 219)

Two airplanes of the trio that made up "The Three Musketeers" were flown throughout the nation-wide tour by these young ladies on the Beech sales staff — Joyce Case (left) and Gene Nora Stumbaugh.

First to
congratulate
Daughter Suzanne
when she soloed
May 20, 1963
in a Beechcraft
Musketeer was
Mrs. O. A. Beech.

Mrs. O. A. Beech
introduced
her grandson
Lowell Jay
to the Musketeer
plane before
the nationwide
introductory
promotion of
this Beechcraft.
(Page 225)

Bjorn Bostad flew
one of the first
Musketeers on a
5,000-mile over-
ocean delivery hop
. . . Wichita via
Gander and Shan-
non to Neuchatel,
Switzerland.
(Pages 220, 221)

228

tion program inaugurated at mid-year. "Work smarter, not harder" was its theme; reduction of manufacturing costs, its purpose. It was a grass-roots effort, enlisting the help of each employee to eliminate waste effort and submit ideas drawn from on-the-job experience to improve methods, processes, tooling and machinery. Useful submissions brought cash awards to many Beechcrafters. And, in less than two months after the plan was established, their proposals resulted in nearly $40,000 in savings to the company. Its immediate and continuing success was to verify that at all times, given opportunity and incentive, Beechcrafters would do their part.

At the Beech-Boulder Division, midsummer completion of a new manufacturing plant of 18,000 square foot size, located on Beech's own 1,500 acre site, provided fully integrated facilities for space systems engineering, testing and limited-volume production matched to the trend of space contracts requirements. The new structure, architecturally harmonized through native stone trim with the exterior of the administration and engineering building, featured full truss construction stressed for an overhead traveling crane, and special chambers permitting contamination-free welding under controlled-atmosphere conditions. Replacing facilities formerly leased at Longmont, Colorado, it was optimally sized and equipped to assure for the Boulder Division a continuing useful and profitable place in the nation's long range space systems developments. Needs were changing in this field, from relatively large-scale production of massive missiles to few or one-of-a-kind articles requiring highly specialized engineering, testing and production efforts. Beech-Boulder would be superbly well equipped to render specialized support services geared to the trend of the future, without extremely heavy and risky investments in excessive facilities.

Another midsummer event was the return of President O. A. Beech from a tour of the Orient. She had been one of a group of prominent persons invited to attend the gala openings of the Tokyo Hilton and Hong Kong Hilton hotels, and accepted their friendly hospitality which provided pleasantly exciting and memorable experiences. Never unmindful of the company's interests, she also visited with the Beechcraft distributors for Japan, and for the Philippine Islands, while on tour. Everywhere, she met a warm welcome for Beech products and for the company's co-founder and chief executive.

The respite from deskbound routines was timely. For a top-level decision of great importance was ready to be made: What should Beechcraft do about a jet-powered business airplane? It was the kind of decision that emphasized the loneliness of command. For, while line and staff members of the engineering, production and marketing teams could submit facts and opinions and projections, the ultimate responsibility rested with the company's president.

There were many factors to be considered. Reactions to the proposed Model 120 Beechcraft turboprop executive transport — displayed in detailed mockup form in December 1962, and the largest Beechcraft ever projected for the business aircraft field — had to be weighed. Balanced with these were comments and evaluations on the suggested Model 85D pressurized piston-powered Queen Air. And there was the competition from other manufacturers — domestic and foreign, actual and potential — to be anticipated.

The time element added urgency. The manufacturer who came up with the optimum design for the largest segment of the market, with the earliest possible delivery dates, would automatically gain a substantial lead.

Judgment and firm choices among the many alternatives came swiftly, yielding to the application of seasoned experience and realistic common sense. On August 14, 1963, Beech announced the availability for firm delivery in Fall 1964 of the new, pressurized twin turboprop Model 90 Beechcraft King Air — a six to eight place business airplane with 270 mph cruising speed, over-the-weather operating capability, and slow-speed landing permitting safe use of small fields and airstrips.

Sound, practical reasons reinforced this decision as to the format of the King Air. In its passenger and crew accommodations, the King Air would very closely resemble the Model 18 Beechcraft — for many years the most popular of all twin-engine executive aircraft — and practically duplicate the almost equally popular Queen Air. On the basis of both historic and probable future market demand, the size was right.

Cabin pressurization, air conditioning and soundproofing

230

would bring new standards of comfort for passengers and crew to the business aircraft field, and permit long-range flights at higher altitudes, above most of the weather and turbulence, without need for oxygen. Turboprop power would be virtually free of vibration and objectionable noise, and would increase cruising speed to a new, timesaving maximum at no sacrifice in range or payload. Compared with pure jet power, it offered many advantages: Great savings in initial and operating costs, ability to operate anywhere without limiting noise factors, and safe, easy, fast transition for the pilot accustomed to handling propeller-driven piston-powered aircraft. The executive who liked to take over the controls himself would have little that was new to learn to handle his company's King Air with the proficiency of a veteran professional.

A firm basis had already been established for the choice of power plants. Since May 15, Beech had been flying a testbed plane equipped with two Pratt & Whitney PT-6 turbojet engines, produced by United Aircraft of Canada and rated at 650 shaft horsepower each. Results of these tests, balanced against test and routine flight reports on the performance of other Beechcrafts fitted with a very good turboprop engine of European manufacture, gave the PT-6 the edge as the best power plant for the proposed King Air design. Later, continued testing was to further confirm the rightness of this choice.

Also important was the fact that the Model 90 King Air was the nearest of all possible designs to an actual aircraft in being. Engineering studies had shown that it could be produced as a modified and strengthened version of the Model 85 Queen Air, with predictably excellent results. Engineering was already well advanced on the changes necessary to pressurize the cabin of the Queen Air, following the interest shown in the pressurized Model 85D proposed some months earlier. All the experience accumulated in building hundreds of Queen Air transports, and most of the existing tooling, could be applied to the efficient production of the King Air. Investments in new tooling would be only a fraction of the amount required to tool up for a wholly novel design. With less investment to amortize, the selling price of the airplane would be sharply competitive in relation to performance and value. And there would be the shortest possible time lapse in getting the King Air off the production lines and ready for delivery, even allowing for the usual extensive Beechcraft flight and reliability testing of pre-production articles. Best of all, there would be the fullest assurance that the King Air, as an advanced version of the thoroughly service-proved Queen Air design, would offer the long-established Beech advantages of docile handling and practical slow landing speeds, permitting the use of the same small landing fields and airstrips as its sister ship — plus a wholly new concept of performance in the high-speed ranges.

Such was the rationale, in condensed form, of the Beech decision to enter the jet aircraft manufacturing field with the Model 90 King Air. It appeared to be sound and well reasoned. But — would it pass the acid test of acceptance in the business aircraft market? Would enough buyers step forward to justify King Air production? The answer was to come before the end of the year.

Meanwhile, closing of the company's books at September 30 on its 1963 fiscal year showed satisfying performance. Sales totalled better than $73.8 million — a more than 9% increase over the preceding year. Commercial and business products accounted for some $45.3 million, and military and aerospace production the remaining $28.5 million of sales. After-tax earnings of slightly less than $2 million were smaller than in fiscal 1962, reflecting large investments in research and development and long-range production start-up costs leading to greater future deliveries and increased sales. It was a good year; but Beech was preparing for a better year to follow.

Fiscal year '64 got off to a good start with the receipt on November 11 from the U. S. Army of a new contract totalling better than $3.2 million for bomb dispensers and containers, extending production of these items through the end of 1964. There was more significance in this award than its dollar size, which amounted to about 3% of the company's projected sales of $90-95 million for the year, might suggest. For, as the third Army order for these highly exacting and critical items, it showed that Beechcrafters were capable of meeting the highest standards of accuracy and performance. That fact was not in dispute; but the confirmation was none the less welcome. As a

232

Three ships of the 8-Queen Air fleet bought by the FAA in 1963 accented the performance and versatility of this Beech design for exacting duties in patrolling the nation's airways. (Page 223)

Optional tricycle gear brought new interest to the Beech 18 series which had featured conventional gear ever since introduction in late thirties. (Page 236)

Advancements in performance, styling and equipment marked the B55 Baron, a series that already led the light twin industry in sales.

Prototype of the King Air turboprop design was the stellar attraction of the Beech 1964 International Distributor-Management meeting.

"Air Force One" took the place of the LBJ Company's Queen Air 80 as the Johnson family airplane when Lyndon B. Johnson became the 36th President of the United States. (Page 237) "warm-up" for the Army award, Bell Helicopter had reordered, a few days earlier, more Beech-built components for its Army HU-1D Iroquois jet-powered helicopter, to the value of $.6 million. And a new member of the Beech target missile family, the Model 1025-TJ, had completed its first flight tests with excellent promise of fulfilling its design capacities of 475 mph at altitudes above 43,000 feet. The turboprop-powered 1025-TJ was planned to fill a gap between existing piston-engine and rocket-powered target missiles.

In keeping with the company's higher goals, "Sell More in '64" was the theme of the Beechcraft International Distributor-Management meeting which convened at the Beechcrafters Activity Center on November 15. Because of the need for peak efficiency in dealing swiftly with a crowded agenda, the group was limited in size, comprising some 100 owners and general managers of Beechcraft sales and service facilities. Members of the "blue-chip" assembly came from all over the free world to see what Beech had in store for the year to come. What they saw provided inspiration that was to help push commercial sales to new record-breaking highs.

Brightest star of the event was the new King Air — most sophisticated of all commercial Beechcraft designs. A preview showing of the production prototype, which was soon to make its first flight, intensified the interest in the 270 mph turboprop design which had already been evidenced by the receipt of customer deposits for future deliveries totalling $10.8 million in value within 90 days after its initial announcement. The decisions made with respect to the Model 90 were beginning to look very sound.

Also unveiled was the new Beechcraft B55 Baron. Sales leader in the light twin field since its introduction in 1961, with more than 500 Barons in use, the new version offered many advancements in performance, style and equipment. Gross weight, upped to 5,000 pounds, provided a useful load of more than one ton. New propellers upped the climb rate to a breathtaking 1,730 fpm and a single-engine ceiling topping 9,000 feet at full gross weight. A longer nose cone enhanced the sleek lines and increased ratio and baggage space by 50%. Equipment and seating options included three-bladed propellers (exclusive with the Baron among light twins), Neumatic omnicoupled auto pilot, and comfort-conditioned accommodations affording ample room for four to six persons.

The all-time flagship of the world-wide executive transport fleet — the Beechcraft Super H18 — stepped forward with a new optional feature that again displayed the tremendous versatility of this time-honored yet perennially fresh design: Factory-installed tricycle landing gear. The new choice between tail-wheel and nose-wheel was the one touch needed to keep the Model 18 up to the minute in style, convenience and handling qualities, as it entered its 27th consecutive year of production. Equipped with tricycle gear, the Super H18 would hold its own in appearance with any of the newest designs fresh off the drawing boards. It would add the convenience of an always-level cabin, a feature to which many passengers had become accustomed from airline travel. It would lose none of the superb aerodynamic and load-carrying qualities which had made it the world leader in its class. And it would gain new appeal to those pilots who preferred the characteristics of tricycle gear.

Historically, the Model 18 tricycle gear option might be said very nearly to mark the end of an era in basic aircraft con-figuration — the era of what was once "conventional," or main-wheels-plus-tail-wheel gear design. That was the era in which an entire generation of design engineers, and pilots as well, had grown up in the years between World Wars I and II. It was the era of small, grassed or unsurfaced airports, when air-planes were slow of speed and light of wing loading; when "tail-first" landings helped the tail skid, predecessor of the wheel, dig into the soft field surface to slow down the landing roll of unbraked main wheels. Later, as speeds and wing load-ings increased and main wheels acquired brakes, it was still the era of the "three-point" landing, with main gear and tail wheel ideally touching down simultaneously.

Shortly before the outbreak of World War II, the design pendulum began its swing backward, toward the use of tricycle gear. (The first successful aircraft, in the opening decade of the century, had used nose-wheel-plus-main-wheel gear, or its equiv-alent.) By the time the war ended, tricycle gear was in almost exclusive use for all but a few special-purpose military planes.

236

And modern postwar commercial designs, led by the Beech Bonanza, featured retractable tricycle gear.

Inevitably, there was a clash of opinion among pilots. Some swore by tricycle gear; others swore at it. With firm interests on both sides, Beech stayed discreetly neutral. For most of the veteran pre-war pilots, and many who had flown the more than 6,000 Model 18 Beechcrafts in military service during the war, the conventional gear would long be favored. The newer generation, trained from solo flight onward in tricycle gear equipment, would favor the type they knew best. Now, both generations could choose whichever they preferred, in the Super H18 — upholding a Beech tradition of many years' standing: "Give the customer what he wants."

Chapter 28

Through a unique chain of circumstances, one of the first Beechcrafts to be delivered in 1964 was forced into competition for the title of "Foremost V.I.P. Transport" in the United States, if not the entire world — with almost no chance of winning. Its competitor was to be the airplane designated as "Air Force One" — actually, whichever one of several Boeing jet airliners or other aircraft was assigned to transport the President of the United States at the moment. While the Queen Air 80 in question could hold its own with anything in the skies, special considerations sharply limited its probable use by the President and other members of the First Family.

The events that created this odd situation started with the receipt in October 1963 of an order from the LBJ Company of Austin, Texas for a Queen Air 80 executive transport, equipped and decorated according to specifications of their board chairman, Mrs. L. B. Johnson. Its notably handsome interior, which among other touches included stylized "J's" and "Texas Lone Stars" custom-worked into curtain and upholstery fabrics, clearly reflected the personal tastes of Mrs. Johnson and her husband, Lyndon Baines Johnson, then Vice President of the United

States. Like many other executive Beechcrafts, this Model 80 would, among other duties, transport its owner's chief executive and family from time to time. It was a pleasing expectation for all concerned.

The assassination of John Fitzgerald Kennedy at Dallas on November 22, 1963 changed many things — this expectation among them. Lyndon Baines Johnson became the thirty-sixth President of the United States; Mrs. Johnson the First Lady of the nation. To avoid any possible conflict of interests that might arise, Mrs. Johnson transferred all of her stock in the LBJ Company to a trusteeship and resigned her position in the firm, which then became the Texas Broadcasting Corporation. The Queen Air which had been so painstakingly planned inevitably yielded its place to other aircraft officially designated for Presidential use.

The introduction on January 13 of two new models which had been in development for nearly two years afforded a promising start toward fulfilling Beech's aim of "More sales in '64." A new version of the Beechcraft Bonanza replaced the Model P35 which had been in production since December 1961. And a bigger, more luxurious Queen Air was offered in place of the Model 80 which had received its Approved Type Certificate in February 1962.

The new S35 Bonanza increased its dominance over the single-engine high-performance field in many ways. A more powerful 285 hp Continental fuel injection engine helped raise the top speed to 212 mph, cruising speed at 75% power to 205 mph, or 200 mph at 65% power, and payload to 1,415 pounds. Extension of the cabin length by 19 inches added more room for occupants, permitting installation of auxiliary family seats for a total of five adult persons, or four adults and two juniors. Baggage area also was upped 50% to 33 cubic feet. A new gear-driven alternator, replacing the former generator, provided ample electric power even at engine idling speeds. A full-flow oil filter, providing 100% filtration, reduced oil change requirements to a normal 50 hours. New cabin heating offered 30% more heat within the cabin. New ring disc brakes produced 35% more braking power. Optional was a new three-blade propeller. All these, plus other advances and refinements, came at a recom-

238

mended $28,750 list price — less than a 4% increase over the former model.

Comments from aviation writers who test-flew the S35 Bonanza were glowingly enthusiastic. Leighton Collins, editor of *Air Facts* magazine and unofficial dean of the business aircraft press corps, summed up the general viewpoint neatly: "In all the years which have slipped by since the Bonanza made its first appearance the wonder each year has been how they could possibly improve the airplane any further . . . A lot of airplane, and when you add the S35's quiet and comfort and small field ability and ease of flying, it comes out to a spectacular airplane — the most spectacular of all the Bonanzas."

Improvements in the new A80 Queen Air were made on such a scale that a new Approved Type Certificate was issued on this model. The wing span was expanded by a full five feet, to 50 feet 10½ inches, and the fuselage was correspondingly strengthened. This made practical a 500-pound increase in gross weight to a new 8,500-pound total, and a 400-pound increase in useful load. In turn a 34-gallon increase in standard fuel capacity provided increased range. Although the Model 80's twin Lycoming geared 380 hp engines were retained, high speed stood at 252 mph, and cruising speed 212 mph at a conservative 65% power rating. An all-new luxury interior, inspired by the forthcoming King Air design, afforded unparalleled passenger comfort. And a redesigned nose compartment permitted the expanded radio installations desired by many owners. Again, Beech had found ways to improve on a design already preeminent in its class.

Hard on the heels of the new model showings at regional meetings throughout the nation came the first flight of the prototype Model 90 King Air. The date was January 20, 1964 — a date that would stand out in the company's annals beside an earlier event dating back 27 years, when on January 15, 1937, the first Model 18 Beechcraft made its initial flight from the selfsame Beech field at Wichita.

This January-based coincidence raised an interesting question: Would the King Air eventually top the records made by the famous Model 18 — beyond question the world's most popular and long-lived airplane design of any class? There was reason

239

to believe that Beech felt this might prove to be true. In a gesture of confidence rare if not unique in the aviation industry, the King Air first flight was not, as customary, barred from close viewing to all but the small group most intimately concerned. Instead, several thousand spectators watched while the newest Beechcraft gracefully took to the skies for the first time, and completed a thoroughly successful test flight. It was a good start for the customary Beech accelerated reliability test program that would continue for the next several months to probe and wring out the slightest flaws that could be detected in the five King Air units assigned for testing. And it confirmed the confidence of buyers who, since the Model 90 was first announced, had sent in firm orders with cash deposits to a total value, as of that date, in excess of $12 million.

That the King Air might also open up new possibilities in areas apart from business and commercial uses became apparent a little later in the year. On March 12, delivery was made at Beech field to the U. S. Army Aviation Test Board, Fort Rucker, Alabama, of the first turbine-powered Beechcraft U-8F Seminole utility transport. Military counterpart of the commercial Queen Air, the twin turboprop was scheduled for a comprehensive three-months "user evaluation," prior to its placement in regular Army service.

The turboprop Seminole, designated as the Army's NU-8F, was already a well-tested airplane. It had served as the testbed aircraft for the Pratt & Whitney PT6A-6 engines adopted for the King Air for nearly ten months. Its test record had validated the reliability of those engines, and had also demonstrated their other advantages: Reverse-flow air intake, virtually eliminating the danger of engine damage through ingestion of pebbles, rocks and other foreign objects thrown up from unprepared fields; and ability to operate satisfactorily on either jet fuels or aviation gasoline. A happy by-product of its uncritical appetite was the fact that occasional use of avgas would purge from the tanks and fuel system growths of algae that had been found to accumulate in jetplanes fueled exclusively with JP-4 and other "jet-only" fuels. The engines could, if necessary, operate for as long as 150 hours during any time-between-overhaul period without penalizing efficiency, using only aviation gasoline.

240

Red-letter dates in general aviation history: First flight of the Model 90 Beechcraft turbo-prop King Air . . . January 20, 1964.

First flight of the Model 35 Beech-craft Bonanza . . . December 22, 1945.

First flight of the Model 18 Beech-craft twin . . . January 15, 1937.

First flight of the Model 17 Beech-craft biplane . . . November 4, 1932.

First design of The Beech Aircraft

U8-F designation was given Queen Air 80 by U. S. Army for its liaison transport. (Page 240)

Astronaut Leroy Gordon Cooper, Jr. and his family first joined the roll of Beechcraft owners with a Bonanza. He is shown accepting delivery of his new Baron. (Pages 196, 247)

The Musketeer II series featured typical Beech refinements ... which were also made available without charge to all owners of the Musketeer I series. (Page 246)

In prospect for the Army's entire fleet of Seminole transports was an eventual rebuilding program which would modernize these, as well as other Army aircraft, with turboprop power plants. It was a pleasing example of military concern for the taxpayers' money; and pleasing also to Beech in affording excellent prospects for participation in the rebuilding program. The Army, as well as other military service arms, had been well satisfied with the results of previous Beech rebuild programs, from both the performance and economy viewpoints. This was, of course, in addition to the Army and other military requirements for new turboprop Seminoles and other adaptations of the King Air basic design that would almost certainly develop in the future. Other military and defense service arms throughout the free world would also represent prime prospects.

Less than a month later, the international scope of Beechcraft's markets was emphasized with the delivery on April 8 of three new Super H18 transports to the Brazilian Air Force. First units of a total of 15 twin 18's ordered by Brazil, they featured the tricycle landing gear announced not long ago as a factory-installed option. Twelve of the twins ordered under a $3 million contract for planes plus spare parts were to serve as flight and navigation trainers and liaison craft; others would be assigned to "V.I.P." transport duties, working out of the capitol city of Brasilia, deep in the nation's interior and accessible primarily by air. The new H18 twins joined one of the largest fleets of Model 18 Beechcrafts operational anywhere, serving the fifth largest country in the world. Twin Beechcrafts were a familiar sight in Brazil's skies; and the Model 18 had long been a favorite in that "Good neighbor" nation, as a reliable and economical airplane fulfilling urgent needs in a country largely dependent on air transportation.

Continuing its program of developing anti-aircraft defense skills second to none, the Bureau of Naval Weapons late in April awarded Beech a new contract for some $9 million worth of Navy AQM-37A rocket-powered, supersonic missile targets. The new contract extended production of the high-speed target in the Beech Aerospace plant through December 1965. Third contract to Beech for this item, it brought to some $40 million the total value of development and production volume for the

243

AQM-37A missile target system. A much-appreciated aspect of this system was the "round-of-ammunition" concept, developed by Beech and carried to the point of completely fueling the rockets at the factory, ready for shipboard launching in minimum time and without need for at-sea or shore fueling facilities.

Beech weapon systems design capabilities met a challenge of another kind, some three weeks later. That was when the Beech proposal was announced in answer to a U. S. Navy competition for the design of a counter-insurgency (COIN) airplane to support ground forces in limited or guerilla warfare of the kind then under way in South Viet Nam. Navy requirements were stringent. The acceptable design would need to have high capabilities for STOL (short takeoff and landing) operation from unimproved runways, jungle clearings, primitive roads and aircraft or helicopter carrier decks without catapults or arrest gear — plus a speed of 240 knots. It would be adaptable to quick installation and interchange of weapons systems and personnel, cargo and litter facilities, for all-around versatility as an attack plane, transport and ambulance. It would ideally be safely operable by crews without extensive training and experience. Economy in first cost and operation would also be a factor.

Of the half-dozen designs submitted by highly respected manufacturers in this competition, the Beech submission was rated well by impartial observers. Two principal features of the Beechcraft PD-183 (its factory designation) were simplicity and low cost. Turboprop engines were the same United Aircraft of Canada T-74 power plants used in the King Air under their commercial designation as the PT-6 Pratt & Whitney. Much of the design stemmed from King Air engineering; and the high speed capability was of practically the same order. Control of the PD-183 was predictably well within the skills of the average pilot trained on any conventional aircraft. However the competition might result, the Beech entry was one to enhance the company's stature and worthily to represent the name of Beechcraft.

May 27, 1964 was a notable day at Beech Aircraft. Coronation Day, it was called — the day when the Model 90 King Air received its Type Certificate from the Federal Aviation

244

Agency. It was a gala affair. President O. A. Beech personally accepted the King Air certification from John M. Beardslee, director of the FAA's central region. Executive Vice President Frank E. Hedrick predicted King Air deliveries to the value of $22 million by the end of 1965 — a conservative figure, considering the large volume of orders on hand. Notable figures in government and industry came from all over the nation to welcome the official crowning of the King Air. Many were rewarded with demonstration flights that confirmed the appropriateness of the event. Further confirmation was supplied on June 8, when Beech announced a firm recommended selling price of $320,000 for the completely equipped, pressurized King Air, less only avionics equipment which would vary from plane to plane with the customer's needs and choices. It was something of a rarity in the aviation industry for an all-new, advanced design aircraft to enter the market at a price so close to its initial estimated price.

The King Air continued to hold the spotlight in the company's activities, with the delivery on July 7 to United Aircraft of Canada, Ltd. of the first Model 90 to a corporate owner. President O. A. Beech personally presented the keys of the airplane to John MacNeil, chief pilot for UACL flight operations. It would serve as an executive transport for UACL; and close watch would be kept over its performance, as a continuation of the accelerated service test program which was still under way at the Beech factory.

Just four days later, on July 11, the center of interest shifted to the Beech plant at Liberal, Kansas, located 200 air miles southwest of Wichita. There, since last February 7, work had been busily in progress on the conversion of 121,000 square feet of floor space at the former Air Force B-24 base to a completely integrated design, production and delivery facility for the new Model A23 Beech Musketeer. The new version of this popular-priced Beechcraft, informally known as the Musketeer II, had made its debut on June 19, featuring a number of refinements not present in the original version. The July 11 event was a public "Open House" for both the Model A23 and the expanded facility at Liberal where it would thereafter originate. Present for dedication ceremonies were President O. A. Beech, Executive Vice President Frank E. Hedrick, and many guests prominent in civic and aviation circles.

The facility at Liberal had been a very busy place for many weeks. At the same time that production equipment was being installed and a skilled labor force being assigned to various duties, the first Musketeer II Beechcrafts were brought to completion. And modifications were also being made there to the first group of Musketeers, which had been produced and delivered by the hundreds to owners all over the nation and in foreign lands. Those first Musketeers, in the opinion of Beech, fell a little short in some details of being fully worthy of their name. Not in any important aspects, nor in any way affecting their safety or airworthiness. No directives had ever been issued by the FAA calling for changes in this respect, as often happened in the case of some generally sound aircraft. But, in striving to produce a low-cost plane that would still be worthy of the Beech nameplate, some small items had slipped through that seemed not quite Beech-like. Action to correct this situation was typical of Beech. All Musketeer owners were notified that they could bring their planes in to the Beech factory, at their convenience for modifications to be made entirely at factory expense. To those owners who found this procedure impractical, Beech offered without charge a modification kit permitting upgrading of the Musketeer I to Beech standards in the field. From the owners' viewpoint, Beech-Liberal was living up to its name. And, in the Musketeer II and future versions, the lowest-priced Beech would be, in every last detail, every inch a Beechcraft. A single facility, dedicated to that purpose, would help to realize this aim.

A review of Beechcraft's standing for the first nine months of fiscal 1964 showed a very bright picture. Total sales that topped $78.7 million represented a 49% increase over the corresponding period of 1963. After-tax net earnings of $2.4 million were up 52%. June was the largest dollar-volume month for business aircraft products in the company's 32-year history, totalling better than $6.3 million. King Air orders on hand with cash deposits exceeded $28 million. It seemed certain that total sales for fiscal '64 would be in the area of $110 million.

Promotions at high levels within the organization bolstered the prospects for continuation of such favorable results through participation in management by persons of fully proved capabilities. Realignment of marketing responsibilities earlier in the year had brought well-deserved recognition to some highly qualified executives in that area. Appointment of four new vice-presidents on July 16, three in manufacturing and one in aerospace marketing and contracts, and all Beechcrafters of long service, further strengthened the top-management team.

The good month of July closed on another favorable note. Issued to Beech on July 30 by Lockheed Aircraft of a $12.4 million contract for Starlifter C-141A ailerons, flaps and spoilers evidenced their satisfaction with previous work performed by Beech for their Marietta, Georgia C-141A production line. Repeat business, earned by efficient performance, spoke for itself.

August, always a hot month in Kansas, showed a quick and early temperature increase in the competitive business aircraft market, following an August 3 announcement by Beech to its domestic and export distributors. Effective at once, the recommended retail price of the twin-engine Model 65 Queen Air would be reduced from its former $126,000 to a new low of $110,000 — a price cut of $16,000. Probably the biggest airplane price-cut in history, at least percentagewise, the reduction made the Queen Air 65 sharply competitive in the price area between the $59,950 Baron and the $140,000 Queen Air A80. It was good news for Beech distributors and dealers — and for business aircraft buyers.

Beechcrafters were used to having plant visitors, many of them owners learning the quality story built into each Beechcraft. A guest many recognized in August was Astronaut Leroy Gordon Cooper who was at the factory to take delivery of a new Baron. He had been flying a Beech Bonanza for the previous three years. He and his wife Trudy, also a qualified pilot, enjoyed Beechcraft ownership for keeping a full schedule of appointments and for family excursions.

Legal counsel, director and member of the executive committee, Dwight S. Wallace died August 28. The 55-year-old attorney had served as a director of Beech Aircraft since December, 1949 and his enthusiasm, experience, and judgment

247

had played an important part in Beechcraft's growth over a 15-year period.

On September 4 the first Beechcraft King Air tour outside the United States began with a 2,600-mile trans-Atlantic flight from Gander, Newfoundland to Paris, France in 9 hours and 50 minutes. Cruising at 19,000 feet, the King Air averaged a 264-mph ground speed. It was the first non-stop Atlantic crossing for an airplane of the King Air's category. Only squawk: the clock lost 30 seconds over the Atlantic.

Thirty-eight countries in Europe, the Middle East and Africa provided a rugged, international "proving ground" as the turbo-prop transport demonstrated exceptional all-weather capability and all-around reliability during the demanding 123-day flight schedule. The 108,000-mile trip, stretching from Helsinki, Finland, to Capetown, South Africa, set an impressive record of 315 scheduled flights without a single delay, without a single cancellation, and without a missed appointment due to maintenance or weather conditions.

Take-off temperatures ranged from -30 degrees to 110 degrees. Operating altitudes varied from below sea level in Holland to more than 30,000 feet over Germany. And the airplane was flown from landing strips as short as 1,420 feet, surfaced with concrete, sand, grass, dirt and steel mats. Despite such challenges, the King Air successfully completed demonstrations for 771 business, military and government leaders, making 454 landings in 91 cities.

The King Air was flown as much as 8 hours, 45 minutes on one day. Throughout the entire trip, 13% of the flight time was at night and 14% on instruments. Yet, due to the reliability of all systems, only 75% of the total maintenance hours scheduled were actually used. The King of Morocco, the Aga Khan and Count Zanon of Italy were among the distinguished passengers. His Highness Prince Karim the Aga Khan later visited Beechcraft to select furnishings for his King Air.

Meanwhile, the first production unit of the King Air rolled from the Plant I assembly line September 9. The sixth King Air to be built, it was delivered to Atlantic Aviation Corporation's New York Division, Teterboro, New Jersey.

Delivery October 19 at Tinker Air Force Base, Oklahoma,

of the first C-141 StarLifter turbofan jet transport to the U. S. Air Force's Military Air Transport Service by the Air Force Systems Command had special significance for attending representatives of Beech Aircraft, a major subcontractor on the program. Beechcraft built inboard and outboard flaps, ailerons, nose landing gear doors, emergency exit doors and spoilers for the giant C-141. Weight was a major consideration on the fast, long-range StarLifter, a transport designed to modernize airlift capabilities of MATS. As a result of this weight-saving design goal, a large portion of the Beech-built assemblies were of lightweight but rugged honeycomb-bonded construction.

Importance of the honeycomb-bonding principle was apparent in the StarLifter's flaps which were exposed to excessive heat from the powerful turbofan engines. Titanium honeycomb-bonded flap panels were proven ultra-heat resistant and were used in the engine wake area of the flaps. To win its major subcontracting position on the important StarLifter program, Beech Aircraft submitted best bids in competition with 11 to 17 other firms on various proposal segments. Because of the giant size of the StarLifter, a specially designed and constructed van carried "ship sets" of Beech-built components 975 miles from Wichita to Marietta, Georgia.

When the fiscal year ended September 30, President O. A. Beech could report total sales in excess of $107 million for 1964. This was an increase of more than 45% over the total 1963 sales! Final earnings after taxes, increased 70%. Aerospace sales totaled $52 million, up 85% over 1963. Commercial sales amounted to more than $54 million, up more than 19%. This history-breaking, all-time high commercial sales volume represented an increase of 160% over 1954 commercial sales.

With such a year behind them, it was a confident, eager group of Beechcraft distributors who gathered for the company's International Distributor Management Meeting November 23 and 24 in Wichita. It was to be a meeting of "firsts."

For the first time, one distributor was recognized for having sold more than $5 million of Beechcraft products in one year. This Award of Excellence went to Atlantic Aviation Corporation — New York. To the usual "Million-Airs" table was added a "Multi-Million-Airs" table to recognize the 13 distributors each of whose Beechcraft sales during 1964 sales year had exceeded $2 million. Beechcraft distributors had become outstanding business leaders in their home states. Modern business aviation facilities with the familiar Beechcraft red, blue and white identification stripes had become the usual, rather than the exception.

For the first time in the five-year history of the Beechcraft Man of the Year Award, the recipient was an export distributor, A. H. Ostermann, president of Travelair G.m.b.H. & Co., KG, Bremen, Germany.

News from the meeting was the introduction of a new model of the Beechcraft Debonair. Sometimes over-shadowed by the better known Bonanza since introduction in 1959, the Debonair nevertheless had earned a place in the product line as an easy-to-fly, thrifty single-engine plane that offered Beechcraft speed and comfort as well. The new C33 Debonair was equipped with more than a dozen refinements. Most noticeable were the large third side windows which added to visibility. Inside, the Debonair offered individual, contoured seating with bucket-style seats and new rich fabrics. Optional three-blade propeller and flight-swept dorsal fin were among the other more noticeable advancements.

Another single-engine Beechcraft was in the news at this time. Beech distributors and their dealers were beginning to stage Beech Family Fun Fairs. This was an event planned by the Beechcraft marketing staff and the distributors to attract non-pilots as well as Beech owners and competitive owners to see the new Beechcraft Musketeer II. Special invitations, facility decorations, signs, newspaper ads and radio spots attracted owner and non-owner alike out to the Beechcraft distributor or dealer facility for a look and perhaps a ride in this new Beechcraft. A special "ladies corner" was included where visitors could get woman-to-woman answers to their aviation questions from Joyce Case or Gene Nora Stumbaugh of the Beech sales staff.

Stockholders in person and by proxy representing 83% of Beechcraft's 2,815,746 shares gathered in Walter H. Beech Hall of the Beechcrafters Activities Center December 17. In presenting the company's programs to stockholders, Mrs. Beech called for reports by Wyman L. Henry, vice president -

marketing; Roy H. McGregor, vice president - aerospace marketing and contracts; and John A. Elliott, secretary-treasurer. A 10-year strengthening of the financial position of the company was disclosed. Since 1954, stockholder's equity had grown by more than 250%. Working capital had increased from $9 million to $29.5 million, while dividends paid increased by 130%.

Beech Aircraft officers elected for 1965 were O. A. Beech, president; Frank E. Hedrick, executive vice president; L. E. Bowery, vice president - materiel; E. C. Burns, vice president - Boulder Division; Leddy L. Greever, vice president - domestic sales; Wyman L. Henry, vice president - marketing; James N. Lew, vice president - engineering; Roy H. McGregor, vice president - aerospace marketing and contracts; William M. Morgan, vice president and assistant to the president; M. G. Neuburger, vice president - export sales; L. L. Pechin, vice president - manufacturing; John A. Elliott, secretary-treasurer; L. Winters, assistant secretary; and R. Warren Fisher, assistant secretary.

And in December *The Beechcrafter* carried the 100th in a series of "I Believe" columns by Cliff Titus. The words of Titus, a member of the industrial relations staff, had special meaning for the Beechcraft organization which had just completed such an excellent year: "I Believe: in God, in Man, in America and the American Way, in Myself, in my Company, in my Work, in Courage, in Honor, in Loyalty, in Gratitude, in Laughter, in Patriotism, in Service, in Discipline, and in the ultimate triumph of Truth."

The Space Age

Chapter 29

Good news came upon good news in the opening months of 1965. First quarter 1965 sales were $28,980,803, a 35% increase over volume one year earlier.

In February Mrs. Beech announced that because of growing acceptance of the Beechcraft King Air it was necessary to accelerate the production rate to meet the demand.

The next day she announced that the U. S. Army had selected the Beechcraft B55 Baron as winner of its competition for a fixed-wing twin-engine instrument trainer. The Army awarded Beechcraft a production contract totaling more than $2.5 million. The selection followed an aircraft evaluation test program involving airplanes from four airframe manufacturers conducted by the U. S. Army Aviation Test Board at Fort Rucker, Alabama. Selection culminated an effort which was started in 1962 by the U. S. Army Aviation School. The Baron would be used as a primary twin-engine instrument trainer by the Army Aviation School Instrument Training Division at Fort Rucker. The secondary mission would be the twin-engine transition of single-engine rated aviators.

With the "Oh Happy Day" flag still flying from the announcement of the Baron order, Mrs. Beech was able to announce a follow-on subcontract in excess of $10 million by McDonnell Aircraft Corporation for production of major subassemblies for the tri-service, multiple-mission McDonnell Phantom II fighter. The new order involved manufacture of center and inner wing leading edge flaps, trailing edge flaps, ailerons, speed brakes, spoilers, main landing gear and nose gear doors for the U. S. Navy/Marine F-4B and U. S. Air Force F-4C and for the reconnaissance versions of both models, the RF-4B and RF-4C respectively. Deliveries under the new contract brought to some $30 million the total value of Phantom II production work received

Queen Air 88 was the first piston-driven Beechcraft to offer pressurization. (Page 259)

Year 1965 marked production of the 8,000th Beechcraft Bonanza . . . and Chief Pilot Vern Carsten's 25th year with the company. (Page 262)

Publisher Merrill C. Meigs accepted delivery of his 10th Bonanza from President O. A. Beech in 1965.

Subcontract work for other major aerospace suppliers is performed at Wichita Plant III.

Unique Beech-craft Display Hangar permits static all-weather showing of Beech-craft product line.

Single-engine Debonairs and Bonanzas and light twin Travel Airs and Barons are assembled at Plant II, Wichita.

by Beech Aircraft. Another mutually pleasing chapter was being written in the Beech-McDonnell production association first started in 1953.

A follow-on contract in excess of $2,760,000 from Textron's Bell Helicopter Company for production of components for the U. S. Army UH-1D Iroquois helicopter was awarded in March. This contract by the Ft. Worth, Texas company brought to more than $8,700,000 the total contracts assigned Beechcraft on the jet-powered helicopter. More than 608 ship sets of panels for the Iroquois, each consisting of more than 70 parts and assemblies, already had been produced at Beechcraft's Plant III in Wichita. This project gave Beechcrafters a direct link with the conflict in Vietnam where the Iroquois was playing a key role.

When one of the four manufacturing buildings at the Liberal Division was destroyed by fire March 18, Beechcrafters took the only road to recovery they knew. They rolled up their sleeves and went to work. While embers of the south fabrication and upholstery building were still smoldering, teams of Beechcrafters were already at the site, planning salvage operations, determining tooling loss, and judging the over-all effect on production. Within hours jigs and tools were trucked to Wichita for rework. Through the efforts of Beechcrafters both in Liberal and in Wichita there was no interruption in the delivery of Musketeers.

The laudatory letter on O. A. Beech's desk late in April was brief and factual. And from the President of the United States. Once again, Beech Aircraft had answered the call from its country, this time for a dollar's worth of defense for every dollar spent.

"It was most gratifying, therefore, to see your company listed among those firms recently called to my attention by the Secretary of Defense as having responded vigorously and effectively to that request," wrote Lyndon B. Johnson in his letter.

"Zero Defects" was what the Department of Defense called this program, a program aimed at improving quality consciousness throughout the entire defense complex. The program took little time to implement at Beechcraft facilities because of the company's own constant concern for quality during the previous three decades. Within days after the program was initiated,

255

99.68 percent of all Beechcraft employees had written their pledge to support the Zero Defects effort. Even Beechcrafters on duty in the Far East, Brazil and Europe sent in signed pledge cards.

A longtime friend earned the admiration of Beechcrafters during these months. Marcellus M. Murdock, 82-year-old president and chairman of the board of The Wichita Eagle and Beacon Publishing Company, earned his multi-engine rating, entitling him to fly his company's Beechcraft Baron.

Through an engineering modification, the licensed gross weight of the King Air was increased in April by approximately 300 pounds, all of which was useful load and meant owners could carry more equipment and luggage or extend their range.

In a demonstration of cooperation among modes of transportation, The Chicago & North Western Railway added a Beechcraft King Air to its corporate fleet during the month of April.

"As significant a milestone in aviation as was the automatic gear shift to the automobile" was the way Wyman Henry described a new factory option made available in May. An automatic safety system for retractable landing gear called the Beechcraft Magic Hand was designed to eliminate the possibility of gear-up landings or inadvertent retraction of the landing gear while on the ground. Beechcraft became the first business aircraft manufacturer to offer such a system on a factory-installed basis. Factory-installed price of the Beechcraft Magic Hand on either the Bonanza or Debonair was only $270, about one third of the cost of the only other comparable system on the market.

The Magic Hand was designed to handle gear extension independently of the pilot's attention. Landing gear was automatically lowered on approach if the engine manifold pressure fell below approximately 20 inches and airspeed had been reduced to 120 miles an hour. The landing gear switch automatically moved to the "down" position on the panel and returned to that position in spite of any effort to move it, always giving the pilot a visual indication of gear position.

On take-off, the Magic Hand kept the gear in the "down" position until the aircraft was airborne and had accelerated to

90 mph indicated airspeed. This feature was designed to avoid premature gear retraction should the aircraft not be ready for flight. In addition, there was a three-position switch to enable the pilot to turn the system on or off, or to perform a functional test. With the Magic Hand system off, the landing gear operation was standard with the usual warning horn and safety switch to prevent accidental retraction on the ground.

"Over the middle of a vast and lonely ocean you have time to contemplate many things. And as we thought of the feeling of safety and security and comfort we were experiencing in flying an airplane that seemed like a small airliner, we thought of those who were responsible for building the plane. We feel deep gratitude toward you for your skill and integrity and conscientiousness. As pilots we bet our lives on you." So wrote Jan and Marion Dietrich to the production line workers of Beech Aircraft following their trans-Atlantic flight of a Queen Air A80 to Bremen, Germany. The attractive twins and the Beechcraft twin made headlines with their routine Atlantic crossing.

Aerospace products were making headlines, too. The Beechcraft-produced AQM-37A missile target set a new altitude record during weapon system evaluation and training operations at the U. S. Navy's Naval Missile Center, Pt. Mugu, California. The target climbed to an altitude of 91,000 feet and maintained a speed of Mach 2.8. The launch was from a Phantom II at an altitude of 47,000 feet and a speed of Mach 1.3. The previous record launch was to an altitude of 86,000 feet set by another Beechcraft AQM-37A some five months earlier.

Superior craftsmanship on the part of Beechcrafters in the development of a missile airframe was recognized by the Radio Corporation of America. RCA presented Beechcraft a Zero Defects award citing the company's role as an associate contractor in the U. S. Army's SAM-D (Surface-to-Air Missile Development) program.

"You're on your way, Molly Brown!" The Gemini GT-4 spacecraft lifted off at 11:15:59 a.m. EDT June 3 at Launch Complex 19, Cape Kennedy, Florida. And the spirits of all Beechcrafters soared with the 7,862-pound spacecraft. A Beechcraft-developed system for loading super-cooled gases played

257

an important role in the success of America's first two-man world-orbiting mission. The Boulder Division completed the important cryogenic system under contract to McDonnell Aircraft Corporation, prime contractor.

Liquid oxygen, supplied by the Beech-built system, provided the vital gases for the cabin's breathing atmosphere and pressurization. The Beechcraft system consisted of three major elements — liquid transport and storage dewars, vacuum-jacketed transfer systems, and control consoles which accomplished the complete servicing operation. Gemini GT-4 completed 62 revolutions during the 96 hours, 56 minutes and 21 seconds it was aloft with USAF Majors Edward H. White and James A. McDivitt. Astronaut White completed a 20-minute extra-vehicular excursion during the flight.

Months of research and technical effort by the creative engineering staff and management of Beechcraft's Boulder Division resulted in Grumman Aircraft Engineering Corporation awarding Beechcraft a contract in excess of $1 million to build aerospace ground support equipment for the lunar excursion module (LEM) of National Aeronautics and Space Administration's Apollo spacecraft system. Under this contract, the Boulder Division would have the responsibility for project direction, including the design, development, final assembly and testing of the supercritical Helium Conditioning Units and the Liquid Helium Storage and Transfer Units. These would be used as ground support equipment for the lunar excursion module descent propellant pressurization system. This system represented one of the first uses of this gas in a supercritical state for spacecraft application.

LEM was the space ferry designed to take two Apollo astronauts down to the moon from the Apollo spacecraft in lunar orbit and then carry them from the moon's surface back into orbit for rendezvous with the Apollo command-service module and return trip to earth. The contract established Beech Aircraft as a vital subcontractor on each of the nation's major space programs — Gemini Program, Apollo Program, and Lunar Excursion Module.

The largest all-time single commercial order for Beech Aircraft was placed June 7 when Stevens Aviation, Inc., Beechcraft

258

dealer in Greer, South Carolina, ordered three King Airs valued in excess of $1 million. The King Airs would be used to fly personnel of two southeastern textile firms.

Beech Acceptance Corporation, Inc., the wholly owned subsidiary formed in December, 1956, experienced one of the largest months in its history during June. Volume rose to $3.1 million and moved BACI past the $150 million mark in total business. This represented 4,047 Beechcraft airplanes financed for distributors and customers. In addition to the basic retail financing arrangements for purchasers, Beech Acceptance offered floor plan agreements for distributors and lease-purchase plans for users.

The Beechcraft name began appearing on a new line of communication and navigation antenna equipment during July. Reason for Beechcraft's decision to market its own antenna systems was to provide a communication system more efficient and more consistent in styling with Beech airplane design and paint schemes.

A new Beechcraft model was introduced to distributors and the aviation press at a special mid-summer meeting at the factory. The Beechcraft Queen Air 88 was presented as a brand new all-weather pressurized transport powered by two Lycoming fuel injection supercharged engines rated at 380 hp each. The six- to nine-place Model 88, third of Beechcraft's high performance business airplanes to carry the Queen Air designation, featured as standard equipment the required avionics instrumentation for all-weather operation, including complete cabin pressurization, air conditioning, super soundproofing, de-icing and anti-icing equipment, oxygen system and electrically-heated windshield.

Recommended delivery price of the Queen Air 88 with these ordinarily optional items as standard equipment was $259,500. Cabin pressurization was identical to that in the Beechcraft King Air, creating 8,000-foot cabin comfort for passengers at 16,500-foot altitude. Performance figures for the Model 88 showed a cruising speed of 221 mph, a range of more than 1,200 miles, and a service ceiling of more than 27,000 feet. The new Queen Air 88 presented businessmen with a choice of five Beechcraft heavy twin-engine corporate aircraft: the pressurized, turbine-powered King Air; pressurized, piston-powered Queen Air 88; and non-pressurized, piston-powered Super H18, Queen Air A80 and Queen Air 65. Prices ranged from $110,000 to $400,000 and speeds from 239 mph to 280 mph.

General Curtis E. LeMay, retired chief of staff of the U. S. Air Force, joined the roll of Bonanza owners. The famed war-time air general, who also commanded the Strategic Air Command and served as chief of staff of the Strategic Air Force in the Pacific, wrote Mrs. Beech, "In all the years I have been flying I have seldom had the opportunity to fly just for fun — always there has been a mission to fly or work to do. The Bonanza is my fun airplane and I am going to just bore a lot of holes in the air and thoroughly enjoy doing it."

The U. S. Army Missile Command at Redstone Arsenal, Huntsville, Alabama, awarded Beech Aircraft three contracts totaling more than $860,000 for continued support of target missile operations. Two of the contracts provided for a continuation of flight service support of the Beechcraft Model 1025 Cardinal target missile at Fort Bliss, Texas. The third contract, and a first for Beech, provided for flight service support of target missiles to be used in missile evaluation programs at the White Sands Missile Range, New Mexico.

The Peruvian Air Force placed an order exceeding $2.5 million in August for 18 twin-engine Beechcraft Queen Air A80's for use as trainers and liaison airplanes. The planes would replace several twin-engine Beechcrafts in service for more than 20 years. And the Paraguayan National Airlines (Lineas Aereas de Transporte Nacional) took delivery of two Bonanzas and two Debonairs to use in air taxi and scheduled passenger service. LATN, which already had six Beechcraft Bonanzas in service, inaugurated its operation with the Bonanza in 1948 and over the years had purchased 17 Bonanzas and two twin-engine D18's.

In the midst of this busy summer, Kansas Governor William Avery asked President O. A. Beech to serve as chairman of the newly announced 14-member Governor's Advisory Commission on Aviation. Once again, Beechcraft's president accepted a call from her fellow citizens.

For the first time in the U. S. space program, a fuel cell for all inflight electrical power was used on the Gemini V manned

260

space flight in August. The fuel cell produced electrical energy from the chemical reaction of hydrogen and oxygen gases loaded aboard the spacecraft in a super-cold liquid state by a Beechcraft-developed and manufactured system. Flown by L. Gordon Cooper, command pilot, and Charles Conrad, pilot, the mission evaluated the spacecraft over a longer duration; the rendezvous, guidance and navigation systems; and the effects of prolonged exposure to space environment on the two-man crew.

Five of the military counterpart of the Baron, the Beechcraft T-42A, were delivered September 2 to the U. S. Army. In making the delivery, Frank E. Hedrick recalled that the occasion marked the continuation of an association with military aviation which dated back 25 years when the first Beechcraft off-the-shelf models were purchased.

In among the Army olive-and-white Barons on the Beechcraft flight line was a distinctive tangerine and off-white King Air. The new owner: Walt Disney Productions, which purchased the King Air to replace a Queen Air 80 being retired after two years and 1500 flight hours of service throughout North America.

Two September events reminded Beechcrafters of their continued growth and change. First, eight Beechcraft Model 17's returned home to the factory for their owners to enjoy a visit. The guests were part of national club of 75 owners and admirers of the famed staggerwing. They were piloting their beautifully preserved Model D17S and G17S Beechcrafts to the Antique Airplane Association meeting at Ottumwa, Iowa. Their appearance at Beech Field brought fond memories to many Beechcrafters who were a part of the Model 17 production force through 1948. Around 250 of the 781 Model 17's built were still flying, reported club members.

Next, the tenth anniversary of the Boulder Division was observed by a weekend of activities. Corporate officials from Wichita joined with Boulder Beechcrafters to commemorate the anniversary. They traced the growth from the first liquid hydrogen test building on the Boulder site to the division's sprawling complex in 1965. A pioneer in cryogenics research and development — the science of the super cold — the Boulder Division engaged in many of the most advanced weapon system and space exploration related programs. Employment had increased from ten in 1955 to approximately 600 by the tenth anniversary.

Soon after the fiscal year ended September 30, Mrs. Beech could announce total 1965 sales in excess of $122 million, an increase of more than 14% over the total sales of the previous year. Commercial sales amounted to more than $74 million. She also announced that the board of directors had declared a regular quarterly cash dividend of 17.5¢ a share for each of the 2,819,820 shares outstanding — the company's 68th consecutive cash dividend.

In October the 8,000th Beechcraft Bonanza rolled from the assembly line. The same pilot who flew the original Bonanza took the controls. Vern Carstens, manager-flight department, recalled, "When I lifted that first Bonanza into the air almost 20 years ago, I and everyone at Beechcraft hoped we had an airplane that would sell 200 units." Taking delivery of the 8,000th Bonanza, a V35 Model, was Norman Larson, president of The Norman Larson Company of Van Nuys, California, which since 1950 had purchased 362 Bonanzas for retail sale!

With a spectacular sales year behind them, Beechcraft marketing officials moved into a "Sales Spectacular" for the coming year. Some 400 distributors, dealers and salesmen attended the annual Beechcraft International Sales Meeting held in the Activity Center. In a new venture for the private aviation industry, the meeting was handled by show business professionals from Broadway and Hollywood. The stars of the spectacular? Edgar Bergen, a Travel Air owner, and Astronaut Gordon Cooper, a Baron owner. And 15 Beechcraft airplanes!

Eight new models were introduced: the Queen Air A80, with greater load-carrying capacity and other refinements; C55 Baron, featuring a new 295 hp Continental engine and 242 mph speed; V35 Bonanza and V35C turbocharged Bonanza, the latter with a 245 mph high speed; C33A Debonair, featuring a new 285 hp Continental engine and top speed of 209 mph; and three new Musketeers, the four-place Super III with 200 hp and 154 mph top speed, the four-place Custom III with 165 hp and 146 mph speed, and the two-place Sport III with 150 hp and 137 mph speed.

Rounding out the display in the newly-constructed airplane showcase on Beech Field were the King Air, Queen Air 88, Super H18, Queen Air 65, B55 Baron, D95A Travel Air, and C33

Debonair. Dan Meisinger, president of Topeka Aircraft Sales and Service, with retail facilities in Kansas City and St. Louis as well as Topeka, was named Beechcraft Man of the Year to conclude the spectacular that lived up to its billing.

First of Beechcraft's 10-place Queen Airliners developed for third level airlines began flying Iowa skies for Commuter Air Lines. Initial routes connected Ames and Marshalltown, Iowa, with Chicago O'Hare International Airport. Passenger demand for this type of airline service and their acceptance of the Queen Airliner caused Commuter President Paul G. Delman to place seven of the Beechcrafts in operation within a few months of the airline's initial operation. Other airlines which quickly followed were Air Executive Airline, St. Louis, Missouri; Executive Airlines, Boston, Massachusetts; ALM, subsidiary of KLM Royal Dutch Airlines; Colombia Aero Taxi S. A.; Trans Australia; and Lapplandsflyg, Sweden.

A Beechcraft King Air transport took its place with Air Force One and other aircraft assigned to Military Air Transport Services' Special Air Missions fleet near Washington, D. C. in November. The King Air, designated VC-6A, would be used for transportation of key United States government and foreign dignitaries.

Soon after the 1,000th Debonair rolled from Plant II production lines in December, Beech export officials were able to announce a contract for 16 new C33 Debonairs to be delivered to Lufthansa German Airlines. Lufthansa would use the new Debonairs as flight and instrument trainers in their aviation college, along with five other Debonairs, two Twin-Bonanzas and one Beechcraft Mentor.

The five-year-old pictured with Santa Claus and a bright red Beechcraft on the cover of the holiday issue of *The Beechcrafter* knew his Beechcraft planes and his way around the Beechcraft Flight Line. A third generation was growing up to share the enthusiasm of Walter H. Beech and Olive Ann Beech for aviation. Five-year-old Lowell Jay was the son of the eldest Beech daughter, Suzanne. Her husband, Thomas N. Warner, was active several years in domestic sales of Beechcraft planes. Daughter Mary Lynn was married to John E. H. Pitt who was active in Beechcraft export sales.

263

Chapter 30

The increased business activity of 1965 gained momentum in 1966. The Beechcraft employment office remained open weekends as hundreds of new employees were added to the Beech work force. Sales records fell, and a completely new satellite facility would be in operation before 1966 was over.

In commercial activities, the year began with the delivery of the 100th King Air to Deering-Milliken, textile manufacturers of Spartanburg, South Carolina. Pilots and maintenance personnel of companies purchasing King Airs all underwent thorough training programs at Beechcraft to insure each owner enjoying the new Beech turboprop's capabilities to the fullest.

The second generation of the King Air, the A90, went into production. Features included increasing cabin pressurization to 4.6 psi, thus maintaining sea level atmosphere to above 10,000 feet and 8,000-foot atmosphere above 21,000 feet. The latest version of the PT6A engine provided 50 additional horsepower for climb-out and cruise speed operations. The A90 would fly higher, climb faster and go farther than any earlier version, and at reduced operating costs.

Vern Carstens, manager - flight operations, retired upon his 65th birthday in January, to be succeeded in this important post by Warren F. Filer. Carstens had been the first person to fly the Beechcraft XA-38 Grizzly, the Model 34 Twin Quad, the Bonanza, the Mentor and the Twin-Bonanza. Two other long-time members of the Beechcraft management team were lost in the early months of 1966. Phil McKnight, 55, manager - corporate relations, was fatally injured when struck by a car. Earl L. "Pete" Endsley, 54, manager - manufacturing hours, died following surgery. The wisdom of Beechcraft's management in depth program again was proved when others could step forward to continue programs initiated by these key executives.

One of the most notable examples of the company's diversification in the field of missile targets was a new contract in February from the U. S. Navy for continued production of the AQM-37A supersonic missile target. The $3.5 million contract marked three years of Beechcraft production on the high speed,

Twins Marion and Jan Dietrich flew Queen Air A80 on trans-Atlantic ferry trip to Bremen, Germany. They are pictured with President O. A. Beech, Frank E. Hedrick, executive vice president, and M. G. Neuburger, vice president - export sales. (Page 257)

Beechcraft VC-6A assigned to Air Force Special Missions (SAM) serving high-level Department of Defense personnel. (Page 263)

Beechcrafters who previously worked at Travel Air Manufacturing gathered to reminisce nearly 40 years later when a Travel Air biplane joined a Beechcraft Model 17 Fly-In at Beech Field. President O. A. Beech is third from left. (Page 261)

Aviatrix Louise Thaden visited with Mrs. O. A. Beech prior to ferrying a new Bonanza to North Carolina. (Page 20)

Lamar W. McLeod, vice president of Westinghouse Electric Corporation, accepted delivery of the 25,000th plane built by Beechcraft, a King Air, from President O. A. Beech and Frank E. Hedrick, executive vice president. (Page 270)

Queen Airliners for Commuter Airlines moved through final assembly at Wichita Plant I. (Page 263) non-recoverable target. Over 1,000 of the missile targets had been delivered. An extension production contract for a second $3.5 million quantity of the missile targets would follow later in the year.

For some 15 years Beechcraft's capabilities had included facilities at Liberal, Kansas. And the Boulder aerospace complex had just observed its tenth anniversary. With the success of such satellite sites proved, Beech announced early in 1966 the opening of a manufacturing facility at the former Schilling Air Force Base in Salina, Kansas to meet current demands for manpower and space. A vocational training school and a technical institute located at the Salina base would provide Beechcraft a labor pool to help ease the tight labor market experienced by industry throughout the nation in 1966.

"Our decision to again diversify our facilities was based on many factors," said Frank E. Hedrick. "In selecting Salina, for example, we cooperated with the Department of Defense in locating in an area where the labor market had been affected by the closing of an Air Force base."

The long term lease for the Salina facilities included immediate occupancy of five buildings which provided more than 265,000 square feet of manufacturing area; 35,000 square feet of air conditioned offices; testing laboratories; and use of an adjacent 13,000-foot runway. Within weeks of the lease signing, Beechcraft's 1025 Cardinal missile target was in production at the Salina site. Wing assemblies for Beechcrafts soon were being fabricated. A modification program to increase altitude capabilities of early King Airs was moved to Salina. By the following August, 300 Beechcrafters were employed at the Salina site in what only weeks before had been quiet, vacated military buildings.

Employment passed 10,000 the summer of 1966 as both Beechcraft's aerospace and commercial marketing programs continued to revise their forecasts upward.

The Lockheed-Georgia Company awarded Beech a new production contract valued at more than $17 million for the manufacture of major assemblies for the U. S. Air Force's C-141 Star-Lifter turbofan jet transport. The first of the new turbocharged Bonanzas, the V35TC, was delivered. The 1000th Model 55

Baron was delivered. Family Fun Fairs featuring the three Musketeer models were sponsored in over 50 cities. The Peruvian government took delivery of the 21st Queen Air to be delivered to that government within a year's time. While the first 18 aircraft were to be used as trainers and personnel transports, the final three were outfitted for aerial photo survey missions.

The Beechcraft honors list continued to grow. First prize in the 1966 Grand Prix International aircraft competition for distance performance was captured by a Beechcraft King Air A90 flown by Transair pilot Pierre Dill and ferry pilot Douglas Hinton. Object of the competition was to travel as great a distance as possible within a 48-hour time limit. The Women's Division of the Washington National Air Races was won by Mrs. Judy Wagner of Palos Verdes Estates, California, flying a 1959 Model K35 Bonanza. Mrs. Wagner, in winning the race, outdistanced another plane which had just established a new world's speed record for planes in its class.

The National Aeronautic Association wired President O. A. Beech: "Pleased to advise that Robert and Joan Wallick flying Beech Baron C55 successfully completed a round-the-world flight Manila to Manila June 7. Official records for speed around the world for piston engine airplanes in Classes C-1 (unrestricted weight) and C-1D (3,858 to 6,614 pounds) claimed with the Federation Aeronautic Internationale. Total elapsed time 5 days, 6 hours, 17 minutes, and 10 seconds." The Wallicks' flight, sponsored by the Beechcraft distributor in the Philippines, Campos Rueda & Sons, Inc., topped a previous record of 8 days, 18 hours, 35 minutes, and 57 seconds.

Beech Aircraft was named one of 15 companies receiving special honors for outstanding product quality performance in the manufacture of parts for the Bell Helicopter UH-1 Iroquois in service with the U.S. Army in Vietnam. Of the literally hundreds of companies supplying parts and assemblies for the Bell Helicopter, only 15 companies were awarded Bell's Gold Rotor.

During these busy weeks there were moments for reminiscing. Beech Aircraft Corporation, President O. A. Beech, and the late Walter H. Beech were honored during ceremonies at the U. S. Naval Air Station, Pensacola, Florida where a scale model Beechcraft T-34 Mentor was presented to the museum. Mrs. Beech was honored as a Naval Aviation Museum Association Life Time Member for her individual contributions to naval aviation. For his contributions to naval aviation — the Model 17, the SNB and JRB series of the Model 18, and the T-34 Mentor — Walter H. Beech was made a Memorial Member. Simultaneously, Beech Aircraft Corporation also became the first Corporate Member of the Naval Aviation Museum.

The Beechcraft Employees Flying Club observed its 25th year, marking it one of the oldest — perhaps, the oldest — continuously active flying clubs in existence. Hundreds of pilots had been trained in the club's airplanes since 1941. On the 25th anniversary, the club's 98 members could boast of a fleet of seven Beechcrafts — two Bonanzas, a Debonair and four Musketeers.

Another Model 17 homecoming in mid-summer attracted much attention to the Beech flight line. In addition to the classic Model 17 staggerwings built in the thirties and forties, a 1929 open cockpit Series D4000 Travel Air biplane joined the display. President O. A. Beech and 16 other Beechcrafters who had been associated with both Travel Air Manufacturing and Beechcraft during Model 17 production particularly enjoyed the Staggerwing Club's fly-in at Beech Field.

"Just for Fun." This was Marion Hart's answer to newsmen who questioned her on why she, a 74-year-old woman, would fly the Atlantic Ocean all alone in a five-year-old airplane. Mrs. Hart possibly became the oldest woman to fly the Atlantic Ocean solo when she made her vacation jaunt to Europe in her Beechcraft Bonanza. She was completely surprised at the sensation she created when she landed at London Airport. The Bonanza was equipped with auxiliary fuel tanks which provided a range of 2,500 miles.

"I just sat back and watched the instruments for most of the 11 hours it took to cross the Atlantic," she said. "I took the easy route by Iceland and Scotland. Nobody could object to what I did. I'm an experienced pilot, I have a well-equipped plane and it's much easier than driving a car."

In September Beech Aircraft concluded the largest fiscal year in company history and delivered the 25,000th Beechcraft. Sales topped $164 million, a tremendous increase over the $122 million of the previous year. Commercial sales alone during fiscal 1966 were $100 million. The historic delivery of the 25,000th plane to be built by Beechcraft took place at the Beechcraft factory when Olive Ann Beech presented a new King Air to Westinghouse Electric Corporation. Accepting the plane was Lamar P. McLeod, vice president.

A 40-month agreement between District No. 70 of the International Association of Machinists and Aerospace Workers and Beech Aircraft Corporation went into effect July 4. A general wage increase of 12¢ an hour and an eighth holiday were among the provisions.

A $9,800,000 U.S. Army contract for production of 48 U-21 utility aircraft of twin-engine, turbine-power design and for training of pilots and mechanics was announced early in October. The planes would be modifications of the Beech NU-8F series developed in 1963.

Salesmen attending the 1967 International Sales Spectacular in Wichita October 24 and 25 honored two longtime members of the Beechcraft domestic sales organization. Jess M. Childress, president of Southern Airways Beechcraft, Inc. at Atlanta, Georgia, was named Man of the Year for 1966. Childress had been a key factor in the development of Southern Airways Beechcraft throughout its 20-year existence. The Beechcraft's President's Award was presented to aviation leader Henry B. DuPont. DuPont, the major stockholder in Atlantic New York — Inc., Beechcraft distributor for the New York area, had been associated with Beech since 1938, longer than any other distributor.

The 600 officials and salesmen were briefed during the musical extravaganza on two new Beechcrafts scheduled to enter the general aviation market within the next few months. The new aircraft were the Model 60 Beechcraft Duke and the 300 mph Turbo Baron 56TC, the fastest piston engine production airplane in the world. Other introductions included a streamlined Beechcraft Queen Air A65 with a swept tail and a six-place, two-door Beechcraft Musketeer III.

On December 29, the Duke, a new pressurized turbo-charged medium twin, completed its first flight following brief ceremonies at Beech Field. Between the Baron and the Queen Air in size,

Record-breaking round-the-world flight of 23,629 miles in 5 days 6 hours 17 minutes was made by Bob and Joan Wallick in their Beechcraft ("Philippine") Baron June 2-7, 1966. (Page 268)

Pictured at the 1967 Sales Spectacular: Henry B. DuPont, Atlantic Aircraft Sales Corp., recipient of President's Award; Frank E. Hedrick, Beech executive vice president; Jess M. Childress, Southern Airways Beechcraft, recipient of Man of the Year Award; O. A. Beech; Frank Hulse, South Airways Beechcraft; and Wyman Henry, Beech vice president - marketing.

Officials of Japan Air Lines took delivery of the first of a fleet of seven Super H18 Beechcrafts — enlarging its existing fleet of 3 Queen Airs and a leased Super 18. (Page 273)

271

Mary Lynn Pitt (at right) was a co-hostess with her mother, Mrs. O. A. Beech, to King Air owners Mr. and Mrs. Reginald Sinclaire.

New Beechcraft Model 60 Duke, a pressurized six-place, turbo-powered twin, completed its first flight December 29, 1966.

Frank E. Hedrick, executive vice president, addressed group attending delivery of first Beechcraft U-21A utility aircraft to U. S. Army. (Page 274)

the Duke had a gross weight of 6,400 pounds and was powered by twin turbo-charged 380 hp Lycoming engines. Range would be approximately 1,000 miles.

The year 1966 would end with Beechcraft offering 15 production models to businessmen, with others such as the Duke in development and testing programs. Orders for the top plane in the line, the King Air, exceeded $24 million alone, with 216 already delivered. Frank E. Hedrick could say with confidence, "The King Air is by far the aviation industry's sales leader among corporate twin aircraft throughout the free world. This enviable sales record has been established in the face of the strongest competition in aviation history. Against new, smaller, lower-cost twins on one hand and the glamorous, high speed pure jets on the other, the King Air has literally flown away from all competition to gain an unparalleled record of popularity and acceptance. And demand for the King Air continues, with an increasing number of customers either placing orders or taking delivery of their second, third, fourth and even sixth King Air."

Textron's Bell Helicopter Company awarded Beech a $2.6 million contract for fabrication of the complete airframe for the new Model 206 Jet Ranger helicopter.

The Beechcraft King Air might be making the current sales headlines but another Beechcraft was making sales history. The Beechcraft 18 series went into its 30th sales year in 1967 with an order from Japan Air Lines for seven tri-gear Super H18s. This classic Beechcraft would be used by the air carrier as a basic multi-engine training plane. This airline also operated three Queen Airs and a leased Super 18 in its training operations.

The first sale of Beechcraft's high performance AQM-37A missile target to a foreign government was announced in February by Michael G. Neuburger, vice president - export sales. The Defense Ministry of the United Kingdom in a $1 million plus contract ordered the missile targets for British guided weapon trials.

Confirmation of her appointment by President Johnson to the President's Commission on White House Fellows was received by O. A. Beech in March. Mrs. Beech succeeded Senator Margaret Chase Smith of Maine on the 12-member commission.

The commission was charged with annually selecting 18 young men and women to serve at high levels within the executive branch of the government, particularly in association with the Vice President and with members of the cabinet.

And in April, Beechcrafters observed the 35th anniversary of the founding of their company. Thousands of employees and their families toured the major facilities at Wichita, Liberal, Boulder and Salina. Displays added interest to the tours which were enjoyed by many guests as well as families. The company's first 35-year service award recipient, O. A. Beech, would later be honored with the gift of a tea set of hammered silver. The company commissioned Rudolph Brom to produce the set for Mrs. Beech.

Three new members were appointed to the executive committee. Wyman L. Henry, vice president - marketing; James N. Lew, vice president - engineering; and John A. Elliott, secretary-treasurer, were already members of the board of directors and joined President O. A. Beech and Executive Vice President Frank E. Hedrick on the executive committee.

A $7,833,000 extension to a contract for production of the new twin-engine turboprop powered U-21A utility aircraft for the U.S. Army was announced in April. The extension covered an additional 40 aircraft. The U-21A was an outgrowth of the Beechcraft NU-8F developed for the Army in 1963 and was capable of accommodating up to ten combat troops or six to eight persons plus crew of two in varied interior arrangements. First deliveries under the original contract were made in May. In August, these Beechcrafts would be serving in Vietnam.

Employment Fellowships were made available for ten school teachers involved in aviation education. The 10-week summer employment program would acquaint the teacher with the aircraft industry through job placement, plus information sessions by specialists in engineering, industrial relations, management, marketing, and manufacturing. The program was created by Beechcraft's newly-organized Aviation Education Department to help teachers in their instruction of aviation classes.

Production plans for the largest airplane yet to be marketed by Beechcraft were announced in May by Wyman L. Henry at a press conference in Washington, D. C. Production of the

17-place turbine-powered Beechcraft 99 airliner — designed specifically for the scheduled airline and scheduled air taxi market — was planned for Spring, 1968. Price of the all-new Beechcraft 99 would range from $350,000 to $400,000, depending on operational equipment programmed by the individual airline operator. The Beechcraft 99 — powered by twin Pratt & Whitney PT6A-20 turbine engines similar to the powerplants of the Beechcraft King Air and U.S. Army U-21A — would cruise at 250 mph fully loaded and offer 24 per cent greater capacity in ton-miles than the venerable Douglas DC-3. The Beechcraft 99 would complement the 11-place Beechcraft Queen Airliner then in service with air carrier operators in 15 countries.

William M. Morgan, retired U.S. Air Force Major General who had served as vice president and assistant to the president, was appointed to the position of vice president - product reliability. He had been associated with development of the weapon system management concept on such projects as the AQM-37A missile target and the SAM-D projects.

Two physicians, Dr. Francis X. Sommer of Barbourville, Kentucky, and Dr. John Rieger of Los Gatos, California, completed an 18,000-mile round-the-world trip in a Beechcraft S35 Bonanza. Earlier the two men had completed the 3,186 nautical mile cross-Atlantic flight, using the same route that Charles A. Lindbergh had flown 40 years previously, in 19 hours, 54 minutes, and 32 seconds. Lindbergh's flight had taken 33 hours, 29 minutes, and 30 seconds from Roosevelt Field, only a few miles from Kennedy where the physicians had departed.

The 1,000th Musketeer to be manufactured at Beechcraft's Liberal Division was delivered in July. Liberal Mayor Lloyd Harp delivered the Musketeer Custom III to David H. Werrett, general manager of Central Bucks Aero, Inc., a Beechcraft dealer in Doylestown, Pennsylvania. This delivery marked the third year of production of the Beechcraft Musketeer at Liberal and the 1,554th production model in the Musketeer series since its introduction in 1962.

A high performance, rocket-powered missile target for the U.S. Air Force's Armament Laboratory at Eglin Air Force Base, Florida, was revealed by Roy H. McGregor, vice president of aerospace marketing and contracts, in late summer. Named

Sandpiper, the new missile was designed to simulate a wide variety of aircraft and missile threats. Powered by a hybrid engine that used both solid and liquid propellants, the Sandpiper would reach speeds up to Mach 4 and altitudes up to 90,000 feet. The test bed vehicle combined the newly-developed engine system with the airframe of the AQM-37A supersonic target missile.

When Mrs. Judy Wagner touched down in her Beechcraft Bonanza K35 at the Torrance, California, airport July 13, the landing marked her second major race victory of the year. With an elapsed time of 12 hours, 27 minutes, and 59 seconds on her flight from Atlantic City to Torrance, Mrs. Wagner had won the 1967 Powder Puff Derby. Earlier in the year, she had captured first place with the Bonanza in the 17th annual Angel Derby race from Montreal to Miami. The tall, attractive blonde and her oral surgeon husband would later attend the Beechcraft International Sales Spectacular where she would receive special recognition.

Beech Aircraft was named by Secretary of Commerce Alexander B. Trowbridge to receive President Johnson's Export "E" Certificate for foreign sales expansion. Presentation of the award to Mrs. O. A. Beech was made on September 25 in the Secretary of Commerce's office with Frank E. Hedrick, executive vice president; Michael G. Neuburger, vice president - export sales; Kansas congressmen; and officials of the Federal Aviation Agency and Department of Transportation present. In response to the award announcement, Mrs. Beech said, "The 'E' Award is a tribute to the Beechcraft export department's past growth, and a challenge to even greater achievements in the future. We are looking ahead to the day when the full potential of the expansion of general aviation throughout the free world is realized." Beechcraft's export sales in the previous five years had increased 168 per cent, from $9,146,286 in fiscal 1962 to $24,522,512 during the year just completed.

Additional honors followed within the week when Beech Aircraft was saluted with a banquet in New York City by the Newcomen Society in North America. Approximately 750 people attended the program at which Mrs. O. A. Beech and Frank E. Hedrick were the guests of honor. Mr. Hedrick addressed the

Beech Aircraft's first 35-year service award was given Mrs. O. A. Beech in the form of a silver tea service, presented by Frank E. Hedrick, executive vice president. (Page 274)

Delivery of the distinguished Newcomen Society Address by Frank E. Hedrick was a thrill for his wife, Betty, surpassed only by his election in 1968 to serve as third president of the Beech Aircraft Corporation.

Five of a fleet of
16 Model 33
Beechcrafts or-
dered by Luft-
hansa Airlines of
Germany for pilot
training formed a
neat echelon.
(Page 263)

U21A turboprop
Beechcrafts headed
for U. S. Army
service in Viet-
nam formed a
precision lineup
at Beech field.
(Page 274)

Three Queen Airs
were among Beech-
crafts purchased
by Lockheed
Missiles and
Space Company.

group, relating the history of Beechcraft. The Newcomen Society is dedicated to the preservation of Material History, and periodically honors leaders from the industrial fields of transportation, communication, utilities, mining, agriculture, finance, economics, insurance, education, invention, and law. The Society's name perpetuates the life and work of Thomas Newcomen, a British pioneer in development of the steam engine in the mid and late 1700's.

Establishment of a major aircraft sales and service center in Denver, Colorado was announced in October. The facility would serve a five-state area. Beechcraft purchased the buildings, fixtures, tools, and other physical property on approximately 16 acres of land on the south side of Denver's Stapleton Airport. Beech Aircraft had previously entered the retail aircraft sales and service market through facilities in Houston, Wichita, and Van Nuys.

A $1 million order for 12 Beechcraft C55 Barons by the College of Air Training at Hamble, England, was announced in early October by Michael G. Neuburger, vice president - export sales. Established in 1960, the College of Air Training was designed as a major flight instruction facility to provide pilots for British airlines. This was the largest single order of Beechcrafts sold to a Great Britain customer.

Record sales in excess of $174 million for fiscal year 1967 which ended September 30, could be reported by Beech Aircraft. Final earnings after taxes were estimated to exceed $3 per share. Of this $174 million total sales, approximately $104 million were commercial sales and $70 million military and aerospace sales. The $174 million total reflected a steady growth when compared with the $164 million total of 1966 and $122 million of 1965.

A new Beechcraft Training Center to consolidate all customer training operations was established in October. The new instruction center for customer maintenance and pilot training was established in a building recently acquired by Beechcraft. The one story facility had been remodeled to include five classrooms, administrative offices, reception lounge, storage facilities, a snack bar, and private office for the use of customers. One classroom was devoted exclusively to the Beechcraft developed King Air cockpit simulator for pilot instruction and to maintenance training aids. Approximately 100 students a month were attending various technical courses offered by the staff of seven full-time instructors.

The largest sales gathering in Beechcraft history brought 900 members of the Beechcraft team from throughout the United States and 15 foreign countries to Wichita in October. The event was the third annual Beechcraft International Sales Spectacular. Those attending heard presentations by product managers as well as by representatives of avionics, parts and service, styling, advertising, and sales promotion concerning the 19-model 1968 lines. The speakers were backed by special stage productions featuring a Broadway cast.

Scheduled for delivery early in 1968, the new pressurized, four to six-place Beechcraft Model 60 Duke was included in a fly-by demonstration during the two-day meeting. Another feature of the meeting was the announcement of the addition to the Bonanza line of the new E33A and E33, refined versions of the former Debonair. The new models would be called Bonanzas, though they would retain the vertical stabilizer rather than the familiar Bonanza V tail. Honored as Beechcraft Man of the Year at closing ceremonies of the Spectacular was Gerald Wilmot, president and general manager of Page Airways, Inc., the company's distributor in Rochester, New York.

As the year ended, Beech Aircraft could announce contracts of $12 million for additional sub-assemblies for the McDonnell Douglas F-4 jet fighter-bombers and $4.7 million for approximately 300 U.S. Navy AQM-37A supersonic target missiles.

At the meeting of stockholders December 21, Frank E. Hedrick, executive vice president, forecast record corporate and commercial product sales for the third straight year in fiscal 1968. Total corporate sales from $175 to $185 million and commercial product sales approximating $120 million were predicted.

Chapter 31

On January 18, 1968, Mrs. O. A. Beech announced an historic move in turning over the presidency of Beech Aircraft Corpora-

Mike Murphy, at left, manager of aviation division, Marathon Oil Company, and pilot Barrie E. Lineken with one of the company's fleet of six Beechcraft King Airs.

Westinghouse Electric Corporation flight crew, from left, R. J. Nagel, Hal Goff and A. Treylinek, took delivery of one of four Beechcraft King Airs purchased by Westinghouse. Don Benes, Beech marketing representative, offers congratulations.

World War II user of government-assigned UC-45A Beechcrafts, General Motors Corporation enlarged its King Air fleet to six Model 90s with the delivery of these four units.

U. S. Senator Mike Monroney of Oklahoma was a speaker at the May 2, 1968 certification ceremonies for the Beechcraft turbo-prop Model 99 17-place airliner. Background: Two of 14 Model 99s ordered by Commuter Airlines of Chicago.

Keys to one of seven Beechcraft King Airs delivered to the Canadian Department of Transport are handed to Moe Louch, second from right, chief of the flight service division, by R. G. Oestreicher, Beech Export Sales regional manager. Jimmy Dale, at left, executive pilot, and W. A. Falconer, of Tele-communications Branch, were crew members on delivery flight.

Instructors and students at Big Bend Community College, Moses Lake, Washington, prepare for flights in the college's Beechcraft Muske-teer training fleet.

tion to Frank E. Hedrick, Executive Vice President since 1960. Mrs. Beech, after nearly two decades of service as President since 1950, would continue as Chairman of the Board and Chief Executive Officer.

Making this step known at the annual management dinner of the Beechcraft Supervisors Club, Mrs. Beech said:

"On behalf of the Board of Directors, I want to introduce to you your new President, Frank E. Hedrick. It is with great pride that I turn the presidency over to him. I know that his able and dedicated leadership of the years past will afford him the inspiration and strength to guide Beech Aircraft to even greater achievements."

There were good reasons for Mrs. Beech's confidence in this choice. Frank E. Hedrick had been associated with the management of Beech Aircraft for nearly 29 years. He joined the company in 1940 as Coordinator and Assistant to the General Manager.

During the stressful World War II period, he was instrumental in establishing one of the most favorable labor-management relationships in American industry and in accomplishing record-setting defense production.

In recognition of his performance he was in 1945 promoted to Vice President - Coordinator. This advancement was followed in 1950 by his election to the company's board of directors and executive committee.

Advanced to Executive Vice President in 1960, Hedrick was a key participant in the long-range planning which guided Beech Aircraft to the fore in diversified aviation and aerospace fields.

Active as an officer and director in all Beech Aircraft subsidiaries, he had also served since 1966 in major capacities with the Aerospace Industries Association of America. Other affiliations included memberships on the directorates of the First National Bank in Wichita, the Southwest Grease and Oil Corporation of Wichita, and the Wichita Area Chamber of Commerce. He was a past president of St. Joseph's Hospital, and active in many other civic and industry-related organizations. Like his predecessor, the third president of the Beech Aircraft Corporation was a person with far-ranging interests and capabilities.

Another event of 1968 seemed sure to rank as a significant milestone in the company's growth. Its Board of Directors, headed by O. A. Beech as Chairman, effected a three-for-two split of its common stock and registered a public offering of $30 million in convertible debentures. The debentures offering was the first major long-term financing in Beech Aircraft's history. The debentures met an excellent market reception and quickly commanded an appreciable premium after their issuance. Funds received from the debentures were to provide financial strength for growth programs affecting immediate and future developments in commercial and military-aerospace production.

The purpose of this step was to provide a solid base for the company's imaginative yet consistently practical planning. Its timing was perfect. Interest rates were climbing fast. Within less than a year, the prime rate for commercial loans was to hit an all-time record high of 8½ percent; and long-term capital funds were to command corresponding premiums. Beech Aircraft had, in one stroke, enhanced the marketability of its ownership equities; and had acquired at reasonable costs the capital funds needed to fulfill its plans. The Beech combination of vision, daring, and good Kansas common sense had scored another winning coup.

Early in the calendar year 1968, it became clear that Beech management planning for full and well-balanced utilization of the company's diversified capabilities would be handily fulfilled. A notable step toward this end came with the receipt on March 27 of a $75 million contract award from Bell Helicopter. This contract called for Beech Aircraft to fabricate the complete airframe for Bell's turbine-powered JetRanger Helicopter in three versions; commercial, U. S. Army's light observation series, and U. S. Navy trainer.

Deliveries on this, the largest single subcontract in Beech Aircraft's history, were to span a five-year period. It was an extension of a $2.6 million contract under which Beech Aircraft was then producing JetRanger 206A airframes for Bell.

A related event explained Bell's choice of contractors for this important production assignment, covering more than 4,000 complete airframes. For the second consecutive year, Beech Aircraft received the Bell Helicopter Company's annual Gold

284

Rotor Award for production excellence. It was conferred for on-time quality deliveries of 74 Beech-built components for Bell's UH-1 "Huey" series helicopter. And it was more importantly reaffirmed a few months later, when in August a $6.3 million follow-on contract came from Bell for more UH-1 components. This brought the total UH-1 volume to more than $25 million.

Another August addition to the company's backlog of subcontracts was a $6 million follow-on contract from McDonnell-Douglas. It extended through December 1969 the Beech Aircraft program of subassemblies production for the F-4 Phantom Jet series; enlarged to $18 million its total of F-4 contracts received in fiscal 1968; and, as the sixth such contract from the F-4's prime contractor, brought to a grand total of more than $66 million Beech Aircraft's participation in Phantom Jet production.

Production for the supersonic F-4 fighter and predominantly military helicopter programs was by no means the whole of Beech Aircraft's contributions to national defense during the year. Events underlined the success of the company's engineering and production diversification into the highly specialized field of target missiles — vital components in keeping America's fighting units "combat ready" as its own and its adversaries' supersonic weapons systems became increasingly complex and sophisticated.

Production of the Beechcraft U. S. Army MQM-61A Cardinal target missile was continued into 1969 with the awarding at mid-year of a follow-on order from the Army. This ground-launched, remote control, recoverable propeller-driven target was a refined version of the original "littlest Beechcraft", the KDB-1/MQM39A, which had won a U. S. Navy design competition in 1955, operating at altitudes above 40,000 feet and speeds of more than 350 miles per hour. The mid-1968 order brought total production to more than 2,000 and revenue, with spares and related services, to more than $43 million since the first order was placed in 1955.

The supersonic Beechcraft AQM-37A was also assured a place in production through August 1970. An add-on contract received from the U. S. Navy in October for $5.8 million enlarged the backlog for this item to $10.5 million. Transfer of production from Wichita to the Boulder Division in June represented a challenge to Colorado Beechcrafters which they met with delivery of the first completed target in August, ahead of schedule.

At that time the fastest and highest-flying target missile in the United States military inventory, the Beech-designed AQM-37A simulated the performance of high speed jet aircraft with a speed of Mach 3 and altitude capabilities of nearly 90,000 feet. The Stiletto, a modified version of this target, which had been ordered by the Defense Ministry of the United Kingdom in 1967, was successfully test flown off the coast of Wales in 1968.

The Sandpiper, Beech-designed replacement for the high-flying AQM-37A, was also produced in a testbed developmental version for the U. S. Air Force Armament Laboratory, and successfully test flown in 1968 at Eglin Air Force Base, Florida. With a newly-designed hybrid engine using both solid and liquid propellants, the Sandpiper seemed sure to make good its planned speed of Mach 4 and 90,000-foot altitude in its production version. Performance of the unmanned Beechcrafts would continue to be outstanding, it appeared — like that of the more conventional piloted Beechcrafts.

Production on U. S. Army contracts for the U-21A utility aircraft, commenced in 1967, was completed in April 1968. A total of 129 units, a military version of the turbine-powered Beechcraft King Air, went into Army service — many into combat zone flying in Vietnam — under these contracts.

In a personal vein, no event of the year could possibly outrank the arrival on March 18 of little Miss Jennifer Gwen Pitt. Daughter of Mary Lynn and John E. H. Pitt, and grand-daughter of Mrs. Beech, the newest member of the Beech family's third generation weighed in at an optimum 7 pounds 4 ounces at birth in Bremen, West Germany. Like any concerned grandparent, the Chairman of the Board of the Beech Aircraft Corporation stood nearby, and was very much relieved and proud of the wholly successful result of the stork flight.

On May 14 the national Angel Flight Award for 1968, a large

286

President Frank E. Hedrick accepted the second Gold Rotor award given by Bell Helicopter to Beech Aircraft as a token of good performance on contracts that were to total more than $100 million ... (Pages 284, 285)

and received for Beech Aircraft the Industry Award for 1968 conferred by the International Exposition of Flight. (Page 290)

Seven weeks old when this picture was taken, Jennifer Gwen was very much the pride and joy of her mother, Mary Lynn and her grandmother, Mrs. Beech.

Mrs. O. A. Beech was honored with a plaque from the Kansas Press Women at the Wichita convention of the National Federation of Press Women . . .

and received the national Angel Flight Award for 1968 from members of Wichita State University's Olive Ann Beech chapter, representing the nation-wide organization.

Welcomed by air taxi and charter operators to the tune of $3.5 million in orders in less than six months was the new 6-place Beechcraft Bonanza Model 36 certificated in May 1968.

288

engraved silver bowl, was presented to Mrs. Beech in recognition of her contributions to that organization. Angel Flight, an auxiliary of the Arnold Air Society honorary scholastic organization for Air Force ROTC members, numbers some 6,000 coed members in the nation's colleges and universities. Members of Olive Ann Beech chapter of Angel Flight at Wichita State University presented the award on behalf of the national staff. The WSU squadron of the Arnold Air Society bears the name of Walter H. Beech.

And at the annual convention of the National Federation of Press Women held in Wichita, Mrs. Beech was honored June 13 by the Kansas Press Women for her support of the organization's scholarship program. A plaque was presented to her in recognition of her active interest.

Beech Aircraft shared in, and contributed to a remarkable triple victory scored by three outstanding women pilots in the 18th Angel Derby held April 22-25 over a 2,403-mile course across five Latin-American countries. First, second and third places in the cross-country competition were swept clean by two Beechcraft Bonanzas and a Beechcraft Musketeer. Judy Wagner won first place in her K35 Bonanza, Janis Hobbs placed second in a Musketeer, and Pat McEwen of Wichita, Kansas won third place in her S35 Bonanza. "Just like old times", observers said, "It takes a Beechcraft to beat a Beechcraft!"

The triple air race win was only one of many highlights in a year that saw the rise of the Beechcraft "Air Fleet of American Business" to new peaks of eminence. New models introduced during the year met with an excellent reception in the general aviation marketplace; orders for Model 18's extended this series into its 32nd consecutive year of production as of 1969; and the Beechcraft King Air, for the fourth year, led all turbine-powered corporate aircraft in sales.

On May 2, at certification ceremonies at Beech Aircraft, the first production model of the Beechcraft 99 Airliner was delivered to Commuter Airlines of Chicago. It was one of 14 Model 99's ordered by that airline; and before the year was over, deliveries of the 17-place turboprop airliner were to exceed a value of $16½ million, to a total of 21 different third-level airline customers.

Also certificated in May was the new six-place Bonanza 36.

Designed specifically for the utility aircraft and air taxi operator, the big new Bonanza combined a top speed of 204 mph with a range of nearly 1,000 miles, including reserves, and a useful load capacity of 1,620 pounds or six passengers. Aft double doors, folding and quick-removable seats, and handsome but sturdy interior trim provided quick convertibility to all or part-cargo carrying service. Offered for sale in mid-June, the Model 36 in less than six months attained a total volume of some $3.5 million to 80 customers.

The International Exposition of Flight on May 25 honored Beech Aircraft with its Industry Award for 1968. Cited by IEF in the award, which was accepted by President Frank E. Hedrick at ceremonies in Las Vegas, were the ". . . imagination and courage which Beech Aircraft has shown in the current controversy for airspace usage and for developing the Beechcraft 99 Airliner . . ."

Orders were received in June for 10 Beechcraft Super H18's for delivery to Japan. Three were from Japan Air Lines (JAL), bringing its fleet of Super H18's to a total of 13. Others were for another major Japanese airline and for three Japanese government agencies, long-time users of the original Twin Beech. The $2 million sale extended production of the Model 18 series into 1969, its 32nd year, making it even more preeminently the longest-lived airplane design in all aviation history. With these deliveries, total sales of the Model 18 series would reach approximately $430 million.

The twin-engine, pressurized Beechcraft Duke was delivered to customers in June and final assembly of the new aircraft was transferred from Wichita to the Salina Division.

Following delivery of the 400th Beechcraft King Air to Gerber Products Company in September, it was revealed that the King Air, for the fourth year, continued as the undisputed sales leader among turbine-powered corporate aircraft, accounting for nearly 77 percent of all deliveries in its class.

Aerobatic versions of the Beechcraft Musketeer Sport and Custom Models and the E33B and E33C Bonanzas, introduced in 1968, offered the convenience of factory package procurement to flight training operators and pilots desiring to maximize their aeronautical skills and enhanced sales of these models. The optional aerobatic package included a "G" meter, quick-release right-hand door, and shoulder harnesses for pilot and co-pilot. It fully certified each model under Part 3 of the Federal Air Regulations for aerobatics, including rolls, Immelman turns, loops, spins, chandelles, limited inverted flight and other maneuvers. No changes were required in the basic aircraft structure, since all Beechcrafts had always been built to meet or exceed FAA strength requirements for utility aircraft — one reason for their preference among professional and highly experienced pilots.

Stellar attraction at the 21st annual convention of the National Business Aircraft Association at Houston, Texas in October was the new Beechcraft 99 Executive corporate transport. The 250 mph turbine-powered Beechcraft was a deluxe 10-place, 3-compartment version of the Model 99 airliner, which at the time had already proved itself in 10,000 hours of flight serving 18 commuter airlines from coast to coast since its first deliveries in May. Available with full airliner equipment, including radar, the Beechcraft 99 Executive held the center of the stage among the 1,500 NBAA members present; and more importantly, developed many future sales for Beech Aircraft.

At the 1969 Beechcraft International Sales Spectacular, held at the Beech Activity Center in Wichita October 20-22, some 1,000 distributors, dealers and guests thrilled to the introduction of the most complete line of Beechcrafts in the company's 36-year history. Twenty single-engine and twin-engine Beechcraft models covered virtually the full spectrum of general aviation and business needs. They ranged in size from two-place trainers to a 17-place twin turboprop airliner and corporate transport. The models available covered all price and performance requirements of the most important segments of the market. There were piston-powered and turbine-powered Beechcrafts. All had one big thing in common. Every airplane was a Beechcraft — with all that the name had come to stand for all over the world. It was not surprising, then, that the meeting was the most enthusiastic in the company's history; and that the 1969 sales goal of $200 million was acclaimed as a realistic one by those present. Knowing that gross sales for 1968 were fulfilling that year's goal, the Beech sales organization left the Sales Spectacular determined to meet and surpass the 1969 projection.

From the viewpoint of the commercial sales that comprised two-thirds of the company's planned dollar volume, the year of 1968 took shape as the best on record. In a wider field possessed of universal historic significance — that of meeting the stated goal of the United States of America to put a man on the moon before the end of the decade — the progress made in 1968, with the help of vital elements designed and built by Beech Aircraft, was consistently excellent.

The successful probing flight of NASA's Apollo 4 spacecraft in November 1967 had earned a "man-rated" designation for the Beech life support system installed in the Apollo service module. This highly sophisticated cryogenic gas storage system, designed and built at Beech-Boulder for North American Rockwell's Space Division, had the task of supplying oxygen to the environmental system of the command module, and hydrogen and oxygen to the fuel cells for electrical power and drinking water. The Beech system was to furnish every breath that the astronauts took, throughout long days and nights in the void of space; and to feed oxygen and hydrogen to assure unfailing electrical power for Apollo's many complex systems from its fuel cells. It was the first of Apollo's 13 major subsystems to be man-rated by the National Aeronautics and Space Administration after the Apollo 4 test results were analyzed.

The follow-on Apollo 5 test flight on January 22 re-verified the performance of the Beech life support system. It also provided an in-use test of the aerospace ground support equipment designed and built at Beech-Boulder under a contract with Grumman Aircraft Engineering Corporation, builders of the Lunar Module (LM) of the Apollo spacecraft system. Beech Aircraft's part was to supply the supercritical helium conditioning units and liquid helium storage units for the LM descent propellant pressurization system. Beech Aircraft's LM equipment operated perfectly in support of the Apollo 5 flight.

The series of manned Apollo flights that followed in 1968 — Apollo 6 in April, Apollo 7 in October, and Apollo 8 in December, marking man's first approach to the moon — thrilled the world. Their success was a special source of pride to Beech Aircraft and its people. At the time the company first entered the

292

field of space vehicle support in 1954, a companion slogan to its then soundly proven phrase, "The world is small when you fly a Beechcraft" had been suggested: "Space is in reach — with support from Beech Aircraft." Fourteen years ago, the new slogan had seemed wildly visionary. Now it was an accomplished fact. And the greatest of all man's adventures seemed assured: his landing on the moon.

Beech Aircraft had aimed high in 1968 — in every way. And hit its targets. In December 1967 management projections called for a total volume of $175 million for fiscal 1968 — $120 million in commercial sales. Closing of the books on September 30, 1968 revealed an actual volume for the fiscal year of $176.8 million — commercial sales of $122.3 million — a new all-time high. And a new quarterly sales record was established in the final three months of the calendar year: Total manufacturing sales of $50,-617,018 and commercial sales of $37,117,428. Export sales of $29,004,401 marked a new record for any one 12-month period. The year was more than good. It was great, in a superlative degree. And the best seemed yet to come.

Chapter 32

Beech Aircraft's thirty-seventh year opened in 1969 with days that were clear, cold and filled with action. Typical of its pace was the 975-mile delivery flight of a new pressurized Beechcraft Duke to York, Pa. at a speed made good of 299 miles per hour. Fast, efficient movement was the order of the day in all divisions and all activities — production, sales, and planning ahead.

Completed at Wichita in mid-January was a new 43,200 sq. ft. paint building that would facilitate the task of turning out Beechcrafts with the most handsome and durable finish known to the industry. Applying the techniques used in designing the controlled-environment "clean rooms" at Beech-Boulder, its entire supply of heated or cooled air was so closely filtered as to be practically dust-free. It used 86 kilowatts of color-corrected illumination to assure rigid quality control and uniform matching of desired colors.

An addition to an earlier evaluation purchase came from the Federal Republic of Germany, calling for $930,000 worth of Beechcraft Cardinal 1025 propeller-driven target missiles. The newest version of the unmanned "littlest Beechcraft" had earned preference in the land where the V-1 and V-2 missiles of World War II had been developed. The add-on order represented a distinct tribute to American technology and to Beech Aircraft in particular.

This tribute was followed in March by a more individualized compliment tendered to the company's co-founder and Chairman of the Board, Mrs. O. A. Beech. It was an invitation to serve on the advisory board of two prominent New York City-based organizations — Marine Midland International Corporation, and Marine Midland Overseas Corporation. Their interests spanned several continents, ranging from Europe to the Far East. In accepting, Mrs. Beech joined a select group whose members included eminent personages in international trade and finance.

The event was a significant measure of the esteem in which Beech Aircraft and its management were held in high-level financial circles. It acknowledged the company's conspicuous success in building up export sales of its products, and the leadership supplied by Mrs. Beech in establishing and maintaining the financial soundness so notably demonstrated in its timely and well-received 1968 issue of $30 million in debentures.

Dedication of a 10,000 sq. ft. addition to the Beechcrafters Activity Center on April 9 brought recognition from the principal speaker, Gordon W. Evans, president of the Kansas Gas & Electric Company, of the active interest shown by Mrs. O. A. Beech in the artistic life of the community and the company. Speaking appreciatively of her services as president of the Wichita Symphony Society and chairman of the board, past president and a trustee of the Wichita Art Association, Evans said Mrs. Beech " . . . has helped Wichita grow into a city which appreciates and fosters art; a city that is interested in more than just business and industry." A plaque was unveiled identifying the warmly attractive new room as the Olive Ann Beech Gallery. Among its purposes would be to serve as a display center for aviation art, photography and memorabilia, and for original paintings by Kansans and other artists. Like the other areas of the Center, it would be

294

open to community service functions when not in use for activities of Beechcrafters and their company.

On April 11 the new Olive Ann Beech Gallery was the setting for the company's annual Service Award ceremonies, honoring employees with 25 years or more of service. The select group who had served Beech Aircraft for 35 years or more grew to a total of 5 persons at this anniversary date. Those with 30 years or more of service totalled 73; with 25 years or more, 954. Attesting the management's high regard for loyal continuity of service and sustained good performance, the new members of the 25-year-and-up group were personally presented with their service awards and gifts by the Chairman of the Board, Mrs. O. A. Beech. It was also noted that at the time, a total of 4481 employees had served Beech Aircraft for 5 years or more — nearly 40% of then current employment. A great many people, the figures suggested, had long considered Beech Aircraft a good place to work. And their loyalty was rewarding to all concerned — to themselves, to the company, and to Beech Aircraft customers all over the world.

Newsworthy examples of mutually rewarding loyalty were also recorded in another vital area — the loyalty of Beech customers to the company's products. Delivery in May of a new Beechcraft Baron D55 to Arthur Godfrey marked the fortieth year of association with Beech-built airplanes on the part of the veteran radio, television, stage and movie personality and life-long aviation booster. The first airplane Godfrey ever flew, in 1929, was an OX-5 Travel Air biplane built by the Travel Air Manufacturing Company when Walter H. Beech was its president. The fast new twin was Godfrey's third Beechcraft. He had previously owned first a Beechcraft Bonanza, then a Beechcraft Travel Air twin.

Another May delivery was that of the 9,000th Beechcraft Bonanza. The V35A model went to Lee D. Hagemeister of Estes Park, Colorado, past president of the International Flying Farmers; and it was the fifth Beechcraft Bonanza he had owned. Beginning his flying career in 1946, he had logged more than 6,000 hours, largely in managing ranch properties in Nebraska, Colorado and Wyoming on which landing strips had been constructed. Bonanza performance had been well tested in Hagemeister's flying over the snow-capped ridges of the Rockies, and high-altitude landings and takeoffs from ranchland strips. It had passed every test.

The Beechcraft Bonanza again made news in June, with the first annual meeting of the American Bonanza Society in Walter H. Beech Hall of the Beechcrafters Activity Center. Like the National Staggerwing Club which had held its first annual convention at Wichita, Kansas in September 1965, this organization was an independent group of aviation enthusiasts, dedicated to the study and preservation of a great classic design in aviation history. The interest of the Staggerwing group centered on the first Beechcrafts – the Model 17 biplanes, of which more than 200 were still in service, out of 781 built during the years from 1932 to 1948.

Unlike the Model 17 Beechcraft, which had been out of production for more than 20 years, the Beechcraft Bonanza was still going strong. First flown in December 1945, it was in its 22nd year of continuous production. Most of the more than 9,000 Bonanzas built were still flying. The Model 35 design had become the symbol of quality among all general aviation aircraft. In both its unique V-tail and conventional empennage versions, its ranking as No. 1 of the world's single-engine airplanes seemed assured for years to come. Now, the loyalty and enthusiasm of its owners was making it a classic – even while the design was still viable and adding further refinements from year to year. The American Bonanza Society was a unique organization. But then, the Beechcraft Bonanza was a unique airplane . . . a classic in its own time.

Deliveries of Super H18 Beechcrafts to Japanese customers in 1969 completed the trilogy of original Beechcraft designs qualified for all-time positions in aviation's permanent Hall of Fame: the Model 17 biplanes, the Model 35 Bonanzas, and the Model 18 twin-engine Beechcrafts. The more than 7,000 Model 18 twins built since 1937, and flown by commercial and military pilots all over the world, had performed in a way to make this design too a classic among the great twin-engine aircraft of all time. And the end was still not in sight for the venerable 32-year-old Model 18, then aviation's longest-lived design by a good 15-year margin over the second-place Piper Cub. In its 1969 version

296

"The air fleet of American business" — twenty outstanding models of Beechcrafts — stood ready for review by Beechcraft distributors and dealers at the 1969 International Sales Spectacular in October 1968. (Page 291)

Arthur Godfrey replaced his Beechcraft Travel Air twin, shown here, with a new Beechcraft Baron in 1969 — continuing his fortieth year of piloting and owning Beech-built airplanes. (Page 295)

Beechcraft Bonanza No. 9,000 was delivered in May 1969 to Lee D. Hagemeister — the fifth Bonanza he had purchased in his 23-year flying career.

On July 20, 1969, man walked on the moon, and came back safely to earth — with support from Beech Aircraft.

The new Beechcraft King Air 100 was introduced on May 23, 1969 as the flagship of the Beechcraft corporate fleet . . . the leader of the Beech Aircraft product line into a future "so exciting it defies definition."

it still had much to offer: a cruising speed of 236 miles per hour, capacity of 11 persons or 4,055 pounds of payload, and a background of countless millions of hours of proven performance and handling ease. Obsolescence overtook such an airplane very slowly indeed. Its engines were the world's best-liked and most fully proven in their class — the 450 hp Pratt & Whitney radial Wasp Juniors. As long as spare engines and parts remained available and production was feasible, the Model 18 Beechcraft would survive — another living classic.

Pleasing as these honors were, Beech Aircraft's major concern was always that of building and selling the finest possible aircraft of the present and the future. If in time they became classics, treasured as examples of man's most nearly perfect artifacts, so much the better. But realistically, production for use and profit was always the name of the game.

An important step in this direction was the unveiling on May 23 of a new corporate flagship — the Beechcraft King Air 100. Introduced at Wichita to more than 300 Beechcraft dealers and distributors and to representatives of national news media, the new series was to be senior companion to the Beechcraft King Air 90 series which had captured 45 percent of the turboprop market since its introduction in 1964.

The Beechcraft King Air 100 would be available with a wide range of executive and airliner interiors, including a 15-place commuter version. With a gross weight of 10,600 pounds, its payload would amount to more than two tons. Featuring twin Pratt & Whitney PA-6A-28 reverse-flow, free-spool turbine engines rated at 680 shaft horsepower each for takeoff, and 620 shaft horsepower for cruising, it would cruise at 287 miles per hour and offer overall performance higher than that of the Beechcraft King Air 90 series, which had earned fame for its ability to operate from short, unimproved fields at elevated altitudes and temperatures.

"It takes a Beechcraft to beat a Beechcraft" was the quarter-century-old saying quoted among members of the Beechcraft King Air 100 preview audience. It was verified by more than $25 million in advance orders placed at the showing for the new models, first deliveries of which were to commence following FAA certification anticipated in July 1969. Another classic

Beechcraft series was in the making. But more importantly, Beech Aircraft was further enlarging the usefulness of its products to its customers.

Joining with other manufacturers in general aviation, Beech Aircraft was a major sponsor of a cooperative industry-wide effort to boost public interest in personal flying throughout the month of June. Under the theme of "Discover Flying", Beech dealers and distributors conducted a vigorous nation-wide promotion which did much to enlist new student pilot starts and publicize the importance of general aviation to the national economy.

Following the introduction of the Beechcraft Musketeer series in 1962, the company's dealers had been in an increasingly favorable position to attract new non-fliers to the pleasures and benefits of personal and business flying. Capitalizing on the experience gained in developing the notably successful Beechcraft Mentor military primary trainers and the Beechcraft Bonanzas, the best of both series had been brought together in Beechcraft Musketeer design — rugged strength to withstand rough use by student pilots, sure and easy response, and typical Beechcraft quality throughout — all at competitive prices. This made it possible for the Beechcraft dealer to invite aviation neophytes to "Go first class — go Beechcraft all the way" from the moment of their first dual training flight to, for some at least, the ultimate moment of Beechcraft King Air flying and ownership. The idea was sound; and it was working well.

America's race for leadership in the conquest of space continued to go smoothly during the moon flights of Apollo 9 on March 4-14 and Apollo 10 on May 18-26. As in previous flights, the support systems and equipment designed and built at Beech-Boulder functioned "A-Okay", as the astronauts would put it. The Beech cryogenic gas storage system located in the Apollo service module performed its vital life-support functions without letup. The lunar module (LM) took on its liquid helium supply from the Beech ground support system without a hitch. All was in readiness for the great adventure.

"It's one small step for a man; one giant leap for mankind." With these words from Apollo astronaut Neil Armstrong as he stepped down from Tranquility Base onto the surface of the moon, the greatest voyage in man's history had reached its goal. The time at Wichita was 3:56 p.m. Sunday, July 20, 1969. As many millions watched and heard the epochal achievement on world-wide television, Beechcrafters felt a special sense of gratitude and pride. With the flight of Apollo 11, America had been first to put a man on the moon; and Beech Aircraft and its people had helped to make it possible. The shape of future voyages into space was not yet firmly predictable. But one thing appeared certain: Wherever man might seek to journey from his home planet Earth, Beech Aircraft would be doing its part to help him arrive and return in safety.

As a prelude to its modest but vital share in the overwhelming Apollo 11 experience, the company had on June 30 reached historic new highs in its own activities. For the first nine months of its 1969 fiscal year, total manufacturing sales of $146,312,355 exceeded by more than 15 percent the $126-plus million of the same period in 1968, and set a new all-time high for the company.

Consolidated sales, including Beech Aircraft and all subsidiaries, totalled $153,319,639 for the nine-month period. Commercial manufacturing sales soared to $111,978,124 for a 31 percent increase over the $85-plus million of 1968, surpassing all previous sales marks for three quarters. Military-aerospace sales zoomed 9.5 percent above the forecast made at the first of the year.

Just when the promise seemed brightest that fiscal 1969 would set new records of accomplishment in all areas, the company's production activities were brought to a halt by the first work stoppage in its history. Spanning the "dog days" of August, a 26-day strike by unionized employees had costly short-range effects on all parties concerned. Its long-range effects, in terms of establishing a more favorable work climate, seemed likely to be, on balance, beneficial. "A fair day's work for a fair day's pay" had been for more than 30 years the essential goal of the contracts negotiated between Beech Aircraft's management and the collective bargaining representatives of its unionized work force. The signing of a new contract, effective through July 1972, reaffirmed and clarified this goal.

Resumption of production at all facilities on September 4 was marked by the inauguration of a carefully planned strike recovery

301

program. Its aims were to make up for lost time by assuring maximally efficient rates of production at the earliest possible time; and to recoup lost earnings and improve long-range earnings prospects through strong cost control practices, including inventory reductions to reduce the costs of money, manpower and facilities. The program was to have the continuing close attention of top management; and its good results were very quickly to become apparent.

Delivery on September 5 of the first Beechcraft King Air 100, which had received its Federal Aviation Administration type certification in late July, marked the full-scale entry of the new flagship of the Beechcraft corporate fleet into the aircraft markets of the world. The $25 million backlog of orders on hand left no room for doubt as to the heartiness of its reception. Its proven capabilities were such as to clearly represent significant advances in the state of the art of turbine-powered aircraft design. The only question was how big and how enduring the markets were to be. Projecting the past and present on even a conservative scale into the future, the King Air 100 was clearly due to enjoy large sales, for a long time to come.

It was therefore with an eye to the future, as well as all due regard to the record of a most illustrious past, that the Board of Directors of the National Business Aircraft Association selected Mrs. O. A. Beech to receive the 1969 NBAA Award for Meritorious Service at its annual meeting in Washington, D. C. on September 24. Earlier recipients of this, NBAA's highest honor, had included Charles A. Lindbergh, Igor I. Sikorsky, Donald Douglas, Sr., and James S. McDonnell.

Acknowledging the universal recognition which had come to Mrs. Beech as the First Lady of Aviation, NBAA President B. Owen Mayfield pointed out that the name of Beech — associated with aircraft since the famous Travel Airs of Walter H. Beech's in the 1920's — is known for "outstanding contributions to business aviation."

"In the 1930's, Walter and Olive Ann Beech's company brought out the famous Beech 18. This transport is to general aviation what the DC-3 was to the airlines", Mayfield said. "After her husband's death in 1950, Mrs. Beech took over management of the

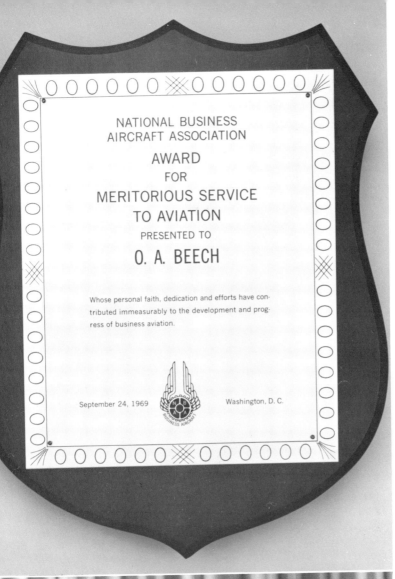

Highest honor of the National Business Aircraft Association — its annual Award for Meritorious Service to Aviation, conferred in previous years on such famous recipients as Charles A. Lindbergh, James H. Doolittle, and Igor I. Sikorsky — went in 1969 to the chairman of the board and chief executive officer of the Beech Aircraft Corporation, Mrs. O. A. Beech.

The award was presented to Mrs. Beech by NBAA President-Elect E. E. Dunsworth on September 24, 1969 during the 22nd annual convention of the National Business Aircraft Association in Washington, D. C.

A great era comes to a close, as Mrs. O. A. Beech views the last three of the many thousands of Model 18 Twin Beechcrafts produced over a 32-year span . . .

and the last three Super H18 Twin Beechcrafts wing their way from Beech Field to serve in the Far East as pilot trainers with Japan Air Lines. (Page 307)

A new era begins for general aviation and for Beech Aircraft, as an affiliation with Hawker Siddeley Aviation Ltd. is announced on December 18, 1969. Shown with the Beechcraft Hawker 125 Corporate Jet Transport — first product of the new joint venture — are (from left) Capt. E. D. G. Lewin, Sales Director for Hawker Siddeley, and Beech Aircraft's Chairman of the Board, Mrs. O. A. Beech, and President, Frank E. Hedrick.

304

Beech Aircraft Corporation and led it in further growth and success."

Many awards and appointments of distinction had been conferred on Mrs. O. A. Beech since she had assumed charge of the enterprise which she and her husband had jointly founded. The most notable included selection as "Woman of the Year in Aviation" in 1951 by the Women's National Aeronautical Association and as "Outstanding Woman in the Field of Business" by Who's Who of American Women in 1965; receipt in 1953 of the Director's Medal of the Freedoms Foundation at Valley Forge and in 1961 of the Max H. Miller Award for outstanding effort in behalf of Junior Achievement; appointment to President Eisenhower's 12-member International Development Advisory Board; appointment by then Secretary of Defense Robert S. McNamara to the Defense Advisory Committee on Women in the Services; appointment in 1967 by President Johnson to the President's Commission of White House Fellows; and most recently, membership in the National Alliance of Businessmen and service on its Business and Industrial Advisory Committee.

Among all these honors, the 1969 NBAA Award was outstanding and unique. "Presented to O. A. Beech — whose personal faith, dedication and efforts have contributed immeasurably to the development and progress of business aviation" was its precise wording. While Mrs. Beech had successfully directed the enlargement of the company's capabilities into profitably diversified fields, she had always placed primary emphasis on the continuance of its leadership in serving the business aircraft world community. The NBAA Award was proof of success in this effort.

Success for Beech Aircraft in a different sphere of operation was verified by the receipt in late September of a follow-on contract of some $6 million for 400 more Navy AQM-37A Beechcraft supersonic target missiles. Extending deliveries through July 1971, the latest contract would bring Beech production of the 600-lb. missile, which had been flown at speeds in excess of Mach 3 and altitudes of nearly 90,000 feet, to a total of more than 2,300 units.

The obligation of successful corporate enterprise to advance the vital cause of education was recognized in actions approved by Mrs. Beech in late September and early October. Southwestern College, Winfield, Kansas, on September 25 acknowledged a gift

305

of $100,000 from the Beech Aircraft Foundation, Inc., the company's eleemosynary affiliate. Proceeds would serve to establish the Olive Ann Beech Chair of Business Administration at the wholly privately supported liberal arts institution. And Beech Aircraft on October 6 announced that the company would make available instrument ground school scholarships to selected high school, college and university staff or faculty members at each of 45 sites where it had scheduled its 3-D instrument training programs in 1970. These concentrated weekend programs, designed to qualify the time-pressed businessman pilot for the FAA written instrument rating examination, were viewed also as a way for personnel involved with aviation education in the nation's high schools and colleges to upgrade their qualifications and keep pace with new developments in general aviation — hence the Beech scholarship grants were established.

Closing of the company's books on the 1969 fiscal year at September 30 revealed total consolidated sales of $187,312,727 — the highest in its history, and nearly $3 millions in excess of the previous all-time 1968 record. Commercial sales of $144,699,015 exceeded the $129,924,363 of fiscal 1968 by more than 11 per cent; and marked the seventh consecutive year of commercial sales increase. Military-aerospace sales of $42,613,712, although below fiscal 1968, exceeded the forecast for the year. The new records were set in spite of the August work stoppage, which with inevitable re-start delays cost at least six weeks of production time. Adding its dollar cost to that of tight money and heavy product development schedules, the effect was to hold down earnings to $1,976,636 for the year. Dividends were continued, however, at the 1968 rate; and a two per cent stock dividend was also declared. The company was keeping faith with its stockholder-owners.

Man's second visit to Earth's moon, via the NASA Apollo 12 lunar voyage, was climaxed with a pinpoint lunar landing on November 19, a mile-long, 4-hour moonwalk, and the recovery of parts of the 1967 Surveyor 3 unmanned space probe, along with many samples of moon rocks and soil. Astronauts Conrad, Bean and Gordon reported flawless performance by the Beech-built Apollo life support system, in spite of lightning striking their craft at takeoff. Theirs was the fifth Apollo "Mission accom-

306

plished" with the help of the Beech-Boulder cryogenic oxygen and hydrogen storage system. Their lunar ferry vehicle "Intrepid", fueled in advance of takeoff by a Beech-built LM ground support system, also functioned flawlessly — thus maintaining Beech's perfect record in space.

Production of the Model 18 Twin Beechcraft at long last came to a close on November 26, 1969 — more than 32 years after the first Model 18 made its initial flight from Beech Field on January 15, 1937. From that same field, the last three Super H18's of Japan Air Lines 10-twin addition to its fleet of multi-engine Beechcraft pilot trainers took off and made a parting pass over Beech Aircraft on the first stage of their long trans-Pacific flight to their new home in Japan.

The unique eminence of the Model 18 Beechcraft in general aviation history had been attested in the 1969 NBAA Award presented in September to O. A. Beech. Well over 9,000 Model 18's, in commercial, military and remanufactured versions, and in a total of 32 variations from the original design, had been produced by Beech Aircraft. Representing nearly one-third of the more than 30,000 Beechcrafts built by the company in its 37-year history, they had accounted for more than $427 million in sales. Exports exceeding $52 million had helped spread the fame of the United States, and of Beech Aircraft and Beechcraft, into the most remote parts of the world. Wherever men flew, the Model 18 Beechcraft had earned recognition and respect. And even though retired from production, the thousands of Model 18 Beechcrafts still in service throughout the world would continue to add to the luster of aviations' longest-lived and best-selling twin-engine airplane design — for many years to come.

Regional sales meetings for Beech distributors and dealers, held early in December at Phoenix, Dallas and Atlanta, took the place of the company's customary annual Sales Spectacular conducted in past years at Wichita for its worldwide sales organization. This break with tradition facilitated concentration on the vigorously pursued work stoppage recovery and cost reduction programs. And it had little or no effect on the presentation of the 1970 line of Beechcrafts, which were greeted as always with high enthusiasm on the part of the dealer personnel who would carry the ultimate responsibility for maintaining the company's leadership in high-performance commercial aircraft sales.

Two new additions to the Beech line of best-sellers in all important categories enhanced sales opportunities for Beechcraft dealers and heightened their favorable outlook for the year ahead. Joining the King Air 100 which had been presented in May, the company enlarged its well-received Musketeer line with a new Super R model featuring retractable landing gear. Offering the advanced performance to be expected from this new feature — top speed 170 mph, cruise 162 mph — and 4-6 place seating, the Super R Musketeer with its 200 hp fuel injected engine promised to establish new standards of excellence and value in the low-priced aircraft field, with sales volume in proportion.

Dealer coverage of the light twin field also was increased with the introduction for 1970 delivery of the new Beechcraft Baron 58. This new version of general aviation's fastest light twin featured a lengthened fuselage offering ample, airline comfort seating for six persons, or corresponding optional loads of cargo or passengers. Double rear doors almost 4 feet wide facilitated loading of passengers or bulky cargo. Designed to meet the specific needs of many business users, the Baron 58 was clearly a model with a very substantial sales potential.

The spirit of excitement and anticipation manifested at the regional sales meetings rose to fever pitch at the annual Beech Aircraft stockholders' meeting, held in the Olive Ann Beech Gallery of the Beechcrafters Activity Center on December 18. For the invitations had stated that at a press conference following the meeting, the Beech Aircraft Corporation would announce its entry into the business/corporate jet airplane market.

What action Beech Aircraft would take in this field and when had been the subject of curious speculation in the general aviation industry for many years. Observers had noted that Beech had tested the market for business jets as long as 14 years ago, when in 1955 the company took over the North American distributorship of the 4-place French twin jet Morane-Saulnier MS 760 "Paris". It was a good airplane for its day; but Beech experience showed that neither the market nor the design was adequate to support continued effort at that time. So a decision was made to concentrate on the development and marketing of superior piston-engine and turbine-powered Beechcrafts until the market for business jets might grow to mature and important size. The trebling of Beech commercial sales in the 1960-1969 decade, under the impetus of continually improved piston-engine designs and the introduction of the industry-dominant propjet King Air Beechcrafts, proved the soundness of this decision.

The judgment seemed equally sound that in 1969, the business jet market was to offer immediate and long-range future volume possibilities justifying Beech Aircraft's entry. Beech distributors and loyal Beechcraft owners had signified their ready acceptance of any design the company might see fit to market. And the state of the art had advanced to the point where it would assuredly be possible to offer a business jet worthy in every way to bear the Beechcraft name. One problem remained: That of the heavy investments in time, talent, money and facilities necessary to design and build a Beechcraft business jet. To start from scratch would take too much time, considering the readiness of the market. And it would call for an investment of not less than $40 million — at the height of a period of tight and high-cost money.

Beech stockholders and members of the working press from international and American aviation publications alike listened with keen interest to the press conference exposition by President Frank E. Hedrick of the course the company was to follow in entering the business jet market. Its management's solution for the problem involved was simple and direct: To promptly take over the marketing through the Beech sales organization of a fully proven business/corporate jet aircraft already in full production.

The airplane chosen to become the first jet in the Beechcraft family was the Hawker Siddeley DH 125 — a design of which more than 200 aircraft were then operational throughout the world. Its characteristics had strong appeal to a broad spectrum of the corporate market: Cruising speed, 510 mph; range with 45 min. reserves, 1,750 statute miles; balanced field length of 4,950 feet; executive seating for 6 to 10 passengers, plus a crew of 2; and gross weight, 23,300 lbs. The price was to be slightly more than $1 million.

Renamed the Beechcraft Hawker or BH 125, the design to be marketed by Beech Aircraft throughout North America would feature improvements with special appeal to American buyers, including exterior and interior redesigns, an outward opening airstair door like the King Air Beechcrafts, and many other features developed jointly by Beech Aircraft and Hawker Siddeley.

Power would be supplied by two Rolls Royce Bristol Viper engines producing 3360 pounds of thrust each. Thus the BH 125 would represent an amalgam of three of the most eminent names in the world of manufacturing — Beechcraft, Hawker-Siddeley, and Rolls Royce.

But this design, President Hedrick explained, was only the immediate market entry of the cooperative effort arranged between Beech Aircraft and Hawker Siddeley Aircraft, Ltd. Future results of the alliance would be the introduction of a whole new family of advanced business jets. The first, then in prototype stage and being prepared for testing, was to be the larger, faster Beechcraft-Hawker 125-600. It would have a larger cabin to provide for 6 to 14 passengers plus a crew of 2, and new, more powerful Rolls Royce Bristol turbojet engines for improved performance. And it would be available in the fall of 1971.

As the calendar year of 1969 came to its close, Beech Aircraft occupied a position unique in the world aviation industry. It was the first and only general aviation company to offer a complete line of airplanes, from a two-place trainer through turboprop corporate aircraft, and in addition, an American-oriented version of a fully proven, sturdy, fast, dependable jet-powered business machine. It had overcome difficulties during the year and established an even firmer foundation for efficient operations in the decade ahead.

Chapter 33

The opening days of 1970 brought good news to Wichita from halfway around the globe. From Australia came word that a Beechcraft 99A Airliner had just won three top prizes in the London-to-Sydney Air Race, one of the oldest and most arduous and prestigious competitions in international aviation.

Covering the 12,000-mile course in 48 hours, 15 minutes and 50 seconds, the Beechcraft not only outsped all other aircraft in its class, but also established a new world speed record for propeller-driven aircraft in the race. Officially sanctioned and later confirmed by the Federation Aeronautique Internationale, the swift flight bettered by 32 hours, 40 minutes and 10 seconds the previous world record of 80 hours and 50 minutes held by a de Havilland Comet DH 88.

The Captain Cook Bi-Centenary Prize, the Dunlop-Australian Prize and the New South Wales (Australia) government trophy, totalling $10,000 in cash plus trophies, all were tokens of victory for the Beechcraft and its crew. Its pilot was Capt. Tom E. Lampitt, chief pilot for Eagle Aircraft Services Ltd., London-based British distributor for Beech Aircraft; its co-pilot, Capt. Roy Bartman of British Overseas Airways.

Theirs was the major, but not the only Beechcraft victory in the hemisphere-spanning race. For three other Beechcrafts were also winners in handicap computed categories. First place went to a Beechcraft Queen Air piloted by Stanley Booker of San Jose, Calif., and fourth place to a Beechcraft King Air 100 piloted by an all-Australian crew, in the twin-engine turbocharged or turboprop aircraft category. And a Beechcraft Baron B55, piloted by two British aviators, placed fifth in the light twin piston-engine category. Once more the results of a major competition validated the maxim that first became current in 1936: "It takes a Beechcraft to beat a Beechcraft."

First place in the pure jet class was won by a Hawker Siddeley 125 owned by Qantas Airways in the dazzling time of 27 hours, 30 minutes and 22 seconds. Its race record suggested that the HS 125, under its new Western Hemisphere identity as the Beechcraft Hawker 125, was to become a worthy companion for the King Air series and other high-performance Beechcrafts.

At Wichita, the company named as its "Man of the Year" for 1969 Mr. Watson E. Richards, president since 1961 of Atlantic Aviation Corporation, Beechcraft distributors on the East Coast and a world leader in the sale of Beechcraft products.

The King Air Beechcraft 99A Airliner again came into prominence when, on February 12, Texas International Airlines took delivery on the first of two new 284-mph 99A's added to its passenger carrier fleet. The sale marked the first use of the

Beechcraft 99A by a regional airline, Texas International, serving 67 cities in 8 states and three cities in Mexico.

On February 19 the company announced the expansion of its board of directors from six to seven members, with the election of Chandler Hovey, Jr. to the board. A general partner in the New York City investment banking and underwriting firm of White, Weld & Co., Mr. Hovey had been closely associated with Beech Aircraft for many years. His more than a quarter century of experience in foreign and domestic business and finance was expected to be, in the words of Mrs. O. A. Beech, "of great benefit to the company."

The month of March opened with the announcement that the time between overhaul for the turbine engines used on the Beechcraft 99 and 99A Airliners had been increased by 30 per cent, permitting these aircraft to be operated 3,000 hours or five years, whichever should come first. This allowed airlines operating the Beechcraft 99 Series to fly 42 per cent longer before pulling the engines for overhaul, substantially increasing the service availability of their Beechcrafts and improving their profits.

From the Liberal, Kansas airport where Beechcraft Musketeer production was based, a mass flyaway was staged on March 13 which represented the largest single purchase of Beechcraft Musketeers on record. The buyer was the Government of Mexico; and its $.5 million contract, negotiated through Aeromex, Beechcraft distributor in Mexico, added 20 bright yellow Beechcraft Musketeer Sports to the pilot training resources of the Air Forces of Mexico. "We wanted the best possible equipment for training our pilots. We have been evaluating aircraft for four years, and the Beechcraft Musketeers meet our requirements." So said Gen. Jose G. Vergara Ahumada, Chief of Staff, Air Forces of Mexico, speaking of the purchasing decision.

Another milestone of the month was the delivery on March 20 at Beech-Boulder to the United States Navy of the 2,000th AQM-37A Beechcraft-designed target missile system. More than a decade had passed since Beech Aircraft in 1959 won a joint Navy-Air Force design competition for the AQM-37A, originally designated as the KD2B-1. In those years the high-performance target missile had been flown to a record altitude of 91,000 feet and to a speed of Mach 2.8; and had made an impressive record for reliability and versatility for combat training functions. The slender 13½ ft., 560-lb. missile, powered by a liquid bi-propellant engine and carrying a programmed self-contained electronic guidance system, had proved itself in both sea and land duty to be every inch a Beechcraft.

The deep personal conviction of Mrs. O. A. Beech and of Beech Aircraft management that every individual should join in appreciating and praising, rather than finding fault with our nation, found expression in a series of messages sponsored by the company in important magazines throughout the year. Started in March, Beech Aircraft advertising was dedicated to the purpose of selling America first. Aerial photographs of typical American scenes, taken by R. James Yarnell from a Beechcraft Bonanza, and accompanying messages emphasized the beauty and the greatness of our land. They brought many favorable comments and, despite the complete lack of any attempt to sell Beech products, provided stronger support for the efforts of the Beech sales organization than more conventional advertising.

As April opened, the company announced the formation of a wholly-owned subsidiary, Beechcraft Hawker Corporation, to market and participate in the design and manufacture of Beechcraft Hawker series executive jets.

Beechcraft Hawker Corporation acquired the aviation assets and personnel of Hawker Siddeley International, Inc., North American marketing and service organization based at LaGuardia Airport, New York City. Named President and Director was Lloyd W. Harris, continuing in the same posts as before. A former executive in the Lockheed JetStar sales program, his background was ideally suited to Beechcraft Hawker requirements.

Named Vice President and sales director at Wichita of fitting Beechcraft Hawker sales into the existing Beech Aircraft dealership network was Stewart M. Ayton, president of Houston Beechcraft, Inc. Active since 1940 with Atlantic Aviation, Inc. and Beech Aircraft in aircraft sales, and well acquainted with distributors, dealers, and customers and prospects throughout the business aviation spectrum, Ayton's appointment gave every sign of putting "the right man in the right place." Beech management's long-range plans for successfully marketing its line of outstanding business/corporate jets were fitting together nicely.

The numeral "13" brought with it in April the ill fortune customarily attributed to it by superstition. On April 13, the moon flight of Apollo 13 was aborted 55 hours into the mission, by the unpredictable failure of two thermostatic switches. In one instant the painstaking craftsmanship of the Beech-Boulder workers who produced the Apollo 13 life support system was rendered futile. In spite of this mishap, crew and spacecraft returned safely to Earth. Beech-Boulder personnel who had built the systems that had worked perfectly on 9 previous Apollo missions, including the Apollo 11 and 12 moon flights and landing, were heartened when they were told later by John L. Swigert, Jr., command module pilot of Apollo 13, on his visit to Boulder: "I will fly again on your tanks any time." Beechcrafters would prove to Swigert that their work on the Beech-built systems for Apollo 14 would vindicate his confidence.

The U. S. Army on April 20 awarded a contract totalling more than $12.3 million for additional RU-21E special electronic surveillance turboprop Beechcrafts. Similar to the U-21 series Beechcrafts, of which 129 were then serving military uses, the RU-21E models would use the same power plants as the pressurized Beechcraft King Air A90 corporate transport.

Next day the Chilean Government approved a $7.1 million contract for a fleet of 9 Beechcraft 99A Airliners, plus spares, to replace its 20-year-old Beechcraft C45 transports. The record made by these and Beechcraft Queen Air and T-34 Mentors in Chilean government service weighed heavily in the contract award.

In a more personal vein, the company's Chairman of the Board was the recipient of new additions to her long list of appointments, honors and citations. Mrs. O. A. Beech was named by President Richard M. Nixon to the advisory Board of the National Air & Space Museum at the Smithsonian Institution. It was a logical choice; Mrs. Beech had been personally involved in many of the notable events in aviation history.

She also became the first woman ever to be honored by election to the Board of Directors of the Chamber of Commerce of the United States — a notable tribute to the ability Mrs. Beech had shown as a business executive.

314

Setting a new world speed record for propeller-driven aircraft competing in the international London-to-Sydney Air Race in 1970, a Beechcraft 99A Airliner piloted by Capt. Tom E. Lampitt (left center, holding pop bottle) won three top prizes for its swift 12,000-mile flight.
(Pages 310, 311)

Delivery of the 500th Beechcraft King Air 90 to Dan L. Meisinger of Topeka Aircraft Sales & Service accented Beech leadership in U.S. and worldwide civil turboprop aircraft production.
(Page 318)

The 30,000th Beechcraft, a King Air 100, was delivered in 1970 to Twin Disc, Inc. Congratulations were extended from Frank E. Hedrick and Mrs. O. A. Beech to John H. Batten, president of Twin Disc, Inc.; Fred Sommer, the buyer's chief pilot; Ira B. Hartzog, president of Hartzog Aviation, Inc.; and Gwen Landry, Hartzog salesman.
(Page 319)

315

Oh, say, can you see ... at 5000 feet.

In aviation, we literally get above the roar. Above the impatience and intolerance on all sides. The illusion below corners your mind back into quiet reason.

For a moment, you even feel that reverent shiver you got shouting the pledge of allegiance back in grade school.

Hard to believe, isn't it, that today our flag is being so shamefully yanked about. It hurts to see it played with, outraged, grounded, stomped on and spat at.

Do we need that?

If it goes on like this, future Americans may wonder what it was we so proudly hailed.

It is still the only flag in the world that is an unassailable guarantee of individual freedom. It is still the symbol of our right to act or react. It is still our protection — regardless of the mistakes we make.

We need to give back its innocence. Perhaps we are still quixotic enough to want to.

To begin, we could run it back up the flagpole where it belongs and, please God, leave it there.

Beech Aircraft Corporation
Wichita, Kansas 67201

Photo by Jim Yarnell from THIS IS MY LAND, Random House, Inc.

The first of a series of multi award-winning messages express-ing the faith in America deeply felt by Beech Aircraft and its people appeared in 1970. Responses were notably favorable. (Page 313, 345)

316

In a poll of 575 business and financial editors in the United States, Mrs. O. A. Beech was named one of the 10 most successful women in American business. It is doubtful if a better-informed group of judges for the selection of this particular "Top Ten" could have been found anywhere.

And Mrs. Beech was cited by the American Mothers Committee, Inc. as "One of the country's most outstanding women", representing the aviation industry in the Committee's categories of selection.

The Beech Aircraft Corporation and its president, Frank E. Hedrick, also were honored in May with a special Award of Appreciation from the National Intercollegiate Flying Association. The award saluted Beech Aircraft and Hedrick "for 22 years of devoted service and cooperation in the cause of collegiate aviation education." It was only the second Special Award ever conferred in NIFA history.

Beech Aircraft support for the Airport and Airway Development Act of 1970 was strong and unhesitating. Both as a matter of public services and enlightened self-interest, the company's executives expressed their convictions of the vital need for more and better airports and air navigation facilities and their long-range value to general aviation, as well as to public air transportation. It took courage to speak out in favor of this not universally popular legislation; but the company saw the course of endorsement as the right stand to take.

On June 4 the U. S. Army completed a review of its aircraft needs, and issued a contract to Beech Aircraft for $6.8 million worth of U-21A Beechcraft utility personnel and cargo-carrying turboprop transports. These were substantially non-pressurized versions of the commercial Beechcraft King Air A90 corporate transports, using the same 500 shp engines.

The U. S. Naval Academy, Annapolis, Md. purchased a Beechcraft Bonanza F33A, which was scheduled for duty as a flying test bed for midshipmen majoring in aerospace engineering. A flight schedule of about 500 hours per year was set up by Academy instructors for its newest "plebe".

Texas International Airlanes increased its Beechcraft 99A Airliner fleet to a total of three units in mid-June. TI reported that 8 of its 9 daily Houston-Galveston round trips were being flown

317

with Beechcraft 99A equipment. Customer demand, they said, prompted the addition.

July opened with receipt of a contract from the U. S. Air Force for development of a new rocket-powered missile target, precisely priced at $1,189,696. Called HAST (High Altitude Supersonic Target), the new target was to operate at altitudes of 90,000-plus feet and speeds in the Mach 4 range. The contract was a follow-on to the successful Beech Aircraft 1966 demonstration of a Sandpiper experimental missile, based on the long-used AQM-37A Beechcraft airframe and using hybrid solid/liquid fuel propulsion.

The month closed with the delivery to Bell Helicopter of the 500th Beech-built complete airframe for Bell's Light Observation U. S. Army OH-58A "Kiowa" helicopter, a military version of the Bell JetRanger. Progress was "on target" at Beech Aircraft on it $75 million contract with Bell for more than 4,000 helicopter airframes.

The "littlest Beechcraft", the U. S. Army Beech 1025 propeller-driven target missile, entered its eleventh year of service around the world in August with a reliability record in excess of 90 per cent. Still in production at Beech-Salina, the Beech 1025 "Cardinal" brought a $474,260 supplement to an existing contract for missile target service support to the company to mark its anniversary year.

A new world's record for turbine-powered aircraft production was set by Beech Aircraft on August 12 with the delivery of the 500th commercial Beechcraft King Air 90 to Dan L. Meisinger, president of Topeka Aircraft Sales & Service, Beechcraft distributor based at Topeka, Kansas. The event established the United States as the world's leader in production of civil turboprop transport aircraft with 67 per cent of all output in the 12,500-pound and below category; and Beech Aircraft as the industry's leader with a commanding share of 51 per cent of the U. S. total.

In the pure jet field, the company's Beechcraft-Hawker subsidiary was also doing remarkably well, considering the lagging market for corporate jet aircraft. At mid-August it had scored a total of 10 Beechcraft Hawker 125 deliveries; and more were scheduled for the future. Progress was good on the larger

318

BH 125-600 model, with a first test flight probable early in 1971.

September 23, 1970 was a very special Happy Day in the life of the Beech Aircraft Corporation. It was delivery day for the 30,000th production airplane, a Beechcraft King Air 100, to Twin Disc, Inc. of Racine, Wisconsin. John H. Batten, Twin Disc president, came to Wichita for the occasion, and received a specially engraved plaque from Mrs. O. A. Beech commemorating the delivery. A Beech customer since 1947, his firm started with a Beechcraft Model 18 and in 1966 added a Beechcraft King Air 90 and a Beechcraft B55 Baron to its air fleet used in conducting its internationally known power transmission business.

President Frank E. Hedrick pointed out that the 30,000 airplanes represented total sales and services of more than $2.5 billion since Beech Aircraft was founded in 1932. He emphasized that it had taken 34 years, from 1932 to 1966, for Beech to deliver its first 25,000 airplanes; but only four years to roll out the next 5,000 Beechcrafts, almost precisely to the day. "We are confident the next 5,000 will be produced in even less time," he said.

Next day, Wichita-based Air Midwest, a commuter airline operating in Kansas, Colorado, Nebraska and Missouri, took delivery on its second turboprop Beechcraft 99A Airliner. It was an event more significant in a way than prior deliveries of Beechcrafts to the far corners of the world; for it showed confidence in Beech Aircraft on the part of its own best friends and severest critics, the people in its own home town. The local delivery made a total of 145 Beechcraft Airliners with turboprop power delivered to that time to 49 domestic and 6 foreign air carriers and other buyers, to a value of better than $59 million.

On October 19 and 20, Wichita was the gathering place for the worldwide Beechcraft distributor, dealer and sales organization as the Beechcraft '71 Bravo International Sales Conference held sway. Beech Aircraft was host to some 700 aircraft marketers in an intensive program presenting the 1971 Beechcraft product line and concentrating on new ideas and techniques for "getting the order".

A major item among many highlights of '71 Bravo was the announcement that the Beechcraft King Air C90 would be completely equipped for all-weather flying, and would feature super deluxe cabin appointments, at no increase in price over its previously announced price of $399,500. It was the first time that any manufacturer had been able to crack the $400,000 price figure with a pressurized, turbine-powered corporate aircraft complete with electronics for instrument operations. The new additions offered a saving of more than $36,000 to the purchaser compared with their cost as optional equipment, and greatly reinforced the already strong position of the Beechcraft King Air C90 in the competitive market.

Throughout the entire line, a host of improvements and refinements showed the results of a continuous effort throughout the year to engineer and build every Beechcraft according to the concept of maximum possible "value-added" to the aircraft purchaser. The Beechcraft Duke A60, recipient earlier in the year of a special citation of excellence from *Flying* and *Business & Commercial Aviation* magazines, offered lighter, longer life turbochargers and design refinements. "More airplane for the money", always a major Beechcraft objective, was never more fully achieved than in every 1971 model.

T. Gail Clark, founder and President of Tulsair Beechcraft, Inc., Tulsa, Oklahoma, was named Beech Aircraft's "Man of the Year" for 1970 at Bravo '71. Starting as a one-man organization in 1945, he had developed his operation to a $5 million business in 1970.

Export Sales earned special commendation for reaching an all-time high of $34,769,139 during 1970, an increase of more than $5.6 million over 1969. Thirteen domestic distributors whose 1970 sales topped $1 million or more each received special honors, well-earned in a difficult year for the nation's economy.

Publication of the company's Annual Report for the fiscal year 1970 in mid-November showed total consolidated sales of $169,806,447 which was $17,506,280 below fiscal 1969 sales of $187,312,727, but still the fourth highest in Beech Aircraft's 38-year history.

Department of Defense and Aerospace sales increased to $53,375,641, a gain of $10,761,929 over last year's $42,613,712. Commercial sales, reflecting a depressed market shared by all General Aviation manufacturers, were $116,430,806, compared

Received in mid-1970 was a seminal initial contract from the U.S. Air Force for development of HAST (High Altitude Supersonic Target), an advanced rocket-powered target missile designed to reach altitudes of 90,000-plus ft. and speeds in the Mach 4 range. (Pages 318, 333)

The 2,000th AQM-37A missile target produced by Beech Aircraft passed in review prior to launch from a Navy F-8 aircraft at the Naval Missile Center, Point Mugu, California. (Page 312)

Special-mission versions of the Beechcraft Bonanza 36, designated by the U.S. Air Force as Type QU-22B, were produced in 1971 for its Pave Eagle data-gathering program with higher-powered turbocharged engines, three-bladed propellers, and both manned and remote guidance controls. (Page 334)

First pressurized aircraft procured by the U.S. Army were U-21F Beechcraft utility transports — "off-the-shelf" adaptations of commercial Beechcraft King Air A100 models. (Page 334)

South of the border, Aeromex, S.A., Beech distributors since 1954, invested over $.3 million in new 44,000 sq. ft. facilities at the Mexico City International Airport. Their expansion enabled complete servicing for all types of commercial aircraft, including corporate jets. (Page 328)

Northward, the Canadian Air Forces took delivery of 25 Beechcraft Musketeer Custom trainers. Off-the-shelf aircraft with aerobatic capabilities, they displayed Canada's maple leaf insignia and bright red and yellow paint styling. (Page 327) with 1969's $144,699,015. Total operations resulted in a net loss of $7,731,899 for the year.

Beech Aircraft nevertheless kept faith with its stockholders, continuing to pay regular quarterly cash dividends of 18¾ cents per share throughout the fiscal year from reserves previously accumulated. The payments represented 22 years of consecutive cash dividends.

On December 1, a realignment of the company's marketing operations and management responsibilities was announced. George T. Humphrey, Senior Vice President, was elected to the Beech Aircraft Board of Directors, increasing its number to a total of eight highly experienced policymakers in all areas of operations. Roy H. McGregor, previously Vice President of Aerospace Marketing and Contracts, was appointed Vice President of Marketing to direct all domestic marketing activities, including Commercial, Department of Defense and Aerospace. M. G. Neuburger, since 1956 Vice President of Export Sales, was appointed Vice President of the newly established International Division. Wyman L. Henry, President of Beech Holdings, Inc., the subsidiary responsible for all company-owned marketing operations, was assigned to give full time to that subsidiary, while continuing as a Vice President and Director of the Beech Aircraft Corporation.

At Beech-Boulder, intensive efforts were successful in completing on-time delivery of the Beech-redesigned cryogenic oxygen tanks to North American Rockwell for the Apollo 14 moon mission scheduled for January 31 launch. A further achievement of the Beech-Boulder Division was the development of a huge prototype cryogenic propellant storage tank for the National Aeronautics and Space Administration. A 7-ft., 7-inch diameter aluminum pressure vessel, the 225-cubic foot or 1,764-gallon capacity tank would store liquid oxygen, hydrogen, helium or methane as required for shuttle vehicles and space stations in future space exploration. Upon completion in a giant metal-spinning lathe at Beech-Wichita, the two massive .75″ thick aluminum hemispheres were found to match within .007 inch when mated for welding.

On December 22, Beech Aircraft celebrated the 25th anniversary of the aircraft industry's most popular and highly regarded high-performance single-engine airplane — the world-renowned Beechcraft Bonanza. The only aircraft of its class to remain in continuous production for a quarter-century, the Beechcraft Bonanza on its Silver Anniversary reaffirmed its standing as a living classic design by outselling all other single-engine retractable gear aircraft in the arduous year of 1970. To date 9,748 Beechcraft Bonanzas had been delivered, 95 per cent of which were of the original V-tailed type.

Marking the event, officers of the American Bonanza Society, a "fan club" comprising more than 2,000 admirers of the Beechcraft Bonanza with a still-growing membership, sent the following telegram to Mrs. O. A. Beech, Chairman of the Board:

"Rarely is a product so conceived, well engineered and manufactured that after 25 years it is still considered to be unsurpassed in its field.

"On this twenty-fifth anniversary of the maiden flight of the Bonanza, please accept our congratulations to you and your company for producing such an outstanding aircraft."

American Bonanza Society
B. J. McClanahan, President
Ralph G. Halzsloop, Executive Director

The eventful year of 1970 came to a close with good news from President Frank E. Hedrick: The combined efforts of all Beechcrafters and their management had moved the company back into a profitable position for the final three calendar months of the year. In spite of inflation, rising costs of labor and materials, and a still unfavorable economic climate for aircraft sales, Beech Aircraft was back in the black and gaining ground. The company's products were better and costing less to manufacture. Its "War on Waste", Zero Defects, Work Simplification, and Value Engineering Programs were showing good results. Plans were in progress to broaden the marketing base for larger and higher performance Beechcrafts through greater penetration of the training aircraft market from which pilots and owners might step up to more advanced Beechcraft ownership. Specifically, development of a two-place commercial Beechcraft trainer was under intensive study, together with studies of ways to launch a new generation of dealers who could enter such a segment of Beechcraft business with minimum capital investment. Taking

324

a long-range view, the vicissitudes of 1970 might on balance prove to be eventually beneficial. Beech Aircraft was in a better position than ever to profit from opportunities that a more favorable economic climate might offer, and to carry forward into the 1970's its projections for growth exceeding that of its record in the 1960's.

Chapter 34

Encouraged by earnings of better than $1.13 millions attained during the final quarter of calendar year 1970, Beech Aircraft entered the new year of 1971 with justifiable confidence in its future.

The company was not alone in its optimistic outlook. One of the most respected financial analytical services, reviewing the prospects for Beech in its January 15, 1971 newsletter, stated:

"The pause in (the world market) growth is believed to be temporary . . . The general aviation boom (based on Federal government studies projecting a doubling in general aviation aircraft in service by 1980) should be well under way by 1973-75 . . . Beech shares can be expected to perform better than most shares over the coming 3 to 5 years . . ."

Optimism was tempered, however, with prudence and due regard for the realities of the immediate economic climate. The market for business aircraft had been subnormal for some time, and would probably continue so for several months, pending a general improvement in all lines of industry and commerce. Substantial inventories of Beechcrafts, ordered and produced in good faith but undelivered to customers whose plans had been altered by adverse circumstances, were being held in dealers' stocks.

So, as the year began, readjustments were made in the company's production and employment schedules. Reductions in working forces at the various Beech facilities brought layoffs to some 9 per cent of the employee complement. Among the remaining 5,100 employees, more than 80 per cent were Beechcrafters with service records spanning five years or more. These people had mastered their skills through experience. They were dedicated to the Beech tradition of quality workmanship; and the company would not freely dispense with their services at any point short of retirement age.

Proof of Beechcraft reliability, and a fitting postlude to the Silver Anniversary Celebration of the Beechcraft Bonanza held the month before, came in a dispatch from Dakar, Senegal on January 20th. Mrs. Marion Hart, age 79, had just completed her third solo Atlantic Ocean crossing in her 10-year-old Model N Bonanza, and was happily wintering in West Africa before taking off on the next in her series of globe-trotting flights. Her "little treasure", as Mrs. Hart affectionately referred to her Beechcraft, was the second Bonanza she had owned in 25 years of flying. The first, a B35 model, had been purchased 17 years ago. Long-range fuel tanks permitted flights of more than 10 hours duration, which Mrs. Hart described as "rather boring", even though "somewhat of a lark."

More good news came from overseas on the following day. At Chester Airfield in England, site of the Hawker Siddeley Aviation works, the successful first flight of the Beechcraft Hawker 125-600 was announced on January 21st. This larger and faster version of the BH 125-400, equipped with higher-powered Viper 601 Rolls-Royce jet engines, was scheduled to be marketed in North America by the Beechcraft Hawker Corporation, a wholly-owned Beech subsidiary.

To round out the happy day, an order came from the Government of Spain for 20 Beechcraft Cardinal 1025 target missiles plus support gear, valued at $866,129. After 12 years in use by armed services of the United States and other Free World nations, the "littlest Beechcraft" was still going strong. Its reliability record of better than 90 per cent continued to enhance the reputation for dedicated craftsmanship established by its builders at the Beech Salina Division.

Over the weekend, the governments of Algeria and Malaysia reached coincidental decisions that the UNACE (Universal Aircraft Communication/Navigation Evaluation) version of the Beechcraft King Air 100 was just what they wanted to carry on a continuous checkup of their airways facilities. Their January 26th orders put into production two UNACE Beechcrafts equipped with special electronic test gear — advanced versions of the design introduced by Beech in 1966 which was in service as a 5-plane fleet with Canada's civil aircraft authority, the Department of Transport.

Another export sale, two days later, set a new record for the largest number of Beechcraft Musketeers ordered at one time by a single customer. On January 28th the Canadian Armed Forces signed an $800,000 contract for 25 aerobatic Musketeers, plus spares and training support, to be used for basic pilot training. The Canadian order topped the previous record sale of 20 Musketeer Sport trainers to the Air Force of Mexico, and affirmed a total of 38 foreign countries relying on Beechcrafts for use in their military training fleets. The management's confidence in promoting Export Sales to the status of a separate division — the Beech International Division — in its December 1970 realignment of operations was being fully justified.

The complete success of the Apollo 14 moon mission that lifted off from Cape Kennedy on January 31st on its ten-day voyage through space to and from Earth's satellite was a vindication of tremendous efforts by Beechcrafters and a good omen for the future. Tireless efforts of the cryogenics team at the Beech Boulder Division had produced a simplified version of the Beech-built life support system that eliminated some valves, motors and switches, and added a third oxygen tank for missions of longer duration. The finished tanks for Apollo 14 were delivered ahead of schedule. Constant on-the-ground simulation of the entire mission was conducted concurrently with the actual voyage at the Beech Boulder facility to assure instant readiness to cope with any possible untoward development — a happily unnecessary precaution. And the Beech-Boulder team continued to keep ahead of schedule on its production of tanks for the Apollo 15, 16 and 17 missions.

The short month of February was remembered mainly as "the time of the big snow." A huge weekend snowstorm, extremely unusual in Kansas, blocked highways and streets and brought almost every normal activity to a halt in the three days following February 21st, including work at the Beech Wichita plants. A notable delivery during the month was that of a Beechcraft 99A Airliner to the U. S. Forest Service of the Department of Agriculture. Its special equipment for multi-purpose missions included adjacent doors with slipstream spoiler for parachuting smoke-jumpers, a special camera hatch also accommodating infra-red scanners, and special FM air-to-ground radio communications gear.

Beech capabilities to meet unusual demands were recognized with the receipt of a contract from the Boeing Company, early in March, to produce a combination probe and drogue mid-air refueling system to be retrofitted to Canadian Armed Forces jet transport planes, equipping them to simultaneously refuel two CF-5 fighter aircraft in flight. Also announced in March was a new "Instant Warranty" program providing immediate settlement in the field for Beechcraft owners on warranty claims of $50 or less. Effective April 1st, it was to cover both parts and labor. Another example of the long-standing Beech concern with "service after the sale", the program was welcomed by dealers and customers alike.

South of the border, there was the grand opening by Aeromex, S.A., Beechcraft distributor in Mexico City for more than 20 years, of a handsome new $350,000 sales and service center handily located at the Departmento Federale International Airport. With three interconnected hangars and 44,000 square feet of enclosed space, the new Aeromex complex provided complete advanced facilities for servicing all Beechcraft models, including the Beechcraft Hawker 125 corporate jet.

On the domestic dealer-owner service front, meetings were held in Wichita for two important groups: Beechcraft parts wholesalers, and Beechcraft service managers from the company's North American distribution network. Discussions and training centered on the theme of "Total Support Through Professional Service" for the quality products of the Beech Aircraft Corporation.

Completion on April 23rd of the first Beechcraft Hawker 125-400 jet to be customized for the North American market at the Beech Wichita plant was the occasion for a special rollout ceremony attended by Wichita's Mayor Jack Greene, who hailed the event as significant for the city as well as for the company. Beechcraft crews had transformed the British-built craft from its unpainted and unfinished interior and unequipped "green" configuration into a brilliantly complete, sleek corporate jet with

328

a cabin customized to meet the most critical executive tastes. They installed instrumentation and avionics of major airline caliber, and provided a flight deck and "front office" engineered to the Beechcraft standards that for many years had led the industry in pilot and crew comfort, convenience and ease and safety of operation.

Throughout the greening months of Spring, customers continued to show their loyalty to Beechcraft, and their satisfaction with the company's products, by placing one repeat order after another for new or additional Beechcrafts of all models. In March the Royal Flying Doctor Service of Western Australia took delivery of its sixth Beechcraft Baron — a Model 58 equipped with the enlarged cargo door which had first been developed to meet its special needs for easy stretcher loading. The new Beechcraft Baron would expand the RFDS air fleet, then flying about 3,500 hours a year providing medical services and transportation to 40,000 persons scattered throughout the 350,000 square miles of Australian Outback.

A Beechcraft King Air B90 delivered to Curt G. Joa, Inc., manufacturers of precision machinery for paper and surgical dressings, became that company's eighth Beechcraft. Curt G. Joa, company president, bought his firm's first airplane, a Beechcraft Bonanza, in 1946 and business picked up immediately, he said. Since then, his company had owned six Beechcraft Bonanzas and one Beechcraft Twin-Bonanza. An avid 10,000-hour pilot, Joa was programming his new King Air for about 400 hours use per year.

Picking up his new pressurized Beechcraft Duke at Wichita, Edmund McGibbon of Barrington, Illinois became a five-time Beechcraft owner. Starting as student pilots in 1965, he and his wife owned in succession a Beechcraft Debonair, a Beechcraft Travel Air, a Beechcraft Baron 55 and a Beechcraft Queen Air 80. Frequent trips to Mexico, Arizona and northern Michigan put some 1,200 hours on his various Beechcraft log books.

In the corporate fleet area, Gerber Products of Fremont, Michigan acquired its third Beechcraft King Air 90, a new B90 model, to provide swift transportation to and from its off-airlines location. No newcomer to the uses of business aircraft, the internationally known baby food manufacturer had operated its own

329

3-aircraft fleet since 1962. The Beechcraft King Air was obviously Number One in their estimation, as with hundreds of other corporate owners.

A new Beechcraft Bonanza, his fifth Model 35 Beechcraft, was the choice of Martin Wilmarth for use in supervising his extensive rice growing operations in Colusa County, California. A World War II fighter pilot, Wilmarth found his Beechcraft Bonanza almost indispensable in his business, and a way to broaden his travel horizons to include winter vacations in the Caribbean, Mexico and Latin America.

A progress report issued in May on two engineered cost reduction programs, Value Engineering and Commonality, which had been initiated at Beech Aircraft on March 1st, showed that a 34 per cent reduction in part numbers and a 50 per cent reduction in engineering prints had been accomplished. The joint program was well launched toward its goal of $2.3 millions in net savings on manufacturing costs over a projected 3-year span, through effecting commonality in design among parts of various models and making engineering changes that would simplify production and increase reliability.

Another May event was the delivery of the 1,000th Beech-built airframe for the U. S. Army OH-58A light helicopter to Bell Helicopter at Ft. Worth, Texas. The delivery marked a total of more than 1,400 airframes built by Beech for Bell's rotating wing aircraft of various military and commercial models.

At almost the same time, the company received on May 15th a $750,000 contract from Bell to supply parts, tooling, engineering drawings and technical assistance for a joint Bell/Government of Australia co-production program involving, at its outset, a total of 21 helicopters.

The company's co-founder and Chairman of the Board, Mrs. O. A. Beech, was the recipient in May and later months of notable additions to an already lengthy list of honors, awards and appointments to important advisory positions.

On May 24th, Mrs. Beech was the guest of honor at the Tenth Annual Service City Invitational Golf Tournament and Distinguished Service Awards Banquet at Dallas, Texas. There she became the first woman to receive the "Wilbur" Award of the Service City group. Presented by George E. Haddaway, publisher of *Flight* Magazine, its symbol was a Steuben glass eagle with wings outspread, mounted on a specially engraved base. The inscription was:

"Olive Ann Beech, the queen of business aviation, gracious lady, patriot, dynamic creator of fine aircraft whose innovative leadership of Beech Aircraft Corporation through 40 eventful years has contributed vitally to the growth and progress of business flying — and whose dedicated service to this industry and to the nation has etched her name and deeds indelibly on the honor roll of great American women. Proudly presented by Airmen representing the Service City International, May 24, 1971."

Following this honor came a series of appointments in close succession. On May 27th Mrs. Beech was named the first woman member of the Awards Board of the Flight Safety Foundation, a group charged with the responsibility of selecting the recipient of the Distinguished Service Award contributed by *Aviation Week and Space Technology* Magazine.

On June 1st Mrs. Beech was named a member of the National Advisory Council of the Army Aviation Museum. On June 2nd she was appointed a Director of the National Executive Committee of Junior Achievement — in recognition of the special interest and encouragement given by Beech Aircraft under her management to these highly constructive youth enterprises. On July 2nd she was appointed by Kansas Governor Robert B. Docking to membership on the NASA Space Shuttle Station Study Committee.

The 42nd annual convention of the International Ninety-Nines, Inc., held at Wichita in August and attended by more than 600 women pilots and their husbands from far and near, brought triple honors to Mrs. Beech. A specially engraved plaque was presented to "Olive Ann Beech and Walter H. Beech for their personal contribution to aviation" by Governor Robert B. Docking from the Ninety-Nines. Mrs. Beech was also given a specially inscribed Amelia Earhart medallion, in recognition of her outstanding contributions to the organization founded by Miss Earhart, and a special certificate of appreciation for her participation in the activities of the Ninety-Nines.

As co-founder of Beech Aircraft and a colleague with Mr. Beech in the business of its predecessor Travel Air Manufacturing Company, Mrs. Beech accepted a certificate issued by the OX-5 Club of America on October 16th, attesting the selection of Walter H. Beech as a member of the OX-5 Club of America Aviation Hall of Fame. The recognition was appropriate; for Walter H. Beech had produced, in his Travel Air designs, the most numerous and demonstrably the most efficient commercial aircraft ever to use the famous OX-5 World War I engine.

The 58th semi-annual meeting of the international Aviation Distributors and Manufacturers Association (ADMA) at Miami, Florida on November 18th brought the presentation of the ADMA Award of Merit to Mrs. O. A. Beech. It was only the eighth such award to be made in ADMA's 29-year history, and the first to be conferred on a woman. G. B. Van Dusen, chairman of the ADMA awards committee and board chairman of Van Dusen Air Incorporated, stated that "In presenting the ADMA Award for outstanding achievement in the aviation industry, we are honored to turn our spotlight on the universally acknowledged First Lady of Aviation."

Meanwhile, the mainstream of Beech Aircraft activities, always the foremost concern of Mrs. Beech and her associates, continued to produce good news. Early in June came a $700,000 follow-on order from the United Kingdom for 20 Beech Model 1072 rocket-powered "Stiletto" supersonic missile targets. Results of the July 1-7 London (England) to Victoria (British Columbia) Air Race showed the 10 Beechcrafts of various models, entered by their owners, placing well in the field of 57 aircraft. A Beechcraft Bonanza 36 flown by ferry pilot Louise Sacchi, the only solo woman pilot in the race, established a new international record in its class, spanning the New York-to-London leg at an average speed of 200 miles an hour. The event marked Miss Sacchi's 165th and 166th Atlantic crossings, about 95 per cent of which she made in Beechcraft airplanes ranging from Musketeers to Queen Airs. A Model 17 Beechcraft Staggerwing biplane built in 1943 and flown by Myron Olson, Montreal, and its rebuilder-owner, George LeMay, Calgary, finished 32nd in the field — not bad for a 28-year-old airplane.

Beechcrafters returning to work on July 19th after a two-week plantwide vacation shutdown found a long-familiar Wichita landmark missing. The company water tower on East Central

Avenue, which had served both Travel Air and Beech Aircraft since 1929, was gone — transplanted to serve the water system of the town of Holcomb, Kansas. One week later, Beech advertising affirming the positive values of America and the American way — a reflection of the personal views of Chairman O. A. Beech and President Frank E. Hedrick — won Award of Merit medals for the company from the Freedoms Foundation at Valley Forge, Pennsylvania.

July 26th was also liftoff day for the Apollo 15 space mission. The 12-day round trip of more than a half million miles to the moon and back was flown with virtually perfect results, aided by liquid oxygen and hydrogen life support systems designed and built at Beech-Boulder.

An additional $8.7 million contract award came from the Department of Defense on August 6th for Beech to continue design and development and to manufacture test articles of HAST — a hybrid-fueled high altitude supersonic target-missile for Army, Navy, and Air Force use. As the prime contractor on HAST, Beech had completed a successful Phase I Design review under a prior contract awarded in July 1970 following keenly competitive bidding. The new award assured the continuation of Beechcraft's work on the Mach 4 and 100,000-ft. altitude missile.

Also received was a $1.8 million Department of Defense contract initiating the development by Beech of a new, highly classified SAGMI (Surface Attack Guided Missile) weapons system. Both this and the target missile contracts seemed to hold strong promise for eventual large-scale production awards.

A new model, the Beechcraft King Air A100 corporate transport, was unveiled on August 23rd. An advanced version of the King Air 100, it offered a wide range of passenger accommodations, with a choice of spacious 8-place to high-density 15-place seating. A 900-pound higher takeoff weight provided a 612-pound gain in useful load; and a 96-gallon enlargement of fuel capacity increased its range by 300 miles to a figure of 1,542 miles at 21,000-ft. altitude. New four-bladed propellers accomplished greater ground/tip clearance and reduced noise; new soundproofing and deluxe interiors further enhanced occupant comfort. Deliveries were scheduled to begin in October.

The Beech Boulder Division displayed on August 26th a high-efficiency thermal protection system for a huge cryogenic test tank developed there for NASA (National Aeronautics and Space Administration) to carry oxygen or hydrogen on 180-day space missions. Capacity of the tank was 16,000 pounds of liquefied oxygen at −297 degrees F., or 980 pounds of liquefied hydrogen at −420 degrees F. Protective insulation layers and a vapor-cooled aluminum shield provided a capability to withstand ambient temperatures exceeding 140 degrees F. A unique suspension system was devised to withstand 7 g's of launch and mission forces. Technology gained from development of the giant tank was expected to find applications in many aspects of future space programs, such as the space shuttle, the space stations and space tugs.

The U. S. Army added pressurized aircraft to its inventory for the first time, with the award on August 30th of a $2.5 million contract for five new advanced versions of its U-21A turboprop utility Beechcrafts, plus field support. Designated by the Army as its U-21F aircraft, the pressurized military Beechcraft would be practically identical with the new commercial Beechcraft King Air A100 model in all major respects.

The Labor Day weekend brought a well-earned holiday to hard-working Beechcrafters, and also marked the completion of two unique special-mission Beechcraft Model 36 Bonanzas. Designated as Air Force Type QU-22B, the Beechcrafts went to the Univac Division of the Sperry Rand Corporation for use in the highly classified USAF PAVE Eagle data-gathering program. Installation of command guidance systems permitted their operation as manned aircraft, pilotless drones, or both.

Like NASA and the U. S. armed services, commercial customers continued to express their approval of Beech Aircraft and its products. A typical instance was that of Macair Charters, a bush flying operation providing air transport into the jungles of New Guinea from a base at Lae. Visiting Wichita with his wife, Cathy, Macair's chief pilot, Graham Syphers, told how their business had grown in four years from one rented aircraft to a fleet of four Beechcraft Barons — with more Beechcrafts in prospect. Their satisfaction was obvious with the performance of the Barons in a country where the annual rainfall is 150 inches, mountains soar to heights of 15,000 feet, and the terrain is all jungle, broken only by a few landing strips often unimproved and not more than 1,800 feet in length.

The profit-making power of the Beechcraft King Air was emphasized in a typical instance of corporate ownership and use by James C. Gorman, president of the Gorman-Rupp Company of Mansfield, Ohio. "In addition to saving travel time between our five plant locations, our company aircraft serve two important functions," Mr. Gorman said. "The first is to bring prospective customers into our factory. Second, and perhaps most important, is to speed the work of our service department for our customers in the field. This often saves them many thousands of dollars." When their Beechcraft King Air is busy, he reported, the firm often uses his Bonanza "and when both of these are tied up, this leaves me my Beechcraft G17 Staggerwing."

Beech Aircraft was host on September 16th to a group of foreign and domestic travel directors making Wichita and Beech their third stop on a 6,500-mile flying trip across the United States. Headed by Assistant Secretary of Commerce for Tourism C. Langhorne Washburn, they were joined at Beech Field by FAA Administrator John H. Shaffer. Their mission was the important task of helping to curb the deficit in the U. S. balance of payments, already exceeding the 1970 total of $2.5 billion in tourism alone, by encouraging foreign travel in the United States. Praising the efforts of the U. S. Travel Service to encourage tourism, President Frank E. Hedrick also pointed out that "The promotion of visits to the interior of the United States would be beneficial in projecting a proper image of America to foreign visitors."

Sustaining the international balance of payments on the plus side in favor of the United States was always a constant concern of the patriotically motivated Beech management. It was an area in which the company could, and did render practical assistance, by promoting export sales of Beechcrafts with all possible diligence and vigor. A summing up showed that from 1946 through the current year, approximately $320 million worth of aircraft and spares had been delivered to foreign customers. This represented some 4,100 Beechcrafts in service in more than

335

a hundred countries, from Afghanistan to Zambia, all over the world.

In mid-September, U. S. Army pilots started to ferry a fleet of Beechcrafts to new homes overseas in Turkey. Ferry flights were begun from Beech Field of five T-42A Beechcraft twin-engine transition, instrument training aircraft for use by the Turkish Army under the Military Assistance Program. Essentially off-the-shelf aircraft (Beechcraft Baron B55's), the trainers were procured by the Army Aviation Systems Command under a $550,000 contract award.

The annual meeting of the National Business Aircraft Association was held September 21st through the 23rd at Minneapolis, Minnesota. There Beech Aircraft, so often a recipient of honors and awards, switched roles and presented an award of its own to the company's largest single commercial customer. Marathon Oil Company of Findlay, Ohio, represented by its aviation division manager, Michael C. Murphy, was the Beech honoree — for excellent reasons. Marathon had just purchased a new Beechcraft Hawker 125 — the 67th Beechcraft bought by Marathon since 1945. Its Beechcraft fleet had included virtually every model from the D17S Staggerwing biplane to Bonanzas, D18 and Super 18 twins, Musketeers and Beechcraft King Air corporate transports. Currently Marathon was operating 18 aircraft, of which 17 were Beechcrafts.

Not only the special Beech award, but also the NBAA annual Award for Meritorious Service to Aviation, was garnered by "Mike" Murphy at the Minneapolis meeting. He was cited by NBAA for "prudence, skill and dedication which expanded aviation's horizons and created a corporate/executive flight operation that is recognized internationally for safety and excellence." His company also earned top ranking as a corporate recipient of the NBAA Flying Safety Award, with a record of better than 26 million safe flying miles. Marathon and Murphy were customers Beech could well point to with pride and satisfaction.

Figures released by Beech at the NBAA meeting showed deliveries at that time of 773 turboprop Beechcrafts, a record unequalled by any other manufacturer in the world. Beechcrafts comprised 52 per cent of all U. S.-built turboprop aircraft in the under-12,500 pounds weight category. It was not surprising, therefore, that the new Beechcraft King Air A100, displayed for the first time outside Wichita at the NBAA gathering, was the star of the show.

To make the meeting even more memorable, there was a presentation by R. H. McGregor, Vice President - Marketing, of Beech Aircraft's first King Air Million Mile Award. Established to honor corporate pilots who verify 4,000 hours (equivalent to one million miles) logged in Beechcraft King Airs, it comprised a set of instruments for the pilot's desk — a suitably engraved clock and a barometer. Rex Shreeve, chief pilot for Miles Laboratories, Elkhart, Indiana, received the first award, qualifying with nearly 4,100 hours of Beechcraft King Air pilot time logged since 1965.

Beechcraft's corporate and business customers were also happy to hear, at the NBAA meeting, that the time between overhaul (TBO) for Beechcraft King Air Pratt & Whitney engines had been increased 300 hours. The effect was to reduce operating costs on these reliable power plants by $2 per hour on the smaller versions, and better than $3 per hour on the larger. The Beech Instant Warranty Coverage was also increased in the customer's favor to cover all claims under $100, or double the previous instant-service warranty amount.

The Beech fiscal year of 1972 opened on October 1, 1971 with the announcement that seven more UNACE Beechcraft King Air A100 aircraft had been contracted for — five by the Canadian Government Department of Transport, and two by the Government of Mexico. Total value of the two contracts was $8 million, including spares and contractor support. This brought to 14 the total number of orders placed for the special mission Nav/Com Evaluation Beechcraft King Air turboprops since 1966 when the configuration was introduced.

Delivery to Beech Aircraft of its 2000th Pratt & Whitney turbine power plant purchased from United Aircraft of Canada was the occasion for the presentation to Chairman Beech and President Hedrick of a unique metal sculpture formed from parts of a PT6 engine by George Jugasz, internationally famous artist. The sculpture, symbolic of important milestones in the histories of both Beech and United Aircraft of Canada, Ltd., was pre-

337

sented in person by UAC President Thor E. Stephenson and his wife, Toni, at a December 17 dinner meeting in Wichita.

Stephenson pointed out that "The combination of Beechcraft airplanes and PT6 engines has produced the majority of the light twin turboprop aircraft in the world. Beech was there in the beginning of the PT6 program, when the prototype was flown in the nose of a Beechcraft Model 18 in 1961. Beech has been there at every successive stage of aircraft and engine development for the light turboprop fleet." It was also brought out that through October 1971, PT6 engines had logged more than 7.1 million flight hours — 60 per cent of which had accrued in Beechcraft commercial and military turboprop aircraft. Purchases of PT6 engines by Beech since 1961 had totalled more than $72 million.

A Beech-sponsored meeting of 44 major suppliers to the company, held at the Wichita plant, brought prompt and productive responses to a challenge from the Beech Materiel Division for a team effort to substantially reduce material costs. The point was made clear that the success of such an effort would produce mutual benefits for all parties concerned. Estimated annual savings ranging from $1,600 to $25,000 each were quickly pledged by twelve suppliers, setting a pattern for cooperative efforts by all participants.

The Beech 1972 Annual Sales Conference, held at Wichita in December 1971, brought good news, joined with a challenge to the distribution organization to prepare for a new decade of general aviation growth. Commercial aircraft sales were regaining momentum. Thirty-eight domestic Beechcraft distributors, dealers and salesmen received special awards and recognition for their sales achievements during the fiscal year. Led by Southeastern Beechcraft of Knoxville, Tennessee, seventeen dealers achieved multi-million dollar sales. The leader's score of more than $4 million was followed closely by three dealers in the plus-$3 million class. Ten Beechcraft salesmen each topped $1 million in sales, with W. F. Work of Southeastern as the leader and "Salesman of the Year" at $3.4 million.

A dazzling array of new 1972 Beechcrafts assured readiness to capitalize to the fullest on sales opportunities in all price and performance categories. Sixteen commercial airplanes were offered, ranging from the new two-place Beechcraft Sport 19 trainer to the ultimate in executive transportation — the Beechcraft Hawker 125 business/corporate jet.

The Beechcraft King Air models of course continued to hold their long-established place at the top of the wholly Beech-built line. At the summit stood the new 285-mph Beechcraft King Air A100, featuring a 612-pound increase in useful load, 96 more gallons of fuel to provide a range of 1,542 miles, new high-styled interiors and quieting, and optional seating plans for 8 to 15 occupants.

The Beechcraft King Air C90 featured the basic advantages and refinements that had enabled it to set new sales records throughout the depressed times since its introduction as an all-weather equipped corporate aircraft at a package price that led the industry in value per dollar invested. Delivered with factory-installed complete de-icing, and anti-icing equipment, weather-avoidance radar, remote compass system, distance-measuring equipment, transponder, private cabin lavatory, air stair door and club seating, its popularity was confidently predicted to continue and increase.

While not a featured model in the 1972 line, the Beechcraft King Air 99 commuter airliner was to be continued in production on an individual order basis.

The Beechcraft Queen Air line was refined for 1972 to offer one model, the Beechcraft Queen Air Model B80. A highly versatile corporate and multi-purpose aircraft, the Beechcraft Queen Air B80 was easily adaptable to either passenger or cargo transport. An optional cargo door facilitated loading of bulky objects; and supercharged 380 hp Lycoming engines provided a cruise speed of 224 mph. With a range of 1,560 miles and a useful load of 3,725 pounds, three basic interior configurations were offered, providing up to 11-place seating capacity.

The 1972 line of corporate aircraft was rounded out with the pressurized, 286-mph Beechcraft Duke A60 model, an airplane suitable for both professional pilot and owner-pilot operation. Recent improvements included a lighter weight turbocharger system integral with its 380 hp Lycoming engines, providing greater fuel economy and cooler operating temperatures for longer engine life; a smoother-working pressurization system to enhance occupant comfort; new interiors; and refinements in cabin fittings. Club seating was optional in a 6-place version.

Three brilliant Beechcraft Barons made up the company's entries in the high performance light twin-engine aircraft market for 1972. Each offered a unique combination of speed, range and payload that, coupled with the luster of the Beechcraft name, had made the Baron line the industry's sales leader in its class during the year.

The Beechcraft Baron 58 — the biggest light twin, with a lengthened fuselage that permitted 6-place club seating — was the year's biggest seller, and seemed likely to hold its lead in 1972. Large dual doors provided easy cabin access for cargo loading and passenger entry, making the Baron 58 ideal for charter and air taxi service. Fuel-injected 285 hp Continental engines permitted over-obstacle takeoffs in less than 1,100 feet. Cruise speed was 230 mph at 7,000 feet; top speed, 242 mph; maximum range with optional tanks, 1,387 miles.

The Beechcraft Baron E55 offered a performance envelope easily outclassing that of its quite respectable competitors in its market. With four to six-place seating, its speeds were identical with those of the Baron 58, using the same engines. Over-obstacle takeoff distance was a mere 968 feet; climb, 1,670 fpm.

The Beechcraft Baron B55, an able performance leader designed to give its owner the most light twin his dollar could buy, had a cruising speed of 225 mph at 7,000 feet and a 236-mph top speed. Its 260 hp fuel injected engines could deliver a 1,225-mile cruising range at economy setting with optional 142-gallon fuel tanks. It was delivered with complete instrumentation and standard avionics.

Four highly refined Silver Anniversary models of the classic Beechcraft Bonanza were offered in the company's 1972 showings. All were ruggedly built to be licensed in the utility category at full gross weight and provide the traditional Beechcraft extra margin of strength under all conditions. All featured new interiors and exterior styling in their 1972 versions.

The classic V-tail was a unique feature of the Beechcraft Bonanza V35B. A direct successor to the original Bonanza, its cruising speed was 203 mph at 75 per cent power from its 285 hp Continental engine. With optional four or six-place seating, a

340

quiet, spacious interior, superb visibility, and solid big-plane feel, it remained the outstanding single-engine airplane in the entire general aviation industry.

The Beechcraft Bonanza F33A practically duplicated the superlative performance of the V35B, while providing a conventional empennage in place of the V-tail. It could cruise at 200 mph, using 75 per cent of its 285 hp. Seating options ranged up to six-place; soundproofing was lavish and interiors luxurious.

The Beechcraft Bonanza A36 continued on its happy way as the industry's most broadly useful single-engine retractable gear high-performance aircraft. Its stretched fuselage provided ample room, and more, for six occupants, large amounts of cargo, or a mixed passenger-cargo loading. Optional double doors made loading easy. Aerodynamic cleanness produced 195-mph cruise speed at 75 per cent of its 285 hp.

The new Beechcraft Bonanza G33 offered high performance coupled with economy. Cruising at 193 mph with 75 per cent output from its 260 hp Continental engine, its 1,015 fpm rate of climb and service ceiling of 16,600 feet made the G33 strongly competitive with the best in its field. It was a true Bonanza in every aspect of its appearance, design, performance and reliability.

The Light Aircraft Marketing Division, established and staffed in 1971 for the specific purpose of advancing Beech penetration into the lower ranges of the general aviation market on a long-range, solid basis, entered 1972 with three new-look, new-name Beechcrafts replacing the former Musketeer models. Activities of this special Division were to be directed toward the acceleration of the growth of general aviation by broadening the market base through innovative techniques. The plan was to establish Beech Aero Clubs at specially franchised existing and new dealerships, emphasizing package pricing for flight training, aircraft rentals and club functions to new pilots and non-owners, some of whom would eventually purchase Beechcrafts of their own. The first step was to offer appropriate aircraft for such operations; and that is what the company did.

The Beechcraft Sport B19 was the basic learn-to-fly and trainer aircraft introduced into the 1972 line. With two to four-place seating and a fixed tricycle gear, it was powered by a 150 hp

341

Lycoming engine. It was licensed in the utility category and built sturdily with big-plane handling qualities and ruggedness.

The Beechcraft Sundowner C23 stepped up a notch in performance using a 180 hp Lycoming engine. Equipment for aerobatic flight and extended cross-country IFR missions was optional.

The Beechcraft Sierra A24R featured retractable landing gear, optional four to six-place seating, and utilized a 200 hp Lycoming engine with a constant speed propeller. In common with the B19 and C23 models, it was equipped with wide optional cabin doors on both sides of the fuselage – a typical Beechcraft quality feature. With its companions, the Sierra completed a line that clearly offered the biggest value per dollar in the entire lower price spectrum of the general aviation market. Beechcraft's creative lightplane sales planning significantly enhanced the spirit of enthusiasm that prevailed throughout the forward-looking Annual Sales Meeting.

President Frank E. Hedrick had good news for stockholders present at the company's mid-December yearly meeting. Beech Aircraft had accomplished a turn-around of better than $20 million in pre-tax earnings in its fiscal year of 1971, compared with the previous year. Through vigilant administration of a number of carefully planned cost management programs, after-tax profits had been raised to a total of $4,753,726 on total consolidated sales of $142,501,041. Earnings per share of stock amounted to $1.04. Adjustment of the quarterly cash dividend during fiscal 1971, from 18¾ cents to 15 cents per share, was offset with long-range compensation in the form of a one per cent stock dividend paid on November 24th.

Commercial sales of $90,079,508 for fiscal 1971 represented a direct reflection of general economic conditions. Of this total, 37 per cent was originated by the company's newly named International Division. Compared with U. S. average exports of approximately 4 per cent of goods produced, Beechcraft's international sales represented a significant contribution to the U. S. balance of payments. The 1971 reorganization and strengthening of the company's North American marketing organization provided full capabilities to make the most of steadily improving domestic economic conditions.

Stockholders were reassured to learn from President Hedrick that the company's vigorous cost controls had achieved their contributions to earnings without any reduction in research and development programs. Instead, R & D had been intensified during the year. The Beech policy of originating continuous improvements throughout its product lines, and planning special-purpose and new model Beechcrafts as commercial and military market opportunities were foreseen, remained in full effect. At Beech-Boulder, work was stepped up in developing next-generation cryogenic storage tanks, holding 50 to 120 times more liquefied oxygen and fuels than prior designs, for use in NASA space missions of up to six months in duration.

Illustrating the importance of Beech research and development to the company's long-range interests, President Hedrick pointed out that in only the specialized field of space exploration, its participation in the Seventies could well exceed the $40 million in space mission contracts during the Sixties. Its many other R & D projects would likewise serve, not only to maintain and advance its competitive position, but also to increase sales. There were good reasons for Beech R & D to retain its high priorities.

Chapter 35

The daily "howgozit" reports that came to the offices of Chairman O. A. Beech and President Frank E. Hedrick throughout the months of October, November and December 1971 had indicated steady gains throughout the first three months of the Beech 1972 fiscal year. Totals for that period, compiled in January, showed actual increases over the same period a year ago of 17 per cent in commercial aircraft sales, more than 10 per cent in consolidated sales, and 15 per cent in after-tax earnings. The year was opening on an upbeat note.

To meet rising costs, the company requested and received Price Commission approval on January 3 for an average 5.9 per cent increase in suggested retail prices for its commercial models. It was no more than a necessary "cost of living" raise that in no way conflicted with the constant Beech aim of giving each customer the most airplane for his money in the general aviation industry. No adverse effects on sales were anticipated, and none occurred, as the year's record was to verify. With the help of the Beech sales organization, alert aircraft buyers could easily see where the best values were to be found.

January 10 brought promotions to four long-time Beechcrafters. John A. Elliott, then entering his thirtieth year of service, was named vice president and treasurer. R. Warren Fisher was appointed to the new post of vice president - administration; and Mrs. Lucille Winters Edwards was named secretary. Both had joined the company in 1937. Mrs. Ila Alumbaugh, a twenty-year employee, became assistant secretary. At the same time, Wyman L. Henry, vice president - marketing, and L. E. Bowery, vice president - materiel, moved into retirement after many years of dedicated and effective service.

The quality built into all Beechcraft products was apparent with the return visit to Beech Field of the first Beechcraft Musketeer to be delivered — serial No. M-4. Since October 1962 it had logged 1,900 hours, and had been successfully rebuilt by its owner, John Lyon of Lorain, Ohio, following an accident in 1969. Its as-new appearance and performance recalled a saying common among pilots over many years: "Those Beechcrafts never wear out." The company's line of light aircraft was carrying on an illustrious tradition.

Important follow-on contracts also brightened the first month of the calendar year. From Bell came another $4.7 million helicopter contract; and from the Department of Defense, a green light for the company to build flight test articles of the Beech-designed Mach 4, 100,000-ft. altitude HAST (High Altitude Supersonic Target). So the tri-service missile target program, which had brought contract awards totalling $9.8 million since its inception in mid-1970, continued in progress.

In February the Royal Flying Doctor Service of Western Australia, which was operating six Beechcraft Barons bringing medical treatment to dwellers in the 350,000 square mile Australian Outback, took delivery of its first pressurized aircraft — a Beechcraft Duke. Pilot/Nurse Robin Miller presented Chairman O. A. Beech with a copy of her recently published book, "Flying

344

Nurse", describing her work with the RFDS and its life-saving Beechcraft fleet.

Film stars and Beech-built products had been famous for getting together as far back as 1928, when Wallace Beery took delivery on a Travel Air 6000 from Walter H. Beech. This trend was renewed in February with the delivery of a new Beechcraft B55 Baron to Academy Award-winning motion picture star Cliff Robertson. A skilled pilot, Robertson immediately put his Beechcraft Baron into use on a nationwide personal appearance tour.

The Beech Aircraft "America First" series of advertisements, conveying a positive view of our nation and its institutions, won a second award from the Freedoms Foundation at Valley Forge, Pennsylvania during the month. Based on the personal views of Chairman Beech and President Hedrick, the winning message, "Oh say, can you see . . . at 5000 feet", featured an aerial photograph taken from a Beechcraft by James Yarnell, Director of Advertising and Sales Promotion. The George Washington Honor Medal Award was a sequel to a companion distinction earned by the company and its advertising agency, Bruce B. Brewer Co., Kansas City, Missouri, in the previous year's Freedoms Foundation competition.

New honors came to the company's products in March. The Federation Aeronautique Internationale (FAI) sent word from Paris that in cooperation with the National Aeronautics Association, official recognition had been given to a new world speed record established June 27-28, 1971 by Miss Louise Sacchi, in flying a Beechcraft Bonanza 36 from New York to London (3,443.56 statute miles) in 17 hours, 22 minutes, 34 seconds at an average speed of 198.17 mph. The speed made good by Miss Sacchi, affectionately nicknamed "The Wichita Lineman" in aviation circles, far surpassed the previous mark of 172 mph established in 1970 for class C-1.d aircraft.

FAI also gave its official sanction to a new world class record for Speed Around the World, established in August 1971 by Trevor K. Brougham, an Australian charter operator, and his co-pilot, Robert N. Dickeson. Flying a Beechcraft Baron B55 over a 24,800-mile course from Darwin to Singapore in five days, five hours, 57 minutes at an average speed of 197.77 mph (including time spent on the ground), the team shaved an hour and twenty

345

minutes off the previous record, which had been set in 1966 by Bob and Joan Wallick in a Beechcraft Baron C55.

There were no records or precedents in existence for the pioneering work in progress at Beech-Boulder on the company's assignments for NASA; the innovative Boulderites were setting new records all their own. A test rig that they devised to conduct hydrostatic testing of a giant 1400-lb. hydrogen thermal tank probably deserved a special award for ingenuity. They simply submerged the big tank in an even bigger standby water storage tank. This procedure served to establish equivalent pressures both inside and outside the tank being tested, and fully verified its integrity at the required ratings.

A significant international delivery was that of a new Beechcraft King Air C90 to the Civil International Aviation Training Center (CIATC), a branch of the Transportation Department of the Government of Mexico at Mexico City. The King Air became the seventh Beechcraft in CIATC's fleet of 16 airplanes and helicopters, joining three Beechcraft Mentor single-engine trainers and three Beechcraft Twin-Bonanzas. It was purchased after an extensive comparison study of turboprop aircraft at manufacturers' facilities that emphasized strict requirements for efficiency and economy. The Mexican Government was the exacting kind of buyer that Beech always welcomed.

Another event of the month held very special personal interest for the company's Chairman. It was the arrival on March 8 at Wesley Medical Center in Wichita of Jeffrey Hanson Pitt — a brand new, 5 pound, 14-ounce Beechcrafter. Jeffrey's mother was the former Mary Lynn Beech, and the proud grandmother was, of course, Mrs. O. A. Beech. The new arrival was Mary Lynn's second child; Jennifer Gwendolyn Pitt celebrated her fourth birthday just ten days after the arrival of her new brother.

Steadily rising commercial sales reached a new high in March; $15 million in deliveries for the month set an early record for the year. Especially gratifying was a sharp uptrend in sales of owner-flown models, ranging from single-engine Beechcraft Sport 19s to twin-engine Beechcraft Barons and pressurized Beechcraft Dukes. The company's products had long enjoyed preference among professional pilots, who were in a favorable position to evaluate the merits of various makes of aircraft. Now that preference was spreading into the ranks of owner-pilots, as the extra value built into Beechcrafts became more widely understood and appreciated. It was a trend rich in promise for strengthening the company's competitive position and further expanding its sales over the full spectrum of the general aviation market.

The end of March marked the midpoint of the Beech 1972 fiscal year. During its first half, sales totalled $80,021,772 compared with $65,580,229 during the first half of fiscal 1971. Earnings were up to $2,848,601 or 62 cents a share, compared with first-half 1971 earnings of $2,198,739 or 48 cents a share. Putting together these results with the distinct outlook for even better business as the year progressed, company directors approved not only the regular cash dividend, but also a special one per cent stock dividend to shareholders.

April 4, 1972 was a most outstanding happy day at Beech Aircraft. One of the company's best-known and most loyal customers came to Beech Field with his wife to take delivery on a new Beechcraft King Air A100; and he had some truly heartwarming things to say about Beechcrafts and their builders.

The company's guest that day was Lyndon B. Johnson, the thirty-sixth President of the United States. Arriving at mid-afternoon from the LBJ Ranch aboard a Beechcraft Hawker 125, he was welcomed by Kansas Governor Robert B. Docking and Wichita Mayor Jack Greene as well as by Beech officials and personnel.

Speaking to an audience that included 1,500 Beechcrafters in Walter H. Beech Hall prior to a tour of Plant I, the former President revealed some keen insights into the character of the company and its people as he expressed his personal confidence in its airplanes. Following are highlights of his talk:

"I came here as a self-invited guest . . . Nobody had to drag me to Wichita. Nobody had to twist my arm. It was my idea to come . . . Why did I want to come?

"Well, there are many reasons. Because all through the years, I have particularly liked the people associated with Beech because I respect their integrity, because I admire their product. But mostly I wanted to come here today to express my personal appreciation while I could for the years of safe, worry-free transportation that all of you have given me and my family.

"I wouldn't attempt to calculate how many thousands of hours of my life have been spent in your hands — have been at the mercy of the airplanes that you've built. Now, my life may not mean much to anyone else, but it always meant a great deal to me. Naturally there is a very warm place in my heart for the Beech Aircraft Corporation and in addition a very strong feeling of confidence in you . . .

"I have been flying in your planes for more than thirty years. I suppose I have either rented or owned or leased every type of commercial plane that you have put out during those years and I never had one cause to ever question the quality or the integrity of your product. I don't say this out of ignorance . . .

"I am not nervous in a Beech. I never have reason to question any of your component parts. I never give any thought to your takeoffs or your landings. I never sit there using body english to help the pilot get the gear up and I don't make that statement about flying any other airplane . . .

"You see, in my judgment, Beech has something that is unique in this modern America of ours, this day of mass production. I guess the experts would call it quality control but down in my country, in the cow country, we just call it plain, old-fashioned integrity — the conscious pursuit of excellence. You don't impose it down on people. You have to develop it from the bottom up; from the man who cleans the floor to the engineers who do the finishing job. It's all a matter of great pride. It's a matter of taking personal satisfaction in doing a job well and doing it competently and doing it accurately . . .

"Ralph Waldo Emerson once wrote: 'The reward of a thing well done is to have done it.' Those words could serve as the motto of Beech Aircraft Corporation. They certainly sum up my own attitude toward Beech.

"To me, Beech is really a part of my family — a very special part. Over the years my family and I have spent a lot of our days and our weeks and our months in your planes.

"I have been with Lady Bird now for more than 37 years and I have been with Beech for a little over 30 and both relationships have been very good.

"Now so I won't add to the credibility gap, I would like to say that there have been some problems with both, but they have

348

Bristling with radar antennae was this special mission U.S. Army RU-21E turboprop — one of 16 produced under a 1972 contract as adaptations of the commercial Beechcraft King Air A100 design. (Pages 314, 354, 355)

Celebrating the 25th Anniversary Year of the classic Beechcraft Bonanza, N25AB ("Anniversary Bonanza") — a blue and silver painted V35B model — made a nationwide "personal appearance" tour. (Pages 352, 353)

The 1,000th turboprop Beechcraft was this King Air A100, which joined Beechcraft King Air 90 and A90 models operated by Miles Laboratories. Checking travel plans at their Elkhart, Indiana base were (from left) Rex Shreve, chief pilot; Dr. Walter Ames Compton, president and chief executive officer; George W. Orr Jr., executive vice president; and John B. Buckley, group vice president. (Page 357)

349

One of Beech Aircraft's best-known and most loyal customers was former U.S. President Lyndon B. Johnson. Gathering when he took delivery in April, 1972 of his new Beechcraft King Air A100 were (from left) Mrs. and Mr. Frank E. Hedrick; Mrs. O. A. Beech; President Johnson and Mrs. Johnson; Kansas Governor R. B. Docking; Mrs. and Wichita Mayor Jack Greene; and (on stairs) Darrell Schneider of Beech Aircraft. (Page 347)

Celebrating forty years of achievement, members of the "Beechcraft Hall of Fame" present at the XL'73 Awards Banquet joined Mrs. Beech in hailing Robert S. Northington, senior vice president of Piedmont Aviation, Inc., Winston-Salem, N.C., as Beech Aircraft's "Man of the Year" for 1972. Upper row, from left: Gerald G. Wilmot, Page Beechcraft; Jess Childress, Hangar One; Dan L. Meisinger, Topeka Aircraft Sales & Service; T. Gail Clark, Tulsair, Inc. Lower row, from left: Tom H. Davis, president and treasurer of Piedmont Aviation, Inc.; Mrs. O. A. Beech; Mr. and Mrs. Northington. (Pages 358, 359)

350

been very rare and I just want to tell you that I hope very much that that relationship between us can continue for a long, long time yet to come. Thank all of you so much for this generous reception."

Praise also came from Preston H. Wilbourne, vice president and general manager of Wisconsin Airlines, with a report that two of the three Beechcraft 99 turboprop airliners in their passenger and cargo commuter service had each passed the 10,000-hour mark in service, becoming the world's first to reach that total. In three years and ten months of operation, the sturdy Beechcrafts had each travelled some 2.15 million miles — equivalent to 86 trips around the world.

"We have operated the 99 Airliners in both passenger and cargo service in our four-state market area since they were purchased in 1968," Wilbourne wrote. "They have been particularly efficient on our longer stage lengths and so reliable that in 1971 we flew them an average of 7 hours, 10 minutes daily."

Export deliveries for the month included a handsome pair of Beechcraft Sport B19s purchased by the Indonesian Flying Academy of Djakarta. They were additions to the Academy's training fleet that already included eleven Beechcrafts — six Sports added in 1969 to an original complement of five Mentor trainers.

The Beech Aerospace Division made a substantial contribution to both immediate and potential future sales by winning a $3.3 million competitive contract award for the design and development of a variable speed training target, the "VSTT" which was later designated the MQM-107, from the Army Missile Command. The VSTT would be called on to operate at altitudes from 300 to 40,000 feet and speeds up to 500 knots. Ten years of work with the Army had preceded the contract award; persistance had finally paid off. The proposed Beech design was considered to have excellent potential as a Remotely Piloted Vehicle (RPV) for many different classified missions, opening the way to possible very substantial future production contracts.

The month closed with the news that the Beech cryogenic life support system had performed very smoothly and with high efficiency throughout the Apollo 16 extended space mission that spanned 11 days from April 16 through April 27. At its end the complete system, designed and built at Beech-Boulder, had totalled more than 6,000 hours supporting manned space flight, with some 400 of those hours in orbit around the moon.

Excitement was in the air not only at Beech Field, but throughout the world of general aviation, on the opening day of May. A new model was being added to the world's most successful and popular line of turboprop aircraft – the Beechcraft King Air E90. It was a pressurized, six to 10-place companion to the Beechcraft C90 and the Beechcraft King Air A100, providing greater speed, altitude capability, and range.

The Beechcraft King Air E90 combined the reliability-proven airframe of the popular C90 with the high-performance turbine engines of the Beechcraft King Air A100 – Pratt & Whitney PT6A-28 turbines of 680 shaft horsepower each, flat rated to 550 horsepower. Reinforced by experience gained in more than 236 million miles of flight by Model 90s, and 13-million plus miles by Beechcraft King Air 100s, the new design offered the highest cruise speeds, service ceilings and ranges of any King Air: Cruise speed at 16,000 feet, 285 mph; service ceiling, 27,620 feet; range at maximum range power, 1,870 miles. An impressive array of standard equipment included engine-driven fuel boost pumps, vertical arrangement of engine instruments for easier scanning, and polarized cabin windows for passenger comfort.

Introduction of the new Beechcraft King Air E90 gave an extra fillip to the celebration of the company's 40th Anniversary which was observed in May. Founded in the depths of a worldwide economic depression in 1932, Beech Aircraft had then seemed a visionary enterprise on the part of Mr. and Mrs. Walter H. Beech, with few chances for survival. Through hard work, persistence and optimism it had grown to the stature of a world leader in general aviation. Such a record deserved commemoration, even though workload pressures ruled out any elaborate and time-consuming observances. Open house was held on a sunny Sunday in May at all of the company's plants for Beechcrafters and their families and friends; then it was back to work as usual the next morning.

It was an anniversary year, too, for the world's most popular high-performance single-engine airplane. The Beechcraft Bonanza was celebrating its 25th Anniversary in 1972 – a quarter century in continuous volume production and sale. In commemoration, the company offered special plaques with its complements to all owners of the 1,229 original V-tailed Beechcraft Bonanzas built during 1947 — most of which were still flying throughout the world.

A specially painted and extensively equipped Beechcraft Bonanza V35B was also dispatched on a "personal appearance" tour of the nation to bring the Silver Anniversary of the Bonanza line to public attention. Finished in bright silvery aluminum urethane paint, it carried the special identification of N25AB (for "Anniversary Bonanza"). Its first appearance came, fittingly enough, at a May 5-7 meeting of Military Aero Clubs hosted by the company in Wichita.

Repeating a stratagem introduced in October 1971, Beech officials were hosts to 56 of the company's suppliers at a one-day cost conference May 10 in Wichita. Discussions led by President Frank E. Hedrick centered on ways to reduce costs, illustrated by Beech experience in achieving economies with no reductions in quality. The previous session with suppliers had produced savings totalling almost a half-million dollars; the May meeting promised to do even better.

Announcement was made that Beech Aircraft had joined with others in forming a subsidiary — Travel Air Insurance Co., Ltd. — to be located at Hamilton, Bermuda. Its purpose was to provide better control over product liability insurance costs, sharing the company's risks with other insurance carriers.

During 1972, Beech Aircraft quietly began making major changes in its domestic distribution organization. In order to strengthen its overall marketing program, the company divided its product line into three separate segments — light aircraft, which included the Beechcraft Sport, Beechcraft Sundowner and Beechcraft Sierra; executive aircraft, comprised of the Beechcraft Bonanza and Beechcraft Baron series, and corporate aircraft, which included the Beechcraft Duke up through the Beechcraft King Air series. Each segment of the product line carried an individual franchise.

After the success of the initial Beech Aero Center franchises, the next step was to refranchise each category in the product line on a direct factory basis and add additional franchisees for greater market penetration.

The terms "distributors" and "dealers" were dropped with the new franchises awarded to Beech Aero Centers, Beechcraft Executive Aviation Centers and Beechcraft Corporate Aviation Centers.

This progressive move was to work to the advantage of the customer, the Beechcraft retail outlet and the Beech Aircraft Corporation.

For the customer, it helped stabilize the aircraft market and provided a broader range of "sales and service" stations to utilize during business and personal travel.

For the Beechcraft retail outlet, the Aviation/Aero Center program provided increased opportunities for profit and stability plus a direct relationship with the Beechcraft factory and all its support capabilities.

For Beech Aircraft, it provided greater expansion of field representation and improved market penetration.

There was no letup in a fast-flowing stream of events at Beech as spring gave way to summer in June. As the month opened, its product display at "Transpo '72", an international transportation display held at Dulles Airport, Washington, D. C., attracted many prospective buyers. Appointment of one of the first franchised Beech Aero Centers — Beechcraft West, Van Nuys, Calif. — and establishment there of the first Beech Aero Club marked the opening of the company's broadened long-range light aircraft marketing program, centering around the single-engine Beechcraft Sierra, Sundowner and Sport models.

Guests visiting Beechcraft during the year included 120 of the more than 250 members of the Staggerwing Club — owners and fans of the classic Beechcraft Model 17 biplane. From 24 states, from Washington, D. C. and from Colombia they came to the club's 1972 fly-in at Beech Field; and a total of 34 Beechcraft biplanes thronged the ramp for the meeting. It was a vivid testimonial to the longevity of Beech products; the Staggerwing Beech had been introduced in 1932, and retired from production in 1948. The oldest biplane there had been built in 1934.

Notable deliveries in June included the last of 16 special-purpose RU-21E turboprop twin-engine aircraft to the U. S.

354

Army. This was the latest version of the RU-21 design, nicknamed the "picket fence" twin because of its bristling array of antennas. Except for its special equipment, it was essentially the same as the commercial Beechcraft King Air A100 — thus providing substantial savings to the Army.

Delivery was also completed of 20 Beechcraft Model 1025 remote-radio-controlled missile targets ordered by the Government of Spain for training service. The Spanish "littlest Beechcrafts" were scheduled for use as tugs to pull Dornier tow targets in anti-aircraft artillery practice — a much safer procedure than that of using piloted aircraft for the towing job.

Commercial sales at the close of the month topped any prior month's totals since October 1969, adding up to $12.3 million on 113 units — 60 twin and 53 single-engine Beechcrafts. The Beechcraft Hawker 125 was adding momentum, too; seven of the 500 mph business/corporate jets were under completion in the Plant I enlarged modification/assembly center during June. Results of the first nine months of fiscal 1972 that closed June 30 showed total sales of $123,278,948, and earnings of $4,740,109 or $1.03 per share. For Beech Aircraft, the recession was over.

To make the most of its fast-growing opportunities, the company enlarged its directorate and top-level management. The board of directors was expanded from seven to ten members with the addition of Robert Martin, the company's chief legal counsel; E. C. Burns, vice president - operations, a 32-year Beechcrafter; and Roy H. McGregor, vice-president - marketing, a Beechcrafter since 1951.

Four new vice presidents were appointed. Harold W. Deets was named vice president - materiel; J. E. Isaacs, vice president - industrial relations; Ed C. Nikkel, vice president - aerospace programs; and Darrell E. Schneider, vice president - government relations. Their combined service records totalled 124 years.

Awards for length of service conferred in July included thirty-eight 30-year honorees, six 35-year honorees, and one 40-year honoree. The recipient of the unique 40-year Service Award was the only Beechcrafter who could have been eligible for such a unique distinction - the company's Chairman and co-founder, Mrs. O. A. Beech. The special service emblem created for presentation by President Frank E. Hedrick to the company's first-ranking senior employee carried a cluster of five diamonds. Of all the countless honors that Mrs. Beech had received throughout an illustrious career, it was probably the most treasured and deeply appreciated.

Always a hot month in Kansas, July set a torrid pace for sales throughout its duration with another record total of $13 million. Export activity was particularly brisk. The Spanish Air Ministry ordered seven Beechcraft Baron B55s for instrument training and liaison, enlarging its fleet of 25 Beechcraft Mentor single-engine trainers. Not to be outdone, the Civil Aviation Bureau of Japan also selected the Beechcraft Baron B55 as its twin-engine instrument trainer, adding a half-dozen twins to its 23-unit Beechcraft Debonair training fleet. The Imperial Air Force of Iran chose 18 Beechcraft Bonanza F33As for its training and liaison work, many equipped for aerobatic flight.

On the domestic front, Beechcrafters were especially happy to welcome another order from the company's most faithful, largest-volume commercial customer — the Marathon Oil Company of Findlay, Ohio. Its newest Beechcraft King Air A100 was the 70th Beechcraft, from Staggerwing biplanes to King Air executive transports, that Marathon had bought from Beech over many years. The Light Aircraft Marketing Program was making good progress, too, with the completion of franchise arrangements for a total of 16 Beech Aero Centers and expanding interest in the Beech Aero Club concept.

Signing by company and union representatives of an improved new three-year contract as the month ended brought wage increases and numerous other benefits to employees, and assured stability for the period of growth ahead. A Beech Employees Bonanza Plan, providing cash gains for the work force in proportion to their increases in productivity, was part of the new agreement.

There was never a dull moment at Beechcraft in 1972, and August was no exception. A strengthening in the position of commuter airlines, recovering from the setbacks of recent mini-recession years, reopened that market for Beechcraft 99 Airliners. The company moved to profit from that happier situation by quietly introducing an improved version — the Beechcraft B99

356

Airliner — incorporating advancements made in its King Air A100 models in the 17-place transport version.

Beech-Salina production workers celebrated the rollout of the 200th Beechcraft Duke by posing with a picture of the historic pressurized twin which they had assembled. It was a big moment for the group, which had achieved a distinguished record for both quantity and quality of output at their division. They had helped put the Beechcraft Duke at the top of its class in sales among pressurized and largely owner-flown fast twin-engine aircraft.

Beech Aircraft Corporation established a new world production record for turboprop aircraft with the delivery of its 1,000th turboprop — a Beechcraft King Air A100 executive transport — to Miles Laboratories of Elkhart, Indiana, at Beech Field. The airplane joined two Beechcraft King Airs, 90 and A90 models, in service with Miles, which had started as a Beech customer in 1959 with a B18 Twin Beechcraft. More broadly, its 1,000th turboprop delivery gave Beech a lead of 655 units over its nearest general aviation rival in turboprop production, and a substantial worldwide lead in commercial turboprop categories, including airliners, over the Russians with 700 IS18s and Fairchild's combined total of 586 F27 and F227 models. Through August the Beechcraft turboprop fleet had logged a massive 2,487,072 hours of utilization — or some 496,664,850 miles of travel, equalling the distance from Earth to the remote planet Jupiter. However viewed, it was a great milestone for Beechcrafters and their company.

The record-smashing Beechcraft King Air turboprops had only one rival for the foremost attention of the business and corporate aircraft fraternity that gathered at the 1972 National Business Aircraft Association convention September 12-14 at Cincinnati.

While occupying a loftier category, that rival still carried the Beechcraft name. It was the new Beechcraft Hawker 125-600 business/corporate jet — a larger, higher-performance, longer-range version of the seasoned BH 125-400 series, of which 270 units were then in worldwide service. Bigger Rolls Royce Viper 601 engines provided 3,750 pounds of thrust each for increases of 20 per cent in payload, 40 knots in speed at 40,000 feet, and 10 per cent in range. A longer cabin provided luxury accommo-

357

dations for eight passengers, or higher-density seating for up to 14; and baggage space was increased by 15 per cent. The joint impact of the new Beechcrafter Hawker 125-600 and the Beechcraft King Airs and Duke aircraft on display served to "steal the show" for Beech Aircraft at the 1972 NBAA meet — not for the first time at that annual event.

Results of the Beech fiscal year 1972 that ended on September 30 were exhilarating. Net earnings — the prime index of any company's performance — totalled $7,086,655 or $1.52 a share, an increase of 49 per cent over fiscal 1971. Consolidated sales came to $174,499,565 for a 22 per cent increase. Commercial sales of $130,280,849 showed a 45 per cent gain. Deliveries of Beechcraft Hawker 125 business/corporate jets and spares were double those of 1971, totalling 13 units or $15,119,966 compared with 7 units or $7,544,251. Export sales during the year totalled $29,857,320 as compared with a 1971 total of $23,305,620. It was a good year; and the directors were quick to share its gains with the company's stockholders, in the form of a ten per cent increase in the quarterly cash dividend rate.

Keeping up the quickened pace of fiscal '72, delivery was made to Page Beechcraft, Inc., Rochester, N. Y.-based Beechcraft Aviation Center, of the largest single order of commercial airplanes ever delivered at one time to a domestic franchisee. The Page "package", representing retail sales of more than $3.3 million, comprised one Beechcraft Hawker 125 jet, two Beechcraft King Air A100s and a Beechcraft King Air E90 — nothing but the best all the way.

There was a touch of nostalgia in a report from the Pensacola Naval Air Station that the oldest airplane in the U. S. Navy's inventory, a Model 18 Twin Beechcraft RC-45J utility transport and trainer, was being retired after a service career of 30 years. Headed for display in the Naval Aviation Museum, old "771" would keep alive the tradition of the thousands of Model 18 Beechcrafts that had served the armed forces of the United States and Free World nations in many ways over many years.

"XL'73" was the title and theme of Beech Aircraft's annual sales meeting that convened in Wichita's Century II convention complex October 23-25; and it was, according to President Hedrick, "a tremendous success and the best introduction of products in Beech's history."

Featuring a $3.5 million exhibit of 14 Beechcraft airplanes and equipment, "XL'73" brought together more than 600 aviation center and aero center franchisees, and foreign distributors representing 68 different countries. It produced commercial aircraft orders totalling $18.3 million, carrying the company into 1973 with a backlog of commercial business that added up to $67.2 million, largest in Beech's 40-year history.

At the annual Awards Banquet, many were recognized for million dollar sales accomplishments. Heading the list was Robert S. Northington, senior vice president and general manager of Beechcraft operations at Piedmont Aviation, Inc., at Winston-Salem, N. C. He was named Beech Aircraft's "Man of the Year" for 1972. Four other aviation centers headed by Southeastern Beechcraft, Knoxville, Tenn., each topped $4 million in 1972 sales.

The title of "XL'73" served to emphasize the company's 40th anniversary year. More significantly for the future, it pointed up a new theme — "The Excellence of Beechcraft" — which was to become the keynote for Beech advertising and sales, just as it had stood throughout four decades as the constant aim of Beech design and production. The new theme was no mere claim or boast; it was simply a concise way to "tell it like it is."

The 14 Beechcrafts on display for sale in 1973 offered visible proof of "The Excellence of Beechcraft." Excellence in value was attested by numerous advancements in design, equipment and appointments — all at no increase over 1972 prices.

The four Beechcraft King Air models on display offered increased aircraft value ranging from $1,395 to more than $13,000, in addition to significantly lower operating costs resulting from an increase to 3,000 hours of the time between overhaul for the Pratt & Whitney engines on all King Airs. Standard equipment added to the King Air C90 included polarized cabin windows, a nose baggage compartment with hinged door, vertical display of engine instruments, a new low-profile glareshield, and deep-pile carpeting. New styling was offered on 1973 versions of the Beechcraft King Air E90 and A100 models. While not on display, the new Beechcraft B99 turboprop airliners offered a total of 66 engineering advancements, headed by a 500-pound increase in gross weight.

The twin-engine, pressurized Beechcraft Duke B60 for 1973 brought the last word in excellence to buyers of high-performance twins, with speeds up to 286 mph, 1,000-mile plus range, advanced pressurization, and short-field capabilities.

Versatility of the 7 to 11-place Beechcraft Queen Air B80, coupled with high performance, economy and a 3,700-pound useful load, maintained its excellence as the outstanding aircraft in the all-purpose twin category for the international market.

The three Beechcraft Baron twins — the B55, E55 and 58 models — offered top performance excellence in the light twin class, with the flexibility and utility of comfortable six-place seating and the ability to operate from virtually any airport or landing strip, improved or unimproved.

Refined to the ultimate as they celebrated their 25th Anniversary Year, the three Beechcraft Bonanzas carried on their classic tradition of excellence. The great V-tailed Beechcraft Bonanza V35B and its sister design, the Beechcraft Bonanza F33A with conventional empennage, again set the industry standard for high-performance single-engine aircraft. The larger single-engine Beechcraft Bonanza A36 topped its class with a useful load of more than three-quarters of a ton and a top speed of 204 mph.

The excellence of Beechcraft was enhanced in its 1973 line of light aircraft with many improvements and refinements. Visibility was greatly improved by adding a new low-profile instrument panel with a padded glareshield. A new engine control quadrant, relocated controls, and an improved door-latching system with new safety contour handles were featured. Control column forces were lightened; and new restyled interiors featured the same materials used in the Beechcraft Bonanza line. All models — the Beechcraft Sierra A24R, the Sundowner C23, and the Sport B19, shared the 1973 advancements, at no increase in cost to the purchaser.

November 15th was the delivery date for the 150th Beechcraft B99 Airliner, which went to Scheduled Skyways, Inc. of Fayetteville, Arkansas. It was the third of the new B99 series to be completed; and more sales were in prospect for the 17-place model, not only for airline service but also for special uses such

360

as simultaneous training of six aircrew navigators or, equipped with electronic remote sensors, for aerial detection of mineral deposits or pollution sources.

Increasing general concern over pollution of the environment revealed that Beech Aircraft had long been active in the abatement of pollution, at all its production locations and also in the design of Beech products. Plant wastes were reclaimed or neutralized, open burning of combustible trash eliminated, and cooling water reused, to cite only typical examples of Beech concern for community ecology. Plant buildings and premises were well maintained and landscaped to look consistently attractive.

Taking a long look ahead, the possibility loomed that both Beech-Boulder and Wichita might become substantially involved in the proposed Space Shuttle System for which North American Rockwell held a $2.6 billion, six-year research and development program. Specific items mentioned for the rocket-like Space Shuttle Orbiter vehicle included the power reactant storage assembly and ground support equipment.

Meanwhile, Beech Aircraft and its Boulder Division concluded an eleven-year involvement with the Apollo spaceflight program as the closing Apollo 17 moonflight of December 6-19 (longest of all Apollo missions) ended with what were termed by NASA "super successful" results. Attention then focused at Beech-Boulder on completion of the tanks to be installed in Skylab for the six-months mission aloft of America's and the world's first habitable space station.

HAST, the Beech-designed High Altitude Supersonic Target, rated high marks in a first development article configuration inspection conducted by a tri-service group of Air Force, Army and Navy representatives near the year's end. The group was highly complimentary of the progress made to date on the $10 million prime contract being fulfilled by the company for design, development and manufacture of the hybrid-fueled HAST flight test articles.

Beech research and development, always strong elements in the company's progress, was engaged among many other items in the design and construction of prototype container systems to demonstrate the practical application of liquefied natural gas

361

(LNG) as a clean-burning fuel for automobiles, trucks and buses. The project drew heavily on Beech-Boulder experience in cryogenics and the storage and use of supercooled hydrogen and other space age gases.

As the year 1972 came to a close, a follow-on contract for $1.9 million assured the continuance in production of the Beechcraft AQM-37A target missile. The Japanese Defense Agency selected the Beechcraft King Air C90 to train Japanese Navy pilots, ordering three aircraft for delivery in the summer of 1973 as the first step in a long range procurement program expected to extend over several years. And Bell Helicopter signed an $8.6 million contract extending Beech production of its Jet-Ranger II components from July, 1973 through August 1974. It included an option for an additional $13.1 million dollar order further extending production through June, 1976.

There were many sound reasons to expect that even from the most conservative possible viewpoint, the year ahead would be the biggest, in both sales and earnings, in the company's 40-year history. Its dedication to excellence was well rewarded in 1972.

Chapter 36

From its opening days onward, 1973 took shape as a year to be long remembered, both in the annals of Beech Aircraft and in the larger context of national and world events.

Shortages of natural gas and fuel oil in Kansas and elsewhere during January foreshadowed the energy crisis that later emerged on a worldwide scale. Beech Aircraft responded by intensifying a company-wide energy conservation program that was originated in 1970 as part of a cost reduction drive. Beechcrafters donned warmer clothing as thermostats were turned down in plants and offices. Sources of heat loss were sealed off, and consumption of electrical power was reduced to the lowest possible level.

The emergency was one for which Beech was well prepared. At the peak of its World War II production in 1943, the company had countered a threatened shortage of natural gas by drilling its own wells to assure a standby source in case of need. Later on, after the wells were exhausted, they were maintained as reservoirs for natural gas purchased in summertime for use during the winter peak consumption period. Fuel oil reserves were similarly maintained, simply as a matter of prudent practice. It turned out well for both Beech and other users of scarce fuels when the real pinch arrived.

In pleasing contrast, there was no shortage of sales and earnings as the new year began. The first quarter of the Beech fiscal year of 1973 set new records: total sales, $49,533,135; after-tax earnings, $2,384,551. Booming sales of commercial aircraft were largely responsible; "the excellence of Beechcraft" was making its imprint in the general aviation market.

At mid-January, Beech Plant III at Wichita made a further entry in its log of subcontract production records. Delivery of the 2000th Beech-built complete airframe for the Army OH-58A light observation helicopter to the Bell Helicopter Company was marked by a brief ceremony. The event didn't take long for more airframes were on the line awaiting completion.

Beechcrafters were saddened by the sudden passing away of two good friends during the month. On January 17 George T. Humphrey, senior vice president and a director of Beech Aircraft, suffered a fatal heart attack at his home. A gifted salesman and seasoned executive, Humphrey had joined the management team in 1969.

Only five days later, on January 22, a massive heart attack took the life of Lyndon B. Johnson at his LBJ ranch in Texas. The former President of the United States had been one of the most enthusiastic boosters for Beechcraft and its products and people. Less than three weeks before he died, he had written a warm letter to President Frank E. Hedrick, reaffirming his appreciation, and recounting his pleasure at visiting the Beech plant in April 1972 to take delivery on his new Beechcraft King Air A100.

On January 23, Miss Louise Sacchi successfully completed her 200th transoceanic ferry flight. Delivering a Beechcraft Sierra to Europe, she made the North Altantic crossing from Boston via Gander, Newfoundland and Shannon, Ireland in 30 hours flying time. About 95 per cent of the over-ocean flights logged

363

by Miss Sacchi had been made in Beechcrafts; and her record verified the acronym "SAFE" that stood for the name of her business — Sacchi Air Ferry Enterprises.

Echoes of that happy acronym resounded in two decisions handed down a few days later by the U. S. District Court in Los Angeles. The court rulings dismissed class action suits filed against Beech Aircraft totalling $273 million in claims against the company. Those decisions disposed of all pending class action litigation. And, while the rulings were based on points of law advanced by Beech counsel, there stood in the background the constant Beechcraft tradition of always designing and building the safest aircraft of their kind that human skills and care could possibly produce.

Closely related to that tradition of care and skill was the semi-annual series of service awards conferred late in January. "There is no substitute for experience" was one of the company's guiding axioms. Awards for experienced, loyal and faithful service went to three 35-year employees and 40 Beechcrafters with 30 years of service. These and other awards brought to a total of 2,808 the number of employees with 10 years or more of service, and 1,858 with 20 years or more, among the total at that time of 5,557 employees.

The month closed with the *good news* that orders received for commercial aircraft from domestic and international buyers during January came to a total of 100 units, valued at more than $13 million. The figure was nearly double the total of commercial sales for January 1972. The new year was off to a great start.

Sales reported early in February included orders for Beechcraft Sierra A24R aircraft for the training fleets of five colleges and universities across the nation. Embry-Riddle Aeronautical University, Daytona Beach, Florida, one of the country's oldest and most prestigious aviation training institutions, bought two Sierras. Ohio State University at Columbus; Rangely Junior College, Rangely, Colorado; Ferris State College, Big Rapids, Michigan; and Central Missouri State College at Warrensburg, also chose the Sierra for their primary and instrument flight training programs.

Beechcrafters welcomed a visit on February 12 from twenty members of the graduating class of the U. S. Naval Test Pilot

School, Patuxent River, Maryland, and staff principals. Commander Douglas P. Dunbar, Jr., chief flight instructor, presented a plaque to Chairman O. A. Beech in appreciation for the company's cooperation with the school programs. Beech Aircraft was the only general aviation manufacturer to be included in the nationwide tour of the class.

The company's reputation for advanced, high-performance designs, solidly established in the Thirties by its distinctive Staggerwing biplanes and highly efficient all-metal Beechcraft Model 18 twins, made Wichita and Beech Aircraft a Mecca for the worldwide aviation fraternity. Throughout succeeding years, the Beech plant enhanced its status as a major attraction for the air-minded, as well as for Kansans and others more broadly interested in one of the state's major industries and in outstanding craftsmanship and advanced manufacturing methods.

Buyers, owners and pilots of Beechcrafts enjoyed a special welcome from the company. They were treated to plant tours whenever their schedules permitted, as well as to luncheons with members of the Beech management team and other manifestations of hospitality. The precedent for these actions was established long ago by Mr. and Mrs. Beech, following the principle of setting up a person-to-person relationship with every customer and doing everything within (and sometimes beyond) reason to assure his complete satisfaction with his Beechcraft. That principle continued, and still remains in full force to the utmost practical extent, even as the list of Beechcraft owners grew to number many thousands.

Reactions of these special guests to their reception brought frequent messages of appreciation. Typical was a letter from Kenneth D. Johnson, manager of aviation sales — north central region, Phillips Petroleum Company, to Chairman O. A. Beech:

"I would like to take this opportunity to thank you and your staff for your gracious hospitality on a memorable occasion.

"This was my second visit (to the Beech factory) and I look forward to each and every one eagerly. I fly a Beechcraft Bonanza 33A for Phillips, and it is great assurance to tour your facility and see the fine workmanship and quality that goes into each aircraft."

A feature of the U. S. Army Worldwide Target Users Conference at Huntsville, Alabama on February 14-15 was a handsome mockup of the proposed Beechcraft VSTT (variable speed training target). Completed through all-out effort on less than a month's notice, the mockup attracted much favorable attention and comments. The Beechcrafters who produced it so quickly kept the company "on target" for a potential decade of large-scale VSTT sales and manufacture.

Extra incentive for all Beechcrafters to put forth extra effort on their jobs was offered soon afterward, with the approval on February 26 by the Federal Pay Board of the Beechcraft Employees Bonanza Plan. Similar in principle to the Beech Efficiency Incentive Plan (BEIP) that had helped to accomplish near-miracles of output during World War II, the Bonanza Plan held forth company-wide bonus payments to all employees for gains in productivity. Its benefits were to become quickly apparent as the year progressed.

With the coming of warmer weather in March, the extent of the company's reliance on its own energy resources throughout the past winter was fully revealed. Reporting on the effects of the general fuel shortage, E. C. Burns, vice president - operations, disclosed that "Since last November 20, we have been required to meet our fuel needs from our own natural gas storage wells and limited fuel oil supplies for 57 per cent of the time". Nevertheless, no shutdowns had been necessary. Production had moved forward on schedule, and the Beech energy conservation program had caused at worst only occasional minor discomfort. Foresight and long-range planning had paid off.

At mid-March Howard "Pug" Piper was retained as a full-time consultant in the Beech light aircraft program. Formerly executive vice president of Piper Aircraft Corporation at Lock Haven, Pa., Piper had been active in lightplane development since 1935.

The company's stature as a major industry in its geographical area became clear as results of a study completed in March were published. Based on its fairly typical 1972 fiscal year, Beech spent a total of $62.3 million for goods and services in the state of Kansas during a twelve-month period. That sum made up 39 per cent of its total out-of-pocket expenses of $160 million during the fiscal year. Its worldwide activities produced a total income of $179 million, 98.9 per cent of which was generated

366

outside the state. Beech was obviously a strong contributor to the economy and growth of Kansas and Wichita.

The news was all good when results of the first half of the Beech fiscal year 1973 that ended March 31 were announced. Total consolidated sales came to $99,276,311, producing net earnings of $4,800,770. A record-breaking year seemed assured, based on commercial aircraft orders that were showing a continuous rate of climb. For the second time in twelve months, directors voted to raise the cash dividend rate — from 66 to 70 cents per share — and, for good measure, approved a one per cent stock dividend.

On April 3, John H. "Jack" Shaffer, former administrator of the Federal Aviation Administration and 1972 recipient of the Wright Brothers Memorial Trophy, was elected to the company's Board of Directors. A graduate of West Point and a World War II combat pilot, Shaffer's distinguished record as an executive with major U. S. corporations and a vigorous and effective FAA chief thoroughly documented his credentials to enhance the capabilities of the Beechcraft directorate. His widely recognized stature also qualified Shaffer as a credible spokesman to the public and to government authorities on matters affecting aviation and aerospace — a circumstance that was to demonstrate special value before the year came to its close.

The April issue of *Fortune* Magazine acknowledged the outstanding leadership of Beech Aircraft's chairman of the board, Mrs. O. A. Beech, in a special article entitled "The Ten Highest Ranking Women in Big Business". Cited as the highest-salaried executive among *Fortune's* group of nominees, Mrs. Beech was given full credit for her constructive guidance of the company's affairs. An illustrative photograph, showing Mrs. Beech at her desk, was appropriately backgrounded by her collection of aircraft models, including some of the famous early-day Travel Air airplanes built by Beech Aircraft's predecessor firm when she and Mr. Beech were first joined in that enterprise.

As the year opened, Beechcrafters had hailed the completion of the 2,000th airframe assembled at Wichita Plant III for the Army's OH-58A Bell light observation helicopter. Echoes of that event resounded in May, with the receipt of a $1.2 million follow-on contract from Bell for the continuation of Beech production of OH-58A airframes.

Commercial aircraft sales continued their upward climb as the benefits of Beechcraft ownership became apparent to increasing numbers of businessmen. Typical was the experience reported by Ernesto DelGato of Aricibo, Puerto Rico, when he came to Wichita to take delivery of his fifth Beechcraft, a new pressurized Duke. Upgrading his equipment as his business grew, DelGato had since 1964 purchased in succession a Musketeer Custom, a Musketeer Super, a used Beechcraft Baron, and a new Beechcraft Baron 58. His purchase of the speedy 286 mph, all-weather Duke would assist the expansion of his Puerto-Rican based Del-Gato Construction Company into Central and South America. And, if business there proved as good as he hoped, he vowed to return to Wichita in a year or two to pick up a newer and bigger Beechcraft. "I worked 365 days a year to get my business built up", DelGato said, "but it took more than just hard work. If it were not for my aircraft, the company would not be where it is today".

Beechcraft cryogenic systems again assumed a vital role in the nation's space programs, with the launching on May 14 from Cape Kennedy of the 100-ton Skylab space station and on May 25 of its Command and Service Modules spacecraft. Storing 639.5 pounds of oxygen and 53.1 pounds of hydrogen in a liquid state, the four double-walled cryogenic Beech-built tanks would supply fuel for the CSM spacecraft electrical power system, life support for the three-man crew, and supplementary power to the earth-orbiting Skylab workshop. Key personnel from Beech-Boulder stood by at the NASA Johnson Space Center at Houston to monitor the launch and help solve any problems that might develop. Their services were not needed. The Beech system functioned flawlessly throughout the flight and the subsequent docking and fulfillment of Skylab Mission I.

Throughout the month of May, commercial aircraft sales kept up their blistering pace. Buyer demand was especially strong for the pressurized Beechcraft Duke — a source of special pride to workers at Beechcraft-Salina, the assembly center for that high-performance twin. The Beechcraft Duke enjoyed its greatest sales month since its introduction in October 1968. Orders

368

for 18 units reached a total at retail figures of $3,377,250, completely selling out the 1973 pressurized Beechcraft Duke production allotment. The production rate was promptly increased for the turbocharged twin. Its popularity came as no surprise. With a top speed of 286 mph at 23,000 feet, the Beechcraft Duke had a service ceiling of 35,800 feet for great over-the-weather capability, and a range in excess of 1,100 miles.

One of the many orders for the Beechcraft Duke was exceptionally gratifying because of the lifesaving services that the airplane was sure to perform. It came from the Royal Flying Doctors Service of Australia; and it represented the second Duke to be delivered to that humanitarian organization, supplementing their existing fleet of six Beechcraft Barons to provide medical services and transportation throughout the far-flung and trackless ranges of the Australian Outback. Like their first Duke, the second RFDS unit would be specially equipped as a flying ambulance, carrying two litters for patients, plus medical equipment and seating for two attendants or passengers. Its pressurized cabin assured the sea level environment vital to the well-being of injured patients, at flight altitudes of 10,000 feet or more needed to avoid rough passage through turbulent air often encountered at lower levels. "Out here, it's an airplane or a grave", said Dr. Harold G. Dicks of the RFDS, quoting a saying long current in the remote Outback of Australia. Beechcraft Dukes and Barons were doing their part to assure the happier alternative for RFDS patients.

Another Beechcraft Duke delivered about that time had the distinction of being probably the most completely equipped medium twin in the entire general aviation industry. Delivered to the Collins Radio Company of Cedar Rapids, Iowa for worldwide service as their demonstrator, it carried an advanced complement of Collins avionics that included dual flight directors, dual VHF communicators, dual VHF navigators, a dual audio system, digital ADF, dual glide slope, marker beacon, dual RMI's, weather radar, radio altimeter and code transponder. As a finishing touch, special promotional lighting similar to that on TWA airliners highlighted the Collins logotype displayed on the vertical tail.

Commercial orders were not the only contributors to the fast-growing Beech Aircraft backlog. The French Air Force contracted for a quantity of Beech Model 1094 supersonic, rocket-powered target missiles, plus spares and support services, and took an option to add on a much larger number of units later. Similar in design to the AQM-37A target missile which had been in production at the Beech plant since 1959, the 560-pound Model 1094 featured Mach 2 speed and 70,000-foot altitude capability.

A significant milestone in the company's aggressive light aircraft marketing program was the grand opening at Beechcraft West, Van Nuys, California, of the world's first Beech Aero Club building. Transported cross-country from Wichita by truck in sections, the handsome modular structure was planned to lead the way for many more of its kind all over the nation as the company's aero club concept became fully activated.

Word had come from the White House on June 29 that the company's president, Frank E. Hedrick, had been appointed to serve as Wichita area chairman of the National Alliance of Businessmen (NAB) for a one-year term. In this post Hedrick would direct area efforts of the NAB — a partnership of business, labor and government organized in 1968 — to secure jobs and job training for Vietnam veterans, disadvantaged people, and needy youth. Functioning principally through the Job Opportunities in Business Sector (JOBS) program, the Alliance had provided jobs or job training during the past year for nearly 2,000 Wichita area residents.

The Beechcraft King Air series made news during the busy summer. Flown solo by Walter Boener of the company's International Division, a Beechcraft King Air A100 returned to Wichita from a worldwide demonstration tour routed to Tokyo by way of Europe and India with only two maintenance items booked in its log — replacement of a landing wheel tire and an engine igniter during a routine 100-hour inspection. The only problem Boener encountered was that of explaining to prospective customers that the Beechcraft King Air needed no copilot, mechanic, or large array of spare parts to complete its 43,100-mile journey in safety and comfort for its one-man crew.

"Nothing can beat aviation when you have to haul people or equipment from place to place in a hurry", said Phillip A. Ryan

370

of Paso Robles, California, as he took delivery at Wichita in August of a new Beechcraft King Air C90. Since the new plane was the second King Air he had purchased, it was logical to infer that in Ryan's estimation, nothing could beat a Beechcraft for his use. Semi-retired as the former owner and president of the Ryan Contracting Company, marine constructors and pioneers in deep-water drilling systems, Ryan had been flying since he was 16 years old in 1936. He expected to continue keeping up his past average of 300 hours flight time per year in his newest Beechcraft, looking after his investment interests and transporting his family which he described as "flying oriented".

Ryan enjoyed the special distinction of receiving the 600th Beechcraft King Air 90 — an airplane that established a production milestone as the 1147th turboprop built by Beech Aircraft since June, 1964. The delivery enhanced the company's distinction of having produced more turbine-powered aircraft in the under 12,500-pound class than any other one manufacturer in the world. The record showed that at that point the entire line of Beechcraft King Airs, 90 and 100 models, made up 52 per cent of the world population of general aviation turboprop aircraft.

Launching of the second manned Skylab mission on July 28 marked the 15th journey into space for Beech Aircraft's cryogenic gas storage system. The Beech system, which had supported every Apollo mission since 1966 — including the air landings on the moon — again performed up to all expectations.

The company further advanced its leadership in the turboprop field with the booking in August of orders for seven Beechcraft B99 Airliners, valued at $3,675,000. All were to enlarge existing fleets of Beechcraft 99 Airliners. Two units for Rio Airways of Killeen, Texas would put nine Beechcraft 99s in service on their mid-Texas commuter routes. Henson Aviation of Hagerstown, Maryland was adding a fifth Beechcraft to its fleet of four.

The largest purchase, that of four Beechcraft B99s through Allegheny Airlines for use by independent operators in the Allegheny commuter system, had been previewed in March with the delivery of a new Beechcraft B99 Airliner to Pocono Airlines, Avoca, Pa. Theirs was the 151st Model 99 delivered since 1968. The new Allegheny order was further reinforced with an option for four additional units.

The Beechcraft Training Center for pilots and mechanics graduated its 10,000th student on September 14, achieving a record unmatched by any comparable facility in general aviation. Garri Warren, the corporate pilot of a Beechcraft King Air E90 owned by Murchison Brothers, Dallas, Texas, received special recognition as Graduate No. 10,000. Organized in August 1964, the Beechcraft Training Center at Wichita, together with its associated Mobile School programs in the field, was making good the company's aims of thoroughly acquainting owners and operators with their Beechcrafts. Its educational follow-through on the long-standing Beech policy of maintaining the closest possible person-to-person relationship with the company's customers was serving to establish increased proficiency and increased safety as a happy end result.

As production and sales kept up a record-breaking pace, Beech Aircraft's continuous research and development program likewise maintained its contributions to the company's progress. President Frank E. Hedrick had reported to stockholders at their last annual meeting that the company's management remained ever mindful of the need not only to improve existing Beech products in every possible way, but also to continue originating and developing successful new products. In keeping with this philosophy, he revealed that a very substantial 8 per cent of the firm's gross revenues was consistently invested in R & D projects.

A progress report on one of the many Beech R & D projects brought a group of distinguished guests to Wichita on September 21. Headed by Assistant Secretary of the Navy Robert B. Nesen, its members included three Rear Admirals: John M. Thomas, Fred B. Koch, and James Ferris. They came to inspect a new Beechcraft T-34C Mentor — an experimental version of the Beechcraft T-34B Mentor trainer that had won high favor with the Navy by virtue of the performance and sturdiness of 1,094 units in military use — that had been equipped with a turboprop engine. Top-level attention to the newly-powered version and a highly successful first flight were good omens for its long-range future.

The most felicitous event of the year was the culmination of four years of intensive research, development and testing. It was the unveiling of an advanced new design that for some months

372

had been designated by the national aviation press as "aviation's worst kept secret" — the new Beechcraft Super King Air turbo-prop executive transport. The new flagship of the company's King Air line had its public showing for the first time on September 14 at the annual National Business Aircraft Association meeting in Dallas, Texas.

An impressive and highly functional T-tail established a new image for the Beechcraft King Air line; and the airplane's performance was completely in keeping with its name. Its maximum speed cruise was 333 mph; its climb rate 2,450 feet per minute; useful load 5,275 pounds; service ceiling above 31,000 feet; and nonstop range 2,172 miles plus a 45-minute reserve. A cabin pressurization differential of 6 psi provided a sea level cabin at 13,820-ft. altitude and a comfort level of 6,740 feet at 25,000 ft. altitude. A takeoff weight of 12,500 pounds and 544-gallon fuel capacity provided highly flexible mission planning.

Power plants were the PT6A-41 version of the thoroughly proven Pratt & Whitney turbines used in all Beechcraft King Air models. The dash 41's produced a maximum power output of 850 shaft horsepower each in the Beechcraft Super King Air, which could be maintained on takeoff on a 106°F day.

Approved and factory-equipped for all-weather and icing flight under air transport certification, the Beechcraft Super King Air featured pneumatic de-icing boots on the wings and horizontal tail, dual electrically heated windshields, heated pitot masts and fuel vents, and complete engine anti-icing devices. Air conditioning complemented the heating and ventilation systems as standard equipment to assure passenger and crew comfort in all seasons and climates. Noise reduction measures that permitted normal conversation throughout the spacious 22-foot cabin included the relocation of engines further outboard, the use of relatively slow-turning three-blade propellers, tri-laminated windows, and computer-guided deployment of sound-absorbing tuned-cell panels. Standard cabin seating comprised six widely spaced, deep-cushioned executive chairs. A wide range of furnishings options was offered, and a high-density configuration was also available.

The new Beechcraft Super King Air made its debut as the most thoroughly tested product ever introduced by the Beech Aircraft

Corporation. Wind tunnel testing alone went on for 375 hours prior to release of the aerodynamic configuration. Actual flight tests consumed a greater span of time, and some 100 hours were devoted to in-flight icing tests, with help from the National Center for Atmospheric Research — many in thunderstorm area icing conditions of particular severity. Additional static testing, flight simulation via computer, pressure cycle testing, systems ground testing, and fatigue testing, brought the man-hours of testing to a total in the hundreds of thousands. The design was not released for public showing and sale until the final report came from Jack L. Marinelli, vice president - aircraft research and development: "The Beechcraft Super King Air has passed all our tests with flying colors".

Its unusual T-tail design was settled on after tests proved it to offer superior controllability, a greater center of gravity range, reduced vibration and longer life. But entirely apart from its intrinsic merits, it also produced a bonus benefit that was sure to have its effect in the corporate aircraft marketplace. The T-tail was eminently distinctive — quite as much so, in its way, as the V-tail made famous throughout the world of aviation on the Beechcraft Bonanza. From as far away as the eye could see, the T-tail would be the prime identifying feature of the Beechcraft Super King Air — an airplane clearly destined to take its place among the foremost products of the general aviation industry.

The "Happy Day" flag on the desk of Chairman O. A. Beech was still waving briskly in the propwash of the new Beechcraft Super King Air when a fresh gust of good news came along. Results of the company's 1973 fiscal year that closed on September 30 were announced. And, precisely as forecast, new all-time records for sales and earnings — topping all previous highs in the firm's 41-year history — were established by the Beech Aircraft Corporation and its subsidiaries.

Consolidated sales totaled $204,661,874 — compared with the previous all-time high of $187,313,727 reached in the 1969 fiscal year. Net earnings of $10,022,584 toppled the record total of $9,036,236 attained in the 1967 fiscal year.

The Beechcraft Board of Directors was quick to share the company's record-smashing earnings with those who had played a part in making them possible. For the stockholders whose

374

Four years of intensive research, development and testing preceded the introduction in 1973 of the Beechcraft Super King Air as the flagship of the company's corporate aircraft fleet.
(Pages 372, 374)

The towering, aerodynamically efficient T-tail of the Beechcraft Super King Air established a new image in general aviation — joining the V-tail of the classic Beechcraft Bonanza as symbolic of the industry's most advanced products.

375

Ranging from outer space to ground level went the span of Beech activities in 1973. Cryogenic gas storage systems designed and built at Beech-Boulder were vital components in the year's NASA Skylab space missions, pictured in a composite drawing and photograph 270 miles above earth.
(Pages 368, 371)

Beechcraft's U.S. Army VSTT (Variable Speed Training Target) roared off from ground launch at White Sands Missile Range in New Mexico to complete a successful 11-minute demonstration flight in May, 1973.
(Page 366)

A company station wagon powered by liquid natural gas demonstrated a fuel supply system and Apollo-type LNG storage tank designed and built at Beech-Boulder in carrying forward Beech research and development of automotive power sources aimed toward fuel conservation.
(Page 387)

376

investments were the foundation of its financial structure, there was an increase in the annual cash dividend rate, from 70¢ up to 75¢ per share, and a concurrent three-for-two stock split.

Employees also came in for their share of rewards. Completing its first year of operation, the Beechcraft Employees Bonanza Plan had produced quantitative increases in efficiency through the cooperative efforts of the company's workers. In return they were given a bonus of nearly $1.6 million, shared among all hands on the basis of a cash payment of 2.91 per cent of each employee's earnings.

New records were established in the 1973 fiscal year for the highest number of orders in one year for three aircraft categories: Beechcraft King Airs, 198 units; Beechcraft Dukes, 57 units; and Beechcraft Barons, 468 units. King Air orders alone totaled more than $90 million. Avionics sales showed an increase of 51 per cent over the 1972 fiscal year, reaching a total of more than $32 million.

In October, the Spanish Air Ministry enlarged its fleet of 11 Beechcraft Baron B55 trainers with a multi-million dollar order for six Beechcraft C90s and two Beechcraft King Air A100s. The Provincial Government of British Columbia in Canada placed the first retail export order for the company's newest model, contracting for two Beechcraft Super King Air 200s equipped for multiple duties that included ambulance service, aerial photography and mapping, and official executive transport.

Unusual, if not unique, was the achievement of a Beechcraft Duke owner who simultaneously earned his private pilot's license and his multi-engine rating as he passed a thorough check ride with an FAA examiner. With only a few hours of flying experience in smaller aircraft, Larry Goshorn, president of General Automation, Inc., Anaheim, California, soloed in his newly purchased Duke after 28 hours of dual instruction. Then he quickly went on and passed his test — all in about two months' time. "It really is a credit to the Duke", Goshorn said, "but I had the advantage of having gone through the factory ground school — and I knew all the systems before I got in the airplane."

Discussions with the Grumman Corporation concerning the possibility of a merger, which had been inaugurated in August, were quietly terminated. After considerable research and review

377

of prospective terms, no mutually acceptable means could be agreed upon for accomplishing such a merger.

A novel twist emerged in one episode of the national game of "sue the manufacturer" that customers of various industries seemed disposed to play during the early Seventies. A Beechcraft owner who had logged more than 650 hours in his Bonanza had an accident in 1971 following an aborted landing. He filed suit against the company for the tidy sum of $785,000, alleging design deficiencies in the fuel control system. Nevertheless, he promptly bought another Beechcraft Bonanza to replace the damaged airplane. A U. S. District Court jury closed out the case with a finding in favor of Beech Aircraft on October 11.

Convening of the company's third annual Supplier Cost Conference on October 19 brought together 115 persons representing 60 per cent of general aviation's leading suppliers, accounting for 70 per cent of all Beech Aircraft's commercial supplies purchases. It was disclosed that through joint planning and research and development, cooperating suppliers had not only increased their own sales and profits, but had made possible savings to Beech that added up to nearly a million dollars during the year. Quality and value improvements through constructive change were producing benefits for all parties concerned – including Beech customers who were consistently gaining more airplane per dollar invested.

November brought a mixed bag of news – some very good, and some that seemed very bad. The month opened with a report from Washington, D. C. that President Frank E. Hedrick had been elected to the Board of Directors of the National Aeronautic Association at their annual meeting. It was a prestigious appointment. The oldest independent, non-profit aviation organization in the United States, the NAA sponsored the aviation interest of 100,000 members in company with a number of affiliated organizations. Its position as the United States representative of the Federation Aeronautique Internationale gave NAA an important voice in world aviation and aerospace councils.

The great success of the Beech 1972 sales meeting – "XL'73" – raised a question that came up often in the course of the company's progress: "What do we do for an encore?" Beechcraft's

378

marketing staff was ready with the answer: "Stage a bigger and better meeting this year." That is what they did — with "Showcase '74", an international exposition that broke all records for sales, attendance, numbers of awards presented, and total value of products displayed.

Wichita's Century II convention complex was again the setting for a showing of Beechcraft products for 1974 valued at more than $5 million. On display were 14 gleaming new Beechcrafts, standing out in luxurious garden settings that included more than 1,000 blooming plants, live evergreens, shrubs and trees brought together from Hawaii and many other states. Special Open House showings for Beechcrafters and their families, and later for the general public, during the November 5-7 International Sales Meeting, attracted thousands of guests.

The excellence of Beechcraft reached new peaks with the 1974 aircraft displayed at "Showcase '74". Heading the array was the widest selection of corporate turboprop airplanes in Beech history — four distinctive models of the pressurized, turboprop Beechcraft King Air series. Refined to the ultimate state-of-the-art through extensive research and development, their handsome lines and luxury accommodations bespoke the firmly established reputation for performance, comfort, quiet flight, reliability and economy that had made Beech Aircraft the world leader in production of general aviation turboprop aircraft.

Towering over all the aircraft on display with its distinctive T-tail, the new Beechcraft Super King Air 200 shared honors at "Showcase '74" with its sister ship, the King Air A100. Identical in cabin size and accommodations, the choice offered to customers by the two big Beechcraft jetprop twins was essentially one of performance. Both could seat six to eight passengers in the executive configuration, plus a crew of two, or up to 13 passengers in higher density arrangements. Both were factory-equipped for all-weather flying and pressurized for high altitudes. And both featured sophisticated sound-reduction engineering techniques that included the use of honeycomb-material tuned panels to maintain a quiet cabin in all operating regimes.

Equally impressive in their category were the newest models in the famed Beechcraft King Air 90 series — the King Air C90, world's value leader in its class, and the high-performance King Air E90. Both shared the same airframe, service-proved for superior reliability in nine years of worldwide flying. Both were factory-equipped for all-weather flight, and offered a wide range of pressurized cabin accommodations to suit individual corporate/executive preferences.

Strongly present in the sales picture, although not on display, were two more popular, high-capacity Beechcrafts — the 17-place B99 Airliner, and the hardy 6 to 11-place supercharged Queen Air B80. Production was under way on more Beechcraft B99 Airliners for several commuter airlines. And the Beechcraft Queen Air B80 continued to renew the perennial appeal of the versatile Queen Air series, particularly to export buyers among whom it had scored increased volume during the past two years.

The latest Beechcraft Duke B60 — the company's winning entry in the pressurized owner-flown business twin high-performance class — attracted keen interest. Almost a new airplane in its 1974 version, the Beechcraft Duke B60 featured a stellar array of advancements and refinements in design and engineering. New chairs retailored for improved comfort and appearance were fitted into a wider, longer cabin interior. Redesigned engine intake valves, an engine overboost relief valve, a Beech-designed electronic ni-cad battery runaway detection system, and a battery air cooling duct, were notable among engineering improvements.

The 1974 Beechcraft Barons put on a three-ring circus all their own. All three models — the versatile Beechcraft Baron B58 with optional 4-place club seating plus two front seats, the high-performance Baron E55, and the economical Baron B55 — drew their share of attention. Significant improvements in the 1974 Beechcraft Baron E55 and B55 models included new single-point fueling at each wing through interconnected fuel cells — a system thoroughly service-proved on the B58 Baron.

Aptly described by one owner as "the ultimate envy machine", general aviation's foremost line of single-engine aircraft — the Beechcraft Bonanzas — was present in full force. The spacious six-place Beechcraft A36 Bonanza, with its optional club seating for four passengers, plus two up front, again displayed its versatility as a station wagon with wings. The classic V-tailed

Beechcraft Bonanza V35B dramatized the effect of continuous refinements in a design that had led the industry since its introduction 27 years ago, with an ingenious cutaway display that revealed the normally hidden details of its very sturdy construction. The Beechcraft Bonanza F33A with its conventional empennage completed the showing with its own special combination of beauty, performance and economy. All three Bonanzas offered refinements for 1974 that included increased headroom, redesigned comfort seating, and rich new sidewall trim with a hand-carved woodgrain effect.

More than ever worthy of the Beechcraft name were the three lightplane models proudly shown at "Showcase '74". The retractable-gear Beechcraft Sierra 200 emerged as a completely recertificated airplane for 1974, featuring a quieter, smoother version of the Lycoming IO-360 engine with an improved oil cooling system, a new design Hartzell propeller, redesigned cowling, and control refinements. Shared with the Beechcraft Sundowner 180 and the Beechcraft Sport 150 were more new-for-'74 features that included restyled, larger windows, a choice of deluxe Beechcraft Baron/Bonanza interior fabrics, a new engine throttle quadrant similar to that offered in twin Beechcrafts, a new easier-to-read engine instrument panel cluster, a higher fuel selector value safety guard, and taxi lights mounted opposite the landing lights to provide on-the-ground lighting on both sides. Reinforcing this brilliant display, the company announced the signing of its 100th Beech Aero Center franchise — 60 days ahead of its target schedule. Adding to all these plus factors was the growing impact of the Beech Aero Club program.

Completing the preview of outstanding offerings for 1974 was a showing of Beechcraft's greatly expanded selection of avionics packages, ranging from ultra-sophisticated airline standard instrument flight control and navigation systems to individual items serving to extend aircraft capabilities during adverse weather. Emphasis was placed on the Beech avionics package concept that enabled customers to save some 11 per cent over comparable equipment purchased separately — a strong factor in the company's worldwide leadership in customized avionics installations.

The annual awards banquet, a highlight of the 1974 International Sales Meeting, produced a new record total of awards and recognition for distinguished marketing achievements. Certifying the international scope of the company's sales, William C. Morales, president of the Beech distributorship, William C. Morales and Company, Caracas, Venezuela, was named the Beech Aircraft Corporation's "Man of the Year" for 1973, in recognition of 19 years of distinguished service to general aviation with Beechcraft in Venezuela.

The Chairman's Award went to Silas King, founder and president for 27 years of Flightcraft, Inc., Beechcraft Aviation Center at Portland, Oregon. Conferring the award, Chairman O. A. Beech said: "Silas King has brought this and many other awards to himself and aviation through his maintenance of high ethical standards in the conduct of a profit-oriented business. In the process, he has earned the esteem of his friends, associates and aviation leaders." King's firm also won three other major awards for sales performance in 1973.

A grand total of 82 awards went to domestic Beech sales organizations and personnel, and 17 awards to international marketing affiliates. Hangar One, Inc., Atlanta, Georgia, led the domestic honorees with FY 1973 sales of more than $10 million; and Transair S.A., Geneva, Switzerland, was the international honoree with better than $5 million in sales. Twenty-five individual salesmen earned special awards for sales in excess of $1 million each.

Arriving in Wichita during "Showcase '74" to take delivery on his 23rd Beechcraft Bonanza, an A36 model, Leonard Hay, a rancher and businessman from Rock Springs, Wyoming, was pleasantly surprised to receive a special award of an engraved plaque "in appreciation of his dedication to the Beechcraft Bonanza". The honor was well-deserved. Hay had bought his first Bonanza, a Model 35, in 1947; and his latest purchase earned him the distinction of having owned more Bonanzas than any other individual in the world. Flying over the vast, rugged ranges of Wyoming, he had logged more than 6,000 hours in his Bonanzas. "I have absolute faith in the aircraft", Hay said in accepting his award. "In over 25 years of flying, I have not had a mechanical failure in a Bonanza."

"Showcase '74" was a stirring spectacle and an appropriate

celebration of the biggest year in Beech Aircraft's history. Most important of all, it was the source of record-breaking advance orders for new 1974 Beechcrafts that totaled more than $33.8 million. The company was off to a flying start on its 1974 fiscal year — a year that held strong promise of bettering its banner year of 1973.

Then came the bad news. Because of the oil embargo proclaimed in October by the Arab states, the United States was confronted with a shortage of refined petroleum products during the coming winter. Allocating anticipated short supplies, the White House Energy Policy Office announced an overall reduction of 42½ per cent in fuel for general aviation uses.

Its impact struck the industry like a bolt of lightning. In Wichita, "the Air Capital" and production center for 70 per cent of general aviation aircraft, reactions ranged from anger to dismay. Throughout the community and elsewhere in aviation, panic was in the air.

Protesting the sweeping cut, industry spokesmen pointed out that only 0.7 per cent of transportation fuel was consumed by all general aviation aircraft, and that their grounding would put 200,000 people out of work. They had a valid point; the cutback was, on balance, unreasonably discriminatory.

The reaction at Beech Aircraft was temperate. There were no "panic buttons" in any of the company's executive offices. Beech had met and overcome many difficulties in its more than four decades of progress; it would take this new emergency in its stride. "Do what we can, then see what develops" was the Beech policy that had been proved sound by long experience. Appearing as a guest on national television network news programs, President Frank E. Hedrick calmly offered a realistic appraisal of the situation.

"What developed" in the current emergency was a readjustment, only one week later, of the amount of fuel allotted to general aviation users. For the time being, the overall reductions were set at a more moderate 25 per cent; and there was a promise of fairer consideration for general aviation in future allocations. Announced by President Nixon on December 1, the readjustment cleared the way for Beech to carry forward its planning for 1974 with only minor and hopefully only temporary reductions.

383

The true importance of general aviation in the nation's economy, and the fuel-conserving benefits of business travel in private and company-owned aircraft, were made clear in an authoritative message from John H. Shaffer, former head of the Federal Aviation Administration, published at mid-December in major newspapers from coast to coast. Sponsored by Beech Aircraft, his timely and factual report included a typical example of fuel and time savings resulting from a business trip made in a Beechcraft Baron twin, compared with the same trip traveling in a standard 1973 automobile. Fuel savings for the business twin travelling at 200-plus mph, Shaffer pointed out, would amount to 14 per cent.

Public and industry response to the message was tremendous in terms of favorable comments. Letters came in by the bushel saying "thanks" to Beech for speaking up for general aviation. Shaffer had scored a coup for the industry and for the company that was wholly in keeping with the constant Beech policy: "Present the facts honestly and let the reader reach his own conclusions."

Meanwhile, business as usual was the order of the day at Beech Aircraft. Beechcrafters hailed the successful launching on November 16 of Skylab III, the modified Apollo Command/Service module carrying a three-man crew of astronauts to the earth-orbiting Skylab workshop for its concluding series of months-long researches and experiments in space. The cryogenic systems designed and built at Beech-Boulder flawlessly continued to fulfill their crucial life support tasks on both space vehicles.

As the company's shareholders gathered at the Beech Activity Center for the annual stockholders' meeting on December 20, they were met with two welcome reports that had come in that morning. The Federal Aviation Administration had just issued certification of the new Beechcraft Super King Air 200. The event was wholly predictable, since the high-powered turboprop was the most thoroughly tested aircraft ever to progress from design onto the Beech production line.

Bell Helicopter Company further brightened the day with a $6.5 million contract award for continued production at Wichita Plant III and Beech-Salina of complete airframes for its Jet-

384

"During this fuel shortage, we can all be thankful for one important activity that helps keep our economy strong and make millions of jobs more secure."

John H. Shaffer, former head of the Federal Aviation Administration

"Throughout the ranks of labor and management, most jobs depend, directly or indirectly, on the flow of necessary business transportation. It is indeed fortunate that General Aviation, the transportation activity that carries one out of every three inter-city air travel passengers, uses less than ½ of 1% of the entire United States petroleum consumption.

But this is only part of a vitally important story. I urge every American who is interested in keeping our country strong during the energy crisis to read the facts on this page.

Business travel is a must

Most business, large or small, has need for some business travel. It may be one professional or businessman who must occasionally make a contact in another city, or it may be hundreds of men on the move daily. The reasons are as varied as the businesses. Sales, purchasing, service or maintenance, supervision, inspection, whatever the reason, most business simply could not operate without business travel. Much of it is accomplished by automobile. But a great deal of it is dependent entirely on the flexibility and speed of flight that saves countless millions of man/hours each month. And this saving is reflected in scores of items we all buy in our private and business lives.

An astounding fact about air travel

There are 12,350 airports in this nation. Over 11,800 of these airports are served only by General Aviation. (General Aviation includes all aviation other than scheduled airline and military operations.) Think of it, over 11,800 airports serving thousands of communities where businesses of many kinds are dependent on General Aviation for air travel, and dependent on air travel for successful business. Communities where many jobs will be lost without dependable air transportation.

Why General Aviation uses so little fuel

As I said previously, this impressive performance by General Aviation, moving one out of every three inter-city air travel passengers, uses less than ½ of 1% of all petroleum consumed in the U.S.A. How is that possible? Here's one reason. About 90% of all General Aviation airplanes are single engine or light twin engine airplanes. On most trips, these airplanes will actually burn *less fuel than a 1973 automobile making the same trip.* For example, a twin engine Beechcraft Baron flying direct from Memphis to Kansas City will burn 41 gallons of fuel. A standard 1973 automobile, traveling by the most direct turnpike route, will burn 48 gallons of gasoline. The Beechcraft Baron will make the trip in 1 hour and 46 minutes. It will take the automobile 9 hours and 35 minutes. The

Beechcraft will save 7 gallons of gas, and if four people are aboard each vehicle, the Baron will save 31 man/hours. On the round trip, it could realistically save 62 man/hours and 14 gallons of fuel. That's a fuel saving of 14%.

The foregoing is but one example of the fuel economy possible with a twin engine business airplane. Even greater economies can be realized with single engine models. A straight line is still the shortest distance between two points, and air routes normally eliminate many miles that topography forces earth-bound vehicles to travel between origin and destination. The airplane is certainly the most efficient travel vehicle man has yet conceived; it goes straight to destination. Most Beechcraft business airplanes will go 1,000 miles or more without refueling. The constant starting and stopping that wastes so much automotive fuel is not a factor in air travel.

Interestingly and factually, if all the fuel used by General Aviation were added to this nation's ground transportation fuel supplies, it would add around two tablespoonsful of gas to each gas tank each day.

There's another reason why General Aviation uses such a comparatively small amount of fuel. There are only 145 thousand active General Aviation airplanes, compared to 120 million trucks, busses and autos on the road. Yet, this small fleet of airplanes carried 80 million passengers in inter-city air travel last year.

Business travel during the fuel shortage

Now, during a period of reduced fuel supplies, the economies of General Aviation can be increasingly more important to business and professional people. Efficient scheduling and operation of business airplane can result in major fuel savings over other travel alternatives. Corporations with men traveling in all directions by car and commercial airlines may find they could operate much more efficiently and economically with their own "anytime-airline." A little extra effort in planning trips and scheduling

appointments, for example, could allow one airplane to accomplish an inter-city travel need that presently keeps four automobiles on the go. You can easily calculate the dramatic reductions in fuel burned, in addition to the man/hours saved. Hundreds of companies, large and small, have been solving business travel problems in a similar manner for years. Talk to some of them. You'll discover what a difference this enlightened approach to business travel can make on the P. and L. statement.

Consider the alternatives

We all recognize the fact that there absolutely must be fuel-use restrictions during the shortage. We must adjust our business and private transportation needs to operate during the present predicament. But we all know that flexibility in business travel is paramount if we are to maintain a healthy economy during the energy crisis. Every transportation mode will be affected by fuel restrictions, making it even more difficult to be *where you need to be — when you need to be there.* Business will have to rely on its own transportation capabilities, and on the private airplane to a far greater degree than ever before.

A business airplane can prove to be invaluable during the current crunch. Of course, fuel for business aviation will be restricted, also. But the economies of operating a company airplane are real and can be capitalized. Careful scheduling, checking fuel availability at destination points prior to departure, operation at reduced power settings and other conservative operating procedures can result in valuable utilization during the fuel shortage. This can make acquisition of a business airplane an important investment. It's a major addition to the total transportation options available to a company.

As the former FAA Administrator, I'm acutely aware of the importance of General Aviation to the economic vitality of this nation. I know that aviation is a vital force which will help keep the business climate healthy and productive during the energy crisis.

Thank you.

[signature]

This space was donated by Beech Aircraft Corporation. Beech pledges its full support to the conservation of fuel during this energy crisis.

A Beech-sponsored message from John H. Shaffer, former head of the Federal Aviation Administration, pointed out the role of general aviation in providing essential business transportation and helping to reduce fuel consumption during the energy crisis that emerged as 1973 ended.

Head start on 1974 came with a $10 million contract from Rockwell International for Beech-Boulder to design, produce and test the power reactant storage assembly for NASA's Space Shuttle Orbiter — world's first re-usable space transportation system — pictured in full-scale mockup form. (Page 388)

Beech Aircraft scored a major coup when the Beechcraft Super King Air was named winner of a joint U.S. Army/ Air Force competition to build and support fleets of Army and Air Force C-12 utility transports in service around the world. (Pages 440, 442)

Five units of a 20-plane fleet of aerobatic Beech-craft Bonanza F33C trainers lined up for delivery under a $1.3 million contract to the Air Force of Mexico. The Bonanzas enlarged Mexico's existing training fleet which included 20 Beechcraft Sport models. (Page 399)

Ranger II high-performance helicopter. Since 1968 Beech had delivered more than 950 commercial and 2,250 defense versions of the JetRanger under subcontract to Bell; and the end was happily nowhere in sight.

President Frank E. Hedrick reported to stockholders that an immediate assessment of the fuel shortage impact on the company's aviation and aerospace activities would be hard to make with any degree of accuracy. Its effect was predictably favorable, however, with regard to the Beech research and development program then under way to apply liquid natural gas and, perhaps later, liquid hydrogen for use in automotive fuel systems.

Displaying the progress made, a station wagon converted at Beech-Boulder to use liquefied natural gas instead of gasoline fuel was demonstrated to stockholders, reporters from various media, and Beech employees. Its cryogenic LNG fuel was stored at -258 degrees Fahrenheit in a special Beech-built vacuum-insulated tank. A simple conversion kit permitted use of LNG, restored to its gaseous state, in the vehicle's carburetor, producing notable reductions in carbon deposits and engine and exhaust pollution.

The year closed on an up-beat note with the announcement on December 31 that the Royal Moroccan Air Force had placed an order for six Beechcraft King Air A100s, variously equipped in executive and high-density configurations. Problems could be foreseen in 1974, to be sure; but the year ahead was also rich in opportunities.

Chapter 37

Industrial nations throughout the world felt the deepening pinch of the Organization of Petroleum Exporting Countries oil embargo as the winter of 1973-74 deepened. In metropolitan centers, traffic jams were frequent around service stations as motorists jockeyed for place in long lines, competing for scarce supplies of gasoline. A nationwide speed limit of 55 mph was legislated in the United States, and other nations took similar steps to cut gasoline consumption. Lights were turned off and heat was turned down to conserve electrical power and fuel. Airline schedules were trimmed and military flights reduced.

In Wichita, the pinch was not as severe as elsewhere. Nevertheless, Beechcrafters and their management willingly cooperated in stepping up conservation measures. Company-furnished bumper stickers that read "55 mph — 65 degrees" blossomed on cars all over the Beech parking lots. Inside the Beech plants, warm dress was popular as heat was reduced to 55 degrees. It was much colder outdoors; the new year of 1974 had dawned clear and frigid, with an outside air temperature of 8 degrees below zero F.

A timely measure of inner warmth soon came to Beech Aircraft. On January 4, a $10 million contract award was made by the Space Division of Rockwell International Corporation, assigning to Beech-Boulder full responsibility for the power reactant storage assembly for NASA's Manned Space Shuttle Orbiter — the world's first reusable space transportation system.

The award had actually been anticipated more than a year ago, when NASA first unveiled its Space Shuttle program. It was the logical consequence of Beech Aircraft's pioneering since 1954 in the field of cryogenics that had produced the company's contributions to the major space programs of Mercury, Gemini, Apollo and Skylab.

The contract called for the Beech-Boulder Division to design, develop, test and produce essential numbers of the two liquid oxygen and two liquid hydrogen storage tanks and associated hardware to supply cryogens to the Orbiter's fuel cells and environmental control/life support systems — items crucial to the successful performance of its missions.

Announced results of operations for the first three months of the Beech 1974 fiscal year also brought good cheer. Commercial sales for the closing quarter of 1973 were up 8.5 per cent over the same period in 1972, to a total of $46,374,937. Total consolidated sales of $49,209,180, while slightly below last year's comparable figure, produced a gain in net after-tax earnings to $2,433,756 for the quarter. Beech efforts to increase efficiency and reduce costs were paying off on the vital bottom line of the company's ledger.

Timely glimpses into the potential radically changed future

of automotive transportation and internal combustion engine fuels came with two showings during the month. On January 16, the Billings Research Corporation, Provo, Utah, staged a demonstration at Santa Barbara, Cal. of a Chevrolet Monte Carlo sedan powered by liquid hydrogen from a Beech-built cryogenic storage tank. Later, at the January 28 annual meeting of the American Institute of Aeronautics and Astronautics at Washington, D. C. the Billings vehicle was displayed, together with a Reynolds Metals Company liquefied natural gas-powered Ford Torino that used a fuel system designed and built by Beech Aircraft.

In another development of futuristic aspect but more immediately realizable nature, a $1 million-plus contract came from Pratt & Whitney Aircraft, West Palm Beach, Fla., for the design and development of components for a gas dynamic laser system. Involving storage assemblies for gases and airborne oxidizer storage and heating assemblies, it was assigned to Beech-Boulder.

The quaint notion that "woman's place is in the home" moved deeper into obsolescence when word came that a Beechcraft King Air professional pilot, Mrs. Claire Phillips of Cincinnati, Ohio had recently received the National Business Aircraft Association's Million Mile Safety Award. In August, 1971, Mrs. Phillips had attended the King Air Pilot School at the Beechcraft Training Center. She was currently chief pilot for the Phillips Supply Company in Cincinnati, owners for the past 2½ years of a Beechcraft King Air. Mrs. Phillips was the first woman pilot thus honored by the NBAA.

Beechcrafters welcomed a fact-finding delegation from Washington, D. C. that comprised staff members of the U. S. House Appropriation Committee and the Department of Transportation, together with officials of the General Aviation Manufacturers Association. The visitation provided an opportunity to acquaint Federal decision-makers with matters of concern to the company and its customers.

As the month ended, the Imperial Iranian Air Force purchased 12 Beechcraft Model F33C Bonanzas — for a total of 30 since 1972 — to become one of the world's largest fleet owners of Bonanzas. Aerobatic versions of the F33 series, the new Beechcrafts would join their predecessors in Iran's highly active primary and advanced training programs and in fulfilling liaison functions.

Some of the uncertainty about the immediate future of general aviation had been dispelled in mid-January when the Federal Energy Office announced overall allocations for aviation gasoline and jet fuels amounting to 95 per cent of 1972 usage. The fuel-saving aspects of travel in business aircraft, as pointed out the month before in the Beech-sponsored message from John H. Shaffer, former FAA Administrator, had been recognized in Washington.

Highlighting the improved outlook was the delivery on February 5 to salesmen and customers of Cutter Aviation, Inc., Phoenix, Ariz. and Cutter Flying Service, Inc., Albuquerque, N. Mex. of more than $1 million worth of Beechcrafts, ranging from Bonanzas to Baron and King Air types. Franchise holders for the full line of Beechcrafts, the Cutter organizations also placed orders for additional Beech planes valued at more than $4 million.

Louison Bobet, former world champion bicycle racer, fulfilled early in February a long-cherished aspiration to pilot his own airplane across the Atlantic Ocean. Bobet and his son, Phillip, took delivery of a new Beechcraft Baron 58 and ferried it straightaway to their home in Quiberon, Brittany, France. There the fast six-place Baron 58 joined a Beechcraft Queen Air B80 used by Bobet to transport clients to his health spas — three in France, and others under construction in Greece and Japan. The new Baron was the sixth Beechcraft Bobet had owned. With 4,300 hours of flying time, he had been honored in 1973 as the European private pilot with the largest number of flying hours.

The safe return to Earth on February 8 of the third and last Skylab astronaut crew completed another phase of Beech Aircraft's participation in the nation's historic space programs. With the Skylab splashdown, the cryogenic gas storage systems designed and built at Beech-Boulder had logged 6,600 hours of space flight. Their latest task had been to provide oxygen for life support, and oxygen and hydrogen for the fuel cells, of the modified Apollo Command/Service module that had ferried astronaut crews to and from their Skylab workshop in its 171 days of globe-girdling space flight. Next, with like support from Beech cryogenic systems, would come the joint US/USSR Apollo/Soyuz Test Project programmed for 1975.

The Spanish Air Ministry joined the growing list of overseas governments operating Beechcraft King Air fleets with its purchase on February 12 of two A100 and six C90 King Air models, equipped for liaison transport and instrument training. The pressurized turboprop aircraft were to join the Air Ministry's current fleet of 11 Beechcraft Baron B55 trainers.

From the Federal Energy Administration at Washington, D. C. came a letter of commendation for Beech Aircraft's vigorous efforts to conserve fuel. Plant Engineering records had shown a 17 per cent reduction in heating fuel use at Wichita, compared with past consumption for the same period. Employee cooperation in a "Share the Ride" program that included the use of company computers to match cars and riders had brought together over 500 Beechcrafters in car pools of four or more persons, and many others in smaller groups.

At San Francisco, Cal., the U. S. Circuit Court of Appeals, Ninth Circuit, sustained on February 14 an earlier U. S. District Court ruling in favor of Beech Aircraft in a $112 million class action damage suit. The plaintiffs had alleged design deficiencies in about 15,000 Beech-built aircraft. Both Federal courts found that the suit could not be brought or maintained as a class action.

Typical of the use of business aircraft to promote industrial and economic growth was the experience recounted by long-time Beechcraft owner Cass S. Hough, a corporation chief executive and also chairman of the Arkansas Industrial Development Commission. A nationally recognized authority on business flying, Hough had logged some 34,000 hours of corporate and military piloting over nearly a half century.

Hough recalled that his company's first business airplane was a 1932 Waco. Later equipment, which he personally chose, came to include a Beechcraft D17S Staggerwing biplane, C18 and D18S twin Beechcrafts, and a Beechcraft Queen Air twin. His current fleet comprised a Beechcraft King Air B90 jetprop and a twin-engine Beechcraft B55 Baron.

Many years of managerial experience had convinced Hough

that there is no acceptable substitute for personal contact. So, as president of the Recreation Products Group of Victor Comptometer Corporation, he regularly paid monthly visits to the headquarters of each member firm. Widely dispersed throughout the Midwest, his charges included Heddon Fishing Tackle, Dowagiac, Michigan; Bear Archery, Grayling, Michigan; Ertl Toys, Dyersville, Iowa; Mission Gymnastic Equipment, Cedar Rapids, Iowa; Victor-PGA Golf, Morton Grove, Illinois; and Daisy/Heddon, Ltd., Cambridge, Ontario.

Flying out of Rogers, Arkansas, headquarters location for his family-founded Daisy Manufacturing Company, Hough was logging about 500 hours a year, and some 50 instrument approaches, in completing his rounds at the controls of his firm's Beechcraft King Air. "I couldn't conveniently do that by any other form of transportation", he said. "And I can be home every evening if I want to."

As in many other cases, Hough's use of business aircraft provided great advantages in terms of corporate flexibility. "We don't feel compelled to locate our plants in major metropolitan centers", he explained. "Instead, we have traditionally located where we could obtain the best work force, with an eye to the proximity of raw materials. Personal transportation is not a factor."

Comments of other corporate Beechcraft owners further accented the benefits of business flying. The 100th Beechcraft King Air E90 twin to come off the assembly line went to Punta Gorda Isles, Inc., a real estate development firm based at Punta Gorda, Florida. Taking delivery of the airplane – his firm's fourth Beechcraft – at Wichita, Alfred M. Johns, chairman of the board of Punta Gorda, commented that his company's travel needs, which spanned much of the nation, would utilize his E90's high performance to its utmost.

"We will be flying our King Air extensively from the air strip at Punta Gorda", Johns said. "If we don't fly our clients out of there ourselves, we would have to take them to Tampa or Ft. Meyers, since there is no local service. By the time we conform to airline schedules and get to the airports, in most cases, we would already have been at the final destination in the King Air."

A mere six months of business aircraft ownership – first of a

Beechcraft Bonanza, and then a twin Beechcraft B55 Baron — sufficed to prove the sales-building power of corporate aviation to the Southwestern Grain and Supply Company of Amarillo, Texas. Taking delivery of a new 286 mph pressurized Beechcraft B60 Duke, Southwestern's president, Robert Bauman, told how flying had brought within easy reach many previously inaccessible customers for his company's line of grain elevator supplies and fumigants.

"The Bonanza enabled us to do a week's work in two and one-half days", said Bauman. "The twin Baron cut the time of a two weeks sales trip to three days, and the entire United States became my territory. Now our new Duke opens a whole world of opportunities."

Reminded of the economic importance of business flying by such examples, multiplied many times over, Federal authorities continued their announced policy of allocating a fair share of the nation's fuel resources to general aviation users. Their action was gratifying, but hardly surprising, to Beech Aircraft. Beech management customarily assumed that, appraised of the full facts in any situation, intelligent people both in and out of government would usually respond reasonably. The assumption held true; business flying, which made up the bulk of general aviation, would not be grounded for lack of fuel.

Members of the Beech sales organization hurried the good news to prospective customers with salutary results, and commercial sales went briskly on. Characteristic was a February mass delivery of more than $2 million worth of Beechcrafts, consigned to customers of Stevens Beechcraft, Inc., Greer, S. C. The flyaway fleet consisted of a Beechcraft King Air A100, a King Air E90, two Beechcraft Baron B58s, a Baron B55, and a Beechcraft Bonanza A36.

On March 29 came the first anniversary of Vietnam Veterans Day, a national observance of the return in 1973 of the last American prisoners of war from Vietnam. In his capacity as White House appointee in June, 1973 to the chairmanship of the Wichita Metro area of the National Alliance of Businessmen, Beech President Frank E. Hedrick reported that Wichita area NAB efforts had produced jobs to date in fiscal 1974 for 1,150 Vietnam veterans, more than double its target goal.

Beech Aircraft, consistent with its own nearly quarter-century-long commitment to give employment preference to the nation's defenders, had filled 15 per cent of its job openings with Vietnam veterans since 1971. Hiring of 520 ex-servicemen in 1973 had boosted that rate to 20.3 per cent. All-out efforts, including the provision of specially fitted work stations, were expanded to provide employment for disabled veterans. "A job is the least we owe these young men", Hedrick said.

There was plenty of work for willing hands. Business was brisk; and the long-range future, too, was bright. Planning ahead, officers of Chaparral Aviation, Inc., Dallas, Texas, signed orders for 28 Beechcrafts, valued at $5.8 million. The commitment brought to $14 million the total value of aircraft in inventory and on order at Chaparral's Corporate Aviation Center bases in Dallas, San Antonio and Victoria.

Federal designation of Wichita, late in March, as a U. S. Customs Port of Entry, emphasized the standing of Beech Aircraft as a major Kansas manufacturer. Statistics supporting the designation showed that in 1972, Wichita area exports came to $145 million, including large amounts of wheat and grains. Beech 1973 export sales were $32.4 million, or more than 20 per cent of that total. Significant contributions to the economy of the state also emerged with the summing up of Beech Aircraft's fiscal 1973 expenditures in Kansas of $82 million — an increase of more than 20 per cent over its fiscal 1972 totals.

At the Beechcraft Training Center in Wichita, the company's wide-ranging educational curriculum was expanded with the first classroom session on April 4 of a new Avionics Training Program. Providing professional quality instruction covering avionics systems and their use, maintenance and repair, it was a timely step. Avionics equipment, which increased the usefulness and enhanced the handling ease and safety of Beechcrafts to their owners and pilots, had grown in popularity to such an extent that it made up an average of more than 20 per cent of the retail price of each Beechcraft delivered. And this ratio continued to increase, as more and more customers took advantage of Beechcraft's money-saving, factory-installed customized electronics equipment.

One week later, Beechcrafters celebrated the delivery of the

1,000th airframe for Bell Helicopter's commercial JetRanger helicopter. On the assembly line at Wichita Plant III stood many more airframes for Bell, in production under a $6.5 million follow-on subcontract that extended through 1975. Workers at Wichita shared honors with employees at the Salina Division, the joint source of many helicopter airframe components, for the JetRanger production mark.

Beech-Salina earned honors all its own in April, too, in its role as the production center for the Beechcraft Duke. Salina Beechcrafters set a new record, completing 12 of the advanced 1974 speedy, pressurized Duke B60 twins during the month. The retail value of their month's work came to more than $2.4 million.

April came to an end in a blaze of glory. New all-time records for sales and earnings alike had been set during the first half of the Beech 1974 fiscal year. Total consolidated sales of $106,531,155 had produced after-tax earnings of $5,337,304. And all past records were again surpassed in April, as commercial deliveries of new Beechcrafts soared to 163 units and commercial sales to $19,350,000.

Beechcraft Hawker Corporation set a new record, too, with the sale of 12 new BH 125 corporate jets, valued at approximately $20 million, during March. This exceptional accomplishment reflected the impact of realignments effected in the Beechcraft Hawker marketing program earlier in the year. Corporate supervision of the BH 125 program was assigned to Roy H. McGregor, vice president - marketing. George D. Rodgers, a former Navy aviator with special training and skills in aircraft marketing, was named director - corporate aircraft marketing to work with McGregor and Beechcraft Hawker President Lloyd W. Harris in developing sales programs for the BH 125.

The effect of the new setup was to provide Beechcraft Hawker with the resources available within the Beech Aircraft marketing organization to further expand jet marketing capabilities. A fourth level of franchising was established with the signing up of seven Beechcraft Hawker Jet Centers. Purpose of the new Jet Centers was to market Beechcraft Hawker 125-600 business/corporate jets in North America. This continued until the marketing agreement with Hawker Siddeley was phased out in late 1975.

At Commencement Day ceremonies of the University of Kansas at Lawrence on May 20, a singular honor came to Mrs. O. A. Beech, co-founder of the company and Chairman of the Board. From the University and its alumni association she received its 1974 Distinguished Service Citation, the highest honor within its power to bestow. The citation was traditionally conferred by the state's largest and most prestigious educational institution on outstanding Kansans "in recognition of significant and life-long contributions to society."

The Distinguished Service Citation was the latest but far from least of the many honors that had come to Mrs. Beech throughout her long and still very active career.

The University of Kansas award, however, held special significance because it came from perceptive citizens of Mrs. Beech's own native state. In reversal of the proverb that "A prophet shall not be without honor save in his own country", it was a signal tribute to the sage and often prophetic insights she applied in guiding the course of Beech Aircraft. Her pleasure in receiving the citation was shared by all Beechcrafters.

Deliveries of two new commercial Beechcrafts at about that time typified some of the "contributions to society" cited in the Kansas University award to the company's Chairman. Peru Pescas, a division of the Peruvian Government Ministry of Fisheries, procured a Beechcraft Queen Air B80 twin for use in spotting schools of fish off the Pacific Coast and guiding fishing boats to catches that, on good days, might amount to as much as 60,000 tons. That Beechcraft Queen Air would play an important part in helping to feed a hungry world.

The second Beechcraft, a King Air C90, went to Aeroambulancia C.A., Caracas, Venezuela. Like many other Beechcrafts fulfilling similar functions all over the world, it would perform lifesaving duties as an aerial ambulance. It was specially equipped as a flying surgical and intensive care facility; and its purchaser, Dr. Alejandro Mendez, anticipated that his King Air's pressurization would provide notable medical advantages for his patients. Dr. Mendez, a pilot for 15 years, had owned two Beechcraft Queen Air twins prior to buying the jetprop King Air.

The company also came up with its own series of awards. In May, following up on its Continuing Quality Support Program,

Treasured by the company's co-founder and chief executive officer was the 1974 "Citation for Distinguished Service" of the University of Kansas, tendered to Olive Ann Beech "in recognition of significant and lifelong contributions to society."

Chancellor Archie E. Dikes presented the University's citation to Mrs. Beech at Commencement ceremonies held on May 20 at Lawrence, Kansas.

397

Sequel to the University of Kansas "Citation for Distinguished Service" tendered to the company's Chairman was the naming in October of Mrs. O. A. Beech as an "Elder Statesman of Aviation" by the prestigious National Aeronautic Association. Cited for "Outstanding contributions to the progress of aviation through the years as co-founder, president, chairman and chief executive officer of Beech Aircraft Corporation," she received the plaque commemorating the award from President Frank E. Hedrick. (Page 411)

Beech Aircraft presented new Certified Service Center plaques to 15 Beechcraft service facilities at various locations. Recertification of existing facilities continued across the nation, as a further step in assuring dependable service to Beechcraft owners everywhere.

At mid-June, all Beechcrafters received a very practical and useful award for their efficient and productive performance throughout the past six months. Checks totalling $905,000 went to 6,220 participants in the Beechcraft Employees Bonanza Plan, bringing to more than $2.5 million the total of incentive payments made, in addition to wages and salaries, under the 18-months-old Plan. The advance payments were distributed just before the customary two-weeks plantwide vacation shutdown, providing extra funds for memorably enjoyable and well-earned holidays.

Beech Aircraft at the same time enjoyed the pleasure of receiving a $1.3 million contract award from the Air Force of Mexico. Our good neighbors south of the border, already operating a fleet of 20 Beechcraft Musketeer Sports aircraft procured in 1970 for primary flight training, were adding 20 Beechcraft Bonanza F33C aerobatic trainers to their air force. The sturdy, reliable Beechcraft Bonanza was gaining increasing preference for rugged training duties. Mexico became the latest in a growing list of users that included the Imperial Iranian Air Force, the Japanese Civil Aviation College, the Venezuelan Civil Training School, and Lufthansa German Airlines and its pilot training center at Southwest Airlines.

All past records fell again as results were announced for the third quarter of the company's 1974 fiscal year. Sales for the quarter totalled $71,813,273, and earnings came to $3,183,132. Progress was also gratifying in Beech Aircraft's lightplane marketing program. Nationwide, a total of 110 Beech Aero Centers had been franchised, and 29 Beech Aero Clubs had become active, since the program began late in 1972.

Entering the service of the U. S. Atomic Energy Commission in mid-July was a uniquely equipped new Beechcraft King Air A100. Serving to collect data for the protection of Americans from possible adverse effects of man-made radiation, the aircraft was factory-equipped with vertical and oblique camera ports and four consoles fabricated for radiation instrumentation. To this the AEC added state-of-the-art radiation measurement and recording devices, an extremely accurate inertial navigation system to pin-point their Beechcraft's geographical location, and infrared scanners, cameras and other optical devices.

A legal precedent of far-reaching importance was established with a decision of the California Supreme Court in August that led to a resolution of five consolidated lawsuits brought against Beech Aircraft. Denying a request by plaintiffs Pease-Evelhoch for a review, the high court in effect upheld a California Court of Appeals finding that punitive damages were not recoverable in actions brought by survivors of accident victims. As a result, a 1971 jury award of $21.5 million in damages was ultimately reduced by court decision to substantially less than $2 million, which was paid by the company's insurance carriers. The decision settled the major claims arising from an accident in 1968 involving a twin Beechcraft Baron.

In other ways, August was also a seminal month in the company's progress. Beechcraft missile target sales soared higher, with the receipt from the French Air Force of a $700,000 follow-on contract for more Beechcraft AQM-37A targets, extending production on an existing $900,000 contract through October, 1975. Introduced into U. S. Navy service in 1963, the AQM-37A subsonic/supersonic target had earned an international reputation for versatility and reliability. More than 2,800 units had been delivered to defense forces in the United States and Europe.

Shortly afterward came a $2.9 million follow-on award for flight testing of the U. S. Defense Department's new tri-service High Altitude Supersonic Target (HAST). Beech had completed the design, ground tests and production of the first HAST targets under previous contracts. The follow-on award strengthened the company's position as the prime contractor on the HAST program and enhanced its prospects for becoming the major production source upon completion of development and testing. Design capabilities of Mach 4 (four times the speed of sound) and an altitude range of 40,000 to 100,000 feet would make HAST the nation's fastest and highest-flying rocket-powered target.

A major event surpassed even those welcome awards. Ten

years of intense competitive effort were crowned with victory for Beech Aircraft, when the U. S. Army announced on August 13 the results of a joint Army/Air Force competition for UX/CX-X utility aircraft. Beech was named the winner, earning a $20.6 million contract to build and support 20 U. S. Army and 14 U. S. Air Force C-12A aircraft — both virtually off-the-shelf versions of the Beechcraft Super King Air 200. A contract option allowed the purchase of 16 additional C-12s by the U. S. Air Force.

Every manufacturer of turboprop and jet aircraft in general aviation with any chance at all of winning had entered the competition. Victory was in itself a rich prize, carrying bright prospects for sizeable follow-on orders from both services. And its rewards in terms of prestige were beyond estimation. The Army and Air Force transports would be operated all over the world, and stationed at embassies in important foreign capital cities. They would display Beech Aircraft's top product at its best, on a global scale, to prospective customers in both government and commercial circles.

The competition specifications were exacting, calling for a multi-mission aircraft capable of carrying passengers and/or cargo anywhere in the world, under all conceivable climatic conditions. Ability to operate from both small, unimproved airfields and into high density traffic areas, and in all-weather IFR regimes day and night, was mandatory. The highest standards of performance, reliability, economy, and passenger and crew comfort were demanded. The total characteristics were precisely those that Beech engineers had striven to attain in designing the Beechcraft Super King Air; and the contract award offered indisputable proof of their success.

Again, Beech Aircraft had come up with the right airplane at the right time in the right place. It was a pattern that had taken shape early in the company's history.

Long experience with Beechcraft jetprop aircraft on the part of both the Army and the Air Force stood behind their selection of the Beechcraft Super King Air 200. More than 160 turboprop Beechcraft U-21 utility aircraft (basically commercial King Air 90s) had been delivered to the Army since 1966. The Army in 1971 put into service its first pressurized airplanes, turboprop

Beechcraft U-21Fs almost identical with the commercial King Air A100. Since 1964, the Air Force had flown a Beechcraft VC-6A (King Air 90) pressurized jetprop in VIP transport and utility service. The August, 1974 contract award was further proof of customer satisfaction.

Good news also came on August 21 to operators of Beechcraft King Airs and Beechcraft 99 Airliners. Time between overhaul (TBO) for their Pratt & Whitney 500 and 650 shaft horsepower turbine engines had been extended by 500 hours, moving from 3,000 up to 3,500 flying hours. The extension produced substantial cuts in direct operating costs. And it gave the King Air engines the highest recommended TBO of any turboprop business aircraft.

There was obviously no cause for dissatisfaction with Pratt & Whitney power plants. Engines rated to function flawlessly without major repairs for 3,500 hours easily met the most exacting demands. A continuing problem for some months, however, had been a recurrent shortage of new engines, because of a protracted labor dispute at the plant of United Aircraft of Canada. This in turn had adversely affected King Air production and deliveries.

To be on the safe side, and also to offer a wider range of choice to its customers, Beech Aircraft chose an additional supplier of power plants for the Beechcraft King Air series. The Garrett Corporation of Los Angeles, a highly respected firm that had built more than 30,000 gas turbine engines for aircraft since 1946, was named. Garrett's 715 shaft horsepower TPE-331-6-251B/252 fixed shaft turboprop engine, which had been foresightedly under evaluation in a company-owned King Air since December, 1972, was the unit selected. An initial order totalling $6 million was placed, with deliveries scheduled to commence next year. Worldwide service support arrangements were included in the Garrett contract.

Beechcrafters mourned the passing away on August 25 of a well-liked and respected colleague. Lloyd W. Harris, president and a director of Beechcraft Hawker Corporation, died following heart surgery at the University of Alabama Medical Center in Birmingham.

For the first time in its long and illustrious history, the Society of British Aerospace Companies, Ltd., in 1974 opened its internationally famous Biennial Flying Display and Exhibition to products manufactured around the world. Seizing this opportunity, Beech Aircraft jointly sponsored a display in the aircraft static park with Eagle Aircraft Services, Ltd., Beechcraft distributor at Leavesden Airport, Watford, England. Throughout the September 1-8 duration of the Farnborough Exhibition, the three Beechcrafts on display — the new T-tail Beechcraft Super King Air 200, the high-performance Beechcraft King Air E90, and the Beechcraft Baron 58 — attracted widespread and favorable attention.

Back home in Kansas, the members of the Beechcraft Duke assembly team at the Salina Division meanwhile hailed the completion of the 300th Beechcraft Duke produced since the sleek twin's introduction in 1968. Sales of the speedy, pressurized Duke had reached a $75 million total.

A recent Beechcraft Duke B60 delivery of note had been to W. Geoffrey Keighly, an Australian legislator, businessman and rancher. A member of the New South Wales legislature, Keighley had previously owned three Beechcrafts — one Beechcraft Debonair, and two Beechcraft Bonanzas. He flew his new Duke home the long way around the world — across the Atlantic to Europe, southeast to Persia, then across the equator and "down under" to Australia.

The company ended its 1974 fiscal year on September 30 with the highest level of sales and earnings in its 42-year history. Consolidated sales in the fiscal year 1974 totalled $241,603,005 — up 18 per cent over last year's record total. Net earnings of $12,479,327 smashed the past record, set in 1973, by 27 per cent. Consolidated commercial sales of $219,259,951 bettered the past peak by 20 per cent. International sales of $51,208,052 were 58 per cent higher than in fiscal 1973.

Defense/aerospace sales of $22,343,054 showed a comparatively modest increase of 5 per cent over the previous year. New contracts totalling $52 million in that area during fiscal 1974 were, however, up by 47 per cent over last year. Sales of Beechcraft Hawker jets and spares completed the pattern of record-breaking increases, reaching $23,064,244 for a 20 per cent increase above the year past.

Added to the company's working capital to sustain future growth was the sum of $9,526,269. Stockholders shared in the gains through a 20 per cent increase in the quarterly dividend rate, effected June 30, and a one per cent stock dividend to shareholders of record October 18. Employees, too, were rewarded pro rata through the workings of the Beechcraft Bonanza Plan.

The record gains were scored in spite of recurrent turbine engine shortages that had reduced deliveries of the top-of-the-line Beechcraft King Air models below the company's projections. To meet that situation and avoid layoffs of loyal employees — an emergency measure of last resort to Beech management — production had been shifted to lower-priced models for which engines were available. The recent selection of an alternate supplier of turbojet engines for the Beechcraft King Air would help to avert future problems in that area.

Augmenting the demonstrated excellence of Beechcraft products and the company's worldwide sales and service network in setting new records were external factors that proved helpful to all builders of business aircraft. The long-term trend toward decentralization of industry, aptly illustrated by the experience narrated by Beechcraft King Air owner Cass S. Hough, was making their company-owned planes virtually indispensable to many corporations. The inconveniences of airline travel, already burdened with "anti-highjack" inspection of all passengers and their belongings by Federal marshals at every boarding gate, were compounded as schedules were cut back to conserve fuel, eliminating many flights and reducing others.

The imposition in 1973 of a nationwide 55 mph highway speed limit had curtailed the usefulness of the automobile for business travel, and further emphasized the time savings and convenience of "go anywhere, any time" travel in business aircraft. Sales rose as businessmen quickly saw the point.

"Placing the company in a better position to capitalize on projected future growth and offering additional flexibility to operate in today's business environment" was the stated purpose of a management realignment involving top-level promotions announced jointly on October 8 by Mrs. O. A. Beech, chairman, and Frank E. Hedrick, president. Elevated to newly created

404

positions as group vice presidents were Edward C. Burns, vice president - operations, and Roy H. McGregor, vice president - marketing. Promoted to new positions as senior vice presidents were John A. Elliott, vice president and treasurer; James N. Lew, vice president - engineering; and Michael G. Neuburger, vice president - International Division. Neuburger was also elected as the eleventh member of the company's board of directors.

"These changes are also being made in recognition of the past performance of these long-service Beechcrafters and as an expression of our confidence in their abilities to manage and direct the course of Beech Aircraft in the years to come", the announcement further stated. The five executives promoted shared a combined span of service with Beech Aircraft totaling 151 years; and the record spoke for itself.

A production milestone was passed next day, with the delivery to Tulakes Aviation Company, Oklahoma City, at Liberal, Kansas of the 3,000th Aero Center Beechcraft manufactured at the company's western Kansas production base. Established in 1951, Beech-Liberal had been responsible since 1964 for building all Aero Center models. The three current types were the Beechcraft Sierra 200, the 4-place retractable gear, top-of-the-line Aero Center model; the Beechcraft Sundowner 180 4-place fixed gear model; and the Beechcraft Sport 2- to 4-place sport and training model. Fitting the event, Liberal's 3,000th Aero Center Beechcraft was a Sierra 200.

The Naval Air Systems Command assigned a challenging mission in mid-October, contracting for the modification of 10 rocket-powered Beechcraft AQM-37A missile targets to perform low-altitude flights. Extremely accurate target performance would be required to maintain pre-set altitude hold as low as 50 feet during use in evaluation of ship defense systems and training of crews. The "Sea Skimmer" missiles, later designated the "Sea Skipper", would face a far more demanding task than prior units soaring to altitudes of 90,000 feet and more. Beechcraft missile makers confidently accepted the challenge, happily noting that the contract provided for the optional purchase of additional precision-performance units. Another opportunity was open to enlarge the total of more than 2,800 AQM-37A missile targets delivered since 1960 in the supersonic version.

Another new Beech product serving in the nation's defense came to notice in October, with the delivery to the U. S. Army of three Beechcraft Super King Airs, specially modified for use in its Cefly Lancer program. Designated as Army type RU-21J aircraft, the antenna-laden Beechcrafts would perform special classified missions.

Commercial deliveries that continued briskly included many items of special interest. Barclays Bank, an international financial enterprise operating from Barbados through the Caribbean Islands, and beyond to the United States and South America, purchased its second Beechcraft King Air E90 for VIP transport service. Barclay's previous Beechcrafts had included a Queen Air B80 and a Baron 55. "We probably fly more long, overwater distances than any other Beechcraft King Air", commented their chief pilot, Derek Leggett.

Water was involved in another King Air purchase – bass fishing water. The Bass Anglers Sportsman's Society of America (B.A.S.S.) took delivery of a new Beechcraft King Air A100 to transport its members to select locations throughout North America where bass fishing would be at its best. Fast, comfortable "door to shore" fishing trips would thus be brought within reach of dedicated bass fishermen by B.A.S.S. regardless of the distances involved.

The eighth Beechcraft purchased to perform lifesaving duties with the Royal Flying Doctor Service of Australia – a new Beechcraft Baron 58 – spanned a wide expanse of water on its way to work. The 6-place twin was ferried across the Pacific on its delivery flight by Dr. Harold Dicks, federal president of the RFDS, and his wife, Robin, a nurse and pilot. For the experienced crew, the trip was routine; and the new Beechcraft soon joined the RFDS aero ambulance fleet of two Beechcraft Dukes and five Beechcraft Barons in use throughout Australia.

Australia was also the terminus of an 80-day flight around the world for a Beechcraft Super King Air – the first model to leave the United States for an international customer. Its arrival also capped a series of "firsts" for its purchasers, Thiess Holdings Ltd., of Sydney, N.S.W. A Beechcraft owner for more than 15 years, Thiess had bought the first Beechcraft Model 18, Queen

406

Air, King Air A90, and then the first Beechcraft Super King Air to be delivered in Australia.

En route, the Beechcraft Super King Air made its international debut at the Hanover Air Show in West Germany. Additional stops were made in Paris, London (at Leavesden), Algier, Ankara, Tehran, Karachi, Madras, Kuala Lumpur, Bangkok, Taipei, Tokyo, Manila, Singapore — for first showings of the Beechcraft Super King Air.

Hawker de Havilland Australia, Beechcraft distributor in Australia, had cooperatively arranged the world tour with Beech Aircraft and Thiess Holdings Ltd. A multi-faceted organization also engaged in manufacturing aircraft components, aluminum boats, and doing manufacturing and overhaul work for the Australian government, Hawker further reinforced the Beech presence in Australia by signing an agreement in October to purchase 1975 Beechcrafts having a total retail value of some $6 million in U. S. funds. David Crompton, general manager - distributor products group for Hawker, conservatively described the commitment as "a $6 million order which may well develop further as the year progresses."

Back home in Kansas, the chief selling tool for Southwest Petro-Chem, Inc., became their new Beechcraft King Air C90, according to H. A. Mayor, chairman of the board and president of the firm. He projected a sales increase from $56 million to $100 million in the next four years, using the Beechcraft to move key people to the right place at the right time. Based in Wichita, Southwest Petro-Chem also owned manufacturing facilities in California, Iowa, Pennsylvania, Nebraska, and northeast Kansas.

Nationwide, Beechcraft franchisees won signal recognition by taking 8 of the top 20 places for excellence of service in a poll conducted by *Professional Pilot* magazine. Replies from some 3,000 randomly selected professional pilots put Hangar One, the Beechcraft Corporate Aviation Center at Atlanta Hartsfield International Airport, in first place among all the nation's fixed base operators. Other Beechcraft affiliates placing in the top twenty were Executive Beechcraft, Municipal Airport — Kansas City; Denver Beechcraft, Stapleton International Airport; Nashville Flying Services, Nashville Metropolitan Airport; Stevens

Beechcraft, Greenville-Spartanburg Jetport; Tilford Flying Service, West Palm Beach International Airport; Mobile AirCenter, Bates Field/Mobile Municipal Airport; and Mitchell Aero Center, General Billy Mitchell Field.

Beechcraft Activity Center was the meeting place for more than 800 Masters of Aircraft Salesmanship from all over the world who met at the 1975 Beechcraft International Sales Roundup on November 4-6. They were there to receive well-earned recognition for their contributions to the company's record-breaking sales year and, more importantly, to profit from a series of product-oriented seminars presenting the newest Beechcraft products, services, and marketing techniques.

Among attendees from the United States, the company's rapidly growing network of Beech Aero Centers was well represented. International outlets in 77 foreign lands, from Aden Protectorate to Zambia, sent conferees from 19 worldwide sales centers. Beechcraft's International Division, which had accounted for $51.2 million of fiscal 1974 sales, was enlarging on the company's long-time slogan, "The world is small when you fly a Beechcraft" with its own version: "The world is wonderful when you sell Beechcrafts."

The new Beechcrafts for 1975 were, as always, the major attraction of the Roundup. There were 17 models on display, plus special added exhibits. For old time's sake, there was a handsomely kept Beechcraft D17S Staggerwing biplane, still airworthy and capable of giving most new current airplanes a run for the money. And, for a glimpse into the future, there were two experimental designs that might well become additions to the company's line.

Heading the showing was the flagship of the fleet, the Beechcraft Super King Air, with its towering T-tail. Fresh from triumphant acclaim on a global tour, and with a record of quick acceptance matched by few if any comparable aircraft, the Beechcraft Super King Air took rightful place as the elegant "big brother" of its companions in the King Air series — the capacious A100, the high-performance E90, and the economical C90 Beechcraft King Airs. New avionics options, dramatized in an operational three-panel display, enhanced the salespower of the 1975 King Air series.

Sharing honors as the company's senior piston-engine twins were the roomy, versatile Beechcraft Queen Air B80 and the sleek, speedy Beechcraft Duke B60. The 1975 Duke offered a new AiResearch Lexan pressurization system with a space-saving mini controller. Lighter in weight, quieter, and requiring less pilot attention, the new system won for the Duke even greater distinction in the pressurized, owner-flown fast twin category.

The first public showing of the new pressurized, air-conditioned Beechcraft Baron 58P was a feature of the Roundup that was joyfully welcomed by the sales force. The pressurized cabin, contributing greatly to crew and passenger comfort at the high altitudes often used in cross-country flight, would surely enlarge the market for the company's light twins. There was extra salespower in the Baron 58P's new air-conditioning system, featuring 16,000 BTU capacity and six individual, adjustable passenger outlets, which was also available on the 1975 Beechcraft Baron 58 and E55 models. A new fuel sight gauge system on all 1975 Barons provided fueling accuracy never before possible.

The 1975 Beechcraft Bonanzas featured an improved heating distribution system, safety switches on both landing gears, an optional 12,000 BTU air-conditioning system, and additional avionics options. And the three Aero Center single-engine Beechcrafts — the Sierra 200, the Sundowner 180, and the Sport 150 — offered in their 1975 versions the ultimate combination of quality and economy.

Throughout the entire 1975 line, the excellence of Beechcraft reached new peaks. Proof came in the fact that the members of the company's sales organization placed orders for more than $23 million worth of new 1975 commercial Beechcrafts during the course of the three-day meeting.

Interest was likewise keen in the two experimental designs previewed at the Roundup. Both were potential additions to the Beech Aero Center line of light aircraft, which had already won thousands of new customers for the company and its sales force.

On display was the completed prototype new Beechcraft PD 289 (later designated the Beechcraft Model 76) a 4-place light twin with 160-hp Lycoming engines that was then undergoing flight testing. Distinguished from all existing production light twins by a towering T-tail, like that on the Beechcraft

Super King Air, its obvious appeal to prospective customers won instant praise from saleswise viewers.

Sketches were also shown of another prototype then under construction — the Beechcraft PD 285 single-engine 2-place trainer. Equipped with a 100-hp Continental engine and sporting a wide-vision bubble-type canopy, it was proposed to provide Beechcraft quality at minimum cost for initial training and personal flying.

Decisions on putting the new PD (Preliminary Design) models into production necessarily awaited the completion of in-depth cost and feasibility studies, followed by the customary exhaustive Beech flight and structures life test series. Hopes were high among all conferees for favorable decisions; the new Beechcrafts looked like sure-fire winners in the worldwide marketplace.

Numerous were the honors bestowed for distinguished sales achievements at the traditional Awards Banquet that brought the three-day product conference and viewing sessions to a close. Domestic sales awards for the most factory deliveries in total units went to Stevens Beechcraft; Hangar One; and Denver Beechcraft; and for highest retail sales within their area to Hangar One; Piedmont Aviation; and Chaparral Aviation. Heading a long list of individual salesmen who earned awards was Bill Simpson of Houston Beechcraft, with both highest total dollar sales and greatest dollar sales of Beechcraft King Airs.

International awards went to Transair France for sales exceeding $9 million; Companhia Carnasciali of Brazil for sales of more than $7 million; and Hawker de Havilland Australia for sales of better than $6 million. Awards for market development were made to the Beech Sales Division of NAFCO, Republic of South Africa; Beechcraft de Guatemala; and Latourrette and Parini S.A.C., Paraguay.

The importance of parts and service support in satisfying customers and reinforcing sales efforts had never been underestimated by the company. Awards for excellence in these categories were also conferred, as customary, on Domestic and International winners.

Joseph E. Farrell, president and general manager of Ohio Aviation, Vandalia, Ohio, was named Beech Aircraft's "Man of the Year" for 1974. The honor came in recognition of Farrell's

410

outstanding services to the Beechcraft organization since 1946, when Ohio Aviation had been organized under his leadership as general manager. Year in and year out, his firm had been among the company's top producers, often leading the entire organization in domestic annual sales. Farrell and his operation alike had won nationwide favor and respect throughout the flying fraternity.

The National Aeronautic Association named the three winners for 1974 of its "Elder Statesman of Aviation" awards. The prestigious NAA, formed in 1905, each year honored in this way outstanding Americans past the age of 60 who, over the years, had made significant contributions to the field of aeronautics and had reflected credit on America and themselves. Past honorees had included Glenn L. Martin, Igor Sikorsky, Eddie Rickenbacker, Richard E. Byrd, Donald Douglas, Sr., and Jimmie Doolittle.

Mrs. O. A. Beech was added in 1974 to this distinguished roster of aviation's Elder Statesmen by the NAA's Board of Directors for her "Outstanding contributions to the progress of aviation through the years as co-founder, president, chairman and chief executive officer of Beech Aircraft Corporation." Sharing the honor with her were Jerry Lederer in the field of flight safety, and Cass S. Hough, Beechcraft customer, in the field of business aircraft flying.

An industry distinction also came to President Frank E. Hedrick, with his election as vice-chairman of the board of directors of the General Aviation Manufacturers Association (GAMA). A founding director of the Association, Hedrick had previously served as chairman of GAMA's Safety and Public Affairs Committee.

In mid-November a legal victory was put on the record for Beech Aircraft by a U. S. District Court in Concord, N. H. There a jury returned a verdict in the company's favor, in a $230,000 product liability lawsuit that stemmed from a June, 1968 aircraft accident.

The steady growth of company-owned sales and service facilities continued with grand opening ceremonies held on December 6 at Fresno, Cal., where Beechcraft West had just put into service a new 14,240 sq. ft. storage hangar. It was the second such expansion for Beechcraft West in 1974. Completed in mid-summer was a new 18,600 sq. ft. service facility at Van Nuys Airport, affording higher efficiency in servicing larger aircraft and turboprop engines. Carrying forward the Beech tradition of excellent, full-scale service to Beechcraft owners, Beechcraft West and other "company stores" functioned as models for independently owned establishments, development centers for marketing concepts like the Beech Aero Club (first opened at Van Nuys in 1973), and controlled sales and service outlets at selected locations.

It was a happy group of shareholders that gathered on December 19 at the Beechcraft Activity Center for the company's annual stockholders' meeting. They came to hear the details of Beech Aircraft's greatest year, and to learn what the future might hold for their company.

After recounting the events and results of 1974, President Frank E. Hedrick told the group that "In 1975 and future years, we will be supplying a greater area of the market with our broadened product line which offers greater strength during fluctuations in the economy.

"The company's present profile is in effect, a conglomerate serving many markets. These include personal and executive aircraft, corporate aircraft, government aircraft, missile and space products, retail marketing including both sales and services, major subcontracting programs, financing and insurance, and international sales involving virtually all of the previously mentioned markets. It is reassuring that we are not dependent upon a single product or customer."

He went on to name a number of new products currently completed or under way. These comprised the new pressurized Beechcraft Baron 58P; the Beechcraft King Air B100 with Garrett AiResearch engines; and the PD 289 (Model 76) T-tail twin and PD 285 single-engine 2-place trainer lightplanes. Also announced for the first time were additional development projects in the works. There would be a turbocharged version of the Beechcraft Baron 58, Hedrick disclosed, providing greater performance and higher altitude capability than the standard Baron 58. Studies also were in process for a number of new aircraft.

For the immediate future, Hedrick forecast sales to increase

412

Beechcrafters at Salina proudly displayed their 300th Beechcraft Duke — general aviation's foremost owner-flown high-performance, pressurized twin-engine aircraft. (Page 403)

Harbinger of success for the company's light-plane marketing concepts was its 3,000th Aero Center aircraft delivery. Dale Erickson, manager — Aero Center Marketing (left) presented a model of the Beechcraft Sierra 200 to Otto Hess, president of Tulakes Aviation Company, before flyaway from the Beech Liberal Division airfield. (Page 405)

The Beechcraft PD 289 displayed at the 1975 Beech Sales Roundup blossomed into the Aero Center Beechcraft Model 76 as development progressed. An aerodynamically superior T-tail was the light twin's most distinctive feature. (Pages 409, 410, 412, 429)

413

Navy T-34C Beechcraft Turbo Mentor trainers maneuvered sportively in Kansas skies, celebrating a $7.1 million letter contract award that presaged likely production of some 400 Turbo Mentors for the Navy's Long Range Pilot Training Syllabus. (Page 419)

Selection of Beech Aircraft by the U.S. Air Force as one of two contractors to design and produce test articles of a new remotely piloted TEDS (Tactical Expendable Drone System) was rich in potential. (Page 424)

Grouped for flyaway from Beech Field were 17 of a 24-plane fleet of Beechcraft King Airs, Barons and Bonanzas purchased by the Spanish Air Ministry. The additions made a total of 62 Beechcrafts procured by Spain since 1972 for civilian and military training. (Page 391)

significantly over the 1974 total of $241.6 million — and a corresponding rise in net earnings. New all-time records were clearly in prospect.

As December came to its close, the feelings of Beechcrafters and their management were succinctly summed up by Walter Gunstream, vice president and general manager of Houston Beechcraft, Inc. He said: "1974 was a good year — but it's gone. Let's get moving with 1975!"

Chapter 38

The challenge to "get going with '75" met a vigorous response as the new year began. For openers, the company started its 1975 fiscal year with sales and earnings that broke all records for any first quarter. The record totals were scored despite lagging economic conditions and slowdowns in engine deliveries from two major suppliers. A very special year was clearly taking shape.

Release of the record-breaking figures coincided with the opening at Washington, D. C., of International Women's Year 1975, focusing attention on the status of women. At a formal dinner held there on January 11 — the 40th anniversary of Amelia Earhart's record-setting flight from Hawaii to San Francisco — Mrs. O. A. Beech was saluted as an honored guest for her role of leadership in the general aviation industry. Co-sponsors of the event were the international organization of licensed women pilots, the Ninety-Nines, Inc., and the international organization of executive and professional women, Zonta International.

Promotions announced in January further reinforced the company's executive talent in depth. Named as corporate officers of Beech Aircraft were three long-time Beechcrafters. C. A. Rembleske was elected vice president - aircraft engineering. L. R. Damon was elevated to the post of controller - cost management. C. W. Dieker attained officer rank as assistant treasurer.

Three executive secretaries were promoted to officer positions in Beech Aircraft subsidiaries. Geraldine Shidler was elected assistant secretary of Beech Acceptance Corporation. Harriett

E. Bulmer was named assistant secretary of Beech International Sales Corporation. Mary Ellen Deets became assistant secretary of Beech Holdings, Inc.

A president-to-president letter addressed to Frank E. Hedrick from the White House conveyed appreciation for the company's continuing cooperation in two national programs — the "WIN" drive to Whip Inflation Now, and the energy conservation program. The letter read:

"May I thank you personally for enlisting as an Inflation Fighter and an Energy Saver for the duration.

"History proves that Americans have overcome many adverse situations in the past. I know we can once again triumph if we work together.

"Keep up the good work." — JERRY FORD

Two projects of the Beech Engineering Research and Development Division took to the air early in the year. A Beechcraft 99 Airliner with modified aileron and rudder controls, designated PD 280, made its first flight from Beech Field in an initial test of a system planned to increase the stability of general aviation aircraft. Its joint originators and sponsors were the University of Kansas Flight Research Laboratory and the NASA Flight Research Center.

Another first flight from Beech Field was that of the prototype PD 285 Beech Aero Center single-engine, 100 hp trainer. Development of the proposed fixed-gear, two-place, low-wing aircraft had evoked keen interest when it was announced at the Beechcraft International Sales Conference in November. Anticipation heightened with the successful completion of the inaugural test flight.

Production of the new pressurized Beechcraft Baron 58P, also announced at the November Sales Roundup, was assigned to the company's Salina Division. First deliveries were scheduled for mid-year.

Highlighting the month of February was the receipt from Bell Helicopter of new contracts of more than $6.5 million for continued production of airframes and spares for the Bell Model 206B JetRanger II helicopter. Since the turbine-powered Bell JetRanger was well established as the fastest-selling rotorcraft in commercial helicopter history, the contract extensions promised well for future relations with Bell, which had already resulted in the delivery of more than 3,600 Beech-built airframes for the JetRanger and its military counterpart, the U. S. Army OH-58A light observation helicopter.

An unusual nine-inch snowfall at Wichita and Salina on Sunday, February 20, posed a challenge that was overcome by massive efforts of Beech maintenance crews. By the time the first shift reported for work at 7:00 a.m. Monday, nearly all the parking lots were cleared and aircraft were able to use the runways.

Deliveries of new Beechcrafts reemphasized the broad range of utility of the company's product lines. The purchase of a new Beechcraft Bonanza V35B by the Chaney Construction Company of Belton, Texas, previously the owner of three Beechcrafts in succession, accented the place earned by Beech airplanes in the nation-wide construction industry. They had earned acceptance as a standard item of money-making construction equipment, expediting the completion of geographically far-flung projects. So much in demand had Beechcrafts become for such uses that the company had become a regular exhibitor at that industry's annual "CONEXPO" international show of essential construction machinery.

Globe Engineering Co., Wichita, a specialized producer of metal formings, and Western Shipping Company, Julesburg, Colo., both prior owners of Beechcrafts, took delivery of new Beechcraft Bonanzas to speed sales and service to customers far and near.

In every instance, the classic Beechcraft Bonanza would fulfill the same basic purpose — to speed face-to-face communication and conserve time and energy. As a bonus, there was a factor aptly summarized by Leighton Collins, reporting in *Air Facts* magazine on his enjoyable experiences in flying a Beechcraft Bonanza F33A on business trips. Collins ended by writing:

"A friend of ours long known in private flying circles told a friend of his who was thinking of selling her Bonanza, 'Don't do it. The day you sell that airplane you're going to be ten years older.' May we suggest that the day you start flying a Bonanza you're going to be ten years younger."

Moving up from its earlier single-engine Beechcrafts, Sea Airmotive, Inc. of Alaska purchased a Beechcraft Super King Air 200 as a companion for its Beechcraft King Air A90 and its president's Beechcraft Bonanza V35B in charter service mainly to the oil fields of Alaska and Canada.

The 1,000th commercial Beechcraft King Air produced also went into duty in the oil fields, although in a warmer climate. A Beechcraft Super King Air 200, it was delivered on January 22 to Pearce Industries, Inc., a Houston-based heavy equipment and engine distributor. It became the third Beechcraft King Air to have been owned by the Texas firm, and it joined their third Beechcraft Queen Air then in service, often into short fields and unimproved ranch landing strips.

Notable among many deliveries of piston-engine twins was the fulfillment of a boyhood dream for Armand Toran, president of Graytor Printing Company, Lyndhurst, N. J., that began when at age 14 he obtained a copy of a Beechcraft catalog. Checking out his firm's new Beechcraft Baron 58, he said that the fast airborne station wagon would expand his sales and services to New England and Midwestern customers.

Expansion of activities over a four-state area prompted the description by Irvin Angel, president of Benner and Fields, Inc., Greensboro, N. C. mechanical contractors, of their Beechcraft Baron B55 as "an indispensable business machine." A former frequent user of chartered Beechcrafts, Angel achieved the distinction of being the first student pilot at GSO Regional Airport to make his initial solo flight in a twin-engine airplane — the Beechcraft Baron.

Speedy new 286 mph Beechcraft Duke pressurized twins winged their way from Beech Field to cover vast territories for their owners. A Beechcraft Duke B60 delivered to Reno-based Kinderfoto International, Inc. was purchased to maintain contact with the firm's 200 outlets throughout the United States and Canada. The entire United States was the operating area for another Beechcraft Duke B60 bought by the Libby Welding Company. Flown from their Kansas City, Mo. base by the firm's father and son team of Hugh H. and Hugh L. Libby, the new twin was their third Beechcraft Duke, and their 14th Beechcraft since 1947. The Libbys reported that their Beechcrafts were

418

definite contributors to their firm's growth — past, present and future.

Sales and earnings as the first half of fiscal year 1975 closed on March 31 showed healthy gains over 1974. The annual cash dividend rate was accordingly raised to 17½¢ per share. Employees' shares in the gains would come through the workings of the Beechcraft Bonanza Plan, which next month reached the highest six-month level ever achieved.

April showers of happy events brought joy to Beechcrafters throughout the month that followed. The company's new version of its stalwart Beechcraft Mentor T-34 two-place trainer, reborn as the turboprop Model T-34C, was crowned with success when on April 8, the U. S. Navy issued a contract for approximately $7.1 million, covering an initial purchase of 18 aircraft. It was expected that Navy requirements for additional T-34C Mentors would amount to some 400 aircraft over the next four years.

The Navy contract followed by four days an award from the U. S. Army Missile Command of a $7.7 million contract for production and contractor operation of the new Beech turbojet-powered Variable-Speed Training Target (VSTT). It was the first of what was estimated to be a $26 million multi-year requirement for 317 of the aerial targets. That award resulted from a three-year Army evaluation of the Beechcraft Model 1089 VSTT in an industry-wide performance and cost competition. The 16 foot-long, 950-pound, remotely controlled Beechcraft would be used primarily as a target tug, operating at speeds ranging from 285 to 575 mph and at altitudes up to 40,000 feet.

A visit to Beech Aircraft by six members of the House of Representatives Sub-Committee on Aviation, headed by its chairman, Glenn M. Anderson, Cal., also included FAA officials from Washington. Their orientation session preceded action later in the month by the House Ways and Means Committee that brought good news to Beech and the entire general aviation industry. Proposals to levy a 20 per cent excise tax on general aviation aircraft, and to tax general aviation fuel at seven cents per gallon, were killed in committee.

The company won a favorable verdict from a U. S. District Court Jury in Salt Lake City in a $1.91 million lawsuit consequent to a 1968 aircraft accident. Punitive damage claims of

$17-plus million arising from the same accident had been dismissed by the court in a prior action.

Elevated to posts as vice presidents of Beech Aircraft were three veteran Beechcrafters. Glenn Ehling was named vice president - manufacturing; Dwight C. Hornberger, vice president - international marketing; and John A. Pike, vice president - production. Their promotions enlarged the company's top-level array of seasoned talent, and also served to facilitate the upward mobility of the second generation of bright young people then in training for higher responsibilities.

Thus the concept of maintaining management in depth, which had often proved its value to the company in years past, was further reinforced. Beech picked good people for promotion at all levels, and gave them the chance to show what they could do. The record spoke for the results.

Acting on behalf of Freedoms Foundation at Valley Forge, Pa., Congressman Garner E. Shriver presented Beech Aircraft with the Foundation's George Washington Certificate Award for Responsible Citizenship Projects. It was the eighth such award received by the company since 1954, in recognition of Beech contributions toward the fulfillment of the non-profit Foundation's goals — "To make Americans proud of America and to develop responsible citizens."

The role of Beechcrafts in checking out the world's airways and airports ground-based navigation and communications facilities was enhanced with the receipt of orders for specially equipped Beechcraft King Airs from the governments of Belgium and the Republic of Indonesia. Introduced by the company in 1963, these flight check Beechcraft King Airs have been put into service in Canada, Mexico and Algeria.

The first Beechcraft Super King Air to be UNACE-equipped was ordered under a $1.6 million contract issued by the U. S. Federal Aviation Administration. Its primary mission would be to inspect air navigation facilities in Hawaii. The Belgian Ministry of Commerce - Civil Aviation contracted for a Beechcraft King Air A100 with UNACE equipment. Orders also came from the governments of Turkey, Chile, and the Republic of Indonesia for UNACE Beechcraft King Airs.

The Indonesian order, in addition to two of the special-mission

420

After delivering the Commencement address to the Class of 1975 of Southwestern College, Winfield, Kansas, President Frank E. Hedrick received the honorary degree of Doctor of Business Administration, presented by Donald B. Ruthenberg, Southwestern College President.
(Page 423)

Honored also was a famous Beechcraft. Restored exactly as on its world record-breaking 1949 nonstop flight of 5,274 miles from Honolulu to Teterboro, N. J. with Capt. Bill Odom as pilot, the 29-year-old "Waikiki Beech" Beechcraft Bonanza 35 was sent to Washington, D. C. for installation as a permanent exhibit in the National Air and Space Museum of the Smithsonian Institution.
(Page 426)

Dedication by the Staggerwing Museum Foundation, Tullahoma, Tenn., of its Walter H. Beech Hangar attested the unique position earned by the company's first products. Aviation progress was emphasized by the arrival of the guests of honor, Mrs. O. A. Beech and Mrs. Louise Thaden, in a turbo-prop Beechcraft Super King Air. Charlotte Parish greeted the guests as they disembarked.

At the celebration banquet, Mrs. Beech was presented by Forrest E. Hood, Tullahoma, with a blown glass Staggerwing replica as W. C. "Dub" Yarborough, Foundation chairman, led the applause.

As a sequel to the dedication, a bronze bust of Walter H. Beech was presented to the Foundation for its permanent collection. Participating were (from left) Thomas N. Warner and Mrs. Warner (Suzanne), daughter of Mr. and Mrs. Beech; W. C. "Dub" Yarbrough, president of the Foundation; John L. Parish, executive vice president of the Foundation, and Mrs. Parish (Charlotte); Mrs. E. C. Burns (Betty) and E. C. Burns, group vice president, Beech Aircraft Corporation.

422

Beechcraft King Air A100s, included 21 Beechcraft Sundowner 180s for primary flight training. The 23 new Beechcrafts were to join an existing fleet of eight Beechcraft Musketeers and two Beechcraft Baron B55 twins in service with Indonesian government agencies. The $5 million contract, which included full support and spares services, was negotiated by the company's Australian distributor, Hawker de Havilland Australia Pty. Ltd.

"Make Your Own World" was the title and the theme of the Commencement address delivered May 18 by President Frank E. Hedrick to members of the 1975 class at Southwestern College, Winfield, Kansas. Affirming that opportunities had never been better than they were at the time, he urged the graduates to make their own decisions as responsible members of society. In recognition of "distinguished service in his field," Hedrick was awarded the honorary degree of Doctor of Business Administration at the ceremonies.

The honor was preceded by the presentation at Washington, D. C. on May 1 of an award to Hedrick by the editorial board of advisers to *Commuterworld* magazine, acting as spokesmen for the nation's commuter airlines, in acknowledgement of Beech Aircraft's contributions to the commuter airline industry. Backgrounded by the performance of the more than 160 Beechcraft 99 Airliners in use, Beech Aircraft was named as "a good citizen in the commuter industry."

From the Jet Propulsion Laboratory of the California Institute of Technology came an assignment for Beech Aircraft to support the study phase of a NASA research project using inflight injection of hydrogen to reduce fuel consumption and pollutant emissions. Savings of better than 15 per cent in fuel flow were expected by project scientists to result from the long-range program.

Fuel conservation had likewise been the aim of an immediately realizable program outlined earlier by the company to aircraft operators. An April mailing to all Beechcraft owners suggested a series of flight management procedures to increase operating efficiency and maximize fuel savings.

A notable era in aviation history was commemorated on June 14 with the dedication of the Walter H. Beech Hangar at the Staggerwing Museum Foundation, Inc. at Tullahoma, Tenn.

Honor guests and recipients of mementos of the weekend event were Mrs. O. A. Beech and Mrs. Louise Thaden. They had made their start together in aviation — Mrs. Beech, then Olive Ann Mellor, as secretary to Walter H. Beech, and Mrs. Thaden, then Louise McPhettridge, as a record-setting pilot, with the Travel Air Manufacturing Company in the Twenties. Subsequently Mrs. Beech, as co-founder of Beech Aircraft, had arranged for Louise Thaden to pilot the Beechcraft C17R Staggerwing biplane that won the 1936 Bendix transcontinental race. More than 300 members and guests of the Staggerwing Club attended the event, hosted by John and Charlotte Parish; and 27 Beechcraft Staggerwing biplanes were flown in by their enthusiastic owners to the dedication.

From that pleasant excursion into the past, Beech Aircraft moved on to make new history. Flown solo by Miss Trina Jarish of Costa Mesa, Cal., an aviation career woman, a modern classic Beechcraft Bonanza A36 took first place in the prestigious All Women's Transcontinental Air Derby July 4-7, with an average ground speed of 204.33 mph. Five other Beechcraft Bonanzas were among the top 20 finishers in the 103-plane field of the 1975 "Powder Puff Derby".

Sales and earnings at the end of the first nine months of fiscal year established new records for any comparable period in the company's history. The company also added $1.7 million to its multi-million-dollar backlog of orders on hand, with the receipt from the Aeronautical Systems Division of the U. S. Air Force System Command of a contract to develop and produce flight demonstration units of a new remotely piloted vehicle, the TEDS (Tactical Expendable Drone System). Beech was one of two companies chosen for the TEDS assignment, which would lead to an Air Force decision as to further engineering and eventual production. Beech test units were to be modified versions of the company's Model 1089 target drone.

From Eglin Air Force Base in Florida came the good news that in a July 9 test by the Armament Development and Test Center of the Air Force System Command, Beechcraft's new High Altitude Supersonic Target (HAST) had been highly successful in carrying out its assigned program in an air-launched test flight.

In an announcement issued July 10, Beech Aircraft and Hawker Siddeley Aviation Ltd. revealed that their joint agreement for marketing Beechcraft Hawker Jet aircraft in North America would not be renewed at its expiration on September 30, 1975. Economic considerations, particularly that of the differing rates in inflation between America and England, were cited as principal causes.

Launching in mid-July of the Apollo Soyuz Test Project — the joint USA/USSR cooperative space flight — marked the 15th journey into space in support of manned flight for Beech life support and power supply cryogenic gas storage systems. The successful completion of the nine-day, 138-earth-orbit mission enlarged the total of 6,600 hours of space flight logged by ultra low temperature systems designed and constructed at Beech-Boulder.

The mission was a timely milestone for the celebration of the 20th anniversary of the Beech Boulder Division which was held on July 20. Started on July 25, 1955 with a modest complement of 75 employees working in leased office space, Beech had built up at Boulder a research, development, design and production center that had contributed significantly to the nation's major space programs. Further contributions were assured by work in progress on the power reactant storage assembly for NASA's Space Shuttle Orbiter and support equipment. Target missile production was moving briskly. And exciting prospects existed with vast potential for helping to ease energy shortages through fuels or liquid hydrogen stored in cryogenic systems originated at Beech-Boulder. There were good reasons why the celebration was a gala event.

Beech-Wichita staged a celebration of its own four days later, with the delivery on July 23 of its first C-12A Beechcrafts to the U. S. Air Force and the United States Army. The Air Force spokesman, Col. Allen F. Learmonth, stated that "The mission for which this aircraft is being procured requires two fundamental characteristics that are fully satisfied by the C-12 adaptation of your very successful Beechcraft Super King Air 200 — these are prestige and safety." Harold L. Bowman, Assistant Secretary of the Army, hailed the C-12A as "a welcome and much needed addition to the Army's aviation inventory."

425

The cordial reception accorded to their C-12A Beechcrafts by both services was more than a formality. On August 5, the U. S. Air Force issued a $10.8 million follow-on contract for 16 additional C-12A Beechcrafts. On August 15 the United States Army followed suit, ordering 20 more C-12A Beechcrafts under a $13.6 million follow-on contract. The two contracts extended production on the military versions of the corporate Beechcraft Super King Air through October, 1977.

Orderly continuation of work on these and all company programs was affirmed with the signing on August 5 of a new three year contract between Beech Aircraft and employees represented by the International Association of Machinists and Aerospace Workers. Providing additional benefits to ease the effects of inflation and economic pressures on workers and their families, the new pact was hailed as fair by employees and management.

Meanwhile, a famous Beechcraft gained an honored place in a permanent exhibition of aircraft outstanding in aviation history. Positioned on August 6 in the new Air and Space Museum of the Smithsonian Institution in Washington, D. C. was the "Waikiki Beech" — the single-engine Beechcraft Bonanza piloted by Captain William P. Odom in a 36-hour nonstop flight from Honolulu to Teterboro, N. J. March 6-8, 1949. Covering 4957.24 officially accredited Great Circle miles and 5273 actual miles, Odom's carefully planned flight was the longest nonstop journey completed by any light commercial aircraft during the first half of the Twentieth Century. Restored by Beech craftsmen to its exact condition as of that historic flight, Beechcraft Bonanza N80040 would serve as an enduring reminder and a source of inspiration to future generations.

Early in September, a Beechcraft D17S Staggerwing biplane also took its place in history as a permanent display in the United States Air Force Museum at Wright Field, Dayton, Ohio. Newly painted in its original military colors, it was one of 338 Beechcraft biplanes purchased by the U. S. armed forces for worldwide service as executive and utility transport aircraft during World War II. Designated by the Air Force as the UC-43, and by the Navy Bureau of Aeronautics as the GB-2, the military Beechcrafts were virtually identical with the commercial Beechcraft Model D17S biplane.

426

The delivery of a new Beechcraft Super King Air 200 to Norfolk Island Airlines of Australia had unique aspects. Equipped with high density seating for 12 passengers, plus crew, Norfolk's Beechcraft went into use on the world's longest commuter hops — 910 nonstop miles over the South Pacific from Brisbane, Australia to Norfolk Island, an exotic tourist paradise only three by six miles wide. An alternate route leg extended south to Lord Howe Island, 485 miles away. The largest Beechcraft replaced a Beechcraft King Air 90 which had been leased by Norfolk.

Record sales and earnings for the third consecutive year were scored when the company's 1975 fiscal year ended on September 30. Total consolidated sales of $267,149,235 were up more than 10 per cent over 1974. Net earnings of $15,611,985 showed a 25 per cent increase over 1974. Shareholders were the happy recipients of a special one per cent stock dividend and an increase in the annual dividend rate from 70 cents to 75 cents per share.

The good news of the company's biggest year was a fitting prelude to the greatest get-together of Beechcraft marketers in its 43-year history — the "Spirit of '76" International Sales Conference. Principals of the worldwide Beechcraft marketing organization met at the Beech Activity Center October 6-8 to celebrate three record years and to plan for a bigger year ahead. Major impetus for their high hopes was provided by the company's 19-model 1976 line of Bicentennial Beechcrafts including three new models, the Beechcraft King Air B100 with Garrett Turboprop engines, the pressurized Beechcraft Baron 58P, and the turbocharged Beechcraft Baron 58TC.

The Beechcraft Baron 58P had been put through a complete type certification under the new and stringent Federal Aviation Regulations, Part 23 and had gone through more than 600 hours of rigorous service flight testing.

A pressurization differential of 3.6 psi gave the Baron 58P a sea level cabin at 7800 feet and a 7800-foot cabin at 18,000. A pilot's door over the wing on the right side and a rear door on the left side, behind the wing trailing edge, gave access to the rear club seating or four forward facing seats and baggage area.

To keep up performance at its 6,100-pound gross weight, the

turbocharged Baron 58P was equipped with 310-hp engines and three-bladed propellers.

The Baron 58P cruise speed was 249 mph at 15,000 feet and maximum speed was 279 mph. Among optional features was an air conditioning system and wide selection of avionics.

The turbocharged Beechcraft Baron 58TC featured speed and range performance similar to the pressurized Baron 58P and a higher payload than the Baron 58. It combined the Baron 58 cabin and door arrangement with the 310-hp turbocharged engines of the 58P to carry sea level performance into the high country and through the summer months.

The Beechcraft Baron B55 with 260-hp engines and the Beechcraft Baron E55 and Beechcraft Baron 58 with 285-hp engines rounded out the five Baron models.

A third new model for '76, the King Air B100 cruised at 306 mph. First Beechcraft to use the highly efficient Garrett turbine engine, the TPE 331-6-252B of 840 shaft horsepower, flat rated to 715 shp, which had accumulated more than 7 million hours of flight experience, the King Air B100 incorporated propeller reversing for short-field operation, negative torque sensing which accomplished automatic, immediate propeller drag reduction in the event of engine shutdown, and electrically activated air-intake anti-icing system employing warm bleed air from the second-stage compressor.

The 16-foot-long walk-around cabin of the King Air B100 offered choices of seating from 6 to 13 passengers. Its pressurization, heating and air conditioning system provided an always comfortable cabin and an 8000-foot cabin at 21,200 feet. Range was 1501 miles, or Houston to New York.

The Beechcraft King Air series of five models included the King Air C90, the lowest priced equipped turboprop, and more powerful King Air E90 with the larger cabin King Air A100 and the Super King Air, with 850 shp engines, higher operational altitude, range of 2,172 miles, 333 mph plus cruise speed, and a 9,840-foot cabin cruising at 31,000 feet.

It was interesting that eleven years ago when the first Beechcraft King Air was introduced it was the consensus in the industry that the jets would take over the turboprop market. But the analysis at Beech was that there was a market for 250-300 cruise turboprop aircraft among owners who had no profitable use for another 100 to 200 mph speed. 1300 King Airs sold to date proved the correctness of the decision.

The pressurized, six-place, 380-hp piston-engined Beechcraft Duke B60 presented a new option for 1976: wet wing tip tanks which held 30 gallons total and increased the range 20 per cent to 1287 @ 65% or 1412 @ 45% sm.

In the single-engine Beechcraft Bonanza line were the Bonanza F33A and Bonanza V35B along with the Bonanza A36 which in 1975 for the first time outsold each of the other model Bonanzas. The F33C, the aerobatic version, available on order, had a good export year. Bonanza sales were reported as having increased by 40 per cent in 1975.

The Beech Aero Center line continued with the Beechcraft Sport 150, the Beechcraft Sundowner 180, and the 200-hp, retractable-gear Beechcraft Sierra 200. All three models included inertia reel shoulder harnesses as standard equipment.

At the Sales Roundup the green light was announced for production of an additional Aero Center aircraft, the four-place, twin-engine Beechcraft Model 76 which will have 180-hp engines and a 185-mph cruise speed over an 800-mile range. As well as filling a need for a multi-engine trainer, the airplane would be attractive as an efficient, easy-to-fly twin for personal and business flying as well as short-haul air taxi.

Still a possible addition to the Aero Center line was the proposed Beechcraft PD 285 two-place trainer, which was being tested in a T-tail configuration. Decision to produce the aircraft was to hinge on evaluation of flight test results.

It was announced that in 1975 Beech Aircraft installed more than $52 million in avionics equipment, an amazing rise from the $1 million sold in 1958 when customized installations were first offered.

In planning ahead, the company shared with its sales force the results of highly sophisticated forecasting techniques. More than two years ago, Beech Aircraft had contracted with Chase Econometrics, a division of Chase Manhattan Bank, to provide national economic forecasts. From these, Beech Marketing Research constructed on econometric model for predicting corporate aircraft deliveries. The model had worked well, though conservatively.

In support of sales, Beech Aircraft's general aviation affairs officer, Marvin B. Small, presented his program "General Aviation Benefits the Nation" in 208 civic club appearances during the past year with notable success. As a public service of the company, its value had been thoroughly proved, as had its merits as a goodwill builder for the local sponsoring Beech sales outlet.

The Conference closed with the presentation of a grand total of 103 awards for distinguished sales and service achievements during 1975. The company's highest honor was conferred on Miguel "Mike" Campos, who was named Beech Aircraft Corporation's "Man of the Year" for 1975. Campos earned permanent placement in the "Beechcraft Hall of Fame" for his achievements during 22 years as president of Liberty Aviation, the Beechcraft distributor in the Philippines. There long known and respected as "Mr. General Aviation", his efforts had proved so effective that more than half of the 96 corporate aircraft owned by the top 55 corporations in the Philippines were Beechcrafts.

Among 16 more sales and service awards presented by the International Division, the International Sales Leadership Award went to Transair France. Hawker de Havilland Australia Pty. Ltd. received the International Sales Accomplishment Award; and the International Market Development Award was earned by Latourrette & Parini S.A.C. of Paraguay.

On the domestic front, Stevens Beechcraft, Inc., Greer, S. C. took top honors for highest factory deliveries in total dollars — $15.9 million. Hangar One, Inc., Atlanta, Ga. was first among Aviation Centers for retail deliveries in their home base area.

Fifty Beechcraft salesmen won awards for achieving "Millionaire" status with more than $1 million in sales. Heading the list was Philip Coleman of Hartzog Aviation, Inc., Rockford, Ill. who produced $5.7 million in sales in 1975. The Awards Banquet was a great finish to a great year.

Midway in the Sales Conference, good news came from Washington, D. C. The Navy issued a letter contract go-ahead on October 7 for the follow-on procurement of 75 additional Beechcraft Mentor T-34C trainers, with an option for purchase of 23 more T-34Cs.

At the 28th National Business Aircraft Association meeting and show in New Orleans, La. October 29-31, the display of five pressurized Beechcraft models for 1976 was a major event.

Featuring a theme of "RSVP" (Reliability, Schedule, Value, Price), the company held its third annual Cost Conference early in November with excellent results. Top management representatives of 60 of its largest suppliers came to exchange ideas on helping to control costs of building Beech products. Almost instant savings resulted from a Beech offer to sign two-year contracts with suppliers who would hold their prices for the next two years. One even cut his prices 10 per cent to get a Beech contract.

As winter neared, energy conservation measures focused on fuel savings at all Beech Aircraft facilities. A company-wide Cold Weather Operations Directive prescribed temperature settings of 55 degrees in shops and 68 degrees in offices as a general standard.

Cooperating in a NASA-sponsored research program, the company delivered to Ohio State University for further flight testing a Beechcraft Sundowner 180 which had been factory-equipped with a new experimental GAW-2 wing. The project was a follow-on of company-funded tests of a new series of airfoils, starting with the NASA GAW-1 wing, that would hopefully provide greater efficiency in use on general aviation airplanes.

Elected board chairman of the General Aviation Manufacturers Association at its directors' Fall meeting was President Frank E. Hedrick. Previously vice chairman of GAMA, Hedrick was a founding member and had served as chairman of its Safety and Public Affairs Committees.

Beechcrafters paused for a moment in their personal preparations for Christmas to take note of December 22 as a special day in their company's history. It was on that date in 1945, thirty years ago that the Beechcraft Bonanza made its first flight from Beech Field, a flight which lasted 20 minutes. Three decades later 12,615 Beechcraft Bonanzas had been delivered to customers around the world. The design had become a living classic among general aviation aircraft. And its future, like that of its builders, was more than ever bright with promise.

Carrying forward the Beech tradition: Mr. and Mrs. William L. Oliver, Jr. (Mary Lynn Beech) with Jennifer Gwen Pitt and Jeffrey Hanson Pitt . . .

and Mr. and Mrs. Thomas N. Warner (Suzanne Beech) with their son, Jay, and Mrs. O. A. Beech.

Honoring the nation's 200th birthday, the company's Aero Center models — the Beechcraft Sierra 200, Sundowner 180, and Sport 150 — appeared in "Spirit of '76" bicentennial colors.

Spearheaded by the Beechcraft Super King Air, the full array of 19 new Beechcrafts for 1976 greeted guests arriving at Beech Field for the "Spirit of '76" International Sales Conference.

New symbols of leadership in general aviation: the distinctive and efficient T-tails of the Beechcraft Super King Air; the Aero Center Beechcraft Model 76 light twin; and the proposed Aero Center Beechcraft PD 285 single-engine trainer.

433

Chapter 39

Welcoming the new year of 1976, Americans everywhere felt a renewed surge of patriotism and pride as the nation prepared to celebrate its 200th birthday. The Bicentennial year was rich with promise, and nowhere more promising than at Beech Aircraft. The first quarter of the 1976 Beech fiscal year had established new all-time records, with sales of $79,412,700 and net earnings of $4,804,000. Prospects were bright for bettering these figures as the year progressed.

So it was not surprising that Chairman O. A. Beech added to her many honors a citation in January by Gallaghers *Presidents' Reports*, a nationally circulated executives' newsletter respected and sometimes feared for its unvarnished candor, as one of the best chief executives of companies with sales under $1 billion per year.

Equally unsurprising were her comments on that citation. In a memo to all Beechcrafters, Mrs. Beech wrote:

"A very fine 'fragile' compliment!

"I am pleased that Beech Aircraft and I are recognized for the accomplishments which were achieved by your dedication and interest in the success of our company . . . Thanks for your part in bringing Beech Aircraft Corporation this timely recognition — and KEEP UP THE GOOD WORK!"

An unquestionably solid compliment, as Beechcrafters saw it, came at about the same time from "Mr. Bonanza" — rancher Leonard Hay of Rock Springs, Wyoming. Taking delivery of his 24th Beechcraft Bonanza, he hailed his new A36 as "the finest Bonanza ever built." He was in a position to speak with authority. Factory records showed that no individual had ever purchased more Bonanzas than Leonard Hay.

U. S. Army and Air Force C-12A Beechcraft Super King Air transports were also earning high praise in worldwide use. The Beech jetprops were then serving in 11 nations, from Argentina to Indonesia. From Turkey came word that the Army's C-12A was saving valuable time for the commander of the Allied Land Forces/Southeastern Europe, transporting him over his entire zone of responsibility without having to make fuel stops.

434

With the delivery to Egypt's Civil Aviation School of two new Beechcraft Baron twins for multiengine pilot training, the company renewed ties with a valued customer whose last purchase was in 1950. Misr Airwork SAE of Cairo had made good use of its Model 18 twin Beech fleet, delivered long ago in trail-blazing transoceanic flights. Now the newest Beechcraft would display the "SU" registry mark of modern Egypt in flight above the pyramids of the ancient Pharaohs.

Hispanic events loomed large at Beech in February. The Spanish Air Ministry accepted 18 aerobatic F33C Beechcraft Bonanzas for military pilot training at the Spanish Air Academy in Murcia, Spain. The new trainers joined 12 Bonanzas then in use at the Academy and 12 Beechcraft King Air models, 19 twin Barons and 24 Bonanzas purchased by Spain's Air Ministry since 1972. In addition to those 85 Beechcrafts, the Air Academy at Murcia had been operating 25 Beechcraft T-34 Mentor trainers since 1962. And Spain's Civil Aviation School at Salamanca had recently taken delivery of 24 new Beechcrafts to offer all-Beechcraft training from primary through jetprop advanced twin-engine stages.

In the New World, the military services of modern Mexico had long concurred with the preference of their Spanish counterparts for Beech-built aircraft. The Government of Mexico had chosen Beechcraft T-34 Mentors in 1958 for both naval and civilian aviation training. These were supplemented in 1970 with a fleet of 20 Beechcraft Musketeer Sports for Air Force use, and in 1974 with 20 Beechcraft Bonanza F33C aerobatic trainers. Mexico's latest additions came in February, with a mass fly-away by its Navy pilots of two new Beechcraft Baron B55 twins and six more Beechcraft Bonanza F33C trainers.

A devastating earthquake that shook Guatemala that month gave Beech Aircraft a chance to show appreciation for the loyalty of its Hispanic friends; and response was instant. On February 10 a donated company-owned Beechcraft King Air E90 took off from Beech Field for a swift 6½-hour flight to the stricken land. On board was one passenger, Dr. Lilia Rodriguez-Tocker, who had volunteered her services in aid, and a cargo of 2,000 pounds of medical supplies given by Wichita area hospitals, firms and individuals. Joined with the services of Beechcraft and other airplane owners in Guatemala, the mercy mission did much to relieve the sufferings of the earthquake victims.

In other altruistic projects, the Beech Aircraft Foundation revealed gifts to various institutions of $120,000 for education, $60,000 for community services, $20,000 for youth services and $20,000 for hospitals and medical research. The company was doing its part as a good citizen. But perhaps even more important to the general public was the total of $108 million that its activities in 1975 had contributed to the Kansas economy. Through its multiple turnover in the channels of trade, that sum would go far to enlarge the prosperity of the state and of Kansans.

A long-standing warm relationship with Bell Helicopter Textron was reaffirmed with the receipt in February of an add-on contract for continued production of Bell's Model 206B JetRanger-II commercial helicopter airframes and assemblies through December, 1977. More than 2,100 commercial Jet-Ranger ship sets had already been bought by Bell. Previous deliveries, starting in 1962 with Beech-built components for Bell's U. S. Army Iroquois jet-powered model, had also included 2,294 airframes for the military OH-58A reconnaissance helicopter.

Recoverable Beech AQM-37A supersonic missile targets were specified in a $2.2 million contract issued February 4 by the U. S. Army Missile Command. Two versions were ordered: a high-altitude target with 1,360-mph and 70,000-ft. altitude capabilities, and a low-altitude modification operable to within 180 ft. above the terrain. A two-stage parachute system would provide soft landings for the flight-controllable targets. Supplementing a prior Army modification contract, the purchase bolstered the future of the versatile Beech-designed AQM-37A target. More than 3,000 units had been delivered to U. S. and other defense forces of the Free World in continuous production since its inception in 1959.

Paired with the AQM-37A purchase was a U. S. Army contract for $1.1 million worth of flight support services and spare parts for its MQM-107 Variable Speed Training Target (Beech Model 1089). Action swiftly followed. The first MQM-107, delivered next month, successfully completed its initial flight test at the Army's White Sands Missile Range, demonstrating controlled

436

speeds of 315 to 515 mph and climbs to 15,000 and 25,000-ft. altitudes. The target was thriftily recovered by use of its ground-actuated parachute system.

In the region of finance, an exacting statistical test requested by President Frank E. Hedrick proved the solid quality of Beech Aircraft's growth over the years. Analysis showed that an investor purchasing 100 shares of Beech stock in December, 1955 would have paid $2,125 at the then current market price for his equity. At March 1, 1976, his holdings would have grown to 922 shares, through stock dividends and splits. Their current market value would have soared to $19,016 — a capital appreciation of 795 percent. In addition, he would have collected $5,927 in cash dividends. It was not surprising, therefore, that *Dun's Review* had recently named Beech Aircraft as one of the 200 best managed companies in the nation, and that *Forbes Magazine* had likewise reported Beech as ranking high in profitability, growth and stock market performance.

All past records toppled as the company closed its books at March 31 on the first half of its 1976 fiscal year. Sales of $162,502,020 and earnings of $10,947,380 prompted an increase to 80¢ per share in Beech's 111th consecutive cash dividend payments to its shareholders.

On the international scene, two new Super King Air Beech-crafts meanwhile spanned half the globe to enter the service of Indonesia Air Transport for charter and utility missions. Removable seating for 12 passengers permitted stretcher installations and cargo space as required. Also delivered in February was the first of two more sister ships — Beechcraft King Air A100s equipped for the Republic of Indonesia with Beech-designed electronic flight checking systems for the growing network of navigation-communications aids that helped link Indonesia's 13,760 islands.

Prospects for general aviation were looking up in both the Far East and the Arab nations of the Near East. Recent sales of 11 twin-engine Beechcrafts (seven King Air, two Queen Air and two Baron models) to Saudi Arabia, Algeria and Egypt prompted the formation by the International Division on March 29 of a new sales region spanning north Africa from Morocco eastward to the Afghan border.

437

Planned construction of a new 58,000 sq. ft. final assembly building at Liberal, Kansas was announced on April 6. Like the existing 113,000 sq. ft. facilities there, it would be leased from the city of Liberal, which showed its confidence in Beech by issuing $1.3 million worth of industrial revenue bonds to finance the project. The addition would enable the Liberal Division to expand its production of the increasingly popular Aero Center line of light Beechcrafts, including the projected Model 76 twin and PD 285 trainer models as well as the current Sierra 200, Sundowner 180 and Sport 150 designs. The work force at Liberal was expected to double when the enlarged plant reached its full capacity.

The Beech concepts of maintaining skilled management in depth and making promotions from within were seen in the promotion on April 13 of Seymour (Jack) Colman to vice president - administration. A Beechcrafter since 1942, Colman assumed responsibility for industrial relations and plant security, succeeding J. E. Isaacs who was moving into retirement.

Taking delivery of his fourth Beechcraft, a new Baron 58, Arthur Godfrey continued an affiliation with Beech products that spanned nearly a half century. The first airplane flown by the famous entertainment personality and aviation booster, long ago in 1929, had been an OX-5 Travel Air biplane built by the Travel Air Manufacturing Company when Walter H. Beech was its president. Godfrey had since owned, in succession, a Beechcraft Bonanza, a Travel Air twin, and a Baron D55.

"Our Million Dollar Club. Still Going Strong." So went the headline on a Beech advertisement published nationally in April, naming 49 salesmen who had each sold more than one million dollars worth of new Beechcraft airplanes in 1975. The message did much to explain the company's success. Its salesmen were making good by the simple process of locating prospects who needed Beech products, and satisfying those needs. Throughout business and industry, the need was clearly great and growing for the swift, safe, flexible and profit-enhancing transportation that Beechcrafts were built to provide.

Next month the point of that advertisement was driven home, as deliveries of commercial aircraft smashed all existing records. Flown from Beech Field in May were 120 new Beechcrafts

438

valued at $21.1 million. As a warmup for that feat, commercial deliveries in April had also set a new record of $20.4 million. A favorite saying of Walter H. Beech came to mind: "Records were made to be broken."

Meanwhile, engineering advancements significantly increased the range capabilities of best-selling twin Beechcrafts. Wet wings became available as options on the Baron 58 models, upping maximum ranges by 18 percent or more. And removable wing tip tanks, developed originally for Beechcraft Super King Air photographic mission aircraft ordered by the Institut Geographique National of Paris, provided a maximum endurance of 10.3 hours at 200 mph at 25,000 ft. altitude. That option was offered to other Super King Air buyers, further widening the market for the company's top-of-the-line product.

Meeting with President Gerald Ford at the White House on May 27, Beech President Frank E. Hedrick acted as spokesman for the General Aviation Manufacturers Association (GAMA). As chairman of GAMA, Hedrick voiced his and the industry's appreciation for Ford's action, announced that day, easing restrictions on general aviation exports. It had, Hedrick told the President, "improved the procedures for exports; potentially expanded . . . employment levels; reduced the cost of government and of doing business; hopefully will improve . . . and add to the U. S. balance of trade."

There were good reasons for Hedrick to applaud President Ford's timely action. Beech Aircraft had just entered two new models in the international sales arena — the Beechcraft King Air B100 with Garrett AiResearch turbine engines, and the pressurized Beechcraft Baron 58P. With seven more Centennial Series Beechcrafts, they had made their overseas debut on May 1 at the German Aerospace Show in Hanover, Europe's largest general aviation show. Then came a month-long tour of Europe, including a showing at Airborne '76, the Gothenberg International Air Show May 12-16 in Sweden. Relaxation of import restrictions would facilitate sales to customers throughout Europe, a prime market for Beech products.

At the same time that President Ford was meeting with Hedrick in the White House, a decision was made at the Pentagon that set the "Happy Day!" flag waving briskly on the

439

desk of Chairman O. A. Beech in Wichita. On May 27, the Naval Air Systems Command named Beech Aircraft as the winner of an industry competition for a planned three-year, off-the-shelf procurement of its new VTAM (X) multiengine advanced training aircraft.

The Navy's initial $8,629,217 fixed price contract called for production of 15 aircraft plus flight demonstration, flight testing and furnishing of engineering data, with deliveries scheduled through October, 1977. Options included purchase of 56 additional aircraft and five years of complete logistical support by the manufacturer.

Competition for the Navy contract had been keen. Three other major manufacturers had submitted meritorious entries. The preparation of the Beech proposal had been typically thorough. To document the fitness of its winning Beechcraft King Air 90 for the Navy's use, engineering and performance data that weighed in at 1,500 pounds of paperwork had been flown to Washington early in the year for the judges' studies.

Hard work had paid off. And the Beech entry was backed by a record amassed over nearly four decades since 1938 by thousands of Beechcrafts in the Navy's service — Model 17 staggerwing biplanes (Navy GB-1's and GB-2's), Model 18 twins (Navy JRB-1's, RC-45's, SNB-1's, 2's, 4's and 5's), and Mentor single-engine trainers (Navy T-34B's and their upcoming successors, the new turboprop Navy T-34C's). Beech was known for building airplanes that measured up to the Navy's exacting demands — demands that, in the case of its newest Navy T-44A Beechcraft advanced twin turboprop trainer, called for a service life of at least 12,000 hours and 30,000 landings by student pilots. Beechcrafters joyfully greeted the new contract as the Navy's way of saying "Well done!" for their efforts.

A series of varied honors and awards followed in the wake of the Navy contract. President Frank E. Hedrick accepted appointments to a second term on the Board of Trustees of the Kansas Foundation for Private Colleges, and to the Kansas Governor's Task Force on Effective Management. At the 1976 Reading Air Show in Pennsylvania, he was named General Aviation's "Man Of The Year" by the Ziff-Davis Publishing Co., which cited "his important contributions to the stature, growth

"Uncommon Citizen" was the title bestowed on Chairman O. A. Beech by the Wichita Area Chamber of Commerce. Its president, H. Marvin Bastian, made the presentation.

Latest additions to the Mexican Government's Beechcraft fleets — two Beechcraft Baron B55's and six Beechcraft Bonanza F33C aerobatic trainers.

One of Indonesia Air Transport's Beechcraft Super King Air transports is prepared for departure to the Far East.

440A

U. S. President Gerald R. Ford and Beech President Frank E. Hedrick reviewed easing of aircraft export restrictions at the White House.

Winning an industry-wide competition, the Beechcraft King Air 90 became the U. S. Navy's T-44A twin turboprop advanced trainer.

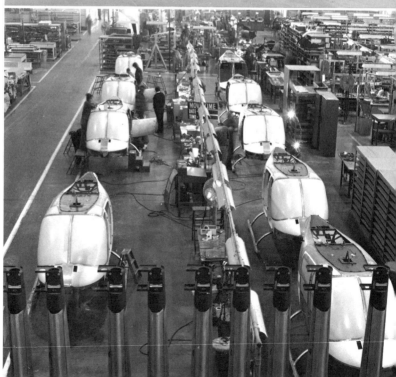

Complete airframes for Bell 206B JetRanger II helicopters continued in production at Wichita Plant III under a new contract.

and stability of general aviation" over the years. This was followed on June 26 by the Golden Plate Award of the American Academy of Achievement, which saluted Hedrick for his "constant aim to do any job better than the job has ever been done before".

Chairman O. A. Beech enlarged her long list of honors with signal recognition by *Business Week* magazine. In its June 21 issue, she was named to head the "Manufacturing" category in the publication's exhaustingly researched listing of "100 Top Corporate Women". And, in a *Life Special Report* shortly afterward, she was chosen as one of 19 "Remarkable American Women" in the category of "Winners in a Man's World". Hers had been one of 1,000 names of women of note considered for honorary listing.

Beech products also earned honors and recognition. The U. S. Air Force placed a handsomely restored AT-11 "Kansas" bombardier trainer on permanent exhibition at the Air Force Museum at Wright-Patterson AFB at Dayton, Ohio. In more than 1,500 AT-11 "flying classrooms", some 90 percent of its World War II bombardiers had learned their skills. The plexiglas-nosed version of the famed Model 18 Twin Beech joined a Model D17S Beechcraft staggerwing biplane UC-43 transport already displayed in the Air Force collection of its distinguished aircraft.

The five Beechcraft Baron twins and eight Beechcraft Bonanzas in use by the Air Training Center of Pacific Southwest Airways at Goodyear, Arizona figured in the receipt by PSA's president, William Shimp, of the Officers Cross of the Award of Merit from the Federal Republic of Germany. One of the highest awards conferred on non-Germans, the decoration recognized PSA's outstanding training of future pilots for Lufthansa, the West German government's airline. "If we hadn't used Beechcrafts, PSA would not have received this award or an extended contract", said Will Ennis, PSA's training director.

A Beechcraft Bonanza A36 took first place for the second consecutive year in the 1976 Women's Powder Puff Derby to win a $10,000 cash prize for its solo pilot, aviation career woman Trina Jarish. Recalling the saying current since 1936 that "It takes a Beechcraft to beat a Beechcraft", second place went to a Beechcraft Bonanza V35 flown by Californians Shirley Cote and Joan

Paynter. Ten of the top 20 finishers in the 176-plane race flew Beechcrafts.

Beech employees were not overlooked in the press of good events. A company-wide Bicentennial Sweepstakes Celebration provided prizes for all. Each employee received a 1976 Bicentennial silver dollar in a souvenir leather case. A man-and-wife pair of Beechcrafters, James and Cindy Mason, won the grand prize — a week-long expenses-paid tour of historic American sites in a Beechcraft Baron twin flown by a company pilot. And a general wage increase, effective August 2 under terms of the company's contract with labor, was garnished with bettered retirement and group insurance benefits that produced a widespread glow of good feeling.

Enhancing the glow was the news of record-breaking sales and earnings for the first nine months and the third quarter of the 1976 fiscal year. Nine-months sales of $248,373,019 were up 26 percent over 1975, and earnings of $16,477,190 up 40 percent. Third quarter sales were up 34 percent at $85,870,999, and net earnings up 34 percent at $5,529,810.

A classic example of the growing use of Beechcrafts by alert business and industrial firms which had fostered new sales records was that of Spencer's Incorporated of Mt. Airy, N.C. For many years, Spencer's had made and sold high quality children's apparel. In 1973 they replaced their first airplane, a small retractable bought in 1972, with a Beechcraft Baron 58 and a Bonanza V35B, and hired a full-time pilot. These were superseded by a Beechcraft King Air C90 in 1974, plus a Baron B55 in 1975.

As Spencer's flying increased, so did their sales — by 30 percent in 1973, 25 percent in 1974 and 1975, and a projected 40 percent for 1976. Providing better access to customers, suppliers, and technological and styling centers, their Beechcrafts played a large part in Spencer's progress.

It was the decision of their co-founder and treasurer, 93-year-young F. L. Hatcher, to buy Spencer's Beechcraft King Air, influenced, he said, because he "didn't want Spencer's executives spending so many nights away from home base". Their firm and a co-enterprise, the Ararat Company, kept on finding new uses for their Beechcrafts to help further their growth.

Beech Aircraft's part in promoting American exports was recognized in Washington with the appointment in August by U. S. Secretary of Commerce Elliot L. Richardson of Michael G. Neuburger, senior vice president - International Division to the Department's new Subcommittee on Export Administration. Neuburger would serve as the representative of the airframe manufacturing industry in dealing with problems affecting export licensing. Neuburger also entered his second consecutive year of service on the U. S. Chamber of Commerce Foreign Trade Policy Panel, an advisory group working to suggest basic import-export guidelines to the government.

Delivery of a new Beechcraft Bonanza A36 to Gerald F. Gruber, president of Trawood Mfg. Co., Inc., Elkhart, Ind., typified the growing fulfillment of expectations for the Beech marketing concepts underlying the Aero Center lightplanes and Aero Clubs. The idea was that by producing Beechcrafts that were inexpensive to buy and fly, and promoting those models through Beech Aero Clubs, customers would be attracted who might well step up eventually to Bonanza, Baron, Duke or King Air ownership. So it went with Mr. Gruber. He had taken his first flying lesson no more than a year ago in an Aero Club's Beechcraft Sundowner 180. Two months later he had his private pilot's license and his own Sundowner; then, in logical sequence, his own new Bonanza which, like most high-performance Beechcrafts, would be used for business and incidental personal flying.

September brought relief from summer's heat, but no break in the procession of good news. The month opened with the receipt from the U. S. Navy of a $36.5 million definitive contract for 98 more T-34C Turbo Mentor trainers, enlarging existing $7.1 million funding for the Navy's initial 18 Mentors, plus engineering services. So the future of the Beechcraft Mentor seemed assured.

At mid-month the U. S. Army Missile Command issued an $8 million-plus follow-on contract for 114 more MQM-107A "Streaker" missile targets, plus field support, that brought its total purchases to more than $18 million. Other services were also evaluating the target's potential. The Beech Model 1089 "Streaker" looked like a sure winner.

Keeping the winning streak going, a Beechcraft Duke 60 set

a new around-the-world speed record for piston-engine aircraft. Flown by Australians Denys Dalton and Terry Gwinn-Jones, its 24,854-mile Brisbane-to-Brisbane run took only five days, two hours and 15 minutes. Officially confirmed by the Federation Aeronautique International, the flight shaved more than three hours off previous world class records set by Beechcraft Baron twins in 1966 and 1971.

The newest Beechcraft Duke B60 was one of five pressurized twins that won keen interest at the annual National Business Aircraft Association convention at Denver, Colo. in mid-September. Formally introduced to NBAA members was the new Beechcraft King Air B100 with Garrett AiResearch turbine power plants, and the latest pressurized twin, the Beechcraft Baron 58P. Completing the display were the Beechcraft King Air E90 and the proud flagship of the company's jetprop fleet, the Beechcraft Super King Air — all-time winner in the corporate aircraft sales market.

Specialized capabilities of Beech Aircraft and its people likewise won recognition. At the rollout of NASA's Space Shuttle Orbiter 101 at Palmdale, Calif. on September 17, its Beech-built power reactant storage assembly shared honors with a ground-based fuel cell support system built for Rockwell International's Space Division under a new $2.25 million contract. This addition raised Beech-Boulder's share in the Orbiter program to more than $11.8 million. Ron Cook, Beech Space Communications supervisor, also won praise as a spokesman for man's voyages into space. On television and radio and in 210 speaking engagements, he had reached an estimated audience of 28,000,000 with inspiring facts about the Space Shuttle and other programs and their wide-ranging public benefits.

Featured with other Beech products at England's Farnborough International Air Show was the latest version of the company's air-to-air refueling system. Introduced in 1960 as the winner of a U. S. Navy design study competition, the self-contained Beech hose-and-drogue system had been adopted in 1971 by the Canadian Armed Forces for their Boeing 707-347 modified transport tankers refueling CF-5 fighter planes. Further orders were in prospect.

444

The best news of all came at the close of the Beech 1976 fiscal year on September 30. New record sales and earnings were scored for the fourth consecutive year: $346,926,203 in sales, up 30 percent; and $20,361,138 in net earnings — up 30-plus percent, in spite of a change to LIFO (last in, first out) inventory accounting that took more than $2.2 million off the actual earnings. Commercial sales were up 18 percent, and defense/aerospace sales more than doubled at $55,626,090. Stockholders welcomed a one percent stock dividend and an increase in the annual cash dividend rate to $1.00 per share — a 25 percent raise.

A grand total of 110 achievement awards went to individuals and organizations making up the company's global sales and service network at the Beechcraft '77 International Sales Conference held October 4-6 at Wichita. Sharing honors with domestic outlets were representatives of 40 international distributors with branches and dealers operating in 127 nations.

For outstanding contributions to the fifth consecutive year of record-breaking international sales, awards were presented to Hawker de Havilland Australia Pty Ltd.; Field Aviation Company Ltd. of Canada; Transair France S.A.; Rene Morel A. of Guatemala; Indamer Company Pty. Ltd. of India; United Beech of Scandinavia A.B.; Avio Beechcraft of Spain; William C. Morales & Co. C.A., Venezuela; Beechcraft Sales S.A. Pty. Ltd., Republic of South Africa; and Wolfgang Denzel GmbH, West Germany.

The company's highest honor, its "Man of the Year" award, became the "Team of the Year" for 1976, recognizing Herb and Arlene Elliott, owners of Elliott Beechcraft, Inc. Celebrating their 40th year in general aviation and their 21st year in Beechcraft sales and service operations, the Elliotts provided distinguished representation for Beech Aircraft from locations covering Minnesota and Wisconsin and parts of Iowa and Illinois.

Top honors for volume sales went to Hangar One (69 Beechcrafts, $20 million); Stevens Beechcraft (57 Beechcrafts, $19.9 million); and Hartzog Aviation (38 Beechcrafts, $15.6 million). Enrolled in the "Millionaires' Club" with $1 million or more in sales were 12 sales managers and 55 individual salesmen. There were awards, too, for outstanding service and parts supply per-

445

formance. The company never forgot what kept customers coming back after their initial purchases.

A unique award was presented by Chairman O. A. Beech to Leonard Hay, the Wyoming rancher famous as "Mr. Bonanza". He was in Wichita to pick up his 25th Bonanza and fifth new Model A36, which would as usual do many chores on his widespread ranches in Wyoming's high country.

A dazzling display of the company's complete line of Beechcrafts featured many refinements for 1977, together with two wholly new models scheduled for future production. Fresh from their triumphs in capturing 54 percent of the general aviation market for American-built jetprops during the year were the Beechcraft King Air models. Headed by the superlative Beechcraft Super King Air 200, the line included the new King Air B100 with Garrett AiResearch fixed-shaft turbine power plants, and the Pratt & Whitney-powered King Air A100, high-performance King Air E90 and economical King Air C90 models. Advancements for 1977 on all models included a wider and superior range of avionics, new exterior and interior decor, and optional lateral-adjustable cabin chairs.

The pressurized Beechcraft Duke entered 1977 with a higher rated cruise speed of 246 knots (283 mph), standard Collins avionics, a 30 percent increase in TBO (time between overhaul) to 1,600 hours for its 380 hp Lycoming engines, wet wing options to extend range, and other new touches. So it became an even more efficient business machine for either an owner-pilot or a professional crew.

Heading the Beechcraft Baron line in 1977 was the pressurized Baron 58P, followed by the turbocharged Baron 58TC, the popular Baron 58, the high-performance Baron E55, and the long-favored, economical Baron B55. All models shared new, simplified fuel management, three-position preselectable flap settings, shoulder harness on all forward-facing seats, styling and decor and other refinements. New wet wing options on the Baron 58 models offered increased range, and six-place club seating was offered on all Beechcraft Barons.

Bidding to hold their place in 1977 as the world's most-wanted, single-engine aircraft, the three Beechcraft Bonanza models — the classic V-tail V35B, the best-selling A36 and the convention-

446

ally configured F33A — featured new-look exteriors and further refinements and options enhancing their customer appeal. Salesmen's reactions made it clear that another record year was ahead — a Bonanza year.

A new look and a new image distinguished each of the three Aero Center models for 1977 — the Beechcraft Sport 150, the Sundowner 180 and the retractable-gear Sierra 200. All featured improved aileron control, larger usable fuel supply, new ventilation systems with optional intake fan and optional autopilots. A larger propeller and new low-drag wheel fairings produced a 7 mph faster cruise speed for the Beechcraft Sierra 200. On all 1977 models, retractable shoulder harness became standard equipment on all forward-facing seats.

Presented as a firm addition to the Aero Center line was the all-new Beechcraft Model 77 T-tail single-engine, low-wing trainer. Under study as the PD-285, it had proved its worthiness and would go into production with first deliveries in the near future.

Also slated for future delivery was the all-new Beechcraft Model 76 Aero Center T-tail light twin with two 180 hp Lycoming engines and counter-rotating propellers. For the first time, orders were accepted for the new twin; and before the Sales Conference ended, more than 200 firm orders had gone on the books. Only the original Beechcraft Bonanza had gotten off to a stronger head start.

Domestic sales outlets were also quick to book 1977 lecture engagements in their areas for the company's two articulate and enthusiastic spokesmen. Marvin Small, Beechcraft's missionary for general aviation, would again deliver his sparkling illustrated talks to hundreds of appreciative audiences in many states. And Ron Cook would continue his programs of enlightenment about America's progress in the conquest of space. Both speakers had been widely well received and had created great goodwill for Beech Aircraft and its sales outlet sponsors.

The naming on October 12 of Charles W. Dieker as Beech Aircraft's secretary treasurer signaled the rise of a new generation of Beechcrafters to major responsibilities. Joining Beech in 1965 as a tax accountant, Dieker earned a series of promotions that led to his election in 1975 as assistant treasurer. In his new post, he succeeded John A. Elliott, senior vice president - treasurer, who after 34 years of service was named senior vice president - investments and a director-consultant as he prepared for eventual retirement. Dieker also succeeded Lucille Winters as secretary, anticipating her forthcoming retirement after 40 years of service. So the Beech tenets of promotion from within and continuity of management were jointly upheld.

Steps taken in October to expand production included leasing a 42,000 sq. ft. hangar located on the Salina, Kansas airport. The total space in use by the Salina Division thus grew to more than 557,000 square feet.

The month closed happily with the receipt from the Naval Air Systems Command of a $1,581,894 add-on contract for more Navy T-44A jetprop twin advanced trainers. Orders on hand for the Navy's version of the Beechcraft King Air 90 thereby increased to better than $10.2 million. And contract options calling for 53 more T-44A's, plus logistical support, held bright promise of additional orders ahead.

Another defense contract followed on November 1 – this time from the U. S. Army Missile Command. Valued at $2 million-plus, it called for Beech-Boulder to produce 100 advanced design rocket-powered AQM-37A missile targets by August, 1977. In its latest version as the Beech Model 1102, the air-launched Mach 2 target featured a solid state autopilot and other technological advancements.

Hedrick Beechcraft, Inc. was the name given a new subsidiary sales and service base purchased November 1 by the company from Maytag Aviation Corporation. Located at Peterson Field, the Colorado Springs principal airport, the Beech president's namesake operation would provide top-flight services to general aviation, and continue supplying fuel to military and airline planes, from its own site of more than 20 acres on the airport.

In a wholly personal vein, the company's chairman added to her long list of honors a unique award from her own community. At its annual meeting on November 10, the Wichita Area Chamber of Commerce presented to Mrs. O. A. Beech its 1976 Uncommon Citizen Award – a citation established "to recognize those individuals who have made 'uncommon' contributions to the community in many fields of endeavor". Engraved on a plaque adorned with a beautiful lalique glass eagle was this inscription:

THE UNCOMMON CITIZEN

OLIVE ANN BEECH

Presented for uncommon citizenship and services to her community, her state and her nation in the areas of aviation progress, cultural development, education, free enterprise and patriotism. She has helped to assure a world of opportunity for future generations.

WICHITA AREA CHAMBER OF COMMERCE

November 10, 1976

Coinciding with that award came a finding that according to a survey covering the 6,300 employees of the Wichita Division, 1.2 million hours of personal time had been given to community services in the past year by local Beechcrafters and their families. The average employee contributed some 86 hours yearly to various civic programs, and family members devoted 109 more hours to community projects. Church activities engrossed an additional 1.1 million hours for a grand total of 2.3 million hours of constructive works. At all levels, Beechcrafters were doing their part as responsible members of their community.

Among its services to education, the Beech Aircraft Foundation announced recipients of its annual scholarship awards. A total of 26 deserving students would attend colleges and universities of their choice, many in Wichita and Kansas, with the help of grants from Beech.

For their contributions to the general aviation industry, two Beech executives were honored by the General Aviation Manufacturers Association (GAMA). President Frank E. Hedrick received GAMA's Distinguished Service Award for his work in founding the organization, and serving as chairman of policy committees, vice chairman of the board in 1975 and GAMA chairman in 1976. Vice President - Corporate Director Leddy L. Greever received a special Recognition Award for "dedicated and devoted" service in GAMA's affairs.

Beech and its people had much to be grateful for as they

observed Thanksgiving 1976. The International Division in particular had fared well. During the year, markets had been reopened in Egypt and the Near East. India, long closed due to currency restrictions, returned as a good customer with $3.3 million in purchases that included five Beechcraft King Air C90's. Scandinavia came on strong with $6 million in sales since May. Business was looking up, at home and around the world.

Beechcrafters found amusement and good cheer in a December news item that a Model 18 Twin Beech was in use to transport captured brown pelicans to new homes in a breeding colony established near Galveston. There it was hoped that the big-billed birds, many injured by entanglements in monofilament fishlines, would recuperate and populate colonies of their own choosing along the Texas Gulf Coast.

The Bicentennial Year came to a glorious close with the receipt on December 27 of a U. S. Army follow-on contract for $16 million more C-12A transport aircraft. It also implied that the Army would exercise its three further options for annual purchases of more C-12A's to expand its worldwide staff and cargo mission capabilities.

The Army's newest contract brought the total value of Beechcraft Super King Air transports ordered by the U. S. armed services to more than $61 million. According to the Department of Defense, Beech Aircraft had moved into 76th place at mid-year among the nation's top 100 defense contractors. Prospects for bettering that distinction were never brighter.

Chapter 40

Productivity was the name of the game throughout Beech Aircraft at the dawn of its 45th year. Efficient production was needed to meet the projected sales goal of $400 million in fiscal 1977. Economies effected in manufacture would assist a corresponding rise in earnings. Improvements in methods, materials and products would give Beech customers more for their money.

Inviting the help of every employee, the company extended

the range of its novel Productivity Council to include all of its facilities. A refined version of the Beech Suggestion System first launched in 1940 to help speed World War II defense production, the new Productivity Council had brought forth a total of 9,896 ideas from employees since its trial activation at Wichita less than a year ago.

The record of suggestion systems in many companies and industries was spotty. All too many suggestions ranged from frivolous ("Go soak your head, boss!") to impractical and unacceptable. Not so at Beech. Out of the first year's entries, 69 percent were accepted, winning cash awards for their originators in proportion to their value.

Some amusing sidelights cropped up. A staff member of the Productivity Council, Don Mock, won a "First Baby of 1977" contest sponsored by the Eldorado, Kansas *Times*, when his wife presented him on January 4 with twin daughters. "That's productivity for you", his friends agreed. And when a Red Cross mobile blood collection unit came to the Wichita plant, 285 Beechcrafters lined up to donate blood at the exceptional rate of 7 gallons per hour. On the job and off, their productivity was high.

The Productivity Council was only one of many ways devised by management to speed production and enhance quality. Beech consistently adopted proven advancements in machinery, methods and equipment of all kinds to speed output and reduce waste of materials and labor.

For example, a new general-purpose computer was installed during the year-end holidays. The latest IBM 370 Model 158 increased computing power by 50 percent over the previous model, which had been outgrown in only four years.

Linked by telephone circuits with all facilities, the computer was performing ever-growing numbers of accounting, order processing, inventory and cost control and other tasks swiftly and accurately. It had become indispensable in the company's growth since 1962, when Beech pioneered in computer usage with one of the largest installations in general aviation. Smartly applied, labor-saving computer power prevented the bogging down of production in a morass of paperwork.

Results for the first quarter of fiscal 1977, announced on Jan-

451

uary 2, revealed record productivity and efficiency. Volume had topped $95.2 million and earnings were up 19 percent to better than $5.7 million, establishing a new all-time first quarter record.

Beech Aircraft's expenditures within its home state in fiscal 1976 also set a new record. The company had added $124 million to the Kansas economy that year in payrolls, taxes and purchases from some 500 Kansas firms. Applying the accepted multiplier factors, the true effect of Beech expenditures came to several times that total.

The U. S. Naval Air Systems Command continued the modernization of its advanced pilot training program with an $11.2 million follow-on contract for additional Beechcraft twin-engine turboprop T-44A trainers, plus testing and engineering data, issued in mid-January.

Beech flight lounge attendants noted that Carlos Mota, Jr. devised a new variation in souvenirs for the folks at home when he headed back from Wichita to his job with William C. Morales & Co., the Beechcraft distributor in Caracas. Mota had made a beeline for the nearest supermarket just before he boarded a new Beechcraft for its delivery flight to Venezuela. When the plane took off, its baggage compartment was crammed full with box after box of Pampers disposable diapers.

February 1977 was Bonanza Month at Beech Aircraft. Its prelude was the rollout from Wichita Plant II of the 1,000th Model A36 Beechcraft Bonanza. Introduced in 1968, the Model 36 had become general aviation's worldwide sales leader in its class, through its versatile performance as a spacious, sturdy deluxe "flying station wagon" for business and charter passenger and cargo transportation. In view of its global popularity, it seemed fitting that A36 No. E-1,000 was scheduled for flyaway over the Pacific Ocean to a businessman owner in Australia.

One week later came a major milestone in general aviation history — the completion at Beech Plant II of the 10,000th Model 35 V-tail Beechcraft Bonanza.

The rollout of V35B Bonanza No. D-10,000 on February 9, 1977 sparked a celebration that, far more than company-wide, spread throughout the nation and the world. In the 31-plus years since the first V-tail Bonanza made its maiden flight from Beech Field on December 22, 1945, the unique design and

452

capabilities of the Model 35 Beechcraft had brought fame and honor to its builders on a truly global scale. An enduring classic, it was everywhere acknowledged to be the world's foremost single-engine aircraft of its kind. On a scheduled nationwide demonstration tour, No. D-10,000 was to reaffirm the unique status of all Beechcraft Bonanzas, past, present and future.

Meanwhile, another illustrious Beech product was making history some 8,000 miles southeast of Wichita. At Umtata in South Africa, Transkei Airways Corporation held ceremonies marking its inauguration of the first international airline services between the newly independent Transkei nation and the South African world gateway Jan Smuts Airport at Johannesburg. After careful consideration of all available aircraft, a Beechcraft King Air A100 was the airline's choice to provide direct daily flights between Transkei's capitol city and the Republic of South Africa. The event was strikingly commemorated with the issuance of two postage stamps by the Transkei government, picturing the new Beechcraft King Air taking off and in flight.

The global range of the company's support for its versatile line of aerospace products was emphasized with the formation in February of a new subsidiary. Beech Aerospace Services, Inc. was founded to expand the logistics support provided for some years by a company department that had grown to number 180 employees. Projected by 1980 was a worldwide complement of 650 technicians factory-trained to service Beech aircraft and other company products everywhere in the field.

At the peak of the coldest Kansas winter in years, Beech-crafters working in Wichita Plant I gained relief with the help of an innovative heat recovery and air makeup unit that reclaimed heat exhausted from a large heat treat and brazing furnace. Tubing filled with Freon gas recovered up to 70 percent of otherwise wasted heat for use in warming work areas. In hot weather the unit would help carry away furnace heat. Its installation was a significant step in the company's continuous overall energy conservation program.

The sales appeal of the pressurized, turbocharged Beechcraft Baron 58P was verified by the rollout at Salina in March of the 100th Model 58P. Introduced late in 1975, the advanced design Baron had rapidly earned favor as a logical step upward

453

for many owners to supercharged, twin-engine high performance plus the comfort and operational advantages of cabin pressurization.

Milestone Beechcraft Bonanza No. D-10,000 completed a press tour in mid-March that presented the historic V-tail craft to the nation's aviation editors and writer-pilots. Throughout its tour, the enthusiasm shown by the working press people who flew, photographed and appraised the epochal Model 35 rivalled that of Beech Aircraft's own officers and employees. The favorable reports of knowledgeable and impartial observers added the final touch to the luster of the Beechcraft Bonanza.

Honors that came to the company and its chairman pleasantly rounded out the month. At the Wichita State University Golden Anniversary Awards Banquet on March 25, Beech Aircraft Corporation received the 1977 Gold Key Award of the College of Business Administration. Out of ten Wichita area business firms nominated for the Award, Beech was judged by the student body to have made the most outstanding contributions to the community and to the University.

Chairman O. A. Beech was honored at a March 16 Awards luncheon for "18 years of dedicated leadership and service to the Wesley Medical Center in Wichita" and elected as a Trustee Emeritus of that institution. Officers of Wesley presented a specially engraved plaque to Mrs. Beech as a permanent memento and token of appreciation.

The month closed happily with new record sales and earnings for both second quarter and six-month periods. Sales of $103,729,185 and earnings of $5,961,043 set an all-time quarterly record. Six-month results of $198,975,407 in sales and $11,662,616 in earnings brought the company's fiscal 1977 goals handily within reach.

To the shrill whistle of the bos'n's pipe and the stirring music of a band, the U. S. Navy's first Beechcraft T-44A was "piped aboard" at the Corpus Christi, Texas Naval Air Station on April 5. The twin turbojet advanced trainer was then formally presented to Rear Admiral Burton H. Shepherd, Chief of Naval Air Training, by Beech Vice President of Aerospace Programs E. C. Nikkel. "A significant event in the history of the Naval Air Station" was a description of the event by Texas Senator John

454

Beech Aircraft employees joined Chairman of the Board O. A. Beech, President Frank E. Hedrick and Group Vice President E. C. Burns for an informal ceremony as the 10,000th Beechcraft Bonanza Model 35 rolled off the final assembly line at the company's Wichita Plant II.

Special edition blue, silver and white Beechcraft Bonanza V35B, serial number D-10,000, made nationwide tour of Beechcraft Aviation Centers in summer of 1977.

President Frank E. Hedrick presents Chairman O. A. Beech the Company's first 45-year service pin.

454A

One of two tip-tanked Beechcraft Super King Airs of Institut Geographique National of Paris shows its special mission photographic equipment.

U. S. Navy adopted Beechcraft UC-12B for its utility transport.

Beechcraft T-34C trainers at Beech Field are bound for U. S. Navy service.

Tower with which Admiral Shepherd concurred. More T-44A's would follow in fast order to replace the Navy's aging piston-engine trainers.

Pilotless Beechcrafts established three "firsts" in service test operations early in April. Beech MQM-107A "Streaker" variable speed training targets completed their 100th powered flight for the U. S. Army at White Sands Missile Range, New Mexico. At the Point Mugu Test Center in California, U. S. Navy crews subjected MQM-107A's for the first time to live firing missions as targets for air-to-air missiles. And near the Arctic Circle, the first target launchings were made outside U. S. territory in a cold-weather oversea flight mission. Beechcrafts engineers and technicians conducted the White Sands launch and supported the others.

Given those proofs of performance, it was not surprising that the U. S. Army Missile Readiness Command issued a $9.9 million follow-on contract on April 18 for more Beech "Streaker" targets, plus accessories, water recovery equipment and furnishing of technical data. MQM-107A production at Wichita, and assembly and delivery from Boulder, would continue through January, 1979, in fulfillment of contracts that had come to more than $33 million.

Beechcrafters applauded the announcement by the Aviation Hall of Fame at Dayton, Ohio on April 28 that the name of Walter H. Beech would be added to its roster of the immortals of aviation. Enshrinement ceremonies would be conducted on July 23 at Dayton. Joining the 70 great figures already enrolled would be Lawrence Bell, James McDonnell, Will Rogers and Alan B. Shephard, in company with Mr. Beech.

In a contemporary vein, the company's most recent achievements won recognition with the issuance of the "Fortune 500", the annual ratings by *Fortune* Magazine of the nation's largest industrial corporations. Beech Aircraft placed 477th in sales with its fiscal 1976 volume of $346.9 million, but ranked 367th in net income. Beech standings in other categories showed superior performance: 130th in total return to investors over the ten-year span from 1966 to 1976; 162nd in net income as a percentage of sales; and an impressive 23rd in net income as a percentage of stockholders' equity.

Contributions of the Beech Aircraft Foundation to education, health, youth and service organizations and institutions during fiscal 1976 were disclosed as exceeding $184,000. In a spirit of responsible corporate citizenship, Foundation grants were largely centered in areas where company facilities were located.

A $3.1 million contract received May 5 from the U. S. Army renewed the company's worldwide field support of the Army's Super King Air C-12A transports through September, 1978. Operating from 20 bases abroad and in the United States, many units of the Army's jetprop Beechcraft fleet were being flown more than their programmed 50 hours per month, while maintaining outstanding readiness records with the support of Beech technicians.

A landmark event was the rollout on May 19 at the Beech Liberal plant of the 500th Beechcraft Sierra Model 200. Foremost of the Aero Center popular-priced single-engine Beechcrafts, the Sierra featured retractable landing gear, roomy 4-place seating and a controllable pitch propeller. In commemoration, Marketing announced a special production run of "Series 500" Sierras. Limited to 100 units, the Special Edition aircraft offered exclusive exterior and interior decorative options, setting them apart from others.

Three world records for speed and distance were chalked up for Beech Aircraft only two days later. In a coast to coast flight on May 21 from San Francisco to Poughkeepsie, N. Y., a Beechcraft King Air C90 set two records for Speed Over a Recognized Course (San Francisco to a refueling stop at Cincinnati; and San Francisco to Poughkeepsie), and a third record for Distance In a Straight Line (2,033.91 statute miles from San Francisco to Cincinnati.) F. T. Elliott Jr. of Visalia, Calif., the plane's owner, and Thomas W. Clements of Beechcraft West at San Jose, were the crew. The records were officially certificated by the Federation Aeronautique Internationale in Paris for turboprop aircraft in the 3,000-6,000 Kg. weight class.

The happy events gave an extra fillip to the celebration of the company's 45th anniversary on Sunday, May 22. Open House festivities at all Beech facilities drew crowds of more than 13,500 Beechcrafters, families, guests and VIP's. Kansas Governor Robert Bennett was a special guest at Wichita — the city where it all began in April, 1932.

There was another noteworthy beginning at Beech Field on Tuesday, May 24. It was the first flight of the first production Model 76 light twin, and it came off like a charm. "Flawless performance" was the word from veteran test pilot Vaughn Gregg.

Juries are more easily impressed than judges, as any good trial lawyer can tell you. A jury trial of a product liability case that alleged fuel starvation as the cause of a Beechcraft Baron accident in 1970 had brought a $14.1 million verdict in favor of the plaintiffs. Reviewing the case, a United States District Court judge in Houston determined the facts did not show that the airplane was at fault. The judge duly overturned the jury verdict and entered judgment in favor of the defendant Beech Aircraft Corporation.

The power of Beechcrafts to help speed up the growth of business was dramatically demonstrated by a Freeport, Texas owner. Albert P. Beutel II was the co-founder and chief executive of Intermedics, Inc., a heart pacemaker manufacturer. As his four-year-old firm started to hit its stride, Beutel had moved up from a Beechcraft Bonanza A36 to a pressurized Baron 58P, then a Duke B60 and most recently to a Beechcraft Super King Air.

Concurrently, the firm's sales increased from $10 million in 1976 to a projected $36 million in 1977, making it the world's second largest in its field.

The growth of his sales force to some 85 representatives nationwide kept Beutel's Beechcrafts constantly on the go, expediting contacts and ferrying doctors to Intermedic's plant to view the manufacturing processes. His Beechcraft Super King Air had logged 300 flight hours in its first month of service. Convinced of its worth as an invaluable sales tool, Beutel was wondering when the purchase of another Beechcraft Super King Air might become necessary.

In a joint program to reduce training time and costs, Beech Aircraft and the U. S. Navy arranged on June 2 for the production of a ground-based operational T-44A flight trainer. A $5.4 million Navy contract named Beech as the prime contractor for the simulator, which would realistically replicate every aspect of the twin turboprop T-44A environment and performance for student pilots at the Navy's Corpus Christi training center. Construction to Beech specifications was subcontracted to Hydrosystems, Inc. of Farmingdale, N. Y.

The deep-throated roar of radial engines heralded the homecoming to Beech Field June 8-10 of a host of classic Model 17 Beechcraft biplanes proudly owned and flown by members of the privately founded Staggerwing Club. Held in Wichita every fifth year, the 1977 meet brought together 42 handsomely maintained Staggerwings, along with three Travel Air biplanes built prior to 1931 when Walter H. Beech headed that company.

Registered as guests of Beech Aircraft for the fly-in were 197 aviation enthusiasts from far and near. Dr. Leland Jones, who piloted his Staggerwing from Anchorage, Alaska, garnered the flew-in-from-farthest-away award.

Highlight of a company-sponsored banquet on June 9 was the presentation to Staggerwing Club members of a model of the Olive Ann Beech Staggerwing. Long-time Beechcrafter Letha Brunk, president of the Beech Employees Staggerwing Restoration Society, made the presentation as a token of the Society's ongoing rebuilding of its Model E17B biplane. In honor of Mrs. Beech, its ultimate home would be the Staggerwing Museum at Tullahoma, Tennessee, near the boyhood home of Mr. Beech.

The Staggerwing meet was an impressive demonstration of the seemingly unlimited service life of properly maintained Beech airplanes. Not one of the 42 Beechcrafts flown to Wichita had been built any later than 1948, and some had left the factory more than four decades ago. All could still provide safe, fast comfortable transportation comparing favorably with that of many new aircraft fresh from the production line. Apart from their value as collectors' items, the classic Staggerwing Beechcrafts were still viable and useful airplanes for their owners.

The days of glory of the Model 17 Beech Staggerwing also loomed in the background of the company's semiannual Service Anniversaries Celebration in June. Of the 55 Beechcrafters honored for completing 25 to 45 years of service, 30 had been active when the classic Staggerwing was still in production.

Four employees had completed their 40th year; G. E. Allen,

The 40,000th Beechcraft, a Baron 58TC, was delivered to Ted F. Brown (left) of Brown Construction, Albuquerque, N. M. With him is Kenn Holzer, vice president and general manager of Cutter Flying Service, Inc., of Albuquerque.

U. S. Navy accepted delivery of first Beechcraft T-44A in ceremonies at Corpus Christi, Texas.

Beechcrafters at Plant II in Wichita roll out the 1,000th Beechcraft Bonanza A36.

The 1,500th Beechcraft King Air, a Model C90, was delivered to R. E. "Bob" Sheriff (left) of TRW, Inc. With him is Rod Rodriguez of Beechcraft West, Van Nuys, Calif.

458A

Classic Model 17 Beechcraft Staggerwing biplanes were displayed on Beech Field by the Staggerwing Club.

Mrs. O. A. Beech stands beside a reproduction of the Walter H. Beech portrait which now hangs in the Aviation Hall of Fame. Milton Caniff was the artist.

Walter H. Beech

Walter H. Beech's enshrinement in the Aviation Hall of Fame was commemorated in a medal presented to Mrs. Beech. Both sides of the medal are pictured.

458B

W. E. Rutledge, F. W. Cantrell and W. A. Utt. 23 had served for 35 years, two for 30 years, and 64 for a quarter century.

The greatest round of applause was reserved for a uniquely special honoree. The company's co-founder and Chairman, Mrs. O. A. Beech, proudly received a one-of-its-kind 45-year Service pin from President Frank E. Hedrick.

Successful teamwork of veteran and newer Beechcrafters produced another round of record sales and earnings for the fiscal nine-month and three-month periods ending June 30th. Sales soared to $307,554,095 and earnings to $18,205,082 for nine months; and to $108,578,688 and $6,542,466 respectively, for the third quarter of fiscal 1977. In keeping with contract provisions, wage increases and Retirement Plan improvements were announced for hourly-paid Beechcrafters, plus increases in other benefit programs for all employees, effective August 1.

Notable performance also emerged in the results of the All Women's Transcontinental Air Race staged July 1-4. Four Beechcraft Bonanzas and a Beechcraft Baron 58 won five of the top six places, with Fran Berra of Beechcraft West, seven times a winner in previous "Powder Puff Derbies", placing second. On its 30th and final staging, the race spanned 2,190 miles, from Palm Springs, California to Tampa, Florida. Entrants came from 36 states, including Alaska, and three foreign countries.

Elected to the Beech Aircraft board of directors on July 21 was L. Patton Kline, president and chief executive officer of Marsh & McClennan, Inc., New York City. His extensive business and management experience as the head of the nation's foremost insurance brokerage firm was to prove highly beneficial in the company's continuing progress.

Anticipating the retirement on August 1 of John A. Elliott, senior vice President - investments, Dan C. Cullinane was elected to an officership as assistant treasurer in addition to his duties as chief accountant. Seven more long-service Beechcrafters were also appointed as officers of Beech subsidiary companies.

Two U. S. Army missile contracts meanwhile enlarged the company's volume of activities for defense. An order for $3.9 million worth of Beechcraft supersonic missile targets was followed by a $3.4 million award for Beech support of target firings in the field. The second award covered air training defense flights of Beechcraft's MQM-107A variable speed "Streaker" targets in the Middle East through September, 1978.

Walter H. Beech, co-founder of the Beech Aircraft Corporation, was enshrined into the Aviation Hall of Fame during ceremonies held July 23 at Dayton, Ohio. Accepting the gold medal emblematic of her late husband's enrollment in the select company of the immortals of flight was the company's Chairman and co-founder, Mrs. O. A. Beech.

The citation that accompanied Mr. Beech's election by a 125-member nominating board detailed "His outstanding contributions as a pilot, instructor, practical aeronautical engineer; and for co-founding Travel Air Manufacturing Company and later Beech Aircraft Corporation which designed, manufactured and sold high-quality, top-performing aircraft for private, commercial and military use that were generally unexcelled in their class; and for his career-long advocacy and activities touching almost every facet of privately-owned and business aircraft use."

Formally presenting Mr. Beech to the organization during the ceremonies was his long-time friend, Lieut. General James H. "Jimmy" Doolittle, USAF (ret). He opened his presentation speech by saying:

"I come to present the first pioneer tonight with great personal pleasure for I have known him for over half a century. I flew and raced his airplanes and remained a close friend for the rest of his life.

"His story is, indeed, the story of the American way of life: success in a chosen field by a dedicated individual who prepares himself well for it and continues to give that extra effort to assure the excellence of his achievements and who, in the end, gives far more to the world than he takes from it."

Recounting the career of his late associate and reviewing his accomplishments with Travel Air and the Beech Aircraft Corporation, General Doolittle said in summation:

"Certainly Walter Herschel Beech has left a valued legacy to aviation. Through personal determination and creativity, plus the will and spirit of a true pioneer, he set the path for his adventures in the skies. In doing so, he created new kinds of aircraft that opened frontiers and brought the benefits of his

460

efforts to all mankind, earning him a cherished niche in the Aviation Hall of Fame."

In affirmation of that honor, a modern version of Walter Beech's pioneering Beechcraft Bonanza made history in a record-setting flight only five days later. Celebrating the Golden Anniversary year of Charles Lindbergh's 1927 New York to Paris flight, German pilot-engineer Dieter Schmitt retraced Lindy's great circle course past Newfoundland and over Ireland to Europe in a new Beechcraft Bonanza F33A.

In striking contrast to Lindbergh's harsh flight of 3,610 miles in 36½ hours, Schmitt completed 4,300 solo non-stop miles from New York to Munich (overflying Paris) in ease and comfort. Cruising at 9,000 feet at 45 percent power, he delivered his Bonanza to Denzel GmbH, Beech Aircraft distributors in Bavaria, in only 25 hours and 37 minutes.

Another Golden Anniversary was also being celebrated halfway around the globe. Hawker de Havilland Pty. Ltd. marked its 50th year in business with special promotions by its General Aviation division, centered on the Beechcrafts which it had distributed for two decades. As a result, HdH substantially enlarged the total of 415 Beechcrafts which it had sold up to that time in the lands "down under."

Meanwhile, the U. S. Navy happily advanced its schedule for training advanced multiengine pilots by one full month. The outstanding performance of its Beechcraft King Air T-44A pressurized turboprop twins at the Corpus Christi Naval Air Station, which had scored an operational readiness rate of 97 percent since April, had produced 60 percent more instructor training missions than originally programmed. So the Navy's schooling for defense moved ahead faster in an important sector.

Echoing the delivery of the 10,000th Model 35 Beechcraft Bonanza in March, Chairman O. A. Beech received an honorary full membership in the American Bonanza Society on September 8th. A unique "fan club" privately founded in 1967, ABS members comprised 70 percent of the total active Bonanza fleet.

The certificate presented to Mrs. Beech identified her, fittingly enough, as American Bonanza Society member No. 10,000. ABS president William Guenther explained that "We feel the 10,000th

Bonanza carries great significance in aviation and is certainly a milestone deserving the highest commemoration."

Another milestone event was the delivery on September 27 of the 1,500th commercial Beechcraft King Air. A Model C90, its purchaser was TRW Inc. of Cleveland, Ohio, a multi-national company with 1976 net sales approaching $3 billion. Little more than 13 years had elapsed since the delivery on September 9, 1964 of the first Model 90 Beechcraft King Air.

The tale of "the great bear chase" amused Beechcrafters at the Boulder Division, where wild life abounds in the nearby Rocky Mountain foothills. It seems Felix Fischer of Dept. 693 was driving to work through Lefthand Canyon, when he met a black bear that would weigh, he guessed, close to 600 pounds. The bear took off in pursuit of Fischer's car, galloping along not the least bit clumsily at a good 25 miles per hour. Luckily for its driver, the car was faster. "Sure glad I wasn't riding my bike to work that day", was Fischer's comment.

The close of the Beech fiscal year on September 30 marked five consecutive years of record sales and earnings. New highs were reached in 1977 of $417,419,646 in sales and $25,482,501 in earnings. Stockholders were rewarded with a 10 percent cash dividend increase to $1.10 per share, plus a two percent stock dividend. And for 1978, sales were projected to top the $.5 billion mark for the first time.

Two executives who had contributed significantly to the year's results were elected to corporate officerships. George D. Rodgers moved up from general manager - commercial marketing to vice president - commercial marketing. Stewart M. Ayton advanced to corporate vice president and continued as executive vice president and general manager of Beech Holdings, Inc., the company's subsidiary which conducted all Beech-owned marketing operations.

Beechcrafters and their company set another new record in October, with contributions at Wichita of $305,111 to the United Way of Wichita and Sedgwick County, and to the Beech Employees Assistance Fund. The cash gifts reached an all-time high in support of the 34 agencies aided through the United Way.

Summer-like weather greeted the 630 Beech salespeople from 25 countries who came to Wichita October 17-19 to view "The

Best Sellers of 1978" at the annual International Sales Conference. Commemorating the record year of 1977, a total of 134 awards for distinguished performance highlighted the convocation.

Named Beechcraft's "Man of the Year" for 1977 was Roland Fraissinet, president of Compagnie Fraissinet which operated Transair France S.A. in Paris and Transair Switzerland in Geneva. Transair distributorships traced their association with Beech as far back as 1946.

Honored for domestic leadership in sales volume dollarwise was Hangar One, Inc., headed by Frank W. "Bill" Hulse; and for top international sales, William C. Morales & Co. C.A. of Venezuela. A Beech distributor for 23 years, its president, William C. Morales, who was the Beech "Man of the Year" in 1973, died soon afterward, leaving his sons to carry on the business.

Awards were presented to 108 domestic and 20 international sales and service people for distinguished achievements in 1977. A special gift was presented to Mrs. Mike Murphy in recognition of her husband, manager emeritus of Marathon Oil Company's aviation division and lifelong Beech friend and booster.

Applying reverse thrust to the flow of awards, the field sales organization presented gifts to Chairman O. A. Beech, President Frank E. Hedrick and Group Vice President Roy H. McGregor "for their support and positive sales management" over the past five years.

The tangible foundation for another record sales year was the company's display of its "Best Sellers of 1978" line of Beechcrafts. On view in their new 1978 colors were 22 gleaming airplanes, from the two-place, T-tail Model 77 trainer to the latest Beechcraft Super King Air, providing inspiration to the sales force. And sales records were broken throughout the model line during the year.

The best-selling Beechcraft Super King Air continued to head the line, and dominate its markets, with its unique capabilities and distinctive, towering T-tail. Also displaying their eminence were the Beechcraft King Air A100, featuring Pratt & Whitney PT6A-28, 680 shaft horsepower turbine engines; and the Beechcraft King Air B100, equipped with AiResearch TPE-331-6-252B, 715 shaft horsepower power plants.

Their companions on display were refined 1978 versions of the perennial favorite Beechcraft King Air 90 series. The high-performance Model E90 combined a maximum cruise speed of 287 mph with deluxe accommodations for four to six or more passengers. The efficient, economical Model C90 afforded equal comfort, together with complete factory-installed equipment for corporate aviation operations.

Contributing to the record-breaking sales year was the Beechcraft Duke B60, the preferred business airplane in the piston-engine, owner-flown category. Many refinements for 1978 were coupled with the announcement of a special "10th Anniversary Edition", honoring the tenth year of production of the popular Duke.

Led by the high-performance Beechcraft Baron 58P and 58TC versions, the five Baron models on display also included the 58, the E55 and the economical basic B55 twin. Together, Beechcraft Barons had accounted for more than $55 million of 1977's commercial sales.

The ten thousandth Model 35 Beechcraft Bonanza, home at last from its nationwide eight-month promotional tour, was the centerpiece for the showing of the three Bonanza models: the classic V35B, the best-selling A36, and the F33A. The top-of-the-line single-engine Beechcrafts, moving into their fourth consecutive record sales year, offered new comfort and equipment options to further increase their sales appeal. Piedmont Aviation was the winner of a drawing held to determine the next owner of the historic Model 35 Beechcraft Bonanza No. E-10,000.

Heading the Aero Center presentation was the freshly christened Beechcraft Duchess, the new Model 76 light twin. Among hundreds of Beech franchise employees who entered a contest to name the aircraft, 25 submitted "Duchess" as their suggestion; and each one was awarded the $250 top prize.

With its distinctive T-tail and counter-rotating propellers that eased pilot transition into twin-engine flying, the Duchess peaked the Aero Center concept of a full line of light aircraft bringing Beechcraft excellence into the lower-cost sector of the general aviation market. Joining it on display were refined 1978 versions of the single-engine Aero Center Beechcrafts: the retractable-

464

gear Sierra 200, the four-place Sundowner 180, the Sport 150, and the all-new Model 77 two-place trainer.

A totally new aircraft combining the best fruits of NASA research and Beechcraft's long experience, the Model 77 incorporated the T-tail first used so successfully on the Beechcraft Super King Air, and a new GAW-1 wing section originated by NASA following their high speed, super-critical airfoil studies. Its spacious two-place cabin afforded full 360-degree visibility — an invaluable feature in a training aircraft — and right and left-hand doors for convenient access. Its four-cylinder Lycoming O-235 engine was rated at 115 horsepower. Auguring well for its future was the receipt of several hundred firm orders for the new Model 77 trainer. So, from one end of the product line to the other, Beechcraft's "Best Sellers of 1978" were already living up to their name.

International recognition of Beech Aircraft was enhanced in October with the receipt of an Honorary Group Diploma from one of aviation's most prestigious institutions. It came from the Federation Aeronautique Internationale world headquarters in Paris, which since 1905 had served as the global governing body for aviation record attempts and competition sanctions. The Diploma stated that the Award was made "In Recognition of Beech Aircraft's contribution to the advancement of general aviation through the development and production of over 38,000 highly efficient aircraft over a period of 45 years. The various models of Beech Aircraft are well known throughout the world for their structural integrity and safety and efficiency of operation."

On the corporate front, discussions of a possible merger with General Dynamics Corporation were discontinued in November. Management's search would continue for a suitable affiliation that would preserve the company's autonomy and protect the interests of stockholders in any contingency.

The first Atlantic crossing of a Beechcraft Turbine T-34C-1 trainer on November 16, en route to a demonstration tour of Europe, was followed next day by the delivery to the U. S. Navy at Pensacola, Florida of the Navy's first T-34C Beechcraft trainers. Welcomed there with fitting ceremonies, the Navy trainers went into immediate service as instructor familiariza-

465

tion units. Student pilot training with T-34C's would follow early next year. Like its predecessor, the Beechcraft Turbine Mentor would be a safe, honest airplane in even the most severe training maneuvers.

As a sequel to the U. S. Navy deliveries, a group of pilots from Ecuador staged a flyaway from Beech Field of six of 14 Beechcraft T-34C-1 trainers ordered by that nation. Ecuador was one of five foreign nations that had placed orders for a total of 69 T-34C-1s and Turbine Mentor 34Cs. The jetprop trainer was on its way, with more than $83 million in U. S. and foreign orders on the books.

Beech President Frank E. Hedrick and Group Vice President E. C. Burns continued to fulfill industry and community duties, in addition to their corporate responsibilities. Hedrick was re-elected to the Finance and Executive Committees of the General Aviation Manufacturers Association, and pledged to serve again in 1978 on GAMA's board of directors. Burns was elected second vice president of the Wichita Area Chamber of Commerce for 1978, and began his second year on the Chamber's board of directors.

Marvin Small, Beechcraft's widely popular traveling spokesman, made ready for his fourth year of crusading from coast to coast, spreading the good word on "How General Aviation Benefits the Nation." In talks to more than 400 non-aviation organizations, Marvin had logged some 20,000 miles in a Beechcraft Sierra, plus thousands more via commercial airlines. A gifted and dynamic speaker, Southern style (he hails from Alabama), Small had built up heaps of understanding and goodwill for general aviation and Beech Aircraft. And, he promised, "That's only the beginning."

Boulder Division Beechcrafters were hosts in December to Space Shuttle Orbiter astronauts Col. Joe Engle and Comdr. Dick Truly. Their guests thrilled the Colorado workers with firsthand recitals of what it was like to pilot the 75-ton space ship "Enterprise" in free-fall flight, and showed film clips of its landing tests. In return, Boulder staff members showed the astronauts the manufacturing processes and hardware involved in developing and building the Space Shuttle's power reactant storage assembly, fuel cell servicing system and freon coolant servicing unit. Keenly anticipated was the eventual flight into outer space of NASA's Space Shuttle with vital systems designed and built by Beech-Boulder.

Two notable production milestones were passed almost simultaneously in mid-December. One was the rollout of the 2,000th Bell JetRanger helicopter airframe manufactured by Beech Aircraft. It marked the 15th consecutive year of producing assemblies for Bell commercial and military helicopters — production that represented a total business dollar volume of more than $170 million for the Wichita and Salina communities.

The 40,000th Beechcraft built by the company since its founding in April, 1932 was delivered on December 14. It was a turbocharged Beechcraft Baron 58TC. And it joined a Beechcraft Travel Air twin that had been in service with its purchaser, Brown Construction of Albuquerque, New Mexico, for 20 years and 3,100 business flying hours.

Both historic events went unmarked by elaborate ceremonies. Beechcrafters were too busy fulfilling their present commitments to look more than briefly to the past. True, their 40,000th airplane rounded out a total of more than $4.6 billion worth of Beech products delivered over a span of some 45 years. Far more important, however, were the deliveries and sales to be made in the days and years ahead.

Defense contracts received in December substantially enlarged the sum of work to be done. From the U. S. Navy came a $1.7 million contractor logistics support award covering its Beechcraft T-44A turboprop twin trainers for fiscal 1978. This brought to a total of $12.8 million the awards to Beech for contractor support during only one month's time.

Ending the year on a happy note, the Navy joined the Army and the Air Force in adding the Beechcraft C-12 to its array of utility aircraft. A $34.2 million contract received on December 28 called for 20 additional U. S. Army C-12 aircraft and 22 C-12 utility transports for the U. S. Navy and the U. S. Marine Corps. Modified versions of the Beechcraft Super King Air, the Navy and Marine Corps C-12's were to operate from 31 sites throughout the world. More work was ahead for Beechcrafters, and more world fame for their products.

Blessings by a Catholic priest were a part of activities at Beech Field as the new year of 1978 unfolded.

The occasion was a formal ceremony honoring the delivery to the Peruvian Navy of a fleet of six Beechcraft T-34C-1 turboprop trainers. It was a Peruvian tradition that every vessel and airplane entering the Navy of Peru do so with the invocation of God's protection for the craft and its occupants.

Accordingly, Father Ken Melaragno, associate pastor of Saint Margaret Mary Catholic Church in Wichita, invoked a blessing on each of Peru's six trainers as part of the acceptance proceedings. Peruvian Navy pilots carried through the flyaway of the Beechcrafts to Peru without incident.

In a more secular vein, Beechcrafters welcomed the news that sound planning and hard work had produced the best quarter in company history. Sales for the first quarter of fiscal 1978 that ended on December 31, 1977 reached $122,291,285. Earnings for the quarter came to $8,388,556. "Try to beat that!" was the challenge they answered with vigor.

The challenge was spiced with fresh multi-million dollar contract awards in January. The U. S. Navy called for $11.8 million worth of additional T-44A turbo-twin advanced trainers, making a total of 61 aircraft to be produced through October, 1979. Bell Helicopter Textron extended its purchases of Beech-built airframe assemblies for its JetRanger III commercial helicopters through December, 1979 with an $11.1 million subcontract. It would enlarge the total number of JetRanger airframes built by Beech at Wichita and Salina since 1967 to more than 2,400.

Beech Aircraft's progress also increasingly enhanced the economy of Kansas. During the company's 1977 fiscal year, it spent a new record total of $136,000,000 within its home state, in the form of payrolls, taxes and purchases from Kansas firms. This represented an increase of 8 percent over the previous year's record total.

The sequence of broken records was not confined to the economic sector. It held good also for product performance. Flying a Beechcraft Bonanza S35, two Colorado pilots decisively shattered the around-the-world speed record for single-engine piston aircraft. Jack Rodd and Harold Benham made the globe-circling flight in 10 days, 23 hours and 33 minutes, bettering the previous record set in 1975 by one day, three hours and 56 minutes.

In their Bonanza, named "The City of Cortez" for their home town of Cortez, Colorado, the two pilots landed in Bangor, Maine; the Azores; Portugal; Munich, Bavaria; Tehran, Iran; New Delhi, India; Colombo, Sri Lanka; Kota Kinabalu, Malaysia; Saipan; Wake Island; Honolulu; and San Jose, California before returning to Cortez and a heroes' welcome from their neighbors.

Notable even though unofficial was the record established by a Beechcraft Super King Air in commuter service with Norfolk Island Airline in Australia. Purchased two years ago, their Beechcraft had flown more than a million miles. NIA's manager of flying operations, H. A. "Tony" Snell, who personally logged 2,000 of the plane's 3,500 flight hours, said the airline had never cancelled a scheduled flight because of aircraft problems. Taking delivery at Wichita of a second Beechcraft Super King Air for NIA, Snell pointed out that both planes would fly what is probably the world's longest commuter route — 910 statute miles over open seas from Brisbane, Australia due east to tiny Norfolk Island.

Not far behind in route length was Advance Airline, another "down under" commuter operation, with an 850-mile over-ocean run from Sydney, Australia to Lord Howe Island, and services also to Temora and Condobolin in New South Wales. Advance budgeted its new Beechcraft Super King Air, equipped like NIA's twins to seat 12 passengers, to fly 2,400 hours per year as a replacement for two older heavy twins. Sales and full support to both airlines originated with Hawker Pacific Pty. Ltd., formerly known as Hawker de Havilland of Australia.

Five months later, Norfolk Island Airline reported a total of 4,500 flight hours for their 30-month-old Beechcraft, and 800 hours for their newer one. Both planes were operating 35 hours a week in maintaining schedules on their long commuter runs.

Beechcraft's own sales and service centers moved into the new

469

year with banners flying. Denver Beechcraft and Beechcraft West at Fresno, California celebrated the completion of massive expansions with open house galas that attracted many VIP guests, customers and prospects. Denver's new 40,000 sq. ft. hangar at Stapleton International Airport enlarged its total floor space to 98,000 sq. ft. for outstanding services to Rocky Mountain area aviators. Fresno opened a new 23,000 sq. ft. hangar, customer lounge and expanded service facility.

Soon afterward, Beechcraft West at Van Nuys doubled the size of its Beech Aero Club facility for better service to its 200 members. Organized in 1974 as the first of all Aero Clubs, the Van Nuys group operated 15 Beechcrafts, including a new Beechcraft Duchess 76 light twin.

Beech Aero Center products also provided good news. FAA certification of the Beechcraft Model 76 Duchess twin came on January 24 as a matter of routine. More impressive was the delivery in February of the 2,000th Beechcraft Sundowner 180. Marking that special event, the company introduced a Special Edition Sundowner series, offering a unique paint scheme and special interiors.

Best news of all was the reaction to the Beechcraft Duchess 76 on its presentation to the aviation press and the public. Designed to fill a dual role as an economical aircraft for both business and twin-engine training, the Duchess won high praise in all its aspects. Peter Lert of *Air Progress* wrote that "the handling . . . rivals that of the Travel Air", referring to the classic Model 95 light twin, first flown in mid-1956, that later evolved into the best-selling Beechcraft Baron series.

The judgment of *Aviation News* was that "While the Duchess is the smallest Beech twin, it gives away nothing in luxury or performance to its bigger brothers. It is, in many ways, more like a smaller Beech Duke than like a bottom-of-the-line economy model . . . Considering the Duke's awesome reputation as a luxury, high performance twin, that is indeed a compliment."

Features that earned praiseful notice for the Duchess included its right- and left-hand cabin doors and large luggage compartment door; easy priming and starting; wide visibility forward and sideward; the comfortable chair-high, adjustable seating; and the well-planned panel and control layout and simple fuel management system. Noted too was its easy handling in both normal and one-engine-out operation, a result of the symmetrical thrust of its counter-rotating propellers and its aerodynamically superior T-tail. One writer cited the Duchess as "the pleasantest twin of all to fly." *Aviation News* summed up the consensus succinctly: "Beech has a winner in the Model 76."

More defense contracts further brightened the frigid Winter months. The U. S. Air Force continued to rely on Beech for worldwide support of its then thirty C-12 turboprop twin transports, issuing a $3.6 million carry-on contract.

The U. S. Navy ordered more T-34C jetprop trainers in March, with a $11.1 million contract that extended production through December. Its record in student pilot training that had begun in January was proving the single-engine jetprop Beechcraft to be just what the Navy wanted.

Missile target production at Boulder and Wichita also got a boost. A $4.8 million contract issued in March by the U. S. Army extended production of Beechcraft Model 1102 (AQM-37A) supersonic, rocket-powered missile targets through December, 1979. They were earmarked for use by the U. S. Navy in fleet training exercises and weapon systems evaluations.

Salina Division Manager Roy Allen and his wife, Marjorie, enjoyed an experience that was to provide them with a conversation "stopper" for years to come. The Allens were seated at the head table at the annual banquet of the Salina Area Chamber of Commerce, in honor of Roy's retirement from the presidency of the Chamber. They had a pleasant chat with the guest speaker who was sitting next to Marjorie — the former Governor of California, Ronald Reagan.

A highlight of early 1978 was the resolution of several lawsuits in the company's favor. Described as "a landmark case" in the area of product liability was a unanimous jury verdict in favor of Beech in the Superior Court of Alameda County California on January 31. The plaintiff had sued for $5 million in damages following a 1973 accident that involved a 23-year-old Beechcraft. A later lawsuit seeking $2.1 million in damages, following a 1972 accident, also brought a verdict favoring Beech from a jury in the Superior Court of California, San Francisco County.

In the procurement area, efforts to prevent Beech Aircraft from fulfilling its Defense Department contracts for C-12 turbo-prope twins were decisively defeated.

Those efforts went as far back as the initial contract awards in 1974. Then, a defeated competitor had filed a complaint with the General Accounting Office, alleging "improper procurement procedures." After a searching investigation, the U. S. Treasury's "watchdog agency" concluded that proper procedures had been followed, and ruled in favor of Beech Aircraft.

The Navy's December 27, 1977 contract for 22 type C-12 Beechcraft utility transports prompted a lawsuit filed by Senators Barry Goldwater of Arizona and Howard Metzenbaum of Ohio on February 3, seeking cancellation on the grounds that the contract had not been competed. Their suit was dismissed by Judge Louis Oberdorfer of the U. S. District Court in Washington, D.C., who found reasonable grounds existed for the contract award. His verdict was handed down on March 23.

The same competitor who had filed the 1974 complaint with the GAO immediately sued for a temporary restraining order to halt Navy C-12 production. Their request was denied by Judge Oberdorfer, and further litigation was eventually dismissed. Production of the Navy's C-12's, halted by a Navy "stop work" order on February 3, resumed "full speed ahead" when that order was lifted on March 24.

Hailing the Government and Court actions, Beech group vice president Roy H. McGregor said the ultimate decision was "right and proper and affirms my faith in the American judicial system, Congressional process and the business judgment of the Defense Department . . . Our only objective was to provide the best aircraft at the least cost to the taxpayers. It's encouraging to see that the Court agreed."

In spite of setbacks from interrupted C-12 production, compounded by the coldest Kansas winter since 1940, sales and earnings for the first half of fiscal 1978 echoed a now familiar refrain. As of March 31, sales of $252,347,965 and earnings of $16,972,286 had set new all-time high records. Stockholders were rewarded with an increase in the annual dividend rate to $1.20 per share, and a three-for-two stock split was approved.

Activated in May was an innovative charter service designed

to appeal to the many American businesses not yet using general aviation aircraft for transportation. Entitled the "Beechcraft Executive Flight Plan", it was aimed to encourage new customers to contract for guaranteed charter service on an annual basis. Starting with 20 Beechcraft Aviation Centers, it was projected to eventually provide nationwide charter service of superior quality. Aircraft used under the Plan would be primarily Beechcraft Baron pressurized 58P and turbocharged 58TC models. Widely promoted to selected prospects, it was another forward step in promoting both general aviation and Beechcraft commercial sales.

Control of Beech-owned and leased facilities totaling thousands of acres worldwide was centralized with the establishment of a new Real Estate Department. Austin "Russ" Rising, a Beechcrafter since 1962 and a company vice president since 1968, was named as its manager.

A second follow-on contract for Navy T-34C turboprop trainers came in May. A $4.6 million award, it extended T-34C production through April, 1979 and brought Navy contracts to a total of $64.8 million.

First deliveries of Duchess 76 twins in May cheered Beechcrafters at the Liberal Division, production source for all Aero Center models. They gathered for a group photo with three twins that were ready to go, then hurried back to work on the hundreds of Duchess orders on hand.

A valued old customer was welcomed home, with the delivery of a new Beechcraft Super King Air to the Republic of China. The Chinese had bought two fleets of ambulance-equipped Beechcraft Staggerwing D17R biplanes in 1938 and 1939, plus a fleet of Beechcraft Model 18R twins modified as light tactical and training bombers. That design evolved into the U. S. Air Corps AT-11 Beechcraft twin trainer, in which 90 percent of World War II USAC bombardiers learned their skills.

The last Chinese orders had come in 1949, when a fleet of 20 Beechcraft Model 18 twin-engine military trainers was delivered to the Republic of China on Formosa (now Taiwan). After nearly thirty years, their welcome back to Beechcraft in May, 1978 was warmly appreciative and sincere.

China's new Beechcraft Super King Air incorporated highly

473

sophisticated systems equipping it for use as a flight inspection aircraft. Its major task would be to check the extensive ground-based navigation systems on Taiwan.

High-time utilization was the keynote of various reports from the field. For example, Advance Airlines of Australia had put 1,850 hours on its Beechcraft Super King Air since its delivery eight months ago. Currently, its 12-passenger jetprop was flying some 65 hours a week in AA's regular commuter airline service.

Northrop Corporation had put 2,530 hours on its Beechcraft Super King Air BB114 flying in Saudi Arabia, a notably harsh environment for aircraft operations, without encountering any problems. Its current flight schedule stood at six hours per day, five days per week — largely to remote locations with primitive airstrips in the Arabian desert.

Dean Pape, head of the Caterpillar dealership for southern Oregon and northern California, reported operating his Beechcraft Super King Air 1,000 hours a year. His average "sales assist flight" was only 40 minutes long, with 12 to 16 takeoffs and landings per day. "It appears the airplane rarely cools down", said an observer. A previous owner of three Beechcraft King Airs and one Beechcraft Queen Air, his company currently operated a Beechcraft Baron 58P and a Beechcraft Bonanza, in addition to its Beechcraft Super King Air. Carefully kept records proved their value in contributing to their owner's sales success.

Heading many more high-utilization owners was Indonesian Air Transport. Flying two Beechcraft Super King Airs in charter service, IAT logged 4,055 hours in 25 months on the first unit, and 3,668 hours in 24 months on their second Beechcraft. Aero Contractors, Inc. in Nigeria, West Africa, countered with a flight log showing 1,477 hours in 18 months for its Beechcraft Super King Air.

Ben Taylor, chief pilot for Oceanic Contractors, Inc. of Brussels, Belgium, got into the game with 3,400 flight hours in 30 months for his company's Beechcraft King Air A100. J. Keith Thompson, aviation department manager for National Medical Enterprises, Inc. of Los Angeles, checked with 4,300 hours in 46 months for his company's Beechcraft King Air A100.

Such reports went far to prove a point that Beech salesmen

474

always drove home to prospective buyers: Beech builds no "hangar queens." Beechcrafts are made to fly . . . and fly . . . and keep on flying.

Good news kept on coming from the company's missile target sector. In May, the Navy reported favorable results from test firings of Beechcraft's HAHST (High Altitude, High Speed Target). It was a step ahead for Beech in the development of a tri-service (Navy, Army and Air Force) vehicle for training and testing highly sophisticated weapons systems.

The U. S. Army followed in June with a $2.1 million contract for more "Streaker" MQM-107A missile targets, bringing its total purchases of that Beech product to more than $48.4 million. Deliveries were scheduled to start in March, 1979 from the Beech Boulder Division.

In a personal vein, the Women's Aeronautical Association of Kansas celebrated its 50th Anniversary June 3-4 and honored four members for their outstanding contributions to aviation. Three were Beechcrafters: Mrs. O. A. Beech, Mrs. Lucille Winters Edwards and Mrs. Marcelline Klein Bowery.

Mrs. Beech was cited as the company's Chairman and co-founder. Mrs. Edwards was the company's secretary, office manager and long-time administrative assistant to the chairman when she retired in 1977 after 40 years of service. Mrs. Bowery, the wife of retired Beech vice president Leroy E. Bowery, founded the company's current 15-member Medical Department in 1939 when she was its first and only nurse.

The fourth honoree was Lillian Whipple, the first woman employee of Stearman Aircraft Company, predecessor of Boeing Wichita. All were charter or long-time members and past officers of Womens' Aero. Their records affirmed the important places held by women in Kansas aviation from its beginning onward.

Good news again greeted Beechcrafters resuming work after the plant-wide midyear vacation period. The purchase by the Japanese Maritime Safety Agency of a 13-plane fleet of Beech-craft Super King Air maritime surveillance aircraft had been confirmed. Deliveries were planned to begin in mid-1979.

In brisk competitive bidding, Beech Aircraft was the winner of a contract with the Forest Service of the U. S. Department of Agriculture for four pressurized Beechcraft Baron 58P aircraft.

475

It was a significant victory. Forest Service flights, mainly for aerial fire control, were conducted at all altitudes, often over mountainous terrain and in turbulent air and adverse weather. High performance, rugged sturdiness and total reliability were mandatory. The top rating earned by the Baron 58P in the Forest Service evaluation competition was convincing evidence of its exceptionally high capabilities.

From spacecraft to Beechcraft was the move made by Alan B. Shepard Jr., America's first astronaut in 1961 and commander of the Apollo 14 mission to the moon. Shepard and his business partner, R. W. "Duke" Windsor, Jr., took delivery of a new Beechcraft King Air for use by their Coors distributorship, the Windward Company of Houston, Texas.

Shepard was inducted into the Aviation Hall of Fame in 1977 at the same time that the late Walter H. Beech was enshrined. His partner was also an airman of distinction. Windsor won the Thompson Trophy in 1956 for being the first man to fly more than 1,000 miles per hour. He set that new record in a Navy Crusader. Not surprisingly, the airplane chosen by the partners was a high-performance model — the Beechcraft King Air E90.

The third quarter of fiscal 1978 closed June 30 with the customary results. Three-month sales of $134,863,338 and earnings of $8,960,811 brought nine-month totals to $378,211,303 and $25,933,097 respectively. All were new 3- and 9-month all-time high records. Hard work was paying off.

Coinciding with the fourth annual Beech Aero Club Round-Up at Wichita in July, membership topped the 5,000 mark at the nation's 100 Beech Aero Centers. William E. Kuechle of Minneapolis, Minnesota was hailed as the 5,000th member. Flown into Beech Field for the three-day gala were 79 aircraft, bringing some 400 members from 29 Aero Clubs near and far.

Shocking to Beech Aircraft and general aviation was the sudden death on July 24 of Roy H. McGregor, group vice president - marketing. A Beechcrafter for 27 years, his passing was mourned not only at Beech, but throughout the industry in which he had been a vigorous but always fair competitor.

It was the third such loss in recent months. Darrell L. Schneider, vice president - government relations and a 36-year Beechcrafter, had died March 24 after a long illness. Dale R. Erickson,

476

Liberal Division Beechcrafters celebrated production delivery of first Beechcraft Duchess.

The 20,000th graduate of the Beech Training Center was honored in the presentation of a Douglas Etteridge signed print of the classic Beechcraft Staggerwing. Celebrating the occasion were (from left) Bob Taylor, Training Center manager, Mrs. O. A. Beech, Dick Todd and Betty Todd.

Moroccan Air Force, Ecuadorian Air Force and Peruvian Navy Beechcraft T-34C-1 trainers were delivered for those countries' pilot training programs. Orders from the Argentine Navy and Indonesian Air Force quickly followed.

The Beechcrafters whose dedication made the Beechcraft Skipper a reality gathered to express their satisfaction just before the Skipper's takeoff on its initial flight.

The Women's Aeronautical Association of Kansas celebrated its 50th anniversary, honoring four distinguished members. At the ceremony were (from left) Marcelline Bowery, Mrs. O. A. Beech, June Harrison Mayer (first president of the association, who presented the awards), Lucille Winters Edwards and Lillian Whipple.

Dr. Forrest Bird, with his daughter Catherine, accepted delivery of the 2,000th Beechcraft King Air.

476B

manager of Aero Center products, had died with his wife, Madge, on April 25 in a weather-induced aircraft accident. The roster closed with the passing on August 13 of Vern Carstens, retired Beech manager of flight operations, who was the first pilot to fly the Beechcraft Bonanza, T-34 Mentor and Model 50 Twin-Bonanza.

On a more cheerful note, new honors were added to the many held by the company's chairman and by its president. With the unveiling on July 22 of a granite plaque bearing her name, Mrs. O. A. Beech was enrolled with aviation's great figures commemorated for all time in the International Forest of Friendship Memory Lane at Atchison, Kansas. Founded in 1976 to honor the city's native daughter, Amelia Earhart, and other aviation immortals, the International Forest of Friendship was planted with trees from America's 50 states and from 33 foreign lands. The Soroptimist International of Wichita sponsored Mrs. Beech for the honor.

At the opening of its new 14,400 sq. ft. hangar and sales/ service complex on Boeing Field in Seattle, Flightcraft Inc. named its Beechcraft Corporate Aviation Center in honor of Beech president Frank E. Hedrick. A bronze plaque with Mr. Hedrick's likeness in bas-relief carried a message of appreciation for his significant contributions to the aviation industry and to the cause of free enterprise.

The 500th Beechcraft delivered to Australia by Hawker Pacific, Pty. Ltd., marked a milestone for the Beech distributor in the important Australasian markets. Hawker had celebrated its 50th anniversary and 18th year with Beech Aircraft in 1977, staging a special promotion of the complete Beechcraft line. Flourishing sales were its fitting reward.

A landmark labor contract in general aviation took effect early in August. Spanning the three years to August 1981, the compact with union-represented workers was the costliest wage and benefits package ever effected by a general aviation manufacturer, and the largest set of increases in Beech history.

Immediate and future wages and numerous benefits alike were scheduled to increase. And consistent with management's constant policy, proportionate gains were also provided for non-union employees. Beech Aircraft was doing well; and while

477

much of the company's earnings were wisely invested in product development and expansion for future growth, and some went to meet its obligations to shareholders, its workers deserved and received their fair share. "Muzzle not the ox that treadeth out the grain" was a Biblical precept traditionally honored by Beech Aircraft's management.

Bell Helicopter Textron sparked a speedup in Beech production of its JetRanger III commercial helicopter airframe assemblies with a $3.7 million add-on contract in August. Larger numbers of airframes would be built within a time frame requiring completion of deliveries in December, 1979.

Two out of six bottles of milk went sour on the way. That was the only problem reported by German pilot Dieter Schmitt, in a 5,000-mile non-stop solo flight August 18-19 over the North Pole from Anchorage, Alaska to Munich, West Germany.

Delivering a new Beechcraft Bonanza V35B to Wolfgand Denzel GmbH, Beechcraft distributors for Central Europe, Schmitt completed the trip routinely in 32 hours and 28 minutes. He became the first pilot ever to complete such a flight solo via the trans-polar route in a single-engine commercial aircraft.

Warming up for his flight over the top of the world, Schmitt had flown a Beechcraft Bonanza F33A non-stop 4,300 miles from New York to Munich last year. His unique Great Circle transit of the Arctic Ocean bettered his previous record by a margin of 700 miles. "There's just no stopping that man Schmitt", fellow pilots agreed.

The company's policy of maintaining management in depth was maintained with a series of high-level promotions as the year progressed. Continuing in charge of its Washington, D.C. office, William G. Rutherford was elected vice president - government relations. He had joined Beechcraft in 1967 after his retirement from the U. S. Army as a colonel.

Dwight C. Hornberger, vice president - international marketing, retired August 31 after 31 years of service with Beech. Reassignment of his responsibilities brought promotions to several International executives. Among them were Robert Staggs, Frank Hutton, Allen W. Snook and Robert G. Oestreicher.

Announcement of his planned retirement December 31 by James N. Lew, senior vice president - engineering, prompted two immediate promotions aimed to preserve the continuity of engineering management. C. A. Rembleske, like Lew a 38-year Beechcrafter, was named vice president - engineering. John A. Pike was named vice president - research and development in his 22nd year of service with the company.

The election of 36-year Beechcrafter Seymour "Jack" Colman to the newly created post of senior vice president - operations in October also brought further advancements. Gary M. Hanssen, who joined Beech in 1962, was named director - industrial relations. James E. Bell, a 22-year Beechcrafter, became manager of the Boulder Division, succeeding Ralph E. Moyer who went on special assignment with Colman.

Leddy L. Greever, vice president and a company director, submitted his plan to retire on December 31 after 37 years of service. His management responsibilities for the company's external communications programs were taken over by William G. Robinson, who was promoted to the newly created post of director - corporate communications. With a background of 25 years in corporate and aviation public relations, Robinson had joined Beech in 1970 as the company's public relations manager. Steve Caine, a former Navy journalist long experienced in general aviation and public relations, became director - public relations.

September 12 was a double "happy day" in Beech history. It was the delivery date of the 2,000th Beechcraft King Air jetprop twin, and the "first flight day" for the production Model 77 T-tail trainer.

Beechcraft King Air No. 2,000 had come off the production line less than a year after the delivery of the 1,500th jetprop King Air. A Super King Air model, it commanded special interest because of its planned use in developing a life-saving airborne intensive care medical system designed by Dr. Forrest Bird.

A biomedical engineer and also an 18,000-hour pilot, Dr. Bird had invented the Bird respirator used in most hospitals. He was the founder-owner of Bird Space Technology, the medical research firm that purchased the 2,000th turbine-powered twin Beechcraft.

Sharing the runway at Beech Field that day was the first prototype production unit of the Aero Center Model 77. Uniquely distinguished as an all-new airplane, rather than an evolution of a previous Beechcraft model, the T-tail trainer fulfilled all the favorable expectations of veteran test pilot Vaughn Gregg in its 50-minute first flight.

In the second half of the company's Name the Planes contest, the two-place Model 77 meanwhile gained the name that would identify it in its worldwide sales career. Five persons in the Beechcraft franchise organization won the first prize of $250 each for submitting the catchiest entry: the Beechcraft Skipper.

A mass flyaway from Beech Field by Argentine Navy pilots meanwhile of 7 Beechcraft T-34C-1 trainers completed the delivery of a 15-plane fleet to Argentina. Like the U. S. Navy, Argentina was updating its pilot training with state-of-the-art Beechcraft jetprops. Old hands at Beech recalled a similar 15-plane delivery in 1957, when Argentina had joined other South American nations in adopting the original piston-engine Beechcraft T-34 Mentor as its basic single-engine trainer.

Results of fiscal year 1978 at September 30 were even better than projected. Handily passing the half-billion dollar mark for the first time, total consolidated sales came to $527,510,511, producing a net income of $35,520,876. New highs in sales and earnings were reached for the sixth consecutive year. In addition to the regular quarterly stock dividend of 20¢ in cash, a one percent stock dividend was declared.

The Beechcraft Training Center graduated its 20,000th student in October. Dick Todd, board chairman of TK International, Tulsa, Oklahoma, received the milestone diploma from Chairman O. A. Beech, together with a special memento, when he completed the 58TC pilot training course in preparation for flying his new Beechcraft Baron on business missions.

Established in 1964, the Beechcraft Training Center had become one of general aviation's most popular institutions. Only four years earlier, it had graduated its 10,000th student. Its current curriculum embraced 22 classes, taught by 18 instructors. Most courses were offered in both English and Spanish. Classes of 2 to 14 days' duration spanned pilotage and maintenance of all models of Beechcraft twins, including avionics. Its primary aim was to promote the safe and efficient operation of Beech customers' aircraft. Their large-scale enrollments and enthusi-

480

astic participation proved that the Training Center was fulfilling its purpose.

Record-breaking 1978 sales brought a record-breaking total of honors and awards to the 646 Beechcraft Masters of Salesmanship who met at Wichita October 16-18 for the company's 1979 Aviation Celebration. Headed by Chairman O. A. Beech, top executives happily handed out a record number of 258 awards to winning conferees.

The traditional "Man of the Year" award changed shape, with the naming of Ed Box and Don Cody, principals of Chaparral Aviation in Texas, as Beech Aircraft's "Team of the Year." The honor was well deserved. Chaparral's outlets at Amarillo, San Antonio, Victoria, and Dallas had together sold $25.9 million worth of Beechcrafts within their market area in 1978 to place first in that category. The runner-up was Hangar One, Inc. with $21 million, followed by Beechcraft West, Van Nuys, with $18 million in sales.

Hangar One, Inc. flew away with the Olive Ann Beech award for the Aviation Center that in 1978 took delivery of the greatest number of Beechcrafts in total dollars. Hangar One led the world with total factory purchases in excess of $26.9 million.

"Millionaire" awards went to 73 salesmen and one saleswoman, Fran Berra, for personal sales totals of one million dollars or more. Their grand total came to an impressive $135 million.

For the second year in a row, the international sales leadership award went to William C. Morales & Co. of Caracas, Venezuela. Their winning total for 1978 was more than $20 million in sales. Ricardo Morales, who had taken over as president when his father died, received the award.

Special recognition for international sales accomplishment was given to Andre Sol, president, Transair France, and Laurie Jones, managing director, Hawker Pacific Pty. Ltd. of Australia; and for international marketing development to W. Eric Hodson, managing director, Beechcraft Sales of South Africa.

Numerous awards were also made for excellence in professional sales management and salesmanship; Aero Club achievement; parts and equipment marketing; franchise business management; and service management. Never overlooked was the importance of good service to customers as a vital ingredient of successful marketing.

Recognition for superior customer service efforts was further provided under a continuous company program through cash grants, matching monies spent by franchises to upgrade their service facilities. A total of 35 such awards went to pleased recipients.

Cash was also the medium chosen to honor franchisees that had actively participated in the company's continuous Order Planning Program by forward ordering and taking delivery as prearranged. Qualifying for cash thus earned were 35 franchisees.

Newly created in 1978 was the "Order of the Silver Eagle." Founded to honor Beechcraft franchise holders of 30 years or more standing, the Silver Eagle Award was presented to eight domestic outlets and seven international distributors at the 1979 Aviation Celebration. It was one way to publicly thank old friends for their abiding support and their loyalty – always a paramount virtue in Beech Aircraft's philosophy.

Domestic Silver Eagle honorees were Hangar One, Inc. (Southern Airways); Tulsair, Inc.; Ohio Aviation; Chaparral/Tradewind; Page Airways; Elliott Flying Service; Topeka Aircraft/Executive Beechcraft; and Cutter Flying Service.

International Silver Eagles were Cogera Industria e Comercio Ltda., Brazil; Hamamcioglu Muesseseleri Tricaret, Turkey; Indamer Company Pty. Ltd., India; Nymba, S.A., Argentina; Pike & Company, S.A., Uruguay; Transair Switzerland S.A., Switzerland; and Hollinda N.V., Netherlands.

The honors and awards, the product information and service clinics, the good fellowship and renewal of personal contacts were always important elements in every Beech sales meeting. But the constant stars of each gathering were always the gleaming new Beechcrafts for the coming year.

So it was with the 1979 Aviation Celebration. The complete lineup of Beechcraft's newest and finest products was a matchless source of inspiration at the opening of the company's seventh record-breaking year.

Replete with refinements and features to heighten their sales appeal, every 1979 Beechcraft from the world champion Super

King Air to the all-new Model 77 Skipper stood ready to inspire each conferee.

Heading the turbine-powered group, the 1979 Beechcraft Super King Air was certificated for operation to 35,000 feet, highest in its class. Sparkling new interiors, plus a new optional cargo/airstair door that greatly enlarged its utility, boosted its salespower. Restyling of its sister ships — the Beechcraft King Air A100 and B100, and the E90 and C90 models — further strengthened Beech Aircraft's grasp on world leadership in the jetprop field.

The Beechcraft Duke B60 stood out with fresh exterior and interior styling and numerous added niceties. Its place as the industry's owner-flown, deluxe high performance twin seemed secure for the year ahead.

The Beechcraft Baron series offered stronger-than-ever competitive values to continue its sales leadership. Alumigrip urethane paint was made standard equipment on all models, and a 14,000-Btu engine-driven air conditioning system featuring simple, unrestricted switch on/off operation was a new option.

Newly equipped with the same turbocharged, fuel injected 325 horsepower engine as the Beechcraft Baron 58TC, the pressurized Beechcraft Baron 58P matched the 58TC's performance with a top speed approaching 300 miles per hour, and a maximum cruise speed of 277 miles per hour. Increased pressure differential provided a sea level cabin up to 8,350 feet, and a 9,200-ft. cabin at 21,000 feet. The Beechcraft Baron 58, E55 and B55 models shared new styling and state-of-the-art touches of comfort and luxury.

A new model Beechcraft Bonanza made its appearance to broaden the 1979 market for that classic series. It was the A36TC, a turbocharged, 300 horsepower version of the best-selling Bonanza A36. In place of cowl flaps, the A36TC featured a series of louvers and grills requiring no adjustment in flight. A new heater with 20 percent more output took the chill off high altitude flight. Shortened propeller tips increased ground clearance and reduced noise. Deliveries were planned to begin in Spring, 1979.

The classic V-tail Beechcraft Bonanza V35B made ready for fresh sales laurels as "the ultimate envy machine" among high performance, single-engine aircraft, with new styling and thoughtful touches here and there. The same held good for the Bonanza A36 and F33A models; a banner sales year was clearly in store for them all.

Top news for the Aero Center line was the availability for 1979 delivery of the all-new Model 77 Beechcraft Skipper two-place trainer. Exciting to look at, with its distinctive T-tail and spacious, full visibility cabin, the Skipper seemed sure to sparkle in the Beech Aero Club system and elsewhere as a deluxe functional, safe and comfortable student trainer. It made a grand companion for the other Aero Center Beechcrafts — the glamorous Model 76 Duchess twin, and the restyled single-engine Sierra 200, Sundowner 180 and Sport 150.

The bottom line of the Aviation Celebration was neatly summed up in the Beechcraft *Marketing Report:* "We rejoiced for '78 but got on with the business of '79."

A source of pride to all Beechcrafters was a letter written to Chairman O. A. Beech by Bill Stone, 1st officer for Air Kentucky of Owensboro, late one night after just returning from a flight. He wrote:

"We operate two Beechcraft 99's and I serve as co-pilot. Tonight we completed a flight from Nashville, Tennessee to Louisville, Kentucky. During the flight we encountered extreme turbulence and hail. Our radar malfunctioned and we had to rely on ATC vectors around the cells.

"Tonight, ATC did not see everything. We, along with nine passengers, were thrown about almost uncontrollably. When we arrived at Standiford Airport in Louisville, the weatherman looked at us like we were ghosts. We were told that we were lucky to be alive. The weather radar showed we had flown through a line of the most intense thunderstorms.

"The Beechcraft 99 we flew was built in the '60's and has 18,000 hours on it. It will begin flying tomorrow morning at 5:15 a.m., as usual.

"Thank you, Mrs. Beech, for building a strong airplane."

Stone's testimonial to Beechcraft's standards of rugged performance might well serve to bolster the spirits of the astronauts who would one day pilot NASA's Space Shuttle Orbiter "Columbia" on its first orbital flight. Its vital systems would rely on

484

the integrity of the Beech-built cryogenic oxygen and hydrogen tanks in its power reactant storage assembly for life support and proper functioning.

The first such tanks were delivered in November, well ahead of the contract schedule, by the aerospace team at the Beech Boulder Division. NASA and Rockwell International, the principal contractor for the Orbiter, stipulated a capability for the tanks of 100 missions into space. Beech-Boulder conducted stringent testing of the tanks' inner vessels and electrical components up to four times the demands of the 100 mission requirement.

Pilot trainers that would never get off the ground were called for in a U. S. Navy contract accepted by Beech Aircraft in November. The company undertook to design and deliver $8.7 million worth of instrument flight simulators to supplement the Navy's actual airborne training in its fleet of Beechcraft T-34C jetprops. Reproducing the handling and movements of an airplane in flight, the ground-based trainers duplicated the panel, controls, seating and operating environment of a T-34C trainer. Construction was subcontracted to the Simulation Systems Design Division of Gould, Inc., Melville, New York.

Pratt & Whitney Aircraft of Canada Ltd. celebrated the completion of its 15,000th gas turbine engine by handing over the milestone power plant, serial #80138, to Beech Aircraft in ceremonies held on November 15 in Montreal. Beech Chairman O. A. Beech and President Frank E. Hedrick were guests of honor, and recipients of special mementoes, at ceremonies held there during Pratt & Whitney's 50th Anniversary observance.

The event paid tribute to the long and successful association of Beech Aircraft with Pratt & Whitney Ltd. P & W gas turbine engines powered more than 2,500 commercial and military Beechcrafts in use all over the world; and the first PT6 engine was still in service in a Beechcraft King Air C90 twin after 15 years.

A new distinction came to Beech president Frank E. Hedrick, with his election to the board of directors of the National Association of Manufacturers. He was chosen to represent the State of Kansas for a one-year term, with elegibility for re-election to two more board terms.

FAA certification of the new Beechcraft Bonanza A36TC on December 13 cleared the way for deliveries to begin early next year. Eagerly waiting for the turbocharged Beech "workhorse of the air" were many operators flying from high altitude sites and over mountainous terrain.

More logistic support and maintenance contracts came from the U. S. Navy in December. A $7.8 million contract covered its T-34C single-engine trainers through a second year. It was followed by a $3.1 million award extending support of Navy T-44A turbo twin advanced trainers through September, 1979.

The contracts accented the growing importance of Beech Aerospace Services, Inc. (BASI), a subsidiary of Beech Aircraft, to the company and its customers. In little more than two years, BASI had enlarged its work force to more than 500 employees, stationed at some 58 locations around the world. Operational readiness rates of 90-plus percent for the far-flung fleet of Beechcraft C-12 transport and utility turbo twins, as well as the Beechcraft T-44A advanced pilot trainer twin jetprops, had been upheld. Even the heavily used Beechcraft T-34C, flown by beginning Navy pilots, were keeping up a readiness rate of better than 80 percent with BASI support. "Your people are saving a bundle of money for the taxpayers", was the gist of unofficial reports that came in from the field.

Good news for communities where Beech facilities were located came with a December 27 announcement of expansion plans. Some 2,600 new employees would be hired in 1979 to help meet the company's projections of $600 million in sales during the year ahead: 2,000 in Wichita, 200 each at Salina and Liberal, Kansas, and 150 at Boulder, Colorado. The current worldwide total of 10,400 employees (subsidiaries included) would thus be substantially enlarged.

A newly leased facility of 58,000 sq. ft. at Selma, Alabama would also initially employ 50 people in modification of nearly completed aircraft for special missions. Prospects for further expansion at Selma's Craig Field, a closed-out military air base, were also seen. Many thousands more square feet of space were available, with much equipment already in place to meet production needs. Beech prudently acquired options for additional space to be occupied as and when needed.

486

Brightening the holiday celebrations, Beech Aircraft received on December 27 a $22.8 million follow-on, ceiling price contract for more Beechcraft UC-12B personnel/utility transports for the U. S. Navy. Deliveries were scheduled between May, 1980 and April, 1981. The award enlarged on a previous $17.9 million contract for C-12 (UC-12B) jetprop military versions of the Beechcraft Super King Air for the Navy and the U. S. Marine Corps. Plans were to station the aircraft at 31 sites throughout the world.

So the books were closed on the company's greatest year of 1978. Greatest, except for the years to come.

Chapter 42

As the New Year dawned, there was no way to predict that 1979 was to develop the largest transaction in Beech Aircraft's entire history. True, the company was well on the way to its seventh straight record year, with new highs of $142,159,801 in sales and $9,396,763 in earnings for the first quarter of fiscal 1979. But that had become almost routine. The great event was still to come.

Good news for stockholders and for a trio of Beech executives came from the January 9 meeting of the board of directors. Annual cash dividends were increased to 92¢ per share, up 11.5 percent from the former 80¢ rate. And three highly qualified Beechcrafters were named officers of the company.

W. D. Wise was elected to the newly-created post of vice president - advanced technology. Joining the company in 1959 as a design engineer, Wise had capably fulfilled many varied assignments, chiefly in product design and development. He had served since 1977 as director of aircraft research and development.

William G. Robinson advanced to the newly-created position of vice president - corporate communications, his second promotion in only three months. He became the company's co-ordinator of General Aviation Manufacturers Association affairs and its representative in other national organizations, and assumed responsibility for all external and internal communications programs, including advertising, public relations, sales promotion, shows and exhibits, aviation education and employee communications.

Wey D. Kenny was named assistant treasurer, taking charge of cash flow which, under his supervision, contributed substantially to the company's earnings. A certified public accountant, he had joined Beech in 1964 as a staff assistant to the treasurer. In addition to carrying out various special assignments, Kenny had served as an officer of the Beech Aircraft Foundation since its inception in 1966.

The first Beechcraft King Air ever sold came home to Beech Field on January 17 so that the pilots for its new owner, Carl Hass, Automotive Imports Inc. of Highland Park, Illinois, could attend the Beech King Air training school. Lined up nose to nose with a Beechcraft Super King Air fresh from the assembly line, it was hard to say which of the two aircraft looked newer. But then, the Hass' Model 90 was only 14 years old — and it was a Beechcraft.

The next day, the U. S. Army issued an $8.2 million contract for continued worldwide support of its 62 Beechcraft C-12 personnel/utility transports through its 1979 fiscal year. Beech Aerospace Services, Inc. had serviced the Army's C-12 Super King Air fleet continuously since the first deliveries in mid-1975, over a span of some 16.2 million flight miles covering every kind of climate and terrain. It seemed the Army was well pleased.

Well pleased, too, was the Space Division of Rockwell International, prime contractors for NASA's Space Shuttle Orbiter program. Cited for "commendable performance" were Beechcrafters at the Boulder Division. Recognizing Beech Aircraft's work on the Orbiter's power reactant storage assembly, models of the Orbiter and commemorative plaques were presented to Boulder manager Ralph Moyer and aerospace manufacturing foreman Claude Stuart.

The continuing progress of the joint labor-management Beech Productivity Council proved even more pleasing to employees and the company alike. In the three years since its start in January 1976, the Productivity Council had received more than

31,000 improvement ideas; and over 13,250 had been put into use. Beechcrafters had taken home more than $550,000 for their submissions, and the gains to the company and its customers more than repaid the cost of the Productivity program.

Ideas of all kinds were encouraged, and submitted at a rate of nearly 40 per day. Some created major savings — like Oscar Gustin's modified jig that increased productivity on the Super King Air assembly line. And R. L. George's system and chart that saved miles of high-cost wire in avionics hookups. Others were varied in subject and method; but all were important to the Productivity program.

Awards to employees were welcome windfalls. "Mine went toward my daughter's braces," said Trudy Kretz, helicopter stockroom clerk. Even more important was the lift to employee morale. "It gets me involved in the entire company," explained three-time winner Fay Smith, flight line electrician.

Warmly welcomed to Alabama by the state's Governor George C. Wallace, on his last day in office, was the Beech Modification Center at Craig Field, at Selma. Managed by 13-year veteran Beechcrafter H. Bruce Addington, a widely experienced administrator and former Navy pilot, Selma's Dixie Beechcrafters received their first assignment on February 3. They began conversion of 13 new Beechcraft Super King Air jetprop twins to the Beech-originated Model 200T Maritime Patrol configuration for the Maritime Safety Agency of the Japanese Government. Beyond that was the prospect of steady employment for some 500 Alabamans on future Beech Aircraft programs; and for the company, an easing of labor and facilities shortages that might impede its progress.

The Beech Aircraft Foundation continued its annual scholarship awards with grants to 28 students. Ten were in Aeronautical Engineering at Wichita State University, in memory of company co-founder Walter H. Beech. Dependents of Beech employees received 16 grants, and two grants were awarded to qualified students at the University of Kansas.

N8616X was the registration number on a new Beechcraft Bonanza A36 that recalled memories of a proud moment for America in its Bicentennial Year. A total of 8,616 points had been scored by U. S. athlete Bruce Jenner when he won the

Decathlon Gold Medal in the 1976 Olympic Games with the highest score in history.

That number was assigned at Jenner's request to his new Beechcraft, which he picked up February 3 at Beech Field. Enriching the event for sports followers was the presence of his friend, football star Bert Jones, who flew Jenner to Wichita in his own Beechcraft Baron 58.

Pro football fans got a further charge from the purchase by Chuck Noll, coach of the Super Bowl winning Pittsburgh Steelers, of a new Beechcraft Duke B60 pressurized cabin-class twin. It was his third Beechcraft; the first was a Beechcraft Bonanza V35B, and the second a Beechcraft Baron 58. All found heavy use in the Steelers scouting program, which each year screened some 3,500 players at widely scattered colleges and universities nationwide to recruit about two dozen eligibles for professional play.

Turning gold into silver was the unique feat performed in February by the Golden B's, an organization of women Beechcrafters with ten years or more of service. The occasion was the celebration of the Golden B's Silver Anniversary.

Founded in 1954 by Lucille Winters Edwards and Margaret Neal, the social and service group had grown from 81 to more than 200 members. Since its founding, the Golden B's had given more than $10,000 to worthy causes, along with many hours of time and personal involvement. Their comradeship and concern for others was typical of the spirit that prevailed among Beech Aircraft employees.

Adding to his many duties, Beech president Frank E. Hedrick accepted an appointment as chairman of the International Affairs Committee of the General Aviation Manufacturers Association. Assisted by Michael G. Neuberger, senior vice president - Beech International Division, Hedrick and his committee were to recommend actions to improve the international market for general aviation products. A top priority item was to work for removal of government restrictions hampering international commerce.

Quoted in a February 26 *Time* magazine article describing Wichita's healthy economy was a trenchant observation by Mr. Hedrick, based on his decades of experience at Beech: "A work ethic still exists in this part of the world. People feel they have to give a day's work for a day's pay."

Beech Aircraft's own contributions to the economic health of Wichita and Kansas communities emerged in the finding that the company's statewide expenditures during fiscal 1978 had reached a new record total of $168 million in payrolls, purchases and taxes. On the basis of U. S. Chamber of Commerce estimates, Beech activities had added more than four times that amount to the economy of the company's home state.

Welcomed to the office of Chairman O. A. Beech in mid-March was a second-generation Beechcraft owner, Dr. Otto Thaning of Johannesburg, South Africa. Dr. Thaning came to Wichita for two purposes: to attend a pilot training course for his new Beechcraft King Air C90, and to fulfill a childhood dream of visiting the factory where his father's first Beechcraft Staggerwing biplane was built.

He shared with Mrs. Beech first-hand memories of records set and racing victories won in Africa by his father, Otto Thaning, Sr., flying the first of his family's six Beechcrafts. Numbered among the earliest Staggerwing Beechcrafts produced, the senior Thaning's biplane was a 225 hp Model B17L. "I learned to fly a Beechcraft before I could drive a motor car," Dr. Thaning revealed.

In addition to the new Beechcraft King Air C90, Dr. Thaning and his company, Fairlie Steels Ltd., also owned and flew a Beechcraft Bonanza V35B and a Beechcraft Baron 58P. All, he said, were vital tools for business transport in support of their activities in South Africa.

Present-day Beechcrafts continued the winning tradition established by the first Staggerwing biplanes. Official confirmation of a world record speed run between Fresno, California and Las Vegas, Nevada provided a fresh example. Reedley, California rancher and owner-pilot Marie McMillan made the record flight in her Beechcraft Bonanza F33A in 1 hour 26 minutes. Her speed run commemorated the Wright Brothers' first flight 75 years ago.

"I'll be doing a great deal of mountain flying, so the Turbo Bonanza is exactly what I need." That was Bill Hane's comment when he took delivery in March of the first Beechcraft Bonanza

491

A36TC, a new turbocharged addition to the Beechcraft Bonanza line of business aircraft. A real estate developer based at Lake Tahoe, Nevada, Hane's high-flying new A36TC was his third Beechcraft. It was preceded by two other Beechcraft Bonanzas, N35 and A36 models. "I like to fly and I like the best," Hane explained.

In preview flights of the new turbocharged Beechcraft A36TC, the aviation press found much to praise. Its ease of operation was noted by *Flying* magazine's Russell Munson, who wrote: "This airplane will delight a lot of owners . . . The pilot never has to touch a cowl flap or install winter baffles. Sufficient cooling is not at the expense of an excessively rich mixture. It is a neat trick that didn't come easy."

Beech Aircraft's "minimum-engine" concept also earned favorable mention. Holding good for all Beechcraft models, this concept simply meant that all performance figures and operating modes set forth in the pilot's handbook (the "Bible") for each airplane were based on the minimum, rather than the maximum horsepower expected to be available from the average engine installed in that airplane.

It was a conservative method of rating that promoted maximum safety, efficiency and economy of operation. For example, the Continental TSIO-520-UB engine used in the Bonanza A36TC was rated for 300 horsepower, plus five percent. There was no minimum tolerance. So the average A36TC engine would reliably deliver 300 horsepower or more.

"These new tolerances," Munson commented, "together with Beech's conservative performance figures, should insure that an A36TC will still meet book figures several years and many hours after purchase."

Leroy Cook of *Aero* magazine concisely summed up the essence of the press comments: "The A36TC is a delightful airplane to fly . . . basically a Bonanza with another 10,000 feet of altitude added to its performance envelope."

New corporate altitude records for sales and earnings were set in the second quarter and first half of fiscal 1979. Sales came to $152,102,872 for the second quarter (January 1 - March 31) and to $294,262,673 for the half-year. Earnings were

$10,499,035 for the quarter, and $19,895,798 at the halfway mark.

The Beechcraft Super King Air kept up its winning ways in industry-wide competitions held by the U. S. Government. This time it was the U. S. Customs Service that evaluated general aviation twin-engine aircraft for operation in its border patrol fleet. The result was a long-term lease of four off-the-shelf commercial Beechcraft Super King Air jetprops, plus field support by Beech Aerospace Services, Inc. So Beech Aircraft would play its part in helping guard the nation's borders against would-be lawbreakers.

A $3.5 million contract from the government of Algeria initiated deliveries of Beechcraft Turbine Mentor 34C trainers and Beechcraft Sierras to its national pilot training school at Oran. Spare parts and ferrying services were included. The new Beechcrafts were to update a training fleet that already numbered four Beechcraft Sierras, in addition to a Beechcraft King Air 100 UNACE (Universal Aircraft Communication/Evaluation) jetprop twin purchased in 1971.

Stepping up Beechcraft King Air production to meet increasing customer demand, Navy T-34C assembly was moved to a 42,000 sq. ft. building at the Salina Division. The move freed space in Wichita's Plant III for final assembly of the fast-selling Beechcraft King Air twin jetprop models.

Coincidentally, Salina proudly rolled out its 500th Beechcraft Duke pressurized cabin twin on March 30. It was the first of a "Special Edition" Duke series featuring a striking silver and black exterior and a harmonizing custom deluxe interior.

Taking delivery of her 15th Beechcraft Bonanza, a Model A36, Evelyn P. "Pinky" Brier proclaimed to one and all that "the Bonanza is the very best airplane in all the world." She was well qualified to judge. Co-owner with her late husband, Joe, of the Tri-City Airport and charter service at San Bernardino, California for 40 years, Pinky had logged 40,000 hours. The first woman in the United States to qualify as a certified flight instructor, she had been assigned the call sign "Pinky One" by the FAA for her many cross-country flights. Her new A36 joined a Beechcraft Twin-Bonanza already in service in her charter fleet.

The company's longest-standing, largest-volume commercial

493

customer justly rated special ceremonies on the delivery of its new Beechcraft Super King Air — the 85th Beechcraft it had purchased over a span of 40 years. Marathon Oil of Findlay, Ohio (formerly Ohio Oil) had purchased its first Beechcraft, a Staggerwing D17S biplane, in 1939. Its flight department had since owned and flown the entire range of Beechcraft corporate and executive models. Fittingly, Marathon's newest Beechcraft was equipped with the historic 15,000th gas turbine engine built by Pratt & Whitney.

Chairman O. A. Beech meanwhile took part as the U. S. Navy's guest of honor in graduation and commissioning ceremonies held April 27 at the Pensacola, Florida Naval Air Station. Mrs. Beech personally presented commissioning certificates to each of the 13 ensigns who had passed their required 13-week basic training course. She was invited to participate in recognition of the thousands of Navy pilots who had learned to fly in Beechcraft trainers, and for her leadership roles in many important government advisory and community positions. It was an honor deeply felt and appreciated by the company's co-founder.

President Frank E. Hedrick's lively sense of humor passed a sharp test following a misprint in the company's employee publication. Introducing a plantwide "Share the Ride" program, Beechcrafters were invited to phone Extension 7734 to ask about carpooling.

It just happened that 7734 was a direct line to Hedrick's office. So a good many prospective carpoolers were startled to find themselves talking with the company's president. "Never knew carpooling was that important," many said. "It sure is," Hedrick responded. "Now, if you'll just call Extension 7234, Plant Security will fix you up."

The departure from Liberal, Kansas on May 8 of the first production Model 77 Beechcraft Skipper to Beechcraft West at Van Nuys, California commenced deliveries of the new two-place, T-tail trainer to the nationwide network of Beech Aero Centers. Certified by the FAA on March 17, the Beechcraft Skipper was afterward test-flown by aviation journalist-pilots eager to gather and report their impressions of the distinctive new Beechcraft. They loved it.

"It's a fun airplane to fly and won't get you into any trouble,"

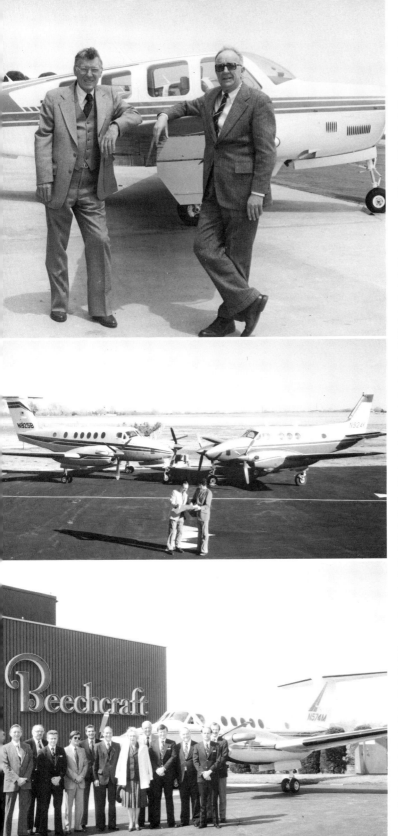

Taking delivery of his 27th Beechcraft Bonanza, a new Model A36TC, Leonard Hay of Rock Springs, Wyoming reconfirmed his title of "Mr. Bonanza" and world champion Bonanza buyer for personal use. With Hay (at left): Denver Beech-craft's salesman Vince Gringas.

At left, the newest Beechcraft Super King Air. At right, the first Beechcraft King Air ever sold, still looking as-new after 14 years. J. D. Weber (left), chief-engineering flight test who test-flew the Model 90 in 1964, with Jan Mann, who flew it to Beech Field for this special meeting.

Participants in the special delivery of Marathon Oil's 85th Beechcraft, a Super King Air, (from left): W. G. Robinson, vice president - corporate communi-cations; E. C. Burns, group vice president; C. G. Parkhurst, manager, sales orders; Steve Sipp, Marathon Oil pilot; Jack O. Ray, director, product marketing, corporate aircraft; Dean Kunselman, Marathon Oil maintenance specialist; Lowell Cress, chief pilot, Ohio Aviation; Mrs. O. A. Beech, chairman; Frank E. Hedrick, president; Jerome Kriegel, Marathon Oil pilot; Bill Merchant, Marathon Oil senior pilot; Jerry Cooke, Marathon Oil pilot; and David Leslie, P & W representative.

494A

Guest of honor at the U. S. Navy's Pensacola, Florida Naval Air Station, Chairman O. A. Beech was assisted by Captain Philip J. Ryan (center) in presenting certificates to each of 23 ensigns officially commissioning them as U. S. Navy officers.

Site of the company's annual display of new models was fittingly designated as Frank E. Hedrick Park. Shown at ribbon cutting ceremonies (from left): Chairman O. A. Beech, President Frank E. Hedrick, his wife Betty, and vice president of domestic marketing George Rodgers.

Deliveries of the new T-tail Beechcraft King Air F90 began in June, 1979, bringing the number of models in the corporate King Air fleet to six.

wrote Jim Summers of *Plane and Pilot* magazine. "Yet it will teach you much about the art of flying."

"I think it's a nice airplane, and one that will fit well into the Beech Aero Club concept of quality and class," was the judgment of *Air Progress'* writer Keith Connes.

"The interior appointments are lavish, but after all this is a Beechcraft," observed LeRoy Cook in *Private Pilot*. That summed it all up neatly.

The dedication on May 8 at Wichita's Wesley Medical Center of its Life Watch helicopter landing pad in memory of John Pomeroy Gaty honored a deceased Beech key executive of nearly a quarter century's standing. John P. "Jack" Gaty had joined the company on March 1, 1937 as its vice president - director of sales. While Walter H. Beech was slowly recovering from a severe illness in 1940, Gaty was named general manager. Jointly, Gaty, Mrs. Beech and Frank E. Hedrick, then the company's coordinator, met and solved the problems of rapid expansion to meet greatly accelerated World War II production.

Gaty made many more contributions to the company's progress up to his retirement in 1960, three years before he died. A gifted engineer and administrator, he was a political conservative with deep humanitarian concerns. He helped bring Beech Aircraft to leadership in the promotion of safe flying, and in 1954 received the Business Flight Safety award of the National Business Aircraft Association.

Excitement ran high at the Reading Air Show in Pennsylvania at its opening on May 24. A showcase event in general aviation, its dominant interest was the presentation by Beech Aircraft of three new models — the turbocharged Beechcraft Bonanza A36TC, the all-new Beechcraft Skipper T-tail trainer, and the new, advanced Beechcraft King Air F90.

The new Beechcraft King Air F90 — a high performance, high payload 7 to 10-place corporate twin offering 307 mph high cruise speed, shared with the Beechcraft Super King Air the distinctive T-tail first offered on that world champion top-of-the-line twin jetprop. Its two 750 shaft horsepower Pratt & Whitney PT6A-135 turbine engines featured slow-turning gear boxes to drive four-bladed propellers at reduced speeds for quiet, smooth, fast flight; a rate of climb of 2,380 feet per minute, and 31,000-ft.

maximum altitude. It was the state-of-the-art aircraft of its class; and not surprisingly, F90 production was sold out well into 1980 only days after its debut.

The company's constant efforts to provide worldwide maintenance and service support of top quality for all Beech products were emphasized with the annual meeting June 5-7 at Wichita of 202 Beechcraft Service Center and vendor personnel from throughout the world. Updates on Beech service-related programs were followed by group seminars covering specialized areas.

Half a century had passed since the Travel Air Model R "Mystery S" ("S" for "Ship") monoplane amazed the aviation world by winning the 1929 proto-Thompson Trophy Race, competing with the fastest military and commercial aircraft of its era over a 50-mile closed course. Other Model R Travel Air monoplanes had gone on to set cross-country world speed records by the dozens in America and Europe in the early 30's.

Those days of glory for the speedy Travel Air, built by Walter H. Beech to designs of Herb Rawdon and Walt Burnham (who later became Beech engineers) sprang to life again with the visit to Beech Field on June 19 of a flying replica of the original "Mystery S." It was a faithful reproduction, right down to the paint scheme (red with black scallops) and the registration number — R614K. Jim Younkin, vice president of engineering for the Mitchell Division of Edo Aire at Mineral Wells, Texas, had put some 4,000 hours into its construction, as the crowning achievement of his lifelong hobby. Beechcrafters shared his pride and joy in his re-creation of the sleek, fast-flying historic Travel Air racing champion.

Eminent connoisseurs of fine aircraft, the nation's airline pilots had stamped their seal of approval on Beechcraft from the days of the first Staggerwing biplanes onward. Many had bought various Beech models for their own use. But the purchase by Captain Tom Dyer of a new Beechcraft Bonanza V35B for his personal business transport was unique.

Dyer, a United Airlines pilot for 25 years, had never flown a Beechcraft Bonanza before he placed his order. Nor had he flown in any light business aircraft since 1946. But the Beech reputation, affirmed by the Bonanza's very high resale value,

496

plus its precise adaptability to his own requirements, was enough for him. "The plane flies great," said Dyer after his first trial run. "And the low speed handling is just superb."

Results of the third quarter of fiscal 1979 that ended June 30 told the same sweet story: Record sales and earnings for the quarter and the year to date. Third quarter sales were $157,591,717 and earnings were $10,824,343. Nine-months sales came to $451,854,390 and earnings to $30,720,141. For the second time in the year, the annual cash dividend rate was increased — up to $1.00 per share from the previous $.92.

Beech Aircraft's management base was broadened on July 10 with the advancement of three seasoned executives. Edward C. Burns, group vice president since 1974, was elected executive vice president and given added responsibility for the engineering division and the entire revitalized commuter airline program. He also remained in charge of all manufacturing operations, procurement and industrial relations activities, quality control, flight test operations and program management.

Burns was well prepared to assume such heavy and far-ranging responsibilities. Joining Beech in 1940 as an engineering apprentice, he had since been involved in every major division of the company, enlarging his experience in managerial positions.

Max P. Eaton was elected vice president - production and Gary M. Hanssen vice president - industrial relations. A 38-year Beechcrafter, Eaton had been director of production since October, 1978. Hanssen, formerly director of industrial relations, had joined Beech at the Boulder Division in 1962 and transferred to Wichita in 1970.

Tapping a fresh source for the skilled labor that was increasingly scarce in Wichita, the company established a new precision parts production facility at Newton, Kansas. Handily located on the Newton Municipal Airport, 20 miles north of Beech Field, it was housed in a 46,000 sq. ft. building formerly occupied by Bede Aircraft. There, 100 Beechcrafters carried on precision assembly of landing gears and other critical units and parts for all models.

A milestone delivery in mid-July was that of the U. S. Army's 100th Beechcraft C-12 personnel/utility transport. It was noted that with the worldwide full field support provided by Beech

497

Aerospace Services, Inc., the Army's and Air Force's C-12 fleets had maintained exceptional operational readiness rates, substantially bettering the services' contract requirement — an impressive testimonial to the quality of Beech products and servicing.

"Here comes Mr. Bonanza!" Word got around fast at Beech Aircraft that Leonard Hay of Rock Springs, Wyoming was taking delivery of his 27th Beechcraft Bonanza, a new A36TC model. Hay was making his annual purchase earlier than usual — a recurring event that won him the affectionate "Mr. Bonanza" nickname as the company's most loyal Bonanza customer. He was, it developed, in a hurry for his A36TC because it was turbocharged. Its outstanding high altitude performance would be extremely useful around his ranch in Wyoming — which is high country any way you go at it.

The Republic of China followed up its 1978 purchase of a Beechcraft Super King Air with a $4.6 million contract issued July 23 for Beech MQM-107A missile targets, plus spares and a ground tracking station. Taiwan's third follow-on missile target contract, the new award brought that nation's MQM-107A purchases to a total of $8.4 million.

In a warm ending to a torrid month, the U. S. Navy issued a $9-million plus contract on July 31 for more Beechcraft T-34C turboprop trainers. Completion of deliveries in April, 1981, would equip the Navy with an all-Beechcraft fleet of 184 T-34C jetprop-powered airplanes for its basic and primary single-engine training program.

The company's foremost franchise holder in terms of dollar volume, Hangar One, Inc. launched an expansion program based on the Beech Aero Center/Aero Club concept. New Centers were opened in Jacksonville, Florida and Monroe, North Carolina, and a new Aero Club was set up at Chattanooga, Tennessee. With the delivery of a fleet of nine Beechcraft Sundowners — one for each of its nine locations — Hangar One went on building for an even greater future with Beech Aircraft.

Within a span of one week, two multi-million dollar contracts were received from perennial Beech customers. Bell Helicopter Textron signed a $12 million contract on August 28 for more Beech-built JetRanger III airframe assemblies. The award would sustain Beech airframe production for Bell, which began in 1967, through the calendar year of 1980.

The Space Systems Group of Rockwell International, principal contractor for NASA's Space Shuttle Orbiter, followed on September 4 with a $13.2 million contract for additional cryogenic liquid oxygen and hydrogen storage assemblies to be produced at Beech/Boulder. The award continued a team effort by Rockwell and Beech that had been continuous since the 1962 Apollo space flight program.

Among many remembrances from friends and well-wishers far and near, Chairman O. A. Beech received a heart-warming armload of greetings and gifts from 5th and 6th grade students at Lincoln Elementary School in Wichita on her birthday, September 25. In addition to wishing her a happy birthday, the students used the occasion to tell Mrs. Beech what they had learned about aviation.

Their teacher, Mrs. Mary Margaret Orsman, had conducted their aviation studies with the help of a new teaching kit prepared by the Beech Aviation Education Department for elementary schools. Comprising three basic units with complete lesson plans and resource materials, it was offered to teachers at a low, non-profit price. The kit was the latest of many teaching aids originated by Marion Stevens, director, and Mary Enstrom, aviation education specialist, since the department's founding in 1967.

Air-minded movie fans at Beech were meanwhile delighted to meet two of their favorite flying characters in person — Superman, and Joe Patroni of the "Airport" movie series. In real life, Superman is star actor Christopher Reeve, and he does his flying much more comfortably in his Beechcraft Bonanza A36. Reeve dropped in on Beech Field at about the same time that Joe Patroni (actually movie star George Kennedy) took delivery on his own new Beechcraft Bonanza — like Reeve's plane, a Model A36. Kennedy and Reeve had one thing more in common: both were ardent Beechcraft fans.

Long-range prospects were favorable for sales of Beech products to the People's Republic of China; and early sales possible for such items as Beechcraft Super King Air jetprops equipped for special missions such as aerial resource surveys and mapping.

That was the judgment of an International Division staff member who visited the world's most populous nation.

Beech Aircraft had been the sole representative of the general aviation industry on a 20-member trade mission, headed by Kansas Governor John Carlin, that met with officials of the People's Republic of China. Their discussions advanced hopes for mutually beneficial trade relations between Mainland China and the United States.

Immediate and long-range prospects alike gleamed brightly for Beech at the 32nd National Business Aircraft Association annual meeting held September 25-27 at Atlanta, Georgia. Displayed at DeKalb Peachtree Airport during the industry's U. S. showcase event were seven Beechcrafts with strong appeal to corporate and business users: a Beechcraft Super King Air, Beechcraft King Air B100, Beechcraft King Air F90, Beechcraft Duke B60, Beechcraft Baron 58P and 58TC models, and a Beechcraft Duchess 76 light twin.

The new Beechcraft King Air F90, fresh from a triumphant 75-day nationwide demonstration tour, was the only commercial airplane on display at NBAA's downtown site in Congress Hall. Commanding attention with its distinctive Beech T-tail, the F90's high performance and payload clinched buying decisions that put many more orders on the books. The Beech goal of a billion-dollar backlog by September 30, announced by president Frank E. Hedrick at Atlanta, seemed sure to be reached.

The shape of things to come drew record crowds to the Beech display. On view was a full-size cabin and nose section mockup of the Beechcraft Commuter 1900, the largest of the company's new models projected for the burgeoning airline and corporate transportation markets.

Foreseeing an era of solid growth for commuter airlines following the 1978 Airline Deregulation Act, as well as continuing decentralization of American business, Beech Aircraft was advancing its long-range plans to renew the leadership earned in past years by its worldwide sales of 164 Beechcraft 99 Airliners. Confirmed at the NBAA meeting, those plans called for deliveries in 1981 of new Beechcraft Commuter C99's, featuring larger 750 shaft horsepower jetprop engines, a longer-life main spar, and other important improvements.

500

The Beechcraft Commuter 1900 would be the ultimate version of the famous series. Equipped with efficient, economical 1,000 shaft horsepower jetprop engines, it would seat 19 passengers in its pressurized cabin and transport them and their luggage at 300 miles per hour for more than 639 miles with IFR fuel reserves.

The Commuter 1900 display at Atlanta was no mere wishful dream. Commitments for the new Beechcrafts-to-be had been made by some two dozen of the larger American commuter operators, plus a number of foreign airlines, to a total of more than $200 million. As to the future, the sky was the limit.

Beech Aircraft's seventh consecutive year of record earnings and sales became an established fact with the close on September 30 of the 1979 fiscal year. Sales of $607,776,654 topped the $600 million goal announced when the year began. Earnings of $41,594,671 were 15 percent higher than in 1978, the previous record year.

Total 1979 commercial sales came to $515,858,173, including $122,292,685 in international sales. Conversions of debentures into common stock totaled $9,337,000, leaving only $11,315,000 of the original $30 million issue outstanding. Long-term debt was thereby reduced to less than $14.8 million, in contrast to assets of $314.6 million and working capital of $173.3 million. Beech Aircraft was in excellent condition, financially and in every other way.

*

Raytheon. "A beam of light from the gods."

Laurence K. Marshall, a founder in 1920 of the Raytheon Company at Lexington, Massachusetts, had coined the name for his enterprise from classical sources. From Old French "Ray", a beam of light; from the Greek "Theon", from the gods.

To Beech Aircraft Corporation, that name fitted perfectly into the context of the largest transaction in the company's history. On October 1, 1979, the managements of Raytheon and Beech reached an agreement in principle to merge.

The merger would be effected through an exchange of common stock. Under the agreement, each share of Beech common stock would be exchanged for .775 of a share of Raytheon stock.

At the normal price range of both stocks, such an exchange

would provide a substantial increase to Beech stockholders in the value of their holdings. Raytheon's principals were quite content to pay a reasonable premium to join hands with Beech. After all, Beech Aircraft was a premium quality company, like their own.

The Beech preponderance of commercial domestic and international sales would give Raytheon a better balance between government-generated and commercial volume. Beech Aircraft's profitable and steadily growing sales would handily enlarge Raytheon's own increasing sales ($3.6 billion in its 1977 calendar/ fiscal year.) Management would impose no burdens. Raytheon consistently upheld a down-to-earth Yankee policy with its other eleven subsidiaries: If it works well, leave it alone.

Beech Aircraft likewise had much to gain in affiliating with Raytheon. Chairman O. A. Beech and President Frank E. Hedrick concisely summed up the gains in a joint statement: "This merger will provide our company with greater technological depth and product development capability to the benefit of our aircraft customers, our employees and our stockholders."

The similarities between Beech and Raytheon were almost uncanny. Beech had scored record results for its seventh consecutive year; Raytheon for its eighth consecutive year. Both companies worked at the frontiers of technology: Beech in high performance aircraft, aerospace support systems and allied products; and Raytheon in highly engineered, sophisticated electronics systems for many defense, commercial and medical applications. Their technology and products were ideally complementary, not competitive. And both stressed top quality in every one of their products.

Basically conservative, the managements of both companies achieved steady, planned growth through extensive research and development of new or improved products, and resourceful marketing on a worldwide scale. Raytheon Chairman Thomas L. Phillips and Raytheon President D. Brainerd Holmes shared with Mrs. Beech and Mr. Hedrick a complete dedication to America and a firm faith in the free enterprise system and the work ethic on which their own corporate and personal success was founded.

Given all these factors, there were obviously no great problems in reaching a meeting of minds on the merger agreement. Nor were any obstacles expected to its consummation. The transaction was ideal: both parties would gain much, and lose nothing. There remained only the matter of working out the details, and gaining the approval of Beech and Raytheon directors and stockholders — approval that seemed as sure as the next day's sunrise.

Addressing all employees on the day the agreement was announced, President Frank E. Hedrick stated: "It is planned that Beech will continue to be operated as a separate entity at its present locations, and Beech's board of directors and management will continue in their present positions." Detailing the advantages of the proposal, he made it clear that it would have no detrimental effects on any employee. "In summation," Hedrick concluded, "we will continue business as usual."

So it went: business as usual, with assured prospects of an even brighter future for Beechcrafters and their company. Marketing people noted that Raytheon President D. Brainerd Holmes, an enthusiastic pilot, had progressively developed a keen taste for Beech products. Starting with the purchase of a Beechcraft Bonanza, Mr. Holmes had moved up to a Beechcraft Baron when he earned a twin-engine rating. He then stepped up to the top of the line, with the delivery in mid-August of a new Beechcraft Super King Air to Raytheon. It was a classic example of the Beech "step-up" marketing concept in action.

In the bustle of great events, Beechcrafters and their company did not overlook their self-assumed obligations to the supportive agencies of their communities. Through the generosity of many, the Beech annual donation to the Wichita/Sedgwick County United Way was the largest cash contribution ever. The 1979 gift of $371,220 exceeded last year's record gift by $30,000. Gifts to United Way campaigns at other Beech facilities were in scale with those at Wichita.

A series of promotions announced on October 9 brought advancement to five thoroughly seasoned Beechcrafters. Charles W. Dieker, the company's secretary-treasurer since 1976, was elected vice president and treasurer. He had joined Beech Aircraft in 1965 as a tax accountant.

W. D. Wise, formerly vice president - advanced technology

and a 20-year Beechcrafter, was named vice president of the company's newly organized Commuter Division. His appointment to head up the Commuter program emphasized its importance in the company's projected growth.

Ila A. Alumbaugh was elected corporate secretary of Beech Aircraft. Mrs. Alumbaugh had joined the company in 1950 as a secretary, and moved up step by step to officership rank in 1972 as assistant secretary.

L. R. Damon was promoted to the corporate post of assistant treasurer and controller. Damon had joined Beech Aircraft in 1950 as a timekeeper and progressed in various finance assignments to an officership in 1976.

Harriette E. Bulmer was elected assistant secretary of the company and continued in her post as administrative assistant to the Chairman. A 35-year Beechcrafter, "Bette" Bulmer had served since 1960 as a secretary to Mrs. O. A. Beech.

"Biggest and best" aptly described Beech Aircraft's International Sales Conference at Wichita October 15-17. Responding to its theme of "US", more than 1,300 came from all over the world to share a record total of 276 awards for outstanding achievements.

Honored as the Beech "Man of the Year" for 1979 was W. Eric Hodson, group managing director of Beechcraft Sales S.A. (Pty.) Ltd., Johannesburg, South Africa. Hodson had directed the expansion of the company's share of market in that area to 40 percent over the past decade.

In domestic sales, Hangar One, Inc. captured two top awards. They nosed out Houston Beechcraft, Inc. and second runner-up Chaparral Aviation, Inc. for the Walter H. Beech Award. And for the fourth straight year, Hangar One, Inc. took home the Olive Ann Beech Award for top volume, with sales of more than $28 million.

A truly "grand" total of 101 Million Dollar sales managers and salesmen were honored for individual sales ranging from $1 to $7 million or more. And the Order of the Silver Eagles (franchises who had "flown" with Beech for 30 years or more) inducted three new members: Central Flying Service, Inc., Little Rock, Arkansas; Air Service, Inc., Greensboro, North Carolina; and Flightcraft, Inc., Portland, Oregon. "Profit Eagle" awards

504

went to Page Beechcraft, Inc., New York state; and Air Service, Inc.

For the third straight year, William C. Morales & Co. of Caracas, Venezuela, won the Olive Ann Beech Award for international sales leadership. Their 1979 sales were approximately $25 million.

The Walter H. Beech Award for outstanding international sales development was shared by three winners: Hawker Pacific Pty. Ltd. of Australia; Transair France S.A.; and United Beech International of Sweden.

A salute to the aviation press for its support of general aviation was a special feature of the Conference. Guests of honor were the deans of aviation journalism, George Haddaway and Leighton Collins. Lifelong friends of Beech, the pioneer editor-publishers of *Southern Flight/Flight Operations* and *Air Facts* magazines received special awards as their careers were retraced for conferees by William G. Robinson, vice president - corporate communications.

As usual, awards and cash grants were made to domestic and international outlets for superior service management and improvement of service and maintenance facilities. Beech did not slight its past customers.

And as always, the new Beechcrafts for 1980 were the top stars of the glittering show. There were 18 great models on display at Frank E. Hedrick Park — the name given to the handsomely landscaped static display area on ribbon-cutting ceremonies on October 15.

From year to year the wonder grew, that clear-cut advancements could be engineered in products so near to perfection as Beechcraft. Yet each year, the challenge was somehow met; and the 1980 lineup was no exception.

A new optional cargo door broadened the utility of the world's best-selling jetprops on the Beechcraft Super King Air 200. The new high-performance F90 advanced the state-of-the-art in the Beechcraft King Air 90 series. Redesigned seating and interiors provided greater comfort and spaciousness in all propeller-driven models, from the Beechcraft Duke to the Skipper Trainer. Mechanical refinements vied with new styling, color and fabric options throughout the line. New exterior styling and detail

505

choices added final touches of distinction. The 1980 Beech-crafts were clearly planned to excel, and they more than fulfilled that plan.

The scope of advanced technology at Beech was also demonstrated with the display of a Pontiac Phoenix sedan, modified by Beech/Boulder to use liquefied methane as its fuel. Test drives by conferees and news media proved the merits of the Beech LM system, comprised of a super-insulated cryogenic, 18-gallon fuel tank and a modified carburetor. Plans were under way for its initial marketing to fleet owners, who would profit most from its added savings and safety compared with conventional fuels.

Beech Aircraft had good news for the Wichita community in November. The recent formation of a special Beech-Wichita Industrial District had opened the way for expanded facilities at its nearly mile-square site at the city's east edge. So plans were announced on November 2 for the immediate construction of a $1 million, 50,000 sq. ft. building at the east border of Beech Field. The new Beech Plant IV would mean more jobs for Wichita area workers, and more money feeding into the community.

In return, good news came to Beech on November 6. After 16 years, the Federal Aviation Administration had decided to replace its faithful 1963 Beechcraft Queen Air Model 80 twins with newer aircraft. In an industry-wide competition, the FAA found its best buy to be (what else?) Beechcraft King Air C90 jetprops. Three new C90's were accordingly contracted for, with options for two more.

"You have a friend at Chase Manhattan" had long held true at Beech Aircraft. The company's relations with the world-famous New York bank were warm and cordial. On November 10, that friend dropped by for a visit. He was David Rockefeller, Chase Manhattan's chairman and chief executive officer. Friend David and other Chase Manhattan officers were breakfast guests of Beech management at the Beechcrafters' Activity Center, and afterward toured the plant. A good time was had by all.

A long and distinguished career came to an end on November

12 with the death of Mrs. Louise Thaden, a pioneer aviatrix who had set many records flying Travel Air and Staggerwing Beech biplanes. A close friend of Chairman O. A. Beech, Mrs. Thaden had learned to fly in 1928 with help from Mr. and Mrs. Beech. She set endurance and speed records in Beech-built Travel Air 3000 and B-4000 biplanes, and with Blanche Noyes as her navigator, flew a Staggerwing Beechcraft C17R to victory over higher-powered twin and single-engine competitors in the 1936 Bendix Transcontinental Speed Dash. A frequent visitor to Wichita in later years, Mrs. Thaden ferried many new Beechcrafts to their destinations. Throughout more than a half-century, Mrs. Thaden accomplished much to advance the progress of aviation.

Late 1979 deliveries to customers of the International Division illustrated the worldwide appeal of standard and special-purpose Beechcrafts. For example, the Republic of Ivory Coast in West Africa came to Wichita for a six-plane fleet of Beechcraft Bonanza F33C's for use as primary trainers by its air force. Strictly "off-the-shelf" models, the aircraft carried high-frequency (HF) radio equipment for long-distance communication.

Royal Air Maroc, the official airline of Morocco, purchased two Beechcraft Super King Air jetprops for final training of its pilots transitioning into its fleet of Boeing 747, 707, 727 and 737 jet transports. Capt. Sala Naji, chief of Royal Air Maroc's Flight Training Center and a 747 captain, had taken his own primary training in a Beechcraft Model D-18 years ago. "We knew the Beechcraft King Air well," said Capt. Naji, "and we needed a good twin-engine training aircraft."

The Austrian government took delivery of a Beechcraft Super King Air equipped for photogrammetry with two vertical aerial cameras and associated special equipment. The full-color, black-and-white and infrared photographs produced by its two 300-lb. cameras would be used for planning highways, locating hydroelectric generating stations, and studying tree usage and replacement in Austria's forests.

Halfway around the globe, the Royal Malaysian Government purchased its second Beechcraft jetprop. A new Beechcraft Super King Air equipped as a flight calibration aircraft, it joined a Beechcraft King Air 100 already serving in flight calibration duties. Malaysia's new plane also became the sixth Beechcraft of the King Air series to be purchased in Southeast Asia for use in flight calibration missions.

Builders of advanced military aircraft, the Northrop Corporation ranked among Beech Aircraft's most knowledgeable customers. Their first Beechcraft Super King Air, based in Saudi Arabia, had logged more than 4,100 hours, operating in the 120-degree heat, gritty dust and sand of the Arabian desert, with almost no shelter and only routine maintenance. Its performance under those harsh conditions prompted a decision by Northrop to purchase two more Beechcraft Super King Air transports for use on their daily shuttle runs between Edwards Air Force Base at Palmdale and Northrop's facility at Hawthorne, California.

So it went the world over. Beechcrafts were the airplanes of choice everywhere that demanding or uncommon missions had to be unfailingly performed. The record they made was a literally priceless asset.

On November 30, directors of Raytheon and Beech jointly approved a detailed draft of their proposed merger agreement. Clearing away one more item, Beech Aircraft issued a call on December 20 for redemption of all remaining outstanding convertible debentures. Their conversion into Beech common stock would produce substantial gains for their holders, just as the merger itself would benefit stockholders of both companies. A great new era was unfolding for both Raytheon and Beech.

Chapter 43

"Raytheon, Western Division."

That's how President Frank E. Hedrick answered a phone call from Thomas L. Phillips, Chairman of Raytheon Company, on the morning of February 6, 1980.

His reply was timely. One hour later, stockholders of Beech Aircraft Corporation approved the company's proposed merger with Raytheon by a majority of 98.82 percent of the votes cast. In an earlier meeting at Lexington, Massachusetts that morning, Raytheon stockholders had taken only 22 minutes to vote their approval of the merger by a 99.7 percent majority — much as expected by the managements of both companies.

The final meeting of Beech Aircraft stockholders that morning was a happy one. Topping the company's seventh straight record year in fiscal 1980 came news that the first quarter of fiscal 1980 (October-December 1979) had reached all-time highs, with $160,690,790 in sales and $10,991,255 in earnings. Ahead were strong prospects for more new records, with corresponding benefits for Beech and Raytheon.

Describing the new affiliation, President Hedrick quipped: "Raytheon is supposed to have $600 million in the bank. You stockholders now own 25 percent of that. So I've already requested our $150 million." Actually, he amended, Beech planned to finance growth from its own operations.

The tally of last-minute votes turned in at the meeting was completed near its end. "It takes longer to count nine million votes than you might think," Hedrick observed. But it was done, and the official results were announced at 11:50 a.m.

The moment passed into history, with Hedrick's assurance that "The Beech name will continue . . . the Beech product identity will be preserved." Looking at his notes, he observed: "It says here that the meeting is over."

With just a trace of emotion, he added: "This is quite a day in our lives. We've worked on it for a long time. We hope it turns out the way we've planned it."

That brought a standing ovation. An outpouring of appreciation greeted the new era.

Formalities were completed February 8, when officers of both companies met at Raytheon's corporate headquarters and signed closing documents effecting the merger. It was a welding of winners. In 1979, Raytheon had earned $179 million on sales of $3.727 billion. Beech sales of $626 million in calendar 1979 had

509

produced $43 million in earnings. The addition of 10,900 Beech employees increased Raytheon's worldwide work force to more than 78,000.

The pooling of interests continued with the election February 27 of Chairman O. A. Beech and President Frank E. Hedrick to Raytheon's board of directors when they attended its regular meeting at Lexington. Their welcome from their 12 fellow directors of Raytheon was warm and cordial. East met West with mutual appreciation.

In turn, directors of the Beech Aircraft Corporation elected Raytheon Chairman Thomas L. Phillips and President D. Brainerd Holmes to Beech's board at its April 8 regular quarterly meeting. The newcomers brought with them a wealth of experience.

Phillips was named Board Chairman of Raytheon Company in May 1965, and chief executive officer in 1968, having previously served as its president since 1964. Earning B.S.E.E. and M.S.E.E. degrees from Virginia Polytechnic Institute, he joined Raytheon in 1948 as an electronics design engineer. Moving upward in engineering and management, he served as manager of the Hawk ground-to-air and the Sparrow III air-to-air guided missile systems and in 1958 received the U. S. Navy Meritorious Public Service Award for his outstanding work on the Sparrow III system. He was elected a vice president of Raytheon in 1960, in charge of its Missile and Space Division, and in 1961 was named executive vice president.

Holmes became president of Raytheon Company in May 1975, having served as executive vice president since January 1969, and a senior vice president and director since 1963. Receiving his B.S.E.E. degree in 1943 from Cornell University, he did graduate work at Bowdoin College and Massachusetts Institute of Technology, then moved into management with Western Electric, Bell Telephone Laboratories, and R.C.A. He came to Raytheon in 1963 from NASA, where he served as the first Director of Manned Space Flight for the National Aeronautics and Space Administration. There he set up the organization that led America's efforts to reach the moon, leaving upon successful

510

completion of the Mercury program. He holds the NASA Medal for Outstanding Leadership, and the Arnold Air Society's Paul T. Johns Award for contributions to aeronautics and astronautics.

With such an aptly complementary amalgam of proven talents and experience to provide direction, Beech and Raytheon became better than ever fitted to move forward together. President Hedrick's hopes were well founded.

Meanwhile, it was "business as usual" at Beech Aircraft. Expanding further, the company exercised a multi-million dollar option in January to buy the former corporate headquarters of Pizza Hut, Inc., after leasing the building for some time. The handsome, modern two-level structure provided 53,000 sq. ft. of working space for 250 employees of Procurement and other departments, handily adjacent to Beech Field. Mrs. Mary Carr of Materiel won an employee contest to rename the building. Her entry: Frank E. Hedrick Center.

A steadfast buyer of Beech-built airframes since 1967, Bell Helicopter Textron placed an order in January for $14.5 million worth of JetRanger III airframe assemblies. Their new order called for deliveries throughout 1981, supplementing an existing contract that carried Beech production of JetRanger airframes through 1980. It brought Bell's purchases from Beech to a total of more than $164 million.

The spirit of comradeship long shared by Beechcrafters was celebrated in the 40th birthday of their own recreational and social organization — the Beechcraft Employees Club. Starting as a flower fund, the BEC (its popular nickname) had grown to include more than a score of special interest groups that ranged from baseball to bridge, the staging of many large-scale events, and operation of the 340-acre Beech Lake recreation and fishing area north of Plant I. The BEC also offered a host of services, from discount tickets to local attractions and vacation tours to the supervision of food and drink vending machines throughout the plants.

Employee-operated, the BEC was self-supporting with a yearly budget topping $175,000. Beech management encouraged the BEC and provided many facilities, on the premise that people who work together should play together. "BEC: a Fellowship of Beechcrafters" was living up to its name.

511

Another "Fellowship of Beechcrafters" was that of alert employees submitting ideas for improvements to the company's Productivity Council. As the year began, 90 employees shared more than $25,000 in cash, handed out in the latest round of semi-annual awards for important betterments.

The company advanced its standing among Kansas' leading industrial firms with a $43 million increase in expenditures in its home state in fiscal 1979, compared with 1978. Beech contributions of $211 million to the economy of Kansas included more than $135 million in statewide payrolls. Beechcrafters and their company had also given more than a half-million dollars to charitable causes during the year.

Productivity was likewise scaling new peaks. The highest single quarter in history was scored in the first quarter of fiscal 1980 (October-December 1979). Sales totaled $160,690,790 and earnings $10,991,225. Volume was projected to exceed $685 million by September 30.

Special efforts were made, and production facilities rearranged, to boost production of the Beechcraft King Air series — long the best-selling jetprop aircraft in general aviation. As a result, new all-time records were set. In December 1979, 39 turbine-powered twins were delivered — a record topped in April 1980 with 43 units. The step-up went on, with completion rates raised from 1.5 to a new high of 1.7 units per day.

The step-up was timely. Commercial, international and military sales of the Beechcraft King Air series were brisk. U. S. government orders included a $25 million follow-on Navy contract for more UC-12B (commercial Beechcraft Super King Air) utility transports in February; U. S. Army orders for new C-12D twins equipped with 850 shp engines and cargo doors to the tune of $12 million in April, and $6.8 million more in July; and two more Beechcraft King Air C90's for the Federal Aviation Administration in March.

The Army also issued a $10.3 million contract in February for continued worldwide support of its C-12's by Beech Aerospace Services, Inc., which had helped to thriftily maintain a high readiness rate for the military's Beechcraft turbine-powered twins. And the U. S. Navy completed its new all-Beechcraft fleet of multiengine advanced pilot trainers, with acceptance in

512

June of its 61st T-44A jetprop twin — a military version of the commercial Beechcraft King Air Model 90 series.

The International Division was setting new records. Its customers accepted a new high number of 13 Beechcraft King Air models in May, bringing total export deliveries of jetprop twins to 51 since the year began. The Navy of Ecuador added three more units to its 20-plane fleet of Beechcraft T-34C-1 trainers, and ordered a Beechcraft Super King Air jetprop for 1981 delivery.

Beechcraft de Mexico became full-line distributors for Mexico, sustaining sales and full service from the strategically located international Benito Juarez Airport. They had bought the excellent facilities of the former Aeronaves de Mexico, S.A. in Mexico City. And a Beechcraft Maritime Patrol demonstrator ended a tour of Central and South America, Africa and Europe in May at the Hanover Air Show in West Germany — a major general aviation showcase event. There, the all-new Beechcraft Skipper T-tail trainer also made its European debut.

Export sales of piston-engine Beechcrafts vied with those of jetprops, covering the entire spectrum of buyers. Typical was a group flyaway southward of five Beechcrafts sold by Latourrette and Parini, distributors for Paraguay. A Beechcraft Baron 58TC went to Paraguayan lumberman Jose Oricchio, and a Beechcraft Baron B55 to cattle rancher Clertan Mereira. One Beechcraft Bonanza A36 was for Yacare, a cattle business, and another for international trader Alerjo Mendieta. And a Beechcraft Duchess went to Cominter, an international coffee and soybean trader.

On the domestic front, commercial sales of the top-of-the-line Beechcraft King Air jetprops continued their steady increase. Creative salesmanship and financing upheld sales of other models, meeting the challenge of inflation-generated high interest rates and a sluggish economy. The company supplied analytical cash-flow computer printouts for individual prospects, based on information sent in by salesmen, that often proved instrumental in closing sales of new Beechcrafts.

The Beechcraft Executive Flight Plan nationwide charter service, plus the fast-growing Beech Aero Clubs, which in March were active on more than 113 airports in 39 states, supplied a

513

steady stream of prospects to Beechcraft's seasoned force of sales professionals. Further support came from the aviation press, consistently speaking well of Beech products. For example, *Plane and Pilot* magazine chose the Beechcraft Bonanza A36TC as its 1980 "Plane of the Year". The lead-in to its test pilot's exhaustive performance report stated that "The Beechcraft Bonanza is considered by many to be the best aerodynamically designed airplane ever offered to the general aviation public."

A historic first flight highlighted activities of the company's Commuter Division in 1980. On Friday, June 20, the prototype Beechcraft Commuter C99 jetprop soared from Beech Field in Wichita on a 45-minute flight that opened its exacting 17-week certification testing program. Senior project test pilot Jim Dolbee reported that "Everything went as planned, with no surprises." Preparations for C99 production at Selma, Alabama moved rapidly forward, concurrently with overall engineering and development of quick-convertible passenger/cargo interiors for the advanced 19-passenger Beechcraft Commuter 1900.

Two company officers received honors early in the year. In February, Michael G. Neuburger, senior vice president - International Division, was cited by *Aviation Week and Space Technology* magazine for his achievements in developing and promoting special mission applications of business. His activities, the magazine reported, had "significantly broadened the market."

President Frank E. Hedrick was initiated in April as an honorary member of the alumni chapter of Wichita State University's business fraternity, Alpha Kappa Psi. His induction came "In recognition of his outstanding involvement in the Wichita business community and for long-time contributions to the Free Enterprise system."

A report to employees published in April gave Beechcrafters a good look at their new parent company. Some highlights:

"In the latest FORTUNE Magazine listing, Raytheon ranks as the nation's 39th largest employer and 73rd largest industrial firm in sales. It ranks ninth on the Defense Department's list of top 100 prime contractors. And DUN'S REVIEW recently ranked Raytheon among the five best managed companies in the nation.

514

"Raytheon is among the leading makers of missile systems, producing among others the Army's Hawk ground-to-air missiles, and for the Navy and Air Force, the Sparrow and Sidewinder air-to-air missiles. A leading producer of radar systems for naval vessels and for air defense, its recent new contracts from the Air Force and Navy call for electronic counter-measure systems designed to jam communications between enemy ships and planes.

"Among major electronic systems, it now produces air traffic control systems for several nations and is a major supplier of missile systems to U. S. allies overseas. Raytheon's foreign sales topped $1.1 billion last year.

"Raytheon produces the data processing systems used by more than 50 airlines for reservations and seat assignments. Other commercial electronic products include X-ray diagnostic systems, marine sonar and other systems, laser welders, and a wide range of transistors, integrated circuits and specialized electronic tubes.

"Now the fifth largest U. S. producer of major appliances, its affiliates make Amana microwave ovens, refrigerators, freezers and air conditioners. Last Fall, Raytheon acquired Speed Queen Laundry Products and Modern Maid built-in ranges. Other members of the Raytheon family include Seismograph Service Corp., Badger Co., United Engineers & Constructors, Inc., D. C. Heath, Caedmon Records, Iowa Manufacturing and El-Jay, Inc. All are ranked topnotch in their respective fields." Clearly, Beech Aircraft was in the best of company.

Presented by Kansas Gas & Electric Company, in cooperation with the Sedgwick County Soil Conservation District, was an award to Beech Aircraft for outstanding conservation efforts at Beech Lake throughout the past 25 years. Beech was cited "For excellence in conservation of soil and water resources on an urban tract of land."

Unique was a June event at the Beech Lake recreation area. Ann Chapman, an Upholstery Department employee, persuaded her husband-to-be, Bill Godwin, that the lakesite would be the perfect spot for their wedding. So the knot was tied at a departmental picnic that provided a host of well-wishers for the happy couple.

The Beechcraft Training Center meanwhile celebrated the graduation of its 25,000th student. Dick Kelly, owner of Kelly Lime and Rock Company at Edina, Missouri was the milestone graduate. A 2,000-hour-plus commercial pilot with single-engine and multiengine and instrument ratings, Kelly was preparing to fly his new Beechcraft King Air F90 — the seventh Beechcraft he had bought for business use since 1966.

Since its founding in 1964. the Beechcraft Training Center had grown to offer 27 pilot, avionics and maintenance courses, taught in both English and Spanish by 24 full-time instructors. Models covered ranged from single-engine Beechcraft Bonanzas all the way to the top-of-the-line Beechcraft Super King Air. Established as a service to customers, the Center had won widespread praise in general aviation circles as another step toward safer flying and better maintenance of Beech products.

New record sales were happily scored as Beech Aircraft moved on July 1 into the final quarter of its 1980 fiscal year. Sales had increased 17 percent for the past nine months, compared with the same period in 1979.

Dollar totals were included in Raytheon's consolidated sales and earnings, which were reported on a calendar year basis. For the first six months of 1980, Raytheon sales of $2.447 billion were up by $279 million, compared with the first half of 1979; and earnings of $137.6 million showed a $20.8 million increase. Acquisition of the Beech Aircraft Corporation shared credit with government electronic systems for the increases. "Beech — a Raytheon Company" was doing well for itself and its corporate parent.

Top management changes early in July enhanced the company's capabilities to continue doing well. Approved by its directors was the newly-created Office of the President, in which responsibility for direction and coordination of all activities and planning would be shared by Frank E. Hedrick, president, and Edward C. Burns, executive vice president.

Stewart M. Ayton was promoted to the post of senior vice president - marketing, taking charge of all domestic commercial marketing activities. A Beech Aircraft vice president since 1977, Ayton had served as executive vice president and general manager of Beech Holdings, Inc., the company's domestic marketing subsidiary, since 1973. Under his leadership, the Beech-owned retail stores and service facilities had grown from one outlet in 1962 to a total of 16 sales and service centers which in 1977 produced $166.347 million in sales. While he formally joined the company in 1961, Ayton's actual field experience in sales of Beechcraft products had been continuous since September, 1940.

John H. (Jack) Funsch was promoted to replace Ayton as executive vice president of Beech Holdings, Inc. from his former post as its vice president. A former Navy pilot, Funsch had joined the Beech marketing staff in 1959.

"War on Waste" was the thrust of a company-wide program that came from the new Office of the President. Executive vice president E. C. Burns pointed out that all Beechcrafters could help curb inflation and control costs by fighting waste of supplies, parts and energy. Careless scrapping of repairable parts, for example, could cause production and delivery delays costing $993 a day in interest alone on just one Beechcraft King Air. And smaller savings, multiplied by the number of workers at Beech, would reach significant totals. Employees quickly grasped the point: Conservation was a logical adjunct to their efforts to uphold maximum productivity.

Colorado Beechcrafters celebrated 25 years of growth in July, with the Silver Anniversary of the Boulder Division. Established on July 10, 1955 as a modest extension of the Wichita engineering department, Boulder had moved in 1957 to its current 1,500-acre site and pioneered in the then top-secret field of cryogenic (super-cold) research, development and production. That specialty won key assignments for Beech throughout the nation's space programs, from its beginnings onward to production of a Space Shuttle Orbiter ground support system under a $2.5 million NASA contract awarded in April, 1980. Production of Beech-designed missile targets, aircraft assemblies and special items also continued, together with development of cryogenic LM (liquefied methane) automotive and aircraft fuel systems.

Boulder Division employees gained more to celebrate in August. Their LM fuel systems offered such attractive prospects that the company established a new Alternative Energy Division, involving both international and domestic markets. Michael G. Neuburger, senior vice president - International Di-

517

vision, was appointed officer in charge of the new division, in addition to his International Division responsibilities.

Many demonstrations of Beech systems using liquefied fuels, most recently in May and July, had aroused widespread interest. "We are excited about the possibilities for Beech in the area of alternative fuels", said Neuburger. "The opportunities are tremendous and the interest in both domestic and international markets is high."

Salina Beechcrafters celebrated, too, with the delivery on July 30 of the 300th pressurized Beechcraft Baron 58P. They were pleasantly surprised to find its purchaser, Ray Carpenter of Indianapolis, on hand to accept his new Beechcraft as it was rolled out. Planned to serve Century 21 and its 250 real estate brokers in Indiana and Kentucky, 58P No. 300 replaced Carpenter's previous Beechcraft Baron B55.

Veteran employees who had helped build the first Beechcraft Bonanzas in 1947 thrilled to a visit in August to Beech Field of D-9, the ninth Model 35 of the original Bonanza series. Western Airlines pilot Bob Picard of San Pedro, California had painstakingly restored the 33-year-old classic to as-new condition and proudly named it his "Cloud Nine."

His visit recalled a statement made by Beech when the Model 35 was introduced: "When the Bonanza was first designed, one of our basic requirements was that the airplane should be able to give approximately 2,000,000 miles of safe operation without unusual maintenance expense." "Cloud Nine" appeared ready to fulfill that requirement and more.

Beech Aircraft's ties with its parent company were reinforced with the election in September of Chairman O. A. Beech to the executive committee of Raytheon's board of directors. And President Frank E. Hedrick joined five other board members on the Raytheon finance committee.

Corporate and business aircraft pilots and owners headed the throngs flocking to view the company's exhibits at the 33rd annual National Business Aircraft Association convention September 23-25 at Kansas City. Experience had taught them to expect much from Beech, and as usual, their expectations were more than met. Outstanding was a fully detailed, "hands-on" concept design cockpit mockup, equipped with a dual cathode

Maj. Gen. Clifton von Kann, president of the National Aeronautic Association, presents Chairman O. A. Beech with the Wright Brothers Memorial Trophy. From left, von Kann, Senator Jennings Randolph, Senator Nancy Landon Kassebaum, Mrs. Beech and Senator Bob Dole, who served as master of ceremonies.

Chairman O. A. Beech received the "Sands of Time" Kitty Hawk Civilian Award, December 5, 1980. From left, Frank E. Hedrick, Vice Chairman; Dr. Allen Puckett, Chairman of the Board, Hughes Aircraft Company; Mrs. Beech and George Moody, President, Los Angeles Area Chamber of Commerce

A milestone in Beech Aircraft history: first flight of the Beechcraft Commuter C99, June 20, 1980.

518A

Dick Kelly (third from right) receives a Beechcraft Staggerwing print signed by Chairman O. A. Beech (second from right), and President Frank E. Hedrick, center, honoring him as the 25,000th graduate of the Beechcraft Training Center. Also participating (left to right): George Rodgers, vice president - domestic commercial marketing; Gary Phillips, Executive Beechcraft salesman; Dan Meisinger, president, Topeka Aircraft Sales; and (far right) Bob Taylor, manager - technical training.

Bob Pickard brings Serial No. D-9, the ninth production Beechcraft Bonanza, his "Cloud Nine," back to the Home of Beechcraft for a visit.

With complete contractor logistics support by Beech Aerospace Services, Inc., (BASI), United States Navy, Marines, Army and Air Force Beechcraft C-12 utility transports maintained high readiness rates for operation worldwide.

518B

ray display Collins EFDS-85 Electronic Flight Director System. Advancing the state of the art in corporate aircraft avionics and instrumentation, it was similar to that developed for the Boeing 757.

Offered for immediate delivery to Beechcraft Super King Air operators was the new Beechcraft Flight Planning Computer. This pocket-sized device provided near-instant solutions for complicated aircraft loading, flight and fuel requirement problems. Coupling a Hewlett-Packard HP-41C computer with a Beech Aircraft-developed plug-in module, it enabled dramatic improvements in fuel efficiency while reducing pilot workload. For example, on a trip from Wichita to Bedford, Massachusetts (1,224 nautical miles), the computer's flight information allowed the crew to save more than 500 pounds of fuel — better than 800 gallons — while extending the time enroute by only six minutes.

New all-time records were set for the eighth consecutive year during Beech Aircraft's 1980 fiscal year that ended September 30. Substantially exceeding projected figures, sales of more than $719 million topped 1979's total of $607.777 million by better than 18 percent. Raytheon's 1980 nine-months sales and earnings were both up by 18.1 percent, compared with those of 1979.

To simplify future reporting, the Beech fiscal year was adjusted to correspond with that of Raytheon, running on a calendar year basis from January 1 through December 31. Beech and Raytheon results were thus placed on common ground.

A landmark long familiar to thousands of pilots vanished from Beech Field in October. The 36-year-old, skeleton frame control tower was dismantled to make room for progress. Replacing it was a new, fully enclosed four-story tower, equipped with the latest state-of-the-art communications gear to expedite the field's more than 40,000 yearly aircraft movements.

The Beech Aircraft Foundation announced $29,000 in college scholarship grants in October to 43 students who were children or dependents of Beech employees. Grades, activities and need were criteria applied by an independent panel of educators in choosing winners. And Beechcrafters and their company pledged a new high of $480,405 to United Way agencies in Wichita,

519

Salina, Liberal and Boulder, largely through the Beech Golden Rule Plan for employees' charitable contributions.

"Winners" was the theme of the 1981 International Sales Conference held at Wichita October 27-29; and it aptly summed up the sales organization's long sequence of record-breaking achievements and the promise of more victories ahead.

Beech Aircraft's highest honor went to Michael M. (Mike) Gordon, named "Man of the Year" for 1980. At the head of Beechcraft West at Van Nuys, California, since 1969, Gordon had led his sales force to many victories, including five awards in 1980.

For the fifth straight year, Hangar One, Inc. earned the Olive Ann Beech Award for highest dollar total deliveries. The Walter H. Beech Award for highest area sales went to Chaparral Aviation, Dallas, Texas, corporate aviation products; Beechcraft West, Van Nuys, for executive aviation products; and Beechcraft West, Van Nuys again, for Aero Center aviation products.

Ten individual salesmen were welcomed into marketing's Legion of Honor; and a total of 97 managers and salesmen were hailed as Million Dollar Salesmen for exceeding or reaching seven-figure totals. Profit Eagle Awards went to Page Beechcraft, Inc. and Mission Beechcraft. Order Planning Program and B-SAF (Service Expansion) cash awards went to 67 Aviation and Aero Centers to the tune of more than $3.7 million.

William C. Morales & Co., C.A., of Venezuela, won the Olive Ann Beech Award for International sales leadership for the fourth time in a row. The Walter H. Beech Memorial Award was shared by four International outlets: C. Itoh Aviation Co. Ltd., Japan; Transair France S.A., France; United Beech International, Sweden; and Young Brothers Development Company Ltd., Republic of China/Taiwan. Legion of Honor Sales Achievement Awards went to 16 individual salesmen all over the world.

Outstanding global parts supply and service operations earned Million Dollar Parts & Equipment Sales Awards for Beechcraft Espanola S.A., Spain; Aero Baires S.A.C.I., Argentina; Transair France S.A., France; and C. Itoh Aviation Co. Ltd., Japan. The Frank E. Hedrick Excellence of Service Operations Management Award winner was Jose Marcelo Re, service manager of Aero Baires S.A.C.I., Argentina. At home and abroad alike, Beech

Aircraft always recognized the importance of good service to its customers.

Winners all the way were the 18 new 1981 Beechcrafts displayed at Frank E. Hedrick Park. Refinements throughout the line enhanced the appeal of each model. New styling, colors and interior options widened the range of choices for repeat buyers and prospective customers. "With products like these, we're sure to win in '81" was the consensus of the sales force.

The Uruguayan Navy mustered in its first turbine-powered airplane, with acceptance at Beech Field in October by Capitan de Fragata Rodolfo Grolero of a Beechcraft Super King Air Maritime Patrol aircraft. First of its kind in the southern hemisphere, the long-range jetprop twin was scheduled to patrol 50,000 square miles of the South Atlantic on fisheries control and search-and-rescue missions. It joined a Model 18 Twin Beech flown since 1961 by the Navy of Uruguay.

Commuter Airline Association of America members enjoyed their first public viewing of the Beechcraft Commuter C99 at their annual convention in November at Phoenix, Arizona. Disclosure of a change to Pratt & Whitney PT6A-36 engines, designed specifically for commuter operations with separate gas generator and power modules to minimize maintenance and spares supply costs, won enthusiastic approval. Prospective buyers, who had already registered firm intentions to buy more than $200 million worth of the new Beechcrafts, also welcomed the new airline-standard seats and overall airline-standard concept integral in the Beechcraft Commuter product line.

The Swedish Defense Administration awarded Beech a $500,000 contract in November for production of digital flight computers. The robot controllers were to be installed in Boulder-built MQM-107A "Streaker" missile targets previously purchased from the company.

Bright prospects intensified for the new Alternative Energy Division, with the passage by Congress of a bill to explore technologies in uses of methane as a transportation fuel. There would surely be a thriving market for Beech liquefied methane systems, following more widespread use of plentiful methane as an alternative to petroleum energy sources.

The Federal Aviation Administration enlarged its fleet of Beechcraft jetprops, with a competitively awarded lease of four T-tail Beechcraft King Air F90's. On delivery in mid-1981, the FAA would be flying nine Beechcraft King Air transports — five C90 models already in use, plus the new additions. Purchase options were included in the lease.

On December 5, Mrs. O. A. Beech was the guest of honor at ceremonies conducted by the Los Angeles Area Chamber of Commerce at Beverly Hills, California. There she received the 1980 "Sands of Time" Kitty Hawk Award, commemorating the 77th anniversary of powered flight and presented to Mrs. Beech in recognition of her contributions to aviation.

The year closed on the happiest of notes. Aviation's highest honor, the Wright Brothers Memorial Trophy, was presented to the company's chairman and co-founder, Mrs. O. A. Beech, at a gala dinner and dance in Washington, D.C.

The guest list of 1,300 included the most prestigious names in aviation — all gathered to honor Mrs. Beech, the first woman to receive the illustrious award.

The trophy itself was a beautifully crafted, authentic replica in miniature of the original airplane built by Orville and Wilbur Wright, which made man's first powered flight on December 17, 1903 at Kill Devil Hill, North Carolina. It was presented to Mrs. Beech by Maj. Gen. Clifton von Kann (ret.), president of the National Aeronautic Association which sponsored the award, "In recognition of significant public service of enduring value to aviation in the United States."

Responding to a standing ovation, the acceptance speech by Mrs. Beech was brief and sincere. "Thank you very much from a grateful heart", she said.

As a fitting postlude to the honors accorded to Mrs. Beech, the company and its corporate parent, Raytheon, together reported record results for 1980 on December 31. Beech Aircraft sales for the calendar year rose to $760.9 million-plus, up more than 21 percent compared with 1979. Raytheon sales of more than $5 billion increased 14.9 percent, and net earnings of $282.3 million rose 17.5 percent, compared with 1979. Beech sales for the fourth quarter (Oct.-Dec.) were the highest in history for any three-months period, reaching more than $262 million.

Many companies had lost ground in the recession year of 1980. Yet it was the tenth consecutive record-breaking year for Raytheon, and the eighth consecutive record year for Beech Aircraft.

Chapter 44

More than 1,000 members and guests of the Beech Supervisors Club witnessed history in the making at their annual management dinner presentation on January 10, 1981 in Walter H. Beech Hall of the Beechcrafters Activity Center.

Near its end, President Frank E. Hedrick electrified the group by saying: "Tonight, it is my special privilege and pleasure to announce a major change in the executive management staff of the Beech Aircraft Corporation."

Breaking the suspenseful silence, he added, "Mrs. Beech and I, with the unanimous consent of the Beech Aircraft Board of Directors, are proud to inform you that Beechcraft's fourth president will be a man we all know and respect — Edward C. Burns".

The response was spontaneous and loudly enthusiastic.

"As of tonight," Hedrick said, "Burns becomes president of Beech Aircraft, a member of the Executive Committee and the Finance Committee of the board of directors.

"Now, in case you are wondering about Mrs. Beech's and my future, Mrs. Beech will continue as chairman of the board, and I will be vice chairman of the board and chairman of the Executive Committee.

"So you're not getting rid of me yet", Hedrick quipped. Again, the supervisors' response was deafening. The audience rose to its feet in a hearty chorus of happy agreement.

It was a moment when history repeated itself. In 1968, Hedrick's election to the presidency had been announced by Chairman O. A. Beech at that year's management dinner of the Supervisors' Club.

The event also marked the continuation of top management in the hands of members of the Beech family. Burns was a nephew of Walter H. Beech. So the Beech tradition of excellence would be carried forward by the individuals most deeply concerned with its perpetuation. It was a matter of family pride and dedication to its founders' principles that Beech Aircraft should go on building "the world's finest aircraft".

The company's new president had been in training for top management throughout nearly 40 years of service in every major division. The final step was Burns' six months of "dual" handling of the controls with Hedrick since July, 1980 in the Office of the President. Taking over as its sole occupant, President Burns assumed responsibility for the management of Beech Aircraft and its subsidiaries. He also continued serving on the three-member Executive Committee with Chairman O. A. Beech and Vice Chairman Frank E. Hedrick, who would devote more time to policies and plans inter-relating between Beech Aircraft and Raytheon Company.

No further changes occurred in the wake of the new presidency. As Burns told reporters who interviewed him, "It's business as usual at Beech Aircraft." Brisk production was spiced with a variety of events that enlivened the early months of the year.

The Beech Employees Club found few takers for a 38 percent discount to members off the $2,750 price of a hot tub, installed. Beechcrafters seemed unimpressed by that fad.

More to their liking were awards presented by the Wichita Aeronautical Historical Association, Inc. to Beech and other local aircraft builders, and by the Continental Casualty Company, Beech's fleet insurance carrier. The Continental award was for 250,000 miles of accident-free driving in 1980, mainly over the road between Wichita and Newton, Salina, Liberal and Boulder, to Beech's safety-minded careful truck drivers.

There were two special treats for President E. C. Burns and other ex-Navy Beechcrafters. In February, the Naval Aviation Museum placed on display a bronze and wood plaque, presented to the company by the Museum Foundation, showing the profiles of Walter H. Beech and Olive Ann Beech. Its text hon-

Congratulatory party was held for new Vice Chairman Frank E. Hedrick and new President E. C. Burns. From left: Mr. Burns, Mr. Hedrick and Chairman O. A. Beech.

Chairman O. A. Beech cuts a ribbon across the doorway to dedicate the company's new Plant Four in Wichita as President E. C. Burns looks on.

524A

Vice Chairman Frank E. Hedrick was awarded a lifetime membership in the General Aviation Manufacturers Association, which he helped to found in 1970. Ed King, at left, chairman of King Radio, presented the special plaque.

Raytheon Company President D. Brainerd Holmes, at right, chatted with Beech Senior Vice President - Engineering C. A. Rembleske after "wringing out" a Beechcraft T-34C-1 jetprop trainer.

Former President Gerald R. Ford toured Beech Aircraft and visited with Chairman O. A. Beech, Vice Chairman Frank E. Hedrick and Mrs. Hedrick.

ored Beech for supplying the World War II Model 18 twin Beechcraft airplanes used in training more than 65,000 pilots, and the later T-34 and T-44A Beechcrafts that trained many thousands more.

Next came the 40th anniversary celebration of the Naval Air Station at Corpus Christi, Texas. Heading the Beech delegation was E. C. Nikkel, vice president - aerospace programs. The newest unit of the Station's 61-plane fleet of T-44A Beechcraft King Air advanced multiengine pilot trainers was proudly on display.

Employees of Beech Aerospace Services, Inc. (BASI) welcomed a $6 million U. S. Navy follow-on contract for continued worldwide support of Navy and Marine Corps UC-12B utility aircraft. Other services later awarded like contracts on C-12 aircraft — the Army for $12.7 million in April, and the Air Force for $6.4 million in November. So BASI's Beechcrafters went on maintaining the services' Super King Air fleets in readiness for takeoff better than the contracted rate of time, and saving large sums for America's taxpayers.

The Army also ordered more utility jetprops that BASI crews would maintain, with an $8.5 million contract issued in March. Specified were C-12D models (newest version of the Beechcraft Super King Air) equipped with wide cargo doors and heavy-duty, high flotation landing gear permitting tonnage operations from unimproved fields and airstrips.

Fitness for rugged duty was a built-in Beechcraft feature. So the Forest Service of the U. S. Department of Agriculture had found, in using its Beechcraft Baron 58P twins in firefighting and heavy hauling, all-weather mountain terrain operations. Their performance prompted another USDA order in March for four more pressurized 58P's, enlarging the Forest Service fleet to include a total of 16 Beechcraft Baron 58P models.

In the Far East, Beechcrafts had long proved their stamina in arduous pilot training service. One such user, Indonesia's Civil Air Training Academy, enlarged its fleet of 23 twin- and single-engine Beechcraft trainers with two new Beechcraft Baron 58P models, flying them off to Java in March.

The Republic of China (Taiwan) placed its fourth order in February for Beech MQM-107A missile targets to the value of

525

$11.9 million. Spare parts and ground support equipment were included in the contract.

Another Beech-Boulder design, introduced in March, offered dual fuel capability to users of the Beech liquefied methane (LM) vehicle fuel system. With the flip of a switch, the operator could select either LM or gasoline power at any time. The new option provided complete flexibility preferred by many fleet operators.

Dedication on March 6 of the new Beech Plant Four continued the company's expansion program in Wichita. Standing at the east edge of Beech Field, the new million-dollar, energy-efficient 50,400 sq. ft. structure housed 120 Beechcrafters, busily completing 26 helicopter airframes each month for Bell Helicopter Textron, a Beech customer since 1962. City and county officials joined Bell and Beech executives in applauding the delivery of the 3,000th Beech-built airframe for the best-selling Bell JetRanger commercial helicopter during the dedication ceremonies.

Spring was in the air as Beechcrafters surveyed the results of their first quarter's work. In March, they had delivered a new record number of 50 Beechcraft King Air jetprops — 25 to U. S. customers, 23 to international buyers, and two to the U. S. military. Total first quarter '81 sales of $198,658,583 set a new record for that period.

How to improve the world's leading business jetprop was a constant question for Beech engineers. They found an answer in the Beechcraft Super King Air B200 with Pratt & Whitney's new PT6A-42 engines — refined versions of the long-proven 850 shp -41 series. Installed in the Beechcraft Super King Air, the more efficient -42 engines increased normal cruise speed at 31,000-ft. altitude to 312 mph (271 knots) and high speed to 322 mph (280 knots). A new double-wide cockpit console, higher cabin pressurization at 6.5 psi and a raise in zero fuel weight to 11,000 pounds were additional improvements. Certificated in March, the improved Super King Air B200 was born; and in nation-wide demonstrations, its popularity continued in a highly competitive market.

Another milestone event was the April 17 delivery of the

526

3,000th Beechcraft King Air, a Model C90, to a longtime Beech owner, Stroehmann Brothers Company of Williamsport, Pa. The new jetprop joined a Model 50 Beechcraft Twin-Bonanza that, coincidentally, had been delivered to Stroehmann Brothers exactly 19 years earlier. Both Beechcrafts would serve as executive transports for the firm's bakery business, which spanned eight states from New York westward into Ohio.

Meanwhile, all America proudly celebrated the successful first space mission of the reusable Space Shuttle Orbiter "Columbia", which completed its two-day flight on April 14 with a dramatic, picture-perfect landing. Nowhere was the anticipation and the pride greater than at Beech Aircraft. Backed by more than a quarter century of experience in cryogenics, the Beech Boulder Division had produced the Power Reactant Storage Assembly (PRSA) that supplied liquid oxygen to the Orbiter's life support system, and liquid hydrogen and liquid oxygen used to generate its electrical power. By-product of the two Beech cryogenic systems was drinking water for the crew.

Boulder Beechcrafters had also built the Fuel Cell Servicing System that supported pre-launch PRSA loading and pressurization of the Orbiter's systems. The part they played in aid of the "Columbia's" mission recalled a prophetic saying that became current in 1954, when the company was first involved in then top-secret cryogenic research: "Space is in reach — with support from Beechcraft." That forecast had become an established fact.

Promotions and added responsibilities were announced April 14 for five longtime Beech executives. Elected senior vice president and treasurer was Charles W. Dieker, who joined the company in 1965 as a tax accountant and rose steadily to become vice president and treasurer in 1979.

Four 40-year Beechcrafters also assumed higher posts. Glenn Ehling was elected senior vice president - operations, succeeding Seymour Colman, recently retired, in that position. Chester A. Rembleske was named senior vice president - engineering, in recognition of his performance since 1978 as vice president - engineering. Harold W. Deets assumed larger duties as vice president - materiel and production, thus coordinating management of those two inter-related functions. He had been vice president - materiel since 1972. Max P. Eaton was elected vice president - satellite operations, with overall responsibility for the company's facilities at Liberal and Salina, Kansas; Boulder, Colorado; and Selma, Alabama. Since 1979, Eaton had served as vice president - production.

Continuing the march of high-level distinctions, Beechcrafters enjoyed a visit from former President Gerald R. Ford, who addressed a dinner meeting of more than 500 Wichita community leaders in the Beechcrafters Activity Center. Ford later met with Beech supervisors and executives. His thesis was the need for stronger national defense programs to counter worldwide Soviet expansionism.

Another VIP guest was Kansas Governor John Carlin. Proclaiming a statewide World Trade Week, the governor pointed out that Kansas led the nation in exports and in aircraft manufacturing and agricultural products. His special host was Michael G. Neuburger, senior vice president - International Division and chairman of the World Trade Club of Wichita.

Beech President E. C. Burns was elected to the board of directors of the General Aviation Manufacturers' Association (GAMA) and named chairman of GAMA's International Committee. And Vice Chairman Hedrick and his wife, Betty, jointly established the Frank E. and Betty E. Hedrick Endowment Fund, to award college tuition scholarship grants to dependents of Beech Aircraft employees.

On a visit to Wichita, Raytheon President D. Brainerd Holmes showed his enjoyment of a 45-minute flight at the controls of a Beechcraft T-34C-1 by performing aerobatic maneuvers that included wing-overs, loops and rolls. Currently the pilot of his own Beechcraft King Air C90, he showed that his commercial, instrument and multiengine ratings had been well earned.

Delivery of three T-34C-1 trainers to the Navy of Uruguay brought to seven the number of countries which had purchased commercial T-34C-1 and Turbo Mentor 34C versions. In addition to Uruguay were Morocco, Ecuador, Peru, Argentina, Indonesia and Algeria. The total of 81 foreign deliveries was in addition to 183 T-34C trainers procured by the U. S. Navy.

Moving to increase its some 30 percent share of Beech product sales, the International Division became a prominent exhibitor at the 34th International Paris Air Show June 4-14. The new Beechcraft Super King Air B200 headed a display of six models that also included full-scale mockups of Beech AQM-37A and MQM-107A missile targets.

On the home front, successful competitive bidding won a notable contract in June from the National Aeronautic and Space Administration (NASA) for a new Beechcraft Super King Air B200 11-place administrative aircraft. It replaced a Beechcraft Queen Air transport plane purchased in 1965 by NASA's Wallops Island, Virginia facility.

Chairman O. A. Beech received two more honors — one from employees, and another from Beechcraft owners. Presented by Wichita employees was a copy of a newspaper ad hailing Mrs. Beech's receipt of the Wright Brothers Memorial Trophy, centered on a large white mat that bore the signatures of countless Beechcrafters. "Congratulations, Boss!! We Love You Too!" was its inscription. The heartfelt tribute went on display just outside Mrs. Beech's office.

At the Staggerwing Museum in Tullahoma, Tennessee, Mrs. Beech was the honor guest in the dedication June 12-14 of the new Olive Ann Beech Gallery and Chapel. With W. C. "Dub" Yarbrough, president of the Staggerwing Museum Foundation, she unveiled a dedicatory plaque naming her "First Lady of Aviation." "This is one of the nicest honors I have ever received", said Mrs. Beech. "I am overwhelmed." World center for the Staggerwing Club, an international group of Beechcraft and Travel Air owners and admirers, the Museum housed an impressive collection of classic Beech Model 17 Staggerwings and memorabilia in its Walter H. Beech Hangar and Louise Thaden Library.

Victory was in the air as the month closed. Two Florida women, Juanita Blumberg and Bonnie Quenzler, flew their Beechcraft Baron to first place in the all-women Air Race Classic June 26-29. They averaged better than 241 mph over the 2,332-mile cross-country course. Winners of last year's Air Race Classic had also flown a Beechcraft — a Bonanza C33A.

Beech Aircraft and Raytheon Company were winners, too, in sales and earnings for the first half of the 1981 calendar year.

529

Beech sales since January 1 came to $420,027,197; and second quarter sales of $221,058,614 reached a new all-time high for any single quarter in history.

Raytheon sales of $2.73 billion produced net earnings of $157.2 million in the first six months of 1981 — up 13 percent over 1980 earnings for the same period. Defense electronic systems, aircraft products and geophysical exploration continued to show greatest growth. A two-for-one stock split, effected June 8, increased investors' access to Raytheon equities.

The Kansas economy shared in the company's progress. In 1980, Beech expenditures statewide came to $236 million. Contributions to education, health care and charitable causes by Kansas Beechcrafters and the company amounted to more than $698,000. Both totals were sure to be surpassed in 1981.

The winning trend went on with the receipt July 1 by the Alternative Energy Division of Beechcraft's first order for a liquefied methane (LM) fuel system. The $272,000 contract with Northwest Natural Gas Company of Portland, Oregon embodied a complete systems approach, including 25 vehicle conversions to optional LM or gasoline fuel, delivery of a complete LM fueling station, and instruction courses for the customer's personnel. Beech alternative energy was on its way, with the promise of cutting fuel costs for LM users, conserving irreplaceable petroleum, and reducing America's dependence on foreign oil.

Development of a Beech LM fuel system for aircraft also neared completion. On September 15, a Beechcraft Sundowner equipped with the revolutionary new system successfully completed a pioneering test flight from the Liberal, Kansas airport. It was the world's first known flight of a methane-powered aircraft; and its potential effects on the future of aviation were beyond estimation. Further feasibility testing and development continued.

Other events likewise made history. On July 25, Chairman O. A. Beech was inducted into the Aviation Hall of Fame at Dayton, Ohio, joining the select company of flight's immortals headed by Wilbur and Orville Wright. Mrs. Beech and her late husband, Walter H. Beech, co-founders of Beech Aircraft, be-

Chairman O. A. Beech, with Mr. and Mrs. George Haddaway, wears the Aviation Hall of Fame medallion. Haddaway, a long-time aviation journalist and friend of general aviation, presented Mrs. Beech at the induction ceremonies.

Aviation Hall of Fame Medallion with plaque which reads, "Awarded To Olive Ann Beech For Outstanding Contributions To Aviation, July 25, 1981."

Prior to Aviation Hall of Fame induction ceremonies, Chairman O. A. Beech gathered with members of her family. Seated, Mrs. Beech with daughters Mary Lynn Oliver, left, and Suzanne Warner. Standing, from left, Jim and Marcia McIlvain; Janet and Craig McIlvain; Bill Oliver, Betty Hedrick, Betty Burns, E. C. Burns, Deana Huntley, Frank E. Hedrick, Bill Huntley and Tom Warner.

Plaque from Beech Aircraft officers and directors honored Chairman O. A. Beech as recipient of these prestigious aviation awards: The Kitty Hawk Sands of Time Award, the Wright Brothers Memorial Trophy and The Aviation Hall of Fame.

530B

came with Charles and Anne Lindbergh the only husband-and-wife teams to be so enshrined.

Chosen by Mrs. Beech to present her credentials for induction was George Haddaway, longtime aviation journalist, general aviation advocate and Beech family friend. Presentations of her fellow inductees — Edward H. Heineman, Charles S. Draper and the late Laurence B. Sperry — preceded Haddaway's account of Mrs. Beech's career.

Consistent with her lifelong principle that deeds count more than words, Mrs. Beech said simply: "Thank you. I love you all."

Beechcrafters enlarged the substance of honors accorded Mrs. Beech with milestone deliveries of illustrious aircraft. On July 30, the first new Beechcraft Commuter C99's were delivered to commuter airline customers in ceremonies at the Selma division assembly facilities in Alabama. Recipients were Christman Air System, serving Pennsylvania, Ohio and West Virginia areas, and Sunbird Airlines, operating in North and South Carolina and Georgia. Sunbird's new Beechcraft was the first of ten Commuter C99's on order and optioned for their commuter services.

Next came delivery from Selma, Alabama of Japan's 13th Beechcraft Super King Air 200T Maritime Patrol jetprop to the Japanese Maritime Safety Agency (MSA). In extended-range missions over the Pacific Ocean, MSA's Beechcraft 200T fleet had already logged more than 7,200 hours. C. Itoh Aviation Co. Ltd., Beech distributor in Japan, received a special commendation from the Japan Defense Agency for distinguished cooperation and after-sales service.

Kansas Beechcrafters then completed delivery of a 21-plane fleet of aerobatic Beechcraft Sundowners to the Canadian Armed Forces. These would replace 25 Beechcraft Musketeers purchased in 1970 and still serving in rugged flight training, after logging 6,000 to 7,000 hours per plane. 1981 deliveries marked the continuation of sales to Canadian government agencies that began in 1938 with an order from Canada's Department of Transport for a Staggerwing Beechcraft D17S biplane.

Flight training among Beech employees was celebrated with the 40th Anniversary Dinner July 11 of the Beechcraft Employees' Flying Club. Started in 1941 with a single much-used,

531

low-powered "Brand X" fabric-covered airplane, the Club had trained hundreds of Beechcrafters to fly, while growing to its current membership of 244 employers flying 13 Club-owned Beechcrafts. It was the world's oldest flying club in continuous operation.

The company's Productivity Council handed out $38,800 in awards to 106 Beechcrafters at its semi-annual midyear presentation. Featured were visual showings of selected "better ideas" to inspire further creative thinking. The sheer simplicity of many very useful suggestions often raised the surprised question: "Why didn't we think of that before?" For example, Jeff Rudock of department 90 collected a well-earned $900 award for suggesting the purchase of diodes in rolls instead of in boxes — a simple idea that saved hundreds of man-hours in electronic assembly.

The largest wage increases and benefit enlargements in company history were awarded to Beech hourly paid employees August 3, in a new three-year agreement between management and labor representatives. Cost-of-living wage adjustments were included, based on the government published Consumer Price Index.

Beech Aircraft stole the show as usual at the 34th annual National Business Aircraft Association (NBAA) convention September 14 at Anaheim, California. Major attractions were two state-of-the-art Beechcrafts. A new Beechcraft Super King Air B200 displayed the latest state-of-the-art in corporate aircraft design. Alongside, a classic Staggerwing Beechcraft D17S biplane presented the state-of-the-art in 1937, the year when the D17 series was introduced. Its owner, Southwest Pacific Airlines Captain Les Deline, had restored his World War II vintage Staggerwing to as-new condition; and the contrast with the freshly minted jetprop Beechcraft was not huge. Old and new designs alike showed the excellence of Beechcraft.

Past records toppled again at the close on September 30 of the ninth month and third quarter of the 1981 calendar year. Since January 1, the company had delivered a record total of 322 commercial and military Beechcraft King Air jetprops. Nine-months sales of $665,032,094 were up 19 percent over 1980's record, and third quarter sales of $245,004,897 reached a new historic high for any single quarter. Raytheon Company's nine-months sales rose to $4.111 billion, and earnings to $244.7 million, with defense electronic systems, aircraft products and geophysical exploration activities continuing to show greatest growth.

Buoyed by this background of achievement, Beech Aircraft's 1982 International Sales Conference was a most happy event. To the theme of "Homecoming '82", the company's worldwide sales team celebrated another record-breaking year and prepared for new challenges in 1982.

Heading a long list of awards to domestic and international sales and service organizations and individuals was the naming as Beechcraft's "Man of the Year" for 1981 of Frank W. Hulse III, chairman of the board of Hangar One, Inc., and vice chairman of the board of Republic Airlines. Active in Beech sales since 1945, Hangar One had grown under Hulse's guidance to number 11 Beechcraft sales and service facilities in Georgia, Florida, Alabama, Tennessee and North Carolina. Hangar One was a consistent winner of top sales volume awards among the company's domestic outlets.

Display of the 1982 Beechcraft line at Frank E. Hedrick Park revealed numerous "fine tuning" touches enhancing the appearance, comfort, convenience and value of every model. Headed by the new higher-performance Beechcraft Super King Air B200 and its 200C cargo and 200T extended-range alternate versions, the four Beechcraft King Air models set new high standards of excellence in the corporate jetprop class.

The Beechcraft Duke B60 added new features and refinements to expand its leadership as a pressurized, owner-flown high-performance piston-engine business machine. Increases in engine time before overhaul (TBO) on four Beechcraft Baron models, and on all Beechcraft Bonanza models, reduced overall operating costs; and 100 percent corrosion proofing became standard on all Beechcraft Bonanzas.

Beech Aero Center models likewise gained new features and wider options of personalized decor. All 1982 Beechcrafts shared a unique distinction — special gold-emblazoned medallions and plaques commemorating "Fifty years of product excellence by Beech", signed by O. A. Beech as co-founder and chairman of Beech Aircraft.

Showings of the experimental methane-powered Beechcraft Sundowner and of a Ford Granada sedan equipped with the Beech liquefied methane fuel system gave glimpses into long-range future possibilities. As to the year ahead, prospects for setting new sales records were never brighter.

The Wings Club of New York City, one of aviation's oldest and most prestigious organizations, recognized the accomplishments of Chairman O. A. Beech at its annual Awards Dinner on October 20. Her name was added to the roll of flight's immortals on The Wings Club Distinguished Achievement Award trophy, kept on permanent display at its New York City headquarters. Mrs. Beech was also presented with a Distinguished Achievement Award certificate and plaque, and given an honorary life membership, as lasting remembrances of The Wings Club honors.

With Vice Chairman Frank E. Hedrick, Mrs. Beech later enjoyed a tour of the U. S. Military Academy at West Point. There Hedrick received two handsome awards – a specially engraved gold watch from Academy Superintendent Lt. General Willard W. Scott Jr., and a cadet dress saber mounted on a presentation plaque. The awards expressed appreciation for the donation of a Beechcraft Sierra to the West Point Flying Club by the Beech Foundation.

As another measure of Beech Aircraft support of U. S. defense services, Vice Chairman Hedrick accepted an appointment as a charter member of the newly formed Naval Aviation Industrial Council (NAIC). An industry-Navy body sponsored by the Association of Naval Aviation, NAIC was established for the betterment of naval aviation, the Navy and the national defense.

Judgment in favor of Beech Aircraft early in November closed out the last of several product liability lawsuits tried during the year. Verdicts favorable to Beech were handed down in each case. So the endless efforts of Beechcrafters and their company to build the highest possible degree of safety into their products won due recognition in the courts of law.

534

Following dedication of the Olive Ann Beech Gallery and Chapel at the Staggerwing Museum, Mrs. Beech and members of her family gathered for this photo in front of the new building. From left, standing, Brian Snart, Tom Warner, Suzanne Warner, Mrs. Beech, Mary Lynn Oliver, Deana Huntley and Bill Huntley; kneeling, Trey Oliver, Jeffrey Pitt, Jeniffer Pitt and Carrie Oliver.

Chairman O. A. Beech with the Wings Club Distinguished Achievement Award Trophy.

United States Military Academy Superintendent Lt. Gen. Willard W. Scott presented a gold watch and cadet saber to Vice Chairman Frank E. Hedrick, as Mrs. Hedrick looks on. Ceremony at West Point was in appreciation for donation of a Beechcraft Sundowner to the West Point Flying Club by the Beech Foundation.

534A

Experimental liquefied-methane-powered Beechcraft Sundowner in flight near Wichita.

First deliveries of Beechcraft Commuter C99s were made to Sunbird Airlines and Christman Air System at the Selma Division.

Native Kansan astronaut Joe Engle and Mrs. Engle visited Beech Aircraft following his historic mission as commander of the second mission of the Space Shuttle Orbiter "Columbia." From left: Vice Chairman Frank E. Hedrick, Mrs. Engle, Chairman O. A. Beech and Colonel Joe Engle.

534B

The International Division welcomed its first commercial customer in South Korea, with the October 29 delivery at Beech Field of a Beechcraft Super King Air B200 to Hyundai Heavy Industries, a firm involved primarily in shipping and trucking. Theirs was the first 1982 model delivered to an international customer. Two Beechcraft Barons had previously gone to the South Korea national police.

Salina Beechcrafters shortly afterward rolled out their 400th pressurized Beechcraft Baron 58P. They completed the milestone airplane a day and a half ahead of schedule, and under budget as well.

Much to the relief of the nation and to Beechcrafters, the "off again, on again" second mission of the reusable Space Shuttle Orbiter "Columbia" was at last completed November 12-14. The collective sigh of relief from the Boulder Division at its successful conclusion was heard as far away as Cape Canaveral.

In mid-December, the west African nation of Gabon became the eighth foreign nation to purchase international or commercial versions of Beechcraft T-34C-1 or Turbo Mentor 34C turboprop trainers. Gabon's initial order for four Beechcraft T-34C-1 single-engine jetprops was scheduled for use by the elite Presidential Guard of the nation's President, Omar Bongo.

The year closed in a flurry of pleasant events. Vice Chairman Frank E. Hedrick was honored with a lifetime membership in the General Aviation Manufacturers Association (GAMA), which he had helped found in 1970. In ceremonies at Phoenix, Arizona, Hedrick received an engraved plaque attesting his 11 years of distinguished service to GAMA.

Delivery to the Southern Gulf Corporation at Houston, Texas of the 1,000th LJ series Beechcraft King Air, a Model C90, marked the 18th year of production for general aviation's most successful line of business jetprops. It was noted that like most of the LJ series and their later, more sophisticated versions, the first Model 90 produced in 1964 was still in daily service. Its owner was a Tulsa, Oklahoma charter operator.

Another milestone delivery was that of the 2,000th Beechcraft Bonanza A36. Long the best-selling business aircraft of its class, the six-place Beechcraft was resplendent in the special blue and

535

gold colors commemorating the company's 50th Anniversary Year.

Warmly appreciative of the quality built into Beech products were two distinguished visitors to Wichita. Rear Admiral Frank Collins, Executive Director of Defense Contract Administration Services Quality Assurance, told how he relied on Beech quality control during 30 years of U. S. Navy service, every time he boarded a Beechcraft, from the classic Model 18 Twin Beech to the current Navy UC-12B jetprops.

Kansas-born Col. Joe Engle, pilot of the second mission of the Space Shuttle "Columbia", acknowledged his reliance on Beech-built cryogenic systems that supplied oxygen for the spacecraft's life support system. Engle's successful completion of the space flight verified the quality workmanship contributed by Boulder Division Beechcrafters to "Columbia's" vital systems.

Whatever the product or its mission, Beechcrafters remained mindful of the admonition of co-founder Walter H. Beech displayed throughout the company's plants from its founding onward:

"Peoples' lives all over the world depend on the quality of your workmanship. Let's be careful!"

Chapter 45

As Beech Aircraft made ready to celebrate the 50th anniversary of its founding in April 1982, the momentum of another record-breaking year swept the company onward at full speed. Calendar year 1981 sales of $907.5 million rose 19 percent over 1980 results, marking Beech Aircraft's ninth consecutive record year.

Raytheon Company, the corporate parent, scored new records in 1981 for the eleventh consecutive year. Raytheon sales of $5.6 billion were up 12.7 percent over 1980; and earnings of $324 million were 14.8 percent higher than in 1980. Raytheon directors raised the quarterly dividend 16.7 percent, to 35 cents per share up from 30 cents per share. Stockholders of record

536

January 8, 1982 welcomed the higher payment, distributed January 26, 1982. The welding of winners was working very well.

The Beech Selma Division continued deliveries of the new Beechcraft Commuter C99s, adding to the total of 16 handed over in 1981 to commuter airlines. Development of the larger 19-passenger pressurized Beechcraft Commuter 1900 pressed forward, with first flight of the prototype planned later in the year.

Irrefutable economics of energy costs continued to work in favor of the company's Alternative Energy Division. Deliveries were in progress on its first quantity order for liquefied methane (LM) fuel systems for truck and car fleets. Development of the pioneering Beech airborne LM fuel system, installed in a Beechcraft Sundowner, continued with encouraging prospects.

Special ceremonies at Beech Aircraft heralded delivery of the 1,000th Beechcraft Super King Air. Delivery of the Super King Air B200 was made through the Beech International Division to National Process Industries Group, a South African firm.

Guided by Chairman O. A. Beech and Vice Chairman Frank E. Hedrick, long-range planning in cooperation with Raytheon took specific shape. Presented to the parent company's board was a five-year action plan charting the course for Beech Aircraft through 1987. For obvious reasons, its details were not made public. Yet in the light of history, it was clear that the future was bright for Beechcrafters and for the Beech Aircraft Corporation.

O. A. Beech
Chairman of the Board

Frank E. Hedrick
Vice Chairman of the Board

E. C. Burns
President

Beechcraft Board of Directors

A total of 270 years of service to the Beech Aircraft Corporation is represented by the members of the company's Board of Directors.

J. A. Elliott
Business Consultant
Wichita, Kansas

Leddy L. Greever
Business Consultant
Wichita, Kansas

D. Brainerd Holmes
President
Raytheon Company
Lexington,
Massachusetts

L. Patton Kline
Chairman & Chief
Executive Officer
Marsh &
McLennan, Inc.
New York, N.Y.

Robert Martin
Senior Partner -
Martin, Pringle,
Davis, Oliver
& Triplett
Wichita, Kansas 538

M. G. Neuburger
Senior
Vice President -
International
Division

Thomas L. Phillips
Chairman of
the Board
Raytheon Company
Lexington,
Massachusetts

John H. Shaffer
Business Consultant
Washington, D.C.

Stewart M. Ayton
Senior
Vice President -
Marketing

C. W. Dieker
Senior
Vice President
& Treasurer

Glenn Ehling
Senior
Vice President -
Operations

C. A. Rembleske
Senior
Vice President -
Engineering

Harold W. Deets
Vice President -
Materiel
& Production

Beechcraft Officers

Corporate Officers not serving on the Board of Directors had at the end of 1981 accumulated a total of 425 years of service with the company.

Max P. Eaton
Vice President -
Satellite
Operations

Gary M. Hanssen
Vice President -
Industrial
Relations

E. C. Nikkel
Vice President -
Aerospace
Programs

Austin Rising
Vice President

Wm. G. Robinson
Vice President -
Corporate
Communications

George D. Rodgers
Vice President -
Domestic Com-
mercial Marketing

W. G. Rutherford
Vice President -
Government
Relations

W. D. Wise
Vice President -
Commuter
Division

L. R. Damon
Controller &
Assistant Treasurer

D. C. Cullinane
Assistant Treasurer

Wey D. Kenny
Assistant
Treasurer

Ila Alumbaugh
Corporate
Secretary

539

TOTAL BEECHCRAFT DELIVERIES

	1932 - 1981 Cumulative		
	Commercial	Military	Total
Total Beechcraft Deliveries	34,408	11,486	45,894

	First Delivery	Commercial	Military	Total
Missiles & Targets	1959	—	6,280	6,280
Bell Helicopter Airframes	1968	3,389	2,287	5,676

COMPLETED PROGRAMS

Beechcraft Model	Production Years	Commercial Units	Military Units	Grand Total
Model 17 Staggerwing (incl. C43 & GC-2)	1932-1948	356	425	781
Model 18 (incl. AT-7, AT-11, SNB, C45, JRB & Mil. Rebuilds)	1937-1971	1,861	7,528	9,389
Model AT-10 Mil. Trainer	1941-1943	—	1,771	1,771
Model 50 Twin Bonanza (incl. L23A-E)	1951-1963	768	206	974
Model 45 Mil. Trainer	1950-1959	318	776	1,094
Model 95 Travel Air	1958-1968	719	—	719
Model 88 Queen Air	1965-1969	45	—	45
Beechcraft Hawker	1970-1975	65	—	65
Dispensers & Containers	1963-1972	—	20,621	20,621

EMPLOYEES' SERVICE RECORD

Employment as of Dec. 31, 1981
10,694

Years of Service — more than:

45	40	35	30	25	20	15	10	5
1	109	217	639	1,076	1,269	2,278	2,949	4,671

Number of Employees

540

Beechcraft
PRODUCTION RECORD — UNITS DELIVERED
1932 - 1981

CURRENT PROGRAMS

Beechcraft Model	First Delivery	Commercial Units	Military Units	Grand Total
Model 35 Bonanza	1947	10,368	—	10,368
Model 65 Queen Air (incl. 70, L23F, U8F)	1959	375	71	446
Model 33 Bonanza	1960	2,405	6	2,411
Model 55 Baron (incl. 56TC, T42A, 58, 58P, 58TC)	1961	5,564	70	5,634
Model 80 Queen Air	1962	508	2	510
Model 19, 23, 24	1962	4,371	—	4,371
°Model 90 King Air (incl. U21A-E, VC6A, T44)	1964	1,511	226	1,737
Beechcraft 99 Airliner	1968	180	—	180
Model 36-36TC Bonanza (incl. 1079)	1968	2,250	27	2,277
Model 60 Duke	1968	578	—	578
°Model 100 King Air (incl. U21F)	1969	366	5	371
°Super King Air 200 (incl. U21J, C12A)	1974	1,027	187	1,214
Model T34C	1976	81	184	265
Model 76 Duchess	1978	399	—	399
Model 77 Skipper	1979	293	—	293
°Total King Air Deliveries		2,904	418	3,318

$\mathcal{B}$eechcraft
HALL OF FAME

Honoring Beechcraft's Man of the Year in Recognition of Their Participation in the Growth of Business Aviation and for Outstanding Achievement in the Marketing of Beechcraft Products

1960 Col. Roscoe Turner (1895-1970) — Roscoe Turner Aeronautical Corporation

1961 W. P. Cutter (1899-1963) — Cutter Carr Flying Service,

1966 Jess Childress Southern Airways Beechcraft, Inc.

1967 Gerald Wilmot Page Beechcraft, Inc.

1973 Wm. C. Morales (1905-1977) — William C. Morales & Co., C. A.

1974 Joseph E. Farrel Ohio Aviation Distributor, Inc.

1978 Edgar G. Box and Don Cody (Team of the Year) Chaparral Aviation, Inc.

Harry B. Combs
os Aircraft, Inc.

1963 *Norman Larson*
(1906-1969) — The
Norman Larson Company

1964 *A. H. Ostermann*
Travelair G.M.B.H.
& Co. KG

1965 *Dan L. Meisinger*
Topeka Aircraft Sales
& Service, Inc.

Tito L. Carnasciali
anhia Carnasciali

1969 *Watson E. Richards*
(1908-1977) —
Atlantic Aviation
Corporation

1970 *T. Gail Clark*
Tulsair, Incorporated

1972 *R. S. Northington*
Piedmont Aviation,
Incorporated

Miguel Campos
ty Aviation
oration

1976 *Herb and Arlene Elliott*
(Team of the Year)
Elliott Flying Service, Inc.

1977 *Roland Fraissinet*
Compagnie Fraissinet

W. Eric Hodson
hcraft Sales (S.A.)
) Limited

1980 *Michael M. Gordon*
Beechcraft West -
Van Nuys

1981 *Frank W. Hulse III*
Hangar One, Inc.

543

Many of the trophies won by planes designed and built by Walter H. Beech are on display in the Trophy Room at Beechcraft today.

544

Beechcraft

Parade of Champions

☆ 1925: First Ford Reliability Tour. Three Beech-designed Travel Air Model 3000s finish one, two, three with perfect scores.

☆ 1925: Tulsa Air Speed Race. Won by Walter H. Beech in Travel Air 2000.

☆ 1926: Ford Reliability Tour. Walter H. Beech won outright first place flying a Travel Air Model 4000J-4.

☆ 1926: "On-to-Sesqui", California-to-Philadelphia cross-country race. First place won by Fred D. Hoyt in a Travel Air Model 2000, in 146 hours.

☆ 1926: "On-to-Sesqui" Races. Fred D. Hoyt in a Travel Air Model 2000 OX-5 won first place in the "free for all" for low-powered planes.

☆ 1926: J. H. Turner Trophy. Won by Walter H. Beech in Travel Air 2000.

☆ 1926: Flint Air Meet Trophy. Won by Walter H. Beech in Travel Air Model 2000C-6.

☆ 1927: First commercial airplane to fly from California to Hawaii. A Travel Air Model 5000 monoplane piloted by Emory B. Bronte and Ernest L. Smith made the 2,340-mile crossing in 25 hours and 36 minutes.

☆ 1927: Pacific Coast Air Derby. Won by H. C. Lippiatt in Travel Air Model 5000 monoplane.

☆ 1927: Western Flying Trophy at National Air Races. Won by Eugene Detmer in Travel Air Model 2000 biplane at speed exceeding 102 mph.

☆ 1927: Dole Race, Oakland to Honolulu. Won by Art Goebel in the famous "Woolaroc" Travel Air Model 5000 monoplane covering the 2,497 miles in 26 hours, 17 minutes, and 33 seconds.

☆ 1928: Oakland-to-Los Angeles Race. Won by a Travel Air Model 6000 piloted by H. C. Lippiatt.

☆ 1928: Atlantic Air Races. Travel Airs entered by Doug Davis won first and second places in every race of the two-day event.

☆ 1928: Civilian Free-for-All 50-Mile Race at National Air Races, Los Angeles. Won by D. C. Warren in a Travel Air Model 3000.

☆ 1929: Portland, Ore.-to-Cleveland Air Derby. Won by T. A. Wells in a Travel Air Model D-4000 in 14 hours and 44 minutes.

☆ 1929: Rim of Ohio Derby. Won by J. O. Donaldson in Travel Air B-4000.

☆ 1929: Toronto-to-Cleveland Race. Won by Herbert St. Martin in a Travel Air Model A-6000A.

☆ 1929: On-To-Tulsa 500-Mile Derby. Won by Billy Parker in Travel Air B-4000.

☆ 1929: International Air Derby, Mexico City to Kansas City. Won by Art Goebel in a Travel Air Model 6000.

☆ 1929: Women's Derby, Santa Monica to Cleveland. Won by Louise Thaden in a Travel Air Model B-4000.

☆ 1929: Endurance record for women of 22 hours, 3 minutes, 12 seconds set by Louise Thaden in a Travel Air Model 3000.

☆ 1929: U. S. altitude record for women, more than 20,000 feet, set by Louise Thaden in a Travel Air Model 4000.

☆ 1929: National Air Races. OX-5 race and relay race won by Travel Airs.

☆ 1929: Experimental ship race at National Air Races won by Travel Air "Mystery S" flown by Doug Davis. Speed: 113.38 mph.

☆ 1929: Thompson Trophy 50-mile closed course Free-for-All Race won by Travel Air "Mystery S" piloted by Doug Davis at record speed of 194.9 mph.

☆ 1929: New York-to-Boston Airspeed Record. Travel Air "Mystery S" flown by Eric Wood made the record run in 52 minutes.

☆ 1930-31: Capt. Frank Hawks in Travel Air "Mystery S" known as "Texaco 13" established more than 200 new speed records in America and Europe and earned the Ligue Internationale des Aviateurs medal as the world's outstanding airman.

☆ 1930: Montreal-to-New York Air Speed Record. Set at 115 minutes in a Travel Air "Mystery S" piloted by Dale Jackson.

☆ 1930: World Speed record for women set by Florence Lowe Barnes at over 196 mph in a Travel Air "Mystery S".

☆ 1933: Texaco Trophy race at Miami Air Races. Won by E. H. Wood in No. 1 Beechcraft Model 17.

☆ 1936: First, second and fourth places in Unlimited Race for Frank E. Phillips Trophy at Denver Mile-High Air Races won by Beechcraft Model 17's. First place winner piloted by Bill Ong.

☆ 1936: National speed record for women set by Louise Thaden in a Beechcraft Model 17 at St. Louis, 197.958 mph.

☆ 1936: Bendix Transcontinental Speed Dash and Bendix trophy. Won by Louise Thaden and Blanche Noyes in a Beechcraft Model 17.

☆ 1936: Beechcraft Model 17 carried to Germany aboard dirigible Hindenberg for Capt. James Haizlip to begin flying tour of Europe.

☆ 1937: U. S. women's speed record — 203.895 mph — set by Jacqueline Cochran in a Beechcraft Model D17W.

☆ 1937: Unlimited Race for Frank E. Phillips Trophy. Won by Art Chester in a Beechcraft Model 17.

☆ 1939: Macfadden Cross-Country Race. Won by Max Constant in a Beechcraft Model D17W.

546

☆ 1939: New York-to-Miami sports record. Won by Max Constant in a Beechcraft Model D17W.

☆ 1939: Seattle-to-Alaska Air Speed Record. The 1,900 miles were flown in 10 hours, 20 minutes by Kenneth Neese in a Beechcraft Model 17.

☆ 1939: National women's altitude record — 30,052.43 feet — set in a Beechcraft Model 17 by Jacqueline Cochran.

☆ 1939: Skis-mounted Beechcraft Model 17 sets altitude record over South Pole in "Snow Cruiser" expedition of Admiral Byrd and the United States Antarctic Service.

☆ 1940: On-to-Miami race for Macfadden Trophy won in a Beechcraft Model 18. (H. C. Rankin, pilot; Walter H. Beech, co-pilot) 1,084 miles in 4 hours, 37 minutes, at an average speed of 234 mph.

Parade of Champions

☆ 1949: World record for non-stop distance flying for planes of Bonanza category. Capt. Bill Odom in a Beechcraft Bonanza from Honolulu to Oakland, 2,406.9 miles in 22 hours, 6 minutes.

☆ 1949: World record for non-stop distance for all light planes. Capt. Bill Odom in a Beechcraft Bonanza from Honolulu to Teterboro, N. J., 4,957.24 miles in 36 hours, 2 minutes.

☆ 1951-52: Around-the-world flight by Congressman Peter F. Mack, Jr., in the same Beechcraft Bonanza Model 35 flown by Bill Odom. Mack covered 30 countries on his solo flight.

☆ 1952: World speed record for light planes — 225.776 km. per hour (140.29 mph) — set by Paul Burniat of Brussels, Belgium, in a Beechcraft Bonanza.

☆ 1953: Beechcraft Bonanzas finished first, second, third and fourth in first annual Jaycee Transcontinental Air Cruise, Philadelphia to Palm Desert, Calif. W. H. Hinselman won first place and O. A. Beech Trophy.

☆ 1953: Beechcraft D18S owned by F. C. Castelli Company, won Wings Field Regatto, at Ambler, Pa. and O. A. Beech Trophy.

☆ 1953: Mrs. Marion Hart, 61-year-old sportswoman, flew non-stop from Newfoundland to Ireland in a Beechcraft Bonanza.

☆ 1954: Mrs. Ann Waddell won O. A. Beech Trophy for fastest speed in annual Skylady Derby, Raton, N.M., to Kansas City, Mo., in a Beechcraft Bonanza.

☆ 1954: Three Beechcraft Bonanzas finished first, second and third in the second annual Jaycee Transcontinental Air Cruise from Philadelphia to Palm Desert, Calif. W. C. Butler won first place and O. A. Beech Trophy.

☆ 1955: Mrs. Ann Waddell flew a Beechcraft Bonanza to win the Skylady Derby, Little Rock, Ark., to Raton, N. M.

☆ 1956: Beechcraft Bonanzas win first and second place in the Powder Puff Air Derby — Winning pilot, Frances Bera, in a Beechcraft Bonanza E35.

☆ 1957: Beechcraft Bonanzas win first and third place in the Powder Puff Air Derby — Winning pilot, Alice Roberts, in a Beechcraft Bonanza C35.

☆ 1958: Beechcraft Bonanza wins first place in the Powder Puff Air Derby — Winning pilot, Frances Bera, in a Beechcraft Bonanza A35.

☆ 1958: World record for non-stop distance flying for all light planes. Capt. Pat Boling in a Beechcraft J35 Bonanza from Manila to Pendleton,

Ore., 6,856.32 miles, Great Circle distance. (Total miles actually flown — 7,090 in 45 hours, 43 minutes.)

☆ 1960: Beechcraft Model 65 Queen Air establishes a new World Altitude Record of 34,862 feet for airplanes in its class — pilot James D. Webber.

☆ 1961: Beechcraft Bonanza wins first place in the Powder Puff Air Derby — Winning pilot, Frances Bera, in a Beechcraft Bonanza E35.

☆ 1962: Beechcraft Bonanza wins first place in the Powder Puff Air Derby — Winning pilot, Mrs. Frances Bera, in a Beechcraft Bonanza F35.

☆ 1966: Beechcraft C55 Baron, piloted by Robert and Joan Wallick, sets round-the-world record for piston-engine aircraft: 23,629 miles; 5 days, 6 hours, 17 minutes.

☆ 1967: Beechcraft Bonanza wins first place in the Powder Puff Air Derby — Winning pilot, Judy Wagner in a Beechcraft Bonanza K35.

☆ 1968: Beechcrafts win first, second and third places in 18th Angel Derby, April 22-25, Managua, Nicaragua, to Panama City, Fla. — Judy Wagner in Beechcraft Bonanza K35, Janis Hobbs in Beechcraft Musketeer and Pat McEwen in Beechcraft Bonanza S35.

☆ 1969: Beech Aircraft cryogenic gas storage system supports Apollo XI spacecraft in putting men on the moon for the first time.

☆ 1970: Beechcraft 99A Airliner wins London, England-to-Sydney, Australia Air Race, in 48 hours, 15 minutes, 50 seconds, piloted by Capt. Tom E. Lampitt and crew.

☆ 1971: Beechcraft Bonanza A36 sets record speed-over-a-recognized-course for Class C-1.d Group I aircraft in flying from New York to London, 3,443.56 miles, in 17 hours, 22 minutes, 54 seconds, at average speed of 198.8 mph — piloted by Louise Sacchi.

☆ 1971: Beechcraft Baron B55 sets Speed-Around-the-World record for piston-engine aircraft — 24,800 miles in 5 days, 5 hours, 57 minutes, at elapsed time average speed of 197.77 mph — Travor K. Broughan, pilot, R. N. Dickeson, crewman.

☆ 1972: Beech Aircraft cryogenic gas storage system supports Apollo 17 spacecraft in the sixth and final manned moon landing mission for the NASA Space Exploration Program.

☆ 1973: Skylab Spacecraft Missions mark 14th, 15th and 16th space flights for Beech Aircraft's Apollo cryogenic gas storage system.

☆ 1975: Beechcraft Bonanza A36 wins first place in Powder Puff Derby at average speed of 204.33 mph. Winning pilot, Trina Jarish.

☆ 1975: Beech Aircraft cryogenic gas storage system supports 138-earth-orbit mission of Apollo-Soyuz Test Project.

☆ 1975: Beechcraft Duke sets round-the-world speed record for piston-engine aircraft covering the 24,854 miles in 5 days, 2 hours, 15 minutes, averaging 198.8 mph. Australian pilots Denys Dalton and Terry Gwynn-Jones flew Brisbane-to-Brisbane.

☆ 1975: Beechcraft Model D17S (C-43) joins Beechcraft AT-11 and Beechcraft C-45H in exhibit of World War II aircraft at the U. S. Air Force Museum at Wright Field, Dayton, Ohio.

☆ 1975: "Waikiki Beech"/"Friendship Flame" Beechcraft Bonanza 35, which set non-stop distance records in 1949, goes on permanent exhibit in the National Air and Space Museum, Smithsonian Institution, Washington, D.C.

☆ 1976: Beechcraft D18S "Twin Beech" added to classic aircraft on exhibit at the National Air and Space Museum, Smithsonian Institution, Washington, D.C.

☆ 1977: Roll-Out of the 10,000th Beechcraft Bonanza Model 35 on February 18, 1977.

☆ 1977: Walter H. Beech, Co-founder of Beech Aircraft Corporation, inducted into the Aviation Hall of Fame.

☆ 1977: Beechcraft Bonanza S35 sets new record for the shortest elapsed time around the world in a single-engine, piston aircraft. Jack Rodd and Harold Benham circled the globe in 10 days, 23 hours and 33 minutes.

Parade of Champions

☆ 1977: Beechcraft Bonanza F33A sets FAI-sanctioned class record for flying 4,300 miles non-stop from New York City to Munich, Germany in 25 hours, 48 minutes – Piloted by Dieter Schmitt of West Germany.

☆ 1978: Beechcraft Bonanza wins All-Women's International Air Race (Angel Derby), from Dallas to Freeport, Bahamas. Pilot, Judy Wagner.

☆ 1978: Beechcraft King Air C90 sets three world records for turboprop business aircraft. Includes record for speed over a recognized course (233.24 mph and 206.21 mph) and distance in a straight line (2,033.91 miles). Pilots F. T. Elliott Jr. and Thomas Clements flying from San Francisco to Poughkeepsie, N. Y.

☆ 1978: Beechcraft Bonanza wins Republic of South Africa's State President's Trophy Air Race. Piloted by Graeme Conlyn and Nigel Forrester of South Africa.

☆ 1978: Beechcraft Bonanza V35B flies 5,000 miles over the North Pole non-stop Anchorage to Munich. Time enroute 32 hours and 28 minutes. Pilot Dieter Schmitt.

☆ 1979: Beechcraft Bonanza F33A sets world speed record for NAA Clc aircraft between Fresno, Calif. and Las Vegas, Nev. Pilot Marie McMillan.

☆ 1979: Beechcraft Bonanza A36 sets world speed record for this class aircraft from Sacramento, to Los Angeles, Calif. Speed 220 mph. Pilot Jeanette Fowler.

☆ 1980: Beechcraft Sundowner wins Republic of South Africa's State President's Trophy Air Race. Pilots Maureen Forrester and Juliett Serrurier were the first all-women team to win the race.

☆ 1980: Turbocharged Beechcraft Bonanza A36TC flies non-stop New York to Munich in 16 hours 18 minutes. Pilot Dieter Schmitt.

☆ 1980: Beechcraft Bonanza C33A wins All-Women's International Air Race (Angel Derby), from Corpus Christi, Tex. to Columbia, S. C. Pilots, Pat Jetton and Elinor Johnson.

☆ 1980: Cutaway airframe of Beechcraft Bonanza joins Bonanza 35 in exhibit at the National Air and Space Museum, Smithsonian Institution, Washington, D.C.

☆ 1980: Olive Ann Beech, Co-founder and Chairman of Beech Aircraft Corporation, accepts aviation's highest honor as the first woman to receive the National Aeronautic Association's coveted Wright Brothers Memorial Trophy.

☆ 1981: Beech cryogenic gas storage system supports first flight of Space Shuttle Orbiter "Columbia."

☆ 1981: Beechcraft Bonanza E33C wins All-Women's International Air Race (Angel Derby), from Los Angeles to Acapulco, Mexico. Pilot, Judy Wagner.

☆ 1981: Olive Ann Beech, Co-founder and Chairman of Beech Aircraft Corporation, inducted into the Aviation Hall of Fame (Walter H. Beech, her husband and Co-founder of Beech Aircraft, was so honored in 1977). With Mrs. Beech's induction, they became the second husband-and-wife team to receive the honor.

☆ 1981: Olive Ann Beech, Co-founder and Chairman of Beech Aircraft Corporation, receives The Wings Club Distinguished Achievement Award for 1981, at its annual awards program in New York City, for "dedicated pioneering contribution to the design and manufacture of personal and business aircraft leading to the development of the world's foremost general aviation industry."

Beech Aircraft Corporation

Subsidiaries

Beech Acceptance Corporation, Inc. ....Wichita, Kansas
Beech Aerospace Services, Inc. ....Jackson, Mississippi
Beech International Sales Corporation ....Wichita, Kansas
Travel Air Insurance Company, Ltd. ....Hamilton, Bermuda
Beechcraft, A. G. ....Kloten, Switzerland
Beech Holdings, Inc. ....Wichita, Kansas
   Baton Rouge Aircraft, Inc. ....Baton Rouge, Louisiana
   Beechcraft East, Inc. ....Facilities at Farmingdale,
      New York and Teterboro, New Jersey
   Beechcraft West ....Facilities at Van Nuys, Fresno,
      Hayward and Bakersfield, California
     Mission Beechcraft (Wholly- Owned
     Subsidiary of Beechcraft West) .... Santa Ana, California
   Denver Beechcraft, Inc. ....Denver, Colorado
     Aircraftco (Division
     of Denver Beechcraft) ....Broomfield, Colorado
   Hedrick Beechcraft, Inc. ....Colorado Springs, Colorado
   Houston Beechcraft, Inc. ....Houston, Texas
   Indiana Beechcraft, Inc. ....Indianapolis, Indiana
   Thompson Beechcraft Of Salt Lake .... Salt Lake City, Utah
   United Beechcraft, Inc. ....Wichita, Kansas
     Fuel and Line Services, Inc. (Wholly-Owned
     Subsidiary of United Beechcraft) ......Wichita, Kansas
Beech Aircraft Foundation ....Wichita, Kansas
   (Non-Profit Charitable Organization)

Facilities

Beech Aircraft Corporation
Corporate Offices ....Wichita, Kansas
   Plant I ....Wichita, Kansas
   Plant II ....Wichita, Kansas
   Plant III ....Wichita, Kansas
   Plant IV ....Wichita, Kansas
   Andover Facility ....Andover, Kansas
   Newton Facility ....Newton, Kansas
Boulder Division ....Boulder, Colorado
Liberal Division ....Liberal, Kansas
Salina Division ....Salina, Kansas
Selma Division ....Selma, Alabama

Four major plants in Wichita, Kansas are centers for Beech research, development and production. With a total Wichita floor area of 2,039,000 square feet and the adjoining Beech-owned airfield, the more than 1,200-acre site provides ample long-range growth capability.

General Offices Adjoining Plant I

Plant II

Plant III

552

Plant IV

Andover Facility

Newton Facility

*Boulder Division
Administration-
Engineering*

553

Liberal Division

Salina Division

Selma Division

554

The Royal Family
of General Aviation...
the 1982 Beechcrafts
The Beechcraft Super King Air B200

Launching a new generation in corporate transportation, the jetprop Beechcraft Super King Air B200 is the flagship and exemplar of all 1982 Golden Anniversary Beechcrafts. Pressurized and air conditioned, its three compartment interior merges handcrafted luxury with total comfort and privacy for all occupants. Available with seating for 8 to 15, its ideally balanced performance profile permits operation at 333 mph maximum cruise speed or 2,272-mile maximum range from small, unimproved airfields all over the world.

All-weather and small-field capability, and a pressurized, air conditioned interior with 8 to 15-place seating, provide great flexibility for fulfilling varied corporate missions comfortably in the jetprop Beechcraft King Air B100. Maximum cruise speed is 305 mph; maximum range, 1,525 miles.

The pressurized Beechcraft King Air F90 jetprop fulfills exacting standards of performance and personal comfort in corporate service. This newest in the King Air 90 series affords optional 6 to 10-place seating. Maximum cruise speed is 307 mph; maximum range, 1,814 miles.

The new Beechcraft King Air C90-1 offers optimum capa-bilities at minimum cost for a wide range of corporate missions. Its comfort-oriented 6 to 10-place interior is pressurized. Jetprop power provides 273 mph maximum cruise speed; 1,497 miles maximum range.

556

The pressurized, turbocharged Beechcraft Duke B60 continues to top the owner-flown light corporate twin field, with its sleek styling, 4 to 6-place deluxe interior, 275 mph maximum cruise speed, and maximum range of 1,344 miles, plus reserves.

Top of the Beechcraft Baron line is the Baron 58P. Pressurized and turbocharged, its 4 to 6-place cabin features optional club seating and a large double rear door. Maximum range is 1,421 miles, plus reserves, and maximum cruise speed is 277 mph.

The turbocharged Baron 58TC, using the same engines as the Baron 58P, has speed, range, and high-altitude performance that parallels that of the pressurized version. A pilot door, plus wide double doors, facilitates loading and access to the 4 to 6-place cabin.

557

Versatility is the keynote of the Beechcraft Baron 58. Its spacious 4-place cabin affords optional club seating for 6, readily accessible through wide double rear doors, plus a pilot door. Maximum cruise speed is 230 mph; maximum range, 1,541 miles, plus reserves.

The Beechcraft Baron E55 couples high performance with affordable operating costs. Seating options provide roomy comfort for 4 to 6 occupants. Its maximum range is 1,306 miles, plus reserves; maximum cruise speed is 230 mph.

Its ideal balance of performance, value and economy maintains the leadership of the Beechcraft Baron B55 among corporate and personal light twins. Seating is optional for 4 to 6 persons. Maximum cruise speed is 216 mph; maximum range, 1,141 miles, plus reserves.

Turbocharging provides the Beechcraft Bonanza B36TC with performance to 25,000 feet for operating in high altitudes and over weather. The 300-hp engine, most powerful in the Bonanza series, delivers a maximum speed of 229 mph. Maximum range is 862 miles.

Combining high performance, luxurious comfort for 4 to 6 occupants, and versatile utility, the Beechcraft Bonanza A36 is the multi-mission sales leader in its category. Its maximum range is 948 miles, plus reserves; maximum cruise speed, 193 mph.

559

The classic V-tailed Beechcraft Bonanza V35B has been in continuous production longer than any other aircraft. Most prestigious in its class, it seats 4 to 6 persons. Maximum cruise speed is 198 mph; maximum range, 1,023 miles, plus reserves.

The Beechcraft Bonanza F33A parallels the Bonanza V35B in performance and its roomy 4 to 6-place cabin. Its maximum cruise speed is 198 mph; maximum range, 1,023 miles, plus reserves.

Combining four-passenger seating with economical operation, the Beechcraft Duchess stands out as both a business airplane and twin-engine trainer. Counter-rotating propellers give smooth, balanced power during takeoff and climb, with maximum cruise of 191 mph and maximum range of 970 miles.

Chieftain of the Aero Center single-engine line is the Beechcraft Sierra. Featuring retractable landing gear, a constant speed propeller, and right and left-side cabin doors, with 4 to 6-place seating, its maximum cruise speed is 158 mph; maximum range, 790 miles.

For business, personal and training use, the 4-place Beechcraft Sundowner combines maximum economy with traditional Beech excellence. Its sturdy tricycle landing gear is fixed — "always down and locked". Maximum range, 737 miles; maximum cruise speed, 145 mph.

Providing unexcelled visibility and comfort for both instructor and student, the T-tail Beechcraft Skipper has set new standards in performance and economy for training aircraft. The Skipper has a maximum cruise speed of 121 mph and a maximum range of 475 miles.

The advanced, 15-passenger Beechcraft Commuter C99 brings another outstanding Beechcraft to the commuter airline field. The Commuter C99 has a maximum cruise speed of 286 mph and a maximum range of 991 miles.

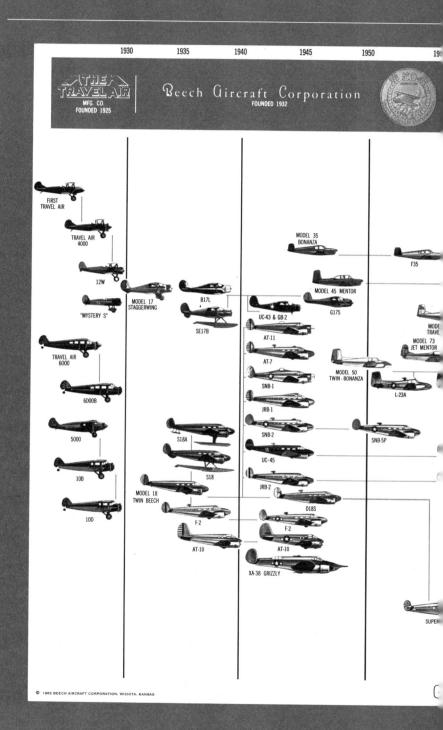

THE TRAVEL AIR
MFG. CO.
FOUNDED 1925

Beech Aircraft Corporation
FOUNDED 1932

FIRST TRAVEL AIR

TRAVEL AIR 4000

12W

"MYSTERY S"

MODEL 17 STAGGERWING

B17L

SE17B

UC-43 & GB-2

AT-11

AT-7

SNB-1

JRB-1

SNB-2

UC-45

JRB-2

D18S

F-2

F-2

AT-10

AT-10

XA-38 GRIZZLY

TRAVEL AIR 6000

6000B

5000

10B

10D

S18A

S18

MODEL 18 TWIN BEECH

MODEL 35 BONANZA

F35

MODEL 45 MENTOR

G17S

MODEL TRAVE

MODEL 73 JET MENTOR

MODEL 50 TWIN-BONANZA

L-23A

SNB-5P

SUPER

Index

Activity Center, Beechcrafters, 200
Addington, Bruce, 422, 489
Admiral Fullam Derby, 2
Advance Airlines, 469, 474
Advertising, early, 16; won awards, 305, 313, 316, 333, 345, 420; re fuel savings, 385; 438
Aero Baires SACd of Argentina, 520
Aero Center/Club concept launched, 211; expanded, 353-4, 381, 399, 408, 438, 443, 447, 456-7, 464, 470, 476, 481, 484, 494, 498, 533 *See also* BEECHCRAFTS, Aero Center
Aerojet-General Corporation, 188
Aero Magazine, 492
Aeromex, S. A., 312, 322, 328
Aeronautical Chamber of Commerce of America, 6, 9, 12
Aeronaves de Mexico, 513
Aerospace, Beech entry into, 130-1. *See also* Military & Aerospace Division; Boulder; Apollo; Gemini; LEM; SSO "Columbia"; Targets
Aerospace Industries Association, 179
Aerovias de Puerto Rico, 31
Ailerons, Beech-built, 114, 118, 120, 143, 181, 182, 206, 217, 252
Aircraft Industries Association, 146, 176
Air Derby, Portland-Cleveland, 10
Air Executive Airline, 263
Air Facts Magazine, 239, 417, 505
Air Force Museum, 441
Air Midwest, 319
Airport Act of 1970, Beech support for, 317
Air races, 2, 3, 5, 6, 7, 9, 10, 11, 14, 15, 19, 20, 21, 22, 23, 26, 27, 34, 35, 79, 95, 96, 118, 128, 149, 154, 205, 268, 276, 328, 310, 311, 315, 332, 345, 365, 424, 441, 459, 484, 529
Air Service Inc., 504
Air Transport Association, 68
Alaska Highway, 32-3
Alert pod system for B-70, Beech-built, 174
Algeria, 326, 420, 437, 493, 528
Allen, G. E., 458
Allen, Roy and Marjorie, 471-2
All American Airways, 66-7
All American Aviation, 75
Allegheny Airlines, 371
Alternative Energy Division, 517, 521, 530, 537
Alumbaugh, Ila, 344, 504
Amana Co., 515

American Academy of Achievement, 441
American Bonanza Society, 296, 324, 461
American Institute of Aeronautics and Astronautics, 389
American Leasing Company, 132
American Mothers Committee, Inc., 317
American Seating Company, 52
Anderson, Congressman Glenn M., 419
Angel Derby, 276, 289
Angel Flight Award, 286-9, 280; Olive Ann Beech Chapter, 289
Angel, Irvin, soloed in Baron, 418
Antenna equipment, Beech, 259
Antique Airplane Association, 261, 265
Apollo program, 196, 218, 258, 292, 314, 327, 333, 351, 360, 368, 371, 384, 388, 390; moon landing, 298, 300-1, 306. *See also* US/USSR Apollo Soyuz Test, 391, 425
Ararat Co., 442
Argentina, 148-9, 174, 480, 482, 520, 528
Arkansas Industrial Development Commission, 391
Army-Navy "E" Award, 50, 55, 62
Arnold Air Society, 289; Paul T. Johns Award, 511
Arnold, General H. H., 36
Atlantic Aviation, 196, 248, 249, 270, 311, 313
Atlee Burpee Seed Co., 76
Australia, 330, 406-7, 423, 427, 440, 452, 461, 469, 474, 477, 481, 505; Outback, 329, 344, 369
Austrian Government, 507
AVCO Corp., Lycoming-Spencer Div., 106
Avery, Kansas Governor William, 260
Aviation Distributors & Manufacturers Association, 332
Aviation education department, Beech, 274, 499
Aviation Hall of Fame, 455, 460-1, 530
Aviation News, 470
Aviation Town & Country Club of Detroit Efficiency Contest, 2
Aviation Week Magazine, 85, 331, 514
Avio Beechcraft of Spain, 445
Avionics sales, 377; packages, 381, 394; options, 408, 409; training program, 394; equipment, 429, 519

Awards, to Beech Aircraft, 50, 55, 130, 149, 268, 276, 287, 290, 305, 316, 345, 371, 420, 454, 455, 465, 515; to O. A. Beech, 106, 115, 131, 161, 214, 268-9, 274, 277, 288, 289, 302-3, 305, 307, 317, 330-1, 332, 337, 355-6, 396-7, 398, 411, 422, 434, 441, 448-9, 459, 461, 463, 522, 530-1, 534; to Walter H. Beech, 331, 332, 455, 460; to John P. Gaty, 136-7; to Frank E. Hedrick, 317, 431, 441, 449, 463, 534, 535; conferred by Beech, 70, 214, 263, 270-1, 280, 295, 311, 337, 350, 359, 364, 381-2, 410, 430, 438-9, 445, 481, 482, 504-5, 520
Ayton, Stewart M., 313, 462, 516

Badger, name for Model 95, 145
Badger Co., 515
Barclays Bank, 406
Barnes, Florence Lowe, 11
Bartman, Capt. Roy, 311
Bass Anglers Sportsman's Society of America, 406
Batten, John H., 315, 319
Bauman, Robt., 393
Bean, astronaut, 306
Beardslee, John M., 245
Beech Acceptance Corp., Inc. (subsidiary), estab. 145-6; 189, 192-5, 206, 259, 453
Beech Activity Center, 209-10, 222, 235, 250, 262, 291, 194-5, 296, 408, 412; Walter H. Beech Hall of, 210, 250, 296, 347; Olive Ann Beech Gallery of, 294-5, 308
Beech Aero Club building, 370
Beech Aerospace Services, Inc., 453, 486, 488, 493, 497-8, 512, 525
Beech Aircraft Company, founded, 13; first design (17R), 15, 241; original plant, 15; 1934 advertisement, 16; upped production, 18; reincorporated, 23
Beech Aircraft Corporation, chartered, 24; bought plant, 24; initial listing of stock, 28; sales topped $1 million, 28, 33; enlarged plant and personnel, 38, 41-2; began incentive payments, 43-4; accelerated production, 44, 50; initiated subcontracting, 48-50; produced glider parts in circus tent, 50; received Army-Navy "E" Award, 50, 55; produced A-26 Invader wings, 51-3; established surplus redistribution subsidiary, 53-4; completed XA-38 Beechcraft "Grizzly", 54, 55, 57-8; qualified for $50 million revolving credit, 59; record praised by Sen-

ator (later President) Harry S. Truman, 62; engineered postwar models and new Beechcraft Bonanza, 65-8, and began deliveries, 71, 75-7; replaced Bonanza wings at no charge, 84-5; began military rebuild programs, 85-6; sought subcontracts, 88; test flew Model 45 Mentor, 89; paid off loans, added $7.2 million to surplus, 89; sponsored world record Bonanza distance flight, 89-90, 91, 93-5; produced first Twin-Bonanza, 95-6; announced 1949 results, 97-8; enlarged facilities and financing for Korean war needs, 100; mourned death of Walter H. Beech, 101-2; set up $20 million revolving credit, 105; won USAF design competition with T-36A Beechcraft, 106, 107, 108; reported 1951 results, 111; built Plant III for T-36A assembly, 107, 112-3; T-36A contract cancellation, 118-9, and effect, 122; reported results for 1953, 122; 1954, 131; 1955, 137-8; 1956, 145; 1957 (Silver Anniversary year), including stock dividend, 157; 1958, including dividend increase, 170; 1959, including stock dividend and dividend increase, 181-2; 1960 record sales, earnings, stock dividend and stock split, 192; established scholarships, 201, 306; announced 1961 results, stock dividend and increased dividend, 205-6; launched Aero Center Beechcrafts, 211; increased working capital and reported 1962 results, 221-2; announced Beechcraft King Air 90, 230, and 1963 results, 232; 1964 results, partial, 246, full, 249; 1965 results, 262; 1966, record sales and delivery of 25,000th Beechcraft, 269-70; 1967, record sales and earnings, 279; 1968, stock split and successful $30 million debentures offering, 284, and record sales, 293; end of Model 18 production, 296, 299, 304; advent of Beechcraft King Air 100, 299; 1969 results, new highs, 301, record sales and stock dividend, 306; 1970 results, 320, 323; 1971 early results and long-range forecast, 325; export sales and Beech policy on, 335; 1971 results and stock dividend, 342; space exploration sales projected, 343; 1972 results, early, 343, earnings and dividend higher, 358; praiseful visit from former President and Mrs. L. B. Johnson, 347-8, 350, 351; introduced Beechcraft Super King Air, 372-3, 375; announced 1973 alltime high results, stock split and increased dividend, 374, 377; reaction to fuel crisis, 383-4, 385; won Air Force/Army utility aircraft competition, 400-2; reported 1974 new high results, stock dividend and increased dividend, 403-4; 1975, greatest year in history, stock dividend and increased dividend, 427; 1976, won U. S. Navy VTAM-X competition, 440; introduced Model 76 Duchess V-tail twin, 447; ranked 76th as defense contractor, 450; fourth consecutive record year, 445; 1977, established BASI, 453; celebrated 45th anniversary, 456-7; produced 10,000th V-tail Model 35 Bonanza, 452-3, 454, 464; delivered 40,000th Beechcraft, 467; declared stock dividend at close of fifth consecutive record year, 462; 1978, introduced Model 77 Skipper V-tail trainer, 465; established Selma (Alabama) facility, 486, declared stock split, 472, and stock dividend at close of sixth consecutive record year, 480-1; 1979, established Commuter Division, announced Commuter C99 and 1900 models, 501; seventh consecutive record year, 501-2; agreed to merge with Raytheon Co., 501-3; 1980, completed merger with Raytheon, 508-11; founded Alternative Energy Division, 517-8; eighth consecutive record year, 519, 523; 1981, elected Edward C. Burns fourth Beech president, 523-4; dedicated Wichita Plant Four, 526; introduced Super King Air B200, 526; hailed Raytheon stock split, 530; delivered first Commuter C99s, 531; made world's first methane-fueled flight with Beechcraft Sundowner, 530; ninth consecutive record year, 532-3; 1982, delivered 1,000th Beechcraft Super King Air, 537; charted five-year action plan, 537; anticipated April 19 Golden Anniversary and next fifty years, 536-7. See also Air races; awards; BEECHCRAFTS; Targets.

Beech Aircraft Foundation, Inc., 305-6, 436, 449, 456, 489, 519

Beech Efficiency Incentive Plan, 43-4, 69-70, 76, 366

Beech Employees Bonanza Plan, 356, 366, 377, 399, 404, 419

Beech facilities, expanded at Wichita, 37-8, 41-43, 50, 105 et seq.; Wichita Plant I, 6, 15, 17, 24, 56, 77, 127, 266, 347, 355; Plant II, 41, 116, 120, 130, 151, 175, 178, 254, 261; Plant III, 107, 124, 125, 133, 254, 363, 367, 384, 395; gas wells, 80; rail spur, 105; water reservoir, 115; display hangar, 254; training center, 279; paint building, 293; Wichita Plant Four, 506. See also Boulder, Herington, Liberal, Newton, Salina, Selma

Beech Holdings, Inc., subsidiary, 323, 416, 453, 462, 516, 517

Beech International Sales Corp., subsidiary, 416, 432, 453. See also International Division.

Beech, Mary Lynn, 56. See also Pitt.

Beech, Mrs. O. A., as Olive Ann Mellor, office manager and secretary of president of Travel Air, 9; married Walter H. Beech and co-founded Beech Aircraft Co., 13; chose Bendix Race pilot, 19-20; viewed production, 45; accepted Army-Navy "E" award, 55; daughters with Mr. Beech, 55; elected president of Beech Aircraft Corporation, 102; named "Woman of the Year in Aviation", 106; received Lady Drummond-Hay Memorial Trophy, 115; stated policy on T-36A cancellation, 119; shown with 1,000th D18S Twin Beech, 124; received honorary doctorate of Science, 131; named "Kansan of the Year", 161; toured European markets, 167; appointed by President Eisenhower to International Development Advisory Board, 172; shown with Travel Air 95 twin, 194; influence on finance, 205; cited for 30 years of service, 214; shown with daughter Suzanne and grandson Lowell Jay Warner, 228; toured markets in Orient, 229-30; hailed first Beechcraft King Air 90, 245; honored at Liberal plant dedication, 245-6; congratulated Merrill C. Meigs on delivery of his 10th Bonanza, 253; named chairman of Kansas Governor's Advisory Commission on Aviation, 260; shown with Dietrich twins, and with veteran employees, 265; shown with Louise Thaden, and with buyer of 25,000th Beechcraft, 266; honored at U. S. Naval Air Station,

268-9; gave out awards at 1967 sales Spectacular, 270, 271; shown with daughter, Mary Lynn, and Mr. and Mrs. Reginald Sinclaire, 272; appointed by President L. B. Johnson to President's Commission on White House Fellows, 273-4; received 35th Service Anniversary award, 274, 277; received Export "E" Award for company, 276; guest of honor at Newcomen Society in North America banquet, 276, 279; handed over presidency to Frank E. Hedrick and continued as chairman of the board and chief executive officer, 280, 283; hailed for civic services, 294; welcomed new granddaughter, Jennifer, 286, 287; honored with plaque from Kansas Press Women, 288, 289; received national Angel Flight award, 286, 288, 289; named to serve on advisory boards of Marine Midland International Corporation and Marine Midland Overseas Corporation, New York City, 294; received NBAA's highest honor, Award for Meritorious Service, 302, 303, 305; viewed last Model 18 Twin Beech, and new Beechcraft Hawker 125 corporate jet, 304; partial list of honors and awards, 305; Olive Ann Beech Chair of Business Administration established at Southwestern College, 305-6; appointed by President Nixon to Smithsonian's National Air and Space Museum Advisory Board, 314; first woman elected to U. S. Chamber of Commerce Board of Directors, 314; shown with 30,000th Beechcraft, 315; named one of 10 most successful women in American business, 317; cited as "One of the country's most outstanding women" by American Mothers Committee, Inc., 317; presented plaque to John H. Batten, 319; received "Wilbur" award from Service City Group, Dallas, 330-1; first woman member of Flight Safety Foundation Awards Board, 331; named to National Advisory Council of Army Aviation Museum, 331; appointed a director of National Executive Committee of Junior Achievement, 331; became a member of NASA Space Shuttle Study Committee, 331; presented by International Ninety-Nines with Amelia Earhart medallion, certificate and plaque, 331; accepted certificate from OX-5 Club of America, 331-2; first woman to receive ADMA Award of Merit, 332; presented with Jugasz metal sculpture, 337-8; shown with Mr. and Mrs. Lyndon B. Johnson, 350; presided at XL-73 Awards Banquet, 350; received 40-year service award, 355-6; received plaque from U. S. Naval Test Pilot School, 365; cited by *Fortune* magazine as heading "Ten Highest Ranking Women in Big Business", 367; received Kansas University "Citation for Distinguished Service", 396, 397; received National Aeronautic Association "Elder Statesman of Aviation" award, 398, 411; honored guest at International Women's Year dinner, Washington, 415; honored at dedication of Walter H. Beech Hangar of Staggerwing Museum, 422-4; honored by Gallagher's *Presidents Reports*, 434, *Business Week*, 441, and LIFE *Special Report*, 441; received Uncommon Citizen Award, 448-9; elected trustee emeritus of Wesley Medical Center, 454; received 45-year service pin, 459; accepted posthumous gold medal from Aviation Hall of Fame for Walter H. Beech, 460; named honorary member of American Bonanza Society, 461; received sales support award, 463; honored by Kansas Women's Aero, 475; enrolled in International Forest of Friendship, 477; presented diploma to 20,000th Training Center graduate, 480-1; thanked for sturdiness of Beech 99 airliner, 485; guest of honor at Montreal, 485; visited with Dr. Otto Thaning, 491; guest of honor at Pensacola graduation, 494; received birthday greetings, 499; commented on merger, 502; elected to Raytheon board of directors, 510, and executive committee, 518; received Kitty Hawk Sands of Time Award, 522; received Wright Brothers Memorial Trophy, 522; honored on plaque in Naval Museum, 524; congratulated by employees, 529; named "First Lady of Aviation" in dedication of Olive Ann Beech Gallery and Chapel at Staggerwing Museum, 529; inducted beside Walter H. Beech into Aviation Hall of Fame, 530-1; received Distinguished Achievement Award and honorary life membership from Wings Club, 534

Beech Research & Development, Inc., subsidiary, estab. 141, 173, 189, 197, 453. *See also* Research

Beech, R. K., 9

Beech subsidiaries, 53-4, 62, 68-70, 87, 141, 145-6, 173, 189, 191-5, 197, 206, 214, 259, 279, 313, 318, 323, 354, 370, 395, 402-3, 407, 410, 411-2, 415-6, 462, 516, 517

Beech, Suzanne, 56, 225, 228. *See also* Warner

Beech, Walter H(erschel), birthplace and background, first solo flight, 1, 2; co-founded Travel Air Mfg. Co., won Ford Reliability Tours, 2, 3; early Travel Air triumphs, 5-6, 7, 8; leader in aircraft industry, 9-12; left Curtiss-Wright, 12; co-founded Beech Aircraft Co., 13; produced first Beechcraft, 14, 15; expanded plant, 15, 17-18; enlarged line, 15, 18; sponsored race entries, 19, 20, 21, and belly landing demonstrations, 22, 23-4; introduced Model 18 Twin Beech, 22, 24-6; redesigned biplanes, 21, 26-7; sales to executives, feeder airlines, 29, 31, Philippine Army Air Corps, 29, Republic of China, 22, 30, 32, 35, 36, U. S. Army Air Corps and U. S. Navy, 22, 30, 32, 36; effect of his experiences on design, 33; co-pilot in MacFadden Trophy race, 32, 34-5; initiated defense production and expansion, 36-8; relationship with employees, 44; viewed production, 45; received Army-Navy "E" Award, 55; shown with daughters, 56; announced conservative production policy, 83; approved Twin-Bonanza plans, 95-6, 107; pledged to meet defense needs, 100-1; suffered fatal heart attack, 101; funeral and memorial, 101-2, 108, 110; left fighting spirit and philosophy as legacy, 150, 156; scholarships and Memorial Wind Tunnel honoring, 201; Walter H. Beech Hall built, 209-10; flying tradition upheld, 225; honored by Naval Aviation Museum, 268-9; honored for "outstanding contributions to aviation", 302; honored with Mrs. Beech by Ninety-Nines, 331; elected to OX-5 Club Hall of Fame, 332; honored at dedication of Staggerwing Museum Walter H. Beech Hangar, 423; enshrined in Aviation Hall of Fame, 455, 460; plaque of in Naval Aviation Museum, 524, 530

Beechcraft A. G., Switzerland, 453

Beechcraft de Mexico, 513

Beechcraft East, Inc., 453

Beechcraft Employees Club, 200, 511, 524

Beechcraft Employees Flying Club, 269, 531

Beechcraft Espanola S.A., Spain, 520

Beechcraft Hawker Corp., subsidiary, estab. 313, 318-9, 395, 402-3, 425; Jet Centers, 395

Beechcraft Hawker, 125, 304, 309-10; 125-400, 326, 328, 336, 339, 347, 358; 125-600, 310, 326, 357-8

Beechcraft Sales S.A. Pty. Ltd., Republic of South Africa, 445, 481, 504-5

Beechcraft Training Center, 279, 372, 389, 394, 480, 516. *See also* Service to customers

Beechcraft West, Inc., subsidiary, 354, 370, 411-2, 453, 470, 481, 494, 520

Beechcrafter, employee house organ, 263

BEECHCRAFTS

Model 17 Staggerwing biplanes:
17R, first Beechcraft, 14, 15, 18, 241; B17L, 15, 17, 18, 28, 136; A17F, 17, 21; B17B, 18; B17R, 18; C17B, 19, 22, 23; C17L, 19; C17R, 19, 20, 21; D17R, 22, 26, 30; D17S, 22, 26, 27, 30, 41, 261, 336, 391, 408, 426, 441, 531; D17A, 26; D17W, 21, 26-7, 34; E17B, 26, 29, 458; F17D, 26; G17S, 87-8, 91, 335; *military versions*, USAAC/USAF UC-43, 22, 30, 41; U. S. Navy GB-1, GB-2, 41; assembly line, 21; B17R round-the-world flight, 18-9; shipment via dirigible, 19. *See also* Air Races; Staggerwing Club; Staggerwing Museum

Model 18 Twin Beech:
Prototype, 18, 22, 24-6, 29, 241; 18A, 29, 31; 18D, 29; 18S, 30, 32, 34, 35; D18C, 66, 67, 75; D18C-T, 75, 76, 77; D18S, 63, 64, 65, 66, 76, 77, 78, 79, 92, 124, 127, 154-5, 199, 202, 260, 391; Super 18, 124, 125, 127, 134, 138, 139, 140, 141, 144, 148, 157, 160, 170, 171, 173, 178, 180; Super G18, 183-4, 186, 193, 336; Super H18, 219-20, 233, 236-7, 243, 260, 271, 273, 290, 296, 304,

307; *military versions*, 18R light bomber, 32, 35, 36; USAF C-45 personnel transports, 37, 39, 48, 114, 223, 314; C-45G rebuilds, 114; F-2 photographic planes, 30, 32, 33; AT-7 navigation trainers, 37, 38, 40, 42, 48; AT-11 bombardier trainers, 36, 38, 39, 40, 42, 45, 46, 48; U. S. Navy JRB-1 utility transports, 40, 41; SNB-1 (USAF AT-11), 39, 86; SNB-2, *see* USAF AT-7; SNB-4 rebuilds, 86; SNB-5 rebuilds, 114, 117, 127-8; RC-45J retired to Naval Aviation Museum, 358; production lines, 45, 63; modernization kits, 172-3; longevity and end of production, 296, 299, 302, 304, 307; flying test bed, 338; AT-11 to USAF Museum, 411; Navy Model 18 trainers, 525

Aero Center Beechcrafts:
Model 19 Sport, 262, 290, 312, 322, 341-2, 351; B19 Sport, 327, 341, 353, 354, 360; Sport 150, 381, 399, 409, 429, 438, 447, 465, 531
Model 23 Musketeer, 208, 211, 213, 216, 218-9, 220-2, 227, 228, free modifications, 246; A23 Musketeer II, 242, 245, 250; Custom III, 262, 275, 282, 290, 344, 368; C23 Sundowner, 342, 353, 354, 360; Sundowner 180, 381, 409, 423, 429, 431, 433, 438, 447, 465, 470, 530-1, 534, 537
Model 24 Musketeer, Super III, 262; Super R, 308; A24R Sierra, 342, 353, 354, 360, 364; recertificated Sierra 200, 381, 401, 405, 409, 413, 429, 433, 438, 447, 456, 465, 534
Model 76 Duchess T-tail twin, proposed as Model PD289, 409-10, 412, 413, 429; introduced, 447, 457, 464, 470-1, 473, 513
Model 77 Skipper T-tail trainer, proposed as Model PD285, 410, 412, 416, 429, 447; introduced, 465, 479-80, 483, 484, 494-5, 496, 505, 513

Beechcraft Bonanzas:
Model 33 Debonair, 178, 179, 183-4, 188, 193, 195; B35, 204-5, 215; C33, 250, 256, 260; C33A, 262-3, 278, 529; F33A, 461, 464, 491; F33C, 389-90, 414, 417, 435, 507
Model 35 V-tail, 58-9, 64, 67, 71-5, 81-5, 89-96, 91, 92, 111, 115, 241, 264, 421, 426, 518; B35, 98; C35, 104; D35, 117, 118, 120; E35, 126, 128-9, 154, 205; F35, 133-4, 137; G35, 138; H35, 148, 5000th Bonanza, 151, 154; J35,

158, 160, 164-5, 170; K35, 170, 6,000th Bonanza, 175, 178, 268, 276, 289; M35, 184, 188, 193; N35, 192, 202, 326; P35, 210, 7,000th Bonanza, 216; S35, 238-9, 8,000th Bonanza, 253, 254, 256, 262, 275, 289, 469; V35, V35C/TC, 262, 267, 441; V35A, 9,000th Bonanza, 295-6, 297; V35B, Silver Anniversary, 323-4, 340-1, 349, 352-3, 380-1, 417, 418, 429, 432; 10,000th V-tail Bonanza, 452-3, 464, 478, 484
Model 36, 288, 289-90, 321, 332; A36, 341, 360, 382, 393, 424, 441, 443, 446, 464, 489, 513; 2,000th Model 36, 535; A36TC, 484, 486, 492-3, 496, 498, 514; *military version* A36, USAF QU-22B, 321, 334
Model 34 Twin-Quad, 68, 87, 91 (Prototype only; not produced. Model number reassigned to commercial/export Turbo Mentor)
Model T-34C Turbo Mentor commercial/export pilot trainer, 372, 465, 466, 467, 480, 513, 528, 535; *military version*, U. S. Navy T-34C, 419, 430, 443, 465-6, 498, 525, 528
Model 45 Mentor commercial/export pilot trainer, 89, 92, 97, 121, 160-1, 181, 351, 356, 435, 525; *military versions*, USAF YT-34, 92, 99; T-34A, 113, 118, 121-2, 127-8; U. S. Navy T-34A, 121-2; T-34B, 123, 128, 268-9. See also Model 73

Beechcraft Piston-Engine Twins:
Model 50 Twin-Bonanza, 95-6, 105-6, 107; B50, 126, 132; C50, 132, 134, 137; D50, 138, 139, 144, 160; E50, 148, 151, 157, 158; F50, 160, 170; G50, 170; H50, 184, 185, 188, 196, 202; *military versions*, U. S. Army YL-23, 111; L-23A Seminole, 113, 117, 120, 123, 126, 135, 144; L-23D, 151, 154, 162-3, 170, 180; RL-23D, 166-7, 180; RL-23F, 180, 186; L-23F, 180, 182, 186
Model 55 Baron, 194, 195, 202; A55, 210; B55, 234, 235-6, 242, 247, 252, 254, 256, 261, 311, 319, 334, 340, 344, 345-6, 356, 360, 369, 377, 380, 384, 385, 391, 393, 406, 416, 418, 423, 428, 446, 464, 483, 513; C55, 262, 267-8, 271, 279; D55, 295, 297; E55, 340, 360, 380, 409, 428, 483; *military version*, U. S. Army T-42A, 261, 336
Model 56 Turbo Baron, 270

569

Model 58 Baron, 308, 329, 340, 360, 368; B58, 380, 390, 403, 406, 409, 418, 428, 438, 439, 459, 483, 529, 533, 535; 58P, 409, 412, 416, 427-8, 439, 444, 446, 453, 464, 473, 476, 483, 518, 525, 535; 58TC, 412, 427-8, 446, 464, 467, 473, 483, 513

Model 60 Duke, 270, 272, 273, 280, 290, 293; A60, 320, 329, 339, 344, 353, 358; B60, 360, 368-9, 377, 380, 393, 395, 403, 406, 409, 413, 418, 429, 443, 446, 464, 483; 500th Duke, 494, 505, 533

Model 65 Queen Air, 178, 179, 183-4, 186, 193, 195, 204, 212-3, 223, 247, 260, 262, 268; A65, 270, 278

Model 73 Jet Mentor single-engine trainer, 135, 139 (Prototype only; not produced)

Model 76, see Aero Center Beechcrafts

Model 77, see Aero Center Beechcrafts

Model 80 Queen Air, 208, 213, 222, 223, 233, 234, 237-9; A80, 239, 247, 257, 260, 261, 262, 263, 265, 266, 268, 311, 329; B80, 339, 360, 380, 390, 396, 409, 418, 506; military version, turbo-powered U. S. Army U-8F, 240, 242

Model 85 Queen Air, 222; 85D, 230, 231-2 (Produced as Model 88)

Model 88 Queen Air proposed, 222, 230, 231-2; introduced, 253, 259-60, 262

Model 90, see Beechcraft Jetprop Twins

Model 95 Travel Air twin, 140, 144, 159-60; B95, 184, 185, 188; B95A, 197, 199; D95A, 224, 254, 262, 295, 297, 329

Beechcraft Jetprop Twins:
Model 90 King Air proposed, 210, 220, 222; announced, 230-2; 234, 235, 239-40, 241, 242, 243, 244-5, 248; 252, 256, 259-60, 261, 262, 440; A90, 264, 25,000th Beechcraft, 266, 267, 268, 270, 273, 279, 281, 282, 290, 299, 309, 315, 318, 357, 418; B90, 329-30, 389, 391; C90, 319-20, 339, 346, 352, 359, 362, 370-1, 377, 379, 391, 396, 407, 408, 414, 428, 446, 456, 462, 506, 512, 527, 528, 535; E90, 352, 358, 435, 444, 446, 476; F90, 496, 500, 505, 516, 522; military versions, USAF VC-6A, 263, 265, 402; U. S. Army U-21A, 270, 272, 274, 278, 286; U. S. Navy T-44A, 440, 448, 452,

545-5, 457-8, 461, 467, 468, 525

Model 95, see Beechcraft piston-engine twins

Model 99 Beech Airliner, 274-5, 282, 289, 290, 291, 351, 416, 484; 99A, 310-12, 314, 315, 317-8, 319, 327, 339; 99B, 356-7, 360, 371, 380, 402, 423, 484-5, 500; Commuter C99, 500, 514, 521, 531, 537

Model 100 King Air, 298, 299-300, 302, 308, 311, 315, 319, 326; A100, 322, 333, 334, 337, 339, 347, 349, 350, 355, 356, 357, 358, 359, 363, 370, 371, 377, 379, 387, 391, 393, 399, 402, 406, 408, 420, 423, 428, 437, 446, 453, 463, 474; B100, 402, 412, 427, 428, 439, 444, 446, 463; military versions, U. S. Army RU-21E, 314, 349, 354-5; U-21F, 322, 334

Model 120, 210, 222, 230 (Produced as Model 90)

Model 200 Super King Air, 372-4, 375, 377, 379, 384, 386, 401, 403, 406-7, 408, 418, 425-6, 427, 428, 433, 439, 444, 446, 469, 470, 474, 483, 493, 505, 507, 508, 521, 531, 537; B200, 526, 529, 532, 533, 535; military versions, U.S. Army/USAF C-12A, 386, 400-2, 425-6, 434, 450, 456, 467, 471, 488, 498, 512; C-12D, 512; U. S. Navy and Marine Corps C-12, 468; UC-12B, 512

Model 1900 Commuter, 500, 514

Model PD183, 244 (Not produced)

Model PD280, 416 (Not produced)

Model PD285, see Model 77

Model PD289, see Model 76

Military Beechcrafts (No commercial versions), USAAC AT-10, 41, 42, 45, 46, 48, 51-2, 60, 112; USAAC XA-38 Grizzly, 54-8, 55, 62, 264; USAF T-36A, 106, 107, 109-10, 112-3, 116-7, 118-9, 120

Beery, Wallace, 7, 345

Beiler, Fritz, 18

Belgium, 420, 474

Bell, A. R., 191

Bell, Donald A., 139

Bell Helicopter, 216, 235, 255, 268, 273, 284-5, Gold Rotor Award, 287; 318, 330, 344, 362, 363, 367-8, 384-6, 395, 416-7, 436, 467, 468, 478, 498-9, 511, 526

Bell, James E., 479

Bell, Lawrence, 455

Belly landing demonstration, 22, 23-4

Bendix Transcontinental Speed Dash, 19, 20, 21, 23, 27, 424; trophy, 20

Benes, Don, 281
Banner & Fields, Inc., 418
Benham, Harold, 469
Bennett, Kansas Governor Robert, 456-7
Berra, Frances, 154, 205, 459, 481
Bergen, Edgar, 262
Beutel, Albert P. II, 457
Bicentennial Year, 434, 450; Silver dollar, 442
Big Bend Community College, 282
Billings Research Corp., 389; vehicle, 389
Bird, Dr. Forrest, 479
Blumberg, Juanita, 529
Bobet, Louison and Phillip, 390
Boeing B-47 ailerons, 114, 119; C-26 generator, 129; fuel tanks, 133, 142, 181; mid-air refueling system, 328
Boener, Walter, 370
Boling, Capt. Marion (Pat), 158, 164-6, 170
Bomb dispensers and containers, 217, 223, 232
Bongo, Omar, 535
Booker, Stanley, 311
Bostad, Bjorn, 228
Boulder Division, estab., 136; growth, 141, 150-2, 177, 186, 202-3, 229; Dewar containers, 152, 163; R & D programs, 163, 169, 196, 198, 217-8, 232; transient heat tower and laboratory, 173, 177, 187; components testing, 183; topping control units, 200; cryogenic systems, 258; anniversaries, 10th, 261, 20th, 425; AQM-37A production, 285-6; 444, 455, 462, 466, 471, 479, 485, 486, 488, 497, 499, 506, 517, 520, 536. See also Alternative Energy; Liquefied gas; Targets
Bowery, Leroy E., 251, 344, 475; (Mrs.) Marcelline, 475
Box, Ed, 481
Bowman, Harold L., 425
Brakes, 4, 15, 134, 216, 238
Brazil, 482; Govt., 35; Air Force, 92, 95, 243
Brewer, Bruce B. Co., 345
Brier, Evelyn P. "Pinky", 493
Brom, Rudolph, 274
Bronte, Emory B., 6, 95
Brougham, Trevor K., 345
Brown Construction, Albuquerque, 467
Brugh, Ken, 139
Brumos Aviation Corp., 215
Brundage, Hubert L., 194
Brunk, Letha, 458
Buckley, John B., 349
Bulmer, Harriett E., 416, 504

Burgerhout, H. A., 149
Burlington Industries, 139
Burma, 154-5
Burnham, Walt, 10
Burniat, Paul, 115
Burns, Edward C(raig), 251; elected to board of directors, 355, 366; named group vice president, 405; pictured with wife, Betty, 422, 466; elected executive vice president, 497; shared Office of the President, 516; declared "War on Waste", 517; elected fourth president of Beech, 523-4; elected to GAMA board, 528
Business & Commercial Aviation magazine, 320
Byrd, Admiral Richard E., 411

Caedmon Records, 515
Caine, Steve, 479
C-26 ground service units, 114, 118, 127
California Institute of Technology, 423
California State Dept. of Fish & Game, 157
Campos, Miguel (Mike), 430
Canadair Ltd., 117
Canada, 31, 34, 76, 77, 113-4, 145, 149, 202, 203, 377, 418, 420, 445, 486
Canadian Armed Forces, 322, 327, 328, 444, 531
Cantrell, F. W., 459
Cape Canaveral, 182
Cape Kennedy, 257, 368
Capsulated ejection trainer, 200-1
Captain Cook Bi-Centenary Prize, 311
Caravan of Beechcrafts to Canada, 201-2
Carco Airservice, 106
Carlin, Kansas Governor John, 500, 528
Carnasciali, Tito L., Companhia Carnasciali of Brazil, 410
CAR.04 Aircarrier transport, Model D18C-T, 75, 76, 77
Carpenter, Ray, 518
Carstens, Vern, 253, 262, 264, 477
Carver, Roy, 130
Case, Joyce, 219, 227, 250
Cassidair Services Inc., 215
Cefly Lancer program, USAF, 406
Centaur space vehicle, 196
Central Airlines, Bonanza fleet, 99
Central American Airways Flying Service, Inc., 154
Central Bucks Aero Inc., 275
Central Flying Service Inc., 504
Central Missouri State College, 364
Century 21, 518

Certified Service Centers awarded plaques, 399
Chamber of Commerce of the United States, 314
Chance-Vought Aircraft, Inc., 188
Chaney Construction Co., 417
Chaparral Aviation, Inc., 394, 410, 481, 504; Chaparral Tradewind, 482-3
Chase Econometrics, 429
Chase Manhattan Bank, 429, 506
Chevrolet D-6 engine, 10
Chicago & North Western Railway, 256
Childress, Jess M., 270, 271, 350
Chile, 119, 145, 161, 174, 420; Govt. of, 314
China, Republic of, 22, 30, 32, 35-6, 92, 97, 473, 498, 520, 525
Christman Air System, 531
Circus tent production facility, 50
Cities Service, 157
"City of Oakland" endurance flight, 6, 95
Civil Aeronautics Administration (CAA), 66, 71, 76, 106, 238, 239
Civil Aeronautics Authority, 30
Civil International Aviation Training Center, 346
Civilian Free-for-All race, 9
Clark, T. Gail, 320, 350
Clements, Thomas W., 456
Cochran, Jacqueline, 21, 26-7, 34
Cody, Don, 481
Coffey, Harry K., 29, 31
Cogera Industria e Comercio Ltda., Brazil, 482
Coleman, Philip, 430
Collecta-data computer system, 191
College of Air Training, 279
Collins, Rear Admiral Frank, 535
Collins, Leighton, 239, 417, 505
Collins Radio Co., 369; Avionics, 446; Flight Director System, 519
Colman, Seymour, 438, 479, 527
Colombia Aero Taxi S.A., 263
Colombia, Republic of, 121, 145, 174
Colorado University, 152
Cominter, 513
Command/Service module, 368, 384, 390. See also Apollo
Commonality program, 330
Communication/Navigation Evaluation, 326, 337
Commuter Airlines, 263, 266, 282, 289; Association, 521
Commuter Division, 504, 514. See also BEECHCRAFTS, Models C99 and 1900 Commuter
Commuterworld magazine, awards spokesman, 423
Compton, Dr. Walter Ames, 349

Computers, 208, 215, 451
Connes, Keith, 495
Conrad, Charles, 261, 306
Constant, Max, 27
Continental Casualty Co., 524
Continental engines, 58, 66, 67, 75, 94, 126, 128, 129, 160, 165, 184, 190-1, 238, 262, 340, 341, 410, 492
Continuing quality support program, 396
Control tower, 519
Convair, 143, 156, 163, 169, 171, 181, 183; topping control unit, 201
Cook, Leroy, 492, 495
Cook, Ron, 444, 447
Cooper, Leroy Gordon, Jr., 196, 242, 247, 261, 262
Cooper, Trudy, 246
Corporate aviation centers, 354
Corpus Christi Naval Air Station, 458, 461
Cote, Shirley, 441
Critchell, Iris, 154
Crompton, David, 407
Cryogenics, 131, 136, 150, 169, 173, 177, 183, 187, 217, 258, 261, 292, 300, 307, 323, 343, 368, 371, 376, 387, 388, 390, 391, 425, 467, 485, 489, 499, 506, 517, 527
Cullinane, Dan C., 459
Cunningham, Dean, 79
Curtis pusher biplane, 1
Curtiss-Wright, 9, 12, 13, 24, 82
Customer service program, 105
Cutter Aviation Inc., Cutter Flying Service, Inc., 390, 482

Daisy Mfg. Co., 392
Dale, Jimmy, 282
Dalton, Denys, 444
Damon, L. R., 415, 504
Danaher, Thos. H., 130
"Dart" tow target, Model 1002, 140, 142
Davis, Arlene, 185
Davis, Doug, 8, 10, 11
Davis, Tom H., 350
Davis, William, 6, 96
Debentures, issuance of, 284; conversion of, 501, 508
Deering-Milliken, 264
Deets, Harold W., 355, 527
Deets, Mary Ellen, 416
Defense Plant Corporation, 89
Del Gato, Ernesto; Del Gato Construction Co., 368
Deline, Capt. Les, 532
Delman, Paul G., 263
Denver Beechcraft, Inc., subsidiary, 279, 407, 410, 470
Denver-Martin "Titan" complex, 152
Department of Defense, 118; con-

tractors, Beech ranked 76th, 450, 472

Detmer, Eugene, 6

Dickeson, Robert N., 345

Dicks, Dr. Harold G. and Robin, 369, 406

Dieker, C. W., 415, 447-8, 503, 527

Dietrich, Jan and Marion, 257, 265

Dikes, Chancellor Archie E., 397

Dill, Pierre, 268

Disney, Walt, Productions, 261

Docking, Kansas Governor Robert B., 331, 347, 350

Dolbee, Jim, 514

Dole races, 6, 7; prize, 96

Donaldson, J. O., 10

Doolittle, General James H., 8, 108-10, 303, 411, 460

Douglas Aircraft Co., 51-3, 60-2, 112, 275, 280

Douglas, Donald, Sr., 302, 411

Dow Corporation, 78

Draper, Chas. S., 531

Drew, Major Adrian, 156

Drones, pilotless target, 414, 424

Dunbar, Douglas P., Jr., 365

Dunlop-Australian Prize, 311

Dun's Review, 437, 514

Dunsworth, E. E., 303

Du Pont, Henry B., 270, 271

Dyer, Capt. Thos., 496-7

Eagle Aircraft Services, Ltd., 311, 403

Earhart, Amelia, Medallion, 331; anniversary, 415, 477

Eaton, John David, 29

Eaton, Max P., 497, 528

"E" Award; Army, Navy, 50, 55; Export, 276

Ecuador, 466, 513, 528

Edwards, Lucille Winters. *See* Winters

Egypt, 78, 79, 435, 437, 450

Ehling, Glenn, 527

Eisenhower, Dwight D., 29, 172, 305

"Elder Statesman of Aviation" Award, 398, 411

Elevons, 176

El-Jay Inc., 515

Elliott Beechcraft, 445, 482

Eliott, F. T. Jr., 456

Elliott, John A., 191, 251, 274, 344, 405, 448, 459

Employees, of Travel Air, 4, 9, 265; of Beech, 41, 43-4, 47, 54, 59, 60, 61, 69, 76, 79, 89, 103-4, 114-6, 117, 125, 153, 168, 204, 209-10, 214, 226, 264, 267, 269, 270, 274, 295, 301, 325, 356, 364, 366, 377, 399, 404, 419, 442, 449, 451, 459, 462, 467, 477-8, 488-9, 504, 512,

520, 529, 532. *See also* Beechcraft Employees Club; Beechcraft Employees Flying Club

Endsley, Earl L. "Pete", 264

Endurance records, 10, 89-96, 164-6

Engines, 2, 5, 10, 12, 15, 17, 18, 19, 26, 27, 35, 66, 67, 94, 106, 126, 128, 132, 136, 138, 144, 148, 159, 160, 165, 170, 174, 183, 184, 190-1, 195, 197, 199, 213, 224, 231, 238, 239, 240, 244, 259, 262, 264, 273, 275, 299, 310, 326, 336, 337, 338, 339, 340, 341, 342, 352, 357, 359, 373, 381, 402, 409, 410, 412, 427-8, 446, 463, 486, 494, 496, 521, 526

Engle, Col. Joe, 466, 536

Enstrom, Mary, 499

Ennis, Will, 441

Erickson, Dale, 413, 476-7

Esso Standard Oil Co., 76

Ethyl Corp., 14

Evans, Gordon W., 294

Executive Airlines, 263

Executive Aviation Centers, 354

Executive Beechcraft, Kansas City, 407

Executive Flight Plan, 473, 513

Experimental Ship race, 10

Export, 33; enlarged markets, 86-7, 113, 116, 273, 279, 286, 323; "E" award, 276. *See also* International Division

Fairchild Aircraft Division, 188

Fairlie Steels Ltd., 491

Falconer, W. A., 282

Farnborough Exhibition, 403, 444

Farquhar, Capt. H. L., 18

Farrell, Joseph E., 410

Federal Aviation Administration (FAA), Authority of, 171; Agency of, 182, 213, 223; FAA, 173, 205, 213, 233, 244-5, 246, 291, 299, 302, 306, 367, 377, 384, 386, 390, 419, 420, 506-7, 512, 522

Federal Energy Administration, 390, 391

Federation Aeronautique Internationale, 186, 268, 311, 345, 378, 444, 456, 465

Ferris, James, 372

Ferris State College, 364

Field Aviation Co. Ltd. of Canada, 445

Filer, Warren F., 264

Firestone, Harvey S., Jr., 172; Tire & Rubber Co., 172

First flights, Beechcrafts, 14, 24, 54, 87, 89, 95, 144, 224, 239-40, 270, 372, 457, 480

Fischer, Felix, 462

Fisher, R. Warren, 251, 344

Fleetways Inc., 140
Flight magazine, 331
Flight planning computer, 519, 521
Flight Safety Foundation, 331
Flightcraft, Inc., 382, 477, 504
Floor plan financing, 137
Florida Airways, 75
Flotation capsules, training, 201
Flying magazine, 320, 492
Fogg, Bob, 21
Forbes magazine, 437
Ford, Jack, 140
Ford Granada, LM-fueled, 534
Ford, President Gerald R., 416, 439, 528
Ford Reliability Tour, 2-3
Fortune magazine, 367, 455, 514
Fourth National Bank of Wichita, 59
Fraissinet, Roland, 463
France, 445, 463, 482, 505, 520
Freedoms Foundation, 305, 316, 345, 420
Free-for-All race, 10
French government, 117; Air Force, 370, 400
Fuel cell servicing system, 527
Fuel & Lines Services, Inc., subsidiary, 453
Fuel tanks, Beech-built, 88, 100-1, 118; for F84-F, 132; for P47, 133, 142, 153, 163, 181; for F104, 163; auxiliary, 144, 165
Fuji Heavy Industries, 122
Funsch, John H., 517

Gabon, 533
Garrett AiResearch engines, 402, 412, 427-8, 444, 446, 463, 495
Gaty, John P., 9, 28, 101, 136-7, 166, 188-9, 495
Geiss safety gear, 144
Gemini spacecraft, 221, 257, 258, 260, 388
General Automation Inc., 377
General Aviation Manufacturers Association (GAMA), 389, 431, 439, 449, 466, 487, 490, 528
General Dynamics Corp., 168, 171, 465
General Motors Corp., 13, 102, 281
Gerber Products Co., 290, 329-30
Germany, Federal Republic of, 220, 225, 294, 441, 445, 478
Glenn, John, 212
Gliders, CG-4A, production of, 50
Globe Aircraft Corp., 51
Globe Engineering Co., 417
Godfrey, Arthur, 296, 297, 438
Goebel, Arthur C., 6, 7, 96
Goff, Hal, 281
Gold Rotor Award to Beech, 268, 284-5, 287

Golden B's, 490
Goldsborough, Brice H., 3
Goodyear Aircraft Corp., 188
Gordon, Michael M., 520
Gorman, James C., Gorman-Rupp Co., 335
Goshorn, Larry, 377
Gothenburg Air Show, 439
Gould, Inc., Simulation Systems Div., 485
Grand Prix International, 268
Grayton Printing Co., 418
Great Britain, 273, 279, 286, 403. *See also* United Kingdom
Greece, 390
Gregg, Vaughan, 457, 480
Greene, Wichita Mayor Jack, 328, 347, 350
Greer Maintenance Award to Beech, 149, 204
Greever, Leddy L., 191, 251, 449, 479
Grolero, Capitan de Fragata Rodolfo, 521
Ground service/support units and vehicles, Beech-built, 114, 118, 127, 129, 130, 133, 135, 140, 142, 144, 147, 155, 161-2, 163, 174, 221. *See also* C-26, MA-3, MD-3
Gruber, Gerald F., 443
Grumman Aircraft Engineering Corp., 258, 292, 377, 435, 445
Guatemala, 435, 445; Beechcraft de, 410
Guenther, Wm., 461
Gunstream, Walter, 415
Gwinn-Jones, Terry, 444

Haddaway, George E., 330, 505, 531
Hadley, Ross, 29
Hagemeister, Lee D., 295-6, 297
Halzslop, Ralph G., 324
Hamamcioglu Muesseseleri Tricaret, Turkey, 482
Hane, Bill, 491-2
Hangar One, Inc., 382, 407, 410, 430, 445, 463, 481, 498, 505, 520, 533
Hanssen, Gary M., 479, 497
Hanover Aerospace Show, 439, 513
Harmon Trophy, 20
Harp, Liberal, Kan. Mayor Lloyd, 275
Harris, Lloyd W., 395, 402
Hart, Marion, 120-1, 269, 326
Hartzell propellers, 138, 184, 381
Hartzog Aviation Inc., 430, 445
Hartzog Ira B., 315
Hass, Carl, 488
Hatcher, F. L., 442
Hawaii, 6, 7, 90, 420; Hawaiian Airlines, 75

Hawk missile system, 510, 515
Hawker de Havilland Pty. Ltd., Australia, 407, 410, 423, 430, 445, 461
Hawker Pacific Pty. Ltd., Australia, 469, 477, 481, 505
Hawker Siddeley Aviation Ltd., 304, 309, 310-11, 326, 395, 425. *See also* Beechcraft Hawker
Hawks, Capt. Frank, 8, 11
Hay, Leonard ("Mr. Bonanza"), 382, 434, 446, 498
Heath, D. C. Pub. Co., 515
Hedrick, Betty, 277, 350
Hedrick, Frank E(dgar), joined Beech as coordinator (1940), promoted to vice presidency, elected to board of directors (1950), elected executive vice president (1960), 189; shown with Queen Air A80, 265; with 25,000th Beechcraft, 266; at 1967 Sales Spectacular, 271; at Army U-21A delivery ceremony, 272; presented 35 year service award to Mrs. Beech, 274, 277; shown with wife, Betty, at delivery of Newcomen Society address, 276, 277, 279; elected president of Beech Aircraft Corp., 280, 283; accepted Bell Helicopter Gold Rotor award, 268, 287, and Industry Award from International Exposition of Flight, 287; shown with Beechcraft Hawker 125, 304; with 30,000th Beechcraft, 315; with Lyndon B. and Mrs. Johnson, 350; appointed by White House to area chairmanship of National Alliance of Businessmen (NAB), 370; elected to Board of Directors of National Aeronautic Association, 378; appraised fuel crisis on national television, 383; reported success of area NAB jobs-for-veterans program, 393-4; presented "Elder Statesman of Aviation" award to Mrs. Beech for NAA, 398, 411; elected vice-chairman of General Aviation Manufacturers Association (GAMA) board of directors, 411; received letter of thanks from President Ford, 416; received honorary Doctorate, 421, 423; delivered Southwestern College commencement address, 423; received award from *Commuterworld* magazine, 423; received 35-year service award, 431; elected board chairman of GAMA, 431-2; analyzed Beech stock appreciation, 437; spokesman to President Ford

for GAMA, 439; accepted second terms on board of trustees of Kansas Foundation for Private Colleges and on Kansas Governor's Task Force on Effective Management, 440; named general aviation's "Man of the Year", 440-1; received Golden Plate Award of the American Academy of Achievement, 441; received GAMA Distinguished Service Award, 449; received sales support award, 463; reelected to GAMA board and key committees, 466; honored by Flightcraft Inc., 477-8; guest of honor at Montreal, 485; elected to board of directors of National Association of Manufacturers, 485; appointed chairman of GAMA's International Affairs committee, 490; quoted in *Time* magazine, 490-1; sense of humor tested, 494; commented on merger, 502-3; elected to Raytheon board of directors, 510, and finance committee, 518; named honorary member at WSU of Alpha Kappa Psi, 514; elevated to vice chairman, 523; honored by U. S. Military Academy, 534; appointed as charter member of Naval Aviation Industrial Council, 534; received lifetime membership and Distinguished Service plaque from General Aviation Manufacturers Association (GAMA), 535
Hedrick Beechcraft, Inc., 448
Hedrick, Frank E. Center, 511
Hedrick, Frank E. Park, 505
Hedrick, Frank E. and Betty E. Endowment Fund, 528
Heineman, Edward H., 531
Helicopters, *see* Bell Helicopter
Henry, Wyman L., 191, 199, 211, 250, 251, 256, 271, 274, 323, 344
Henson Aviation, 371
Herington, Kan. air base facility, leased by Beech, 99-100; enlarged, 109; produced C-26 units, 114, and modified Model 18s, 114; produced fuel tanks, 142
Hess, Otto, 413
High altitude supersonic target (HAST), 317, 321, 333, 344, 361, 400, 424
Hinton, Douglas, 268
Hisso engine, 10
Hobbs, Janis, 289
Hodson, Eric W., 481, 504-5
Hoerner-type wing tips, 184
Holliinda N V, Netherlands, 482
Holmes, D. Brainerd, 502, 510, 528

Honeywell 400 computer, 215
Hood, Forrest E., 422
Hornberger, Dwight C., 420, 478
Hough, Cass S., 391-2, 404
Houston Beechcraft, Inc., subsidiary, 214, 279, 313, 410, 415, 453, 504
Hovey, Chandler, Jr., 312
Howe, Jack, 157
Hoyt, Fred D., 5
Hudson's Bay Company of Canada, 34
Hughes Tool Co., 188
Hulse, Frank, 271, 463, 533
Humphrey, George T., 323, 363
Hussein, King of Jordan, 158
Hustler Mach 2 B58 bomber, 200
Hutton, Frank, 478
Hydro-Systems Inc., 458
Hyundai Heavy Industries, Korea, 535

Ianiszewski, Col. Rene, 174
Indamer Co. Pty Ltd of India, 445, 482
India, 445, 450, 482
Indiana Beechcraft, subsidiary, 453
Indonesian Air Transport, 437, 474
Indonesian Flying Academy, 351
Indonesia, Republic of, 420, 423, 525, 528
Industry Award of International Exposition of Flight, 287, 290
In-flight refueling system, Beech-designed, 149
Inspect & repair as necessary (IRAN) program, 136
Instant Warranty program, 328, 337
Institut Geographique National, Paris, 439
International Air Derby, 10
International Air Salon, Paris, 199; Air Show, 529
International Association of Machinists, 168, 204, 226, 270, 301, 426
International Development and Advisory Board, 172
International Division, 323, 327, 342, 358, 370, 394, 408, 416, 430, 432, 437, 450, 479, 500, 507, 513, 528, 535, 537. See also Export
International Exposition of Flight Industry Award, 278, 290
International Flying Farmers, 295
International Forest of Friendship, 477
International merchandising fair, 213
International Sales Spectacular, 291, 297. See also Meetings
International Training Center for Civil Aviation, Mexico, 160-1
Iowa Mfg. Co., 515

Iran, Imperial Air Force of, 356, 389, 399
Iroquois U. S. Army helicopter, 216, 235, 255, 268, 285
Irving Airchute Corp., 76
Irwin, Capt. Walter W., 163
Isaacs, J. E., 355, 438
Itoh, C., Aviation Co., Japan, 520, 531
Ivory Coast, Republic of, 507

Jackson, Dale, 11
Jacobs engines, 17, 18, 19, 26
Japan, 122, 145, 149, 161, 174, 181, 229, 290, 296, 307, 390, 520; Civil Aviation Bureau of, 356; Maritime Safety Agency of, 475, 489, 531; National Defense Agency of, 212, 362
Japan Air Lines, 271, 273, 290, 304
Japanese Civil Aviation College, 399
Japanese Coast Guard, 141
Jarish, Trina, 424, 441
Jaycee Cross Country Derby, 128; Transcontinental Air Cruise, 118
Jenett, Lieut. R., 90
Jenner, Bruce, 489-90
Jet-assisted takeoff (Jato), 157, 171, 178
Jet Propulsion Laboratory, California Institute of Technology, 423
JetRanger helicopter, 273, 284, 318, 362, 384-6, 395, 416, 417, 436, 467, 468, 478, 498, 511, 526
Joa, Curt G., 329; Inc., 329
J.O.B.S. NAB program, 370
Johns, Alfred M., 393
Johnson, Kenneth D., 365
Johnson, President Lyndon B., and Mrs. (Lady Bird), 234, 237-8, 255, 273, 276, 305, 347-8, 350, 363
Jones, Bert, 490
Jones, Dr. Leland, 458
Jones, Laurie, 481

Kann, Major Gen. Clifton von (Ret.), 522
Kansas Foundation for Private Colleges, 440
Kansas Gas & Electric Co., 515
Kansas Governor's Task Force On Effective Management, 440
Kansas University, 396, 397; Flight Research laboratory, 416
Karim, Prince, the Aga Khan, 248
Keighly, W. Geoffrey, 403
Kelly, Dick (Lime & Rock Co.), 516
Kendrick, H. E., 223
Kennedy, George, 499
Kenny, Wey D., 488
Kinderfoto International, 418
King Air Million Mile Award, 337

King, Silas, 382
Kiowa U. S. Army helicopter, 318, 330, 363, 367-8, 417
Kline, L. Patton, 459
KLM Royal Dutch Airlines, 78, 263
Knudsen, Lieut.-General Wm. S., 102
Koch, Fred B., 372
Korea, conflict in, 99-103, 114, 117, 118
Koss Construction Co., 186
Krupp Co., Essen, 141
Kuechle, Wm. E., 476

Labor contract, record-setting, 532
Lady Drummond-Hay Memorial Trophy, 115
Lampitt, Capt. Tom E., 311, 315
Landing gear, 17, 19, 23, 25, 29, 31, 57, 66, 67, 72, 75, 100, 122, 128, 134, 219, 233, 236-7, 243, 256-7, 308, 324, 341-2, 498, 525
Landry, Gwen, 315
Lapplandsflyg, Sweden, 263
Larson, Norman, Man of the Year, 439; Co., 262
Latourrette & Parini S.A.C., 410, 430, 513
Lawsuits, 400, 411, 419, 457, 471-2, 534
LBJ Company, 234, 237
Learmonth, Col. Allen F., 425
Lederer, Jerry, 411
Leggett, Derek, 406
Le Grand Prix de France competition, 149
LeMay, General Curtis E., 260
Le May, George, 332
Lert, Peter, 470
Lew, James N., 191, 251, 274, 405, 431, 478
Lewin, Capt. E.D.G., 304
Libby, Hugh H., Hugh L., 418; Libby Welding Co., 418
Liberal (Kan.) Division, 109, 114; Musketeer production center, 208, 211, 245-6, 255, 267, 274; 1,000th Musketeer from Liberal, 275; mass flyaway, 312; 3,000th Aero Center Beechcraft delivery, 405, 413; 500th Sierra, 456, 473, 486, 494, 520
Liberty Aviation, Philippines, 430
LIFO inventory accounting, change to, 445
Light Aircraft Marketing Division, 323, 341, 356, 405, 413
Ligue Internationale des Aviateurs, 11, 20
Lindbergh, Charles A., 6, 275, 302, 461, 531
Lineken, Barrie E., 281
Lippiatt, H. C., 6

Liquefied gas, research into, 136, 261; containers, 151, 152, 163, 258; liquefied natural gas (LNG), 361-2, 376, 387; liquefied methane (LM), 506, 517-8, 521, 525, 530, 534, 537
Lockheed, components for, 112, 114, 118, 132, 135, 142, 143, 156, 163, 180-1, 188, 216, 247, 267
Lockheed Missiles & Space Co., 187, 278
London-to-Sidney Air Race, 310, 315
London to Victoria Air Race, 332
Longmont, Colo., 163, 203, 229. See also Boulder Division
Louch, Moe, 282
Lufthansa Airlines trainers, 188, 263, 278, 399
Lunar excursion module (LEM, LM), 258, 292, 300, 307
Lycoming engines, 126, 132, 138, 144, 148, 159, 170, 183, 197, 213, 239, 259, 273, 339, 341-2, 381, 409, 446, 447, 465
Lycoming Spencer Div. of AVCO Corp., 106
Lyon, John, 344

MA-3 ground service vehicle, 140, 142, 155, 161-2, 221
Macair Charters, 334
MacFadden race, 27, 35, 79; trophy, 32, 35
Mack, Congressman Peter F., Jr., world tour in Bonanza, 110
MacNeil, John, 245
Magic Hand landing gear, 256-7
Malaysia, UNACE Beechcraft for, 326
Marathon Oil Co., 63, 124, 281, 336, 356, 463, 494
Marcelo Re, Jose, 520
Marine Midland International Corp., 294; Overseas Corp., 294
Marinelli, Jack, 374
Marketing Division, 189-90, 192, 218, 222, 323, 353-4; research, 429. See also Export; International Division
Marshall, Laurence K., 501
Martin, Glenn L., 411
Martin, Robert, 355
Mason, James and Cindy, 442
Material Distributors, Inc., subsidiary, 53-4, 62, 68-9, 70, 87, 141
Maxwell, Shelby, 139
Mayfield, Owen, 302
Maytag Aviation Corp., 448
Mayor, H. A., 407
McClanahan, B. J., 324
McCullough engine, 136, 190
McDivitt, James A., 258

McDonnell Aircraft, 120, 135, 142-3, 149, 156, 162, 163, 181, 188, 198, 200, 216, 221, 252, 255, 258; McDonnell Douglas, 280, 285
McDonnell, James S., 302, 455
McEwen, Pat, 289
McGibbon, Edmund, 329
McGregor, Roy H., 251, 275, 323, 337, 355, 395, 405, 463, 472, 476
McKnight, Phil, 264
McLeod, Lamar W., 266, 270
McMillan, Marie, 491
McNamara, Robert S., 305
McNaughton, Major-General K. P., 109
MD-3 ground service units, 129, 133, 135, 144, 161
Meigs, Merrill C., 253
Meisinger, Dan L., 263, 315, 318, 350
Meetings, Beech sales, 1953, 117; 1954 Plane-O-Rama, 124, 125-7; 1955, 133; 1956 International Sales Meeting, 138; 1957, 147-8; 1958, 159; 1959, 170; 1960, 183; 1961, 192; 1962, 209; 1963, 222; 1964, 235; 1965, 249; 1966, 262; 1967, 270, 271; 1968, 280; 1969, 291, 297; 1970 regional meetings, 307; 1971 Bravo International, 319-20; 1972, 338-42; 1973 XL-73, 358-9; 1974 Showcase '74, 379, 381-2; 1975 Round-up, 408-11; 1976 Spirit of '76, 427-30, 433; 1977, 445-7; 1978 Best Sellers, 462-3; 1979 Masters, 481-3; 1980 International, 504-6; 1981 Winners, 520-1; 1982 Homecoming, 533-4
Melaragno, Fr. Ken, 468
Mellor, Olive Ann, 9, 13, 424
Mendez, Dr. Alejandro, 396
Mendieta, Alerjo, 513
Menzi, Col. Hans, 185
Mercury capsule, 196, 198, 388; program, 511
Mereira, Clertan, 513
Merger, Raytheon, 501-2-3, 508-11
Mexico, 18, 160-1, 174, 312, 322, 327, 328, 337, 346; Air Force fleet, 386, 399, 420, 435
Miami Air Races, 14, 15; Air Show, 22, 23
Mile-High Air Races, 19
Miles Laboratories, 337, 349, 357
Military Aero Clubs, 353
Military Air Transport Service (MATS), 263
Military and Aerospace Division, 206, 216. See also Boulder Division; military Beechcrafts; subcontracts, targets
Military Assistance Program, 336

Miller, Max H., 305
Miller, (Pilot/Nurse) Robin, 344
Million Dollar Club, sales, 147, 192, 222, 249, 430, 438, 445, 481, 504, 520
Misr Airwork (Egyptian airline), 78, 79, 435
Missile targets, see Targets, missile
Mission Beechcraft, Inc., subsidiary, 453, 520
Mitchell Aero Center, 408
Mitchell Division of Edo Aire, 496
Mobile AirCenter, 408
Mobile training school, Beech, 204, 372
Mock, Don, 451
Modern Maid, 515
Monroney, Senator Mike, 282
Morales, Wm. C., 382; Co., 382, 445, 452, 463, 481, 505, 520
Morane-Saulnier Co., 135. See also MS760 twin jet
Morgan, Major-Gen. Wm. M., 199, 251, 275
Morocco, 507, 528
Morrell & Co., John, 194
Morris, W. B., 215
Mota, Carlos Jr., 452
Moyer, Ralph E., 479, 488
MS760 twin jet executive plane, 134-5
Munson, Russell, 492-3
Murchison Bros., 372
Murdock, Marcellus M., 256
Murphy, Mike, 124, 281; Beech honoree, 336; Mrs. M., 463
Murray, Lt. Col. Loren P., Jr., 164

NAFCO, Republic of South Africa, 410
Nagel, R. J., 281
Naji, Capt. Sala, 507
Napalm drop tanks, 114, 118
Nashville Flying Services, 407
National Advisory Committee for Aeronautics, 169
National Advisory Council of the Army Aviation Museum, 331
National Aeronautic Association, 186, 268, 345, 378, 398, 411, 522
National Aeronautics and Space Administration (NASA), 169, 214, 218, 221, 292, 306, 323, 334, 343, 346, 361, 368, 376, 386, 388, 416, 423, 431, 444, 465, 467, 484-5, 488, 499, 510, 511, 517, 529; Johnson Space Center, 368
National Air Fair, Chicago, 97
National Air Races, 6, 10, 19, 22, 268
National Air Transport, Inc., 4, 5, 7
National Alliance of Businessmen (NAB), 305, 370, 393

National Association of Manufacturers, 485
National Bureau of Standards, Boulder, 152
National Business Aircraft Association (NBAA), 136, 291, 302, 303, 305, 336-7, 357-8, 373, 389, 431, 444, 495, 500-1, 518, 532
National Center for Atmospheric Research, 374
National Executive Committee of Junior Achievement, 331
National Federation of Press Women, 288, 289
National Intercollegiate Flying Association, 317
National Medical Enterprises Inc., 474
National Process Industries Group, 537
National Safety Council Award of Merit, 130
National Staggerwing Club, 296. See also Staggerwing Foundation, Museum
Naval Air Missile Center, 152
Naval Air Stations/Training, see U. S. Navy
Naval Aviation Industrial Council, 534
Naval Aviation Museum, 524
Neal, Margaret, 490
Neelands, T. D., 9
Nesen, Robert B., 372
Netherlands, 42, 76, 117, 149, 482
Neuburger, Michael G., 251, 265, 273, 279, 323, 405, 432, 443, 490, 514, 517, 518, 528
Newcomen Society in North America, 276-9, 277
New South Wales Trophy, 311
Newton, Kan. production facility, 497
New York Times, 94
New York to Miami Sports (race), 27
Nigeria, 474
Nike-Hercules mission, 203
Nikkel, Ed C., 355, 454, 525
Ninety-Nines, 331, 415
Nixon, President Richard M., 314, 383
Noll, Chuck, 490
Norfolk Island Airlines, 427, 469
North American Aviation, Inc., 173-4, 188, 200, 218, 292
North American Rockwell, 361
North Atlantic Treaty Organization (NATO), 117, 225
Northington, Robert S., 350, 359
Northrop Corp., 474, 508
Northwest Natural Gas Co., 530
Noyes, Blanche, 20, 507

Nymba S.A., Argentina, 482

Oakland to Los Angeles Race, 9
Oceanic Contractors Inc., 474
Odom, Capt. Wm. P., 89-96, 91, 110, 150, 164-5, 166, 426
Oestreicher, Robt. G., 282, 478
Ohio Aviation, 410-11, 482
Ohio Oil Company, 63, 124. See also Marathon Oil Co.
Ohio State University, 364, 431
Olson, Myron, 332
Ong, Bill, 19, 22
On-to-Detroit Race, 2
On-to-the-Sesqui Cross Country Race, 5
On-to-Tulsa Derby, 10
Operation Turnkey, 195, 215; "B" package plan, 215
Oricchio, Jose, 513
Orr, George W., Jr., 349
Ostermann, A. H., 250
Outside production department, 49-53, 117. See also Subcontracting
OX-5, 2, 5; OXX-6, 2
OX-5 Club of America, Aviation Hall of Fame, 332

Pacific Coast Air Derby, 6
Pacific Southwest Airways, 441
Page Airways, Inc., 280, 350, 358, 482
Page Beechcraft, Inc., 505, 520
Pape, Dean, 474
Paraguay, 410, 430, 513
Paraguayan National Airlines, 260
Paris, Wilbur, 154
Parish, Charlotte and John, 422, 424
Parker, Billy, 10
Parker Pen Co., 76
Paynter, Joan, 441-2
PAVE Eagle USAF program, 321, 334
Pearce Industries Inc., 418
Pechin, L. L., 251
Pelicans, 450
Peruvian Air Force, 260; Government, 268; Pescas, 396; Navy, 467, 528
Philippine Baron, speed record, 268, 271
Philippine Bonanza distance flight, 164-6
Phillips, Mrs. Claire, 389; Supply Co., 389
Phillips, Frank E. Trophy, 19
Phillips, Thomas L., 502, 509, 510
Photography, aerial, 30, 32, 154
Picard, Bob, 518
Piedmont Aviation, Inc., 350, 359, 410, 464
Pike, John A., 420, 479
Pike & Co. S.A., Uruguay, 482

Pitt, Mary Lynn (Beech), 263, 272, 287, 298, 346; Jennifer Gwenn, 286, 287; Jeffrey, 346
Pittsburgh Plate Glass Co., 76
Pizza Hut, Inc., 511
Plainsman gas-electric car, 129-30, 142
Plane & Pilot magazine, 495, 514
Pocono Airlines, 371
Polaris missile, 187
Pontiac Phoenix sedan, LM-fueled, 506
Powder Puff Derby, 154, 205, 276, 424. *See also* Women's Derby
Prairie Airways, 29, 31
Pratt & Whitney Aircraft, Fla., 389
Pratt & Whitney engines, Wasp Jr., 26, 27, 35, 75, 299; R-2800, 106; of Canada, turbo prop, 224, 231, 240, 244, 264, 275, 338, 352, 373, 446, 463, 485, 494, 495-6, 521, 526; *also* 336, 337, 359, 402
Private Pilot magazine, 495
Productivity Council, 451, 489, 512, 532
Professional Pilot magazine, 407
Propellers, Beech-built, controllable pitch, 58, 62, 64, 67, 79; constant speed, 128, 148, 160, 342; Hartzell, 138, 184, 381; 3-bladed, 183, 235, 238, 250, 321, 333, 373; 4-bladed, 333
Puerto Rico, 29, 31, 368
Punta Gorda Isles, Inc., 392

Qantas Airways, 311
QU-22B USAF Bonanzas, 321, 334
Quetzler, Bonnie, 529

Races, *see* Air races
Radar, 166, 172, 180, 184, 198, 291; systems, 515
Radio Corporation of America, 257
Rangeley Junior College, 364
Rankin, H. C., 35
Rawdon, Herb, 10
Raytheon Co., 501-2-3, 508, 509, 510, 515, 516, 522-3, 529-30, 533, 536, 537
Reading Air Show, 495
Reagan, (President) Ronald, 471
Real Estate Department, 473
Reconstruction Finance Corporation, 36
Records, altitude, 10, 21, 34, 152, 169, 171, 186, 193, 257; distance, 6, 10, 89-96, 110, 158, 164-6, 170, 268, 421, 426, 456; endurance, 10; speed, 8, 10, 11, 12, 17, 19, 20, 21, 26, 27, 34, 35, 79, 115, 118, 156, 162, 163, 268, 276,

315, 332, 345, 444, 456, 461, 469, 491. *See also* Speed Around the World
Reeve, Christopher ("Superman"), 499
Refueling system, Beech air-to-air, 190, 328, 444
Relay Race, 10
Rembleske, C. A., 415, 479, 527
Rene Morel A. of Guatemala, 445
Republic Airlines, 533
Republic Aviation Corp., 120, 132-3, 135, 143, 181, 182, 190, 206, 217
Research, 141, 163, 169, 173, 177, 179, 232, 396, 397; and development, 343, 372, 387, 412, 416. *See also* Boulder Division
Retail finance plan, 137
Reynolds Metal Co., 389
Richards, Watson E., Man of the Year, 311
Richardson, Elliot L., 443
Rickenbacker (Capt.) Eddie, 411
Rieger, Dr. John, 275
Rim of Ohio Derby, 10
Rio Airways, 371
Rising, Austin, 473
Roberts, Alice, 154
Robertson, Cliff, 345
Robinson, Wm. G., 479, 487-8, 505
Roby patent, propeller, 58
Rockefeller, David, 506
Rockefeller, Arkansas Governor Winthrop, 193
Rocketdyne, div. of North American, 200
Rockwell International, Space Div., 386, 388, 444, 485, 488, 499
Rodd, Jack, 469
Rodgers, George D., 395, 462
Rodriguez-Tocker, Dr. Lilia, 435
Rogers, J. A., 157
Rogers, Will, 455
Rohweder, Ralph A., 141
Rolls Royce Bristol Viper engines, 326, 357
Roosevelt, President Franklin D., 36
Royal Air Maroc, 507
Royal Canadian Air Force, 113, 123, 174, 181, 202
Royal Canadian Mounted Police, 76, 77, 202
Royal Flying Doctor Service of Western Australia, 329, 344-5, 369, 406
Royal Malaysian Government, 507
Royal Moroccan Air Force, 387
Ruthenberg, Donald B., 421
Rutherford, Wm. G., 478
Rutledge, W. E., 459
Ryan, Phillip A, 370-1; Contracting Co., 371

Sacchi, Louise, 332, 345, 363-4; Air Ferry Enterprises, 364
St. Louis *Post-Dispatch*, 76
St. Martin, Herbert, 10
Safety Merit Award, 130; suggestion program, 137
Salina Chamber of Commerce, 472
Salina Division, 267, 274, 290, 318, 326, 357, 368, 384, 395, 403, 413, 416, 417, 448, 453, 467, 469, 486, 493; completed 500th Duke, 493, 518, 520, 535
SAM-D project, 257, 275
Sanford Mills, 21
Sands of Time Kitty Hawk Award, 522
Saturn program, 187
Saudi Arabia, 437, 474, 507
Scandinavia, 445, 450. *See also* Sweden
Scheduled Skyways Inc., 360
Schmitt, Dieter, 461, 478-9
Schneider, Darrell, 350, 355, 476
Schoech, Rear Admiral W. A., 155
Scholarships, Beech-funded, 201, 305-6, 449, 490, 519; Hedrick Endowment, 528
Scott, Willard W., Jr., 534
Sea Airmotive, Inc., 417-8
Sedgwick County Soil & Conservation District, 515
Seismograph Service Corp., 515
Selma (Alabama) Division, 486, 489, 514, 531, 537
Semi-trailers, Boulder-built, 202-3, 207
Sidewinder missile, 515
Serralles, Sucesion J., 29
Service awards, 70, 214, 295, 355-6, 364
Service City International, 330-1
Service to customers, 105; Clinic program, 149, 172, 203-4; after the sale program, 328. *See also* Beechcraft Aerospace Services, Inc.; Beechcraft Training Center
Shaffer, John H., 335, 367, 384, 385, 390
Sharp, W. F., 139
Shealy, Geo. A., 10
Shell Aviation, 8
Shepard, Alan B., Jr., 198, 212, 455, 476
Shepherd, Rear Admiral Burton H., 454, 455
Shidler, Geraldine, 415
Shimp, Wm., 441
Shreeve, Rex, 337, 349
Shriver, Congressman Garner E., 420
Sikorsky, Igor I., 302, 411
Silver Anniversary, Beech, 153, 156
Silver Eagle, Order of the, 482, 504

Simpson, Bill, 410
Sinclaire, Mr. and Mrs. Reginald, 272
Skelton, Betty, 92, 97
Skylab, 361, 368, 371, 376, 384, 388, 390
Skyphone, 219
Small, Marvin B., 430, 447, 466
Smith, Earnest L., 6, 95
Smith, Senator Margaret Chase, 273
Smithsonian Institution, 110, 314, 421, 426
Snell, H. A. "Tony", 469
Snook, Allen W., 478
Sol, Andre, 481
Sommer, Dr. Francis X., 275
Sommer, Fred, 315
Soroptimist International, 477
South Africa, 17. 410, 453, 481, 491, 504
South Korea, 535
Southern Airways Beechcraft, Inc., 270
Southern Gulf Corp., 535
Southeastern Beechcraft, 338, 359
Southern Flight/Flight Operations magazine, 505
Southwest Airlines, 399
Southwest Pacific Airlines, 532
Southwest Petro-Chem, Inc., 407
Southwestern College, 131, estab. Olive Ann Beech Chair of Business Administration, 305-6; 421, 423
Southwestern Grain & Supply Co., 393
Space Shuttle System, 361; Orbiter, 386, 388, 424, 488; "Enterprise", 466, 484, 517, 527, 535, 536
Space Technology magazine, 331
Spain, 174, 326, 355, 445, 520
Spanish Air Ministry, 356, 377, 391, 414, 435
Sparrow III missile system, 510, 515
Spencer's Inc., N. Car., 442
Speed Around the World records, in C55 Baron, 268, 271; in B55 Baron, 345; in B60 Duke, 444; in S35 Bonanza, 469
Speed Queen Mfg. Co., 515
Sperry, Lawrence B., 531
Sperry Rand Corp., div. of Univac, 334
Staggerwing Club, 261, 265, 269, 354, 424, 458
Staggerwing Foundation and Museum, 422, 423-4, 458, 529
Staggerwing Restoration Society (at Beech), 458
Staggs, Robt., 478
Stalin, Joseph, 88, 118
Starratt Airways & Transportation, Ltd., 29, 31

Stephenson, Thor E. and Toni, 338
Stevens Aviation, Inc., 258
Stevens, Marion, 499
Stock, common, 24; stock issued as dividends, 181, 192, 205, 306, 342, 404, 427, 462, 480; stock splits, 192, 284, 377, 472; appreciation over 20 years, 437; exchanged at merger, 501-2, 508, 509; stock split, Raytheon, 530. See also Debentures
Stone, Bill, 484-5
Strategic Air Command, 129, 155
Stroehmann Bros. Co., 527
Stuart, Claude, 488
Stumbaugh, Gene Nora, 219, 227, 250
Subcontracting, performed for Beech, 48-53, 117; by Beech, 51, 88, 100, 112, 114, 120, 129, 132-3, 135, 142-3, 155, 156, 163, 168, 171, 173-4, 176, 179, 180-2, 183, 187, 190, 198, 200-1, 206, 216-7, 221, 235, 247, 249, 252, 255, 258, 267, 273, 280, 284, 285
Suggestion System, 451. See also Productivity Council
Summers, Jim, 495
Sunbird Airline, 531
Sun Oil Co., 78
Supervisors Club, Beech, 283, 523
Supplier cost conference, 378
Surface attack guided missile (SAGMI), 333
Swallow Airplane Corp., 1, 2, 150
Sweden, 439, 505, 520, 521. See also Scandinavia
Swigert, John L., Jr., 314
Switzerland, Republic of, 220-1, 482
Syphers, Graham and Cathy, 334

Tactical expendable drone system (TEDS), 414, 424
Targets, missile, supersonic, (X)-KD2B-1, USAF/Navy AQM-37A, 174-5, 203, 207, 212, 220-1, 223, 225, 312; XKD2B1/Q-12, 200, 212, 312; KD2B1/Q-12, 207, 221; AQM-37A, 225-6, 243-4, altitude record, 257, 164-7, 273, 275, 276, 280, 285-6, 305, 312-3, 318, 321, 362, 370, 400, 405, 436, 448, 471, 529; "Sandpiper", 276, 286, 318; "Stiletto", 332; SAGMI Mach 4, 333; Model 1094, 370; "Sea Skimmer/Skipper", 405; HAST, 424; HAHST tri-service, 475
Targets, pilotless aircraft, U.S. Navy XKDB-1, 136, 141-2, 152; Model 1013, 152; KDB-1, 139, 163, 169, 171, 174-5, 179, 180, 190, 198, 225; Navy KD-300, 172; Model 1025, 198, 207, 225, 267; Model

1001, 220, 225; Model 1025-TJ, 235, 260; Model 1025 ("Cardinal" U. S. Army MQM-61A), 285-6, 294, 318, 326, 351, 355, 370; Model 1089 "Streaker" (US AF TEDS), 414, 424; as U. S. Army MQM-107, 436-7; MQM-107A, 443, 455, 459-60, 475, 498, 525, 529
Targets, tow, "Dart" Model 1002, 140, 142
Taylor, Ben, 474
Texas Co., Texaco, 8, 11, 13
Texas International Airlines, 311-2 317
Texaco Trophy, 14-5
Textron, see Bell Helicopter, Div. of
Thaden, Louise McPhettridge, 10, 20, 21, 266, 422, 424, 506-7
Thaning, M., 17; Dr. Otto, 491
Thiess Holdings, Ltd., 406-7
Thomas, John M., 372
Thompson, J. Keith, 474
Thompson Trophy, 8, 10, 19, 156, 476; race, 10, 19
Tilford Flying Service, 408
Time magazine, 490
Timken, Henry H., Roller Bearing Co., 167
Titan ICBM, 153, 169, 187; Titan II, 202-3
Titanium, 143, 187, 218, 249
TK International, Tulsa, 480
Tobey, O. George, 151; Tobey, Inc., 152
Todd, Dick, 480
Topeka Aircraft Sales, 315, 318, 350; with Executive Beechcraft, 482
Topeka Daily Capital, 161
Topping control units, 201
Toran, Armand, 418
Toronto to Cleveland Race, 10
Tower, Senator John, 454-5
Trainer, seat escape procedure, 200
Transair, 206, 268, 382, 410, 430; of France S.A., 445, 463, 481, 505, 520; of Switzerland, 463, 482
Trans Australia (airline), 263
Transient heat tower and lab, 174, 177, 187
Transkei Airways Corp., S. Africa, 453
Transpo '72, 354
Travelair G.m.b.H., 187-8, 193, 206, 250, 286
Travel Air Co., history and record flights, 2-12; also 13, 15, 17, 24, 29, 95, 96, 265, 269, 295, 331-2, 458, 496-7
Travel Air Insurance Co., Ltd., subsidiary, 353
Trawood Mfg. Co., 443

Treylinek, A., 281
Trophies, 8, 10, 14, 15, 19, 20, 32, 35, 115, 156, 311, 367
Trowbridge, Alexander B., 276
Truly, Dick, 466
Truman, Senator (President) Harry S., 62, 99
T-tail, 373, 374, 375, 403, 408, 409, 412, 413, 429
Tulakes Aviation Co., 405, 413
Tulsair, Inc., 350, 482
Turbine power, 199-200
Turbomeca engines, Astazou, Bastan, 199
Turkey, 145, 161, 174, 336, 420, 434, 482
Turner, J. H., 20
Twin Disc, Inc., 315, 319

UNACE Beechcrafts, 326, 337, 420
United Aircraft of Canada, Ltd., 231, 244, 245, 337, 402
United Beech of Scandinavia A. B., 445
United Beech International of Sweden, 505, 520
United Beechcraft, Inc., subsidiary, 453
United Engineers & Construction, Inc., 515
United Fruit Co., 76
United Kingdom, 332; Defense Ministry of, 273, 286
United Nations, 103, 160
U. S. Army Air Corps, 22, 30, 32, 35, 36, 39, 40, 41, 46, 155; see also BEECHCRAFTS, military
U. S. Army, Aviation Museum, 331; Aviation Systems Command, 336; Aviation Test Board, 180, 240, 252; Field Forces, aircraft for, 117 et seq. See also BEECH-CRAFTS, military; Materiel Command, 260, 419; Missile Command, 436, 443, 448, 450, 455, 459, 475; Munitions Command, containers for, 217, 224; Ordnance Department, 198; VSTT/MQM-107 target missile system, 351, 366, 376, 419; White Sands missile range, 190, 260, 376; Worldwide Target Users Conference, 365-6
U. S. Air Force, aircraft for, 54 et seq. See also BEECHCRAFTS, military; Air Materiel Command, 173; area offices, 127, 133, 200; Armament Laboratory, 275, 286; HAST target missile, 317, 321, 333; Inspection Board, 109; Military Air Transport Service, 249, 263, 265, 424; Systems Command, 249, 424; Training Command, 109, 111; Museum, 411. See also ground service units; trailers
U. S. Atomic Energy Commission, 399-400
U. S. Chamber of Commerce, 443, 491
U. S. Customs Service, 493
U. S. Department of Commerce, 432
U. S. Department of Defense, 118, 179, 333, 344, 450, 472
U. S. Department of Transportation, 389
U. S. Forest Service, Dept. of Agriculture, 327, 475-6, 525
U. S. Marine Corps, 467, 487, 525
U. S. Military Academy, 534
U. S. Navy, aircraft for, 33 et seq. See also BEECHCRAFTS, military; Bureau of Aeronautics, 121, 127, 151, 155, 169, 174, 181, 426; Bureau of Naval Weapons, 190, 221, 223, 243. See also Targets; Ordnance Test Center, 142; Naval Academy, 317; Air Systems Command, 405, 440, 448, 452; Air Training Command, 123, 128, 155; Missile Center, 152, 212, 257, 321, 455; Aviation Museum, 358; Test Pilot School, 364; Training Center, Pensacola, 209, 223, 268, 494
US/USSR Apollo/Soyuz Test Project, 391, 425
United Way, 503, 519
Unlimited race, 19
Uruguay, 482, 521, 528
Utility Aircraft Council, 206
Utt, W. A., 459

Value Engineering program, 324, 330
Van Dusen, G. B., 332; Van Dusen Air, Inc., 332
Variable speed training target (VSTT), U. S. Army, 351, 366, 376, 419
Venezuela, 161, 174, 181, 382, 396, 399, 445, 452, 463, 481, 505
Vergara, Jose G., 312
Vetterlein, Wayne, 120
Volkswagen, 194
Voodoo F-101 fighter, 120, 135, 143, 162, 181
V-tail, 58, 67, 71, 82, 87, 152, 175, 280, 296, 324, 340-1, 353, 360, 374, 375, 380-1; missile, 136, 152, 225

Wagner, Judy, 268, 276, 289
Waikiki Beech Bonanza, 89-96, 91, 110, 164-5, 421, 426
Walker, Harold, 157
Wallace, Dwight, 191, 247

Wallace, Geo. C., 489
Wallick, Joan and Robert, 268, 271, 346
War bonds, 47, 61
Warner, Lowell Jay, 228, 263
Warner, Thomas N., 263, with wife, Suzanne, 422
War on Waste program, 324
Warren, Garri, 372
Washburn, C. Langhorne, 335
Wasp Jr. engines, see Pratt & Whitney
Water supply, standby, 115
Water tower, Travel Air/Beech, 333
Webber, James D., 186
Wells, T. A., 9, 10, 41
Werrett, David H., 275
Wesley Medical Center, 495
Western Flying Trophy, 6
Western Shipping Co., 417
Westinghouse Electric Corp., 266, 270, 281
Weyerhauser Co., 139
Whipple, Lillian, 475
White, Edward H., 258
White House Energy Policy office, 383
White, Weld & Co., 311
Who's Who of American Women, 305
Wichita Area Chamber of Commerce, 448-9, 466
Wichita Aeronautical Historical Association, 524
Wichita Industrial District, Beech, 506
Wichita Plant Four, 506, 526
Wichita to Hartford Speed Record, 79
Wichita State University, Olive Ann Beech chapter of Angel Flight, 288, 289; Golden Anniversary Awards, 454
Wilbourne, Preston H., 351
Wilbur Award to Mrs. Beech, 330
Wildhaber, A. J., 139
Wilmarth, Martin, 330
Wilmot, Gerald G., 280, 350

Windsor, R. W., Jr., "Duke", 476
Wind tunnel, Walter H. Beech Memorial, 201
Windward Co., Houston, 476
Wings, Beech, 25, 51-4, 60, 62, 84-5, 112, 114, 118, 132, 135, 143, 180-1, 431
Wings Club, the, 534
Winters, Lucille (Mrs. Edwards), 251, 344, 448, 475, 490
Wisconsin Airlines, 351
Wise, W. D., 487, 503-4
Wolfgang Denzel GmbH, 445, 461, 478
Woolaroc Travel Air, 6, 7
Women's Aeronautical Association, 475-6
Women's Derby, 10; Washington, 268
Women's International Association of Aeronautics, 115
Women's National Aeronautical Association, 106, 305
Women's Powder Puff Derby, 441
Wood, E. H., 14
Work simplification program, 226-8, 324. See also Productivity Council
Work, W. F., 338
Work stoppage, 301
World Trade Club of Wichita, 528
Wright Brothers Memorial Trophy, 522
Wright engines, 2, 10, 12, 15, 17, 18, 19, 26
Wright, Orville & Wilbur, 522, 530

Yacare, 513
Yankey, C. G., 9
Yarbrough, W. C. "Dub", 422, 529
Yarnell, James R., 313, 345
Yellow Air Cabs, Inc., 120
Young Bros. Development Co., Ltd., 520
Younkin, Jim, 496

Zero Defects, 255-7, 324
Ziff-Davis Publishing Co., 440
Zonta International, 415